compliments of *Look* Magazine

Admiral Richardson, Commander-in-Chief, U.S. Fleet, 1940.

On the Treadmill to Pearl Harbor

THE MEMOIRS OF
ADMIRAL
JAMES O. RICHARDSON
USN (Retired)

as told to
Vice Admiral
GEORGE C. DYER, *USN (Retired)*

Introduction by
Vice Admiral Edwin B. Hooper, *USN (Retired)*
Director of Naval History

Naval History Division
Department of the Navy
Washington, D.C., 1973

Introduction

Those who, for the benefit of the future, seek the lessons of the past will be indebted to Admiral Richardson for making available his recollections spanning half a century of distinguished naval service, and in particular, for recording so fully and frankly views concerning events and decisions with which he was associated in the months preceding war in the Pacific.

Quite naturally there is a tendency for naval and other military history to focus on operations, strategy, and tactics in times of war. Comparable attention deserves to be paid to the roles and employment of the Navy and other forces as a part of national strategy in times of peace. Not only is the effectiveness of diplomatic interplay on major matters largely dependent on the posture of overall military power, but peacetime deployments and operations have often played direct roles in fulfilling national objectives on the international scene.

This has been particularly true in the case of maritime powers such as the United States. The effectiveness of sea power as a determinant in foreign affairs has stemmed from such factors as: the global expanse of the oceans and their international character; the world's high degree of dependence on the seas for resources and for the movement of materials and goods; the use of the seas for resources and for the movement of materials and goods; the use of the seas for the projection of power to distant areas; the decisive effects of control of the sea; and the inherent mobility and flexibility of naval forces. Success or failure has depended on how well sea power has complemented diplomatic and economic acts and other means of influencing international decisions. Success or failure also has depended on such factors as potential strength of the Fleet vis-a-vis the enemy in terms such as numbers and capabilities of ships, aircraft, and weapons; manning levels; training; material readiness of the Fleet for war; geographic disposition; and employment of Fleet units. Without consideration of factors such as these, the naval strategy adopted as a part of a peacetime national strategy may be faulty.

Insofar as lessons for the future are concerned, no historical example is of greater importance than that of the decisions and events in the period leading up to the Pearl Harbor Attack.

As had others before him, President Franklin Delano Roosevelt directed deployments of the Fleet as a part of his overall national peacetime strategy. Rather than deterring the Japanese from aggressive actions, the maintenance of a major portion of the Fleet at Pearl Harbor was viewed by the then militaristic leaders of Japan as an opportunity to cripple U.S. naval power in the Pacific. As she decided to launch the devastating carrier air attack of 7 December 1941, Japan had memories of the decisive results of the Battle of Tsushima in the Russo-Japanese War and of territorial acquisitions made possible by the diversion of the western navies to meet the needs of warfare in Europe and the Atlantic during World War I. In 1941, with Europe again in the throes of all-out war, only the American Navy could prevent fulfillment of ambitions of establishing a "Greater Asia Co-prosperity Sphere."

In this volume, completed (except for editorial work) in 1958, Admiral J. O. Richardson records his recollections and views, concentrating mainly on the years from 1939 to 1942. He devotes considerable attention to war plans, to his efforts to obtain adequate manning for the Fleet, to his concern over the effects of the prolonged Hawaiian deployment in degrading Fleet readiness for war, and to the disagreement with the President that led to his being relieved as Commander-in-Chief, U.S. Fleet.

Regretfully, many of the official records of Commander Battle Force during Admiral Richardson's tour were lost at Pearl Harbor. Rear Admiral John B. Heffernan, as Director of Naval History, in 1955 did much to help counterbalance the losses when he arranged for Vice Admiral George C. Dyer to work with Admiral Richardson and assist in compiling these memoirs. Enjoying a close personal and official relationship with his commander, Admiral Dyer had served as Aide to Admiral Richardson when the latter was Chief of the Bureau of Navigation. He served also as the Admiral's Aide and Flag Secretary during three tours; first, when the latter was Commander Destroyers, Scouting Force; second, when he was Commander Battle Force; and finally when he was Commander-in-Chief, United States Fleet. In addition to being close to many of the critical events recorded in this book, Admiral Dyer had played a key role in staff actions to do with plans and their implementation.

While the primary value of this book has to do with decisions and events in the months before the Japanese attack, Admiral Richardson has included material on other periods of his long and eventful naval career, thus providing valuable insights with regard to a changing Navy from the turn of the twentieth century to World War II.

Mr. Edward J. Marolda of our Operational Archives, working under the direction of Dr. Dean C. Allard, located and verified sources that were cited, undertook a number of editorial tasks in conjunction with Vice Admiral Dyer, and performed other functions associated with the publication of this book. However, the Naval History Division has made no attempt to pass judgment on the views expressed in this volume; they are solely those of Admiral Richardson. With the full realization that, for a complete picture or an overall evaluation of the decisions and events of the time, it will be necessary to draw also upon additional source materials and the opinions of others involved, the work is published, in the expectation that it will provide valuable contributions to naval history.

EDWIN B. HOOPER
Vice Admiral, U.S. Navy (Ret.)
Director of Naval History

Preface

Primarily, this book is the story of a Naval officer, Admiral J. O. Richardson, who commanded the United States Fleet during the year 1940 and until January 31, 1941, and of his unsuccessful efforts, subsequent to May 1940, to keep the main strength of that Fleet from being regularly based at Pearl Harbor, Hawaii.

A bit of the story of the growing United States Navy and of the development of a midshipman into a four-star admiral during the forty-one-year period from 1898 to 1939 is related. And, an effort is made also, in an early chapter, to create for the reader the "spirit of the times" of 1939, not by telling it as it is known *now,* but, insofar as it could be reconstructed in 1956, by telling it as it was known *then* (1939).

Examined are the details of the effort by the Commander-in-Chief, United States Fleet to obtain from the Chief of Naval Operations additional naval air-patrol aircraft for the naval air squadrons based at Pearl Harbor, as well as the institution, by Admiral Richardson, of daily long-range search air reconnaissance. It is particularly noted that the Chief of Naval Operations did not give his approval, on a continuous basis, to even this minimum security precaution for the United States Fleet.

And, at long last, the details are made public of the final conference of Admiral Richardson with President Franklin D. Roosevelt in October 1940, which Admiral Richardson firmly believes led to his detachment from command of the United States Fleet.

Work on the manuscript commenced in 1956 in close collaboration with Admiral Richardson. I will attest that throughout his seventies and into his mid-eighties, Admiral Richardson had an inexhaustible memory for facts and figures and personalities.

In addition to drawing upon his memory and material in his possession, I researched some 70,000 incoming and outgoing despatches of the Navy Department. Countless pieces of naval official and personal correspondence were read to provide a fully factual basis for the account of the effort to prepare the United States Fleet for war during the June 1939 to January 1941 period.

After Admiral Richardson had approved a rather detailed outline, I paid bi-weekly visits to his home. The usual procedure was for him to review what I had reduced to writing in draft form, as a result of the previous reviews and related research. Then, many times holding the outline in hand, he would relate a further part of his story.

Often he retained between visits my double-spaced rough draft and wrote in extensive, but clarifying amplifications, suggested possible additional research leads, or made corrections.

When we reached the part of the story dealing with Admiral Richardson's meetings with President Roosevelt on July 8, 1940, and October 8, 1940, I suggested to Admiral Richardson that he draft the manuscript himself, and this he did.

His diary is mentioned a number of times in the text. I never saw even the reduced diary, but from time to time Admiral Richardson produced pages from his "little black book," which I did read, use, and return to him.

When the manuscript for this book neared completion in 1958, Admiral Richardson prepared this statement:

> Off and on during my Naval career, I had kept a diary. It was kept most regularly during my early years on the China Station [1902–1904], and later during the period [in 1939–1941] when I was Commander Battle Force and Commander-in-Chief, United States Fleet.
>
> When it became apparent that I would probably be called as a witness before the Congressional Pearl Harbor Investigation, it seemed to me that this record might become known and be subpoenaed.
>
> Since in the diary I expressed frank and sometimes offhand opinions (some of them highly critical) of various officers of the Navy, and of officials of the Government for their actions or inactions during the 1939–1941 period, I thought it best that the diary be burned. So, I burned it, after extracting some non-critical parts. I also burned some of my personal letters and various naval communications carrying my pithy comments.
>
> The [complete] diary would have been of great help in preparing this book and, in this respect only, I regret the burning.

George C. Dyer

11 December 1972 GEORGE C. DYER

Contents

Illustrations and Charts

(Illustrations identified by numbers preceded by 80-G are official U.S. Navy photographs in the National Archives; those numbered with NH prefixes are in the Naval History Division, Washington, D.C.)

Chapter I

"To Sea"

I walked out of the White House.

I held in my hand a piece of paper. It had just been handed to me by President Franklin D. Roosevelt.

Typed on this piece of paper was the President's Slate of officers for the principal command billets of the Navy, both afloat and ashore.

The date was March 9, 1939.

Admiral William D. Leahy, USN, who held the number one billet in the professional Navy, the Chief of Naval Operations, was due to retire on May 6, 1939 because he would reach the legal retirement age of 64 on that date.

Throughout January and February of 1939, I had been pressing my superior to decide on his relief as well as a slate for all the senior command

\- PRESIDENT'S SLATE -

Office		Relief
C.N.O.	Leahy-retire one month after Congress adjourns.	Stark
CINCUS	Bloch - remain until next winter.	Richardson
CINC A.F.	Yarnell	Hart or Watts
Battle Force	Kalbfus - relieve in June.	Richardson
Scouting Fon.	Andrews - remain.	- - - -
Battleships	Greenslade	Snyder
AirBatFor	King	Blakeley
BuNav	Richardson	Kalbfus or Wainwright or Anderson or Nimitz

billets in the Navy, because as the Chief of the Bureau of Navigation (now designated as the Chief of Naval Personnel), I had a legal responsibility for, and a deep professional interest in, the assignment of the seagoing officers of the Line of the Navy. The end result I earnestly sought was the highest efficiency and teamwork in the Fleet and supporting Shore Establishment.

And, finally, here the slate was—all typed out on a piece of paper. How well would it support the end result sought in the critical years ahead? I didn't know this, but I did know that the sun was shining brightly outside, and I felt a warm glow inside. It was surely "R" Day; "R" for Richardson, for my name occupied a prominent part in the "New Slate."

The events building up to the moment described above had been crowded into the first three months of 1939 and are detailed below to give a better understanding of this period.

Fleet Operations Early 1939

The United States Fleet was scheduled to move from the Pacific for a visit to the Atlantic in early 1939, as indicated in the following extract from the Annual Report of the Navy Department:

> On January 4, 1939, . . . the Fleet sailed from West Coast bases for the Canal Zone. The Fleet made a mass transit of the Canal on January 13, 1939 and proceeded to base in the Guantanamo-Culebra Area. Fleet Problem XX was conducted in February and March in the Caribbean Area and off the Northeast Coast of South America. The latter phase of the problem was witnessed by the President of the United States and the Chief of Naval Operations in *Houston.* [1]

February 1939 Conference With President

In connection with this visit to the Fleet and the prospective slate of three and four-star Flag Officers, Admiral Leahy and I visited the President in early February 1939.

Following the discussion of the details of the President's visit to the Fleet

[1] U.S., Navy Department, *Annual Report of the Secretary of the Navy for the Fiscal Year 1939* (Charles Edison, Acting) (hereafter cited as SECNAV, *Annual Report,* with year) (Washington, D.C.: GPO, 1939), p. 8.

in the heavy cruiser *Houston,* I asked the President if he had made up his mind about the "New Slate." He said, "Well, even if I had, I wouldn't tell you" and then added that he would come up with a slate after he had watched the actual performance of the Fleet during the Fleet Problem and of the principal Flag Officers now in it.

The President then took off his desk his personal copy of the 1938 Naval Register (containing the names of all professional naval officers in order of seniority) and, going down the list of 74 Line Flag Officers, commented on or queried Admiral Leahy or myself with regard to a number of them.

Two comments that the President made during this visit have remained in my memory. The first was:

> Adolphus Andrews—I probably know him better than I do any other officer of Flag rank on the Navy List, and I think very highly of him, but he does not have what it takes to be a Commander-in-Chief.

Vice Admiral Adolphus Andrews currently was in command of the Scouting Force in the United States Fleet. He had been my predecessor as Chief of the Bureau of Navigation for three years. Prior to that, he had been Chief of Staff to Admiral Joseph M. Reeves (1902),[2] Commander-in-Chief of the United States Fleet during 1933 to 1935. He had been Naval Aide to Presidents Harding and Coolidge. Vice Admiral Andrews was a fellow Texan, one year senior to me, being of the Naval Academy Class of 1901.

The second comment related to myself:

> As for you J. O., you can relax. You aren't going to go to sea this year. I think that the Chief of Bureau [of Navigation] should be in his job at least two years.

I fully concurred with this comment and had not nourished the hope of an early sea assignment. I had been in the billet only seven months and had just begun to feel fully familiar with the multiple personnel problems of a rapidly expanding Navy.

During this interview, I originated only two major comments to the President in regard to the various Flag Officers. I said, "Admiral Hart is too able, too young, and too capable to be overlooked for a billet at sea," and, "In my opinion, Peck Snyder should be given serious consideration

---

[2] Year dates shown in parentheses after officers' names in this and subsequent chapters are those of initial commissioning in the Navy or Marine Corps.

for one of the top billets. He has amply demonstrated his superior qualifications."

Rear Admiral Thomas C. Hart, Naval Academy Class of 1897, was currently Chairman of the General Board. He was a classmate of Admiral Leahy's. It had been my observation that classmates become jealous of each other when they are competing for high honors, so I believed if anything was to be said in Admiral Hart's favor, that I would have to say it.

Rear Admiral C. P. Snyder, Naval Academy Class of 1900, was two years senior to me and currently President of the Naval War College. He had been a very successful Chief of Staff to Admiral David F. Sellers when the latter was Commander Battleships and later Commander-in-Chief of the United States Fleet from 1932 to 1934. Prior to that, he had been a very successful Commandant of Midshipmen at the U.S. Naval Academy, Annapolis.

The President did not ask me for a recommendation as to who should be the next Chief of Naval Operations, nor did I volunteer such a recommendation to him.

In fact, neither Admiral Leahy, the Chief of Naval Operations, nor the Secretary of the Navy, asked me for my opinion or recommendation in this particular matter. Had I been asked for my suggestion, I was of a mind to recommend Admiral C. C. Bloch, currently the Commander-in-Chief of the United States Fleet. I would have recommended Admiral Bloch because of his outstanding professional capabilities and because of his wide experience in, and familiarity with, the Navy Department.

Admiral Bloch had served as Chief of the Bureau of Ordnance, Budget Officer, and Judge Advocate General. He had no peer in the handling of committees of Congress.

Some time previous to this February meeting, Secretary of the Navy Claude A. Swanson had asked me and Captain Frank Jack Fletcher, USN, his former personal Aide, and then the Assistant Chief of the Bureau of Navigation, to luncheon at the President's camp at Rapidan. Just previous to this visit, I had talked with Admiral Leahy about his relief as Chief of Naval Operations and had said it would be very helpful to me to know whom it would be, so I could work up a realistic slate for the shifting of two-star Flag Officers. He said, "J. O., when I leave this job, I am going to completely sever my connections with the Navy, and I am going to do this so completely that when I go, I am not even going to recommend my successor." I was surprised at this statement, for it was contrary to precedent and the natural procedure.

While at Rapidan, I told Mr. Swanson that he ought to make up his mind soon about the new CNO, and I told him what Admiral Leahy had said to me in this connection. He said, "J. O., did Leahy say to you he would make no recommendation to me in regard to his successor when he leaves? Huh; he doesn't have to—he has already recommended Stark."

I knew Rear Admiral Harold R. (Betty) Stark (currently Commander Cruisers, Battle Force, U.S. Fleet) very well. He was very capable, hard working and one of the best-intentioned officers in the Navy, as well as one of the most likable. I believed then, and believe now that his capacities, although marked, were not equal to those required by the Chief of Naval Operations billet, under conditions then existing.

I believe also that few, if any, other senior officers in the Navy could have served the President so long and so satisfactorily as did Admiral Stark.

President's Visit to Fleet

That the President's visit to the Fleet, in February 1939, was important from a personal point of view was well understood by the senior officers of the Navy. This is factually set forth by Fleet Admiral E. J. King, U. S. Navy, in his *A Naval Record,* as follows:

> The President's visit to the Fleet was inevitably associated in the minds of most senior flag officers with the choice of a new Chief of Naval Operations, for it had been known since the beginning of the year that Admiral Leahy was due to retire in May 1939 when he reached his sixty-fourth birthday. The choice of his successor was a matter of the keenest interest. Although King had little conviction that it would fall to him, he thought that they might do worse, and could not help hoping that lightning might strike. In looking back over his forty-two years in the Navy he reflected that he had had service in destroyers, very little in battleships except staff duty on board battleships, and none in cruisers. He had spent a year at sea in submarines, three years in command of the Submarine Base at New London [Connecticut], and had raised two sunken submarines. His forte was in naval aviation, where he had served twelve varied years and was now reaching the end of a three-year tour of sea duty. It was not too bad a record, although at that time service in battleships appeared to weigh heavily. Moreover, he had never closely associated himself with the clique centering around the Bureau of Ordnance—and consequently known as the "Gun Club"—that maintained prac-

NH 77347

President Franklin D. Roosevelt and Admiral C. C. Bloch at an earlier Fleet Review, July 1938.

tically a monopoly of the top posts both in the Navy Department and at sea, to the exclusion of others including naval aviators. As King had passed sixty in November 1938, and had less than four years of active service ahead before retirement, it was clearly "now or never." Under existing circumstances "never" seemed the more probable, but he still could not help hoping.

On the afternoon of 28 February 1939 King and Halsey went together on board *Houston* where some twenty or more flag officers of the United States Fleet had been summoned to pay their respects to the Commander in Chief of the Army and Navy. President Roosevelt was in high spirits, for he loved the Navy and always visibly expanded when at sea. As the admirals greeted him, he would have some pleasant, half-teasing personal message for each. King, when his turn came, shook hands and said that he hoped the President liked the manner in which naval aviation was improving month by month, if not day by day. Mr. Roosevelt seemed pleased by this, and after a brief

> chat, admonished King, in his bantering way, to watch out for the Japanese and the Germans.
>
> King made no attempt to hold further conversation with the President, even though Admiral Bloch urged him to do so. . . . It seemed that the die was already cast, although the President's decision would not be known for some weeks.[3]

Admiral Bloch, Commander-in-Chief, U.S. Fleet, told me, when he visited the Navy Department in April 1939, that Admiral Leahy had seen to it that no Flag Officer had had a chance to talk to the President alone during the Fleet visit.

Admiral Leahy later told me that Vice Admiral Andrews had been particularly desirous of talking alone with the President. He said he told Andrews, "You don't have a thing to worry about, because I heard the President say just the last fortnight that he probably knew you better than any other Flag Officer in the Navy and thought very highly of you." He failed, however, to tell Andrews the most important part of the President's remark.

March 1939 Conference with President

When the President handed me this piece of paper with the "Slate" on it, I said to him, "Is this something you want to talk about, or is this something you want done?" He said, "It's final—I want it done."

I noticed, however, that he had listed three officers as reliefs for me (Kalbfus, Wainwright, and Anderson). The multiplicity of names made me realize that, in fact, he had not finally made up his mind in regard to the officer to relieve me, and that this offered me an opportunity to make a recommendation of my own. As I believed there was a fourth officer better qualified to handle the Navy's personnel problems than any of the three listed, I said, "None of the three officers listed possess the confidence and respect of the mature officers of the Navy to the extent that would fully qualify them to hold the BUNAV job. In my opinion, Chester Nimitz is the best qualified officer to come into the Bureau as my relief. He is one of the best young Flag Officers in the Navy today."

The President said, "Well, what then will we do with 'Old Dutch' (Kalbfus)—I suppose we can send him to the Naval War College?"

[3] FADM Ernest J. King and Walter Muir Whitehill, *Fleet Admiral King: A Naval Record* (New York: W. W. Norton and Co., Inc., 1952), pp. 291-92.

The President then took back the piece of paper, drew a line thru the names of Kalbfus, Anderson, and Wainwright, and wrote "or Nimitz."

That ended my discussion of the "President's Slate." He had drawn the line thru "or Watts" after "Commander-in-Chief, Asiatic Fleet," before he handed the Slate to me, and, as I fully agreed with this decision, I said nothing about it.

Reactions to New Slate

The President then instructed me that, while I could inform each officer named in the slate of his own particular assignment, I could inform no others. Accordingly, I informed Rear Admiral Hart who was on duty in the Washington area; those at sea I informed by confidential letter.

When Hart, Chairman of the General Board, dropped in to see me at the Bureau, he said, "J. O., you are the one that should be going to China instead of me, because you know far more about American relations in the Far East than I do. If you can arrange matters at this end, it will be perfectly agreeable to me for you to come out and relieve me after I have one year in command."

I thought that this latter remark was typical of Tommy Hart. He was an extremely competent, although not a "showy" officer. He had always sought to further the interests of the Naval Service, as he saw them, and never pushed himself forward for any purpose. His personal standards of duty-performance were very high, and he sought to have his juniors emulate them.

The first time that Stark came to Washington after my letter to him, notifying him of his future appointment, he came into my office and in the course of the conversation asked, "Where are King and Kimmel going to be detailed?" He added, "In my opinion, and with present company excepted, they are the two best Flag Officers in the Navy today." I told him that Kimmel was going to relieve him (Stark) as Commander Cruisers, Battle Force and that King was coming in to the General Board. Stark said, "Fine. There is no one I would prefer to be relieved by than Kimmel."

I shared fully Stark's high opinion of both King and Kimmel, but King was overdue for shore duty, so he had been slated by me for the General Board, which acted many times as the Bureau of Navigation "Receiving Ship for Admirals." That is, it was a place where an Admiral might be brought and usefully employed, but kept available for an important detail, without the necessity of an immediate sight relief for him on detachment from the General Board.

In October 1940, when serving as Commander-in-Chief, U.S. Fleet, I was ordered to Washington to see the President. During this visit, I said to Nimitz, the Chief of the Bureau of Navigation, "We are likely to be in a war at any time now, and if we are, it may turn out that some of us in high command may not be able to measure up to our jobs. You should have your mind all made up, now, as to the officers who should step into our shoes in this circumstance." Nimitz said, "I would like to have a list from you of four or five who you think are particularly well qualified for the CINCUS billet." Later (October 29, 1940), when I sent him my list, it included the names of King and Kimmel, but I added that, because of his seniority, I thought King should relieve me when the need for a successor arose.

King was not unaware of the efforts of his admirers to return him to a suitable high command in the Fleet. As stated in King's *Naval Record*:

> Stark, ever since his appointment as Chief of Naval Operations in the previous year, had shown a friendly consideration for King, and had made various attempts to fit him into a command at sea.[4]

As a result, after less than eighteen months of shore duty, King went to sea again on December 17, 1940, when he relieved Rear Admiral Hayne Ellis, USN, of command of the Patrol Force of the United States Fleet. He fleeted up to four stars when the Patrol Force became the Atlantic Fleet on February 1, 1941.

In retrospect, it probably was best for the nation that King was assigned in the Atlantic. For, in the Atlantic Fleet Command, King's talents were not exposed to the possibility of a December 7th tragedy and were available to give drive and direction to the whole Naval Establishment during World War II.

Woman's Intuition

My prospective detail as Commander Battle Force, U.S. Fleet, with the prospect of becoming Commander-in-Chief, United States Fleet, came as a

[4] *Ibid.*, p. 308.

considerable surprise to me in view of the President's previous statement, less than a month before, that I was to remain as Chief of the Bureau of Navigation for another year. In view of the many personnel problems that were arising with the expansion of the Navy, it was my belief that a longer period in that duty, by any Chief of Bureau, would have been beneficial to the Navy.

In February 1939, before the departure of the President from Washington for his visit to the United States Fleet, Mrs. Richardson had received a call from Mrs. Charles Edison, the wife of the Assistant Secretary of the Navy, asking if our engagement calendar would permit us to come over that evening for dinner and bridge. As our calendar was clear, we were happy to accept.

During the course of the evening's conversation, and appropriate to the trend of the conversation, Mr. Edison said to me, "If you had your choice of details, would you prefer to be Chief of Naval Operations or Commander-in-Chief of the U.S. Fleet?" I readily answered that I thought every officer with a real love of the sea and the Navy, and a little salt in his veins, would prefer the Fleet billet, and that I certainly would.

On the way home, Mrs. Richardson had said that she thought the Assistant Secretary was sounding me out on a future detail. I scoffed at the idea, saying that he was just asking a question normal to the conversation and in an effort to get the viewpoints of a senior naval officer on how Departmental billets were viewed.

However, it turned out that she was correct.

I still have no regrets for my reply, insofar as my Naval career is concerned, but I do believe the United States Fleet would not have been in Pearl Harbor on December 7, 1941 had I been the Chief of Naval Operations at that time.

Detail of Seagoing Line Officers

In view of present day practices, I believe it important to point out that during my tour (June 11, 1938 to June 15, 1939) as Chief of the Bureau of Navigation, the Bureau actually determined the assignments and detailed the seagoing officers of the Navy of the rank of Captain and below, with the exception of personal aides of Flag Officers. These latter were

NH 54876

Rear Admiral Richardson as Chief of the Bureau of Navigation, June 1938.

largely determined by the Flag Officers themselves, and then detailed by the Bureau, if at all practicable.

In regard to the seagoing Flag Officers in the rank of Rear Admiral, the highest permanent rank of any active duty officer (commonly called two-star Flag Officers), their detail was largely in the hands of the Chief of the Bureau of Navigation. As long as he knew accurately the unofficial opinion of the Chief of Naval Operations and the Commanders-in-Chief of the Fleets in regard to particular officers, it was not too difficult a task to do this well, without interference from the Secretary of the Navy or Assistant Secretary of the Navy, who generally had only a brief and cursory knowledge of the seagoing capabilities of the seagoing Line officers of the Navy.

It does not seem to me that any officer detail system which permits civilian officials, with only one or two years association with officers (and mainly in an administrative capacity), to determine the selection or assignment of officers to subordinate commands in the fighting Fleets, can be other than to the detriment of the professional standards of the Navy and to its leadership for combat operations.

Three and Four-Star Billets 1939

The seven billets carrying advanced rank and their occupants in February 1939 were:

Chief of Naval Operations (4 stars): Admiral William D. Leahy, USN
Commander-in-Chief, U.S. Fleet (4 stars): Admiral C. C. Bloch, USN
Commander-in-Chief, Asiatic Fleet (4 stars): Admiral H. E. Yarnell, USN
Commander Battle Force, U.S. Fleet (4 stars): Admiral E. C. Kalbfus, USN
Commander Scouting Force, U.S. Fleet (3 stars): Vice Admiral A. Andrews, USN
Commander Aircraft, Battle Force (3 stars): Vice Admiral E. J. King, USN
Commander Battleships, Battle Force (3 stars): Vice Admiral J. W. Greenslade, USN[5]

During the 1933-1939 period, when I was in a knowledgeable status in regard to these matters, the final determination in regard to assignments to these seven billets was made by President Franklin Delano Roosevelt,

---

[5] Note: Admiral Leahy would be 64 in May 1939 and Admiral Yarnell the same age in October 1939. Admiral Bloch had been at sea for well over two years. Kalbfus, King, and Greenslade had been in their present sea commands since January 1938 and at sea since January 1937, June 1936, and January 1937 respectively. Under the normal procedure of two years at sea, they were all overdue for shore assignment.

Andrews had gone to sea only the previous June and was to remain at sea another year, although not necessarily in the same assignment.

who knew, or was acquainted with, and in either case, had very decided views on, nearly all senior naval officers, particularly of the seagoing branch.

While the President was most active and the final arbiter in this field, the Secretary of the Navy, the Assistant Secretary, and the Chief of Naval Operations all voiced opinions to the President, in addition to an occasional opinion the President received from the Chief of the Bureau of Navigation.

And a very real effort was made by all of these subordinates of the President to assure that the President should not substitute his arbitrary judgment or his personal likes and dislikes for that of the normal naval processes in picking officers for high command. These efforts were far from being 100 percent successful.

Mr. Swanson, the Secretary of the Navy, was Secretary from March 4, 1933 to July 9, 1939, and had known many naval officers during his previous long service as a Senator on the Naval Affairs Committee.

By the time Mr. Swanson had been Secretary for four or five years, he knew reasonably well a large percentage of the 73 Line and Staff admirals which the Navy was allowed in those days. However, his acquaintance with the approximately 475 captains was limited, in general, to those captains who had served in the Navy Department or in the few ships in which he had cruised.

He saw a good deal of the senior officers in the Staff Corps, as the Staff Bureaus were directly under his administrative control, and, of course, practically all of the Staff Corps senior officers served ashore and a large percentage in the Departmental bureaus. So, it probably is a reasonable assumption that by 1937 or 1938 Secretary Swanson was well qualified for making the final determination for the heads of the Staff Corps bureaus in the Navy Department since, for some of the bureaus, there were only 12 captains from whom to chose. In any case, I believe that his was the final determination.

As for Line officers, with their much greater numbers and with half of them serving at sea all the time, he was far less well-qualified to select them for important assignments, either afloat or ashore, so he listened to the advice of his naval advisors and passed this along to the President.

However, his long personal friendship with the President, as well as his opinions formed as the Secretary, frequently worked to the advantage of officers with service in the Navy Department when they were due for sea duty. It certainly had so worked out in my case, and in the case of

Stark, who had done an outstanding job as Chief of the Bureau of Ordnance just previous to going to sea as Commander Cruisers, Battle Force, United States Fleet.

The purpose of the next four chapters is to orient the reader back to 1939 with some details of:

(a) The world political scene in 1939

(b) The national political scene in 1939

(c) The approved and promulgated policies under which the Navy operated in 1939

(d) The organization, composition, and distribution of the 1939 Navy

Chapter II

The World Political Scene in 1939

I know, from my talks with naval officers who have come to maturity subsequent to World War II, how greatly they lack, and how difficult it is for me to recreate for them in clear and vivid pictures "the spirit of the times" of the long years between World War I and World War II.

While I think a full appreciation of this "spirit of the times" is most desirable for understanding the naval history of the period, I believe its exposition would require a book of its own. And I am not going to write that book.

However, it does seem desirable for me to log a few of the major world politico-military events of this period and add a few comments, even though this will in no way represent a balanced or adequate or historical treatment of the events. Primarily, the events logged will be the ones which I remember now as affecting my thinking, as they happened.

In this chapter, I will include events taking place from 1930 until I took over command of the Battle Force of the United States Fleet in late June of 1939.

Subsequent world politico-military events, which affected my thinking or actions in a major manner, will be referred to in the appropriate later chapters.

Because of their greater interest to me, and my fuller knowledge thereof, I am going to separate the events occurring in the Far East from those in Europe, and cover the former somewhat more fully.

The Far East

In the light of after knowledge, I suspect now, that the dual-headed national government in Japan, one military, one civilian, really underwent its first modern trial in September 1931. For it was on September 18, 1931, when under the pretext of suppressing local disorders which had culminated in the killing of a Japanese Army officer by Chinese soldiers, that Japanese troops, acting without the approval of the Japanese Foreign Ministry, commenced the occupation of various cities, including Mukden, in southern Manchuria. While the world meekly lamented, the occupation expanded, during the next three months, to all of Manchuria.

These Japanese acts of war were in direct violation of the Covenant of the League of Nations, the Nine-Power Treaty (1922), and the Kellogg-Briand Pact (1928) for the renunciation of war as an instrument of national policy. Japan had signed all of these documents.

In January 1932, the United States policy of non-recognition of any of the results obtained in China by the Japanese, thru their illegal use of force, in violation of existing treaties, did not receive immediate support by other signatories of the Nine-Power Treaty. It was my understanding that initially it was turned down by the government of Great Britain and subsequently, by France, Italy, and the Netherlands, although on March 11, 1932, the League of Nations resolution creating a Commission of Inquiry into the matter was supported by these four nations. I was made painfully aware that the majority of the governments and peoples of Europe were uninterested, or unwilling to be greatly interested, in China or in maintaining the sacredness of their signed word.

The Japanese military operations for the seizure of the city of Shanghai, with its large international population and world-wide commercial interests, which commenced on January 28, 1932, seemed to me to be Japan's answer to the failure of Europe and America to take a strong military stand against the Manchurian adventure.

As Secretary of State Stimson has written:

> He [President Hoover] said he would fight for Continental United States as far as anybody, but he would not fight for Asia. . . . In taking this position Mr. Hoover was squarely in line with the whole tradition of American foreign policy in the Far East. Even Theodore Roosevelt had always insisted that American interests in the Orient were not worth a war.[1]

The comparative disinterest of the American people in this strong, first move of the Japanese militarists toward the conquest of Asia and the closing of the long-existing "Open Door" to China was disheartening to me,

---

[1] Henry L. Stimson and McGeorge Bundy, *On Active Service in Peace and War* (New York: Harper and Brothers, 1947), pp. 243-44.

and somewhat of a surprise, for I had believed our attachment to China was firm.

By February 24, 1933, seventeen months after the start of Japan's aggression, the League of Nations finally bound its members not to recognize the new state of Manchukuo, created by Japan from Manchuria and the additional Chinese province of Jehol. A month later, March 27, 1933, Japan withdrew from the League of Nations.

These events made plain to me that, even when it was aroused, the united moral condemnation of the world was not a force which could be relied upon for success in dealing with the strong expansionist policies of the Japanese Government.

Japan's next major step was on December 29, 1934, when she announced that she would withdraw, at the end of 1936, from the Naval Limitation Treaty signed at Washington on February 6, 1922. Six months after having been released from her obligations to limit the size of her Navy, Japan began direct war on the central government of China, the initial fighting taking place west of Peiping (Peking). Tientsin, the main port of northern China, was bombed on July 29, 1937. Peiping, the old capital of China, was occupied on August 11th. Shanghai was evacuated by the Chinese Army on November 8th, and Hankow was established as the new capital of the central government of China on December 12. That same day, *USS Panay* (PR-5) was sunk in the Yangtze River by Japanese bombers.

The *Panay* Incident, which will be detailed somewhat more fully later, since I had a personal part to play therein, greatly affected my future interests and my then current opinions. It deepened my interest in our Navy's war plans. It made me realize that our Navy was most inadequate in size to wage war successfully against the Japanese Navy of that period.

The *Panay* sinking, and the almost universal approval by the press and the people of what seemed to me in 1937, to be the administration's conciliatory, if not meek and supine reaction to the incident, strengthened my belief that it was not so much the counsels of prudence and restraint which were governing our actions in world affairs, as the desire of the American people for a quiet and pleasurable life, and the reaction of the administration to this desire.

By October 1938, the Japanese had occupied Canton, the main Chinese port in southern China and, worse yet, Hankow, the year-old capital of the Chinese central government. On the last day of 1938, Secretary Hull sent

NH 54765

USS Panay *in Chinese waters.*

another of this government's many notes to Japan. This one categorically denied "the validity of the conception of Japanese authorities of a new situation and a new order in East Asia."

I could not see that our "word war" with the Japanese was having any success.

On February 10, 1939, the Japanese landed armed forces on the Chinese island of Hainan. This large island, lying off the northern part of French Indochina and on the western flank of the sea route from Hong Kong to Singapore, marked the most southern penetration of the Japanese up to that time.

Seven weeks later, on March 31, 1939, Japan announced the annexation of the Spratly Islands. These islands, lying 700 miles southwest of Manila and between the southern Philippines and Indochina, had been previously claimed by France, and their annexation presaged further pressure on France in connection with Japanese interests in Indochina.

As Japan pushed further and further into Southeast Asia, the execution of our current war plan against Japan became more and more impracticable with the naval forces available. These plans implied a capability of the Fleet to be moved further westward by the President, should Japan move further southward.

Despite this lack of war capability, the United States Fleet's schedule was suddenly changed by the President, and in mid-April 1939, it was ordered back to the Pacific.

The first good Far Eastern news for many, many months came in May 1939, when open border fighting between Japanese and Soviet troops was reported near Lake Bor Nor.

I hoped that these border skirmishes between Japan and the Soviet Union would blossom forth into a full-blown war between these nations. Such a war, I believed, would stop the southward expansion of Japan and divert Soviet strength and efforts from its subversion of democratic countries.

Shortly after this border war between Japan and the Soviet Union was reported, I started to pack my bags for leaving Washington. News on the military and political alliance of Germany and Italy was crowding the developments in the Far East off the front pages of the newspapers. All eyes were turned towards Europe by the signing, between Germany and Italy on May 7 and 22, 1939, of the political alliance and the ten-year military pact known as the "Pact of Steel."

Europe

Just as there is a strong affinity between communist nations in the post-World War II years today, in the past there have been periods when there was strong affinity between nations controlled by dictators, even though the political philosophies of the individual dictators might be aimed in quite different directions.

The eastern periphery of Europe (Russia) acquired a dictator in 1917. The southern and southeastern peripheries of Europe acquired three dictators in 1922-1923 (Mussolini in Italy in 1922, Kemal Ataturk in Turkey in 1923 and Primo de Rivera in Spain in 1923).

On the northern periphery, Chancellor Adolf Hitler of Germany acquired dictatorial powers in 1933 and 1934 and merged the chancellorship and the presidency on the death of President Von Hindenburg on 2 August 1934.

When this latter event happened, there seemed to me to be a strong possibility that these dictators might all join arms in a circle and squeeze the center of Europe. If they did this, something was bound to pop. The actual joining of dictatorial arms never included the Turks or the Spanish, and attained its maximum squeeze only during a couple of years (1939-1941). But there were some fairly significant poppings, during the short era of dictators, on the northern and southern anchorage positions of Europe's periphery: Austria, Czechoslovakia, Poland, the Baltic States, and Albania to mention only the obvious.

I think there is a point in the way these "birds of a feather" flocked together—not only for the present, but the future.

The almost continuous round of disarmament conferences which had occupied the energies and attention of the world since World War I, finally was made completely futile when, on October 14, 1933, Germany withdrew simultaneously from the League of Nations and the Geneva disarmament conference. In retrospect, 1933 was a very bad year for the League of Nations. Hitler had come to power as Chancellor of Germany on January 30, Japan had withdrawn from the League on March 27, and now Germany was to be a non-member.

Although in 1934 the Soviet Union joined the League of Nations, on September 18, this accession of strength did not balance-out previous losses. In 1934, the gong was to sound for the beginning of the final round for the League. For on August 2, 1934, President Von Hindenburg died, and

Adolf Hitler took over as President of Germany, in addition to his duties as Chancellor. On December 9, 1934, the first clash between troops of Ethiopia (Abyssinia) and Italy occurred.

On March 9 and 16, 1935, Hitler announced the re-creation of the German Air Force and the introduction of conscription for the German Army, both in contravention of the Versailles Treaty. A month later, nineteen countries in the League of Nations registered their disapproval of the unilateral repudiation of treaties by Germany. Stronger action against Germany failed of support by League members.

It seemed to me that each of the countries in the League of Nations which refused to take any stronger action than to vote for the resolution expressing disapproval of the unilateral violation by Germany of the Versailles Treaty and the Locarno Pact, was expressing its willingness that the League of Nations should never become an effective instrument for world peace.

On October 3, 1935, Italian troops invaded Ethiopia. On November 14, the Conservative Party won the British election by a large majority, running on the platform that "there must be no war" against Italy over Ethiopia, and that "there must be no large rearmament program" by the British to match growing German strength.

This seemingly impressive election victory for "peace and pacifism" brought home to me the attraction of such debilitating slogans for political parties in the English speaking nations.

The British action during and subsequent to the Italian-Ethiopian War was ineffective and difficult to understand. It seemed to me that their verbal condemnation of Italy merely irritated the Italians and seemed certain to alienate Italy from helping to maintain the future integrity of Austria. During 1935, when Germany tried to expand into Austria, Italy's concentration of 48,000 troops on the Austrian border had tipped the scales against Germany. And Germany had backed down from its then current intention of annexing Austria. It didn't seem possible to me that Italy would help the British and French again in this manner.

The British failure to support strong measures by the League of Nations in the Italian-Ethiopian War put the final nail in the coffin of the League of Nations, long before Italy completed its conquest of Ethiopia in May 1936 and withdrew from the League on December 11, 1937.

The Anglo-Italian agreement of April 16, 1938, in which the British confirmed Italy's conquest of Ethiopia, and the British pressure on Czechoslovakia in late September 1938 to accept German proposals for local autonomy for German populated areas in Czechoslovakia (and later the cession of Sudetenland to Germany), cost the British heavily, in my estimation. For my money, the British had lost markedly more in moral stature than Germany and Italy had gained in physical stature, even after Germany had forced the Republic of Czechoslovakia to dissolve in March 1939, and German troops had occupied Bohemia and Moravia.

The willingness of the British to appease the Italian aggressor in Ethiopia and the German aggressor in Czechoslovakia, by urging the smaller nations to accept the penalties of being weak, was an unpleasant surprise to me.

These actions, coupled with what I thought was the British failure to support, even diplomatically, the United States moral position versus Japan in the early days of the Manchurian crisis in 1931, led me to question whether Great Britain could be relied upon to fight, with arms, for a world moral cause.[2]

I did not believe that the United States could be expected to go to war unless directly attacked.

So, it seemed to me it would be more appropriate for our leaders to leave pious pronouncements or belligerent statements, in regard to the world's moral causes, to others, and to confine our main attention to matters close to home.

Summary

In summary, the "Spirit of the Times" in world affairs was such that the nations which wanted major changes in the status quo did something about creating these changes, and the nations which wanted the world to remain largely as it was, seemed willing only to diplomatically protest these changes, to moralize about them, and to wring their hands.

Peace was still the major password to political success.

At times, it appeared as if political party success in this country and in Great Britain was considered more important by the leaders (Roosevelt, Baldwin, and Chamberlain) than the strong medicine necessary if the long-range security of their nations was to be fully maintained.

---

[2] Alfred E. Zimmern, *The League of Nations and the Rule of Law 1918-1935* (London: Macmillan and Co., Ltd., 1939), p. 428; Felix Morley, *The Society of Nations: Its Organization and Constitutional Development* (Washington, D.C.: The Brookings Institution, 1932), p. 442.

Chapter III

The National Scene in 1939

In June 1939, when I left the Bureau of Navigation for sea duty, I did so with a wonderful feeling of pleasurable relief from the politically surfeited atmosphere of Washington and with an old sailor's anticipation of soon breathing some good clean sea air into his lungs.

In Washington, it seemed to me, I was well ahead of my contemporaries, political bosses, and the Congress in my feeling of urgency to get our Navy ready for war by getting the necessary men into it for proper training. In the Fleet, I felt sure, there would be plenty of officers and men who single-purposedly would be giving all their time and energy to preparing their commands and personnel for war. I would be much happier to be working with them.

The political temper of the country appeared to vary sharply from section to section and even from state to state. Opinions ran the gamut, from those who believed that the United States should take sides in the quarrelings of Europe's communist, socialist, fascist, and democratic governments, to those who believed we should not even have an interest in these quarrels, except to ensure keeping them out of our doors. A few would even have closed the windows to keep out the noise of the quarrels.

As a Chief of Bureau, I daily scanned the *Congressional Record,* which an aide had marked up and placed on my desk. I looked at the speeches, as well as the editorials and other cut-outs which appeared therein at the behest of some member of Congress.

It seemed to me that very large segments of the American people had hypnotized themselves into believing that what they wanted to happen in international affairs would happen. The American people wanted peace; therefore there would be peace. The American people wanted an end to bad nazism and bad fascism; therefore, there would be an end to bad nazism and bad fascism. The American people wanted communism to stay clear of their shores; therefore, communism would stay clear of their shores. The way for the United States to have peace was to have no international obligations, to mind one's own business, and to tell others to mind theirs.

It was easy and simple and stupid. But the strength of this feeling tempered every new measure taken in the national defense field during my two years in the Navy Department from 1937 to 1939.

In early June, I had just finished a very pleasant chore, acting as aide to the King (George VI) and Queen (Elizabeth) of England during their visit (June 7-11, 1939) to the United States. It was quite obvious that their visit, or even the opening of the World's Fair in New York City (April 30, 1939), had carried a higher billing in the newspapers than the signing of the military and political alliance by Germany and Italy, the Pact of Steel, on May 7, 1939.

I didn't like this—I wasn't sure I fully understood why. But I was sure that in real significance to my country, there was no comparison between the events.

But, maybe a selfish interest inside me kept hoping that this isolationist philosophy of disinterest would turn out to be a correct one. For a professional sailorman, with a strong distaste for war (because it leads to the killing of so many of the best young men of the coming generation and the diversion of so many of our material resources to this business of killing), it would have been just wonderful, if true, that Europe's and Asia's power struggles were no concern of the United States. For the German and Japanese navies were getting larger, and proportionally much faster than our own Navy.

To make it short, I will discuss only three of the many matters which I might cover to illustrate the "spirit of the times."

The first will be disarmament, and the major events I logged are as follows:

DISARMAMENT

1919 Versailles Treaty providing for disarmament of Germany

1922 Washington Naval Treaty limiting naval armaments of France, Great Britain, Italy, Japan, and the United States

1928 Kellogg-Briand Pact of Paris, by which all the major powers renounced war as an instrument of national policy

1930 London Naval Reduction Treaty further limiting naval armament of Great Britain, Japan, and the United States, effective January 1, 1931

1931 Five-year holiday on all capital-ship construction (until 1936)
1932 Geneva World Disarmament Conference (No agreement reached)
1932 Herriot Disarmament Plan (No agreement reached)
1933 MacDonald Disarmament Plan (No agreement reached)
1934 Japanese denounce 1922 Washington Naval Limitations Treaty
1936 London Naval Arms Limitation Treaty between France, Great Britain, and the United States, initial effective dates January 1, 1937, to December 31, 1942

The advocates of disarmament were strong during this period, and their cause was popular. All senior naval officers, of course, were vitally concerned about the continuous proposals and the three agreements reached in the field of naval disarmament (1922, 1931, and 1936).

It did not seem logical to me, then or now, that our political leaders should continue to accept some reductions and many limitations in the field of sea power, when the great land powers of the world were not accepting similar reductions or limitations for their armies. Such a policy was altering the relative overall strength of the nations in favor of the land army powers.

The land army powers were continually examining the proposal for world security thru land power disarmament and continually finding it unacceptable. At the same time, the major sea powers, the United States, Great Britain, and Japan, were examining the same proposal for world security through sea power disarmament, and the first two named were finding it quite acceptable. For, even after Japan refused to continue to support further sea power disarmament proposals, the political leaders of Great Britain and the United States continued to agree to change downward the relative ratios of overall strength of their countries versus the land power countries.

In the early years of the decade (prior to September 1934), when the Soviet Union was not a member of the League of Nations and not participating in the disarmament talks, it didn't make sense to me for my country to be urging the French to reduce their land power. For that would change the scales of world power in favor of world communism, centered in the Soviet Union. After Germany had withdrawn from the League of Nations and was rearming in violation of its treaty obligations, it made even less sense for the other countries to continue to urge the French to reduce their land power. But they did.

I was one of the many who greatly overestimated the caliber of the French Army during this period. But the fact that this Army was a major factor acting in restraint of Germany and the Soviet Union remains correct, whether or not it was good or indifferent in caliber.

But the "spirit of the times" was disarmament for the sake of disarmament. And anyone who talked for maintaining the basic security and relative strength of his country was likely to find himself labeled a warmonger.

Neutrality Acts

The second matter which I have selected to illustrate the "spirit of the times" is our neutrality acts of the middle and late 1930's.

Firstly, it seems desirable to look back at our old logs in order to have available a few essential facts and dates before commenting on the subject.

I believe it can be said honestly that the Neutrality Act of August 31, 1935 had as its purpose an impartial arms embargo. The Act embargoed the export of arms, munitions, or other implements of war from any place in the United States to any port of the declared belligerents. In addition, it embargoed the transportation of similar exports by American ships, not only to belligerent ports, but to any neutrals who might be of a mind to pass them on or resell them to the belligerents. It did not forbid the export of other sinews of war such as oil or scrap iron. It did not provide for any action during undeclared wars, unless the President took affirmative action and found that a state of war existed.

The February 1936 Neutrality Act extended until May 1, 1937 and amended the 1935 Neutrality Act, leaving some provisions intact. It contained strengthened financial provisions including one which forbade the making of loans or granting of credits to belligerents by U.S. citizens, banks, or corporations. It gave the President discretion to decide whether or not a state of hostilities existed.

The second Neutrality Act was on the statute books when the outbreak of the civil war in Spain occurred in July 1936. Nothing happened until President Roosevelt, at a press conference in December 1936, suggested the extension of neutrality legislation to the civil war in Spain. Upon its reconvening, the Congress promptly set to work.

In early 1937, an emergency addition to the 1936 Neutrality Act became law. It forbade the export of arms to both sides in a civil war.

President Roosevelt, who had applied the previous Neutrality Acts to the

Italian-Ethiopian War, now placed an embargo on munitions for the Spanish Civil War.

There was a further revision to the Neutrality Act, in May 1937, which, in some respects, weakened the previous Act, although the provisions which made it illegal to export arms to any belligerent, or to either side in a civil war, or to transport such material on United States ships, were continued.

In the May 1937 revision, the President received authority to establish a list of prohibited goods which could not be exported, except on a "Cash and Carry" basis. Cash and carry goods could only be exported in non-American bottoms. The President could extend or diminish the list of prohibited goods at his discretion. This "Cash and Carry" provision, under which foreign ships could load in our ports a wide range of essential war material, other than arms and munitions, provided title had passed out of the hands of U.S. citizens, became the most important feature of the 1939 Neutrality Act.

The Navy was one of the agencies involved in the enforcement of the Neutrality Acts. Copies of the acts were duly distributed to the naval commanders concerned. But the "spirit of the times" was such that the Navy had to learn that words did not necessarily mean what they said.

For the Italian-Ethiopian War, the United States neutrality legislation was strictly enforced.

For the Chinese-Japanese War, a far larger and more important war so far as United States interests were concerned, the legislative provisions were not even placed in effect. The U.S. Government never found that a state of war existed.

It seemed to me that the United States' word should be as good as its bond. If there is a law on the books, covering our dealings with foreign nations, which is not in our national interest to carry out, the law should be repealed. I believe that the standards of fascism, nazism, and communism are that the end justifies the means and that a lie which serves the purposes of their creed is a worthy matter. I did not believe that a Christian democracy should adopt the standards of an atheistic dictatorship, and it grieved me when our President apparently publicly engaged in subterfuge.

From 1938 to 1940, I was much concerned when we continued to ship oil and scrap iron and many similar war-making materials to the Japanese. I believed that these sinews of war would help Japan destroy our friends the Chinese or, worse yet, would be saved for use against us, should we continue to intrude with our freewheeling advice on Japan's territorial expansion.

Had the United States, in 1937, placed the Neutrality Act in effect on both Japan and China, we would not have created a series of crises in our relations with Japan, as we did when we took step-by-step action in 1940. I do not believe that the end result for China would have been any different than it turned out to be.

In the Neutrality Act of 4 November 1939, the provisions of the Neutrality Acts of 1935 and 1937 were markedly weakened by not repeating those parts therein relating to the arms embargo.

World War I Influence

As we moved toward World War II, the beliefs of the American people in regard to our entry into World War I influenced American actions greatly. These beliefs were a real part of the "spirit of the times" and will be my third illustration.

Secretary of State Stimson summed it up well in these words:

> . . . many Americans were persuaded by a new school of writers that in 1917 they had gone to war not because of unrestricted submarine warfare, and still less because Imperial Germany threatened the world's freedom, but because of the munitions makers, the bankers, and the sly propagandists of England and France.[1]

One of the extensive Congressional investigations and debates which occurred in the middle 1930's, was in regard to the munitions industry. Senator Gerald P. Nye from North Dakota, during a Senate investigation of the munitions industry, developed and gave widespread publicity to the "bamboozlement" that the reason the United States entered World War I was to provide profits for those who operated the munitions industry. And then he went one step further and said there was no reason for war at any time, except to provide profits for those who operated the munitions industry. These pronouncements reportedly were accepted by many as gospel truth.

So, in 1937-1939, the munitions industry was considered by many to be in bad odor. During this period, the entry of many concerns into new contractual relations with the Navy was highly desirable in order to provide

[1] Stimson and Bundy, *On Active Service*, p. 308.

a broad logistic base for naval mobilization. The "spirit of times" was such that the run-of-the-mill management could let some concern, other than their own, acquire some of the bad odor surrounding the munitions industry and keep away from taking steps essential to the industrial preparedness of the United States.

A further aspect of this "spirit of the times" was reflected in 1937 by the Ludlow Resolution in Congress. The Ludlow Resolution provided that a national referendum would be required before a declaration of war by the Congress, under any circumstances except a direct armed attack. A Gallup poll showed that seventy-five percent of the people questioned approved this severe restriction upon the constitutional authority of the Congress. The impossibility of bringing all the facts to the attention of all the electorate, so that they might make a knowledgeable decision, and the lessening of the strength of the United States in the councils of the world that would take place, were the executive and legislative branches of the government to be so hamstrung, did not deter the many supporters of this resolution. Fortunately, the resolution was defeated in the House.

The expansion of our Military Services was under constant attack from neutralist and pacifist groups in and out of the Government. As a result, our Armed Forces were small enough to be almost puny.

Our foreign policy, which, according to the statements of the nation's political leaders, had its basis in justice and morality, did not have the strengthening influence which would have come from a strong Navy and a strong Army.

Our President, in the 1937-1939 period, had made frequent statements critical of the actions of Japan in Asia and of Germany in Europe. But it followed, as night does day, that this nation, which did not have at hand the military power to support its professed high standards of conduct which it desired to control in the international field, was not listened to with respect. And at times, it seemed to be listened to only with derision.

Another indication of "the spirit of the times"—even more so than today—was a constant urgency by the Congress and by the public to reveal all the details of our limited military preparations, presumably on the assumption that the other nations of the world would be impressed by our strength. I did not believe that they were so impressed.

As we learned during and after World War II, the Germans and Japanese were able to hide from us tremendous increases in their numerical strength and technical features of their armed forces made during this period. These hidden resources gave our enemies real advantages which could not be balanced in the early days of the war.

The Acting Secretary of the Navy, Charles Edison, was to say in his annual report to the President for the fiscal year ending June 30, 1939 that:

> The Navy is prepared to exercise its vital function of bringing the enemy to our terms as quickly as possible, while keeping him at a safe distance from our shores.[2]

When I left Washington in June, I had heard no responsible naval officer voice such an opinion, and I didn't believe this to be anything like the truth. But I hoped that it might become true before war was thrust upon the United States.

The Secretary's statement just couldn't be true because the ships of the Fleet were considerably understrength in officers and in men. The Fleet was lacking, almost entirely, the auxiliary ships needed if the Fleet was to move away from home base " . . . to bring the enemy to our terms. . . ."[3]

Such all-encompassing statements as these in the *Annual Reports of the Secretary of the Navy* can rarely be true in time of peace. They are a disservice to the country, if war occurs, and can only bring criticism on the Navy by the citizens of the country, who have no real knowledge of its actual strength and readiness. However, this statement was typical of the times. It was what many American citizens would want to be true, and so by saying it, the Secretary apparently hoped it would be true.

In 1939, I believe that many Americans were in a dream world where they believed "an apple a day keeps the doctor away."

[2] SECNAV (Charles Edison, Acting), *Annual Report,* 1939, p. 1.

[3] *Ibid.,* p. 1.

The Approved and Promulgated Policies Under Which the Navy Operated in 1939

In the fourteen and more years that have elapsed since the Pearl Harbor disaster, it has been easy and it has been common, to overlook:

(1) the Governmental and Departmental (Navy) policy fundamentals which closely controlled the Forces Afloat (the operating Navy) during the pre-Pearl Harbor decade, 1930-1940

(2) the organization, composition, and manning levels of the Forces Afloat during the pre-Pearl Harbor decade, 1930-1940

Also unknown to many now, but of tremendous importance then, in influencing the actions and decisions of a Commander-in-Chief were:

(3) the annual pattern of Fleet training operations

(4) the annual pattern of officer and enlisted personnel movement which had developed within the Forces Afloat (the operating Navy) during this same 1930-1940 period

U.S. NAVAL POLICY 1930-1940

Presidential and Congressional Policies

What were the fundamental policies approved by the President and the Congress and written into law or treaties, under which the Navy operated in the 1930-1940 period?

In the main, these were sixfold and contained in the:

(A) 1922 Washington Naval Treaty and concurrent agreements
(B) 1930 London Naval Treaty
(C) 1934 Vinson-Trammell Naval Bill
(D) 1936 London Naval Treaty
(E) 1938 Naval Expansion Act
(F) 1940 Naval Expansion Acts[1]

(A) The 1922 Washington Naval Treaty designated by name the capital ships which each nation might retain and established future basic ratios of naval strength between the United States, Great Britain, Japan, France, and Italy in the categories of capital ships and aircraft carriers at 5-5-3-1.67-1.67 (525,000 tons of battleships for the United States and Great Britain, 315,000 tons for Japan, 175,000 tons for France and Italy; 135,000 tons of aircraft carriers for the United States and Great Britain, 81,000 tons for Japan, and 60,000 tons for France and Italy). It restricted the displacement of future replacement battleships to 35,000 tons and replacement aircraft carriers to 27,000 tons. It left cruisers, destroyers, and submarines unrestricted as to total tonnage or numbers, but restricted each of these types to not more than 10,000 tons displacement and their armaments to a gun no larger than 8″. It established the useful life of capital ships and aircraft carriers as twenty years and authorized their replacement with new ships at that time, providing the total treaty tonnage in that type was not exceeded. United States insular possessions in the western Pacific Ocean (Samoa, Guam, and the Philippines) were required to remain in their status quo as to fortifications and naval bases. No increase could be made in repair or maintenance facilities, of any kind, at any of the British, Japanese, or United States naval bases in this area, west of the 180th meridian and north of the equator to 30 degrees north latitude.

(B) The 1930 London Naval Treaty in all its provisions governed only the navies of Great Britain, the United States, and Japan, since France had opposed the concept of ratios and Italy was unwilling to accept any inequality. No capital ships were to be laid down during the 1931-1936 period. The battleship strength already afloat was to be further reduced by

[1] Actual authorization for the construction of eight scout cruisers was contained in the act of 18 December 1924 and for fifteen light cruisers in the Act of 13 February 1929. Authorization for the use of funds for the purpose of construction of naval vessels, within the terms and/or limits established by the London Naval Treaty of 1930, was contained in the National Industrial Recovery Act of 16 June 1933.

NH 61253

USS Delaware *(BB-28) about 1920, one of the battleships scrapped under the terms of the Washington Naval Treaty.*

the early scrapping of five ships by Great Britain, three by the United States, and one by Japan. This agreement established two types of cruisers; heavy cruisers mounted with 8″ guns and light cruisers mounted with guns of 6″ or smaller. Limits for total cruiser tonnage were established (U.S., 323,500 tons, Great Britain, 339,000 tons, Japan, 308,850 tons). All future cruisers were limited to a maximum of 10,000 tons displacement.

Submarines were limited to 2,000 tons displacement and to guns not larger than 5.1″. Destroyers were limited to 1,850 tons displacement and to guns no larger than 5.1″.

The useful life of new cruisers was established as 20 years, of destroyers as 16 years, and of submarines as 13 years. Replacement was to be made only after these periods. The ratio of cruiser strength established changed the overall ratio of naval strength to approximately 5, 5.2, and 3.25 for the United States, Great Britain, and Japan. Provisions of the treaty on the regulation of submarine warfare were accepted by France and Italy.

(C) The 1934 Vinson-Trammell Naval Bill envisaged the United States Navy being built up to reach its authorized treaty tonnage strength by 1942. While it authorized building to this strength, funds were to be provided in the future in annual naval appropriation bills. It was labeled the "Full Treaty Navy" Bill.

(D) The 1936 London Naval Treaty governed only the navies of the United States, Great Britain, and France, as the Japanese delegation had been withdrawn by Japan when its demand for parity in naval strength with the United States and Great Britain had been stated by these nations to be unacceptable.

The 1936 Treaty provided for a six-year building holiday for cruisers above 8,000 tons. It carried forward the provisions for the maximum permissable sizes of the various types of combatant ships and of the guns which the various types of ships could carry, contained in the 1922 and 1930 treaties. These provisions were about to expire. Maximum displacement of aircraft carriers was reduced from the 27,000-ton limit provided in the earlier 1922 treaty to 23,000 tons, and they were forbidden to carry a gun above 6.1″ in caliber.

On November 10, 1939, the Secretary of the Navy notified all ships and stations that all obligations of the 1936 London Naval Treaty had been suspended by all parties to that treaty.

(E) The 1938 Naval Expansion Act authorized the gradual building of the Navy over the next ten years but provided no funds. The Act authorized a total tonnage of 600,000 in capital ships, 412,500 in cruisers, and 175,000 in aircraft carriers. This was an increase of only 75,000 tons in battleship tonnage, 89,000 tons in cruiser tonnage, and 40,000 tons in aircraft carrier tonnage. It was popularly known in the Navy as the bill to provide a "Navy Second to None."

(F) There were two 1940 Naval Expansion Acts. The first was introduced early in the Congressional session and called for a twenty-five percent increase in authorized naval tonnage. Strong opposition by isolationist and pacifist groups delayed the passage of the bill for months and reduced its authorization to an 11 percent increase in tonnage. It was signed by the President on June 14, 1940, the day German troops entered Paris. Its provisions authorized an increase of 167,000 tons in the current overall total of carrier, cruiser, and submarine tonnage (combatant ships), as well as an additional 75,000 tons of auxiliary ships.

Three days later, on June 17, 1940, and just five days prior to the signing of the French-German armistice, Congressman Carl Vinson of Georgia introduced a second 1940 Naval Expansion Act. Its provisions authorized a further twenty-four percent increase in naval tonnage. To meet the request of the Chief of Naval Operations, Admiral Harold R. Stark, USN, based on the realities of the world situation, it was changed by the Congress to provide for a seventy percent increase in naval tonnage and a "Two Ocean Navy."

When this act was made law by the President's signature on July 19, 1940, a month and two days later, the Congress had established a modern speed record for action on a naval expansion bill.

What had been the effects of these Presidential and Congressional naval policies?

The Overall Effect of Presidential and Congressional Policies

It was my opinion in 1939 that the United States, through its participation in these naval limitation agreements, had suffered a substantial loss in relative naval power from that which had existed on January 1, 1922.

I did not believe that this adverse trend in relative naval power would be reversed by the United States taking the initiative toward a new or definite national power policy objective. Such a trend reversal had been accomplished by Japan, Germany, and the Soviet Union during the previous decade thru internal decisions, arrived at independently, but I thought a reversal would be accomplished in the United States only in reaction to some real hurt which another nation would inflict on us.

It was my opinion that Japan's:

1931 occupation of Manchuria
1932 (January to March) occupation of the Japanese district, Hongkew, Shanghai with Japanese troops
1934 notice of her termination of adherence to the 1922 Washington Naval Treaty (effective December 31, 1936)
1936 withdrawal from the London Naval Treaty conference
1937 (December 12) bombing of Peking, and launching of the China campaign
1937 sinking by bombing of *USS Panay*

had sounded a proper death knell to a noble experiment in naval limitation, but that many Americans had not heard the tolling of the bells. This was evidenced by the strong opposition to the limited aims of the 1938 Naval Expansion Acts.

It was not until I had been at sea a year that the Second Naval Expansion Act of 1940 had at last brought plans for naval building abreast of the realities of the then current world situation. But, it was two or three years too late to bring actual naval strength up to the requirements of the then current world situation.

Effect on Naval Technical Matters

The seventeen-year period (1922-1939) during which the various types of naval ships were limited in their displacement and armament was one of intense international competition between naval architects to realize the maximum offensive power and defensive strength out of each ton of naval displacement.

The competition increased markedly the previous rate of progress in ship design and ship building practices. Its effect, in this respect, was very good.

But, when the United States really started to get ready for World War II, it was found that our ships did not have characteristics and capabilities required by our prospective fighting needs. We had to begin to design and build new cruisers, carriers, and destroyers with the required capabilities. These ships did not get into service until the middle of the war.

Our pre-World War II ships were designed with no spare tonnage for new equipment normal to naval progress. When war needs required larger airplanes (and more of them), extensive voice radios, radars, degaussing installations, and strengthened antiaircraft batteries, the ships rapidly became badly overloaded. They became less capable of staying afloat after severe underwater damage and less capable of fighting well in bad weather. Due to extensive overcrowding with personnel needed for the additional equipment, poor habitability became an adverse morale factor.

On balance, the adverse effects of building to a "treaty ton" were far greater than the advantages in my viewpoint.

Departmental Naval Policies

What were the fundamental policies, approved by the Secretary of the Navy, under which the Navy operated during the 1930-1940 period?

Three comprehensive statements of United States Naval Policy were approved by the Secretary of the Navy during this decade on June 1, 1931, May 10, 1933, and July 23, 1940.

A recommended statement of U.S. Naval Policy submitted by the General Board of the Navy on February 18, 1937 was "noted" by the Secretary of the Navy and published to the Naval Service—but not officially approved.

So, the 1933 statement of Naval Policy of the United States remained in effect for seven years. Since it contained only minor changes from the 1931 statement of Naval Policy, its principles can be said to have had a controlling influence during the 1931-1941 decade.

It should be pointed out that one of the more pressing reasons for these formalized statements of Naval Policy was the requirement to obtain money annually from the Congress to operate the Navy. During the Congressional appropriation committee hearings, as well as the more detailed earlier hearings before the Bureau of the Budget, and before the Navy Department Budget Officer, each proposed expenditure had to find justification within the statement of Naval Policy.

One of the first steps within the Navy in the preparation of new budget estimates, was for the Secretary of the Navy to call upon the General Board to frame a statement of Naval Policy. This statement, if approved by the Secretary of the Navy, was then circulated throughout the Navy Department for use by all officers responsible for preparing budget estimates.

It was quite usual for the Secretary to play it safe by not accepting a new statement of Naval Policy, submitted by the General Board, even if concurred in by all Chiefs of Naval Bureaus and by the Chief of Naval Operations, but to reutilize the previous year's statement, particularly if this statement had met the pleasure of the Congress. This explains, in part, why only three new statements of U.S. Naval Policy were approved in a ten-year period.

Fundamental Naval Policy

When I went to sea in 1939, the Fundamental Naval Policy of the United States was:

> To maintain the Navy in sufficient strength to support the national policies and commerce, and to guard the continental and overseas possessions of the United States.[2]

In support of the Fundamental Naval Policy, there were fourteen General Policies. All these directly affected the United States Fleet and all the other Forces Afloat, but the four most important to the Fleet were:

> (1) To develop the Navy to a maximum in battle strength and ability to control the sea in defense of the Nation and its interests.
> (2) To make war efficiency the objective of all development and training and to maintain that efficiency at all times.
> (3) To encourage and to lead in the development of the art and material of naval warfare.
> (4) To organize the Navy for operations in either or both oceans so that expansion only will be necessary in the event of war.[3]

---

[2] "U.S. Naval Policy" (hereafter cited as "Naval Policy"), General Board (GB) no. 420-2, serial 1569 of 27 Apr. 1932, GB Files, Operational Archives Branch, Naval History Division (NHD), Washington, D.C., p. 1.

[3] *Ibid.*

Fleet Operating Policies

In further support of the Fundamental Policy of the U.S. Navy and its General Policies, there were ten Fleet Operating Policies. The more pertinent were as follows:

> (1) To organize forces afloat so as to obtain maximum administrative efficiency, tactical and strategical flexibility and mobility, decentralization and unity of command.
>
> (2) To operate forces afloat under balanced schedules designed to secure proficiency, discipline and contentment of personnel, and general excellence as to condition of material, administration, and technical, tactical and strategical performance.
>
> (3) To assemble the United States Fleet for a period of not less than two months at least once a year.[4]

Were these statements of fundamental policy important?

These statements of policies were very important in that they set up guidelines for specific directives issued by Navy Department authorities and Fleet commanders. These were the doctrine, well known to all senior officers in the Navy.

I believe this can be illustrated by pointing out some of the more important changes between the 1933 Naval Policy and the 1940 Naval Policy, changes dictated by world events.

They represented the policy difference between a Navy expecting a long period of peace and a Navy expecting war in the near future.

The 1940 Statement of Naval Policy

The 1940 Naval Policy, issued only four days after the President signed the 1940 Naval Expansion Act for the creation of a "Two Ocean Navy," took cognizance of this fact by stating as a new General Policy, in lieu of that stated in subparagraph (4) above of the 1939 Policy, the requirement:

> To organize and maintain the Navy for major operations in both the Atlantic and Pacific Oceans.[5]

Thus, the basic organization of the United States Fleet was changed from one fleet for two oceans to one fleet in each ocean. The change in basic Fleet

[4] *Ibid.*, p. 4.

[5] "Naval Policy," serial 1915 of 18 May 1940, chart.

guidelines, in the new Naval Policy, was also marked. The requirement, in subparagraph (1) of the 1933 Policy above, " . . . to organize the forces afloat so as to obtain maximum *administrative* efficiency . . ." was dropped completely—and the rest of the requirements of this paragraph were amplified and strengthened so as:

> To organize the forces afloat to obtain maximum flexibility, mobility, and effectiveness in strategical and tactical operations.
>
> • • •
>
> To give full effect to established command principles stressing unity of command and appropriate decentralization in both execution and administration.[6] (author's italics)

Thus, the "Unity of Command" principle was brought to the fore.

The change in emphasis in Fleet Operating Policies was even more marked. Instead of the policy being "To operate the forces afloat under balanced schedules designed to *secure proficiency, discipline, and contentment of personnel . . .* " the basic requirement was changed to, "To operate the forces afloat under balanced schedules formulated *to secure* excellence in strategy and tactics, gunnery, engineering and other technical performance and in material upkeep; and also *to promote* proficiency, discipline and contentment of personnel." (author's italics)[7]

Effect of Departmental Naval Policies

What had been the effect of these Departmental naval policies?

It is my opinion that these Departmental policies had contributed to formation of a well indoctrinated and cohesive personnel in the Navy, contented and well disciplined.

They had created a Navy intensively devoted to competition in aviation, gunnery, seamanship, communications, damage control, and engineering, and with a very high degree of technical skill in these areas of the naval profession.

They had led to very broad and very detailed studies of the strategy and tactics that would be entailed in a war with Japan and to a more limited study of the strategy and tactics entailed in a war with Germany.

---

[6] *Ibid.*

[7] *Ibid.*

They had led to a full integration of naval aviation and those officers particularly skilled in aviation into the Navy and the Fleet.

They had encouraged a marked development in amphibious operations and the use of the Fleet Marine Force in island operations.

I consider that the policies were sound and reasonably progressive.

The policies would have been even more progressive, if the Secretaries had not been so responsive to the strong isolationist and pacifist minorities in the United States Congress and amongst the American people.

The Commander-in-Chief, U.S. Fleet in his 1939 Annual Report stated:

> In April 1939, the *Ranger* [CV 4] was transferred to the Atlantic Squadron and Patrol Squadrons ELEVEN [San Diego] and TWELVE [San Diego] were transferred from Patrol Wing ONE [Pacific] to Patrol Wing FIVE [Atlantic]. The naval air strength assigned to the Atlantic was greatly increased.
>
> • • •
>
> In June [1939] Cruiser Division SEVEN was transferred to the Atlantic Squadron, leaving twelve heavy cruisers in the Pacific.
>
> • • •
>
> Effective 10 October 1938, the forces in the Atlantic, formerly designated as Training Detachment, U.S. Fleet became Atlantic Squadron U.S. Fleet [The four battleships of the Training Detachment became Battleship Division FIVE.][8]

Further indication of awareness of things to come, by the professional high command of the Navy, may be gleaned from recalling that 1939 was the fifth year in which large-scale amphibious operations were carried out;[9] that the annual summer cruise of the midshipmen of the U.S. Naval Academy, instead of following the normal pattern of visiting Europe, was in home waters;[10] and that one of our five carriers was transferred from the Pacific to the Atlantic Ocean.[11] All these decisions were taken prior to the summer of 1939 and months before war broke out in Europe on 1 September 1939.

---

[8] "Annual Report to the Commander-in-Chief, United States Fleet," (C.C. Bloch), for the period 1 July 1938 to 30 June 1939 (hereinafter cited as CINCUS, "Annual Report," with year), serial 01105 of 4 Aug. 1939, World War II Command File (WWIICF), NHD, p. 2.

[9] This was Fleet Landing Exercise Number Five.

[10] Halifax and Portland, Maine were the liberty ports.

[11] *USS Ranger* and attached squadrons were reassigned 15 April 1939.

ANNUAL PATTERN OF OFFICER AND ENLISTED PERSONNEL MOVEMENT 1930-1940

During this decade, the Navy had developed a very firm annual pattern of officer and enlisted personnel movement. This originated from the necessities of extreme austerity in the use of men and money. It was strongly supported, by those responsible for personnel management, because it ameliorated, to the extent possible, the family strains which arose when moving personnel from the Pacific to the Atlantic (or vice versa) or from either of these oceans to the inland naval stations in the United States.

I consider that this annual pattern was one of the major factors which kept resignation of professional officers at a low ebb and reenlistment of professional sailormen at a high flood during this decade. So, I will describe one of the major phases of the pattern.

The Naval Academy classes graduated in the first week of June each year. By and large, their numbers somewhat exceeded the vacancies which were to be caused in the officer corps on June 30 of each year by forced retirement of those officers who had twice failed of selection as best fitted for promotion to the next higher rank, as well as by resignations, physical retirements, and deaths.

The young ensigns from the Naval Academy were so distributed amongst the ships of the Fleet as to fill the vacancies in ship's officers complements about to be caused by the bringing ashore, for instruction in aviation or submarines, of ensigns in their second year of service, or of other officers of from five to seven years service who had been selected for postgraduate work. Considering the number of officers and men in the Navy, an extremely high percentage was kept under instruction at all times, either at naval schools or at various universities around the country.

The previous groups of postgraduate students were completing their two or three years under instruction in the various branches of the engineering profession or in advanced communications, aeronautics, or other diverse subjects during the same June period. They were available to fill vacancies in the Fleet, normally to occur when their postgraduate school predecessors, who by now were sea-trained specialists, were brought ashore into the various technical Bureaus.

It was a daisy chain of huge proportions.

Similarly, married enlisted personnel, whenever possible, were moved to long-term technical schools, to shore duty, or to duty on ships with new home ports, during the summer quarter.

All this personnel shifting was timed to permit personnel to move together with their families during the grade and high school summer vacation periods.

Each June and July about half of the officers of each ship or aircraft unit were changed. As soon as the new officers and men were aboard, a new year of training of the ship's company started.

This pattern of personnel movement, so conducive to high morale amongst naval personnel, had its disadvantage in that the battle efficiency of the individual ship or aircraft unit and of the Fleet as a whole was at its lowest ebb each June and July and at its highest peak each April or May of the year.

But I believe, on an overall basis, that it paid tremendous dividends to the Navy, for it trained and retained in the Navy a very high-grade corps of professional officers and sailormen.

ANNUAL PATTERN OF FLEET TRAINING OPERATIONS 1930 - 1940

During these ten years, a very effective competition was held throughout each year between individual ships, and between individual aircraft units for the improvement of the technical proficiency of each ship and aircraft of the Fleet. The details of the competition varied from type to type of ship or aircraft and from year to year, but covered the skills in airmanship, gunnery, communications, engineering, and damage control.

Officers' reputations were made or lost, and selection to higher rank influenced by the capabilities which commands or ship departments or units displayed in the various competitions. The competition could be classified as largely clean and keen—on occasion, it was cutthroat.

The competition year was from July 1 to June 30. As the teams on each ship started to break up in early June due to personnel transfers, it was desirable that the competitive exercises should be completed by June 1 each year.

During the first half of the competition year, competitive exercises were designed to train and test individuals and teams in the more elementary professional skills. Highly complicated exercises were scheduled in the second half of the training year, culminating in experimental exercises for advancing technical skills into new and untried areas. Ships or aircraft units were specially designated for these latter purposes.

During a large part of each competitive year, ships left port early Monday morning for the training areas and returned Thursday evening or Friday afternoon for a weekend in port, with inspection on Saturday morning. This regular schedule had a high morale value for the married personnel.

The competition detailed above was largely for the training of individual ships or air units or the lowest subdivision of ships or air units.

Fleet training at the Type and Force level was carried along simultaneously by the holding, each month or six-week period (depending on the plans of the Fleet or Force Commander), of minor tactical exercises. They were for the training of ships or aircraft of the same type, or the intertype or intratype training of ships or aircraft of various types, and covered the waterfront in their variations. A few of these were: search and scouting exercises by appropriate type planes and destroyers; air attacks of all types, and air defense against all types; night destroyer attacks, submarine attacks, and submarine defense; battleline attacks and defense.

Once each competition year, a large-scale Fleet Problem was held. All units of the Fleet, not under overhaul in navy yards or air stations, were gathered together in one large ocean area. The Fleet Problem lasted from six weeks to two months. During this period, the ships were kept in a modified war status of alertness for the unexpected.

The Fleet Problem to be solved was carefully set forth in considerable detail by the Fleet Commander. The major features had been worked out in the office of the Chief of Naval Operations and by various officers of the Fleet staff in order to test new capabilities or new theories of naval operations, or to retry old theories.

The Fleet was divided into appropriate task forces to permit realistic war operations to be carried on. Umpires were appointed at the unit and higher levels. The war games or war operations were fought with zest and determination, although only with modest realism (as real bullets or bombs could not be used) and great risk to life, limb, and government property could not be taken.

Naval aircraft training off Diamond Head. NH 77057

Following the games, individual Force critiques were held and then finally a Fleet critique. All officers of command rank and many of lesser rank attended the critiques. The battles of the Fleet Problem were vigorously refought from the speaker's platforms. The Fleet Commander summed up at the end and everybody was told to apply the lessons learned. Voluminous data were collected and voluminous reports issued.

Like the Army-Navy game, there was always a next year to get back at a more fortunate opponent. The annual Fleet Problem stimulated thought on operational problems and was one of the foundation stones of our naval readiness for war.

Chapter V

The Strength, Organization, and Distribution of the 1939 Navy Afloat

The Actual Operating Navy (the Forces Afloat) in 1939

Having considered the policy fundamentals, the next requirement is to consider the organization, composition, and manning levels of ships and aircraft of the operating Navy (Forces Afloat).

Some people shrink from the realities of facts and figures. But to me, facts and figures seem essential to any adequate understanding of the steps taken, during the 1939, 1940, and early 1941 period, to prepare for war tasks that part of the United States Navy assigned to the Forces Afloat. I believe that there must be readily available to the reader, in some detail, the data regarding:

(a) the ships and aircraft in the Forces Afloat of the Navy

(b) the organization of the Forces Afloat into fighting units

(c) the distribution of the Forces Afloat amongst the Seven Seas

The question always arises in the military student's mind—"Did a naval commander do the best practicable with what he had?" To judge this, it is essential in any study of naval history to know, not only what ships and aircraft a commander controlled, but what personnel he had to work with—numbers, personalities, and quality.

Since the above groups of basic naval data for the 1939-1941 period are but several of the omissions from Morison's *History of United States Naval Operations in World War II* (the current semiofficial naval history of the war), they are, in part, given in this and other chapters and, in part, added to this book as an appendix, with the hope of rounding out the 1939-1941 naval picture a bit.

This appendix (A), is a copy of a United States Fleet Notice showing the organization of the U.S. Fleet at the time of the last major reorganization of the Fleet prior to the date of my detachment as Commander-in-Chief.

This Notice also names the principal subordinate commanders in the Fleet. These are the officers of the Navy and Marine Corps team who strove, during 1939 and 1940, to prepare the Fleet for prospective war missions.

Naval Combat Strength and Organization

The story of the organization of the fleets and the distribution to them of the new or recommissioned ships and aircraft, during the 1939-1940 period, had its elements of improvising and temporizing, since there never were enough ships or aircraft or personnel to meet the actual needs of the occasion.

Each fleet commander and each of his principal subordinates advanced very logical reasons as to why his particular command should be bolstered. The Navy Department authorities could not meet these demands with the resources which the President and the Congress made available, except in a very minor way.

Strength of the 1939 Forces Afloat

January 1, 1939 seems a logical date to start my digest of the facts on this subject.

On that date, ships and district craft in the Navy were designated in either of two general classifications, "in commission" or "out of commission."

Ships in each of these two general categories were subject to further special classification such as, 'in full commission," "in reduced commission," "in commission, in reserve" or "out of commission, in service" or "not in service."

The category of "out of commission, in service" covered a multitude of types of district craft, from self-propelled garbage lighters to seaplane wrecking derricks and from ferry boats to fuel oil barges.

Old combatant ships, assigned to training the Naval Reserve, such as the old gunboats *Dubuque* (PG-17), *Wilmette* (IX-29), and *Wilmington* (PG-8), were generally maintained out of commission, in service, or when enough officers and men were available, in commission, in reserve.

The seagoing Navy (Forces Afloat) on January 1, 1939, nine months before World War II started in Europe, approximated the same number and strength in ships and aircraft as had been planned for in the Chief of Naval Operations "Operating Force Plan, Fiscal Year 1939" issued in the previous May. This strength was 329 ships and 1,030 aircraft. 254 of the 329 ships were combatant and 75 were auxiliaries.

231 of the 236 combatant ships of the 1939 Navy, which were in full commission, and 1,030 of the 1,583 operating aircraft in the Navy were assigned to the Forces Afloat, together with three battleships and fifteen destroyers in reduced commission with partial (50%) crews on board.[1]

The combatant ships (249) and aircraft in the Forces Afloat were as follows:

5 aircraft carriers with a total of 360 combatant aircraft embarked
15 battleships with a total of 46 aircraft embarked
18 heavy cruisers (8″ main battery guns) with a total of 68 aircraft embarked
18 light cruisers (6″ main battery guns) with a total of 50 aircraft embarked
104 destroyers
4 light minelayers
17 minesweepers
1 minelayer, second line
11 patrol ships and gunboats (all 2,000 tons or less)
5 patrol wings with a total of 204 patrol aircraft
56 submarines, including 1 minelaying submarine
9 squadrons of Fleet Marine Force aircraft with a total of 112 aircraft

48 of the 104 destroyers, 28 of the 56 submarines, and the 4 light minelayers were well overage and by the provisions of the Naval Limitation Treaties which we had signed with Great Britain, Japan, France, and Italy, during the 1921-1936 period, could have been replaced by new ships some

[1] Unless otherwse indicated, data in this chapter is from (a) *Navy Directory: Officers of the United States Navy and Marine Corps,* January 1939 (Washington, D.C.: GPO, 1939); (b) "Operating Force Plan, Fiscal Year 1939," Chief of Naval Operations (CNO), serial 38770 of 10 May 1938, 1st revision, serial 38790 and 2nd revision, serial 14723, WWIICF, NHD; (c) "Assignment of Vessels in the Organization of the Seagoing Forces of the U.S. Navy, Fiscal Year 1939," CNO, serial 380509 of 9 May 1938 and serial 380511 of 10 May 1938; (d) "Annual Report of the Chief of the Bureau of Navigation" (James O. Richardson) for the fiscal year 1939 (hereafter cited as CHBUNAV," Annual Report," with year) in *Annual Reports of the Navy Department;* (e) CHBUNAV (Chester W. Nimitz), "Annual Report," 1940; (f) SECNAV, *Annual Report,* 1939.

NH 77060

USS Argonne *(AS-10), a Fleet submarine tender, servicing submarines V-1, V-2, and V-3.*

years previously, had Congress been willing to provide the funds. 7 of these overage destroyers were scheduled to be decommissioned, largely during the second half of fiscal year 1939. 4 submarines, in addition to the 56 listed above, were in the process of being placed in commission in reserve.

51 of the 75 auxiliaries, including all of the major auxiliaries in full commission, were assigned to the Forces Afloat. These included 6 destroyer tenders, 5 submarine tenders, 2 large seaplane tenders, 2 transports, 2 repair ships, 8 oilers, and 2 store ships, but only 1 ammunition ship, the *USS Nitro* (AE-2).

Other auxiliaries in full commission included small seaplane tenders, survey ships, and submarine rescue ships.

Nearly 200 utility aircraft were assigned to various units of the Forces Afloat, in addition to the 840 combatant aircraft whose assignment is detailed above. 553 aircraft were assigned to the Shore Establishment, largely for training purposes.

Besides 5 minesweepers and 24 auxiliaries, listed basically as belonging to the "seagoing forces of the Navy" and included in the 329 ships so designated, there were 194 other ships and self-propelled craft assigned to the Shore Establishment. In general, these were either small combatant ships, such as 75′ patrol craft (61), submarine chasers (11), and eagle boats (8) or the logistic support craft of the naval districts, such as station ships, ocean-going tugs, harbor tugs, water barges, or fuel oil barges. The submarine chasers, eagle boats, and patrol craft were employed by the district commandants for the general shipboard training of the Naval Reserve, and for intensive training of selected Naval Reserve units in inshore antisubmarine operations. Nearly all these small ships and craft had reduced or skeleton crews on board, and many were not in full commission or in reduced commission, but were "out of commission, in service."

The 553 aircraft assigned to the Shore Establishment were engaged largely in training regulars (288 aircraft assigned) and reserves (182 aircraft assigned) to fly, and in performing experimental work, or as a means whereby already qualified naval aviators on shore duty could maintain their essential flying proficiency.

In the Reserve Fleet, not in commission, and with no crews on board, were 208 ships and craft.

On January 1, 1939, the Navy Department, due to personnel and money limitations established by the Congress, was planning on keeping the Forces

Afloat at the same strength throughout the remaining six months of fiscal 1939, but some of the older ships were to be replaced with new ships coming out of the building yards.

Organization of
Six Subdivisions of Forces Afloat

In the Forces Afloat, all the combatant ships and aircraft, and most of the auxiliaries, were distributed amongst:

(1) The United States Fleet
(2) The Asiatic Fleet
(3) The Special Service Squadron
(4) Squadron 40-T

The rest of the auxiliaries were assigned to:

(5) The Naval Transportation Service
(6) Special Duty

Each of these six major subdivisions operated directly under the orders of the Chief of Naval Operations in the Navy Department at Washington.

The United States Fleet, the largest subdivision of the Forces Afloat, was largely in the Eastern Pacific Ocean. Except for the submarines and the Atlantic Squadron, all units were based on Long Beach and San Diego, California. The submarines of the United States Fleet were based at New London, Connecticut, Coco Solo, Canal Zone, San Diego, California, and at Pearl Harbor, Territory of Hawaii. The newly renamed and expanded squadron of the Fleet, maintained in the Atlantic Ocean, was based on Norfolk, Virginia, and Newport, Rhode Island, as reported in the Secretary of the Navy's Annual Report.

> The Atlantic Squadron, United States Fleet was organized in January, 1939, and includes the former training detachment, United States Fleet, in addition to certain other vessels.

The Asiatic Fleet, the second largest subdivision of the Forces Afloat (38 ships, 6 VSO planes [Scouting], and 2 VJ planes), was in the Western Pacific Ocean and based on the Philippines and China.

The Special Service Squadron, consisting of two gunboats and two destroyers, operated along the coasts of Central America and was based on Panama.

Squadron 40-T, consisting of one light cruiser and two destroyers, was in Spanish waters as a result of the necessity of having protection closely available for United States citizens and interests during the Spanish Civil War.

Naval Transportation Service

The Naval Transportation Service consisted of ten ships, oilers, ammunition ships, and transports that carried fuel oil and ammunition to the ships of the various fleets, and distributed personnel and supplies from the Shore Establishment to the fleets.

Special Duty

The twenty-one Special Duty ships were all small. They varied from hydrographic survey ships to experimental ships under the Bureau of Ordnance or Bureau of Engineering. They included the station ships at Guam, Samoa, and at the headquarters of the various continental naval districts, as well as the yachts for the President and Secretary of the Navy.

The United States Fleet

The great majority of combatant ships and fighting aircraft of the Navy were in the United States Fleet during 1939. This is shown in the following table, which indicates the number of ships and aircraft in the United States Fleet out of the total in commission in all the Navy:

5 out of 5 carriers (375 aircraft)
5 squadrons of VB (bombers)
5 squadrons of VF (fighters)
4 squadrons of VT (torpedo)
6 squadrons of VS (scouts)
embarked in the carriers
(each squadron had 18 planes)
15 out of 15 battleships
16 out of 18 heavy cruisers (8″ guns)
15 out of 18 light cruisers (6″ guns)
85 out of 104 destroyers
46 out of 55 submarines
1 out of 1 minelayer, second line

1 out of 1 minelaying submarine
4 out of 4 light minelayers
4 out of 17 minesweepers
0 out of 11 patrol ships and gunboats
5 out of 5 patrol wings (204 aircraft)
20 squadrons of VPB (patrol bombers)

Subdivisions of United States Fleet

The United States Fleet had five major combatant subdivisions:

The Battle Force
The Scouting Force
The Atlantic Squadron
The Submarine Force
The Fleet Marine Force

and a sixth major subdivision was made up of auxiliary craft:

The Base Force

The Battle Force was the largest unit of the U.S. Fleet and had:

5 out of 5 carriers
360 combatant aircraft, 15 utility aircraft
12 out of 15 battleships
14 out of 15 light cruisers
68 out of 85 destroyers
1 out of 1 minelayer
4 out of 4 light minelayers

The Scouting Force had:

12 out of 16 heavy cruisers
1 out of 15 light cruisers
4 VCS squadrons with a total of 64 planes
5 patrol wings out of the 5 patrol wings, with a total of 20 squadrons having 204 patrol planes

The Atlantic Squadron had:

3 out of 15 battleships
9 out of 25 destroyers[2]

[2] Each battleship division had a squadron of 9 observation and scouting planes (3 VOS planes per ship), and each cruiser division had a squadron of from 4 to 16 scouting and observation planes, depending upon the newness of the cruisers (4 VSO on each of the new cruisers) and the number of cruisers in the division. There were 4 VOS squadrons, totalling 36 planes, in Battleships, Battle Force and 4 VSO squadrons, totalling 40 planes, in Cruisers, Battle Force.

It is apparent from the above that, in June 1939, I was about to command the third most important subdivision of the Forces Afloat—the Battle Force of the U.S. Fleet—and that if all went well, I would then have the Number One billet afloat, command of the United States Fleet; a sailorman's dream come true.

Operating Force Plan 1940

Just before I went to sea duty in June of 1939, the Chief of Naval Operations issued the latest version of his "Operating Force Plan, Fiscal Year 1940"[3] and his "Assignment of Vessels in the Organization of the Seagoing Forces of the U.S. Navy, Fiscal Year 1940."[4] Perhaps I should add that the "Operating Force Plan" each year, amongst other things, prescribed the authorized allowance of enlisted personnel for each ship, aircraft unit, and unit of the Fleet Marine Force.

This Operating Force Plan provided for operating, during the 1940 fiscal year, 368 ships and 1,714 aircraft in commission, and a Fleet Marine Force of 5,243. Of the 116,000 enlisted personnel in all the Navy, 89,403 were to be in the Forces Afloat.

The 368 ships included:

15 battleships, 3 of which were in reduced commission
6 aircraft carriers
18 heavy cruisers
19 light cruisers
127 destroyers, 28 of which were in reduced commission
64 submarines, 6 of which were in reduced commission
1 minelayer
22 minesweepers
10 patrol craft
5 submarine rescue ships
81 auxiliaries

Of the 99 destroyers in full commission,

13 were 1,850 tons
60 were 1,500 tons
26 were 1,200 tons (all overage)

[3] "Operating Force Plan, Fiscal Year 1940," CNO (W. D. Leahy), serial 14788 of 2 June 1939, WWIICF, NHD.

[4] "Assignment of Vessels in the Organization of the Seagoing Forces of the U.S. Navy, Fiscal Year 1940," CNO, serial 390523 of 23 May 1939, WWIICF, NHD.

All of the 28 destroyers in reduced commission were overage. Of the 64 submarines, 32 were overage.

As given previously, the comparative figures for the 1939 fiscal year had been 329 ships in commission, 1,583 aircraft, and a Fleet Marine Force of 4,731 men (out of a total of 18,000 Marines). 200 ships and craft, not in commission, remained in the Reserve Fleet. Roughly speaking, the June 1939 plans for fiscal 1940 were to have 40 more ships and 130 more aircraft in commission, and 1,000 more Marines and 6,000 more naval personnel than in fiscal 1939.

With the major nations of Europe feverishly building up their armed strength, it seems incredible now that the United States, in mid-1939, was so unaware of this buildup, or so unafraid of it, that the Navy (at that time our first line of defense) was allowed only a 6,000-man increase in its enlisted strength, and the Marine Corps was given only a piddling 1,000-man increase, by the Congress and the President.

It is apparent that, at that late date, the President, the Budget Office, and the Congress had permitted for fiscal 1940 somewhat less than the small average percentage increase in naval personnel (5 percent to 10 percent) which had been authorized during the previous three years.

The actual enlisted personnel strength of the Navy during the fiscal years 1936-1939, and as planned at the start of fiscal year 1940 was as follows:

Appropriation Year	Average Enlisted Strength	End of Fiscal Year
1936	88,000	93,077
1937	96,500	100,180
1938	102,500	105,000
1939	107,550	110,100
1940 (initial appropriation act)	113,050	116,000 [5]

In naval personnel preparedness, we were losing ground steadily, relative to our material preparedness, as evidenced by the following extracts from official SECNAV Annual Reports.

> During the fiscal year ending June 30, 1939, new construction both for the orderly replacement of overage vessels and aircraft and for the orderly augmentation of existing strength, authorized by the act of May 17, 1938, was continued with the view to bringing our naval strength up to that authorized by the Vinson-Trammell Act of 1934 and the Naval Expansion Act of May 17, 1938. Work was started on . . .

[5] CHBUNAV, "Annual Report," 1936, 1937, 1938, 1939, and 1940, pp. 1, 8, 1, 1, and 9 respectively.

2 battleships
2 cruisers
8 destroyers
6 submarines

. . . provided for in the Naval Appropriation Act of April 4, 1938, and, in addition, work was also started on the . . .

2 battleships
1 aircraft carrier
2 cruisers

. . . provided for in the Second Deficiency Act of June 25, 1938.

The 1940 Appropriation Act contains funds for commencement of further replacements and augmentations of . . .

2 battleships
2 cruisers
8 destroyers
8 submarines

This Act also contains funds for the modernization of the aircraft carriers *Lexington* and *Saratoga.* By the act of April 20, 1939, authorization was obtained for the modernization of the three large submarines, *Argonaut, Nautilus* and *Narwhal.*

On July 1, 1939 there were 105 ships under construction.

. . . the following new ships were placed in commission during the year [1939]

2 aircraft carriers
1 heavy cruiser (8″ guns)
3 light cruisers (6″ guns)
8 destroyers
4 submarines
1 oil tanker

Other ships (not new) placed in full commission . . .

2 minesweepers
1 cargo ship
1 harbor tug

v

Aircraft Carriers

I have heard some post-World War II criticism that the pre-World War II Navy should have had more aircraft carriers in it. The answer to this is that the 1922 Washington Naval Treaty was still in effect up until

January 1, 1937. By this treaty, the United States, contrary to the advice of its naval advisors, had agreed to limit itself to 135,000 tons of underage aircraft carriers. The 1938 Naval Expansion Act, the first naval expansion act after the expiration of the "22" and "30" Naval Limitation Treaties, to obtain the approval of the Congress, increased this aircraft carrier tonnage to only 175,000 tons, despite urging by naval representatives for a much higher total tonnage. Underage aircraft carriers of 175,000 total tonnage were either in commission in 1939 or building by late 1939. All were available when the war started in December 1941. If there is any blame to be assigned, it belongs to the Congress.

Naval Auxiliaries and Amphibious Types

In July of 1939, the Secretary of the Navy bluntly advised the President that, "The status of our naval auxiliaries is still very unsatisfactory."

For reasons not understandable to me, President Roosevelt always had it in his mind that, by and large, our merchant marine overnight could become our Fleet Base Force or Fleet Train and be available immediately for an overseas movement of combatant and expeditionary forces. Even had the immediate changeover from merchant service to naval service been a practicability, the overall sea power problem would not have been solved, for the United States still would need these same ships for our merchant marine in time of war. By the most optimistic ship-building estimate, it would take a year to expand the shipbuilding industry and build the first of the replacement merchant ships in the new facilities, and there would not be a year to spare.

The Navy knew that many passenger-carrying merchant ships, within weeks, could be converted so as to carry troops from dock to dock in friendly ports. But the Navy also knew that major and time-consuming alterations were necessary to change these passenger ships into amphibious attack transports required to handle the various types of small naval landing craft needed for landing troops or special army equipment, in a ground swell on a hostile shore.

And as for some of the types of auxiliaries which accompany the Fleet to the combat zones, such as repair ships, ammunition ships, or refrigeration ships, they have to be naval built from the keel up to be fully effective for use in combatant zones of operation.

It was undoubtedly correct reasoning that, as the Fleet was expanded during a war, by adding combatant ships laid down subsequent to the war's start, ships of the Fleet Train to serve them, could be converted from merchant ships and replacements built as fast as needed. But this concept was wholly fallacious with respect to the existing Fleet, which had to carry out the initial overseas operations.

Although President Roosevelt had done marvelous things in building up the combatant Navy during the period 1933-1939, he just could not or would not do much about providing the Fleet with the necessary ships for amphibious operations and for the Fleet Train, in advance of an immediate need.

Manning Levels 1930-1940

During this decade each ship and aircraft unit was furnished with a prescribed "complement" sheet, which gave the total number of officers and men and listed the various ranks and ratings and special qualifications, which the Chief of Naval Operations and the Chief of the Bureau of Navigation considered would be adequate to man the ship or aircraft in battle.

Each ship and aircraft unit also was furnished with a prescribed "allowance" sheet, which was the number of officers and men which the Chief of Naval Operations was able to allot as its honest share of the total number of personnel authorized and appropriated for the Navy, by the Congress, in the current fiscal year.

The personnel complement was presumably based on the minimum number of personnel needed to fight the ship or aircraft, that is, to man all guns, torpedoes, or other armaments and to steam the ship at full power for four hours, or to fly the airplane for its limit of endurance in the air.

The personnel allowances, except for submarines and single aircraft, were markedly less than the complements. The latter varied from year to year, depending on the appropriations of the Congress. In general, however, during the period 1930-1939, the allowances for major combatant units were from 80 percent to 85 percent of the complement. For less important ships and units, they varied between 50 percent and 80 percent of complement, with the average about 65 percent.

Men for Ships

It was a naval truism that, when the threat of war was slight, it took longer to build ships and aircraft than it took to train the personnel to man them.

It is part of the naval tradition that this truism reverses itself during the period just prior to a war, or during a war, when shipyards and aircraft factories are manned by three shifts of workmen around the clock, but the individual officer or sailorman cannot receive instruction in a school or on a ship around the clock. During such emergency or war periods, ships can be built faster than officers and men can be brought in from civilian life and trained to fight them *effectively.*

So, during the 1930-1939 period, it had been considered, by a succession of Chiefs of Naval Operations, far better to train at one time 100 Commanding Officers, 100 pilots, 100 navigators, 100 chief boatswains mates or chief watertenders, or even 100 leading seamen in 100 ships and aircraft, with only partial crews, than it was to train only 85 of the same personnel in 85 ships and aircraft, even though the latter arrangement would provide each ship with a full crew and would provide replacement crews for a number of aircraft.

By the chosen arrangement, every officer and man was, in effect, training in a little better billet, or getting into the billet at a younger age than if the ships had been fully manned, or each aircraft provided with a crew to keep it in the air whenever it would fly. It was a very limited way of training for the expected war-expansion of personnel, ships, and aircraft.

During the 1930-1940 decade, most ships and aircraft units operated year in and year out with even less than their prescribed allowance of personnel actually on board, to say nothing of less than the prescribed complements.

This was due to a reluctance of the Congress to admit that there would always be a considerable number of personnel in the Navy in transit between duty stations, sick in hospitals, attending short-term schools, or on reenlistment or other leave, and to provide adequately for this percentage of personnel (about 8 percent) over the total of the allowance of all ships, aircraft, and stations to be kept in commission.

So, the Navy learned to do the best it could with what it had, and operated short-handed.

Inadequacy of Enlisted Complements

By 1937, every seasoned naval officer realized that the complements had more than an aura of unreality about them because of:

(a) the twenty-year period since our Navy had been in combat operations
(b) the tremendous technical developments during this twenty-year period which had not been put to the actual test of combat operations
(c) long continued inability to overcome Congressional reluctance to authorize the funds necessary for increased naval personnel.

The result was that the "paper" war complements became very unrealistic.

It might well be asked why the individual Commanding Officer of a ship did not do more letter writing on the subject.

A Commanding Officer of a destroyer, whose complement of enlisted personnel was 132, and whose allowance was 112 or 106 or 83, and who spent many hours trying to obtain an allocation of additional seamen or firemen from higher authority so that his ship would have its authorized 112 or 106 or 83 men actually on board, could not get very interested in trying to obtain an increase in a theoretical "paper" complement for his ship from 132 to 140 or 150. The complement was a "heaven" far in the future from the day-to-day heavy tasks of the present, which had to be accomplished with the number of officers and men actually on board.

The unreality of the allowances and complements is succinctly illustrated by the following data.

On July 1, 1940, the allowance of men for the heavy cruiser *Indianapolis* (CA-35) was 588 men. The complement was 685 men.[6] On July 5, 1940, the CNO increased this allowance by 11 percent, or 68 men, to a total of 656.[7] Twelve weeks later on September 28, 1940, the CNO increased by 184 men the allowance over the July 1 allowance to 772, or a 31 percent increase.[8] A week later, on October 4, 1940, the CNO indicated that the allowance of the *Indianapolis* was to be further increased on July 1, 1941, to 876, or 49 percent greater than the allowance had been a year previously.[9]

[6] "Operating Force Plan, Fiscal Year 1940," p. 3a.

[7] "Operating Force Plan, Fiscal Year 1941," CNO (H.R. Stark), serial 107738 of 5 July 1940, WWIICF, NHD, p. 3a.

[8] "Revised Operating Force Plan, Fiscal Year 1941," CNO, serial 150638 of 28 Sept. 1940, WWIICF, NHD, p. 3a.

[9] "Revised Operating Force Plan, Fiscal Year 1941, CNO, serial 154438 of 4 Oct. 1940, WWIICF, NHD, p. 3a.

Thus, in the short space of four months, the Chief of Naval Operations showed an appreciation of the necessity of increasing the number of men aboard the heavy cruiser type of ship by nearly 50 percent. Even this marked increase turned out to be inadequate, as the wartime complement of the *Indianapolis* and all similar types of heavy cruisers was 1,024, roughly 75 percent more men than the ship had on board for its training for war in 1939-1940.[10]

These paper changes were indications of a belated recognition of the need for a vastly increased allocation of personnel. But, the paper changes couldn't produce men. The Commanding Officer of the *Indianapolis,* in submitting his report on the December 7, 1941 Japanese attack on Pearl Harbor said, "The ship was 170 men under its allowed complement." This statement indicated that the ship had on board only a few men more than her July 1, 1940 complement."[11]

My successor as the Chief of the Bureau of Navigation (Rear Admiral C. W. Nimitz, USN) softly summed up this very serious enlisted personnel shortage situation in his 1939 Annual Report:

> To man the ships in commission during the fiscal year 1939, the annual appropriation provided funds for a total enlisted strength insufficient to fill the various complements.[12]

Quality and Morale

Despite the very inadequate numbers of enlisted personnel, their quality and morale were very high.

The quality of the 1939-1940 sailorman was evidenced during World War II when tens of thousands showed themselves so well qualified in their professional navigating, engineering, gunnery, communications, or supply duties as to be able to fleet up to officer rank and to discharge their duties in an extremely capable manner.[13]

---

[10] "Operating Force Plan, Fiscal Year 1944," CNO (H. R. Stark), serial 0308623 of 22 July 1943, WWIICF, NHD, p. 5a.

[11] Commanding Officer, *USS Indianapolis* (CA-35) (E. W. Hanson), serial 0155 of 14 Dec. 1941, letter to CINCUS, WWIICF, NHD.

[12] CHBUNAV (C. W. Nimitz), "Annual Report," 1939, p. 8.

[13] 20,652 enlisted personnel were advanced to officer rank in 1943; 58,000 in all by 1 March 1945.

The height of the morale of the enlisted man was evidenced by the very large percentage who reenlisted regularly in the Navy, despite the fact that the period from July 1, 1934 to June 30, 1940 (except for the sharp recession in the latter half of 1937) was a six-year period of generally decreasing national unemployment.

The Chief of the Bureau of Navigation in his Annual Reports provided the following figures:

Fiscal year	*Percentage of reenlistments*
1935	80.86
1936	83.67
1937	81.75
1938	72.21
1939	80.81
1940	75.48 [14]

Officer Shortage

On June 30, 1939, there were 6,877 Line officers on the active duty list, 700 under the allowed strength of 7,562. The increase during the year had been only 346.

By and large, I viewed the 1939 officer shortage with far less concern than the enlisted shortage. The ordinary college graduate in the United States can be taught the bare fundamentals of naval leadership in four months. He can be taught the technique of one particular subordinate billet in another six months, and he can be adapted to the seagoing life in a year. But, it takes four to six years to make the ordinary grammar or even high school graduate into a leading petty officer, skilled in diagnosing the ills of an aircraft engine, a radar, a radio, a torpedo, a gun, or a fire control instrument.

I knew that our 1939 Line officer corps in the Navy was of extremely broad professional competence. A rigid selection up system of promotion had been in effect for twenty-three years for the promotion of the seagoing officer to the three highest grades of officer. Selection up for the more junior grades had been in effect for five years. Our Selection Boards had acquired

[14] CHBUNAV, "Annual Report," 1935, 1936, 1937, 1938, 1939, and 1940, pp. 10, 9, 8, 11, 8, and 10 respectively.

a well earned service-wide reputation for fairness. By and large, they had weeded out all the incompetents and a large percentage of the barely competent.

Elimination from active duty of from 20 percent to 30 percent of those remaining in each Naval Academy class, as they acquired service enough to be considered for selection to the next higher grade, had accentuated in nearly all seasoned seagoing officers an urgent desire to become thoroughly qualified in all aspects of their part of the naval profession.

In 1939, I was sure that we could fill our junior officer ranks in the Navy with large-scale promotion of our leading petty officers to officer rank—to give high-grade technical direction—and with large-scale appointment directly from civil life for general leadership purposes. It would take two or three civilians in uniform to do one young regular officer's job, but it could be done.

The 7,000 regular Line officers would provide the overall leadership and direction for the naval campaigns of the war, which would be needed for victory. I did not visualize the great extent of the expansion that lay ahead, but I was extremely confident of my fellow officer and the professional sailorman.

As aptly put by Commodore Dudley W. Knox in his *A History of the United States Navy,* in speaking of World War II:

> By 1945 the regular was spread very thinly through the Navy. Yet the original officer corps had managed to transfuse its high spirit as well as its basic War College and Naval Academy indoctrination and training to the much larger group of reserve officers to a truly astonishing degree.[15]

A long line of my predecessors had done their work well, and when, in June 1939, I left the Bureau of Navigation and went to sea, it was with confidence regarding the officer situation, but with many doubts in regard to the enlisted situation. New ships were being built faster than we could man them with thoroughly competent crews.

---

[15] Dudley W. Knox, *A History of the United States Navy* (New York: G. P. Putnam's Sons, 1948), p. 631.

Chapter VI

My First Thirty Years 1898-1928

Young officers may logically ask whether there is any real relationship between the early years of an officer's career in the Navy and the attainments or accomplishments of his mature years.

I am one of those who think that there is such a direct and logical relationship, and that the earlier a young officer, even as a midshipman, gives all that he has to the full performance of his duty, the higher the later return on his investment.

And so I believe my formative years are a logical part of this book.

When I left the Naval Academy, the Navy, although growing, was very small by present standards. There was no thought of a war, within the foreseeable future. No drills on board ship were held in the afternoon except fire drill on Friday afternoon. Among the forenoon drills were such antiquated ones as bayonet exercise and single sticks for all deck divisions.

General Quarters was held once a week but no regular loading and pointing drills were held except for a short period just before annual target practice.

The target practice had been most amateurish, with only a flag on a barrel as a point of aim, until the Navy was awakened in 1902 by Lieutenant William S. Sims (1880), with the ardent support of President Theodore Roosevelt, under the slogan "It is only the shots which hit that count."

Undoubtedly, Sims, as Gunnery Officer of the Asiatic Fleet, where the modern target practice first started, and then as Director of Gunnery Exercises in the Department, did much to develop improved gunnery and fire control. Later, he did much to develop the interest of our senior naval officers in the Naval War College.

In those days, and until 1916, promotion was by seniority, so that all an officer had to do to ensure reaching Flag rank was to:

(a) enter the Naval Academy very young
(b) graduate
(c) remain reasonably sober
(d) avoid being court-martialed with possible loss of numbers
(e) pass the rather cut and dried professional examinations for promotion
(f) safeguard his health to avoid physical retirement
(g) make a record as good as average so as to avoid being plucked by the annual "Plucking Board."

I entered the Naval Academy on 21 September 1878. So, I was three days over the limiting age of nineteen years when I entered. If an officer entered as the oldest man in his class with many seniors younger than he, as I did, there was absolutely no chance of his reaching Flag rank, assuming the then current system of promotion continued in effect, and the Navy remained with a thousand-man officer corps.

Under these conditions, it was natural that many officers, old for their classes, when due for shore duty, sought duty at the Naval Academy where quarters were available for many, or rents in town were cheap, the work very light, leisure plentiful, responsibilities almost nil, and the social life delightful. To a somewhat lesser degree, similar conditions prevailed at the navy yards and naval training stations. On isolated stations like recruiting, inspection offices, and ammunition depots, the life was not arduous, but there was little contact with Navy friends.

Duty in the Navy Department was arduous and confining, and some billets carried responsibility. Living was expensive and recreation facilities were available to only a few, but there was a wonderful opportunity to become known to the officers and officials who were running the Navy.

After promotion by selection became effective, most officers of the Navy believed that their chances of selection for promotion were enhanced by being known to many senior officers who might be members of the Selection Board. In fact, while I was Director of Officer Personnel, I had several senior captains say to me, "Joe, I have always had duty in the sticks (obviously of their own choice). I shall have little chance of selection unless you can find for me a billet in the Navy Department."

If a young officer happened to be ordered to duty in the Department and made a good impression, he was likely to return to the Department many times. In my own case, in 1914, I was slated for duty as the Officer-in-Charge of the experimental oil-burning plant in Philadelphia, when Lieutenant Commander David F. Boyd (1897), on duty in the Bureau of Steam Engineering, persuaded the Chief of the Bureau to accept me as his relief in order that he might be ordered to other duty. Thereafter, I never performed shore duty elsewhere than in Washington, with the exception of one year at the Naval War College and two and a half years at the Naval Academy. In my whole career I lived only two and a half years in government quarters.

To the Asiatic Station

When I graduated from the Naval Academy in 1902, the Navy planned to keep one half of our heavy fighting ships on the North Atlantic Station and one half on the Asiatic Station. With this distribution of ships, and consequently of personnel, I realized that it was almost certain that I would be ordered to the Far East within a few years. My father was sixty-five years old, and I wished to be reasonably near home when his final illness came. Consequently, I requested duty with the Asiatic Fleet so as to increase my chance of being in home waters in the subsequent years.

This request was granted. I believe that thirty-nine others of the fifty-nine members of my class also were sent to the Asiatic Station at this time, and two others saw duty on the Asiatic Station during their first year after graduation.

The 1902 Navy

In early 1902, our Fleet was expanding rapidly due to warship construction which had been initiated during the Spanish-American War and continued after the war's successful termination. This increased Fleet strength and national strength was needed to provide security for the responsibilities and interests of the United States acquired since 1898 in the Philippine Islands, Cuba, Puerto Rico, and Guam. The rapid growth was well portrayed by the Secretary of the Navy who, in his Annual Report to the President, stated with pride that during the fiscal year 1902, the following ships were accepted into the Navy:

Battleships	*Torpedo Boats*
Alabama (BB-8)	*Bailey* (TB-21)
Wisconsin (BB-9)	*Bagley* (TB-24)
Illinois (BB-7)	*Barney* (TB-25)
	Biddle (TB-26)
	Shubrick (TB-31)
	Stockton (TB-32) [1]

On June 30, 1902, there were under construction for the Navy by contract:

8 battleships
6 armored cruisers
9 protected cruisers
4 monitors
13 torpedo boat destroyers
7 torpedo boats
7 submarine torpedo boats [2]

• • •

> The country approves, with hardly a dissenting voice, the policy of strengthening our power upon the sea.[3]

The need for the fifty-nine "passed midshipmen" that constituted my class of 1902 was such as to cause the "Powers That Be" to graduate the class on May 2, 1902, instead of in the traditional month of June. This step was taken unwillingly but:

> The shortening of the course at the Naval Academy is forced upon the Department by the urgent demand for officers on board seagoing vessels.[4]

An additional fifty-nine passed midshipmen represented a sizeable increase, since on July 1, 1902, the total officer corps of the Line of the Navy, including passed midshipmen, was only 1,023. The number of enlisted men was 21,433. The Marine Corps consisted of 278 officers and 6,062 men.

Along with a number of my classmates, I took passage in the hospital ship *Solace* (AH-2), from San Francisco and arrived at Manila, Philippine Islands, in June 1902.

Forty-one of the fifty-nine members of my class saw duty on the Asiatic Station during their first year after graduation.

En route to Manila, the *Solace* coaled in Pearl Harbor, and visited Guam.

[1] SECNAV (William H. Moody), *Annual Report,* 1902, p. 6.
[2] *Ibid.,* p. 5.
[3] *Ibid.,* p. 14.
[4] CHBUNAV (H. C. Taylor), "Annual Report," 1902, p. 21.

The Navy was then in the process of acquiring the land upon which, over the next forty years, was to be built the magnificent Pearl Harbor Naval Base. At a cost of $58,140.00, 719 acres were acquired.[5]

The *Quiros*

My first duty was on an ex-Spanish ship, converted into a "fourth class" gunboat, the USS *Quiros* (PG-40). She was composite-built, steel framed, wooden hulled, copper sheathed, displacing 350 tons, and propelled at a maximum speed of eleven knots by a single screw. The *Quiros* was powered by a vertical, triple expansion reciprocating engine and two Scotch boilers, and her battery consisted of six rapid-fire guns; 2 six pounders, 2 three pounders, and 2 one pounders. She was 137 feet from stem to stern, and had been built in Hong Kong in 1895.

The complement was one lieutenant, two passed midshipmen, and forty enlisted men. The *Quiros* had no electricity, no refrigeration, a single dry compass, and a bunk for me five and one half feet long, even though I measured six feet two inches.

The *Quiros* patrolled in the Southern Philippines along the southern coast of Mindanao and in the Moro Group of the Sulu Islands. The latter area was one of the more active patrol zones, as the Moros provided the last large bandit forces in the Philippines who remained active after the organized Philippine Insurrection, under Aguinaldo, had been crushed.

From an operational point of view, the duty was fine for a young officer, for there was a spirit of adventure about and things happened. One *Quiros* foray even made the Annual Report of the Chief of the Bureau of Navigation to the Secretary of the Navy, as indicated in the following extract:

> *QUIROS* November 20, [1902] left Zamboanga for Pandan-Pandan to investigate an armed Moro expedition of 200 men reported proceeding to that place. [Ship's party] . . . proceeded in an armed boat from Pandan-Pandan to Talusan and encountered two armed bintas . . . ascended the Cabacsilan and Ciay rivers in search of the expedition, which had dispersed. Captured three rifles and a supply of ammunition from one binta.[6]

And, the Secretary of the Navy found a place in his Annual Report to the President to say kind things about the patrolling gunboats.

[5] SECNAV, *Annual Report,* 1902, p. 31.
[6] CHBUNAV (H. C. Taylor), "Annual Report," 1903, p. 557.

NH 67130

USS Quiros *(PG-40) on the Yangtze River.*

> So far as conditions ashore in the Philippines are concerned, there has been a general state of peace and the Navy has not been called upon to take part in active operations, with the exception of the patrol of the southern coast of Mindanao and the Sulu Islands to assist the Army in checking supplies for the Moros and the suppression of illicit traffic of all kinds by means of boats. The vessels engaged in the patrol work have done their work thoroughly and their presence has been of material assistance in maintaining a state of peace among the Moro coast tribes, such tribes having a great fear of and respect for a gunboat.[7]

Early Commanding Officers

Nearly every officer, whom one serves under or with, has some effect on one's future career. Those officers of strong character or with marked professional abilities, or with both, are doubly important. The example of the top leadership is most important. Does this man in the leadership spot really lead?

So, it is necessary for me to relate who these officers were, and how they stimulated or stultified.

In the *Quiros,* during the short space of fifteen months, I served under four Commanding Officers, the last three of whom were of the Naval Academy class of 1887. My first Commanding Officer, and a competent one, was Lieutenant William Bartlett Fletcher (1881) who, at that time was forty years old and, thru the workings of the Navy's slow promotion system of that era, still a lieutenant. Years later, he commanded the squadron of Armed Yachts (Squadron Three, Patrol Force, U.S. Atlantic Fleet) which operated out of Brest, France, during World War I, as well as the Naval Base at Brest, at which the squadron was based. He is now—December 1956—the oldest living Flag Officer graduate of the Naval Academy—ninety-four years of age.

However, Lieutenant Fletcher was soon ordered home from the Asiatic Station, and Lieutenant Levi C. Bertolette (1887) succeeded him. About half a year later, Bertolette was succeeded by Lieutenant Francis Boughter (1887), and he by Lieutenant Benton C. Decker (1887).

The last three lieutenants firmly believed that the only way to convert a passed midshipman into a worthwhile ensign was to give him "Hell" every minute of the day and a fair share of each night.

[7] *Ibid.*, p. 476.

They practiced what they believed, with the result that, when I was detached, I believed that I had the dubious distinction of having been under suspension more than any other passed midshipman in the Navy. I never even requested to be excused from morning quarters during all this period. For the younger reader, I will add that, in that hard-working period, the Navy held morning quarters and inspecton each Sunday, in addition to the other six days of the week.[8]

Despite this basic policy of indoctrination, which had its successes and failures amongst the passed midshipmen of my era, I learned a most valuable lesson; namely, how to get along with seniors, particularly "sundowners." I learned not to be, or want to be, a martinet. I learned the importance of being able to handle sailormen, and in the international field, I learned of the tranquilizing effect that a man-of-war can have on a disturbed political area. I learned to enjoy reading while aboard ship and I read much about the countries of the Far East.

From my reading in regard to China and the Chinese people, I learned a few proverbs which I have quoted to my friends all the rest of my adult life, such as:

> A wise turtle keeps the pain inside.
>
> Leprosy may be cured, but the enmity of an official underling can never be dispelled.

At that time (1902), the Navy had no radio, no gyro compass, no internal combustion engines, no steam turbines, no oil-burning boilers, no range finders, few telescopic sights, no directors, no semaphore, no damage control, no radar, no large-scale War College attendance, no "P.G." school, no specialization, no promotion by selection; many officers had served thirteen years or more as ensigns. Only two thirds of the petty officers were native-born citizens.

I felt that in the *Quiros,* I was not learning anything about the material or the technical side of the Navy, so I requested transfer to a battleship. This request was not granted (and many similar requests were not granted,

---

[8] This was changed to: "The commanding officer's inspection of ship and crew shall not be held on Sunday. The inspection of the ship shall be held on such other day of the week as may be most expedient and the inspection of the crew on Saturday before noon, if circumstances permit; if not, as soon after the dinner hour as practicable." See *Instructions for the Administration of the Naval Establishment of the United States (Naval Instructions)*, 1913 in *Regulations for the Government of the Navy of the United States (Navy Regulations)*, 1913 (Washington, D.C.: GPO, 1913) Art. 2602 (6), p. 153I.

until over nine years after my graduation). My Commanding Officer said to me:

> Young man, there is nothing in the Navy more important than the enlisted man, and you can learn more about how to handle him on a small ship than you can on the larger ships in the Navy.

As the subject of handling enlisted men is the most difficult and most important thing for a young officer to learn, I consider that this was good advice. At first, the young officer is either too severe, through fear of being too lenient, or too lenient, through fear of being too severe. Eventually, he should learn that there is a time to be lenient and a time to be severe, but that a man likes to serve under a taut officer who is always fair.

I should also add that I am now convinced that service on small ships is best for the rounded development of a young officer.

USS New Orleans

Although my request for transfer to a battleship was not granted, on August 3, 1903, I was transferred as a Watch and Division Officer to the protected cruiser *New Orleans,* Commander Gottfried Blocklinger (1868) commanding, with Lieutenant Albert L. Key (1882) as Executive Officer. These officers were later relieved by Commander Giles B. Harber (1869) and Lieutenant Commander Hugh Rodman (1880), respectively.

The *New Orleans* was a veteran of the Spanish-American War and a new ship of 3,437 tons, 10 guns, twin screws, 7,500 horsepower, and capable of 21 knots. Built at Newcastle-on-Tyne, England, for the Brazilian Navy and purchased by the United States at the time of the Spanish-American War, she had engine order telegraphs, name plates, and other markings in Portuguese, together with the Brazilian Coat of Arms on the gangway ladder headboards and on the wardroom silverware, including napkin rings. She was purchased on 16 March 1898, commissioned two days later, and fitted out at the Navy Yard, New York. She became a member of the Flying Squadron off Santiago de Cuba, but was absent from the Battle of Santiago because of the necessity of coaling at Key West.

Despite the fact she was only five years old, her 6″ guns were fitted with open rifle sights, and a single pointer at each gun had to train, elevate, and fire the gun.

80-G-1035122

A later view of USS New Orleans.

I joined the *New Orleans* at Chefoo, China. Soon after I joined this ship, she proceeded to Tsingtao, where the Germans were building a naval base and rebuilding parts of the port, then to Nagasaki where the ship was coaled by coolies, largely women, and finally to Yokohama where we witnessed an Imperial Review of Japanese troops in Tokyo and had separate gun training and elevating gear and makeshift telescopic sights installed by a Japanese machine shop.

As I remember one of the very interesting occurrences of this cruise, the *New Orleans,* in company with three other cruisers, *Albany* (CL-23), *Cincinnati* (C-7), and *Raleigh* (C-8), and three battleships, *Kentucky* (BB-6), *Wisconsin* (BB-9), and the famous *Oregon* (BB-3), were peremptorily ordered by cable to proceed at the highest practical speed from Yokohama to Honolulu. On this trip, the *Oregon* maintained a higher speed than she did on her famous cruise around the Horn during the Spanish-American War. She was burning 100 tons of coal a day and arrived in Honolulu with less than 100 tons.

This movement of the Asiatic Fleet was mentioned by the Chief of the Bureau of Navigation (George A. Converse) in the *Annual Report of the Secretary of the Navy* to President Theodore Roosevelt:

> It had been intended to rendezvous [the Asiatic Fleet] in Manila Bay for squadron work in winter, as had been done during the previous winter, and at Chefoo during the summer, but instead of this the Department ordered the commander in chief to proceed, as soon as convenient, with the Battle ship and Cruiser squadrons on a cruise to Honolulu. . . . The readiness with which all the instructions for this cruise were executed and the creditable performance of the vessels themselves evoked the hearty commendation of the Department.[9]

However, the Secretary of the Navy did not add the political background of the naval movement, which added great interest at the time.

In August 1903, the Senate of the Republic of Colombia rejected the treaty which had been negotiated with the United States, providing authority for the United States to build a canal across the Colombian province of Panama. Early in November 1903, the revolution, which was to lead to the independence of Panama from the Republic of Colombia, broke out.

In December 1903, President Theodore Roosevelt ordered all naval ships of combat value in the Atlantic to Culebra Island, Puerto Rico, West Indies, and in the Eastern Pacific to Magdalena Bay, Lower California. As

---

[9] CHBUNAV (George A. Converse), "Annual Report," 1904, p. 487.

described above, he ordered the major portion of the combatant strength of the Asiatic Fleet to Honolulu. These movements were initiated in order to have the United States Fleet close to Panama, should any European nation seek to bring its naval pressure to bear to divert his planned course of events in the Panama area.

It was a splendid example of the dispositions and use of naval strength which, coupled with that of a year earlier during the Germany-Venezuela-United States controversy greatly impressed my youthful naval mind, in regard to the uses of sea power.

During the previous year's Germany-Venezuela dispute, it was widely reported in our Navy that, when Germany had insisted she was going to collect money owed by the Venezuelan Government on a bonded debt, by means of a military occupation of Venezuela, President Roosevelt had informed the Kaiser that he would place Admiral George Dewey in command of the Atlantic Fleet and send it to Venezuela to prevent any landing of German forces. This threat of the use of the big stick was alleged to have been a major factor in obtaining a German decision to arbitrate the dispute.

Shortly after the return to the Philippines of the *New Orleans* from Honolulu, I was ordered to the Naval Hospital, Yokohama for a short period because of illness.

The Japanese merchant ship, *Kumano Maru,* which took me to Yokohama, was diverted to troop-carrying duty soon afterward, as the Russian-Japanese war broke out on February 8, 1904. I arrived on the dock in Yokohama just in time to witness the Russian Minister, Baron Rosen, boarding a ship to return to Russia.

The surprise attacks made by the Japanese, before a declaration of war, on the detachments of the Russian Fleet in the harbors of Port Arthur and Chemulpo, were a shock to my susceptible mind, conditioned by the code of honor methods of warfare taught at the Naval Academy. The remembrance of these "foul blows" stuck in my "craw" all thru the pre-Pearl Harbor period and showed up in some of my letters on our War Plans, as may be observed later in this book.

USS Monadnock

Not very long after my return to the *New Orleans* from the hospital, I was transferred, in July 1904, to the double-turreted monitor *USS*

Monadnock (BM-3), the station ship of the Asiatic Fleet, generally moored in the Whangpoo (Hwang Pu) River at Shanghai. The Commanding Officer of the *Monadnock* was in general charge of the gunboats operating in the Yangtze River and its tributaries.

The *Monadnock* had been originally launched March 23, 1863, at the Navy Yard, Boston, rebuilt completely with a new iron hull at the Continental Iron Works, Vallejo, California, and relaunched on 19 September 1883, but not commissioned for nearly thirteen years until 20 February 1896. She had two horizontal, triple-expansion, reciprocating engines and a theoretical speed of 12 knots. Her armament was four ten″ breech-loading guns, two in each water hydraulic turret mount. The Captain of the *Monadnock* was Commander Dennis H. Mahan (1869), USN, the younger brother of the very famous naval writer and philosopher Alfred Thayer Mahan (1859). Dennis Mahan claimed that he was a practical naval officer, while his brother, for whose great talents he had little or no respect, was a theoretical officer. Amongst the officers on board, who later became Flag Officers, were Lieutenant Joseph W. Oman (1886) and Lieutenant James J. Raby (1895). The paymaster son of the famous Commodore Joseph Fyffe (1853), was also a shipmate.

I was still a midshipman when reporting to the *Monadnock* but was

NH 60658

The Monitor Monadnock *(BM-3)*

assigned to be the turret officer of Number One Turret. This was a detail much to my liking, since at that time:

> The task which is employing the highest energies of the Navy, and receiving the greatest attention . . . is the work of training . . . particularly in "gun pointing. . . ." [10]
>
> • • •
>
> Commencing in 1902 under the leadership of then Lieutenant Commander W. S. Sims and Lieutenant R. McLean, a great reform in gunnery training had been made and carried forward with steady progress, until the accuracy and rapidity of fire was truly remarkable as measured by former standards.[11]

The competition between ships in gunnery was beginning to catch hold, and I was very fortunate that, during the gunnery year 1904-1905, the Number One Turret in the *Monadnock* stood first in the turret competition of all monitors in the Navy. As noted by the Secretary of the Navy (Paul Morton) in his 1904 Annual Report to the President:

> It is gratifying to note that an increase in efficiency [and in marksmanship] is reported as a result of the year's [gunnery] practice, especially in the case of the heavier guns, namely, those from 8 to 13 inches in caliber installed in turrets.[12]

I received the following letter from the Chief of the Bureau of Navigation:

> August 11, 1905.
>
> Sir:—
>
> The Bureau is pleased to note that the turret which you commanded aboard the U.S.S. Monadnock on the record target practice, 1905, attained the highest final merit of any 10- or 12-inch turret aboard vessels of the monitor class, thereby winning the first Navy prize for monitors' turrets.
>
> The Bureau therefore commends the zeal and ability displayed in the discharge of your duties as a turret officer.
>
> A copy of this letter has been filed with your record in the Navy Department.
>
> Very respectfully,
> G. A. CONVERSE
> Chief of Bureau
>
> Midshipman J. O. Richardson, U.S.N.,[13]
> U.S.S. Nashville.

---

[10] SECNAV (William H. Moody), *Annual Report,* 1902, p. 4.

[11] Knox, *A History of the United States Navy,* p. 355.

[12] SECNAV (Paul Morton), *Annual Report,* 1904, p. 12.

[13] CHBUNAV, 11 Aug. 1905, letter to MIDN Richardson, "Naval Records Special (NRS)" microfilm file no. 1M, NHD.

To accomplish this record, many things had to be improvised in the Number One Turret of the *Monadnock.*

The *Monadnock* was still firing the old brown-powder ammunition and not the new "smokeless powder." There was no gas ejection system.

The turret chamber and handling room were open from the deck of the handling room to the top of the turret.

To increase the rate at which the guns could be fired safely, we rigged canvas bags on the guns and secured them to the front armor plate of the turret, closed the access to the handling room with a rugged wooden door, and to this wooden door connected the discharge of a powerful electric blower. With the blower running at full speed, the handling room, turret chamber, and turret were put under air pressure, so that when the breech plugs were opened, everything except the molten brown powder was blown out of the gun. Within my knowledge, this was the first instance of providing a means of clearing the bore of a gun of hot gases after firing the gun.

In order to safely load the powder more rapidly, we rigged wet blankets over the openings of the ammunition hoists, so that the burning grains of powder, which frequently fell back into the turret as the breech was opened, would not get into the ammunition hoist where the next powder charge was exposed.

When we reached Manila Bay and had our scheduled overhaul, the *Monadnock* received new breech plugs and primer locks for the turret guns and a full allowance of the new "smokeless powder."

USS Nashville

Upon completion of my three years on the China Station, I was ordered back to the United States, via the collier *Zafiro,* which had been purchased by Admiral Dewey in Hong Kong just before sailing to attack the Spanish Fleet in Manila Bay. I proceeded then, in July 1905, to the *Nashville* (PG-7) as Watch and Division Officer. The *Nashville,* a small gunboat of 1,371 tons with eight 4" guns, had been built in 1894-1897 and commissioned 19 August 1897. Placed out of commission on 30 June 1904, she was just going back into commission at the Navy Yard, Boston, to be assigned to the Atlantic Fleet.

As I mentioned before, the Navy, at the time I entered it, was served by a very large number of foreign-born enlisted men. But, by the summer of

1905, the nationality of the enlisted personnel had commenced to change rapidly. As reported by the Secretary of the Navy (Charles J. Bonaparte) in his 1905 Annual Report to the President:

> The percentage of American citizens among our seamen has steadily risen, and it may be said that for practical purposes the corps of petty officers is now composed exclusively of Americans.[14]

The *Nashville* spent the latter months of 1905 thru June 1906 in Santo Domingan waters. According to the Secretary of the Navy's report:

> Owing to the exigencies of the political situation in Santo Domingo the sixth division of the Atlantic Fleet, augmented from time to time by additional gunboats, has been almost constantly required in Santo Domingan waters.[15]

My Captain was Commander Washington I. Chambers (1876), who did so much to promote the interests of naval aviation in its early years. One historian noted:

> Widely known as a keen-minded engineer, the captain [Washington I. Chambers] had been concerned in most of the developments that were remaking the Navy.[16]

Shipmates, who were selected to be Flag Officers later, were Ensign John Downes (1901) and Midshipman Halsey Powell (1904). Robley D. Evans (1864) was Commander-in-Chief of the North Atlantic Fleet and continued on as Commander-in-Chief of the Atlantic Fleet when this Fleet was constituted on January 1, 1906.

USS Tennessee

When the *Nashville* was placed out of commission on July 23, 1906, I was transferred to the big, fast, and brand-new armored cruiser (14,500 tons—22 knots) *Tennessee* (ACR-10). "The *Washington* [ACR-11] and *Tennessee;* the finest ships that sail the sea" were part of the old Armored Cruiser Squadron which was commemorated in naval song and verse for thirty years.

Despite the boasts of the song, the 1908 *Jane's Fighting Ships* said:

[14] SECNAV (Charles J. Bonaparte), *Annual Report,* 1905, p. 10.

[15] CHBUNAV (George A. Converse), "Annual Report," 1906, p. 399.

[16] Archibald D. Turnbull and Clifford L. Lord, *History of United States Naval Aviation* (New Haven: Yale University Press, 1949), p. 7.

NH 76320

USS Tennessee *(ACR-10) in the Panama Canal.*

The *Washington* Class when designed were very fine cruisers [four 10″ 40-caliber guns; 5″ side armor], but that was many years ago. Since then ideas have moved forward, and they make but a poor show besides such vessels as the [Japanese] TSUKUBA [four 12″ guns 45-caliber; 7″ side armor] completed about the same time.[17]

My cruise in the *Tennessee* was a pleasant one. I was assigned as Watch and Division Officer and commanded Number One Turret, at a time when it was reported that:

The records of gun pointers for this year show that both the rapidity of fire and the percentage of hits are greater than in any preceding year, though the conditions governing the test of gun pointers and gun crews were more difficult than heretofore. . . .

This increase in efficiency is largely due to the personal initiative of commanding, gunnery, and division officers, actuated by a spirit of loyal competition between individual ships. . . .[18]

---

[17] *Jane's Fighting Ships* (London: Sampson Low Marston and Co., 1908), p. 428.

[18] CHBUNAV (W. H. Brownson), "Annual Report," 1907, p. 374.

Besides having a trip to France, the *Tennessee* was an escort for the battleship *Louisiana* (BB-19), which had President Theodore Roosevelt aboard on a voyage from Piney Point, Maryland, to Colon, Panama, and thence via Ponce, Puerto Rico and back to Piney Point (November 9, 1906 to November 26, 1906). My Captain was Albert G. Berry (1869), later a Flag Officer, and my shipmates included Ashley H. Robertson (1888) and Samuel M. Robinson (1888), both headed for advanced rank in the Navy.

USS Tingey

On May 2, 1907, five years after graduation, I made lieutenant and was soon (October 3, 1907) ordered in command of the twin-screw torpedo boat *Tingey* (TB-34). The *Tingey* had had its keel laid way back in 1899, but was not commissioned until 1904. She displaced, on a six-foot draft, 165 tons, had 3 torpedo tubes and had 3,000-horsepower engines, which gave her 26 knots speed.

The Chief of the Bureau of Navigation reported in July 1907:

> . . . we have not a sufficient number of officers to man properly the ships of the fleet and vessels of the torpedo-boat type.[19]

Due to this officer personnel shortage, the *Tingey* was in the Reserve Fleet and had no officer in her when I reported aboard.

I recommissioned the *Tingey* on December 11, 1907, and stayed in her for almost two years. During that period, I had the distinction of commanding one of the smallest combatant ships in our Navy and to participate in the organization of torpedo boats into flotillas, which were organized in the Atlantic and Pacific that year. Further, the *Tingey* had the good luck to win the Gunnery and the Engineering competitions, and was, I think, the first ship in the Atlantic to fly the newly created Battle Efficiency Pennant.

By the spring of 1909, I had been out of the Naval Academy almost seven years and, under normal conditions, could expect to go to shore duty. However, the Chief of the Bureau of Navigation (Rear Admiral W. H. Brownson) in his 1907 Annual Report to the Secretary of the Navy had said:

---

[19] *Ibid.*, p. 369.

NH 66926

USS Tingey *(TB-34) off Camden, New Jersey.*

> Under present conditions the younger officers of the line [lieutenants, lieutenants (junior grade), and ensigns] can not be spared from the fleet for assignment to duty on shore until after they have served at sea for at least ten years. This condition, however, results in increased efficiency of the personnel, for it is in the fleet that an officer receives the most important part of his training. . . .[20]

Since I was soon to go into engineering work, perhaps a few official statements on the subject may be appropriate:

> At the Naval Academy all line officers are given what is probably the best technical education furnished by any school in this country. The graduates of such a school are naturally fit to undertake subordinate engineering duties of all sorts. This theoretical education is supplemented, at least during the first five years of service, by alternate periods of duty on deck and in the engine room. . . . Almost every act of the line officer aboard ship has to do with machinery and with engineering.
>
> • • •
>
> This excellent general education and practical experience has not, however, qualified officers for the important work of designing the machinery of our vessels, and the department has met this need at an opportune time by the establishment of a post-graduate school of engineering at Annapolis that will, it is believed, provide fully for the needs of the service in particular.[21]

Postgraduate School

In the spring of 1909, I had been put on notice that I would be ordered ashore during the late summer.

In early April 1909, I had received a personal letter from Captain F. W. Bartlett (1878), USN, Head of the Department of Marine Engineering at the Naval Academy, saying that he had asked that I be ordered to the Naval Academy for duty in the Department of Marine Engineering. I politely replied that I had had no engineering assignments at sea and didn't want to teach marine engineering at the Naval Academy.

In order to avoid being ordered to the Naval Academy to teach a subject which I knew little about, I submitted the following letter requesting Post Graduate Instruction at the Massachusetts Institute of Technology, where our naval constructors had been receiving their basic post-Naval Academy instruction:

[20] *Ibid.*

[21] SECNAV (George von L. Meyer), *Annual Report,* 1909, p. 27.

U.S.S. TINGEY
Navy Yard, Pensacola, Fla.
April 12, 1909.

Sir:—

1. I respectfully request that I be detailed for the course of instruction in Marine Engine Design at the Massachusetts Institute of Technology, Boston, Mass.

2. My reasons for making this request are that I am interested in engineering work, and I am so old for my position in the Line that there is no hope of my ever reaching command of a division.

Very respectfully,

U.S.S. TINGEY
Navy Yard, Pensacola, Fla.
April 12, 1909.

The Secretary of the Navy.
Bureau of Navigation.[22]

My squadron commander forwarded my application with this endorsement: "Disapproved. This officer is too valuable to waste his time going to school."

In justice to the Navy, I should add that this officer, from the class of 1895, was later dropped from the Navy for repeated drunkeness. In justice to this officer, I should add that, as a bachelor officer, he was bored by the routine peacetime duties. Since he had plenty of nerve, was an expert handler of ships, and an excellent leader, he might, in my opinion, have been a war hero, had war occurred at the right time in his career in the Navy.

After my letter had started up the chain of command, a circular letter came out from the Department stating:

> The Department is of the opinion that to keep an officer out of contact with the Fleet for three years would be to so discriminate against him as to make it impossible for him to keep up to date, and, at the same time be practical in the execution of the various duties of his grade.

So, I promptly sent off the following letter, hoping that I could stall off going ashore at all:

U.S.S. TINGEY
Navy Yard, Pensacola, Fla.
April 26, 1909.

Sir:—

1. I respectfully request that I be relieved from command of the U.S.S. Tingey on her arrival at Charleston, South Carolina, and ordered to the U.S.S. Minnesota or one of the ships of her class.

[22] LT Richardson, 12 Apr. 1909, letter to SECNAV, microfilm NRS No. 1M, NHD.

NH 77342

James O. Richardson as a lieutenant.

2. My reasons for making this request are that I have never been on duty on a battle ship, have never been in the fleet, and "the Department is of the opinion that to keep an officer out of contact with the fleet for three years would be to so discriminate against him as to make it impossible for him to keep up to date, and, at the same time, be practical in the execution of the various duties of his grade."

Very respectfully,
J. O. Richardson
Lieutenant, U.S. Navy.
Commanding

The Secretary of the Navy.
Bureau of Navigation.
Thru the Flotilla Commander.[23]

The Department did not grant either of my requests.

Shortly thereafter, I was transferred to command of the torpedo boat *Stockton* (DD-73) and the Third Division of the Atlantic Torpedo Boat Flotilla. Harold ("Betty") Stark (1903) and Charles A. Blakely (1903) commanded the other two divisions in the flotilla. It was fun steaming at 20 knots in a three-boat wedge formation, so close together that one could toss a pack of cigarettes from the bow of the wing boats to the fantail of the leader, and I was most reluctant to go to shore duty.

Nevertheless, although I had no regular detail in the engineering departments of any of the ships I had served in since graduation, I was one of the ten officers selected for the first postgraduate marine engineering class at the United States Naval Academy and reported there September 29, 1909. It was stated later that:

> The basis of selection is professional ability, as evidenced by records of service of those officers who are candidates for detail to this school. There were considerably more than 200 applicants for detail to the classes now at the school, thus necessitating nice discrimination among officers whose claims to selection were, in many cases, nearly equal.[24]

My postgraduate classmates included a number of officers who were to make their mark in the engineering branch of the Navy; S. M. Robinson (1903) O. L. Cox (1905), and Albert T. Church (1905). Harry L. Brinser (1899) made his mark in the Line as well.

---

[23] *Ibid.*, 26 Apr. 1909.

[24] SECNAV, *Annual Report,* 1910, p. 27.

USS Delaware

Upon completion of my postgraduate course in 1911, I was ordered to the newly commissioned *Delaware* (BB-28) as Assistant Engineer Officer, and later Senior Engineer Officer. The *Delaware* was the first battleship to be built with boilers that could use oil as well as coal and the first to have forced lubricating for its reciprocating engines. She was a lucky ship for me as I had the good fortune to have among my Commanding Officers, both Captains John Hood (1879) and Hugh Rodman (1880), and her engineering plant functioned to the satisfaction of my Captains and the Department, as the following quotation indicates.

NH 60559

USS Delaware *(BB-28) firing during battle practice.*

> To test the reliability of the reciprocating engine in its present [stage of] development under conditions which might obtain in time of war, the *DELAWARE* . . . immediately upon her return to Boston from an extended South American cruise, was subjected to a surprise full-power run of 24 hours. Prior to this trial she was in port only 22½ hours for the purpose of coaling, during which time no examination or adjustment was made about her main

> engines. Her average speed for the 24 hours trial, burning coal alone, was a little better than her contract speed. There was no derangement of the main engines or auxiliaries during the trial or during the standardization runs which followed.
>
> Subsequent to these trials the *DELAWARE* steamed from New York to England, remained there 12 days, and returned to Boston, having completed the round trip without taking aboard any fuel during the trip and with 600 tons of coal left in her bunkers at the conclusion of the trip.[25]

During my cruise in the *Delaware,* there were two Fleet Reviews. At the second of these reviews, on October 15, 1912, President Taft said:

> A Navy is for fighting, and if its management is not efficiently directed to that end, the people of this country have a right to complain.[26]

Every naval officer could say "Amen" to this ever-vital truth, and it should be carved on the overhead of the offices of the civilian Secretaries and their assistants.

The Changing Navy

The Navy had continued to grow and, ten years after my graduation, had more than doubled in size. With an increase of 4,000 men during fiscal 1911, the total enlisted strength reached 51,500.

To illustrate the fact that shortages of technicians are a constantly recurring difficulty in the Navy, I quote from the 1910 Annual Report of the Chief of the Bureau of Navigation (Rear Admiral R. F. Nicholson [1875]):

> Much difficulty has been experienced in recruiting sufficient machinists' mates for the needs of the service. This is due in a large measure to industrial conditions, as there is a great demand for machinists at good wages throughout the country.[27]

Despite this difficulty with obtaining technicians, the overall quality of the enlisted personnel had continued to improve. The number of foreign-born in our Navy continued to decrease to a negligible number, and the American character of both the petty officers and non-rated men in our Navy was definitely established by 1912.

---

[25] *Ibid,* 1911, pp. 46-47.
[26] *Ibid,* 1912, p. 18.
[27] CHBUNAV (R. F. Nicholson), "Annual Report," 1910, p. 293.

Due to the inability of the Navy to recruit technicians directly into the Navy, in adequate numbers, the Navy Department, stimulated by demands from the Fleet and by the social philosophy of its new Secretary, laid a firm foundation during this period for the technical training of the officers and enlisted personnel of the World War I and World War II Navy. The Secretary of the Navy, Josephus Daniels, said with enthusiasm in his 1913 Annual Report to the President:

> It is my ambition to make the Navy a great university with college extensions, afloat and ashore.[28]

Bureau of Steam Engineering

On May 11, 1914, I reported into the Bureau of Steam Engineering. R. S. Griffin (1878) was the Chief of Bureau and Samuel S. Robison (1888) was his assistant. Arthur J. Hepburn (1897), later to hold the same billet as I—Commander-in-Chief of the United States Fleet—was also on duty in the Bureau. There were just twelve officers in the whole Bureau.

In addition to my duties as Aide to the Chief, I was Personnel Officer and Bureau representative, both in connection with fuel contracts and in connection with Naval Petroleum Reserves. This latter duty brought me into contact with the Secretary of the Navy, Josephus Daniels, and his assistant, Franklin D. Roosevelt.

The day I reported, I was informed that I would represent the Secretary of the Navy in complying with a Resolution of Congress requiring the Secretary of the Navy and the Secretary of the Interior to investigate and report on the feasibility, advisability, and expense of the Government owning a pipeline to the coast from oil-producing properties in the mid-continent fields, for the purpose of supplying fuel oil for the Navy.

Fuel oil was expensive, and its use was expanding rapidly. The Secretary (Josephus Daniels) had definite ideas in regard to fuel oil for the Navy, which he frequently set forth. A couple of quotes from the *Annual Report of the Secretary of the Navy* to the President will suffice.

> I desire to recommend to Congress the immediate consideration of providing fuel oil for the Navy at reasonable rates, and the passage of legislation that will

[28] SECNAV (Josephus Daniels), *Annual Report,* 1913, p. 6.

> enable the department to refine its own oil from its own oil wells and thus relieve itself of the necessity of purchasing what seems fair to become the principal fuel of the Navy in the future, at exorbitant and ever-increasing prices. . . .[29]
>
> • • •
>
> The recent trial tests of the *NEVADA,* the first dreadnaught equipped for the exclusive use of oil as motive power, emphasize the growing need of a large supply of oil for the Navy.[30]

On May 19, 1914, in company with Cato Sells, who represented the Secretary of the Interior, I left Washington to visit the mid-continent fields. After several months study, and based on the same information reported by Mr. Sells and myself, the Secretary of the Interior reported to the Congress that the project was feasible and desirable, while the Secretary of the Navy reported that it was feasible but not desirable.

Congress did nothing in regard to the project.

Somewhat later, at my request, Dr. George Otis Smith, the Director of the Geological Survey, selected an area, in the public lands, believed to contain large oil deposits. The Secretary of the Navy, in a letter prepared by me, requested the President to set this area aside as a Naval Petroleum Reserve. In 1915, it was reported that:

> A step in the right direction was taken when the President, on April 30, 1915, by Executive order, created naval petroleum reserve No. 3, containing 9,481 acres of probable oil-bearing land.[31]

Naval Petroleum Reserve No. 3 later became widely known as Teapot Dome.

Mr. Daniels' interest in oil for the Navy remained at a high level throughout his service as Secretary. In two later reports, he wrote:

> . . . it is of vital importance that the Navy protect every barrel of oil within these [petroleum] reserves in order that at least an adequate supply [of oil] shall be available within the continental limits of the United States in the event of war.[32]
>
> • • •
>
> The war on sea and in the air as well as on land has depended so much on transportation that it can be laid down as a basic principle that no nation that does not control an adequate oil supply can successfully maintain its forces in the field.[33]

[29] *Ibid.*, p. 14.
[30] *Ibid.*, 1915, p. 62.
[31] *Ibid.*, p. 65.
[32] *Ibid.*, 1916, p. 35.
[33] *Ibid.*, 1918, p. 138.

During this time, at the direction of the Secretary, I appeared many times before the Committees on Public Lands of the House and the Senate, to speak for him during hearings on proposed legislation that would affect the Navy's interest in the Naval Petroleum Reserves. It is seldom that such opportunities come to a junior lieutenant commander, and I believe that I greatly profited by the experience. I learned that, to be effective, a witness must be honest and forthright.

I had been promoted to lieutenant commander on July 1, 1914, and in 1916 was anxious to get to sea after my two and a half years of regular shore tour. This was particularly so in view of the war going on in Europe. However, I was held over by the Secretary until June 1917.

At one time, Admiral Griffin (Chief of the Bureau of Steam Engineering) told me that I, a young lieutenant commander, would be appointed as his successor. I said that I would refuse the assignment, believing myself unqualified.

The Secretary was anxious for me to become an Engineering Duty Only officer, a "new breed of cats" just created by Congress, and frequently urged me to request such transfer from the Line of the Navy. However, I hankered for sea duty, not a set of quarters on shore. We finally settled for having me draft a list of officers who would profit the Navy, if they were to devote all their talents to engineering work. This list was drafted for the signature of the Chief of the Bureau of Steam Engineering, who signed the letter. I then took this letter to the Secretary, who approved the recommendations, and then to the Bureau of Navigation. I do not remember all the names on this short, first list of EDO's, but among them were some good engineers, such as Joseph O. Fisher (1902), Samuel M. Robinson (1903), Ormond L. Cox (1905), and Albert T. Church (1905).

The Secretary was thoughtful enough to have the following letter placed in my record:

To: Lieutenant Commander
James O. Richardson, U.S.N.
Bureau of Steam Engineering,
Navy Department,
Washington, D. C.

Subject: Work in connection with the Naval Petroleum Reserves.

Upon your detachment from duty at the Bureau of Steam Engineering the

Secretary of the Navy desires to express his appreciation of your excellent work in connection with the Naval Petroleum Reserves.

The fact that you undertook this work in addition to regular duties and handled it in such a competent manner is a matter of satisfaction to the Navy Department.

The importance of this work and your knowledge of the questions involved warranted your retention on shore duty after December 1, 1916, and were it not for the fact that a continuation of shore duty at this time might adversely affect your chances for promotion, you would be retained for work in connection with pending Oil Land Legislation.

Josephus Daniels

Bureau of Steam Engineering,
June 25, 1917 [34]

USS Nevada

As the Secretary of the Navy reported to the President:

> The business of a naval officer is on the sea.[35]
>
> • • •
>
> Since April 6 [1917] the Navy of the United States has been undergoing the test of war.[36]
>
> • • •
>
> From a force of 4,500 officers and 68,000 enlisted men in January, 1917, the Navy has expanded to 15,000 officers and 254,000 enlisted men. . . . Further expansions are inevitable.[37]
>
> • • •
>
> The day of promotion by seniority in the line of the Navy has forever passed.[38]

On June 27, 1917, I reported to the battleship *Nevada* (BB-36) as Navigator and spent the remaining seventeen months of World War I in that fine ship. Captain Joseph Strauss (1885) was the first of four captains I served under in the *Nevada.* William D. Leahy (1897) was the Executive Officer when I reported and, when he was detached in early April 1918,

---

[34] SECNAV, 25 June 1917, letter to LCDR Richardson, Personal File, Military Personnel Records Center, St. Louis, Mo.

[35] SECNAV, *Annual Report,* 1913, p. 19.

[36] *Ibid.,* 1917, p. 1.

[37] *Ibid.,* p. 2.

[38] *Ibid.,* p. 14.

I fleeted up to Executive Officer, having been promoted to temporary commander as of October 15, 1917.

During the first year of World War I, the *Nevada,* along with all the other larger combatant ships on this side of the Atlantic, acted as a training school for the expanding Navy. She cruised a contingent of midshipmen from the Naval Academy during the summer of 1917 and conducted training of armed guard crews for U.S. merchant ships and Army-Navy transports, turning out qualified gun crews every six weeks.

It was not until August 1918, that the *Nevada* moved into the European War Zone. She came at the urgent request of Vice Admiral William S. Sims (1880) (Commander U.S. Naval Forces in European Waters) with headquarters in London. He described the need as follows:

> Despite all the precautions which I have described, there was still one danger which constantly confronted American troop transports. By June and July, 1918, our troops were crossing the Atlantic in enormous numbers, about 300,000 a month. . . . A successful attack upon a convoy, involving the sinking of one or more transports, would have had no important effect upon the war, but it would probably have improved German morale and possibly have injured that of the Americans. There was practically only one way in which such an attack could be made; one or more German battle-cruisers might slip out to sea and assail one of our troop convoys. In order to prepare for such a possibility, the department sent three of our most powerful dreadnaughts to Berehaven, Ireland—the *NEVADA* . . . the *OKLAHOMA* . . . and the *UTAH* . . . the whole division under the command of Rear-Admiral Thomas S. Rodgers (1878).[39]

Operating out of Berehaven, Bantry Bay, Ireland, escorting convoys and on one occasion, searching for the German battle-cruiser *Von der Tann,* the *Nevada* finished out the war.

On November 18, 1918, the *Nevada* left Berehaven to join Battle Squadron Six, Grand Fleet, and arrived at Rosyth, Scotland, November 23, 1918, two days after the surrender of the German Fleet.

1919

In the period immediately following World War I, the Navy expanded and its objectives were changed. As reported by Secretary Daniels in his report to the President:

---

[39] RADM William S. Sims and Burton S. Hendrick, *The Victory At Sea* (Garden City, N.Y.: Doubleday, Page and Company, 1920), p. 354.

NH 57232

USS Nevada *(BB-36) in European Waters.*

The United States Navy emerged from the war incomparably stronger and more powerful than ever before—second only to that of Great Britain. . . .[40]

• • •

On January 8, 1919, the "United States Fleet" was formed. . . .[41]

• • •

In the summer [of 1919], after careful consideration, the American Fleet was organized, in two divisions, one under the command of Admiral Henry B. Wilson [1881], known as the Atlantic, and the other known as the Pacific, under the command of Admiral Hugh Rodman [1880].[42]

In the next nine years after World War I, I served as Head of the Department of Steam Engineering at the United States Naval Academy, as Commander South China Patrol, and the Commanding Officer of the gunboat, USS *Asheville* (PG-21), in the Asiatic Fleet, as Assistant to the Chief of the Bureau of Ordnance, and as Commander Destroyers, United States Naval Forces in Europe and as Commander Destroyer Division Thirty-eight.

These nine years were important to the Navy and to me, but I pass

[40] SECNAV (Josephus Daniels), *Annual Report,* 1919, p. 5.
[41] *Ibid.,* p. 17.
[42] *Ibid.,* p. 9.

over them lightly, noting only a few of the red marker buoys of naval progress and matters relating to my own naval experience:

1920

The former collier *JUPITER* is being converted into an aircraft carrier and will be ready for commissioning during the winter. This craft, renamed the *LANGLEY*, will give the fleet an opportunity to develop the usefulness of vessels of this character.[43]

• • •

. . . it has become imperative as a matter of national defense to provide for the maximum possible development of aviation . . . in the Navy.[44]

1921–1922–1923

The Navy Department is fully alive to the demand of the country for economy. . . .[45]

The department has during the year given great attention to the matter of . . . economy, in accordance with the expressed wishes of the President.[46]

• • •

There were no combined maneuvers on account of lack of appropriations.[47]

• • •

Economy has been enforced in every branch of the Naval Establishment. . . .[48]

• • •

Due to inadequacy of funds . . . to meet all upkeep needs, the material condition of the fleet has not improved during the past year.[49]

1924–1925

. . . there is concerted effort for economy of operation and consequently a much stricter supervision over all activities.[50]

Contrary to the reflected opinions of certain portions of the press, the bureau

---

[43] *Ibid.*, 1920, p. 44.

[44] SECNAV (Edwin Denby), *Annual Report*, 1921, p. 3.

[45] *Ibid.*, p. 7.

[46] *Ibid.*, 1922, p. 10.

[47] *Ibid.*, p. 3.

[48] *Ibid.*, 1923, p. 2.

[49] *Ibid.*, 1924, p. 12.

[50] "Annual Report of the Chief of the Bureau of Ordnance (C. C. Bloch)," for the fiscal year 1924 in *Annual Reports of the Navy Department*, p. 263.

is of the firm opinion that our Navy afloat is in a highly efficient condition and that much progress has been made during the past year in gunnery.[51]

The high percentage of reenlistments, the decrease in percentage of net desertions, the reports on personnel from unit commands . . . [all] are indicators of a general improvement in the character and skill of the personnel and its administration.[52]

• • •

. . . The fiscal year 1925 has been marked by a return to stabilized personnel conditions. . . .[53]

1927–1928

The United States Naval Forces in Europe acting in cooperation with the State Department [were engaged primarily in showing the flag along the entire] . . . European and North African Coasts.[54]

• • •

The *USS MEMPHIS* [CL–13] and Destroyer Division 25 were relieved by the *USS DETROIT* [CL–8] and Destroyer Division 38 in June 1927.[55]

• • •

Destroyer Division 38 returned to the United States in February [1928] without replacement, leaving only the *DETROIT* in Europe.[56]

• • •

During the past few years the personnel [of the Navy] has been gradually reduced from 86,000 to 83,250. For the past year the funds appropriated for the pay of enlisted men was not sufficient to support the numbers required to man vessels necessary to accomplish all the duties required of the Navy.[57]

Commander South China Patrol

I will relate only one personal incident during this period and I relate

[51] *Ibid.*, 1925, p. 239.

[52] CHBUNAV (W. R. Shoemaker), "Annual Report," 1925, p. 140.

[53] *Ibid.*

[54] SECNAV (Curtis D. Wilbur), *Annual Report*, 1927, p. 6.

[55] *Ibid.*, p. 7.

[56] *Ibid.*, 1928, p. 6; Destroyer Division Thirty-Eight was recalled from Europe to make available an adequate number of destroyers in the Fleet in order to handle the rapidly growing requirements for plane guards.

[57] "Annual Report of the Chief of Naval Operations (C. F. Hughes)" for the fiscal year 1928 (hereafter cited as CNO, "Annual Report" with year) in *Annual Reports of the Navy Department*, p. 91.

NH 77341

Commander Richardson (left) visiting the Sphinx in Egypt while en route to the Asiatic Station. With him (left to right) Lieutenant W. B. Young (SC) and Lieutenant R. W. Hayworth (MC).

it because I think it points out the great value to juniors of serving under an understanding senior.

Lieutenant Thomas Washington (1887) was on the staff of Admiral Robley D. Evans (1863), Commander-in-Chief, U.S. Asiatic Fleet, during my first tour of duty on the Asiatic Station. Later, when I was Commander South China Patrol in 1923-24, he was Commander-in-Chief, Asiatic Fleet.

I have never served under a finer officer.

There was always something of interest happening on the Asiatic Station, and 1923 was no exception. According to the Secretary of the Navy's Annual Report:

> In December, 1923, Sun Yat Sen, President of the Republic of South China, threatened to seize the customs in Canton, hitherto under international control. In concert with [the movement of] . . . forces of other nations the United States sent six destroyers to Canton. The firm stand and cooperation shown by the various naval forces compelled Sun Yat Sen to recede from his threat to use force and the customs continued to be administered as formerly.[58]

Sun Yat Sen's proposed action was a serious threat to all of the Treaty Powers, whose loans to China were serviced by the revenues of the Chinese Maritime Customs.

During the ensuing crisis, there assembled at Canton, naval forces whose senior officers held naval rank as follows:

British	—vice admiral (Sir Arthur Leveson)	Italian	—captain
Japanese	—rear admiral	Portuguese	—captain
French	—rear admiral	U.S.A.	—commander (James O. Richardson, USN)

In the early days of this crisis, I had available to me no statement of the policy of our State Department and no specific instructions from my Commander-in-Chief in regard to it. However, I believed that it would be to the best interests of the United States if my efforts were devoted to securing close cooperation between the representatives of the Treaty Powers in the firm protection of their mutual interests.

Vice Admiral Sir Arthur Leveson, RN, was Commander-in-Chief of the British Eastern (China) Fleet at this time. He was in Canton only part of the time but was close by in Hong Kong during the whole incident.

Every evening I reported by radio to the Commander-in-Chief of the Asiatic Fleet and the American Minister to China what had occurred during the day and closed each despatch with—"In the absence of other instructions, I propose to do. . . ."

Each day, I anticipated receiving a statement of policy from Washington. I scanned the radio operators' log of the Cavite Broadcast Schedule several times each day. After about ten days, I found that the *Asheville* had copied

[58] SECNAV, *Annual Report*, 1924, p. 7.

from the Cavite broadcast a coded despatch from the Navy Department in a code not held by me. The despatch was not addressed to the Commander-in-Chief, nor was my radio call in the heading as an information addressee, but, by changing one letter in each radio call or address, the despatch would be addressed to the Commander-in-Chief for action and for information to myself.

I informed the Commander-in-Chief that I believed this despatch contained instructions for him. Within an hour, this despatch was repeated to me by the flagship, in a code which I held. It read:

> TO: CINC ASIATIC
> INFORMATION: COMMANDER SOUTH CHINA PATROL
>
> CONCENTRATE NECESSARY FORCES AT CANTON AND PREVENT SUN'S SEIZURE OF CUSTOMS BY ALL MEASURES SHORT OF WAR.[59]

On the following day, I met, as usual, with the senior naval officers of the various nations whose ships were in the harbor and the consul generals of the interested foreign powers. The British Consul General, as usual, said to me, "Well, Commodore have you received any instructions?" I said, "Yes," and read the despatch. The British representative said "How do you interpret that language?" I said, "If Sun tries to seize Custom House here, I shall stop it by force, but my men will not pursue his when they flee." That reply was satisfactory to all hands.

After a few tense weeks, during which I, the junior force commander present, had at my command by far the largest naval force, but having no daily detailed instructions, the situation became normal. No attempt to seize the customs was made, and the assembled forces dispersed.

At the start of this incident, the Commander-in-Chief was in the Southern Philippines. I was told, by what I consider an authoritative source, that he said to his Chief of Staff, "Richardson knows more about this than I do; there is no need for me to go to Canton and stick my neck out."

During this incident, I had more responsibility, independence, and power of decision than usually come to an officer of the rank of commander. I loved it and I believe that it was conducive to my development.

During my cruise in the *Asheville* I was present in the harbor of Tsingtao when Japan relinquished the former German-leased territory of Kiaochow in Shantung Province to China as a result of the Chinese-

[59] Quoted from ADM Richardson's diary.

80-G-1034878

USS Asheville *(PG-21), Flagship of the South China Patrol on the Yangtze.*

Japanese Shantung Agreement (1922). There was fear that disorder would follow the removal of the firm Japanese control, but quiet prevailed.

The *Asheville* was present in Amoy, in the Min River below Foochow, and in Swatow during the "War of the War Lords." I saw these cities change hands one or more times and met several of the contending war lords.

My cruise on the South China Station was capped by the *Asheville* winning the Gunnery Trophy, the Engineering Trophy, and by a despatch from the American Minister to China, reading as follows:

> 8615 . . . . . I LEARN THAT COMMANDER RICHARDSON IS TODAY RELINQUISHING COMMAND OF SOUTH CHINA PATROL AND DESIRE TO RECORD EXPRESSION MY ADMIRATION FOR THE EFFICIENT MANNER HE HAS DISCHARGED THE DUTIES OF THAT DIFFICULT POST AS WELL AS MY THANKS FOR HIS VALUABLE ASSIST-

ANCE TO AND HELPFUL COOPERATION WITH THE AMERICAN LEGATION AND CONSUL OFFICIALS IN CHINA WHICH WILL BE GRATEFULLY REMEMBERED BY ALL CONCERNED SIGNED SCHURMAN 1320

Toward the end of my *Asheville* cruise, I applied for duty under instruction at the Naval War College. I was informed by Admiral H. B. Wilson (1881) (Superintendent of the Naval Academy) that I would be ordered to the Naval Academy, and by C. C. Bloch (1899) that I would be ordered to the Bureau of Ordnance, but I was actually ordered by radio to proceed to Washington by the first available transportation. Leave was denied me, although I had had only nineteen days leave in the preceding nine years. When I arrived in Washington, I learned that I had been ordered home peremptorily, for duty in the office of the Assistant Secretary of the Navy in connection with the Naval Petroleum Reserves and the pending Congressional investigation. But Bloch interceded for me, and I went to the Bureau of Ordnance.

To BUNAV

After my duty in the Bureau of Ordnance, at my request, I was ordered to command Destroyer Division Thirty-Eight, slated for one year's duty in Europe, but after about seven months, the division was ordered to Guantanamo Bay. Arriving on 13 February 1928, we conducted one year's target practice in less than two months. Thence, the division proceeded to San Francisco, where I was detached after a cruise of less than a year. Over my repeated personal protests, I was ordered to duty in the Bureau of Navigation. However, the Chief of the Bureau of Navigation promised me that my next cruise would be a long one, and his successor kept the promise.

My prospective chief had the following official letter addressed to me—which encouraged me to believe that my short sea cruise would not adversely affect my future promotion:

9 March 1928

From: Chief of Bureau of Navigation
To: Captain J. O. Richardson, U.S. Navy,
U.S.S. WHIPPLE.
Subject: Detail to Duty

1. After careful consideration of the fact that you have only been at sea on your present cruise about one year and also of the fact that your average sea service is fifteen years compared to that of about sixteen for your contemporaries, it has been decided to order you to duty as Director of Officer Personnel in the Bureau of Navigation.

2. In issuing these orders to you the Bureau has given very careful consideration to the fact that this limits your present cruise but feels that the best interests of the Service will be served at the present time by detaching you and

3. The change in duty will take place shortly after the arrival of the Division of Destroyers under your command on the West Coast.

assigning you to the duty as above stated.

R. H. Leigh[60]

After Thirty

In 1924, the Annual Report of the Secretary of the Navy contained this note on one of my former ships:

> The *QUIROS*, an old gunboat no longer serviceable on the rivers, was placed out of commission.[61]

Like the *Quiros*, I was getting on in years, but instead of being placed out of commission, my first thirty years in the Navy were ending on a note of hope for the future.

---

[60] CHBUNAV, 9 Mar. 1928, letter to CAPT Richardson, Personal File, Military Personnel Records Center, St. Louis, Mo.

[61] CNO (Edward W. Eberle), "Annual Report," 1924, p. 71.

Chapter VII

Preparation for Four-Star Assignment 1928-1939

I do not believe that any senior naval officer ever received a forewarning that he was about to be ordered to a command assignment in the Navy, without such notice giving him a few qualms as to his qualifications for the billet. If not qualms, then certainly he would go thru some inward questioning or perhaps a quick listing on a balance sheet of his own abilities or deficiencies, previous training or lack of it, which he would need or miss in meeting his future responsibilities. For a Flag Officer, this balance sheet, in addition, provides information on those special talents which he should seek to provide within his staff or command.

I know it was this way with me.

My Qualifications?

What were my qualifications to take over an important billet in the United States Fleet in June 1939? The only way this can be judged is by a review of some of the training, experience, and study which had been undergone in the ten years immediately preceding.

Senior Detail Officer

In May 1928, after having been in the Navy for thirty years and having reached the age of fifty, I was a captain, number 125 in grade, out of 243 captains. I was fortunate enough to be the Director of Officer Personnel in the Bureau of Navigation. The Chief of Naval Operations was Admiral Charles F. Hughes (1888), USN, and Admiral William V. Pratt (1889), USN, was Commander-in-Chief of the U.S. Fleet.

My billet was as fine a shore billet as there existed in the Navy then for a young captain. It was a billet calling for a very extensive knowledge of the individual capabilities of the seagoing, command-rank officer personnel, the laws governing the promotion of officers, the rules and regulations that had been laid down under these laws, and the customs which had grown up to ensure fairness to the individual officer, as well as fairness to the Navy as a whole.

During this period (1928-1931), I served under Rear Admiral R. H. Leigh (1891), USN, and Rear Admiral Frank B. Upham (1893), USN, who were the Chiefs of the Bureau—two very fine and thoroughly capable officers.

There were many problems, a number of them recurring, as indicated in the following quotations from official reports:

1928

> A shortage [of personnel], requiring the reduction of vessels' allowances of personnel below the point of efficiency exists during the current fiscal year, and will increase in the future unless adequate measures . . . are taken to forestall it.[1]

1929

> As certain classes of vessels in the fleet require full complements, it is necessary that the remaining vessels operate with greatly reduced complements in order to provide the men necessary in the interest and progress of aviation.[2]
>
> • • •
>
> . . . the contentment of the personnel, and, therefore, its fullest efficiency, has suffered because of the situation in respect to service pay.[3]

1930

> The decommissioning of vessels will permit the reduction of the enlisted force of the Navy during fiscal year 1931 by 4,800 men.[4]
>
> • • •
>
> The increased pay which the services have received since 1908 is only 11 percent over that received in 1908, whereas during the same period of time the cost of living has more than doubled. The officers of the service are men whose lives have been consecrated to the service of their country; they are the first

[1] SECNAV (Curtis D. Wilbur), *Annual Report,* 1928, p. 21.
[2] SECNAV (Charles F. Adams), *Annual Report,* 1929, p. 3.
[3] *Ibid.,* p. 15.
[4] *Ibid.,* 1930, p. 4.

line of defense in time of war, and their country should recompense them adequately, even generously, for their service and hardships which they are forced to undergo—hardships which the layman can not properly appreciate unless he actually sees them.[5]

USS Augusta

My three years of duty as Director of Officer Personnel, were extremely busy but pleasant years. And, near the end of my shore duty, I was slated for command of one of our new 10,000-ton heavy cruisers which was nearing completion, the USS *Augusta* (CA-31). According to a report from the Chief of Naval Operations:

> The *Augusta* was commissioned at Norfolk on January 30, 1931. Her original shakedown cruise was curtailed due to damage to one of her turbines. She did, however, make a cruise to Colon and return. The *Augusta* became flagship of the Commander Scouting Force on May 21, 1931.[6]

After ordering that no civilians and no ladies could be present, because I believed that this was the opportunity for a Commanding Officer to impress his ideas on the officers and men of his ship, I assumed command with these words:

Officers and Men of the *Augusta*:

> Today we take over a new ship of the Navy just delivered by the builders. Now she is an inanimate thing, without life, without spirit, without record and without reputation; what she becomes depends upon us.
>
> We have the opportunity to so play our parts that in the future officers and men of the Navy will take pride in recalling their service on the *U.S.S. Augusta.*
>
> I pledge myself to do my best. I could demand no more of you. I expect no less.

I remained in command of the *Augusta* over two years (from January 30, 1931 to May 20, 1933), the longest command cruise of a large ship by any naval officer within my memory. My immediate seniors were Vice Admiral Arthur L. Willard (1890), USN, then Vice Admiral Frank H. Clark, Jr. (1893), USN, each serving as Commander Scouting Force, and Vice Admiral William H. Standley (1895), USN, Commander Cruisers,

---

[5] *Ibid.*, p. 15.

[6] CNO (William V. Pratt), "Annual Report," 1931, p. 115.

80-G-466398

USS Augusta *(CA-31), 1933.*

Scouting Force. Her first four Commanding Officers (Richardson, Ingersoll, Nimitz, Gygax) eventually wore a total of fifteen stars.

These years, 1931 to 1933, were bleak ones for the Navy, as evidenced by Secretary of the Navy, Charles Francis Adams, in his Annual Reports:

> Curtailment of expenditures has been made principally at the expense of the fighting fleet.[7]
>
> • • •
>
> The act making appropriations for the fiscal year 1932 provided funds for an enlisted strength of 79,700 men. This is the lowest number of men appropriated for in any year since the World War.[8]
>
> • • •
>
> Neither is there economy in our example of disarmament, which has not been followed by others. It is extravagance.[9]

Naval War College

In my opinion, my real preparation for high rank in the Navy can be said to have begun in 1933. For on June 20 of that year, when I was a captain with thirty-one years of service after graduation, I reported to the Naval War College at Newport, Rhode Island, for duty under instruction as the senior member of the senior class.

For many years, a vigorous minority of the senior officers of the Navy felt that a course at the Naval War College tended to make one a theoretical officer.

As late as 1930, I said to the Chief of Naval Operations that, although I had applied many times, I had never gone to the War College. He replied, "Failure to attend the War College has never hurt anyone."[10]

It was often said, by the detractors of higher learning in the Navy, that the only senior captains ordered to the Naval War College were those whom the Navy Department could not find, elsewhere, any duty to which to assign them. From my experience as the Director of Officer Personnel in the old Bureau of Navigation, I learned that there was some truth in this jibe.

[7] SECNAV (Charles F. Adams), *Annual Report,* 1932, p. 4.

[8] SECNAV, *Annual Report,* 1932, p. 22.

[9] *Ibid.,* 1933, p. 3.

[10] I note that on 1 January 1930, 36 of the 57 Line Flag Officers were graduates of the Naval War College, one was there under instruction, and another of these Flag Officers attended the next year (65%). On 1 January 1924, only 25 of the 49 Line Flag Officers were graduates of the Naval War College (50%). On 1 July 1941, 83 of the 84 Line Flag Officers were graduates.

But, the Bureau also ordered to the senior class at the Naval War College:

(a) captains of uncertain caliber

(b) as many top-caliber captains who earnestly sought the War College assignment as could be pried away from the clutches of various Flag Officers seeking to have these top-caliber officers assigned to duty under them

(c) captains whom it was desired to put "on ice" for a year, awaiting the opening up of a particularly desirable or appropriate assignment

My experience was that the three classifications were about equal in number in each senior class.

I had sought assignment at the Naval War College for some years, and I was delighted when ordered there. I enjoyed and benefited from the course. I recommend attendance at the Naval War College to all seagoing officers of the Navy who aspire to serve their Navy well in time of war.

On the last working day of my course at the Naval War College, when the members of the graduating class were asked to make any remarks they might wish to make, because I was the senior member, and no one else had risen to speak, I rose and said, "Today an ambition of long standing is being realized. I am completing the course at the War College for which I have applied periodically during the past fifteen years. When I first applied for this assignment, I had a definite idea as to the value of the course here. That idea has not changed. I think that the course makes 'a good officer a better officer, but that it tends to convert a fool into a damn fool.' "

Senior Thesis

The subject assigned to the Senior Class of 1934 for writing their thesis was: "The Relationship in War of Naval Strategy, Tactics, and Command."

In my thesis I observed that, "An industrious and gifted writer might, somewhat inadequately, cover the subject in a lifetime."

Among my "random ideas" submitted, there were some that stood the test of World War II, and I believe will stand the test of any future war.

ON STRATEGY

> If the enemy has a Fleet, and a superior geographical position for attacking our vital trade routes or for protecting his own, our first Naval aim will be to improve our geographical position, and then contest for the control of trade routes.

• • •

In peace, the role of Naval strategy is to so prepare the Navy for the support of the National Policy, that other Nations, whose policy may conflict with ours, will be loath to resort to war; yet if war should unhappily eventuate, our Navy will be so prepared and so disposed, with properly equipped and adequately defended bases so located, as to enable it to attack successfully the vital trade routes of the enemy, while defending our own.

• • •

Naval Strategy begins in time of peace. A large part of the work of strategy should be completed before war begins.

ON NATIONAL POLICY

At best, our foreign policy is nebulous and improvised. However, its developments and changes should be the subject of constant study by naval personnel, in order that in the absence of more authoritative information, such an estimate may serve as a basis for the development of American Navy Strategy.

COMMAND

Naval Command does not formulate policy, but since it has the duty of supporting policy, it should have some voice in seeing that the means provided are in harmony with the policy to be supported.

INDOCTRINATION AND TRAINING

The only time during the past twenty years when I have been conscious of any effort to indoctrinate me has been at the Naval War College.

• • •

I believe that indoctrination is an aid to the success of any organization in peace and is essential to its success in war; that the higher command in the Navy does not realize that the failure to indoctrinate subordinates during peace may have grave consequences in war.

PLANNING

The Navy as a whole is exceedingly weak in planning. Nearly everyone is so concerned with doing the job in hand that he devotes little thought to the future. The larger the organization, the more necessary that a fair portion of its time and intelligence be freed from considerations of the here and now, in order that the requisite time and intelligence may be devoted to plans for the future.

Having hit the nail on the head a good many times, it was certainly human to hit my fingers at least once—and I surely did, for I said:

It would probably be safe to assume that our Navy will not, in our lifetime, be employed in escorting large troop movements across the Atlantic.[11]

[11] James O. Richardson, "The Relationship in War of Naval Strategy, Tactics, and Command" (Senior class dissertation, Naval War College, 7 May 1934).

Amongst the members of my Naval War College class who became Flag Officers were:

Captain William R. Furlong (1905)
Captain John H. Towers (1906)
Captain Harold M. Bemis (1907)
Commander James L. Kauffman (1908)
Commander Samuel A. Clement (1908)
Commander Arthur S. Carpender (1908)
Commander Frank T. Leighton (1909)
Commander Robert G. Coman (1909)
Commander Charles M. Cooke (1910)
Commander Augustine H. Gray (1910)
Commander Herbert R. Hein (1910)
Commander Ralph F. Wood (1911)
Commander Elliot B. Nixon (1911)

Of the five Line captains in my class, four became Flag Officers. Of the thirty-four Line commanders, ten became Flag Officers. This seems to me to indicate that the Bureau of Navigation did an acceptable job in picking the Class of 1934 at the Naval War College.

Pre-High Command Training

Officer's careers are now greatly shortened from what they were when I was active in the Navy. In my days, the midshipman entered younger (at ages 16 to 20), and, on the average, the officer retired later (after 35 years of service for non-selection to Flag rank; or at age 64 after selection to Flag rank).

Therefore, many of our most distinguished Line officers served from 40 to 44 years after graduation from the Naval Academy, and every thoroughly capable officer of good health was available to serve the Navy and the government for 35 years.

With selection to Flag rank taking place after 33 and 34 years service, instead of after 23 to 28 years as of now, it was possible to do some realistic training of mature officers for high command, officers who had shown a high level of performance after maturity, not just those who had shown a high level of performance in reaching maturity (ages 45 to 50).

Admiral W. H. Standley says of this:

> During my almost continuous service of six years [1924-1930] [in the Navy Department] . . . I had often thought about and discussed with other officers the difficult problem of selecting properly qualified officers for the big com-

> mands in the Navy—Chief of Naval Operations; Commander-in-Chief, United States Fleet; Commander-in-Chief, Asiatic Fleet; Commander, Battle Fleet; Commander, Scouting Fleet; and others carrying with them the higher temporary rank of Admiral or Vice Admiral. In talking this over with Rear Admiral J. O. Richardson, who was then Assistant Chief of the Bureau of Navigation, which had the responsibility for the detail and orders of officers, we hit upon what we thought would be a better plan. The Bureau of Navigation would arrange for certain flag officers to be assigned such duties from the time of their selection that several of them would be qualified for a certain job to which it was expected they would be assigned, culminating in the top job as Chief of Naval Operations. When this plan was explained to Admiral Charles F. Hughes, then CNO, he heartily approved and Joe Richardson set about putting the plan into effect.[12]

This statement has several minor errors in it. Instead of being a rear admiral and Assistant Chief of the Bureau of Navigation, actually I was a captain and Director of Officer Personnel in the Bureau. My promotion to Flag rank did not take place until December 1934, and I never held the job of Assistant to the Chief of the Bureau of Navigation.

But in any case, this decision of the Chief of Naval Operations led to the practice, during my tenure as Director of Officer Personnel, of making up a "Training Slate" for Flag Officers. I believe the practice was carried on for some years and that it paid good dividends to the Navy.

I believe I was the recipient of such training in Flag rank, since I was given six different details in six years, all very helpful in training an officer for a broad knowledge of the Naval Establishment.

Budget Officer

When I completed the War College course in the summer of 1934, I had been ashore one year. I was ordered to the billet of Director of Naval Communications in Naval Operations. Rear Admiral Claude Bloch, who was Budget Officer and at that time a rear admiral of the lower half, found that there was an unexpected vacancy as Judge Advocate General, a billet carrying the pay of a rear admiral of the upper half, so he arranged to get that job and suggested that I be ordered as Budget Officer to relieve him.

---

[12] ADM William H. Standley and RADM Arthur A. Ageton, *Admiral Ambassador to Russia* (Chicago: H. Regnery Co., 1955), p. 24.

I received this change in my orders just as I was leaving the Naval War College.

This was an excellent detail, since, at that time, the Budget Officer played a very real part in shaping up the proposed allocation of funds within the Naval Establishment. The detail is one that is extremely instructive to the officer who holds the billet, and as well, is one that can be extremely useful in guiding funds into naval channels, where in his judgment they are most needed, for the proper development of the Navy. In order to defend the requests of the Navy before the Budget Bureau and before the Congressional appropriation subcommittee, it is necessary for the budget to be sound and for the Budget Officer to have all the necessary detailed knowledge of the various projects, to show that it is sound when it is closely examined before military seniors and vitally concerned Congressional inquirers.

In my opinion, the Budget Officer should be a seagoing officer. I do not see how an Engineering Duty Only Officer can possibly have the overall naval knowledge and perspective needed to promote constantly the long-range interests of the operating forces of the Navy.

When I reported as Budget Officer, I found that Captain Frank Jack Fletcher (1906) was Aide to the Secretary of the Navy, Claude Swanson. As I did not know the Secretary well, with Jack's assistance I sold myself to the Secretary. In a few months, the Secretary asked me to stay with him as long as he was in office, which I promised to do.

In the spring of 1935, both the Secretary and the Assistant Secretary (Henry Latrobe Roosevelt) told me that I would be appointed Chief of the Bureau of Navigation to relieve Rear Admiral "Bill" Leahy (1897). I told both of them that I did not want the job but would do any assigned job to the best of my ability. Shortly thereafter, "Bull" Reeves, who was CINCUS, came to town and obtained the BUNAV billet for Adolphus Andrews, who was his Chief of Staff.

The last of May 1935, I heard that Rear Admiral Horne would be taken out as Commander Cruiser Division Six, so I went to the Secretary and said:

> Mr. Secretary, I would like to have your advice. I have just learned that an unexpected vacancy will occur in the command of a division of cruisers. I know that I have promised to stay with you, which I will do, but if I am ever going to have a high command at sea, I should go to sea now. What do you advise me to do?

The Secretary put his arm around me and said, "Joe, I never stood in anybody's way; of course you may go to sea." Later, he told me that this agreement to let me go to sea was predicated on the understanding that I would find a wholly satisfactory relief for myself. I proposed Captain Husband E. Kimmel to Admirals Standley and Bill Leahy, and they both agreed to recommend Kimmel for the job. Kimmel was so assigned.

THE NAVY IS REVIVED—THE FISCAL YEAR 1935-1936

As indicated in the following quotes, the Navy was revived during 1935-1936.

> During the year ended June 30, 1936, the purpose of our Government to bring the Navy to full treaty strength in under age vessels of the combatant categories which are limited by the Washington (1922) and London (1930) agreements has been brought measurably nearer to accomplishment.[13]

• • •

> The additional vessels provided for by the 1937 Appropriation Act are 12 destroyers and 6 submarines, all to be built as replacements for existing vessels which are over age or which will become so before completion of the new units.[14]

• • •

> Legislation is greatly needed to give authorization for an adequate continuing plan of improvement in fleet auxiliary vessels.[15]

Service Pay

> In other words, in 28 years, wherein the cost of living has increased materially and the pay of other Federal officials and of State officials has been largely increased, only a slight increase has been granted Naval officers and men. In consequence considerable hardship has been and is being experienced by naval personnel and, while the morale of the service remains high, inadequacy of pay necessarily affects the efficiency of the service.[16]

Chief of Staff to CINCUS

In June 1935, I traveled to the Pacific Coast and reported as Commander Cruiser Division Six at Bremerton, Washington. The division left Bremer-

[13] SECNAV (Claude A. Swanson), *Annual Report,* 1936, p. 1.

[14] *Ibid.*

[15] *Ibid.,* p. 2.

[16] *Ibid.,* p. 17.

ton the last day of August and arrived in Long Beach the day before Labor Day. When I went ashore to the Villa Riviera, my wife's first words to me were, "Do you know that you are going to be ordered as Chief of Staff to 'Bull' Reeves?" Reeves was the Commander-in-Chief, U.S. Fleet (CINCUS). I said, "Not if I can help it." Next morning, Labor Day, 1935, I went off to see Admiral "Bill" Leahy who had reported as Commander Battle Force. He said, "Joe, I recommended you for this job, and you can not refuse, because you are now under Reeves' command and you must take the job." While I was talking to Bill, the barge of CINCUS came alongside, and an aide came on board and said that CINCUS wanted to see me at once. I went over in the barge and, a few days later, was ordered as Chief of Staff. It was the best sea billet I ever had as preparation for high command, even though I found "Bull" Reeves a difficult man to work for.

The need for a new Chief of Staff to CINCUS was caused by the fact that Rear Admiral S. W. Bryant (1900), who had relieved Adolphus Andrews, had developed tuberculosis and had to be relieved.

BUILDING CONTINUES—THE FISCAL YEAR 1936-1937

With the support of Congress and the President, Secretary of the Navy Swanson was able to report real progress in the building up of the Navy in his 1937 Annual Report.

> Naval development during the fiscal year ending June 30, 1937, continued the new construction and orderly replacement of over age vessels and aircraft as authorized in the Vinson-Trammel [sic] Act of 1934.[17]
>
> • • •
>
> Preliminary plans for the two new battleships [*North Carolina* (BB-55), *Washington* (BB-56)] provided for by the 1937 Appropriation Act have been completed and work will start on them in the near future.[18]
>
> • • •
>
> . . . the following new ships were placed in commission during the year: 1 heavy cruiser, 25 destroyers, 6 submarines and 2 gunboats. . . 21 destroyers, 7 submarines and 2 patrol vessels . . . were placed out of commission. . . .[19]
>
> • • •
>
> The United States Fleet continued to remain concentrated on the west coast during the fiscal year. During the first quarter of the fiscal year the Fleet visited

[17] *Ibid.*, 1937, p. 1.
[18] *Ibid.*, p. 1.
[19] *Ibid.*, p. 7.

Alaska, the Hawaiian Islands, and ports of the Northwest. . . . The fleet carried out tactical . . . training . . . and fleet landing exercise No 3 during the second and third quarters. Fleet Problem XVIII was conducted in the Hawaiian Pacific area during April and May. On completion of the problem the fleet returned to west coast bases late in May and early June, the heavy ships of the fleet attending the opening of the San Francisco Golden Gate Bridge on May 28. . . .[20]

• • •

. . . the pay of officers of the Navy is on the average but approximately 10 percent over their pay under the act of 1908, and that of enlisted men approximately 35 percent. The cost of living has increased 80 percent meantime and at this writing is visibly rising. . . . At present inadequate pay is occasioning discomfort and hardship to naval personnel of all ranks. . . .[21]

Commander Destroyers Scouting Force

When Admiral Reeves hauled down his flag as CINCUS, I was ordered as Commander Destroyers, Scouting Force (June 1936).

This was a force consisting of thirty-eight destroyers, a light cruiser flagship, and two destroyer tenders. Its wartime tasks were primarily in antisubmarine work and in the night search and torpedo attack area, since our naval aircraft were not yet in possession of radar, and their searching was limited to the daytime.

My squadron commanders were Captain David W. Bagley (1904) and Captain W. R. Munroe (1908) (both later Vice Admirals, USN), so I was well served. My immediate senior was Vice Admiral W. T. Tarrant (1898), a wonderful naval officer and boss.

This command was an interesting and instructive job. The year I spent in it was highlighted by a very well conceived and well played Fleet Problem (Number XVIII). My command had task assignments which tested the individual ship and composite-type capabilities to the utmost. The considerable amount of night work showed me how great our Navy's deficiencies were in this area of capabilities.

---

[20] *Ibid.*, p. 8.

[21] *Ibid.*, pp. 16-17.

USS Richmond (*CL-9*), *Flagship of Commander Destroyers, Scouting Force, 1936.* NH 77340

NH 77339

Commander Destroyers, Scouting Force and Staff: First row, left to right, Captain A. S. Carpender, Rear Admiral Richardson, Commander Smith Hempstone (SC); Second row, left to right, Lieutenant W. E. Linaweaver, Lieutenant Commander F. R. Dodge, Commander G. B. Vroom, Lieutenant Commander W. P. Davis, Lieutenant Commander George C. Dyer.

NAVAL PROGRESS CONTINUES—THE FISCAL YEAR 1937-1938

Important steps up the progress ladder were highlighted by the Secretary of the Navy in his 1938 Annual Report.

> I am happy to report that the efficiency, morale, and spirit of the Navy have never been higher.[22]
>
> • • •
>
> Congress, by the Act of May 17, 1938, . . . increased by 20 percent the authorized composition of the United States Navy in under age vessels as pro-

[22] *Ibid.*, 1938, p. 1.

vided for by the Vinson-Trammell Act of 1934, and authorized a naval aircraft strength of not less than 3,000 useful naval airplanes.[23]

The status of our naval auxiliaries is only slightly improved.[24]

• • •

. . . the *USS PANAY* was bombed and sunk by Japanese aircraft while anchored in the vicinity of Hoshien on the Yangtze River.[25]

Pay Effort

The Chairman of the House Committee on Naval Affairs has requested the Navy Department to prepare and present a pay bill for the Navy and Marine Corps to the Committee at the forthcoming session of the Congress.[26]

Assistant Chief of Naval Operations

In June of 1937, I was relieved as Commander Destroyers, Scouting Force by Rear Admiral W. S. Pye (1901), USN, and returned to duty in Washington as Assistant to the Chief of Naval Operations, Admiral William D. Leahy (1897), USN. At that period, there existed no Vice or Deputy Chief of Naval Operations billets and only one billet for an Assistant Chief of Naval Operations. I was very much pleased with this assignment. I knew my boss very well and I believed that we worked well together.

The major naval event, in which I had a direct part in handling the aftermath, was the sinking, in the Yangtze River by bombs from Japanese military planes, of the river gunboat, *USS Panay* (PR-5), Lieutenant Commander James J. Hughes (1919), USN, Commanding. This foul blow occurred on December 12, 1937.

When news of this attack reached Washington, Admiral Leahy was out of the city. There was a wide divergence of opinion amongst the various civilian and naval officials as to what this attack portended. Some believed this attack was the unannounced blow by which Japan commenced her modern wars. Others claimed the bombing was purely accidental in

[23] *Ibid.*
[24] *Ibid.*, p. 2.
[25] *Ibid.*, p. 9.
[26] *Ibid.*, p. 16.

character and of no present or future significance. The latter viewpoint was the prevalent one and, as now known, quite inaccurate. It seemed highly desirable to me to strengthen further the hand of Admiral Yarnell, Commander-in-Chief of the Asiatic Fleet, and the man on the spot. I had been instrumental in getting out a despatch sending the Sixth Regiment of Marines to China for his support in September 1937, but was unable, in December 1937, to have a division of heavy cruisers, requested by Admiral Yarnell sent. Only a single 7,500-ton light cruiser, the USS *Marblehead* (CL-12), was ordered out in January 1938.

Another event that made the headlines and a headache for the Navy was the large-scale naval search for Amelia Earhart. The *Lexington* (CV-2) made a 4,000-mile high-speed run from San Pedro, and the tremendous expenditures for gasoline, used by searching planes, put a severe strain on our aviation funds.

Chief of the Bureau of Navigation

Between the middle of January 1938 and the last of March 1938, my civilian or military seniors, including the President, talked to me sixteen different times, by actual count, regarding the possibility that I would be appointed the Chief of the Bureau of Navigation. But the President did not give his official decision to the Navy Department until April 8, 1938.

A few extracts from my diary of that period may be of general interest.

20 January 1938

At 1550 the SecNav sent for me and in the presence of Leahy and Andrews said "Joe, we three have agreed to recommend to the President your appointment as Chief of the Bureau of Navigation." I said, "Mr. Secretary, I had hoped that this job would not be offered me but if you and the Navy want me to have it, I will, if the President wishes, take it and do the best I can with it."

23 March 1938

At 1105, in reply to a call from White House, called Mr. Caney who informed me that as arranged by Admiral Andrews with Mr. McIntyre yesterday, I had an appointment at the Executive Office of the White House at 1115.

I arrived at the Executive Office at 1115 saw McIntyre and was told that I had a ten minute appointment. I told McIntyre I did not care how long I waited but I must have ten minutes.

I entered the office at 1145. The President said: "Joe, I have decided to ask

NH 54881

Admiral William D. Leahy, Chief of Naval Operations, congratulates Rear Admiral Richardson at his swearing in as Chief of the Bureau of Navigation. Rear Admiral Adolphus Andrews, at the right, has just been relieved.

you to take on the duties of head of Navigation and I want to talk to you. First I want to talk about the White haired boys which you and I know all about. "At times BuNav has been the worst offender." Acting on the advice of Admiral Leahy as soon as possible I broke in and said "Mr. President before you make your decision final I would like to talk for five minutes, because I do not want this assignment, I would never have sought it and I hoped to avoid it for many reasons but I would like to present three of them."

"First, I firmly believe that no one should be assigned this duty unless it is the intention that he should remain in it at least two and possibly three years. On 1 July 1938 I will have but 4 years and 3 months remaining of active duty. If I remained Chief of BuNav for three years I would then have only 1 year and 3 months to serve so that appointing me as Chief of Bureau would effectively destroy what prospects I might have for future assignment to sea duty or any hope of eventually attaining high command in the Fleet."

"Second, while I do not believe that officers should ever repeat in the same assignment on shore or that large numbers should repeat on Department duty;

the billet of Chief of BuNav is difficult at best and would be rendered impossible if the appointee were forced to rely, for assistants in the Bureau, entirely upon officers with no previous experience. If I should be appointed I would not expect to have many repeaters in the Bureau but I would count upon having a few in key positions."

"Third, there is now being presented before the Naval Committee of the House a Naval Line Promotion Bill. I have not had time to study this Bill, a copy of which I received yesterday, but a hurried and somewhat superficial examination of the Bill inclines me to the belief that I could not honestly support it, as it appears that its enactment might be prejudicial to the efficiency of the Navy because of the large number of officers that would exist in the upper grades. If my impending appointment were announced I would most certainly be called before the Committee for a hearing and I would then, without adequate study, be in a position where I would either have to support a bill that I did not believe wise; or possibly injure the prestige of the Navy Department by causing the Committee to believe that the Navy does not know its own mind in regard to officer personnel legislation."

The President said that none of my objections were valid except the denial of opportunity for sea duty and that he would look out for that by releasing me.

I then said "Mr. President, unfortunately I am of a temperament that does not turn lose of a difficult task once undertaken until it appears that the job is done."

I know of several instances of this kind when it took two months for the President to make up his mind—yes or no—on a rather low-level appointment in the large-scale governmental machine in Washington. In one case, the officer, who really desired the appointment, became so upset he was stricken with the shingles.

THE GOOD AND THE BAD—THE FISCAL YEAR 1938-1939

As the Navy expanded in combatant ships, its problems in other areas became more visible, as a new Secretary of the Navy reported to the President:

> The Navy has suffered an irreparable loss in the death of Secretary of the Navy Swanson. Under his leadership, the sea defense of the Nation has benefited by its greatest peacetime expansion and has made great progress toward reaching an adequate strength for the defense of this country.[27]

[27] SECNAV (Charles Edison, Acting), *Annual Report*, 1939, p. 1.

Work was started on the two battleships [*South Dakota* (BB-57), *Indiana* (BB-58)] two cruisers [*Atlanta* (CL-51), *Juneau* (CL-52)], eight destroyers, and six submarines provided for in the Naval Appropriation Act of April 4, 1938, and, in addition, work was also started on two battleships [*Massachusetts* (BB-59), *Alabama* (BB-60)], one aircraft carrier [*Hornet* (CV-8)], and two cruisers [*San Diego* (CL-53), *San Juan* (CL-54)] provided for in the Second Deficiency Act of June 25, 1938.[28]

• • •

The status of our naval auxiliaries is still very unsatisfactory.[29]

• • •

The year's [tactical] training culminated in fleet problem XX, comprising operations in the Atlantic Ocean, east of the West Indies.[30]

• • •

A scheduled visit of the fleet to New York to attend the opening of the World's Fair was canceled. . . .[31]

• • •

. . . 8,671 line officers are necessary to fully man, with peacetime allowances, the Navy now authorized and building. . . . On June 30, 1939, there were 6,877 line officers on the active list.[32]

• • •

While the 85 percent allowance is sufficient for the peacetime requirements of certain types, . . . the total personnel is inadequate in experienced men to provide for mobilization of the Fleet.[33]

Again Pay

. . . fairness and equity warrant a proper adjustment of the pay schedules.[34]

I had a number of experiences as Chief of the Bureau of Navigation which I feel carry a lesson for those who, in the future, may hold a similar billet.

[28] *Ibid.*
[29] *Ibid.*, p. 2.
[30] *Ibid.*, p. 14.
[31] *Ibid.*, p. 10.
[32] *Ibid.*, p. 17.
[33] *Ibid.*
[34] *Ibid.*, p. 19.

The Personnel Bill

Some days after my appointment as Chief of the Bureau of Navigation, the President sent me a copy of a letter he had written to Senator David Walsh, the Chairman of the Senate Naval Affairs Committee. In this letter, the President said that the Personnel Bill, if the changes which he outlined in his letter were made, would be acceptable to him. The Personnel Bill was so passed by the Senate; the House accepted the changes, and the bill reached the President for approval.

On a Sunday, I received a telegram from the President at Hyde Park asking for a recommendation as to whether he should or should not sign it. I replied in substance as follows:

> From my point of view the bill is unacceptable. If you believe you can secure a better bill from the next Congress, or prevent the passage of a worse one, I recommend you veto it.
>
> However, I believe that in your letter to Senator Walsh, you committed yourself to approve it, if certain changes were made. These changes were made.

The President signed the bill.

Franklin D. Roosevelt had a very marked interest in the Navy. He had a considerable knowledge of its problems and credited himself with a complete knowledge of these problems. He loved to tinker with the assignment of the senior officer personnel, and, since the Chief of the Bureau of Navigation, by law and regulation, was charged with this responsibility, my relations with the President during the year 1938-1939 were close.

My problems in dealing with him during this period arose from his habit of rapidly changing his mind and decisions, and from his carelessness in not always making his word his bond.

Policy of No Repeaters in Washington

The last six words the President had spoken to me in the White House before my appointment as Chief of the Bureau of Navigation were: "Now remember, no repeaters in Washington." And I had replied, "Mr. President—I don't think you should deny the Chiefs of Bureau the right to employ those who know something about the Washington job."

For years, the Bureau of Navigation had ordered top-flight young officers into the lower echelon billets in Washington, during their first or second shore duty, and then in subsequent years, reordered the best of these back to Washington for assignment to head up the various divisions and sections of Naval Operations and the Bureaus. A sure way to preferment for Flag rank, for many years, was up the ladder in the Office of Naval Operations and in the Bureaus of Navigation and Ordnance.

The number of naval officers assigned to duty in the Navy Department, in the late 1930's, was only about 520, or less than seven percent of the commissioned officer strength of the Navy.[35] Many of these officers were "Washington Repeaters." Consequently, a large majority of the capable officers of the Navy were not tagged with the "Washington label" and had never had an assignment in the Navy Department. This group objected to the rigidity and continuity of some of the Departmental policies and they particularly objected to the fact that the BUNAV repeaters so frequently received the top-flight assignments at sea and reached Flag rank.

So, the President had lent his support to the group who believed that there should be "no repeaters in Washington."

Within the first week after I had taken over as Chief, I received a telephone call from Marvin McIntyre in the White House. He said, "Admiral, the President wants Lieutenant Commander Walter R. Jones detailed to command the *Potomac* (AG-25) (the President's yacht)." I said, "Why, Jones (1921) had that detail once before, and the President has just told me with great firmness that there were to be 'no repeaters in Washington.' " And then I added, "And, I don't think the detail would be a fair one for Jones, as he had that detail as a lieutenant and now he is a fairly senior lieutenant commander."

McIntyre said he would check back with the President. The next day he called again and said, "We want Jones." So, "Jones" it was. The "no repeater" policy hadn't lasted a week.

New Presidential Aide

The day after I became Chief of Bureau, I had a call from the President and he said, "As you have probably heard, I am appointing 'Sal' to be the JAG, so I need a new aide." "Sal" was Captain Walter B. Woodson (1905),

---

[35] *Navy Directory*, Jan. 1937, P.520, Jan. 1938, P.534, Jan. 1939, P.517.

the President's Naval Aide. Woodson had failed of selection by the regular Flag Selection Board, and the President, by his appointment as Judge Advocate General, would assure Woodson the rank and pay of the upper half rear admirals on retirement. "I have here the names of five officers who have been recommended to me as my Naval Aide and I have examined summaries of their fitness reports. Whom do you recommend I take?" He then read to me the names, and I recommended that he take Commander Daniel J. Callaghan (1911), one of the five named. The President accepted the recommendation. Appropriate orders were issued by the Bureau for Woodson and Callaghan.

I was appointed on June 11, 1938, and Woodson's appointment was made effective on June 20, 1938.

In the President's office a day later, I asked the President if it would be agreeable to have Callaghan report to him at San Francisco, as Callaghan was currently on duty on the Pacific Coast and the President was soon to go to San Francisco. The delay in Callaghan's reporting would lessen the rush of getting the officer relieved, who was to relieve Callaghan, and in getting Callaghan to Washington before the President left Washington for San Francisco. The President agreed.

So then I said, "Woodson is needed here in Washington as Judge Advocate General. He tells me you have agreed to a change in his orders so he can travel with you to the Pacific Coast and then go fishing with you in the Galapagos." The President said, "I did tell him he could go with me, but I have done enough for him. You tell him he can't go." So, I had the unpleasant task of telling Woodson that he could not go with the President, without being able to tell him that this was the President's decision.

This was entirely characteristic of the President. He wanted about him an aura of praise, approval, and happiness and, insofar as he could, he avoided seeing an associate whom he had doublecrossed, a favorite who had offended him, or one whose services he wished to dispense with.

Admiral Leahy and the Personnel Requirements of the Navy

For many years, in the period between World War I and World War II, representatives of the Navy gave testimony before the Congressional appropriation subcommittees, in regard to the number of men which the

Navy needed. They would testify, in substance, that the Navy couldn't be operated efficiently and effectively without a certain number of men, generally about 100,000.

Each year, the Congress would appropriate for considerably less than this number of men, and, each year, the Navy would continue to operate, to all outward appearances, in quite a satisfactory manner.

Under the Constitution, the Congress is charged with the responsibility of raising and maintaining a Navy. There are restrictions placed by law on official testimony given before Congressional appropriation committees—limiting testimony to that in support of the Bureau of the Budget estimates.

But I believe there is an innate responsibility for officials of the Executive Departments to give all the facts to these appropriation committees. "All the facts" during this period was that over 100,000 men were needed to man the ships and stations to be kept in commission, and, when the Congress appropriated for only 85,000 men or 90,000 men, the Navy was forced to operate at only 75 percent or 80 percent effectiveness in carrying out its assigned peacetime missions and tasks.

When I became Chief of the Bureau of Navigation, I told the Head of the Enlisted Personnel Section of the Bureau to determine the total number of enlisted personnel needed to man the Fleet and the Shore Establishment, so that each unit could carry out its assigned duties one hundred percent.

This requirement, when approved by me, was sent to the Budget Officer (Rear Admiral Husband E. Kimmel, USN). The Budget Officer showed it to the Chief of Naval Operations (Admiral William D. Leahy, USN). Admiral Leahy sent for me. He said, "You can't do this (after what I have said to the Congress before). I would be stultifying myself if I were to ask for one hundred percent of the men needed by the Navy."

I thought the readiness of the Navy was the more important of the choices available to the CNO.

NH 54879

Admiral Richardson, fisherman par excellence, about 1938.

Chapter VIII

Picking the Fleet Staff

Picking the Staff

Every officer in command in the Navy is anxious to have competent subordinates. Most officers in command are desirous of having only the best that are available. As I was slated to go from command of the Battle Force to command of the Fleet, six or seven months after going to sea, I believed it would be highly desirable from a Fleet viewpoint to have my staff move along with me to the CINCUS billet.

I wanted a staff amongst whose members a high degree of teamwork and mutual respect and understanding would exist. I wanted officers whose reputations for personal professional competence was of the very best. I wanted very much to avoid having on the staff any officer who thought the mantle of the Commander-in-Chief descended on him (i.e., who sought to arrogate to himself the power and authority of a four-star admiral). In picking the staff, these considerations had to be kept in the forefront.

I had had an instructive experience when serving as Chief of Staff to Admiral Joseph M. Reeves, who had been Commander-in-Chief of the United States Fleet in 1935 and 1936. About two weeks before Admiral Reeves was to be detached, I prepared the following memorandum to be circulated to the staff:

> I have a few things I want to tell you before the Staff breaks up and I hope that what I have to say will prove helpful to you in the future because that is my purpose in talking.
>
> In order that I may certainly say what I feel should be said, and in order that there may be no doubt as to what I have said, I have written my remarks.
>
> You have rendered long, faithful and highly valued service to the Admiral and from his point of view your performance of your duty to him has been of the highest order.

From remarks made to me by many officers both Afloat and Ashore, I am constrained to believe that there is a relatively large group of officers who rightly or wrongly do not hold the same high opinion as to the manner in which you have performed your duty to the Navy.

This group believes that the good of the Navy demands that there should exist as far as is possible a spirit of understanding, good will and cooperation between the higher officers of the Navy; that no officer does his full duty to the Navy who does not do his utmost to foster this desirable relationship; and that if friction, discord and ill will unhappily do enter this relationship any officer who seizes every opportunity to aggravate the existing unfortunate situation is woefully lacking in his conception of the duty he owes to the Navy. Are you proud of your record in this respect?

As a result of the manner in which you have performed your duty to the Admiral you have received superb reports of fitness couched in terms of fulsome praise. My knowledge of the Navy and of the experience of other officers in similar circumstances leads me to believe that the full value of these excellent reports of fitness will not accrue to you unless they are confirmed and substantiated by subsequent reporting seniors to whom your relationship is less personal.

In practically all the remarks you have heard me make incident to courtesies shown the Admiral prior to his detachment, I was speaking in the capacity of Chief of Staff; but in what I am about to say to you I am speaking as a Rear Admiral in the Navy.

During my association with you on the Staff on many occasions you have taken up matters directly with the Admiral without my prior knowledge and without informing me of the circumstances after action had been taken. This has been done when neither the urgency of the case, its confidential nature nor its routine character rendered such procedure necessary or proper. Furthermore on other occasions after a matter had been fully discussed with the Admiral and decision reached in my presence as to the course of action to be taken, some of you have later, without my knowledge, made different recommendations, resulting in a change in the decision without your subsequently informing me.

You have proceeded in this way, in some cases through ignorance, in others through thoughtlessness, and in others deliberately and intentionally. Such action indicates lack of proper conception of Staff work, or heedlessness, or bad manners.

I finally decided not to circulate this memorandum to the staff, believing that it would disrupt and markedly lessen the effectiveness of the turnover of the business of the Fleet command to the members of Admiral Hepburn's staff, some of whom were already on board preparing themselves for taking up the staff work. I realized also that it would mar the harmoniousness of the various staff get-togethers normally held at a change-of-command time.

The decision not to circulate the memorandum did not change my belief that it was a sound statement of professional naval standards and well justified in the circumstances. I also was convinced that one "bad apple" on a staff could expose a fleet commander to much eyebrow raising by his subordinates—both in high and low positions. I was determined to avoid "bad apples."

My staff as Commander Battle Force, on the day I took command, on June 24, 1939, was as follows:

Captain Sherwoode A. Taffinder (1906) Chief of Staff and Aide
Captain Bernhard H. Bieri (1911) Force Operations Officer
Commander Osborne B. Hardison (1916) Aviation Aide
Commander Thorvald A. Solberg (1916) Force Engineer
Commander Ernest E. Herrmann (1918) Force Gunnery
Commander George C. Dyer (1918) Aide and Flag Secretary
Commander Marcy M. Dupre (1919) Assistant Operations Officer
Lieutenant Commander Maurice E. Curts (1919) Force Communications Officer
Lieutenant Commander Thomas J. Raftery (1922) Force Aerological Officer
Lieutenant Daniel T. Eddy (1927) Aide and Flag Lieutenant
Lieutenant David T. Ferrier (1929) Radio Officer
Lieutenant (jg) Harry B. Stark (1936) Communication Watch Officer
Ensign Newell E. Thomas (1937) Communication Watch Officer
Ensign Earl W. Cassidy (1937) Communication Watch Officer
Ensign Joseph A. Dodson, Jr. (1937) Communication Watch Officer
Ensign John C. Patty, Jr. (1937) Communication Watch Officer
Captain Kent C. Melhorn (MC) (1908) Force Surgeon
Captain William N. Hughes (SC) (1904) Force Paymaster
Commander Sidney E. Dudley (CC) (1916) Force Constructor
Lieutenant Colonel Le Roy P. Hunt (USMC) (1917) Force Marine Officer

Hughes, Hardison, Solberg, Dudley, and Hunt were nominated to me by the Bureau of Supplies and Accounts, Aeronautics, Engineering, Construction and Repair, and the Commandant of the Marine Corps, respectively. After a review of their records and after making inquiry in regard to them, I accepted the nominations.

The five young communication watch officers were nominated to me by Commanding Officers of ships on which they were serving with the Battle Force. Raftery, the aerologist, was already on the staff of Admiral Kalbfus, the current Commander Battle Force, and the Bureau of Aeronautics desired that he stay on the Battle Force staff, as he had gone to sea only in June 1938. I picked Taffinder, Bieri, and Dyer. Dyer recommended Hermann, Dupre, Curts, and Eddy to me.

I chose Captain Sherwoode A. Taffinder as my Chief of Staff because I believed that a Fleet or force commander should be free of all details, and yet, these details should be forcibly and effectively handled with sound judgment. The Chief of Staff must be both a self-starter and an expediter, yet he must have such a personality that he welds the members of the staff together and does not drive them apart, or permit them to fly apart from constant friction. He must be able to compromise opposing professional opinions without losing the meat of new ideas. Taffinder had all these qualities to a very high degree.

I chose Bieri as my Operations Officer because he had an extremely keen mind and extremely broad professional knowledge and training, as well as a very fine grasp of naval operations, both in the strategical and tactical fields. He had a wonderful sense of what was practical and what was not. His interests were in the Navy and not in himself. He had a tremendous capacity for effective work. His standards were very high; he had plenty of iron in his system—and moreover, young officers looked up to him with adoration.

When the Surgeon General of the Navy (Percy S. Rossiter) asked me whom I wanted as Force Surgeon and Fleet Surgeon when I became Commander-in-Chief, I said, "Commander Joel T. Boone." I had a very high opinion of Boone's capabilities, but I knew he was slated for duty in Guam following a very serious stomach operation. After some discussion, Rossiter agreed to nominate Boone for a more appropriate assignment and proposed Captain Kent C. Melhorn (Medical Corps) for the sea assignment.

I accepted with alacrity because I had known and liked Melhorn since 1909. I had a high opinion of his professional ability and would have asked for him in the first place, except for a desire to help Boone, and the knowledge that Melhorn had already served as Fleet Surgeon with Reeves.

Of the nine seasoned Line officers on the staff, lieutenant commander or above, seven became Flag Officers of the rank of two stars or above; i.e., Taffinder, Bieri, Hardison, Solberg, Hermann, Dyer, and Curts.

It is interesting to compare this with the staff on which I served as Chief of Staff, and which I did not believe had been loyal to the Navy, in addition to being loyal to their admiral. Of the nine seasoned Line officers, lieutenant commander or above, on this staff, three later became Flag Officers of the rank of two stars or above.

The captains of this 1939 Battle Force staff had had from 28 to 35 years of commissioned training, the commanders from 20 to 23 years, the lieutenant commanders from 17 to 19 years. They had a far greater knowledge of the Navy, and particularly of the Fleet, than the nineteen-year captains and twelve-year commanders of today. And they still had tremendous drive to take full advantage of their professional knowledge and their skill as officers and leaders.

So while their ranks were low and their numbers were quite insignificant, in comparison with present day Commanders'-in-Chief staffs, they were a top-notch outfit and served the Fleet and the Navy well.

Chapter IX

Command of the Battle Force, United States Fleet 1939-1940

On March 9, 1939, when I learned I was to command the United States Fleet in early 1940, I honestly was far more interested and concerned about Asiatic nations and the Pacific Ocean area and far better prepared to deal with these problems, than with those of European nations and the Atlantic Ocean area. Most naval officers were so minded and so prepared, since the major portion of the Forces Afloat had been operating in the Pacific Ocean areas for nearly ten years, and, for much longer, Japan had been pinpointed as our next enemy.

I realized that the world situation was worsening and that the United States Fleet had responsibilities in both the Atlantic and Pacific Oceans. I also realized from my conversations with the President, and with those from whom I learned of his conversations second and third hand, that the President was greatly concerned with the growing power of Germany and the deteriorating position of the western democracies.

So, I kept my ear to the ground and sought to leave Washington as much abreast of the situation as possible.

However, whatever my other qualifications, I was not one of those whose foresight, at the June 1939 stage of events, could foretell the swift shift of the Soviet Union to the side of the fascist Hitler or the crushing German attack on Poland in September of the same year. I left Washington fearing that war in the Pacific would come upon the United States before the Navy could be prepared for it, but not expecting the war in Europe to occur as soon as it did.

The Records Went Down With the Ship

The assembly of anything like a complete record of my tour as Commander Battle Force has been prevented by battle damage to the official files, occurring on December 7, 1941, and subsequent water damage occurring as the flagship, the *USS California,* rested on the bottom in Pearl Harbor, T. H., for a number of months. The following letters tell the story:

December 12, 1941

From: Commander Battle Force
To: Commanding Officer, U.S.S. NEVADA
Subject: Correspondence—destruction of
Reference: (a) C.O. Nevada Ltr. BB36/A6-4 Nev-2 dated December 10, 1941

1. In view of the fact that nearly all of the files of Commander Battle Force were recently destroyed, it will not be practicable to supply the NEVADA with any correspondence from this office.

H. S. COVINGTON
By direction[1]

January 24, 1942

From: Commander Battle Force
To: The Secretary of the Navy
Subject: Destruction of the 1939 and 1940 files of Commander Battle Force—report of
Reference: (a) Article 2039 U.S. Navy Regulations 1920.

1. It is reported that the official files for the year of 1940 of Commander Battle Force were destroyed in action on Dec. 7, 1941. Due to the stowage location of the 1939 files, and the inaccessibility thereto at the present time, destruction of these files cannot be definitely determined, but it can be assumed with reasonable certainty that they were also destroyed.

2. All correspondence pertaining to aircraft or structural aircraft accessories and parts, prior to 1941, and retained in accordance with various directives of the Secretary of the Navy, were destroyed together with the files reported above.

H. C. TRAIN
Chief of Staff[2]

---

[1] Commander Battle Force (COMBATFOR), serial 1681 of 12 Dec. 1941, letter to Commanding Officer, *USS Nevada,* box 291529, General Correspondence Files of Commander Battle Force, Records of Naval Operating Forces, Record Group 313 (hereafter cited as BATFOR Files, RG 313), National Archives (NA).

[2] COMBATFOR, serial 042 of 24 Jan. 1942, letter to SECNAV, box 290722, BATFOR Files, RG 313, NA.

NH 61542

USS California *(BB-44) in Lahaina Anchorage, 1940.*

There are no 1939 or 1940 files of Commander Battle Force, U.S. Fleet in the Federal Records Management Centers, in the National Archives, or in the Operational Archives Branch of the Naval History Division of the Office of the Chief of Naval Operations.

The Command Setup

I took over command of the Battle Force from Admiral Edward C. Kalbfus (1899), USN. He had been in the command for eighteen months. A classmate of Kalbfus' (Claude C. Bloch) had been his immediate senior and another classmate (John W. Greenslade) had been his senior subordinate commander.

I was faced with a different situation, since my senior subordinate commander (Commander Battleships, Battle Force) was Vice Admiral Charles P. (Peck) Snyder, USN.

C. P. Snyder (1900), graduating fourth in his class and one year younger than I, although two years senior, was a very able and talented officer. As

NH 54892

Admiral Richardson on 24 June 1939, as he took command of the Battle Force. Captain R. M. Brainard, Chief of Staff to Admiral Kalbfus, is on the right.

NH 77345

U.S. Fleet Commanders, 1939. Left to right: Commander Battle Force, Admiral Richardson; Commander-in-Chief, U.S. Fleet, Admiral C.C. Bloch; Commander Scouting Force, Vice Admiral Adolphus Andrews; Commander Battleships, Battle Force, Vice Admiral C. P. Snyder.

far as I can recall, his shore duty prior to World War II was largely spent at the Naval Academy, Naval War College, and Navy Yard, Portsmouth, N.H. In early 1939, when President Roosevelt was going over the list of senior Flag Officers available for high command, we came to Snyder's name. I said, "Mr. President, there is an officer who can not be ignored; he is extremely able, talks well on his feet, is young, and has had much experience at the Naval War College." The President said, "I do not know him." However, he became Commander Battle Force and, had the President known him, he might have gone higher in the Fleet. He did invaluable service during the war as Inspector General.

Temporary inversions of rank in the military service are always difficult to digest and generally most distasteful to the former senior. However, "Peck" Snyder said from the first that he would serve me loyally and he did. He was an extremely able and talented naval officer, a tower of strength in the days ahead, and, from my point of view, we were a good team.

My other principal subordinates were Vice Admiral Charles A. Blakely (1903), Commander Aircraft, Battle Force, Rear Admiral William S. Pye (1901), Commander Destroyers, Battle Force, Rear Admiral Edward J. Marquart (1902), Commander Minecraft, Battle Force, and Rear Admiral Husband E. Kimmel (1904), Commander Cruisers, Battle Force.

I have frequently expressed my high opinion of Admiral Kimmel in other chapters of this book. In regard to the others, Blakely had served with me in the Third Torpedo Boat Flotilla back in 1908-1909. He was a good ship handler and a good leader in those days. After he became an aviator, our paths did not cross again until this later period, during which poor health was creeping up on him and hampering his effectiveness.

Pye had done much work of marked value to the Navy by his continued study and writing on strategy and tactics. He had made a major contribution to Naval War Plans. In his work as a member of the "Knox, King, Pye Board" on Line officer education, he made and left his mark on the Navy. He was more a thinker and planner than a leader and doer, but I was pleased to have him assigned to serve under me, although he was my natural senior.

E. J. Marquart (1902) devoted most of his talents to the field of industrial work, materiel administration, and logistics in the Navy. He did these tasks extremely well. He was not an outstanding leader but, in later life, he was one of my most loyal classmates. I valued highly his support.

The Fleet in 1939

It seems to me that before describing what I did or tried to do as Commander Battle Force, a few excerpts from the official letters or reports of some of the senior officers in the Fleet, during the period 1937-1939, might be helpful in establishing a picture of the Fleet of 1939, as it was seen by its commander and other senior officers.

> The close of the fiscal year marks the end of a five year period during which the major forces of the U.S. Fleet have been concentrated in the Pacific. During that time many additions have been made to the Fleet, the

Scouting Force in particular having been greatly increased in strength, and new construction now building or authorized will result in still further expansion in all forces. Much of the new construction is of radically new design, with capabilities and tactical qualities far different from the prototypes of earlier days. During recent years several important changes have been made in fleet organization; notably, the Control Force has disappeared; all submarines have been placed under single command and they now constitute an independent force; the Base Force organization has been consolidated and simplified by abolishing the division into Train Squadrons One and Two; Destroyer Squadrons have been reorganized into two four-ship divisions each; effective July 1, 1937 the Training Squadron will be removed from the Scouting Force and made an independent detachment. All these changes have been of unquestioned value.[3]

• • •

Very considerable advances have been made in the following relatively new tactical fields:

(1) Development of tactics based on the employment of underwater sound.

(2) Development of doctrine for coordinate [sic] operation of patrol plane squadrons and combatant surface craft, particularly destroyers.

(3) Development of doctrine for coordinate [sic] offensive operation of aircraft carriers and heavy cruisers.

(4) Development of doctrine for the employment of light forces as anti-aircraft screens for the battle line.[4]

• • •

The demand for destroyer services for high speed target set-ups, plane guards, and experimental work of various kinds, is rapidly mounting. The extent of these demands is such as to cause serious interference with their own training as destroyers.

• • •

The general policy of providing two three-day tactical periods each quarter has been continued. Experience shows that these periods are of too short a duration for satisfactory training in advanced tactical operation and for progress in the ever expanding field of experimental tactics. By utilizing some of the time allotted to "enroute" and "miscellaneous" to move units to initial positions for tactical exercises, and to return to bases from final positions, it has been possible to provide for progressive tactical training without seriously detracting from other important activities. Insistence upon rigid adherence to tactical periods of three days each does not afford sufficient flexibility to meet the varying needs of tactical training.

---

[3] CINCUS (A. J. Hepburn), "Annual Report," 1937, WWIICF, NHD, p. 3.

[4] *Ibid.*, p. 4.

The policy of providing for at least one protracted flight operation each quarter for all units of Aircraft, Base Force, was continued, and the benefits of this policy are reflected in the increased effectiveness of this unit of the fleet, as demonstrated during tactical exercises and Fleet Problem XVIII.[5]

• • •

A Night Battle Practice [was inaugurated] in which pyramid targets were used to simulate enemy destroyers attempting to pass through a screen. The practice incorporated the element of surprise as to moment of disclosure, bearing and number of targets and required simultaneous firing on multiple targets.

• • •

[Cruiser gunnery practices included] a "duel" engagement with the *Richmond* in which each light cruiser towed a sled target at which the other cruiser fired. The firing vessels were permitted to maneuver at discretion within certain safety limits and were penalized in rate of fire for hits received on their own target.

Certain heavy cruisers further investigated night aircraft spotting and the use of aircraft illuminating flares in night firing. While aircraft spotting at night is practicable, the hazard of landing and recovering planes at night does not appear to be warranted in time of peace.[6]

• • •

Night flying has been regularly scheduled as a routine operation at the Fleet Air Detachment, San Diego.[7]

• • •

Successful experimental night catapult and recovery operations were conducted by the planes of the *Chicago* on 8 and 9 February [1937].[8]

• • •

The Fleet submarines as a whole have not been satisfactory.[9]

• • •

The desirability of voice radio equipment for maneuvering purposes in submarines to supplement visual signalling equipment has been stated in separate correspondence.[10]

• • •

[5] *Ibid.*, p. 3.
[6] *Ibid.*, p. 5.
[7] *Ibid.*, p. 6.
[8] *Ibid.*, p. 8.
[9] *Ibid.*, p. 14.
[10] *Ibid.*, p. 10.

Excessive turnover in commissioned personnel continues to affect adversely the efficiency of the fleet. The problems of the Bureau of Navigation regarding the assignment of personnel are fully appreciated but it is hoped that some system can be devised to increase the permanency of personnel on combatant ships. It is considered especially important that commanding officers of the new destroyers remain in command a sufficient length of time to afford them ample opportunity to develop fully the capabilities of these vessels.[11]

• • •

The delays in new construction joining the Fleet have sharply emphasized the shortage of destroyers actually with the fleet: whereas, the "Assignment of Vessels in the Organization of the Seagoing Forces of the U.S. Navy," provided for four squadrons in each of two flotillas, making in all a total of sixty-nine ships, the actual numbers present have been at all times appreciably less than this figure. The suitability of new destroyers has also been brought into question by the difficulties encountered in their engineering plants.

• • •

As compared with modern merchant practice and based on the requirements of the fleet, it is apparent that all existing train and repair vessels are overage, obsolescent and definitely lacking in speed. Provision, ammunition, repair, hospital and oil ships should be able to maintain the fleet speed; if they are not, the fleet will be required to slow down to the speed of the train.[12]

• • •

Numerous exercises were held in which all available aircraft squadrons made air attacks on the fleet disposed in cruising dispositions. A new cruising disposition for defense against air attacks has been devised as a result of this experience.

• • •

The demands for developing measures against aircraft and submarines are becoming greater each year, requiring increased time and increased services.[13]

• • •

The introduction of a new [antiaircraft gunnery] practice simulating [defense against] a dive-bombing attack has met with indifferent results. Difficulties in towing the target so as to represent a diving plane are largely responsible. Solution of the problem of repelling this type of attack is recognized as being vital, and every effort will be made to effect it. Improvement in results in future firings is confidently anticipated.[14]

---

[11] *Ibid.*, p. 17.

[12] CINCUS (C. C. Bloch), "Annual Report," 1938, WWIICF, NHD, p. 1.

[13] *Ibid.*, p. 4.

[14] *Ibid.*, p. 7.

The tactical training of carrier aircraft has stressed group tactics with particular emphasis on rapidity of rendezvous and departure on assigned missions and on coordinated development of available attack strength against objectives assigned. The progress made in group tactics and in the general tactical control of large flights of carrier aircraft by their assigned flight leaders has been most satisfactory.[15]

• • •

On several occasions during the past year, the value of radio-telephone equipment for coordinating aircraft and surface-craft operations was demonstrated. The forthcoming installation of modulation units for use with the Model TBL series of transmitters will provide destroyers with a means of satisfactory voice communications for tacical operations of this kind.[16]

• • •

The increased number of exercises to be accomplished each year, brought about by the growth of the Fleet and the development of new equipment, makes it progressively more difficult to provide the necessary services and areas, and to complete the exercises in the time available. Ships whose overhauls occur between August and January, will have great difficulty in completing their scheduled practice during the year.

The orderly and progressive training of the Fleet requires adequate time for a thorough analysis of each exercise conducted in order that lessons may be determined, absorbed and applied.

• • •

The shortage of experienced personnel continues to be acute.[17]

• • •

The situation with regard to adequacy of the Fleet for its war mission has been definitely improved during the year by the joining of new construction. The carrier and cruiser types have received new additions which have brought them markedly nearer the strength required for balance in those types. Real improvement in destroyer and submarine strength has resulted from replacement of obsolete vessels by modern craft.

Fleet auxiliaries as a group have continued to be unsatisfactory in numbers and in cerain characteristics, notably in their speed.

• • •

The experience of the past year has demonstrated that the proportion of fighting planes in the Fleet is too low by comparison with other aircraft types. Remedial measures are being initiated.[18]

---

[15] *Ibid.*, p. 8.

[16] *Ibid.*, p. 12.

[17] "Annual Report of the Commander Battle Force" (E. C. Kalbfus), (hereafter cited as COMBATFOR, "Annual Report" with year) for the fiscal year 1939, serial 0623 of 17 Jun. 1939, box 74, Commander-in-Chief, U.S. Fleet, Correspondence Files, 1939-1940 (hereafter cited as CINCUS Files), RG 313, NA, p. 5.

[18] CINCUS (C. C. Bloch), "Annual Report," 1939, p. 1.

Because of the large annual turnover of personnel, the Fleet Employment Schedules must necessarily be based each year upon a plan which will provide basic training and indoctrination of new personnel, with refresher opportunities to those occupying new stations after absences from the Fleet, and will thence be progressive to advanced training in all phases of Fleet operations. This applies not only to the internal organization of each ship but to the higher echelons as well.

The growth of the Fleet itself and the increasing complexities arising from advances in material, in operational methods, in tactical uses and coordination of types have led to expansion in the number and variety of training exercises considered essential to development of the capabilities of the Fleet. Thus, though many discernible avenues for advancement of effectiveness remain not fully explored, the activities prescribed and undertaken are each year more numerous and varied. Closely coordinated schedules become more important as well as more difficult. Time and availability of required services, especially for ship and type training requiring services from other combatant types, are important limiting factors.

• • •

As much time and effort as possible is given to advancement in tactical coordination through fleet and inter-type exercises. Test and evaluation of new tactical methods and concepts by these means are most important and lead to consolidated advance in the tactical knowledge and capability of the Fleet. The periodical fleet tactical exercises and the annual concentration for the major Fleet Problem are most valuable and are essential portions of the fleet employment.[19]

• • •

Fleet Exercise Number 5 demonstrated the urgent need of an aircraft weapon, such as a depth-charge, for attacking submerged submarines.[20]

• • •

Efforts to attain and maintain a satisfactory state of battle efficiency throughout the year have been adversely affected by an unstable personnel situation. The turnover of officer personnel, in general, has been inordinately high; that of enlisted personnel, too great. The results of this situation are that a satisfactory state of training for battle is not reached until the inexperienced personnel are trained, and that it cannot be maintained at a uniformly high level because of the constant loss of trained personnel through transfer to other units, frequently outside the Fleet. *Representations have been made to the Department for remedying or alleviating this situation, but, to date, no constructive action has been taken.*[21]

---

[19] *Ibid.*, p. 3.
[20] *Ibid.*, p. 6.
[21] *Ibid.*, p. 7.

> The importance of antiaircraft defense has received the full attention of all responsible officers of the Fleet throughout the year. Fleet training exercises have been held, in which carrier and shore-based aircraft were exercised in making attacks on the Fleet, and the units of the Fleet were exercised in defending against those attacks.[22]

A Six-Month Job

When I took over command of the Battle Force in June 1939, I had the word of the President that I could anticipate fleeting up to the number one job afloat in six months, if all went well. I was anxious to make this short six-month period a fruitful one for the Battle Force but, above all, I wanted to obviate creating any impression that I was the Crown Prince just waiting for the mantle to fall around my shoulders.

80.G-345179

Rear Admiral Chester W. Nimitz relieves Rear Admiral Richardson as Chief of the Bureau of Navigation. Rear Admiral Walter B. Woodson, Judge Advocate General, is to the right.

[22] *Ibid.*, p. 11.

One thing that my previous experience on the Fleet staff had taught me was the deleterious effect of friction between the members of the staffs of the major U.S. Fleet commands or between these staffs and the officers handling the more important desks in Naval Operations.

So, one of the first things that I did was to get my staff together and set forth my policy in this respect. Then I set my eagle eye to scanning the dozens of letters which went out each day over the signatures of subordinate members of the staff so as to smack down the first sign of violation of this policy.

1939 Problems

The problems facing the Navy afloat were greater in number than the count of ships in the Fleet. I shall not attempt to list or discuss them all, and any omission from mention does not indicate that the problem was not important or urgent.

However, there were certain problem areas where my previous training drew my interest more than others. I believed that:

(a) A vastly increased and more efficient shipboard training schedule was necessary if competent ship companies were to be available for the new ships being built, since, under the then current policies, officers and men could not be brought into the Navy and trained as fast as ships could be built for them to man.

(b) The cruising dispositions of the Fleet had to be vastly improved in antiaircraft and antisubmarine defense if the Fleet was going to be able to make a trans-Pacific crossing in the early days of an "ORANGE War."

(c) The work of creating and bringing to full usefulness the Pacific island air bases, which had been added to the ORANGE War Plans back in 1937, had to be fully supported by the Fleet. The Fleet would need these bases if it was to be adequately informed by air reconnaissance regarding Japanese forces, during its westward offensive effort.

(d) The logistic support forces of the Fleet had to be vastly improved in numbers and quality and efficiency of operation.

(e) The efforts and capabilities of the officers and men of the Fleet had to be brought fully into tune with those requirements essential for successful war-making. This included such variables as operating at high speeds for long periods of time, operating large formations darkened at night, operating for long periods with radio silence, operating in very rough weather, preserving adequate security in regard to ships' movements, etc.

(f) The personnel of the Fleet had to have additional time to develop their seagoing and professional capabilities, and this would have to be gained firstly, by an increased effort by all hands and secondly, by a large-scale reduction in time devoted to writing letters and reports. Too much emphasis had been placed upon the accounting of every dollar spent by the Forces Afloat (just as too much emphasis had been placed by the President upon the amount of money spent on the Armed Forces and the material things to be produced for them), and too little attention had been paid to the creation in the minds of the Naval Service, of the fighting spirit necessary for successful war-making.

(g) The personnel of the Battle Force should be held to a very high standard of discipline and effort.

I set my staff to work along these lines. I resolved that, during the time I was Commander Battle Force, I would work hard towards these objectives within my current area of authority and responsibility.

Paper Work

One of the first administrative jobs done was to review the current instructions of the Battle Force and to revise and bring them in accord with the policies of higher authority, as I knew them, or with my own policies. There were currently in force some forty-five standing orders and instructions. These were reduced to an even dozen by incorporating the bare essentials of the remainder (when considered necessary) into a new edition of the basic Battle Force Instructions, thus facilitating indoctrination of officers newly reporting to the Battle Force.

A list of some of the subjects of the reissued standing orders indicates the area of administrative effort with which I was immediately concerned:

(A) Delineation of Operating Areas for Battle Force ships in the San Pedro-San Diego Area

(B) Annual Military and Surprise Inspections, conduct of

(C) Organization and Equipment of Landing Forces

(D) Fuel oil and Supplies, minimum quantities to be carried on board ships of the Battle Force; Battle Force Fueling Policy

(E) Mileage and Fuel, expenditure for fuel and reporting of miles steamed

(F) Annual Physical Examination of officers, delegation of authority to certain subordinates to convene Boards for this purpose

(G) Motor Vehicle Accidents involving Naval Personnel, action to be taken in connection therewith

The basic objective for the board I established, to consider the paper work of the Fleet, was not what paper work should be done away with as useless, but what paper work was indispensable for the operation and administration of the ships and aircraft. The work of this board, as well as the efforts of the Navy Department, bore their first fruit just before I was detached as CINCUS, when the Chief of Naval Operations directed that fifty-eight reports be discontinued.[23] No real solution to this paper work problem can be effected throughout the Naval Service without changing certain administrative procedures by a redelegation to subordinates of authority, now held in Washington, to take final action in many matters.

Discipline

I had always believed in a taut ship and a taut organization, and the first opportunity to let my subordinates know this occurred only a few days after taking command, as indicated in the following letter:

San Pedro, California,
28 June 1939

BATTLE FORCE LETTER 5-39

From: Commander Battle Force
To: BATTLE FORCE
Subject: Uniform worn at Change in Command Ceremonies
Reference: (a) Article 121, U.S. Navy Uniform Regulations

1. In a recent change of command ceremony in the Battle Force, service uniform was worn and ladies were present.

2. The U.S. Navy Uniform Regulations are specific as to the uniform to be

[23] CNO, serial 20713 of 29 Jan. 1941, letter.

worn at these ceremonies and shall be strictly complied with, within this command.

3. Ladies shall not be present when the ceremonies take place on board ship.

J. O. RICHARDSON

GEORGE C. DYER
Flag Secretary [24]

Pacific Island Bases

To provide early information of the movements of Japanese naval forces over the broad expanse of the Pacific Ocean, the Navy had developed during a period of twenty years a marked ability in the search of water areas by seaborne patrol planes. The planes were excellent, and the officers and men who manned them were superb in their skill.

But, the United States lacked the necessary shoreside base facilities to utilize these patrol planes in the area which should have been searched, if Japanese naval attack forces were to be located moving eastward across the Pacific toward Hawaii, the mainland of the United States, or the Panama Canal. And, the United States lacked anything like adequate numbers of the necessary patrol planes.

Admiral William D. Leahy, Chief of Naval Operations, on May 28, 1939, in a broadcast over the Columbia Broadcasting System, said:

> The Navy at the present time is much in need of bases in both the Atlantic and Pacific Oceans, in order that we may more easily and successfully keep any possible overseas attack at a distance from our shores. Congress is aware of the situation and last year ordered that a board of experts make a comprehensive study, and recommend what was needed in respect to naval bases. A Board of which Rear Admiral Hepburn [USN, formerly Commander-in-Chief of the United States Fleet] was President made this study and reported directly to the Congress. With the exception of some harbor work at Guam and Wake . . . Congress approved this report, and appropriated money to start work on the most urgently needed of the bases. Work will commence this year on base facilities at or in the vicinity of
>
> Kaneohe Bay, Hawaii — San Juan, Puerto Rico
> Midway Island [Pacific Ocean] — Pensacola, Florida
> Johnston Island [Pacific Ocean] — Jacksonville, Florida

[24] COMBATFOR Letter No. 5-39, serial 1773 of 28 Jun. 1939, letter to BATFOR, box 10, CINCUS Files, RG 313, NA.

Palmyra Island [Pacific Ocean]
Kodiak, Alaska
Sitka, Alaska
Pearl Harbor, Hawaii
Tongue Point, Oregon [25]

Admiral Leahy's broadcast statement did not inform the American public that the Navy had been urging on the Congress for three years the building of these bases before even partial success was achieved, that the bases would take several years to build, and that the number of patrol planes needed to make adequate over-the-water searches from these bases was nowhere in sight.

Admiral Leahy in no way knew at the time he made his radio report to the American people that the failure to have an adequate number of naval patrol planes on hand to permit regular around-the-clock and around-the-circle air searches from Kaneohe Bay, Hawaii, would be a major factor in the successful surprise Japanese attack on Pearl Harbor thirty months later. However, I believe that a more accurate statement by him of the urgent naval need for patrol planes and bases might have properly been his contribution to arousing the American people to a more determined effort to attain war readiness.

On the Treadmill as the World Moves Along

I had been at my endeavors as Commander Battle Force only a little over two months when, on September 1, 1939, Germany invaded Poland and, on September 3, 1939, Great Britain and France declared war on Germany.

The Naval Attache at Paris had given a final alert to the Navy Department when, on August 24, 1939, he reported as follows:

FROM: ALUSNA PARIS 24 AUG. 1939
TO: OPNAV
0024 ESTIMATE ALL GERMAN FORCES IN POSITION ENTER POLAND NOT LATER THAN FRIDAY NIGHT X TODAY ACTION DANZIG APPEARS HOSTILITIES INEVITABLE WITH DRIVE TO SOUTHEAST THROUGH HUNGARY POSSIBLE X MY OPINION ENGLAND AND FRANCE WILL FIGHT X FRENCH MOBILIZATION PROCEEDING RAPIDLY WITH REQUISITION LAW NOW EFFECTIVE AND GEN-

[25] ADM William D. Leahy, CBS radio broadcast of 28 May 1939, microfilm NRS No. 136/8, NHD.

ERAL MOBILIZATION IMMINENT X FRENCH FLEET STILL AT NORMAL BASES X SPANISH CHARGE PARIS TOLD ALUSNA TODAY SPAIN REMAINS ABSOLUTELY NEUTRAL 1830

Neutrality Proclaimed

Shortly after the war started in Europe, the President (on September 5, 1939), in accordance with existing law previously approved by him, issued two Neutrality Proclamations. From one of these proclamations I wish to quote and then discuss it a bit, as this was a typical Rooseveltian action; i.e., he proclaimed one thing publicly and meant and did something quite different.

In his proclamation ". . . proclaiming the Neutrality of the United States in a war between Germany and France; Poland; and the United Kingdom, India, Australia and New Zealand. . ." the President said:

> AND WHEREAS the laws and treaties of the United States, without interfering with the free expression of opinion and sympathy, nevertheless impose upon all persons who may be within their territory and jurisdiction the duty of an impartial neutrality during the existence of the contest;
>
> • • •
>
> . . . I do further declare and proclaim that the statutes and the treaties of the United States and the law of nations alike require that no person, within the territory and jurisdiction of the United States, shall take part, directly or indirectly, in the said war, but shall remain at peace with all of the said belligerents, and shall maintain a strict and impartial neutrality.[20]

The same day, the President issued an Executive Order (8233) directing the Navy Department and other Executive departments to enforce this Neutrality Proclamation. The Navy Department complied immediately by originating the following messages:

FROM: ACTING SECNAV 5 SEP 1939
TO: ALNAV

INFO: BUREAUS AND OFFICES OF NAVY DEPARTMENT

4005—COMMANDERS INSURE STRICT OBSERVANCE OF NEUTRALITY BY THEIR SUBORDINATES X — 1615

[20] *Documents on American Foreign Relations, July 1939 to June 1940,* Vol. II, S. Shepard Jones and Denys P. Myers, eds. (Boston: World Peace Foundation, 1940), pp. 630-31, 637.

Five minutes later, the following despatch went out:

FROM: ACTING SECNAV 5 SEP 1939
TO: CINCUS / COMBATFOR / COMSCOFOR / COMSUBFOR / COMBASEFOR / COMATRON / CINCAF / COMSPECRON

0005 EXECUTE NAVY BASIC PLAN NEUTRALITY MINIMUM FORCE SUBJECT PROVISIONS ALNAV 40 1620

On September 3, 1939, the President, in a radio address to the nation, had said:

> I hope the United States will keep out of this war. I believe that it will. And I give you assurances that every effort of the Government will be directed toward that end.[27]

Most naval officers take any President's word as his bond, and so, naval personnel started out believing that the United States was to act as an impartial neutral in this great struggle of the European powers.

I hoped the President meant what he had proclaimed to the world; i.e., that the United States would act as a neutral but I was less sure of it than many of my associates. I do not wish to imply that I was an isolationist. Because of their knowledge of the interdependence of all peoples, gained by continuing travel around the world, few naval officers are isolationists. Certainly, I was never such. But, until the rise of international communism, I was one of those "Americans [who] habitually viewed their country as a land of special destiny with opportunities and interests fundamentally different from those of European Nations." [28]

I believed that the failure to build up an effective Army and Navy, during the four-year period 1935-1939, had reduced to a negligible quantity the weight of our voice in the world's affairs. And I felt that until our military power was such that it commanded universal respect, we should maintain an impartial neutrality.

If we did not maintain an impartial neutrality, I believed we would suddenly find ourselves in war due to disrespect of our military strength, and a desire by one of the antagonists to reduce us to a second-rate power, while our military strength was still second rate.

I did not wish to be dragged into war by our own violations of neutrality.

---

[27] *Ibid.*, p. 5.

[28] Donald F. Drummond, *The Passing of American Neutrality 1937-1941* (Ann Arbor: University of Michigan Press, 1955), p. 2.

I wanted my country to become strong and then make a free choice of its destiny.

NH 77084

Lighter moments with Charlie McCarthy, in Long Beach, California, September, 1939. (left to right) Captain E. M. Zacharias, Charlie McCarthy, Edgar Bergen, Admiral Richardson, Commander Dyer, and Bill Henry (Los Angeles Times *reporter*).

The Forces Afloat Start "Neutrality Patrols"

The Forces Afloat moved rapidly to carry out the President's Proclamation, and, on September 6, 1939, the Commander Atlantic Squadron, Rear Admiral A. W. Johnson, USN, was ordered by the Chief of Naval Operations to form up the Neutrality Patrol for the Atlantic Ocean.

The initial naval orders for the Neutrality Patrol were quite appropriate:

FROM: OPNAV 4 SEP 1939
TO: COMATRON
INFO: CINCUS

0004 AT EARLIEST PRACTICABLE DATE ESTABLISH COMBINED AIR AND SHIP OUTER PATROL FOR OBSERVATION APPROXIMATELY

ALONG LINE EAST FROM BOSTON TO LATITUDE FORTY TWO THIRTY LONGITUDE SIXTY FIVE THENCE SOUTH TO LATITUDE NINETEEN THEN AROUND EASTWARD OUTLINE OF LEEWARD AND WINDWARD ISLAND TO TRINIDAD X OBSERVE AND REPORT IN CODE MOVEMENTS COMBATANT VESSELS OF NATIONS IN STATE OF WAR 2359

These instructions were constantly modified, but the first major breach in "impartial" neutrality was made when the movements of German merchant ships were required to be reported and those of merchant ships of the Allied Nations were not. The following is a typical order which came out of the Office of the Chief of Naval Operations:

FROM: OPNAV 26 OCT 1939
TO: COMATRON
INFO: CINCUS / COAST GUARD HEADQUARTERS / COM 6

0026 DESIRE LOCATE AND OBSERVE EMMY FRIEDERICH EARLIEST PRACTICABLE TIME X IN ADDITION YOUR PROSPECTIVE PLAN DESIRE AUGMENT SEARCH GROUP BY AT LEAST ONE HEAVY CRUISER PLUS RANGER [CV-4] WITH TWO PLANE GUARD DESTROYERS SUBSTITUTING DESTROYER FOR HEAVY CRUISER ON STRIKING GROUP PATROL AS DESIRED X SEARCH TO COVER MEXICAN GULF COAST AND CONTIGUOUS WATERS X PENSACOLA [NAVAL AIR STATION] AND ARMY AIRCRAFT SEARCHING CONTINENTAL GULF COAST, FLORIDA KEYS AND OFF SHORE WATERS AS FAR AS PRACTICABLE AND AS WEATHER PERMITS 2235

In mid-December 1939, the *USS Tuscaloosa* and other ships trailed the German liner *Columbus* out of Vera Cruz and, acting under OPNAV orders, gave regular broadcasts of her position so as to furnish a point of contact for British combatant ships seeking to locate and sink the *Columbus*.

After the sinking of the *Columbus*, the Department sent the following despatch to the *Tuscaloosa*:

THE COMMANDING OFFICER OF THE *TUSCALOOSA* WILL BE ASKED TO MAKE A BRIEF RADIO ADDRESS ON A NATIONWIDE BROADCAST WHEN YOU ARRIVE IN NEW YORK X THIS IS AUTHORIZED FROM COMMERCIAL FACILITIES X THE ADDRESS SHOULD BE LIMITED MERELY TO THE HUMAN INTEREST ACCOUNT OF THE RESCUE OPERATIONS X THE DEPARTMENT HAS TOLD THE NEWSPAPERS THAT YOUR SHIP WAS NEAR THE SS *COLUMBUS* WHILE

ON NORMAL DUTIES IN CONNECTION WITH THE NEUTRALITY PATROL AND WAS ON HAND DURING THE SCUTTLING BECAUSE OF THIS FACT AND THEREFORE WAS IN A POSITION TO RESCUE SURVIVORS X ALSO INFORM THEM THAT AN ENGLISH DESTROYER WAS NOTED CLOSE AT HAND BUT THAT SHE GAVE NO SIGN OF STARTING ANY NAVAL ACTION X WE DO NOT DESIRE YOU TO MAKE PUBLIC THE DETAILS OF THE WORK OF OUR NEUTRALITY PATROL

That action was wholly and completely incompatible with "impartial neutrality," but the order for impartial neutrality still stood for every naval officer to read. The public in general had the President's word in regard to impartial neutrality, but the Forces Afloat of the Navy were being ordered to act otherwise than in conformance with the President's public word, and with the laws of the country.

The First Four Months of War Preparations

The four months between the commencement of the war in Europe, and my assumption of command of the United States Fleet, were crowded with interesting problems and decisions as the Forces Afloat gradually stepped up their tempo of preparations for war. I shall discuss only two of these, and these because they particularly affected the United States Fleet and because of the lessons they teach for the future:

(a) The recommissioning of the ships of the Reserve Fleet

(b) The establishment of the "Hawaiian Detachment" in the United States Fleet

Recommissioning of Reserve Fleet Destroyers

During the 1937-1939 period, the high command of the Navy in Washington (of which I was a part) had tried with little success to obtain from the Budget Office and from the Congress the men and materiel needed to improve the materiel condition and to modernize the equipment of the out of commission ships which were in the Reserve Fleet.

The Reserve Fleet was largely made up of destroyers built during or soon after World War I. Some of them had been in the Reserve Fleet for a goodly number of years and, consequently, their antisubmarine gear was either obsolescent or obsolete, and their antiaircraft batteries (other than hand-manned machine guns) were either nonexistent or obsolete. But, these destroyers, properly modernized and improved in operating condition, were essential if there was to be any antisubmarine protection of our coastal merchant shipping and if the overseas movements of our ORANGE (Japan) War Plan were to be practicable.

For accuracy's sake, it should be added that the Reserve Fleet also included out of commission submarines, tenders for destroyers and submarines, and some ancient oil tankers, provision ships, repair ships, and other ships of the Fleet Train.

While I had been the Chief of the Bureau of Navigation, the problem of where to obtain the necessary active duty personnel to provide the leadership nuclei for the planned reserve-manned ships of the Reserve Fleet, without closing the Navy's officer educational institutions ashore and stripping the United States Fleet afloat, had been the constant concern of my principal subordinates and myself.

I had told anybody and everybody who would listen to me, including the President and the Chief of Naval Operations, that the Active Fleet needed to have more officers and men in its ships, so when the time came to mobilize the Reserve Fleet, the necessary personnel could be taken out of the ships of the Active Fleet without crippling effect. But, all such pleas fell on deaf ears, and the President said such action would alarm the country.

Commander Battle Force had a real interest in the Reserve Fleet, since many of the destroyers were assigned as antisubmarine protection for the troop ships and logistic support ships which were to be convoyed westward across the Pacific, under the protective wing of his combatant ships in the D+60-day movements of a war with Japan.

On September 7, 1939, the Navy Department, having issued somewhat conflicting despatch orders on September 5, clarified its intentions regarding the Reserve Fleet, upon which so much of the feasibility of our ORANGE War Plan was based.

FROM: ACTING SECNAV 7 SEP 1939
TO: ALNAVSTA
INFO: CINCUS / COMATRON / COMBASEFOR

0007 IN ORDER TO CLARIFY MY RECENT DISPATCH INSTRUCTIONS FOLLOWING RECAPITULATION OF TASKS IS PRESCRIBED: FIRST PREPARE FOR ACTIVE SERVICE AND RECOMMISSIONING

AS SOON AS POSSIBLE ALL PRIORITY ONE DESTROYERS, LIGHT MINE LAYERS AND PATOKA [AO-9] REQUESTING FUNDS FROM BUREAUS FOR THIS PURPOSE, ORDERS REGARDING COMMISSIONING OF THESE VESSELS WILL BE ISSUED AT EARLY DATE; SECOND AS SOON AS PRACTICABLE AND FUNDS ARE AVAILABLE, RAISE PRIORITY TWO AND THREE DESTROYERS TO MATERIAL CONDITION OF PRIORITY ONE AND PREPARE FOR ACTIVE SERVICE AND RECOMMISSIONING REMAINDER PRIORTY TWO OIL TANKERS PLUS DENEBOLA [AD-12] AND BRIDGEPORT [AD-10] PARAGRAPH PRIORITY OF WORK AT YARDS ASSIGNED AS FOLLOWS: FIRST WORK ON PRIORITY ONE DESTROYERS, LIGHT MINE LAYERS AND PATOKA: SECOND NEW CONSTRUCTION AND APPROVED AVAILABILITIES OF SHIPS IN COMMISSION; THIRD PRESCRIBED WORK ON PRIORITY TWO AND THREE DESTROYERS, TANKERS AND DESTROYER TENDERS PARAGRAPH CLASSIFICATION OF COMMUNICATIONS CONCERNING ABOVE EXCEPT SUCH AS ARE NORMALLY CLASSED AS SECRET OR CONFIDENTIAL IS CHANGED TO RESTRICTED 2100

On September 8, 1939, the President proclaimed a state of "limited emergency" and ordered an increase of naval enlisted strength from 110,813 to 145,000.

Under the "State of Emergency Laws," the President had the necessary authority to authorize an increase in Naval enlisted strength to 191,000. I was very disappointed when he chose a much lower figure. I believed that he had violated the advice, not only of his current naval advisors, but of one of the most respected of naval writers, A. T. Mahan, who believed in "the relatively far greater importance of personnel, compared with weapons."

But, ordering an increase, and having an increase of enlisted strength were two quite different things. In effect, the Navy was given the one-two punch: (1) In order to obtain officer personnel for these ships, 129 of the 207 officers at the Postgraduate School and of the Line officers attending the junior class at the Naval War College were ordered to sea; and (2) the Fleet was directed to supply a draft of 1,728 petty officers. Plans also were made for 1,000 retired officers, 670 reserve officers, 3,000 enlisted Fleet Reservists, and 2,750 enlisted reserves to be called to active duty.

According to the Chief of the Bureau of Navigation:

This Bureau deplores the necessity of withdrawing personnel from the Fleet,

> but it will be compelled to increase its demands should more vessels be ordered in commission. C. W. Nimitz[29]

At a period when the Navy should have redoubled its educational efforts, it closed its General Line School, the Junior Courses at the Naval War College, and its operating engineer and applied communications postgraduate schools. And, when it most needed its skilled enlisted leadership in the Fleet to handle the increased influx of recruits, large numbers of petty officers had to be transferred to the Reserve Fleet.

The recommissioning of the destroyers did not go "according to plan," despite the all-out endeavor of thousands of officers and men who gave their best efforts in long days and nights of work. The Chief of Naval Operations wrote:

> The Department assumed that Priority I destroyers at San Diego could be ready for service in approximately 30 days, or at least a considerable percentage of them could. Instead it has taken 80-90 days.[30]

This delay was primarily caused by the refusal of the Budget Office and the Congress to provide funds for men and material for these ships during the long years of peace between 1919 and 1939.

As I see it, the lesson for all future naval planners to be learned from this incident is:

(a) A ship of the Reserve Fleet must be kept reasonably modernized or else should not be considered in the War Plans.

(b) Ships of the Active Fleet, during periods of strained relations or a cold war, must have on board an adequate nucleus of regular naval personnel for the ships of the Reserve Fleet.

Perhaps the saddest part of this recital is the fact that the President did not learn from this lesson that, with the institution of a tremendous ship and aircraft building program for the Navy, skilled naval personnel would be needed to man these vehicles of war-making before they could be used

---

[29] BUNAV, serial 292 of 6 Sept. 1939, letter to CINCUS, box 78, CINCUS Files, RG 313, NA; BUNAV, serial 295 of 12 Sept. 1939, letter to CINCUS, box 78, CINCUS Files, RG 313, NA; BUNAV, serial 296 of 13 Sept. 1939, letter to CINCUS, box 78, CINCUS Files, RG 313, NA.

[30] CNO, serial 6297 of 14 Nov. 1939, letter to CINCUS, Central Classified Records of the Secretary of the Navy/Chief of Naval Operations, 1940-1947, (hereafter cited as CNOCF), NHD.

against the enemy, and that such personnel should be trained ahead of time in the ships, planes, and schools of the Navy.

Establishment of Hawaiian Detachment

On September 22, 1939, the following despatch was received by the Commander-in-Chief of the United States Fleet and by him relayed to his principal subordinate commanders:

> FROM: OPNAV 22 SEPT 1939
> TO: CINCUS
> INFO: COM 11 / COM 12 / COM 13 / COM 14 / CINCAF
>
> 0022 IN ORDER FACILITATE TRAINING IN THE FLEET, DEPARTMENT DESIRES FOLLOWING UNITS WITH APPROPRIATE TASK GROUP COMMANDER BE TEMPORARILY TRANSFERRED HAWAIIAN AREA BASING PEARL HARBOR; TWO HEAVY CRUISER DIVISIONS ONE FLOTILLA FLAGSHIP CARRYING FLOTILLA COMMANDER TWO DESTROYER SQUADRONS ONE DESTROYER TENDER ONE AIRCRAFT CARRIER OF CARDIV TWO AND SUCH BASE FORCE UNITS NECESSARY FOR SERVICING ABOVE TASK GROUP X ISSUE NECESSARY ORDERS AND INSTRUCTIONS INFORMING DEPARTMENT UNITS DESIGNATED AND PROSPECTIVE DATE OF DEPARTURE 1815

Commander Scouting Force, Vice Admiral Adolphus Andrews, USN, whose flag was in the heavy cruiser *Indianapolis,* was designated Commander Hawaiian Detachment and sailed with his large detachment for Pearl Harbor on October 5, 1939.

In my opinion, this despatch (and the decisions which it indicated) was important for two reasons:

(a) It was the forerunner of the Washington hierarchy's thinking, which found its fruition in the stationing of the major portion of the United States Fleet in Hawaiian waters and its presence there on December 7, 1941.

(b) It was the beginning, for me at least, of receiving official despatches with double talk in them. For, it was obvious to every "polly wog" in the Fleet that the stationing of a major portion of the Fleet in Hawaii would not "facilitate training in the Fleet." Had no reason been assigned for the movement of a task force to Hawaii, there would have been only normal

> speculation as to the reason. But when a false reason was assigned by Naval Operations, tongues were really set to speculating, and the normal reaction was to question everything associated with the movement because of its false foundation. It was built on "sinking sand."

My belief is that "false cover plans" have a place in cold wars and warm wars. But cover plans have to offer to the intelligent a reasonable or rational explanation for the assigned operation. If there is no reasonable or rational explanation, other than the real reason, then a cover plan should not be used.

This is an important lesson for future planners.

In regard to the establishment of the "Hawaiian Detachment," this was certainly a case of the camel getting his nose under the edge of the tent. At a time when the Forces Afloat were quite unready to undertake war operations in the Western Pacific, not having stripped ship for war operations, nor filled up with either the war allowance of ammunition or personnel, a naval movement was ordered which, presumably, the President and the State Department assumed would act in a cautionary manner upon Japan. This move weakened rather than strengthened the deterrent power of the Fleet.

Once our Hawaiian Detachment was established and its deleterious effect upon our naval readiness for war became patently apparent to all, the Washington hierarchies were unwilling to suffer the loss of face which they believed would have resulted from the withdrawal of the Hawaiian Detachment to normal mobilization bases.

It seems to me that the important lesson for the Navy to learn from this unfortunate operation is firstly, that the difference between the readiness of the Navy to conduct peacetime operations and its readiness to conduct war operations must be narrowed, as far as it is practicable to do so; and secondly, that the Chief of Naval Operations and all his supporters must place great emphasis on this readiness difference in their advice to the civilian heads of the Government.

First Four Months of World War II

While things were moving along in the Fleet, things were also moving along in the world;

(a) The short-term aims of the unnatural alliance of Germany and the Soviet Union had been disclosed.

(b) Poland had been conquered by Germany in twenty-nine days and then partitioned by Germany and the Soviet Union.

(c) Estonia, Latvia, and Lithuania had been subverted and threatened by the same unholy pair and had disappeared as independent nations.

(d) And, on November 30, 1939, Finland had been attacked by the Soviet Union in a further effort to reestablish the 1915 national borderlines of old Russia.

On our side of the Atlantic, delegates from the United States and twenty other nations of the Western Hemisphere had assembled in Panama. In October 1939, the assemblage proclaimed to the belligerents that no warlike act should be committed within a paper security belt, which extended eastward 600 miles from the Atlantic coastline.

The *Graf Spee* action off the River Plate in the South Atlantic led to paper protests to Great Britain, Germany, and France and exposed the ineffectiveness of the "American Security Belt."

January 1940

As the time approached for the big change in my status to that of Commander-in-Chief, a quick look back indicated that I was a long way from accomplishing all the things which I had hoped to do in my six-month tour as Commander Battle Force.

I believed that my objectives had been good and that they should be pushed with renewed vigor throughout the Fleet. I felt the Forces Afloat were making good progress in a material sense, but less progress in mental readiness for the realities of war. But, I found myself in opposition to the restraints which were being exercised by the President and the Congress in making this country strong enough to wage war, if war came upon us. I strongly objected to the restraints being exercised in trying to arouse the people to meet war's trials. I believed that the sort of middle course, which was adopted by the President for reasons of political expediency and a desire to maintain an uninterrupted tranquility, was leading directly to the bull's eye of future war, and that we must step up the tempo of preparing for it.

I believed: (1) The President had a responsibility to arouse the country to face up to the unpleasant fact of Hitlerism in the world and, (2) the vital interests of the United States were more important than the President's personal popularity or any political party's continuance in office.

I believed then and believe now that only an uninformed or misinformed people clamor for peace at the price of their present or future well-being.

Chapter X

I Assume Command of United States Fleet and Face Up to the Problems of Preparing it for War; January 6, 1940

The Situation in 1940

Some major aspects of the World and United States naval situation were set forth in the *Annual Report of the Secretary of the Navy*:

> The international situation is such that we must arm as rapidly as possible to meet our naval defense requirements simultaneously in both oceans. . . .
>
> • • •
>
> The auxiliary shipbuilding program is progressing. However, the status of naval auxiliaries is still unsatisfactory and emphasis must be placed on the increased need of this type of ship and the vital necessity of acquiring and converting or constructing additional auxiliaries as rapidly as possible.[1]
>
> • • •
>
> To man these ships and their attached and assigned aircraft the annual and supplemental appropriations provided funds sufficient for a total enlisted strength of 145,000 men. . . . with this number of men the complements could not be filled. . . . The battle efficiency of a fleet is dependent upon its personnel and its material readiness. The adequacy of the personnel, both officers and enlisted men, is of paramount importance. . . . the price of . . . shortage should be clearly understood as unreadiness for war.[2]

---

[1] SECNAV (Lewis Compton, Acting), *Annual Report,* 1940, p. 2.

[2] *Ibid.,* pp. 5-6.

. . . fairness and equity warrant a proper adjustment of the pay schedules.[3]

I was four months past sixty-one when the responsibility of the Fleet command was entrusted to me. This will seem pretty old to the officers of the Navy today.

But, it may be worth pointing out that age is an individual matter with each one of us and that the naval officers in the leadership and principal fighting billets throughout World War II were along in years. For, when the war ended, the ages of those who had occupied the principal administrative and fighting commands were as follows:

Commander-in-Chief	King (67)
Commander-in-Chief, Pacific	Nimitz (60)
Commander-in-Chief, Atlantic	Ingersoll (62)
Fleet Commander	Halsey (63)
Fleet Commander	Spruance (59)
Fleet Commander	Kinkaid (57)
Fleet Commander	Hewitt (58)
Fleet Commander	Mitscher (58)
Fleet Commander	Turner (60)
Fleet Commander	Fletcher (60)
Fleet Commander	McCain (61)

Only the unknowing and brash would assert that age handicapped these officers in the exercise of their great skills, acquired and seasoned by long experience.

Change-of-Command Ceremony

I considered very carefully the remarks that I should make upon the occasion of the change-of-command ceremony.

One of the questions which I believed the newspaper reporters would ask would be, "Is the Fleet ready to fight?"

It was a pertinent question, and one to which the correct answer, in my humble opinion, was "no." But no Commander-in-Chief could afford to give such a short and unqualified answer, unless he were ready to have the concerted wrath of his superiors upon him. I decided to avoid mention of "readiness to fight" in my relieving remarks, and to turn that question aside when questioned by the reporters later. I did not know, when I made up

[3] *Ibid.*, p. 18.

NH 67585

USS Pennsylvania (*BB-38*), *the Fleet Flagship.*

my mind in regard to this, that my predecessor would publicize quite a contrary point of view.

I came aboard the Fleet Flagship *Pennsylvania* (BB-38) from the *California* (BB-44). The band played the Admirals' March. I inspected the Marine Guard. I talked a bit with my old friend Claude Bloch, whom I was relieving. The ceremony began. Bloch made his farewell remarks and read his detachment orders.

Extracts from the *New York Times* of January 7, 1940 reporting the event, read as follows:

> The United States Fleet was turned over to a Texan today with its retiring chief saying "This Fleet is ready to fight."
>
> "Two years ago on this same quarterdeck," said Admiral Bloch just before he ordered his flag hauled down, "I said to you officers and men that our only excuse for being was to be ready to fight. It is my firm conviction that this fleet is ready to fight, and for that condition, full credit is given to the officers and men of the fleet, who have worked so intelligently during our two years of service together." [4]

It was now time for my part in the formalities of the "Big Moment." I stepped to the microphone and made the following remarks:

> Officers and men of the Fleet.
>
> Before reading my orders I would like to express my appreciation of the kind things the Commander-in-Chief has said about me.
>
> I have been more closely associated with Admiral Bloch, and have known him more intimately than any other officer in the Navy.
>
> His superior qualities of mind and character and his broad professional attainments distinguish him as one of the outstanding officers of my time.
>
> Under him the Fleet has been brought to a high state of efficiency, but like any other living organization it can not remain in a static condition.
>
> It must either improve or deteriorate.
>
> Whatever the form of an organization, or whatever the qualities of the individuals having a place therein, no organization can maintain or increase its efficiency unless its members are imbued with mutual respect, good will, understanding, and an earnest will to cooperate, and unless each individual loyally performs his allotted task.
>
> A Navy can be no better than its officers' conception of duty.
>
> In these serious and disturbed times the people of the United States confidently rely upon the Navy as their first line of defense.

---

[4] *The New York Times,* 7 Jan. 1940, L-39.

> We can not honorably discharge our obligation to our country unless each of us voluntarily contributes the last bit to his assigned task.
>
> I pledge myself to perform my duty in this way to the limit of my abilities. The people of our country can demand no more of you,—they will be secure with no less.

As usual, I meant what I said.

A few seconds later, I said, "I relieve you" to Admiral Bloch, and I became the Commander-in-Chief of the Fleet of the largest Navy in the world not currently at war.

As soon as the force commanders and their staffs had left the flagship, I met the "gentlemen of the press." I told them this:

> From my earliest experience in the Navy, to the present, I have learned to distrust and fear the press.
>
> But I realize that you make your living by informing the American people of what is happening. They have a perfect right to know what is happening with their Fleet. And I shall be pleased to give you any information, that is not, in my opinion, inimical to national security.
>
> *Personally,* I do not care what the press says about me, because the only people on earth who care anything about me are three old ladies. If you should say anything favorable about me, they would think "the press is learning what we have always known." And, if you should say anything unfavorable, they would think that "this is an example of the lying press."
>
> *Officially,* I am most anxious to receive favorable press attention because the officers and men of the Fleet like to feel that their Commander-in-Chief is worthy of the position he occupies. And the extent to which you can give me favorable press notice, will assist me in the discharge of my duties.

My remarks in regard to distrusting and fearing the press diverted the attention of the "gentlemen of the press" from asking me whether I agreed with my predecessor's estimate that "The Fleet is ready to fight." They led to an "off the record" discussion of those phases and events of my naval experience which had created distrust and fear of the press, rather than far more pertinent questions.

Second Thoughts

When the "hubbub" of the day was finally over, after the long hoped for summit of the seagoing Navy had been reached, I couldn't help but have a few "second thoughts."

My broad responsibilities were welcome ones. I did not feel them to be a burden; I hoped that each future day I would feel that they were offering me a greater opportunity.

The calendar indicated we were at the end of a decade, of which it has been said:

> For ten long years . . . [civilized man] had suffered grievously from financial panic, industrial depression, political revolution and bloodshed. He had witnessed the disappearance of stable money, the strangulation of foreign trade, the deterioration of democratic government, and the rise of new and passionate ideologies. International relations had broken out of their framework of morality, religious persecution was rife, and brute force proclaimed its empire from the throne of unreason.[5]

Officially, the United States was neutral in the war in Europe, but the neutrality of its officials appeared to have broken out of a "framework of morality" and to vary from official to official, and from day to day.

I realized that there were many things which I must do and many more about which I must counsel my seniors and juniors. Some of my advice or counsel would affect directly our neutrality, and the readiness of my country and the Navy for the coming war. I hoped that I would have the necessary judgment and show the necessary intestinal fortitude in counseling and in doing what would be best for the future of the Fleet, the Navy, and my country.

My Bosses

On January 2, 1940, just four days before I had stepped up to a bigger job, Mr. Charles Edison had similarly stepped up to become Secretary of the Navy. He had been Acting Secretary of the Navy since July 7, 1939, when Mr. Swanson died, and Assistant Secretary of the Navy before that. Lewis Compton, who had been a special assistant to Mr. Edison, became the Assistant Secretary. Admiral H. R. Stark had been the Chief of Naval Operations since August 1, 1939. Franklin Delano Roosevelt had been the Commander-in-Chief of the Army and Navy for nearly seven years.

[5] Whitney H. Shepardson and William O. Scroggs, *The United States in World Affairs: An Account of American Foreign Relations* in series *Council on Foreign Relations* (New York: Harper and Brothers, 1941), p. 1.

My Principal Helpers

When I fleeted up to CINCUS, Peck Snyder took over my four-star billet as Commander Battle Force, and Bill Pye took over Snyder's three-

NH 77338

Commander-in-Chief U.S. Fleet with his Chief of Staff, Captain S. A. Taffinder.

star billet as Commander Battleships, Battle Force. Bill Halsey was soon to be promoted to vice admiral and to relieve Blakely as Commander Aircraft, Battle Force. Rear Admiral G. J. Meyers, Commander of the Base Force, had died suddenly in early December 1939. I offered the billet to F. H. Sadler (1903). When he refused it, I asked for Bill Calhoun (1906), who accepted and did an outstanding job. The rest of the force commanders continued on in their assignments. I felt that I had my fair share of the talent of the top echelon of the Navy on deck and working for me.

Fleet Staff

The staff of the Commander-in-Chief of the Fleet was small, numbering twenty-one officers of whom five were Communication Watch Officers, but it was a highly competent one and devoted long hours to its duties.

I had taken with me from the Battle Force staff to the Fleet staff; Taffinder, Melhorn, Bieri, Hardison, Herrmann, Dyer, Dupre, Curts, Raftery, and my Flag Lieutenant, D. Tom Eddy. Commander Vincent R. Murphy was picked to take over the War Plans billet. I asked Captain R. R. Thompson of Admiral Bloch's staff to remain on as Fleet Maintenance Officer. In the spring of 1940, Commander Arthur C. Davis was requested as a relief for Commander O. B. Hardison as Fleet Aviation Officer, in view of Davis's superior abilities and the increased role of aviation in the Fleet's operations.[6]

Preparing the Fleet for War

I must admit that frequently in my previous thirty-eight years of service, when some broad problem arose, I had looked up the echelon of command of the Fleet and, fixing a mental eye upon some superior, from the Commander-in-Chief on down, I had asked a mental question: "Why doesn't *he* do something to solve this problem?"

I realized that, now, many of my subordinates would be looking up at me with the same question in their mind's eye, and I resolved to do something about their problems for, now, their problems very much belonged to me.

---

[6] CINCUS Fleet Memo. 1M-40, serial 24 of 6 Jan. 1940, memo to Fleet, WWIICF, NHD.

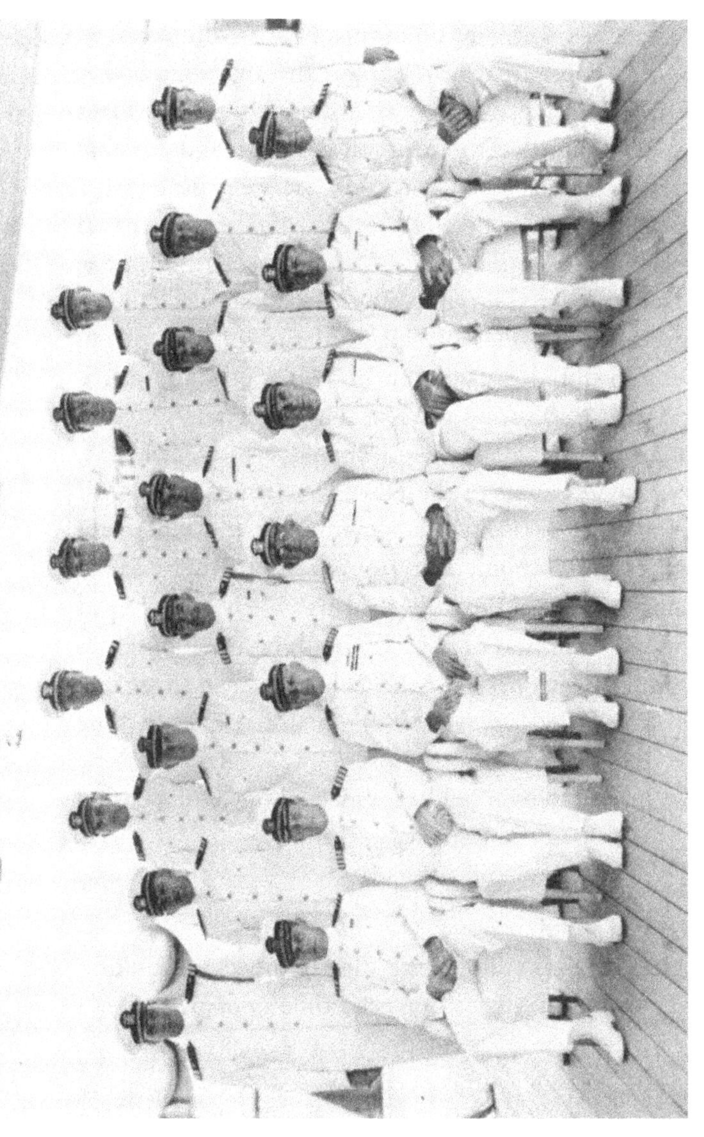

NH 77337

Staff of Commander-in-Chief, U.S. Fleet on 2 July 1940. First row, left to right, Commander V. R. Murphy, Captain R. R. Thompson, Captain K. C. Melhorn (MC), Admiral Richardson, Captain S. A. Taffinder, Captain B. H. Bieri, Commander, O. B. Hardison; Second row, left to right, Lieutenant D. T. Eddy, Lieutenant Commander T. J. Raftery, Commander M. E. Curts, Commander G. C. Dyer, Commander E. E. Herrmann, Commander M. M. Dupre, Jr., Lieutenant W. B. Goulett, Lieutenant A. L. Reed; Third row, left to right, Lieutenant (j.g.) L. H. Marks, Ensign C. R. Johnson, Ensign L. J. O'Brien, Jr., Ensign R. H. Burgess, Jr., Ensign R. G. Bidwell.

Objectives

The Seven Point Program toward which I had directed the energies of my principal subordinates and my staff, as well as my own energies while I was Commander Battle Force, was applied to the whole U.S. Fleet and stressed at the various conferences with my subordinate force commanders.

And, I added several other points to my program, the most important of which was in the War Plan field, for it was essential that the Fleet should assist mightily in the early development of a sound and feasible ORANGE War Plan, one that I was convinced could be successful.

In late October 1939, when the first detailed reports of the early naval actions of World War II started coming to Commander Battle Force, my Intelligence Officer (Commander George C. Dyer), had started a Force Intelligence Bulletin. Requests for copies of this Bulletin rolled in from afloat and ashore, and from an initial distribution of 100 copies, the distribution was soon running over 1,000 copies a week. The Fleet was quick to sense the tremendous changes in tactical and technical fields which lay ahead.

In accordance with the General Orders of the Navy Department, technical matters in the ships had for years been largely a matter for the type commanders (aircraft carriers, cruisers, submarines, minecraft, battleships, destroyers etc.) who had done their jobs superbly well. Now, these technical matters largely affected the war readiness of the Fleet and, by the longstanding instructions, were an immediate concern of the Commander-in-Chief. So, keeping the Fleet abreast of new developments in the material field became another essential objective, and was added to the program.

Three of the programs I made my own field for personal day-to-day attention and effort:

(a) Developing the War Plans
(b) Obtaining more personnel
(c) Getting the leadership personnel of the Fleet attuned to thinking in terms of war operations, instead of peacetime operations

In the first two of these areas, success could not be obtained except by favorable action outside of the Fleet; i.e., by the Navy Department or the President or the Congress. I was the agent of the Fleet to make its needs and desires known to these higher authorities.

These efforts, during the prosecution of which I placed my own head on the block and had it neatly chopped off, are detailed in the following chapters.

Chapter XI

Command and Personnel Problems

Command Problems

It is human nature to want the best of subordinates. And in 1939 it had been a naval practice of longstanding for each senior naval commander afloat to make a real effort to obtain the best of subordinates to support him in carrying out his assigned tasks.

It also should be mentioned that the hierarchy in the Navy Department always viewed their own personnel needs as being just a bit special. Since the Navy Department occupied the controlling position in the detail of personnel, it was something more than happenstance that the Department generally had more than a proportionate share of top-flight naval talent.

I had been on both sides of the fence in this struggle. When in the billets of Director of Officer Personnel and of Chief of the Bureau of Navigation, I had been on the fence in the middle of the struggle trying to meet equitably the demands of the Forces Afloat and of those in the high command ashore. My sympathies always lay with the Forces Afloat, which I think contributed to the favorable point of view with which it seemed to me the Naval Service viewed my occupation of these particular billets. Many times the Forces Afloat find themselves facing a contrary wind in the Bureau.

In my day also, there was a longstanding naval custom of assigning each Line officer, at certain intervals as he moved along thru the increasingly more difficult knotholes of promotion, an appropriate sea command, so that he might demonstrate his qualification for further selection and promotion. The Navy, as a whole, believed each officer was entitled to a fair share of opportunity to display his seagoing naval talents.

The Navy, as a whole, also believed that the Shore Establishment existed only for the purpose of supporting the Fleet and that victory in war would be won by the Fleet. It seems to me that basically, while the Shore Establishment can lose a war, it can't win a war. Only the Fleet can win a war. The best officers should be where victory can be obtained, and they must train at sea and in the air to obtain this competence.

So, competence afloat was a prime essential, and, when this competence was combined with a high degree of administrative talent ashore, a successful naval career was in the making.

I believe it will also be pertinent for the present-day naval officer to learn of some of the customs and policies which largely governed selection in the period from 1916 to 1939. For, these norms exercised a strong influence upon the assignment of officers to the Forces Afloat.

Selections to lieutenant commander were generally based on the demonstration of a pronounced aptitude in the specialty the officer had chosen or a marked capability in a variety of general assignments.

The first real break with technical proficiency was made on selection to commander, when all specialists, whether in naval aviation, submarines, gunnery, engineering, or communications, as well as all non-specialists, had to demonstrate qualifications for the rank of commander by a previously really successful command afloat. This could be command of an aircraft squadron, a destroyer, a minecraft, a submarine, or an auxiliary, or whatever else in the command line that was available.

To qualify for captain, an officer normally sought to have on his record a successful cruise in command of a patrol wing, a large auxiliary, a destroyer division, a submarine division, or as executive officer of a battleship, carrier, cruiser, or large tender.

Selection percentages varied from year to year and grade to grade but roughly 65-75 percent of the officers completing 14, 20, and 26 years of service were selected each year to the respective grades of lieutenant commander, commander, and captain. This percentage of selection, when applied three times, resulted in a rather severe overall attrition, especially when added to the usual deaths and physical and occasional voluntary retirements.

In a period of about 12-14 years, 200 hotly-competing senior lieutenants found their ranks thinned to 150 lieutenant commanders, to 105 commanders, and then to 70 captains. From these 70 captains, 10-12 Flag Officers would be selected upon the completion of 32 to 33 years service.

But, the effect of this selection process on naval efficiency in these ranks was markedly favorable.

All this is pertinent to the statement that, as Commander-in-Chief, I knew that I would have a lot of "eager beavers" under me, anxious to make their mark by getting their part of the Fleet fully ready for the war ahead. They would be intelligent enough to want and to recognize good strong leadership, and they would respect deeds on my part more than words.

Personnel Problems

Before discussing the Fleet's major personnel problems, it seems desirable to drop in a few facts as a departure point and as a matter of record.

On the last day of the fiscal year 1939, just after I left the Bureau of Navigation, there were 10,597 officers of all grades of the Line, Staff Corps, and warrants on the active list of the Navy.[1] A year later, despite nine months of war in Europe, there were just 10,817—a gain of 220. In addition, only 539 retired officers and 1,806 reserve officers were on active duty.[2]

The number of enlisted men in the Navy on certain occasions during the eighteen months I was afloat in 1939-1941, was as follows:

30 June 1939	110,187	all regulars
30 June 1940	144,824	139,544 regulars
1 January 1941	192,173	172,991 regulars[3]

The initial appropriation act for the fiscal year 1940 had provided appropriations to pay for an initial enlisted strength of 110,100, an average strength of 113,000, and a final enlisted strength, on June 30, 1940, of 116,000.[4]

The revised appropriation act for the fiscal year 1940 had provided money for an average enlisted strength of 124,829, beginning the year with 110,100 and ending with 145,000.[5]

---

[1] CHBUNAV (C. W. Nimitz), "Annual Report," 1939, p. 5.

[2] *Ibid.*, 1940, p. 5.

[3] U.S., Congress, House, Subcommittee of the Committee On Appropriations, *Navy Department Appropriation Bill for 1942.* (77th Cong., 1st sess., 1941) (Washington, D.C.; GPO, 1941), p. 66.

[4] U.S., Congress, House, Subcommittee of the Committee on Appropriations, *Navy Department Appropriation Bill for 1940.* (76th Cong., 1st sess., 1939) (Washington, D.C.: GPO, 1940).

[5] CHBUNAV (C. W. Nimitz), "Annual Report," 1940, p. 1.

The President did not have to abide by this limit once a national emergency had been declared by him. He had authority to increase naval enlisted strength to 191,000 and to overexpend authorized appropriations for this purpose.

In case the definition has been changed since the 1930's, I should also state that the complement of a ship or aircraft was the number of officers and men, of varying degrees of individual skill and experience, required to meet the demands for battle. The allowance of a ship or aircraft was the number of officers and men that could be assigned to the ship or aircraft in time of peace, based on the total number provided for the Navy by Congress.

On the day before I took over as Commander-in-Chief, the Chief of Naval Operations issued a major revision of the Navy's Force Operating Plan for the fiscal year 1940, based on the President's Executive Order of September 1939, proclaiming a state of "limited emergency" and directing that the Navy be built up to 145,000 men from 110,000 men, as soon as possible. As I have indicated earlier, the Navy's previous Operating Force Plan for fiscal year 1940 was issued three months before war started in Europe. This subsequent one was issued four months after the war started.

By this new plan, the number of ships to be in full commission was raised from 368 to 452 by activating 70 1,200-ton World War I destroyers, 12 old auxiliaries, and 2 patrol craft.[6] 112 ships (including 35 destroyers and 36 submarines) were still to be left out of commission and in the Reserve Fleet.[7] These omissions were far too many considering the spreading menace of Hitler and Stalin. Poland had been gobbled up, Finland was fighting to keep from being brought into the Soviet orbit, and the Baltic States were losing their independence day by day.

Fleet aircraft were to be increased only from 1,111 to 1,118, but the training aircraft ashore were to be increased from 296 to 468 in order to handle the expanding air training program.[8]

Other major changes for the operating forces were incorporated in subsequent plans issued by the Chief of Naval Operations and briefly outlined below.

---

[6] "Revised Operating Force Plan, Fiscal Year 1940," CNO, serial 238 of 5 Jan. 1940, WWIICF, NHD, p. 1a.

[7] *Ibid.*, p. 1c.

[8] *Ibid.*, pp. 21a-22a.

On May 10, 1940, the proposed naval aeronautical organization for the fiscal year 1941 was promulgated. This showed plans for assignment of a sizable increase in aircraft for the fast-growing training activities of the Shore Establishment, and a modest increase in the aircraft to be assigned to the Forces Afloat for the 1941 fiscal year. A total of 1,283 aircraft were assigned to the Forces Afloat, 677 to the regular Shore Establishment and 264 to the reserve establishment ashore. The breakdown of planned assignments of aircraft to the Forces Afloat was as follows:

U.S. Fleet Commander—1
Battle Force—519
Scouting Force—417
Fleet Marine Force—162
Atlantic Squadron—91
Base Force—63
Asiatic Fleet—26
Submarine Force—2
Special Service Squadron—2 [9]

Just after the fiscal year 1941 commenced, the CNO issued his Operating Force Plan for the new fiscal year. This new plan raised the total number of ships planned to be in commission to 602 and retained the number of Fleet aircraft at 1,283.[10]

Only 31 ships of the Reserve Fleet were not to be put back in commission. A number of these were so ancient and useless that they were about to be stricken from the Navy list and sold as of no naval value for modern war. Others were either real or virtual naval relics. In effect, all of the naval resources in ships finally were to be in commission, but only 87.6 percent of the needed complements of enlisted personnel were to be aboard.[11]

This 1941 Operating Force Plan went thru two major revisions, while I was in the Fleet. The revision of September 1940 increased the number of assigned ships and aircraft, and subsequent despatches changed the name of the Atlantic Squadron to Patrol Force, and established Type Commands within the Patrol Force. At the same time, the Submarine Force Command was abolished and the submarines in the Pacific Ocean and Atlantic Ocean were assigned to the Scouting Force and the Patrol Force respectively. The

[9] "Naval Aeronautical Organization-Fiscal Year 1941," CNO (H. R. Stark), serial 61238 of 10 May 1940, box 16, CINCUS Files, RG 313, NA, pp. 12-13.

[10] "Operating Force Plan, Fiscal Year 1941," pp. 21a, 2d.

[11] *Ibid.*, pp. 2a, 2d.

new Fleet organization is shown in Appendix A.

The January 1941 revision became effective on the day I hauled down my flag as CINCUS, so I will leave it to others to discuss the details.

The percentages of enlisted allowances to enlisted complements for the Fleet for fiscal years 1939 and 1940 were as follow:

Fiscal year	*Number of ships*	*Percentages of enlisted complements on board*
1939 Operating Plan	329	85.6
1940 Operating Plan	368	84.7
1940 Operating Plan (Revised)	452	87.2
1941 Operating Plan	602	90.0 [12]

The number of enlisted personnel actually on board was as follows:

	Total [enlisted] allowance of all ships and aircraft of Fleet	*Total [enlisted] on board*
June 1940	68,874	63,167
December 1940	81,927	79,377
April 1941	84,021	79,587 [13]

Truer words were never written, nor more disregarded during this period, than the following by the Acting Secretary of the Navy:

> One of the greatest single steps towards preparedness which can be taken in time of peace or strained relations is the authorization of funds for sufficient men to man the fleet to full complement and to provide sufficient additional personnel for ships under construction.[14]

In fact, when I read this, I was sure that Mr. Compton had cribbed it from one of my letters, but I find it was taken from the report of the Chief of the Bureau of Navigation (C. W. Nimitz).

The personnel problem had many ramifications, but most of them could be included in the two general categories of:

(a) quantity
(b) quality

[12] *Ibid.*, p. 9; CHBUNAV (Chester W. Nimitz), "Annual Report," 1941, p. 1.

[13] "Annual Report of the Commander-in-Chief, U.S. Pacific Fleet" (H. E. Kimmel), for the fiscal year 1 July 1940 to 30 June 1941 (hereafter cited as CINCPACFLT, "Annual Report" with year) serial 01275A of 15 Aug. 1941, WWIICF, NHD, Part IV, p. 35.

[14] SECNAV (Lewis Compton, Acting), *Annual Report*, 1940, p. 6.

The quantitative deficiencies were the more urgent in 1940. However, this factor was bound to have an expandingly deleterious effect upon the technical quality of personnel, when war actually occurred and a necessarily more rapid expansion of the Navy finally got underway.

Deficiencies in quantity existed because:

(a) Ships had entered the President's "State of Emergency" well under their war complements.

(b) New equipment, such as degaussing, radar, and voice radio, was being added to ships.

(c) Additional equipment or weapons, such as antiaircraft or antisubmarine, were being added at each regular or special navy yard overhaul of ships.

(d) Modernized versions of old weapons or equipment were being installed at frequent intervals, such as new directors for gun batteries. These modernized versions always seemed to require additional personnel.

(e) New tasks, such as manning all antiaircraft batteries all the time, or providing separate air and surface lookouts, or continuous damage control patrols, were being found necessary in the interest of self-preservation. These required additional personnel.

The cumulative effect of these quantitative deficiencies was snowballing, and had been handled piecemeal. In June of 1940, I established personnel boards for each type of ship and for aircraft, to conduct a comprehensive study of the shortages and then to recommend new complements for ships and air units of the Fleet. Admiral Snyder (Commander Battle Force) pointed out that there really was no allowance figure which could be trusted as a realistic base to start adding to, when he reported:

> There have been no means of definitely determining the adequacy of present allowances during the past year. Ships of all types have operated in short of allowance status, which was caused primarily by the unusual demands made on the Force to supply personnel for new construction, recommissioned destroyers, and outlying stations.[15]

Vice Admiral Andrews (Commander Scouting Force) reported:

> The officer allowance for Cruisers, Scouting Force, when filled is inadequate from the viewpoint of ship efficiency, continuity of training, and permanency of personnel at battle stations. . . . A shortage of peace time allowances of general line officers averaged five (5) per heavy cruiser in the Hawaiian Area in June

[15] COMBATFOR, "Annual Report," 1940, serial 0698 of 17 Jul. 1940, box 74, CINCUS Files, RG 313, NA, p. 34.

1940. . . . Enlisted allowances were not maintained generally at the full 85% of complement allowed; in itself inadequate.[16]

Extracts from the report of the Destroyer Board also pointed up the personnel quantity problems:

1. Pursuant to the instructions set forth [in CINCUS Confidential Letter P16-1/S80 of June 16, 1940] an exhaustive analysis has been made of the complements of the various classes of destroyers included in Destroyers, Battle Force, based upon the consideration that the modern air threat will require an advanced condition of readiness for protracted periods.

2. . . . the increase in complements recommended herein is based on the maximum total number of enlisted men which can be accommodated without sacrifice of reasonable standards of comfort and sanitation.

3. Based upon berthing limitations, the following increases in complement are recommended:—

Class	*Present Complement*	*Increase*	*Recommended complement*
DD 384-385	191	44	235
386-393	178	57	235

4. Recent intelligence reports indicate that British antiaircraft destroyers keep all guns manned at all times when air attack may be expected . . . . increases recommended [herein] are justified as follows:

One additional AA Director Crew	11 seamen
Additional gun crews to man all 5″/38 caliber guns continuously	28 seamen
Additional battle lookouts	6 seamen
Additions to ammunition party	10 seamen
Crew for ten additional machine guns	20 seamen[17]

It seems impossible to believe, but allowances of ships and staffs were still being reduced in 1940—instead of increased. The Commander Scouting Force noted in his 1940 Annual Report to the Commander-in-Chief:

The allowance of machinists was again reduced to two for this fiscal year. . . . The allowance of communication watch officers on the Staff of Commander Cruisers, Scouting Force, was reduced to one lieutenant (junior grade) and one ensign. . . . The allowance of aviators . . . was reduced to one regular line aviator.[18]

[16] "Annual Report of the Commander Scouting Force" (A. Andrews), for the fiscal year 1 July 1939 to 30 June 1940 (hereafter cited as COMSCOFOR, "Annual Report" with year), serial 1931 of 13 July 1940, box 74, CINCUS Files, RG 313, NA, pp. 45, 47, 48.

[17] Commander Destroyers, Battle Force (COMDESBATFOR) (M. F. Draemel), serial 4209 of 7 Sept. 1940, letter to CINCUS, box 145, CINCUS Files, RG 313, NA, pp. 1-2.

[18] COMSCOFOR, "Annual Report," 1940, p. 45.

So much for the quantitative deficiencies.

The quality deficiencies in the personnel of the Fleet in 1940 were minor compared with the quantitative deficiencies and tended to be more in the aviation arm than in the other arms of the Fleet. For officers, they arose largely from the basic personnel problem and were well stated in the 1939 Annual Report by Commander Scouting Force.

> The turnover of officers in cruisers, due to selection, non-selection, and rotation of duty for the training of the individual, is extremely high and does not lend itself to obtaining maximum efficiency. . . .[19]

This condition was known and deplored at all levels of command, as the following quotation will show:

> I think that the average efficiency of officers in all departments could be materially higher and the efficiency of the ships could be materially raised by stabilizing details and requiring officers to remain in a ship and in a station long enough to acquire efficiency, responsibility, and personal professional interest and pride in achievement, which in my opinion is not now generally the case.[20]

The failure to use the officer quality available, in a stable manner, led to a further dilution of quality. This failure was set forth in a letter by me to the Chief of the Bureau of Navigation in September 1940:

> In recent years frequent and strong representations have been made to the Department on the matter of instability of officer details to key gunnery positions, especially in antiaircraft batteries, but up to the present time no appreciable decrease in turnovers of these important details has materialized. . . . the basic policy of officer assignment recently promulgated in reference (a) [BUNAV Circular Letter No. 52-40] makes no provision for promoting greater permanence of details to key gunnery positions.[21]
>
> • • •
>
> With our Navy confronted at one and the same time with unparalleled expansion, increasing complexity of materiel, decreasing opportunity for school training, and the necessity of maintaining a high degree of readiness for action, the importance of developing to the highest possible degree the proper assignment of trained personnel cannot be overestimated. . . .[22]

---

[19] *Ibid.*, 1939, serial 1125 of June 1939, box 75, CINCUS Files, RG 313, NA, p. 41.

[20] Commander Cruisers, Scouting Force (COMCRUSCOFOR (G. J. Rowcliff), serial 2245 of 1 July 1940, letter to COMSCOFOR, box 150, CINCUS Files, RG 313, NA, p. 1.

[21] CINCUS, serial 1606 of 19 Sept. 1940, letter to CHBUNAV, box 144, CINCUS Files, RG 313, NA, sec. 1, p. 1.

[22] *Ibid.*, sec. 4, p. 4.

Quality dilution thru increased personnel in the Fleet, during a period of training for war, was a prospect genuinely welcomed by the Commander-in-Chief. During the fiscal year 1940, the daily average total number of recruits at the four Naval Training Stations increased from 4,000 to 7,500. Had the necessary Presidential authority been granted, I believe that 1,200 additional recruits could have been crowded into the Naval Training Stations each week, at this stage of the "emergency" period, and could have been trained there for three months. In the nine months left in the fiscal year after the emergency was declared, this increase would have filled the pipeline and produced more than 35,000 vitally needed seamen second class ready for further training in the Fleet. As it was, the Fleet did not receive large numbers of recruits until fiscal 1941.[23]

On January 24, 1940, the Navy Department Budget Officer informed the Chief of Naval Operations that, based on building programs for which Congressional authorization and appropriations were already in hand, the Navy needed 226,483 men to man the ships on a 90 percent of complement basis.[24] And yet, no steps were actually in hand to provide the number of men ahead of the actual commissioning of the ships.

The Fleet's attention was directed to the current personnel situation in the following memorandum:

FLEET MEMORANDUM 26M-40

From: Commander-in-Chief, United States Fleet
To: FLEET.

Subject: Education and Training of Officers and Enlisted Personnel

1. During the past few years, in which many new units have been added to the Fleet, the difficulty in maintaining a stable organization of trained personnel in ships has been forcibly demonstrated. The condition was one that could not be avoided. New units must have a reasonable proportion of experienced officers and trained enlisted personnel. The main source of supply is the Fleet. The only replacements are newly commissioned officers and re-

[23] The Fleet received 3,750 recruits between July and September 1940, 10,527 from October through December 1940, 6,190 from January through March 1941, and 3,401 from April through June 1941. "Annual Report of the Commander Base Force," for the fiscal year 1 July 1940 to 30 June 1941 (hereafter cited as COMBASEFOR (W. L. Calhoun), "Annual Report," with year), serial 0775 of 19 July 1941, WWIICF, NHD, p. 28; CINCPACFLT, "Annual Report," 1941, p. 35.

[24] Budget Officer (E. G. Allen), 24 Jan. 1940, letter to CNO.

cruits. Recently commissioned ships, which for a time enjoy a degree of immunity from certain forms of attrition of personnel, must be prepared as time goes on to experience in increasing degrees the effects of drains similar to those which their own commissioning put on older ships.

2. With the condition of international affairs as it exists at present, the Navy must be ready to meet a large and rapid expansion on short notice. Such an expansion means that trained personnel of the Fleet will be severely depleted. Of a necessity, a large number of both officers and men will be transferred for the purpose of serving as a nucleus to the new units added to the Navy. The only replacements possible are officers now serving or those who will later be commissioned in the lower grades, the lower rated petty officers, non-rated men, and recruits.

3. To meet this possible situation adequately and to maintain the Fleet in a satisfactory state of readiness it is necessary that every ship and unit in the Fleet devote maximum efforts to the training and education of the officers and men in order that all will be ready to fleet up to duties of greater responsibilities, that properly qualified reliefs will always be available for personnel detached or transferred, that a nucleus of properly trained personnel will be assured for the purpose of instructing inexperienced personnel sent to ships as replacements for experienced ones lost, and that the Fleet will be kept mobile.

4. During this particular time, between the end of one gunnery year and the beginning of the next, an excellent opportunity for conducting schools and courses of instruction is available. It is urgent that it be utilized.

S. A. TAFFINDER
Chief of Staff

GEORGE C. DYER [25]
Flag Secretary

At the end of May 1940, I received a "personal and confidential" letter from Rear Admiral Nimitz, my relief as Chief of the Bureau of Navigation. The pertinent parts of this letter were:

In connection with the recent turn of events, it is probable that additional vessels will be recommissioned for active service as follows:

35 Destroyers
3 Oilers
36 Submarines

At the present time there is . . . [an overall] shortage in the [Navy in the] ranks of Lieutenant Commander and Lieutenant of approximately 343.

• • •

With reference to the Aviation situation it is apparent that in order to

[25] CINCUS Fleet Memo, serial 1752 of 27 May 1940, memo. to Fleet, WWIICF, NHD.

implement the emergency training program to provide more than 15,000 Naval Aviators by the end of the fiscal year 1944, the most drastic steps must be taken to augment the number of Naval Aviators required as flight instructors.

• • •

This student input rate will require a staff of more than 2,000 Naval Aviators to carry on this training.

• • •

Your comment is desired in regard to the proposed infiltration of Reserve Officers into the Fleet to replace regulars, especially in reference to the number of Reserve Officers each type of combatant vessel can take without unduly upsetting the organization of the ships. In requesting this comment I assume that sufficient information is now available as to the value of Reserve Officers now serving on active duty in the Fleet.

• • •

I, of course, desire to spare the Fleet as much as possible and will appreciate your recommendations, even if such recommendation takes an entirely new form.[26]

I replied to this personal letter with an official letter, as I believed that official business should be transacted officially and should be a matter of record. After stating that the Commander-in-Chief recognized that (a) experienced Line officers must be drawn from the combatant units of the Fleet for the requirements of new construction that can not be met with officers ordered from shore duty and (b) that Fleet units must supply aviators to be used as instructors at Pensacola, I commented on our experience with reserve officers up to that period. It seems to me that these comments might be helpful in future war planning, and so I quote them in full.

(a) In auxiliaries, merchant marine reserves compare favorably with regulars of equal rank except that they require more supervision and are weak in initiative and maintenance of discipline.

(b) Young technical specialists who have volunteered for active service are very good and become more quickly useful than non-specialists.

(c) While some are excellent, few reserve officers, now on board voluntarily for one year, are considered qualified to relieve regular line officers in line duties.

(d) It is estimated that it will require from three months to one year to

[26] RADM C. W. Nimitz, letter, 25 May 1940, to ADM Richardson, Nimitz Personal File, NHD.

qualify in line duties young reserves who volunteer for active duty and that many will be found inept.

(e) On the whole, reserve officers now in the Fleet are not as good as the reserve officers available during World War I after a short course at the Naval Academy.

• • •

In regard to the "proposed infiltration of Reserve Officers into the Fleet to replace regulars," it should be recognized that the Fleet is already short of officers; that a large turnover of officers is in progress; that Fleet efficiency has already been impaired; that any immediate replacement of regulars by reserves will further reduce the efficiency of the combatant units of the Fleet.[27]

I knew that the Bureau of Navigation was being faced with many tough, and some unsolvable, problems, so my recommendations ranged over a wide area and included the following:

Since the Navy is being brought to war time strength without regard for the Bureau's war plan, formulate tentative plans for putting the war plan in effect without entirely upsetting Fleet personnel.

I do not believe this was done. However, many of my recommendations, which are appropriate to any emergency or war period, were carried out.

Cancel the September leave for Naval Academy Class of 1941, have this Class pursue an abbreviated first class course, graduate it early in January and immediately replace it with a new fourth class.

(This was done, except the class was commissioned on February 7, 1941.)

Modify the courses for classes remaining at the Naval Academy so that each class would graduate after a three year course and maintain four classes under instruction except immediately after graduation.

• • •

Make every effort to secure for active service as reserve officers mature men who are qualified engineers, as they could soon qualify for duty and replace regulars as electrical officers and assistant engineers on large combatant ships.

• • •

Replace regular officers in auxiliaries with reserves where practicable.

• • •

For the duration of the emergency, on carriers, replace all ship heads of departments, except air officers, by non-flying officers.[28]

---

[27] CINCUS, serial 0953 of 4 June 1940, letter to CHBUNAV, box 442, BATFOR Files, RG 313, NA.

[28] *Ibid.*

Aviation Personnel

On June 15, 1940, the General Board recommended to the Secretary of the Navy what it considered to be the most desirable allocation of aircraft in the 10,000 Plane Program. On June 24, 1940, the Secretary of the Navy approved the recommendations, and on June 27, the Chief of Naval Operations distributed the information to the Navy. This program provided for the expansion of aircraft in the Navy from the then current 1,836 operating aircraft (with 1,016 more on order) to 7,646 operating aircraft, with 2,354 planes designated as spares awaiting future assignment. More importantly, it called for the Navy to have 16,000 pilots.[29]

I should probably state right here that, with the approval of the program, the shortage of aviation personnel became the most severe of all the shortages of personnel in the Navy. This shortage appeared astronomical, since it had been found necessary to provide duplicate crews for all operating aircraft in the Forces Afloat. This training of duplicate crews for aircraft had been commenced somewhat earlier in 1940.

The shortage of qualified aviators was so severe that even the battleship and cruiser type commanders did not have, and I could not get for them, aviators assigned to duty only on their staffs and wing commanders for the numerous aircraft in their commands.[30] This lack of regularly detailed aviation advisors became more disadvantageous when task group operations became the normal method of operation.

Racial Integration in the Navy

The Navy has been confronted with some of the more difficult aspects of integration of the races for many, many years, as everyone in a ship, except the captain, works, sleeps, and eats in close and constant contact with others. Racial antagonisms, if allowed to crop out, could soon disrupt the efficiency of the Ship's Company.

Despite the fact that I was born and raised in Texas, I believed that the efficiency of a ship was more important than the prejudices of individuals,

[29] Bureau of Aeronautics (BUAER) Memo, 11 July 1940, box 78, CINCUS Files, RG 313, NA.

[30] CNO, serial 59638 of 30 Apr. 1940, letter; CHBUNAV, serial 6/00/55 of 19 Apr. 1940, letter.

and that the Navy should be in the clear on any charges of race prejudice or racial discrimination. The following extracts from a memorandum to the Fleet will demonstrate this belief.

> There have appeared recently in the public press several articles which alleged that the mess attendants of the Navy are not provided with messing and living accommodations comparable with those provided other ratings. . . . In order that there may be no factual basis for these allegations each Commanding Officer is directed to examine the living and messing conditions of the mess attendants in his ship and take such remedial measures as may be necessary and practicable.
>
> • • •
>
> Mess attendants should receive the same considerate treatment that is accorded to other ratings in the Service, in order that no charge of race prejudice or discrimination can be justly made.[31]

New Tropical Uniform

Due to the operation of the Fleet in semi-tropical waters, the adoption of a cooler working uniform for officers and men seemed desirable. The British Navy in the tropics had worn a white "shorts" uniform for many years, and on the Yangtze River, white shorts and short sleeves had been worn on our gunboats since the mid-1930's. After some correspondence with the Navy Department, approval was received for trial of a "white shorts" uniform within the Fleet. I joined in by personally wearing the uniform during the trial. Reports from all hands were highly favorable, and on October 26, 1940, the uniform was authorized throughout the Fleet operating in Hawaiian waters. It was a splendid peacetime uniform but a very bad one for use in war, not only because it made ships more easily sighted, particularly at night, but because of the undue exposure of body surfaces to flash burns from explosions.

Horne-King-Compton Board Reports

In 1940, the reports of three high-powered boards, dealing with personnel problems, were submitted to the Fleet for comment.

The most important of these was the Horne Board, convened by the

[31] CINCUS Fleet Memo, serial 3911 of 31 Dec. 1940, memo. to Fleet, WWIICF, NHD.

Secretary of the Navy on June 29, 1939, "to study matters concerning the regular and reserve aviation personnel of the Navy and Marine Corps."[32] The Board submitted its report to the Secretary of the Navy on December 22, 1939, after nearly six months of fruitful effort.

The rapid expansion of aviation in the Navy had created a need for pilots far beyond the supply available from the graduates of the Naval Academy. Back in 1925, as a result of the Morrow Board report, the Congress authorized for the naval aeronautical organization a 1,000-plane program to be completed in five years. In 1925, there were only 376 commissioned officers qualified as naval aviators. By 1934, when there were 801 naval aviators, Congress authorized an expansion of the naval aeronautical organization to 1,910 aircraft, needing 1,950 naval aviators. In 1938, a further expansion to 3,000 aircraft by 1945 was authorized. This latter program would require 4,300 aviators and there were, in June 1939, only 1,059 commissioned naval aviators. It was this specific problem, as well as the possibility of further expansion, that the Board had to deal with.

The Horne Board wisely decided that a basic premise should be that "Naval aviation is an essential part of the fleet. A comprehensive knowledge of Naval operations is necessary for the effective performance of all duties that may be required of Naval aviators," and that, "Naval Aviators should be required to maintain qualification for general duty in the line."[33] These declarations appealed to all non-aviation Line officers and to a very large proportion of the naval aviators. The Board thrust aside arguments for a separate "Aviation Corps" in the Navy, as well as the suggestion of designating officers for "Aviation Duty Only"[34] but it recommended strongly the commissioning in the regular Navy of a number of reserve naval aviators and placing them in the same status as graduates of the Naval Academy.[35]

The Horne Board report was distributed by CINCUS to all force, type, flotilla, wing, group, squadron, and division commanders, as well as to the Commanding Officers of all aircraft carriers and air bases in the Fleet chain of command, for their comment.

---

[32] RADM Frederick J. Horne, USN; CDR George D. Murray, USN; CDR Edwin T. Short, USN; LTCOL L. C. Merritt, USMC; LCDR Walton W. Smith, USN; "The Regular and Reserve Aviation Personnel of the Navy and Marine Corps," General Board, serial 350102-7 of 29 June 1939, box 191, CINCUS Files, RG 313, NA.

[33] *Ibid.*, pp. 14, 27.

[34] *Ibid.*, p. 34.

[35] *Ibid.*, p. 35.

Although a basic change in the procurement of Line officers of the Navy was involved, the Board's report met with wide agreement and acceptance. In my comments to the Secretary of the Navy, I said, "I consider the Horne Board Report to be an outstandingly excellent one and recommend that the report be approved."[36]

One comment that I made at the time, which I believe will be pertinent when severe selection once again starts to take hold in the Navy, was as follows:

> Experience with the selective system has indicated that when officers from non-Naval Academy sources fail of selection that many of these officers voice the opinion that their failure was not due to any of their own short comings, but due to discriminations because of their original status. No amount of facts or figures have been able to dispel this feeling. These officers have also shown a great tendency to take their grievances to Congress and to air them in the public press.
>
> There is no reason to anticipate that the experiences of the future would be different from that of the past.[37]

By and large, the Horne Board Report was placed into effect by the Navy Department. To provide for transferring reserve aviators into the regular Line of the Navy, Congressional approval was obtained.

King-Compton Boards

The King Board was convened by the Secretary of the Navy on June 30, 1939, to consider the question of distribution, promotion, and retirement of officers of the Staff Corps of the Navy, as well as officers designated for engineering duty only, or for aeronautical engineering duty only.[38] The Board submitted its report to the Secretary of the Navy on December 9, 1939, and the report was sent by him to CINCUS on January 16, 1940. CINCUS distributed it widely throughout the Fleet for comment, requesting 100 additional copies of the report from SECNAV for such distribution.[39]

[36] CINCUS, serial 749 of 29 Feb. 1940, letter to SECNAV, box 104, CINCUS Files, RG 313, NA, p. 2.

[37] *Ibid.*

[38] RADM E.J. King, USN; CAPT L.M. Atkins, USN; CAPT R.D. Workman, USN; CAPT Garland Fulton, USN; CDR W.J.C. Agnew, USN; CDR F.S. Low, USN; CDR K.B. Bragg, USN; CDR W.B. Young, USN; CDR D.H. Cark, USN; "Distribution, promotion, retirement, etc., of Staff Corps and Officers designated for Engineering Duty Only and for Aeronautical Engineering Duty Only," General Board No. 421, 9 Dec. 1939, GB Files, NHD.

[39] CINCUS, 221900 Dec. 1940, despatch to SECNAV.

NH 77050

Commander-in-Chief, U.S. Fleet with his personal staff. Left to right, Captain S. A. Taffinder, Commander George C. Dyer, Admiral Richardson, and Lieutenant D. Tom Eddy.

In 1916, the original selection system for officers' promotion to the three command ranks was applied only to the Line of the Navy. It was not applied to the Staff Corps for another ten years. When the "best-fitted selective system" was applied in 1934 to promotion to the ranks of lieutenant and lieutenant commander in the Line of the Navy, it was not applied to the Staff Corps.

During the period 1916-1939, the sentiment of the officers toward selection within each staff corps, varied from that of the officers in every other staff corps. All staff officers wanted promotion at the same time as their Line contemporaries, but in some of the corps, the majority of officers did not want this promotion to be accompanied by the hazards of selection similar to those experienced by the seagoing officers of the Line. These sentiments were reflected in the King Board report.

Of the nine members of the King Board, only two were seagoing Line officers. As each of its recommendations was based on the approval of six of the nine members, the majority appeared to have been based on political logrolling by the various Staff Corps members and the non-seagoing Line officers. The report carried three minority reports.

The Board's report aroused marked critical comment within the Fleet. I believe this criticism was aroused because the Board advocated to the Secretary of the Navy that he accept measures which were based on the principle of the greatest good for the greatest number, insofar as Staff Corps promotions were concerned. Certainly few of its proposals seemed to be based on what I had considered a guiding principle of naval personnel legislation, —"what is best for the Navy and the nation." I recommended flatly to the Secretary of the Navy that he disaprove the Board's report.[40]

In view of the wide-scale adverse reaction to this report, the Secretary of the Navy, on May 20, 1940, convened a new board to consider the same subjects, with Assistant Secretary of the Navy Lewis Compton as senior member and Admiral Joseph M. Reeves, USN (ret.), as the only other member.[41]

The Compton Board report was submitted on October 10, 1940, but not forwarded to CINCUS by the Chief of the Bureau of Navigation until November 20, 1940. Fleet comments were asked, but it was stated that the Department's recommendations in the matter had to be submitted to the Congress within ten days of the beginning of the next session of Congress, so that there was little time to gather any real cross section of opinion in the Forces Afloat.[42]

The Compton Board in its report missed no opportunity to stress its reliance upon the axiom "best interests of the Navy as a whole," although it appeared to me that this fine principle was considerably diluted in its final recommendations. The Board advanced and strongly supported the proposition that the duties and functions performed in any particular rank in the Staff Corps are not peculiar and restricted to that grade alone. For this reason, it stated that no rigid distribution of staff officers to the various

---

40 CINCUS, serial 728 of 27 Feb. 1940, letter to SECNAV, box 191, CINCUS Files, RG 313, NA.

41 SECNAV, serial 463 of 20 May 1940, letter to Asst. SECNAV, box 191, CINCUS Files, RG 313, NA.

42 BUNAV, serial 468 of 20 Nov. 1940, letter, box 191, CINCUS Files, RG 313, NA.

ranks was necessary and that a large percentage of Staff Corps officers in the command ranks was fully acceptable and desirable.[43]

Since this principle has been accepted and written into law, I wish to record my opinion in regard to it:

> There is no justification for a higher percentage of staff corps officers in the upper grades than exist in the line, except for the increase in contentment with the career of a staff corps officer that results from increased rank and pay.[44]

By and large however, the Compton Board report was an excellent one and, subject to major disagreement on this one point, I recommended its approval.

The Horne Board and Compton Board reports were major milestones in personnel matters in the rapidly changing conditions in the Navy in 1940, and I believe their implementation assisted in meeting some of the difficult personnel problems of the war years.

On June 19, 1940, when it appeared that my trip to Washington might be postponed indefinitely because of the French crisis, I sent off the following message to the Bureau of Navigation:

> BASED ON EXPANSION OF NAVY ALREADY AUTHORIZED AND THAT NOW PROPOSED ABSOLUTELY ESSENTIAL THAT IMMEDIATE STEPS BE TAKEN TOWARD OBTAINING AND TRAINING NEW OFFICERS AND MEN NECESSARY TO MAN THESE SHIPS OTHERWISE NAVY WILL HAVE ALL SHIPS INADEQUATELY MANNED BY UNTRAINED PERSONNEL X ARE ANY FURTHER REPRESENTATIONS DESIRED FROM ME TO SUPPORT YOUR RECOMMENDATIONS TO THIS END

The answer I found upon my arrival in Washington was that recommendations were a "dime a dozen," but what was needed was some way to change the mind of the President in the vital matter.

It was not until October 2, 1940, that CNO recommended to the Secretary of the Navy that the Operating Force Plan 1941 be revised and ". . . that immediate steps be taken to permit an estimated total enlisted personnel of 253,000." This was approved by the Secretary the same day.[45] The plan

[43] "Distribution, promotion, and retirement of officers of the Staff Corps of the Navy," General Board No. 421, 10 Oct. 1940, GB Files, NHD, p. 203.

[44] CINCUS, serial 3598 of 8 Dec. 1940, letter to CHBUNAV, box 104, CINCUS Files, RG 313, NA, p. 1.

[45] CNO, serial 400614 of 2 Oct. 1940, letter to SECNAV, box 20, CINCUS Files, RG 313, NA; SECNAV, serial 010012 of 15 Apr. 1940, letter to Navy Department, box 119, CINCUS Files, RG 313, NA.

authorized 115 percent of complement on major ships with the purpose "of providing trained personnel" for ships and aircraft of the expanding Navy.

On December 12, 1940, I informed the Fleet that 220 graduates of the First Reserve Midshipmen's School, the *USS Illinois,* were under orders to ships of the Fleet. This was the first increment of a large number of new reserve officers to be received in the years ahead. It had taken the Navy fifteen months from the start of the war in Europe to get this essential program underway. I, for one, was greatly pleased that the officers, who would have to carry a very large part of any future war, had started to arrive in the Fleet to be actually trained on the job for their job. Soon thereafter, January 16, 1941, I expressed my thanks to the Chief of the Bureau of Navigation for ". . . substantial increases in complements of gunnery ratings, thus laying the foundation for long felt and much needed improvement in the quality and permanence of personnel immediately connected with the operation and control of armament."[46]

Personnel problems are never solved. Sometimes the star of hope for such resolution appears a little nearer than at other times. I felt that, at long last, this might be one of those times.

I have touched herein on just a few of the personnel problems. The greatest problem was the shortage of personnel. It was also the easiest of correction. All that was needed, when the war started in Europe in September 1939, was a willingness of President Roosevelt to accept the advice of his naval advisers to expand the Navy to 191,000, its legal authorized strength for a national emergency, instead of the figure of 145,000 he personally chose. Every subsequent expansion of naval personnel which he authorized during my tenure was too little and too late.

As late as January 1941, with a "Two-Ocean Navy" being built that required nearly 600,000 men to man it, the Bureau of Navigation reported to Congress that "We expect to end [fiscal 1942] with 258,000 men."[47] The Navy Department Budget Officer estimates, prepared in the month of May in the peacetime year of 1941 for the fiscal year commencing July 1, 1942, showed a need for 587,000 men and 102,750 Marines to man the

[46] CINCUS, serial 068 of 16 Jan. 1941, letter to BUNAV; BUNAV serial 632 of 12 Nov. 1940, letter to CINCUS, box 146, CINCUS Files, RG 313, NA.

[47] *Navy Department Appropriation Bill for 1942,* p. 67.

ships and aircraft that would be available at the end of the fiscal year 1942.[48]

These were the men we should have been training in 1940.

---

[48] SECNAV, serial 400200 of 22 May 1941, letter.

Chapter XII

New Developments, Materiel Problems, and their Impact on the Fleet 1940-1941

According to the newspapers, more is now being spent by the Navy Department each year on naval research alone, than was spent on a yearly average during the fiscal years 1935-1940, by the whole Naval Establishment for all purposes.

Since, I presume, there is some relation between money put into materiel research and progress obtained, it seems probable that naval materiel progress during this 1935-1940 period was at a considerably lesser rate than now seems to be the accepted norm. But, in looking back at that period of the late 1930's, the Navy was moving along in the materiel field at what seemed to me, then, to be a highly acceptable rate of progress.

Most new developments in the naval materiel field have an influence on naval tactics. Two of the pre-World War II materiel developments, which were to have tremendous impact in the naval tactical field in World War II, were radar and voice radio. My participation in these developments was limited to pressing to get them installed in ships and aircraft of the Fleet, but a little of their history, as to when they were available in the Fleet, may not be amiss.

Radio Telephone

The possibility of large-scale use by the Navy of radio telephone—or voice radio—first became widely known throughout the Fleet as early as 1933. On November 1, 1933, CINCUS (D.F. Sellers) informed the Fleet[1]

[1] CINCUS (D. F. Sellers), serial 3121 of 1 Nov. 1933, letter to Force Commanders; CNO, 25 July 1933, letter to CINCUS.

that he had received a comprehensive study made by an informal "Departmental Radio Telephone Board." This thirty-page study was dated September 20, 1933, and concluded with the recommendation that all aircraft and aircraft carriers and one squadron of destroyers be equipped with radio telephones. The Commander-in-Chief concurred with this basic recommendation and urged early installation in the destroyer squadron, so that tests could indicate future policy in regard to its wider use in the Fleet.

The CINCUS recommendation was approved by the CNO and established as a policy. From that date forth, there was a constant effort, by a limited number of farsighted communication officers in the Navy Department and afloat, assisted at important moments by other officers in command billets, to get voice radio into the Fleet.

I do not have any detailed records available on the installation of voice radio in the Fleet, but I do know that money for such secret developments was scarce during the period and that progress was not rapid. However, by September 1939, the use of voice radio by the planes of the Fleet was quite general. During the September 1939 tactical exercises, the CINCUS reported that the use of voice radio was excellent, and planes with voice radio installed were superior to those using only key and code.[2] From that time forward, the use of voice radio increased by leaps and bounds, although in early June 1940, the Commanding Officer of the *Lexington* noted that the *Lexington* was fitted with an "insufficient number of modern transmitters for voice transmission for carrier operations." [3]

A few more extracts from official reports may be helpful in setting forth its exact status during this period:

> Experimental voice recording equipment has been in use throughout the year with excellent results. It has proved valuable in providing a permanent record of important transmissions and in improving voice circuit discipline.
>
> • • •
>
> There has been a marked decrease in unnecessary radio traffic on aircraft circuits, particularly the voice circuits.[4]

---

[2] CINCUS (C. C. Bloch), serial 01769 of 11 Dec. 1939, letter to Fleet, box 103, CINCUS Files, RG 313, NA, p. 8. ("Fleet Tactical Exercises, September 1939—Report of Exercise No. 207.")

[3] Commanding Officer *USS Lexington* (A. D. Bernhard), serial 763 of 7 June 1940, letter.

[4] "Annual Report of the Commander Air, Scouting Force" (A. L. Bristol), for fiscal year 1940 (hereafter cited as COMAIRSCOFOR, "Annual Report" with year) serial 0451 of 7 Jan. 1940.

Commander Base Force was interested in having Base Force ships equipped with voice radio and was unhappy that:

> The model CXL radio telephone installed in the *Argonne* was removed during the past year and transferred to the *Nevada.*[5]

In early January 1941, Commander Destroyers, Battle Force reported on and recommended increased use of voice radio transmissions in destroyer night search and attack,[6] and Commander Battle Force noted in his Annual Report that, "Installation of TBS equipment in destroyers was completed during the year."

Radar

Radar and IFF (Identification Friend or Foe) were well behind voice radio in reaching general Fleet use. Up until the time of my detachment, the recommendation by the Forces Afloat for the installation of radar in all combatant ships of the Fleet had not been approved by the Navy Department,[7] but, during 1940, radar installations were approved for all aircraft carriers and many of the major combatant ships.

As an illustration, the Bureau of Ships reported in 1940 that radar equipment would be installed on the *Saratoga* (CV-3), *Lexington* (CV-2), *Enterprise* (CV-6), *Pennsylvania* (BB-38), *Idaho* (BB-42), and *West Virginia* (BB-48), commencing in June 1941.[8] The *California* had a search radar installation installed prior to my detachment from the Fleet, at the end of January 1941.[9]

Installation on heavy cruisers was also proceeding apace, and, by June 30, 1941, Commander Scouting Force could report to CINCUS that radars were installed in four heavy cruisers.[10]

---

[5] COMBASEFOR (W. L. Calhoun), "Annual Report," 1940, box 74, CINCUS Files, RG 313, NA, p. 11.

[6] COMDESBATFOR (M. F. Draemel), serial 027 of 7 Jan. 1941, letter to CINCUS, with COMBATFOR End., serial 068 of 29 Jan. 1941.

[7] CNO, serial 07023 of 27 Jan. 1941, letter to SECNAV, CNOCF, NHD, p. 2.

[8] Bureau of Ships (BUSHIPS), 4 Dec. 1940, letter to Navy Yard Puget Sound, box 171, CINCUS Files, RG 313, NA.

[9] Commander Battleships (COMBATSHIPS) (W. S. Anderson), serial 096 of 13 Feb. 1941, letter to CINCUS.

[10] COMSCOFOR (Wilson Brown), "Annual Report," 1941, p. 19.

NH 77350

The first ship-borne radar, in USS New York *(BB-38), about 1938.*

COMBATFOR noted in his Annual Report:

> The greatest change in tactical ideas is taking place through the use of RADAR. This instrument is installed in only a few ships, but the schedule requires many more ships to receive it in the next four months.[11]

Other Materiel Developments

The early naval actions in the European Theater of World War II indicated the particular urgency of further materiel developments in our Navy to meet more effectively previously unknown developments in mine warfare and unexpected aspects or developments of air-sea warfare.

Our ships had been equipped since World War I with minesweeping apparatus (paravanes), which effectively protected ships from anchored mines, and with antiaircraft batteries, which had a fair capability of shooting down single airplanes at moderate altitudes and speeds when delivering bombs or torpedoes at our ships.

But early in World War II, the magnetic mine was brought into wide-scale use. The magnetic mine was not anchored but lay on the bottom of the ocean bed and was activated by magnetic waves created as ships passed near or over them.

And the marked increase in the number of aircraft in the armed forces of all nations made possible attacks on naval ships by swarms of aircraft. This fact, coupled with the considerable increase in the capabilities of all aircraft built in 1939 and 1940, indicated plainly that the aircraft bomb menace would be a more frequent and hazardous menace to our ships than the shell of the major caliber gun of other ships.

Degaussing Equipment

The new magnetic mine menace was met by the installation of degaussing equipment. In a nutshell:

> The purpose of degaussing equipment is to counteract the high magnetic permeability of a ship's hull with an electromagnetic coil. This prevents a change of the earth's magnetic field due to the presence of a ship.[12]

The large-scale program for the installation of degaussing equipment in the ships of the Fleet started in mid-July 1940. The installation consisted

[11] COMBATFOR (W. S. Pye), "Annual Report," 1941, serial 0651 of 12 July 1941, WWIICF, NHD, p. 7.

[12] BUSHIPS, serial 6-25-ME-DE of 9 July 1940, letter to Navy Yards, WWIICF, NHD.

of large coils of wire running completely around the outside hull of the ship, and other large coils in the forward and after parts of the ship. Every ship of the Fleet had to proceed to a navy yard to have this equipment installed. Then, the effectiveness of the new installation had to be calibrated on a degaussing range and checked at regular intervals thereafter.

As with all new installations, some difficulties arose with the degaussing installations, as the following despatch reports:

> FROM: COMBATFOR
> TO: BUSHIPS
>
> THE DEGAUSSING COILS OF ALL FOUR BATTLESHIPS GROUNDED DURING THE PASSAGE TO HAWAII FROM THE WEST COAST, WITH MODERATE WEATHER. THESE COILS ARE NOW INOPERATIVE, AND IT IS CONSIDERED IMPERATIVE THAT BETTER INSTALLATIONS FOR BATTLESHIPS BE DEVISED. A LETTER FOLLOWS.
>
> THE 5 DESTROYERS AND 4 CRUISERS IN COMPANY WITH THE BATTLESHIPS WERE NOT AFFECTED.

But fortunately, once the original degaussing installations were made, tested and calibrated, the menace of the magnetic mine could be largely removed from the "worry list."

Antiaircraft Program

Steps to meet the far greater bomb hazard were more numerous and complicated and not nearly so satisfying. Depending on the type of ship, the antiaircraft program consisted of:

> Additional 1.1″, 3″50, or 5″38 antiaircraft guns installed with accompanying new directors, magazines, clipping rooms, and ready lockers, to increase protective capabilities against multiple plane attacks. Additional .50 machine guns and ready service ammunition boxes. Rearrangement or elimination of boats and boat stowages which interfered with area of fire. Reduction of bridge structure.[13]
>
> • • •
>
> Twenty-five pound S.T.S. splinter protection installed topside around gun and ship control party areas, so as to protect topside personnel and equipment from bomb fragments of near misses. These personnel were provided with helmets.[14]

---

[13] SECNAV (Charles Edison), serial 400525 of 1 June 1940, letter to CNO, box 181, CINCUS Files, RG 313, NA, pp. 1-3.

[14] CINCUS, serial 01815 of 12 Nov. 1940, letter to CNO, WWIICF, NHD; CNO, serial 093923 of 23 Oct. 1940, letter to CINCUS, CNOCF, NHD.

• • •

SKY LOOKOUT STANDS INSTALLED SO AS TO BE ABLE TO PROVIDE PROPER PLATFORMS FROM WHICH SKY LOOKOUTS COULD BETTER SIGHT AND KEEP TRACK OF INCREASED NUMBERS OF AIRCRAFT. THESE LOOKOUT STATIONS WERE PROVIDED WITH SPLINTER PROTECTION.[15]

Other improvements undertaken to improve combat capabilities included:

(a) Additional depth charge rack facilities and depth charges provided.

(b) Depth charge projectors installed.

(c) Chemical Decontamination Centers established in areas where shower facilities existed and then provided with isolating compartmentation.

(d) Improved means for darkening ship, with light-tight locks in all access hatches provided.

Some of the more prosaic materiel improvements undertaken were:

(a) Camouflage of submarines underwater.

(b) Hot plastic paint applied to ships' bottoms to reduce the rate of fouling.

(c) An increase of berthing and messing facilities and the introduction of the cafeteria system of messing to handle a larger ship's company.

(d) Nonskid deck treads provided to handle heavy personnel traffic in darkened ship areas during rough weather.

(e) Additional life rafts were rigged so as to float off in case of sudden sinking of ship without time for "abandon ship" procedure.

(f) Damage control material provided for all compartments below main decks.

(g) Chemical Defense equipment including gas masks, protective clothing, woolen gloves, and decontamination gear distributed to all ships, and stowage provided.

(h) Removal or blanking off of all air ports below the main deck to increase watertight effectiveness.

(i) Metal shelving placed in dry provision store rooms and spare part store rooms in order to eliminate the fire hazard previously arising from stored provision crates and wooden spare part boxes.

All these alterations and provision of additional equipment could not be undertaken on each ship of the Fleet without removing compensatory weight, so as to keep the ships stable and the top of the armor belt of armored ships well above the water line. The discussions in regard to what could best be spared were warm. The recommendations varied widely with

[15] CINCUS, 312350 Dec. 1940, despatch to CNO; CNO, serial 07023 of 27 Jan. 1941, letter to SECNAV, CNOCF, NHD.

various types of ships, but included marked modifications to the upper structure of the ships and elimination of many of the ships' boats in all types.

There was always more gear than every one could agree should go on the ships, than there was gear that even two or three subordinate commanders could agree could be taken off.

Fueling at Sea

One of the earlier experiments, developed and brought to a general Fleet capability in 1940, and which paid large-scale dividends during World War II, was the broadside fueling-at-sea procedure for large combatant ships. This required the installation on all fleet oilers and major types of combatant ships of the necessary broadside fueling-at-sea equipment.

Some of the pertinent events in this development seem worth recording. On January 11, 1924, the *USS Cuyama* (AO-3) fueled the 7,500-ton light cruiser *USS Omaha* (CL-4), as well as the minesweepers *Tern* (AM-31) and *Kingfisher* (AM-25). The fueling took place in a calm sea and was by the alongside method using 4″ fuel oil hose lines. The *Cuyama* was making turns for 4 knots and the *Omaha* was making turns for 1 knot. In four hours, 221,878 gallons of fuel oil were transferred. This is the first recorded instance of a fueling-at-sea exercise in the post-World War I period for fueling a large combatant ship from a tanker by an approximation of the broadside method.[16]

This success with a light cruiser was followed by the fueling of a battleship towed astern by the tanker. In the 1924-1926 period, the *USS Kanawha* (AO-1) fueled the battleship *USS Arizona* (BB-39) four times at sea by the astern method of transferring fuel. The *Kanawha* towed the *Arizona* by towing engine, making turns for speeds up to 10 knots for the *Kanawha* and making turns for speeds up to 8 knots by the *Arizona*. Rates of transfer of fuel oil varied between 13,000 to 17,000 gallons per hour.

The Commander-in-Chief of the Battle Fleet, in commenting on the astern fueling tests stated that:

> The quantity of oil which it was possible to transfer by means of the equipment on the *Kanawha* was too small to warrant the fitting of other oilers with equipment of this capacity.

[16] Naval Operations, serial 38831 of 20 Oct. 1938, letter to CINCUS; ÇOMBATFOR, serial 01275 of 10 Nov. 1938, letter to COMBASEFOR.

As a result of this recommendation, the CNO established a policy of:

> Continue experiments with a view to increasing the rate of delivery of fuel when the tanker is the leading vessel. In overseas movements, it may be necessary to fuel vessels of the train by this method.[17]

The fueling-at-sea experiments were continued, but only by having large ships—battleships and carriers—fuel destroyers by the broadside method. A fueling of destroyers at sea exercise became almost a standard part of each Fleet Problem during the late 1920's and early 1930's.

In late 1938, the Chief of Naval Operations (W. D. Leahy) stated that:

> In considering an overseas movement in force, the Department has noted that there is practically no data on file, in connection with the fueling at sea underway of battleships, carriers and cruisers by tankers.
>
> • • •
>
> It is desired that further tests be made at the convenience of the Commander in Chief; that the necessary equipment be obtained and the technique developed.[18]

The CNO letter was based on a memorandum to him from the Director of War Plans (R. L. Ghormley) which said:

> The War Plans Division believes that an existing deficiency in our readiness for war, is the lack of equipment for and lack of training in fueling large ships at sea,—particularly cruisers and carriers.[19]

The Fleet was due shortly to proceed to the east coast of the United States for Fleet Problem XX. CINCUS directed his two principal subordinates as follows:

> Commander Battle Force will please submit plans and recommendations for tests with at least one battleship, one carrier, and one light cruiser of each class.
>
> Commander Scouting Force will please submit similar plans and recommendations for tests with at least two heavy cruisers.
>
> No opportunity prior to arrival of the Fleet in the Guantanamo Area on January 21, 1939 is foreseen. However, tests prior to arrival in Hampton Roads on April 14, 1939 are desired. Commander Battle Force should give consideration to holding all these tests, or such as may be practicable, with ships remaining on the West Coast, completing prior to June 15, 1939.[20]

---

[17] CNO, serial 270328 of 14 Apr. 1927, letter; Bureau of Construction and Repair, 13 Apr. 1931, letter to SECNAV.

[18] OPNAV, serial 38831 of 20 Oct. 1938, letter to CINCUS.

[19] Director, War Plans Division (DWPD), 29 Sept. 1938, letter to CNO (with draft of proposed letter to CINCUS).

[20] CINCUS, serial 3941 of 27 Oct. 1938, letter to COMBATFOR and COMSCOFOR.

Subsequently, the Commander-in-Chief turned the fueling-at-sea chore over to Commander Task Force Seven, Commander Battleship Division One (C. W. Nimitz) who was slated to remain as the Senior Officer Present Afloat on the West Coast during the absence of the Fleet.

Commander Battleship Division One must have taken a dim view of the project, for in a letter to CNO he recommended as follows:

> Inasmuch as the broadside method of fueling at sea is not considered practicable for battleships, carriers, and other heavy ships, it is recommended that the Bureau of Construction and Repair proceed at once with the development of "over the stern fueling gear" that will have a minimum capacity of 50,000 gallons per hour. . . . "Not until such equipment has completed satisfactory shore tests should it be submitted for sea tests."
>
> It is recommended that the fueling experiments required [by the CNO] be limited to the fueling of a heavy cruiser at sea under favorable weather and sea conditions by the broadside (or some approximation thereto) method.[21]

Commander Base Force (W. C. Watts) was not quite so firm against the broadside method of fueling large combatant ships. He opined:

> It is considered that alongside fueling of battleships and carriers should not be attempted unless any similar experiment with heavy cruisers proves successful to an unexpected degree.[22]

The CINCUS (Bloch) had also expressed a dim view of the need, for the present, of including battleships in the project of developing fueling-at-sea procedures for large ships.[23]

After long consideration, CNO (W. D. Leahy) disapproved COMBATDIVONE's recommendation and directed that the fueling-at-sea of carriers by the broadside method be undertaken. He stated:

> The Chief of Naval Operations feels that tests for fueling carriers at sea (including replacement of aviation gasoline) should be accomplished at the earliest practicable date. . . .

Admiral Leahy indicated that the fueling-at-sea tests of battleships by the broadside method was of less urgency than that of carriers, but he did not authorize the cancellation of his previous order for a tanker-battleship test.[24]

[21] Commander Battleship Division One (C. W. Nimitz), serial 963 of 13 Dec. 1938, letter to CNO.

[22] COMBASEFOR, serial 01429 of 17 Dec. 1938, letter to COMBATFOR, box 128, CINCUS Files, RG 313, NA, p. 4.

[23] CINCUS, serial 4286 of 25 Nov. 1938, letter to CNO; CINCUS, serial 01888 of 15 Dec. 1938, letter to CNO.

[24] CNO, serial 4010 of 14 Apr. 1939, letter to CINCUS, box 168, CINCUS Files, RG 313, NA.

Accordingly, the Fleet initiated the tests in the months and days just before I broke my flag as Commander Battle Force. The *USS Kanawha* (H. J. Reuse) successfully fueled the *USS Saratoga* (CV-3) (A. C. Read) by the broadside method on June 12-13, 1939. The *Saratoga* steamed at 6-7 knots, and the rate of transfer was at 115,500 gallons per hour. The report of this fueling operation came up the chain of command to me soon after I became COMBATFOR and, based on this success, I recommended to the CINCUS that all carriers be fueled during Fleet Problem XXI and that the *Kanawha* be designated to conduct an initial test with a battleship.[25]

On August 19, 1939, I directed that the type commanders of the Battle Force revise their procedures for fueling destroyers at sea and submit the revised procedures to Commander Battle Force prior to December 18, 1939. It was further directed that, after my approval, the procedures should be printed and distributed to all destroyers. This was done and, when completed, provided destroyers, for the first time, with detailed instructions permitting them to receive fuel from any type of large combatant ship.

On October 13, 1939, CNO approved the purchase of the necessary fueling gear and directed that the tanker-battleship test recommended by me be proceeded with.[26] It took another nine months to manufacture, obtain, and install the special fittings and gear and to conduct the tests, despite much diligent effort both afloat and ashore to accomplish these tasks more quickly. A major step forward occurred when, on January 17, 1940, the Chief of the Bureau of Ships approved the type plans for fueling battleships at sea from a tanker, and directed that the plans be distributed to the Forces Afloat.[27]

Although the *USS Brazos* (AO-4) (H. W. Need) had successfully fueled a 10,000-ton heavy cruiser (*USS Chester*) (CA-27) (W. K. Kilpatrick) by the broadside method, during the period April 6-11, 1939 in the San Pedro-San Clemente area, no ship of the 10,000-ton light cruiser

[25] COMBATFOR, serial 0726 of 15 July 1939, letter to CINCUS, box 168, CINCUS Files, RG 313, NA; COMBATFOR, serial 0842 of 17 Aug. 1939, letter to CINCUS, box 168, CINCUS Files, RG 313, NA.

[26] CNO, serial 6233 of 13 Oct. 1939, letter to Chief of the Bureau of Construction and Repair, box 168, CINCUS Files, RG 313, NA.

[27] CHBUSHIPS, 17 Jan. 1940, letter to Commandant Mare Island Navy Yard, box 168, CINCUS Files, RG 313, NA.

type completed the operation until the *USS Brazos* (C. S. Isgrig) fueled the *USS Philadelphia* (V. D. Chapline) on September 14, 1940. This delay in the 10,000-ton light cruiser fueling-at-sea experiments was occasioned, in part, by a difference of opinion regarding the fueling fittings and equipment with which the 10,000-ton cruiser should be fitted.

CNO was opposed to, and disapproved, the recommendations of the Forces Afloat for fitting most of the heavy cruisers and all the 10,000-ton light cruisers with connections for fueling more than one destroyer at a time, stating:

> . . . Heavy cruisers of, and subsequent to, the *Minneapolis* [CA-36] class, and the 10,000 ton light cruisers have a radius of but 10,000 to 11,800 miles at 15 knots. On the other hand, the 1500 and 1800 ton destroyers have radii of from 7,000 to 8,800 miles at 15 knots. Thus, in any overseas operations any extensive fueling of destroyers from cruisers would result in the latter being dangerously depleted in oil.[28]

As a result of the delay inherent in this minor difference of opinion between the Forces Afloat and those ashore, it was not until January 5, 1941, that COMCRUBATFOR was in a position to issue CRUBATFOR Letter 2-41 prescribing a standard fueling-at-sea bill for the 10,000-ton light cruiser fueling from a tanker. This was the last of the type commands to reach this stage of readiness.

In March 1940, the type commanders of the Fleet were directed to inform CINCUS and COMBASEFOR when ships under their type command were equipped and ready to conduct fueling-at-sea exercises with tankers. CINCUS stated he would then schedule a fueling-at-sea exercise for each ship.[29] Commander Base Force had stated a little earlier in the month that:

> the Commandant Navy Yard Mare Island has advised that special equipment, including quick couplings and light weight smooth bore fuel oil hoses, will not be available for use in projected fueling tests during the current quarter.[30]

[28] DWPD, serial 21241 of 5 Apr. 1940, letter to Director, Fleet Maintenance Division, CNOCF, NHD; Bureau of Construction and Repair, 23 Apr. 1940, letter to COMCRUSCOFOR and Commander Cruisers, Battle Force (COMCRUBATFOR), box 168, CINCUS Files, RG 313, NA.

[29] CINCUS, serial 0504 of 25 Mar. 1940, letter to Force Commanders, box 169, CINCUS Files, RG 313, NA.

[30] COMBASEFOR, serial 0402 of 7 Mar. 1940, letter to CINCUS, box 169, CINCUS Files, RG 313, NA.

So, it was evident that the holding of the tests was going to have to be after completion of Fleet Problem XXI.

In due time, a summary of the information received from subordinate commands was passed on to the Navy Department. In early June 1940, CNO informed the CINCUS that approved alterations had been issued for providing carriers, heavy cruisers, and fleet tankers with fueling-at-sea installations and equipment at the next regular overhaul of the ships concerned. The CNO stated that funds for the work had been asked for in the emergency budget then under consideration by the Congress. The CNO again urged that the battleship and tanker tests be held.[31]

It was not until after the Fleet was stationed in Hawaiian waters that the designated battleship, the *Maryland* (BB-46) (G. C. Logan), received the necessary fittings and equipment and fueled from the *Brazos* (C. S. Isgrig) on July 31, 1940. The fueling exercise was successfully completed but, while subsequently conducting zig zag exercises alongside, the rudder on the *Brazos* jammed and she was slightly damaged forward in a collision with the *Maryland*. Despite the previous trepidation, this was the only mishap in all the fueling-at-sea tests.

With the battleship test accomplished, the 10,000-ton light cruiser represented the last major hurdle before it could be definitely stated that the Fleet had the capability to go to sea and stay at sea, once the necessary equipment and fittings were provided the ships. This task the Forces Ashore pressed to accomplish.

In September 1940, the Forces Afloat (COMBASEFOR) issued standard procedures for "Fueling Heavy Combatant Ships at Sea from Fleet Oilers,"[32] and this materiel problem, which controlled the mobility of the Fleet, was finally on its way to solution.

Much of the progress made during this period came from the Commanding Officers of the fleet tankers who constantly sought to develop the technical equipment, as well as the seamanship features of this initially hazardous operation. I believe special credit is due their boss, who urged them along and backed them up, Commander Base Force (Admiral W. L. Calhoun), and to the Commanding Officers of the *Kanawha* (Commander

[31] CNO, serial 03838 of 7 June 1940, letter to CINCUS, CNOCF, NHD.

[32] COMBASEFOR (W. L. Calhoun), serial 0827 of 28 Aug. 1940, letter, box 169, CINCUS Files, RG 313, NA; CINCUS, serial 01612 of 22 Sept. 1940, letter to COMBASEFOR, box 169, CINCUS Files, RG 313, NA.

H. J. Reuse) and *Brazos* (Commander H. W. Need and later Commander C. S. Isgrig).

Materiel Readiness

The longer the major portion of the Fleet remained in Hawaiian waters, and the more our Navy learned from the experience of the British Navy in the European phase of World War II, the larger the number of essential military alterations for each ship became and the more difficult their accomplishment.

The Pearl Harbor Navy Yard was working very well and at full capacity, but steadily falling behind in keeping those ships of the Fleet operating from Pearl abreast of the desired materiel readiness. In January 1941, a general survey of this materiel situation was directed by me, in order that full information would be available at Fleet Headquarters, which generally did not deal with the details of materiel matters.[33]

It was further anticipated that this survey would result in recommendations to the Navy Department to provide additional interim navy yard overhauls at West Coast navy yards for those ships which had not been brought up-to-date in increased antiaircraft batteries, degaussing installations, splinter protection, and similarly vital alterations. I have been told that this premise proved correct.

Characteristics of New Ships

Another major matter of concern to the CINCUS in the materiel field was in regard to the characteristics of the new ships which were on the drawing boards in the design sections of the Departmental bureaus. Comment, in regard to light and heavy cruisers and battleships, was carefully prepared and submitted to the Department.[34]

Merely for the record, I note that CINCUS recommended against 70,000-ton battleships and for 45,000-ton battleships, and against 26,500-ton car-

---

[33] CINCUS, serial 0101 of 21 Jan. 1941, letter to Force and Type Commanders.

[34] CINCUS, serial 0543 of 29 Mar. 1940, letter to CNO, box 156, CINCUS Files, RG 313, NA; COMSCOFOR, serial 1200 of 8 May 1940, letter to CINCUS, box 156, CINCUS Files, RG 313, NA; CINCUS, serial 0366 of 7 Mar. 1940, letter to Chairman General Board, box 156, CINCUS Files, RG 313, NA.

riers and for 33,000-ton carriers, and stated a further increase in carrier tonnage "may be warranted" to handle new and larger types of bombers.[35]

Auxiliary Aircraft Carriers

In order that it would not be necessary to use a first-line carrier to ferry carrier aircraft, as was being done by the *Lexington* (CV-2) at the time of the Pearl Harbor attack, Commander Aircraft, Battle Force, U.S. Fleet, Vice Admiral Halsey, in late 1940, recommended that merchant ships be converted into auxiliary aircraft carriers for this function and for training purposes.

I endorsed this proposal with these words:

> Forwarded, strongly concurring with the basic letter. Procurement and conversion of XCV's *after* commencement of hostilities has always seemed to the Commander-in-Chief to be an over-optimistic plan with respect to time factors. The basic letter points out the practical necessity for action along this line *now*. . . .[36]

However, Naval Operations rejected the idea as impracticable, stating that minimum conversion time would be 720 days.

Considering the speed with which the "jeep" carrier program was carried out during World War II, using merchant ship hulls, it has always been a matter of regret to me that the Navy did not get this successful program started at the time of the receipt of Bill Halsey's letter and my endorsement. These ships would have been more than useful in the early days of the war.

Aircraft Materiel Problems

I have not included in this chapter very much about the materiel problems of naval aircraft of this 1939-1940 period. Although always interested, I was never an expert in the technical details of the airplane. One aspect of the aircraft materiel problem, however, should be mentioned.

---

[35] *Ibid.*, 0366 of 7 Mar. 1940.

[36] Commander Air, Battle Force (COMAIRBATFOR) (W. F. Halsey), serial 01078 of 13 Dec. 1940, letter to CNO, box 156, CINCUS Files, RG 313, NA; CINCUS, serial 01983 of 29 Dec. 1940, letter to CNO, box 156, CINCUS Files, RG 313, NA; CNO, serial 07423 of 29 Jan. 1941, letter to CINCUS, CNOCF, NHD.

At the time I became CINCUS, our airplanes did not have leak-proof gasoline tanks or armor protection for the pilot. In the Fleet, the necessity for all replacement aircraft to have these two characteristics was considered a matter of urgency. My aviation advisers counseled me that fitting the new aircraft with these two improvements should have overriding priority over earlier dates of delivery or over speed and range characteristics in new aircraft.

I came away from the CINCUS billet with the feeling that the Bureau of Aeronautics was still favoring early delivery dates, and speed and range characteristics, at the expense of toughness in fighting capability, long after the Fleet had turned this corner into the street of reality.

Personnel Handling Materiel Matters

The Navy was blessed with excellent technical bureaus, attuned to the needs of the Fleet during a major portion of my active career. I attribute to this factor major credit for the rapid progress made in materiel war readiness matters during 1940.

I believe that the practice of rotating general Line officers with technical postgraduate training, between sea billets and these bureaus was, to a considerable extent, responsible for this excellence.

With the very great increase in influence, which technical and materiel matters have on the fighting capabilities of our ships and aircraft today, the necessity of having general Line officers with recent seagoing experience occupying positions of decision in the bureaus appears to me to be even greater than formerly.

Chapter XIII

Training for Battle Efficiency and Fleet Problem XXI

The Navy had for many years softly said that its operational training was "for battle efficiency," instead of using the broader and, to the American people, more alarming term of "training for war."

The unprovoked Japanese attack on China in 1937 and the unwarranted German attack on Poland in 1939 tended to draw back the veil for the individual seagoing officer of the Line of the Navy, as far as the immediate essential purpose of our training was concerned, but many seemed reluctant to face the issue squarely.

Conditions Governing Training

For, in our training during the long period between World War I and 1939, the safety of the individual and the conservation of the property and funds of the Government had been the two overriding considerations in our operational training, all but blotting out all other considerations.

To illustrate the earlier point, the first tactical exercises held after I became CINCUS contained this safety rule:

> Weather conditions and weather forecasts will be given careful attention and flights will be cancelled or discontinued promptly upon the approach of unfavorable flying weather.[1]

In this same exercise, to save fuel oil money and wear and tear on

[1] "Operation Order No. 1-40," CINCUS, serial 01776 of 12 Dec. 1939, box 22, CINCUS Files, RG 313, NA, Annex C, p. 1.

NH 77063

Battleship maneuvers in the 1930's.

machinery, cruisers and destroyers were limited to speeds of 24 knots, battleships and submarines to 15 knots.

Tactical exercises were planned carefully and well in advance. They were designed so that they could be conducted in a money-saving manner. High-speed steaming was tabu, and the necessity for large-scale negative air searches was avoided in setting up the exercises. It was an accepted fact of life that our tactical and battle efficiency progress should be conditioned by the necessity for strict financial economy, but the Navy still sought to obtain steady progress.

The money restrictions for fuel oil, gasoline, and ammunition expenditures stemmed from the annual appropriation bills, where the Bureau of the Budget or Congress always set the levels markedly below those desired by the high command of the Navy.

During 1940, increased but far from unlimited fuel oil and gasoline funds were made available to the Fleet. This made it practicable to lengthen, or to make more frequent the periods devoted to tactical exercises or to steaming at higher speeds. I chose to increase the number of tactical periods. As one of my subordinates reported:

> The results achieved from the increased periods of tactical exercises were gratifying but restrictions as to use of fuel at times necessitated lower speeds than would otherwise have been used.
>
> The progressive minor tactical exercises, culminating in the Fleet Problems were of the greatest benefit in the training of officers.[2]

As we got nearer to war, more realistic training was a must. While not prepared to accept the adage "one should not hope to achieve in war, something which one has not learned in peace," it did seem to me that this adage would govern during the early days of any war operations.

Moving the officer corps toward more realistic training was difficult but necessary. It was difficult because too many officers had observed or felt the sad consequences to the violators of the ever-present "play it safe" considerations during the previous twenty years.

My efforts to get our tactical and gunnery training on a more realistic basis bore some excellent fruit. Bill Halsey stated the problem re aircraft and gunnery training succinctly:

---

[2] COMSCOFOR, "Annual Report," 1941, serial 0498 of 12 July 1941, WWIICF, NHD, Part II, pp. 9-10; Commanding Officer, *USS Lexington*, serial 763 of 7 June 1940, letter to COMAIRBATFOR.

> It is hardly necessary to state that the fundamental objectives of aircraft gunnery training will be the highest possible state of readiness for war of each aircraft squadron. It must be realized that, in the early stages of war, the success of our air operations will depend upon the battle efficiency of the squadrons now organized. New or better airplanes and additional pilots may not be available immediately upon the outbreak of hostilities. The gunnery proficiency of an aircraft squadron will be measured in terms of its performance in combat rather than in terms of scores and merits. Any emphasis on gunnery competition between squadrons must now be shifted to emphasis on probable actual competition with an enemy who will have the advantage of recent extensive experience and training under fire.[3]

I do not intend to relate the details of the tactical training in the Fleet during 1939-1940. But, I believe some mention of the particular training operations upon which the Fleet concentrated its energies, as well as my mention earlier of the limitations under which the training was carried out, will be of interest to those officers who have entered the Navy since World War II started.

The basic pattern of training of the Fleet in the pre-World War II period has been set forth in Chapter Four. I did not alter this pattern. I did seek to intensify the effort within the pattern and to conduct operations in a manner far more nearly approaching those which were bound to exist in war.

As the appropriated funds for the Navy increased, I recommended, and it was practicable for the Department to make available, more target-practice ammunition, so that the guns and gun crews could be tested under conditions approaching those in battle.

As reports came in from our observers in the European Theater, it was possible to work up experimental practices based on their observations. Some of the earliest of these were antiaircraft firing by condition watches rather than General Quarters crews, and firings at night against star shell and searchlight illumination.[4]

In addition to the experimental exercises, many of the standard gunnery practices fired during the calendar year 1940 were modified so as to include advances toward realistic battle conditions. For years, the Navy had

[3] COMAIRBATFOR (W. F. Halsey), serial 0617 of 9 July 1940, letter to AIRBATFOR, box 39, CINCUS Files, RG 313, NA, p. 1.

[4] CNO, serial 04522 of 26 Apr. 1940, letter to CINCUS, CNOCF, NHD, CINCUS, serial 0329 of 2 Mar. 1940, letter to CNO, box 169, CINCUS Files, RG 313, NA; CINCUS; serial 0527 of 28 Mar. 1940, letter to CNO, box 38, CINCUS Files, RG 313, NA.

introduced casualties into gunnery practices, but, in general, these were casualties which could be corrected in seconds, if the designated procedures were carried through. In 1940, practices were actually fired after casualties had been imposed for the duration of the practice, such as:

(a) the hydraulic systems for the guns shut off
(b) non-automatic operation of breech mechanism
(c) hand ejection of empty cartridges
(d) local control in train and manual control in elevation.[5]

The scoring system for the gunnery practices was changed by the Chief of Naval Operations to give an extra bonus for hits on the first salvo, which was helpful in accentuating this important part of our gunnery.

The problem of training a fleet, in any age and in any navy, is a complex one. To give some idea of the training in the year 1940, I list the purposes of a series of exercises the Fleet as a whole carried out during one five-day period of one month in that year.[6]

To train surface-ship personnel in detecting and recognizing submarines and aircraft

To test visual means of transmitting warning of approach of hostile aircraft

To coordinate operations of submarines and patrol planes in both day and night search and attack

To coordinate attacks of carrier air groups

To test measures for repelling coordinated air attacks

To familiarize lookouts, fire control, and ship control parties of all types of ships with the rudiments of night attack and defense

To exercise in night search and in repelling night destroyer attack

To develop and test coordinated minelaying with fast mine layers and patrol planes

To exercise in minelaying and minesweeping ahead of a disposition

To examine effectiveness of darkening ships and aircraft

It also should be stated that the increasing number and variety of training exercises, and the complexity thereof, which the 1939-1940 tactical developments entailed, too often resulted in inadequate time for study of

[5] Commander Cruisers, Battle Force (COMCRUBATFOR) (H. E. Kimmel), serial 5220 of 6 Aug. 1940, letter to CINCUS, End. of CINCUS, serial 01465 of 28 Aug. 1940, letter to CNO, box 37, CINCUS Files, RG 313, NA, pp. 1-2.

[6] These are the September 1940 Tactical Exercises.

results, and their proper evaluation.[7] This lack of thorough analysis, coupled with the strict application of peacetime safety rules, always contained the real hazard of sometimes arriving at erroneous conclusions.

During 1940, emphasis was given to the following in the tactical training of the Fleet.

(A) Training by task force, task group, or task unit
(B) Training for night action
(C) Defense of fleet against attack by aircraft
(D) Air operations

I will discuss each of these very briefly.

(A) Training by Task Force, Task Group, or Task Unit

One of the things, which I look back upon with particular pride, is the accentuation which was given during 1940 to task force training. The task force concept—a temporary grouping of units of various types under one commander, formed for the purpose of carrying out specific operations or missions—had existed in our Navy for a good many years. The question, as to whether the Fleet should be organized on a task force or type basis, had been discussed for years and resolved with what I believe was the correct decision; i.e., to organize it on both the task force and type basis.

Although force commanders were, as a general rule, senior to type commanders, the organization on the type basis exercised the predominant influence, because the type commanders largely controlled the money spent by individual ships.

By and large, throughout the 1930's, the Fleet's normal operations were carried out by types of ships or aircraft. Commander Patrol Wings trained the patrol aircraft, Commander Destroyers trained the destroyers, Commander Minecraft trained the minecraft, while other type commanders trained aircraft carriers and their embarked aircraft, battleships, heavy cruisers, light cruisers, and submarines.

The regular semi-quarterly tactical periods were devoted to type exer-

[7] "The orderly and progressive training of the Fleet requires adequate time for a thorough analysis of each exercise conducted in order that lessons learned may be determined, absorbed and applied." COMBATFOR, "Annual Report," 1939, serial 0623 of 17 June 1939, box 74, CINCUS Files, RG 313, NA; p. 5.

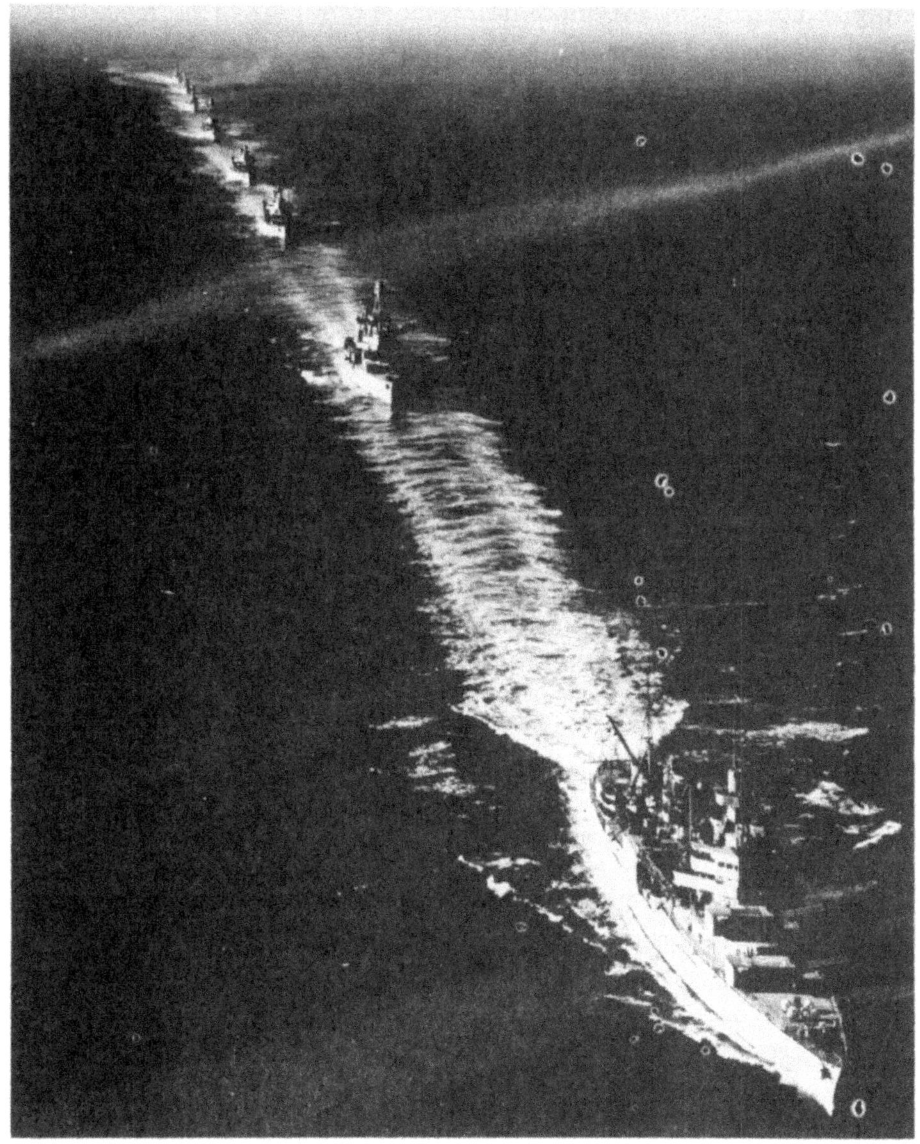

NH 77333

Heavy cruisers of the Scouting Force.

cises under the type commanders, and to task force exercises employing two or more types under a designated task force commander.

In 1940, the need was very great for inter-type training to give subordinate Flag Officers in the Fleet operational functions and responsibilities fully comparable to the probable operations of war. This requirement, coupled with the further need to train the units of ships and aircraft for carrying out specific parts of the War Plans, led to the establishment in June 1940 of numbered task forces, the very early forerunners of the actual task forces and task fleets of World War II.

My staff then sought to so design the tactical exercises that these numbered task force organizations would operate together again and again, so as to gain experience and training in the tasks they would be called upon to carry out in war. I have been told that this accentuated task force training which was continued by my successor, paid off large dividends during World War II.

Numerical designations of components of task organizations also were initiated by CINCUS in early June 1940.[8] These numerical designations were a great step forward over the previous system of using the name and number of the predominating units of normal fleet organization, such as Patrol Wing Two, Destroyer Squadron Ten, or Submarine Division Nine. They simplified the command organization and indicated on their face the chain of command. They made easier the drafting of communications plans for the task force organization, and made quite self-evident to which subdivision each of the type units therein was assigned, thus making communications much more flexible.

These numerical designations were used throughout World War II. The famous task fleets, task forces, task groups and task units became well known by their numbers throughout the military services, as well as to many others who maintained a close interest in the war. In 1940-1941, their simplicity contributed markedly in facilitating the inter-type training in the Fleet. Such training became highly popular in the Fleet, and was pushed cheerfully by the appropriate subordinate commanders.

(B) Training for Night Action

One of the weaknesses of our Fleet in 1940 was in the field of night action by ships larger than destroyers. In the era before radar, close-in night action brought great risk of collision, loss of life, and expensive ship repairs.

---

[8] "U.S. Fleet Tactical Bulletin No. 4-40," serial 0996 of 10 June 1940, WWIICF, NHD.

If collisions occurred, it was believed that the repercussions from the Navy Department and the public would be sure, swift, and severe. Consequently, training in this important field of major combatant ship action was approached gingerly and on a step by step basis.

The Second Phase of Fleet Problem XXI had culminated in a confused night battle between the two fleets, with some near collisions, undesired illuminations, and missed gunnery and torpedo opportunities. This battle led to a strong awareness in the Fleet that improvement in night-fighting capabilities was necessary, but the desire to take immediate radical training action was tempered by an appreciation of the fact that radar was "just around the corner." Many thought that the Fleet would have radar before the Fleet would have to fight at night.

However, as soon as the Fleet commenced its new training year, training in existing night exercises, and additionally experimental testing of new night exercises were held.

By late fall of 1940, although radars in the Fleet were very few and far between, steady training had rendered it possible to hold simple night actions between major combatant types, with a reasonable approach to reality. A new set of Fleet Training Exercises was issued on October 26, 1940. These carried forward the former night-training exercises for light combatant ships and added several new night-attack exercises for heavy combatant ships. Tactical Bulletins covering cooperation of light forces in night attacks were issued and these doctrines were "used with success." [9]

We did not go far, but at least we started.

(C) Defense of Fleet Against Attack by Aircraft

In 1940, the Navy was as concerned over defense of the Fleet against attacks by enemy aircraft bombing, as the United States today (1958) is concerned over attacks by intercontinental ballistic missiles with nuclear warheads.

In 1940, the very vocal believers in the strategic use of air power stated that the only method of dealing with enemy aircraft was to destroy the means of their production or mobility. It was quite obvious that even if this were true, the military air forces of the United States were not in

[9] COMCRUSCOFOR, serial 0520 of 20 June 1941, letter to COMSCOFOR.

sufficient strength, or so positioned, as to accomplish this at the start of any war in the near future.

The next method most talked about was to destroy the enemy carriers or air bases from which enemy planes might attack our Fleet. It was obvious that this also was not a possibility at the start of any war in the near future.

The two remaining, and largely "unballyhooed," methods were defense by the aircraft the Fleet carried with it and, when this method was less than 100 percent effective, close-in defense by the antiaircraft-gun action of the ships themselves.

There was common agreement by all, however, that major improvement in defense against aircraft bombing attacks was essential if the Fleet was to be able to maintain its command of the seas.

A study of the results of antiaircraft firings by the ships of the Fleet, from July 1, 1938 to June 30, 1940, gave little cause for cheer or hope for solution in this area. This study showed that in 307 firing runs by 1.1″, 3″, and 5″ antiaircraft guns against high-altitude, horizontal-bombing drone aircraft, dive-bombing drone aircraft, and low-altitude, horizontal-bombing drone aircraft, only 5% of the drone target aircraft had been hit seriously enough to stop the bombing attack and only 17% hit at all.[10]

Increased numbers of guns on the ships of the Fleet, and putting increased skill into using them would undoubtedly improve results, but it did not appear this action would provide the protection sought.

As early as February 1940, after the conclusion of the minor Joint Army-Navy Exercise of January 1940, the problem of defense of a group, a force, or a fleet against air attack was put in proper perspective by Commander Carrier Division One (Rear Admiral W. F. Halsey, USN). He reported:

> A Fleet can be afforded a higher degree of protection from air bombing attack by properly coordinated aerial pickets and combat patrol.[11]

As I read the history of our Fleet in the Pacific during World War II, it seems to me that the early acceptance of this principle by the officers of the Fleet was one of the basic steps taken toward its future success in maintaining itself at sea and thus controlling the waters and islands of the Pacific.

---

[10] "Defense of the Fleet Against Attack by Aircraft," General Board No. 420-11, serial 1952-A of 12 June 1940, GB Files, NHD, p. 1; CNO, serial 085323 of 12 June 1940, letter.

[11] Commander Carrier Division One, Feb. 1940, letter to CINCUS.

The question of where the balance lay, between the antiaircraft defense within the ships themselves and the antiaircraft defense provided by our own aircraft on carriers or at bases, was a hotly debated matter. The proper balance between fighters, scout observation aircraft, scout bombers, torpedo bombers, bombers, and patrol planes which could be accommodated within Fleet resources, was subject to strong, special pleading by each particular interest represented. It seems to me that the balance, as determined in the final analysis by Naval Operations, and which increased fighter aircraft strength, was an excellent one.

Antiaircraft-gun firings by ships of the Fleet were increased during 1940 by leaps and bounds, but had to be strictly controlled due to the great danger to the plane towing the target or to the plane controlling a drone target. It was not until late January 1941 that enough antiaircraft firing under controlled "surprise" conditions had developed adequate skill and safety rules to permit me to issue the following letter representing a further step forward in preparing the Fleet against a more realistic surprise aircraft attack:

From: Commander in Chief, U.S. Fleet
To: All Type Commanders
Subj: Radio Controlled target airplanes, firing on

1. In order that the problems of establishing effective antiaircraft fire under conditions of surprise attack may be examined in connection with actual firing, it is desired that the Type Commanders addressed formulate and schedule for their respective Types, a practice conforming to the following general requirements.

(a) That the firing ship have advance notice of the time of the attack only to the extent that the attack may occur at any time within a stated two hour period.

(b) That the attack may be made from any direction, and that it be made insofar as practicable and safe, in such manner as to seek the advantages that would be sought by hostile attacking aircraft. . . .

• • •

5. Steps shall be taken to prevent knowledge of these firings from becoming available to unauthorized persons. In this connection attention is invited to U.S. Fleet Letter 3L-40 Revised.

J. O. Richardson

George C. Dyer
Flag Secretary [12]

[12] CINCUS, serial 0168 of 20 Jan. 1941, letter to Type Commands.

By the standards of 1939, this directive indicated the Fleet had made great progress in a little more than a year. However, I was sure that much more progress would be needed to be made under the actual attacks of the enemy.

(D) Air Operations

During 1940, the following principles were evolved and recommended to higher authority in the field of aircraft operations:

Flight and maintenance crews should be separate.

Ground officers should be attached to squadrons for administrative duties.

Duplicate plane crews are a necessity.[13]

These three principles stood the test of war. Dive-bombing practices on the mobile target ship, the *USS Utah,* had been held for several years, generally under quite favorable conditions of wind. But in 1940, the *Utah* (AG-16) was dive-bombed downwind, crosswind, as well as upwind.

As early as October 1940, carrier air groups were directed to undertake the development of a standard doctrine for divided carrier air group attacks on enemy formations.[14] Previous to this, the Fleet air arm had concentrated on simultaneous high-level and dive-bombing and torpedo attacks, massing air strength for a concentrated and coordinated attack on the target.

Development of a doctrine for carrier launching and recovery operations in submarine waters was pushed.[15] This development had started much earlier, when the British carrier *Courageous*, while steaming on a steady course recovering her aircraft, had been sunk by a submarine.

One problem in 1940 that was carried to its initial fruition was the establishment of doctrine and procedures for the joint operation of submarines and patrol planes.[16] The procedures and doctrines developed as

---

[13] "Operation Plan No. 1-40 (Change No. 1), Commander Patrol Wing Two (COMPATWINGTWO), of 13 Dec. 1940, box 33, CINCUS Files, RG 313, NA; Commander Patrol Wings, U.S. Fleet (COMPATWINGS), 21 Jan. 1941, letter.

[14] COMAIRBATFOR, serial 0921 of 19 Oct. 1940, letter to AIRBATFOR, box 20, CINCUS Files, RG 313, NA.

[15] "Operation Order No. 7-40," CINCUS, serial 01361 of 8 Aug. 1940, Plan File, NHD; Bulletin of Tactical Information No. 1-40," AIRBATFOR, 18 Oct. 1940, box 102, CINCUS Files, RG 313, NA.

[16] Commander Surface Forces, serial 0326 of 18 May 1940, letter.

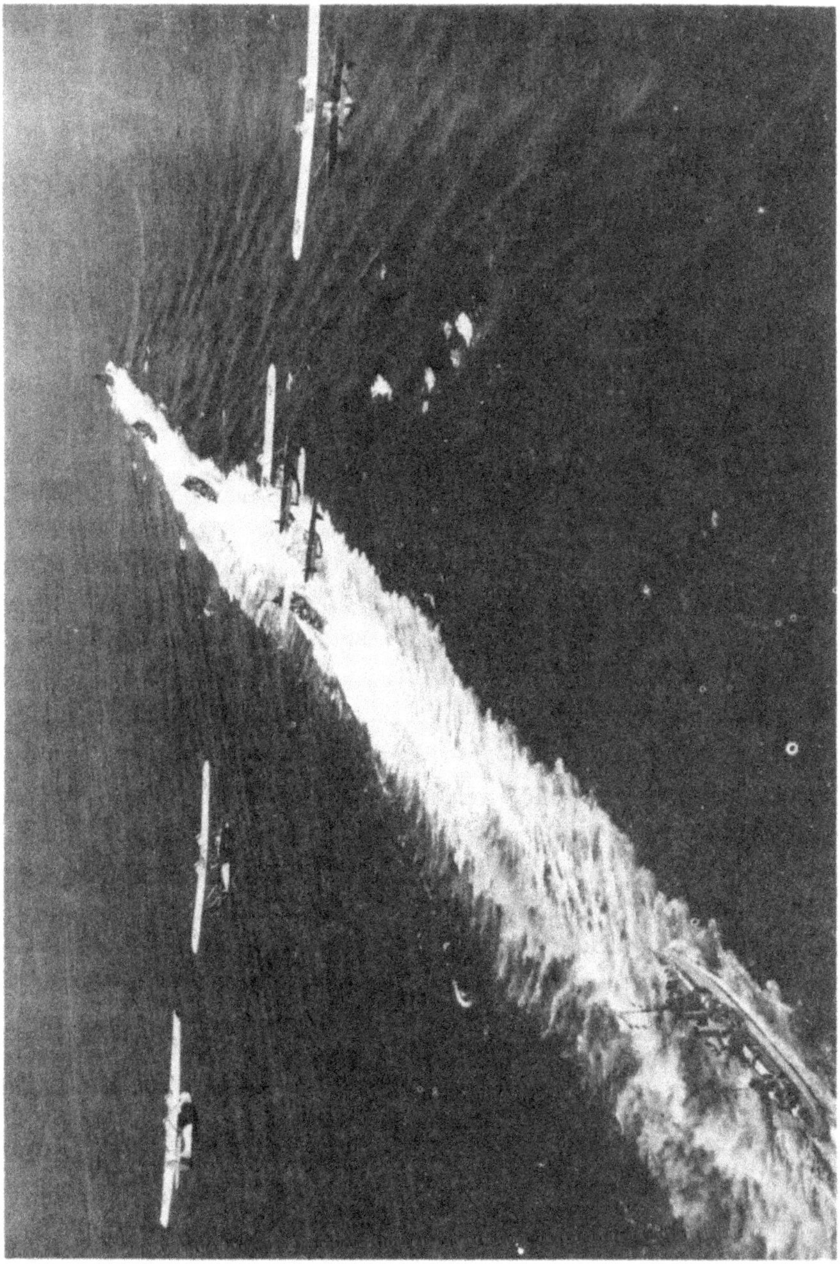

NH 77332

Flying boats and destroyers in the 1930's.

indicated in the following reports paid dividends during the war, not only in combat operations, but in air-sea-rescue operations:

> Type tactics with submarines and light surface vessels have been conducted by Patrol Wings One and Two for furthering the policy of the Commander-in-Chief to develop and perfect joint tactics amongst various types.[17]
>
> Considerable advance has been accomplished in fueling patrol planes from submarines and such exercises have been frequently conducted by the units of Patrol Wing Two.[18]
>
> Patrol Wing One conducted night horizontal bombing practice using the *Utah* as a target. This was the first occasion that a ship target had been used for such a practice.[19]

Major Changes in Fleet Operating Schedules

A measure of the effort being put into training the new personnel in the simple skill of learning to function in all kinds of weather and conditions at sea is indicated by the miles each ship steams during a twelve-month period. By June 30, 1940, the battleships had steamed an average of about 24,000 miles during the fiscal year, with the high ship, the *Oklahoma,* having covered 33,022 miles. The average was about twice the previous peacetime total.

I believed strongly in keeping the Fleet at sea and so kept two thirds of it operating at sea as a routine measure. Major changes in the operating schedules—which showed up strongly in the number of ships in port on December 7, 1941—took place after my detachment. These changes resulted in normally keeping only a little more than one third of the Fleet operating at sea. The reasons this change was made by Admiral Kimmel are stated in the following reports, made long after I had left the Fleet:

> From July 1, 1940 to January 28, 1941, all vessels operated under the general policy of operating four weeks out of every six week period. From January 28, until March 25, 1941, this command was organized into two task forces, one force operating while the other force was in upkeep. Since March 26, 1941 all vessels have been organized into three task forces, each force has operated one third of the time, thus allowing two thirds of the time for upkeep, exclusive of Navy Yard overhauls.[20]

• • •

[17] COMAIRSCOFOR, "Annual Report," 1940.

[18] *Ibid.*

[19] *Ibid.*

[20] Commander Submarines, Scouting Force (W. L. Friedell), serial 0458 of 18 June 1941, letter to COMSCOFOR.

> Under this [previous] system, ships averaged four operating weeks . . . to two weeks in upkeep. With increasing necessity for basic war training and security measures in Fleet operating areas, transition to a Task Force operational program was effected. Two Task Forces were employed at first, each at sea and in port alternate weeks. This arrangement proved impracticable because of large fuel expenditures and loss of extended upkeep periods essential to material maintenance. With the organization of the Pacific Fleet, a three Task Force assignment was adopted to insure necessary coordinated Task Force training for war, to provide for instant transition to full war operational status, to conserve fuel, and permit most efficient use of repair ship upkeep facilities. Under this reassignment, Task Forces averaged 8 days at sea to thirteen in port.[21]

By this action, Admiral Kimmel reduced the time the Fleet spent at sea from 66 percent under Admiral Richardson to 38 percent.

Tactical Publications

One of my last acts as CINCUS was to approve many changes to our Fleet tactical publications, so that the new CINCUS would at least have a temporary doctrinal platform from which to advance. In doing this I said:

> The Commander-in-Chief is aware that current war developments have been leading, and will continue to lead, to many revisions, both minor and major, in conception as to the optimum methods of employing aircraft. He also realized that the present proposed changes are susceptible, as they stand, of further improvement, both in arrangement and in detail. It is essential, however, to have a better basis than currently exists for development and improvement of the publications under consideration, and he desires that the revisions as now proposed be undertaken at once.[22]

Command of the Fleet from a Carrier

One of the experiments carried out in the fall of 1940 was the exercise of tactical command of the Fleet from an aircraft carrier. Some of the younger members of my staff believed that the nerve center of the Fleet in the next war would be in the carriers and stated that the tactical command of a task fleet could more appropriately and effectively be exercised from a carrier.

When the opportunity arose, due to the absence of the regular flagship of the Fleet for overhaul, I authorized the shift of the Fleet Flag to the *USS Enterprise.* The *Enterprise* had not been built for duty as a fleet

[21] CINCPACFLT, serial 01275A of 15 Aug. 1941 letter to SECNAV; as cited in *Pearl Harbor Hearings*, part 33, p. 1246.

[22] CINCUS, serial 0153 of 30 Jan. 1941, letter to COMAIRBATFOR.

flagship. She lacked communication equipment, both radio and visual, for handling expeditiously the heavy Fleet traffic. This was particularly a handicap when operating tactically. The spaces for the various Fleet staff functions were cramped. The personal accommodation problem was unusually complicated when Secretary Knox was aboard during part of this period.

So, after some three-weeks trial and a period of tactical exercises at sea, the flag was shifted back to a battleship, the *USS New Mexico,* on September 21, 1940.

When Commander Battle Force, I was Commander White Fleet during a tactical exercise held in September 1939. Perhaps it is worth recording that, during one phase of this tactical exercise, I placed the only carrier in the White Fleet (*USS Enterprise*) and her plane guards (*USS Cummings* and *USS Tucker*) at the center of the White Fleet disposition. The *Enterprise* was protected by the antiaircraft fire of four battleships, disposed ahead on the axis, of seven cruisers, spaced on circle two, and of eighteen destroyers, spaced on circle three. Circle spacing was one mile.[23]

I believe that this was the first time that both of the following occurred:

(1) the carrier occupied the key spot in a cruising formation
(2) all the antiaircraft resources of the formation were disposed for the protection of the carrier

While the formations used by the task groups of the Fast Carrier Task Force during World War II were based on countless variants of the formation used by me on this occasion, still, the basic principles of the September 29, 1939 formation largely governed these variants.

My predecessor, Admiral Bloch, thought highly of this positioning of the carrier and, commenting on the usual practice of separating the carrier from the main body of the Fleet, said:

> One of the disadvantages of operating carriers at a distance from the Main Body is that not only is the carrier deprived of effective antiaircraft defense by guns, but the Main Body is deprived of effective antiaircraft defense by carrier fighters.—It is important that we realize the ability of fighters to interpose and to punish severely unprotected flights of bombing planes and that we train them for that duty.[24]

---

[23] CINCUS, serial 01769 of 11 Dec. 1939, letter to Fleet, box 103, CINCUS Files, RG 313, NA, p. 23. ("Fleet Tactical Exercises, September 1939—Report of Exercise No. 207.")

[24] *Ibid.*

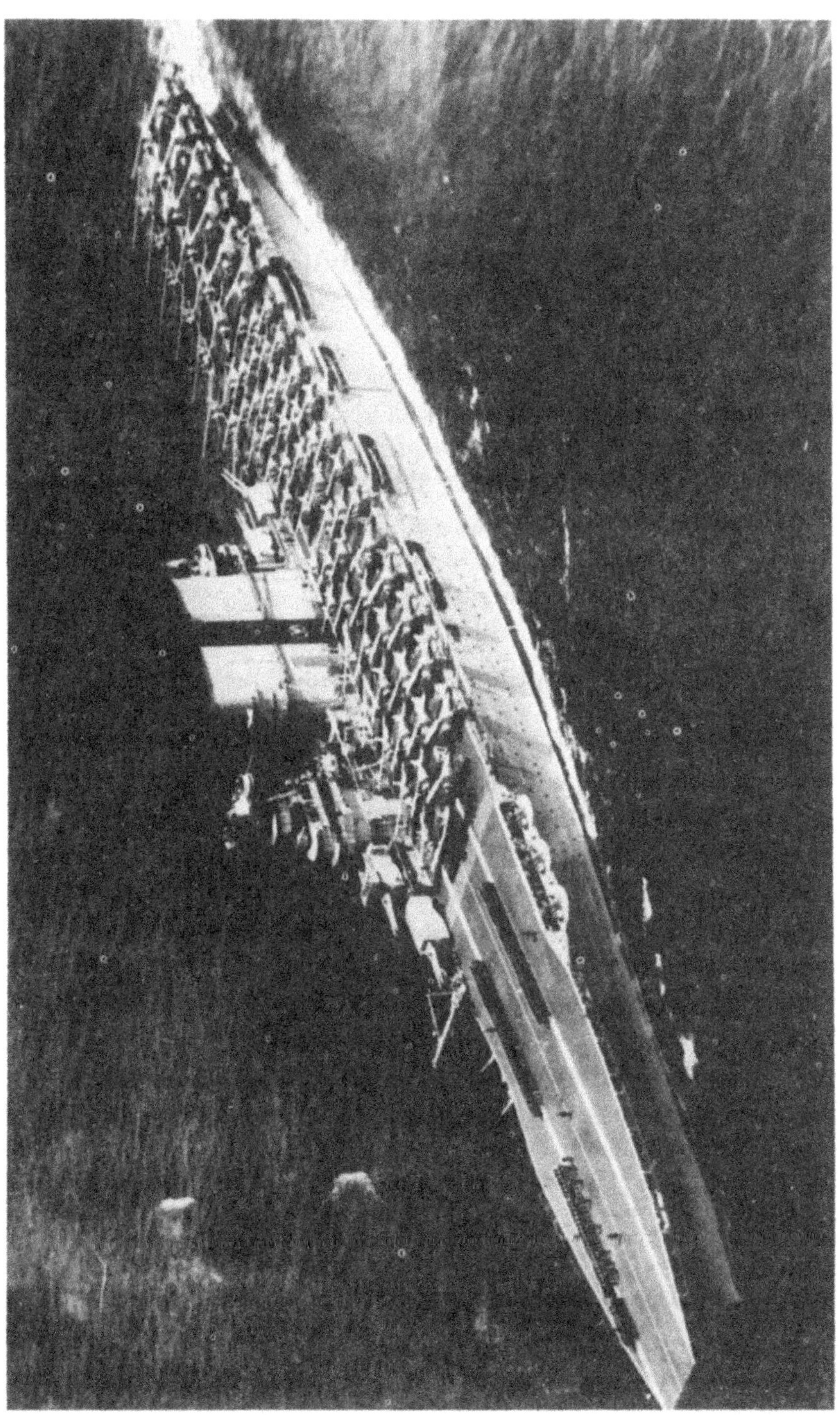

NH 681

USS Saratoga (*CV-3*).

I used a similar formation again in November 1939 when the *Saratoga* was in the Fleet center. This time I placed the battleships on circle three, the cruisers on circles four and five, and the destroyers on circles five and six.[25]

The carrier commanders were slow to accept the advantages of a position within the main body.[26] They were quick to point out the extra ease with which enemy carrier aircraft could locate carriers when with the main body, and the limitations on carrier movement when within any large formation.

As late as the tactical exercises of September 1940, the Commander GREEN Fleet, who had tactical command of battleships, cruisers, destroyers, submarines, and patrol planes, assumed in his estimate of enemy intentions that Commander BROWN Fleet would separate his carriers from the BROWN main body, and from each other, but keep them close enough to be able to provide carrier aircraft to protect the BROWN main body from the GREEN patrol plane air attacks.[27]

Amphibious Training

Urged on by the Marine Corps, the Navy had made steady progress in training for amphibious operations during the 1930's.

As Commander Battle Force, I had participated in the planning for a Joint amphibious exercise, which was held from 15 to 22 January 1940 in the Monterey, California, area. It was a miniature edition, in many respects, of the amphibious operations of World War II. As stated by the commanders concerned, the main objectives of the Monterey exercise, besides training both the Army and the Navy in planning and executing Joint operations, were to train the Army in embarking and disembarking one of the new triangular divisions, and to provide an opportunity for the General Headquarters Air Force and naval patrol squadrons to work together and with ground forces.[28]

[25] CINCUS, serial 01787 of 14 Dec. 1939, letter to Fleet, box 103, CINCUS Files, RG 313, NA, Encl. B. ("Fleet Tactical Exercises November 1939—Report of Exercise No. 306.")

[26] Commander Air, Pacific, serial 086 of 11 Apr. 1940, letter to COMBATSHIPS.

[27] "Operation Order No. 16-40," COMBATFOR, serial 0880 of 12 Sept. 1940, box 102, CINCUS Files, RG 313, NA. ("Comments and Recommendations on September Tactical Exercises and Report of Minor Problem [Exercise 129]"), CINCUS, serial 01928 of 16 Dec. 1940, CNOCF, NHD.

[28] Commanding General, 4th Army (J. L. DeWitt, USA), serial 0193 of 8 Dec. 1939, letter to COMBATFOR.

Commander Battle Force (C. P. Snyder) conducted the Navy's part of the exercise. Upon its completion, I reported to the Navy Department:

> . . . the Fleet profited in the recent exercise from its association with the Army in planning and in demonstrating that the two services can cooperate.[29]

The exercise was excellent training for all the forces assigned. Particularly, it might be mentioned that the Army's Third Division, the new triangular division, later participated in the initial Allied landings in North Africa and in the invasion of Sicily.

Soon after completion of the Monterey Exercise, Fleet Landing Exercise VI was conducted (February 26, 1940–March 12, 1940) in the Caribbean area, although the Neutrality Patrol reduced the number of ships which normally would have participated.

Another landing and base defense exercise was held in the San Clemente area from May 25, 1940 to June 1, 1940. As a result of the Monterey exercise, the War Department requested that Army officers be assigned temporary duty with the Fleet. The Chief of Naval Operations, in advising the Commander-in-Chief of this request, said that the Army had stated:

> The recent minor Joint exercises on the West Coast during the period January 15th-January 20th showed that the knowledge possessed by many Army officers of the tactics and techniques of Fleet operations is not sufficient to secure the most efficient results from Joint operations.[30]

I favored close cooperation with the Army, and eight Army officers were so ordered during Fleet Problem XXI.

One further matter in the field of amphibious operations is worth mentioning. In August 1940, in a letter to the Department, I stated, "It is considered that the technique of aerial photographic reconnaissance, by means of which complete and usable maps of landing areas may be furnished attacking forces immediately prior to a landing, should be developed at an accelerated rate."[31] I have been told that this was done.

Advanced Light Force Practices

Two Advanced Light Force Practices and Advanced Submarine Force Practices were conducted in the San Diego-San Pedro area, in the several

[29] CINCUS, serial 0194 of 9 Feb. 1940, letter to CNO, box 82, CINCUS Files, RG 313, NA.

[30] CNO, serial 400227 of 2 Mar. 1940, letter to CINCUS.

[31] CINCUS, serial 01474 of 29 Aug. 1940, letter to COMBATFOR, box 81, CINCUS Files, RG 313, NA, pp. 25-26. ("Aerial Photographic Reconnaissance of Beaches")

NH 77086

Submarines surfacing during training exercises.

months before the Fleet sailed westward on Fleet Problem XXI. These practices called for the conduct of attacks and the actual firing of exercise torpedoes by light cruisers, submarines, aircraft, and destroyers at fast-steaming, surface-ship formations, during heavy and well coordinated strafing, dive-bombing, and horizontal-bombing attack exercises. All combatant ships and aircraft in the San Pedro-San Diego area, which were operative, participated in the exercise.

The destroyers and light cruisers fired 42 torpedoes from ranges of 7,000 to 13,900 yards and made 10 actual hits. The aircraft fired 24 torpedoes from ranges of 2,500 to 5,000 yards and made 11 actual hits. The submarines fired 10 torpedoes at estimated ranges of 900 yards to 2,040 yards and made 3 actual hits.

Ships maneuvered to avoid torpedoes. The usual peacetime restrictions on maneuvers of surface craft, in waters where our own submarines were operating, were suspended in the interests of greater realism. But a considerable number of artificialities had to be retained as safety measures, because of the necessity of the screening destroyers to act as recovery ships for the expensive torpedos which were fired.These artificialities limited the use of smoke, set up minimum distances between light forces, and required the submarine attacks to be made by sound. But the exercises were more realistic than any held previously when I had been in the Fleet.

There was only one confirmed report of the sighting of a periscope during the early stages of the submarine attack and no reports of the sighting of deeply submerged submarines by the very heavy antisubmarine air patrols. This was a precursor of much wartime experience.

The report of these exercises—forty-two pages in length—is an interesting document. One lesson pointed out, unfortunately, was relearned at the Battle of Midway. The report noted that the torpedo planes had been subjected to " . . . several attacks by large numbers of opposing fightars at 0930, 0932, 0935, 0936, and 0940, and it appears that they would have suffered greater losses than indicated [by the umpires] prior to the delivery of their [torpedo] attack . . ."

The report further noted, "In either case the estimate of [torpedo plane] losses exceeds the total of 24 VTs which actually operated as torpedo planes," and commented, " . . . it appears that a relatively small number of the 24 torpedo planes would have succeeded in launching their attacks under similar circumstances in a real engagement."[32] This was what happened at Midway.

Mining

It was extremely difficult to work up any enthusiasm for training in mining operations in the Fleet, until the impact of the magnetic mine started to be appreciated, and stories of the tremendous damage caused by mines became widely known. However, our Navy was still training only with the moored mines. Our state of skill with this weapon was only passably satisfactory, as the following report, submitted in January 1941 by Commander Minecraft, Battle Force shows. He stated that mining practices had continued their "modest improvement" and presented the following statistics:

	No. mines planted	*Percent effective*	*Percent mines firing premature*
1938–1939	358	84.3	5.0
1939–1940	342	89.0	2.6
1940–1941	358	89.9	1.7 [33]

Fleet Problem XXI

The Fleet Problem, during the twenty-three year period between World War I and World War II, was the big event of the Navy's year. Fleet Problems were expensive in time, money, and effort, but they led to the great advances in strategical and tactical thinking which marked our naval development during this period.

The first Fleet Problem was held in 1923 in the Canal Zone area. Its purpose was "estimate training, study of war plans, ascertain defensive condition of Panama Canal."

In order that the professional officer personnel would give time and study to the war problems of both the Atlantic and the Pacific Oceans, the problems were held in both oceans, although the Pacific was the favorite. The 1934 and 1939 problems were held in the Atlantic and Caribbean, while the 1935, 1937, 1938, and 1940 problems were held in the Pacific.

[32] CINCUS, serial 0686 of 19 Apr. 1940, letter to CNO, box 48, CINCUS Files, RG 313, NA, pp. 5, 27.

[33] Commander Minecraft, Battle Force (E. J. Marquart), serial 0351 of 20 Jan. 1941, letter to CINCUS.

The 1936 problem was held in the Panama and west coast of Central America area.

The story of Fleet Problem XXI in 1940 might as well start with a January 1940 despatch which conditioned some of the things we did during the planning and playing of the Fleet Problem:

> ALUSNA [NAVAL ATTACHE] TOKYO
> OPNAV [OFFICE OF CNO]
>
> ACCORDING TO INFORMATION I HAVE, THE JAPANESE NAVY IS MAKING PLANS WHICH ARE UNUSUALLY ELABORATE TO COVER OUR FLEET PROBLEM. IN THE OPERATING AREAS THEY WILL HAVE TANKERS IN ADDITION TO SUBMARINES AND DESTROYERS.

The presence of Japanese ships in the general area of our Fleet Problem would mean that all the thousands of radio messages sent during the Fleet Problem would be copied and that there would be a heavy strain on the security of our naval communication system. Errors were bound to be made as officers and men pressed to save seconds in putting messages into cryptographic systems, and hurriedly transmitted them. One error could provide the key to Japanese cryptographic experts, which might spell insecurity for our communication system in a future war.

Additionally, plain language radio messages were a necessity during a great deal of the close-in action occurring in Fleet Problems, particularly those connected with air operations. A skilled Japanese naval officer could learn a great deal of the doctrine and procedures being used in the United States Navy by a study of these plain language messages or by listening in when voice radio was being used. So, effective measures against prying eyes and ears were desirable.

The Commander-in-Chief issued the basic order on the problem, on January 15, 1940.[34] The forces involved were to be assembled at normal bases by March 31, 1940, and the problem was to last from April 1, 1940 to May 17, 1940.

During Fleet Problems, simulated damage to ships and aircraft was applied by umpires in accordance with a complicated set of rules governing

[34] Unless otherwise indicated, all subsequent quotations in this chapter are from the following references; "Operation Order No. 2-40," CINCUS, serial 073 of 15 Jan. 1940, Plan File, NHD; Commander WHITE Fleet Operation Order 2W-40 of 3 Apr. 1940, Commander MAROON Fleet Operation Order 3S-40 of 20 Mar. 1940, Commander PURPLE Fleet Operation Order 7P-20 of 19 Mar. 1940, Commander BLACK Fleet Despatch Plans and Orders, Critique statements, reports, and recommendations, umpire rules, and estimates of the situation by the Commanders, boxes 91-96, CINCUS Files, RG 313, NA.

damage from various types of weapons—guns, bombs, torpedoes, or mines. These rules were issued by the Chief of Naval Operations. There was an umpire on each ship and an additional umpire in each unit of ships or aircraft. The umpires had full authority to see that ships or aircraft were placed out of action or operated in accordance with the damage assessed.

The Commander-in-Chief, as Chief Umpire, was greatly interested in seeing that the problem was played realistically, so that false conclusions would not be drawn.

No Commanding Officer of a ship or aircraft liked to be "put out of action," so the pressure on each ship and aircraft umpire was strong to view softly the theoretical damage received by his own ship or aircraft. Under date of March 4, 1940, I opined to my subordinate commanders:

> The prompt and intelligent assessment of damage, and the report thereof, in Fleet Problems and Exercises, not only have an important bearing on the conduct of the exercises, but also contribute materially to their realism.

The Commander-in-Chief further directed that every officer in the Fleet be informed:

> Umpire rules shall be applied promptly and rigidly.
>
> Every effort shall be made to simulate actual war conditions as closely as possible.

Fleet Problem XXI had two major phases. Each was a possible ORANGE War situation, distinct and complete in itself. During each of these two major phases, the Fleet was divided into two forces of comparable but not equal strength. Appropriate subordinate commanders were designated as their "Fleet Commanders" and exercised complete operational control over the units assigned to them. The Commander-in-Chief, U.S. Fleet was Chief Umpire and an intensely interested observer of the operations.

In order that the Commander-in-Chief, U.S. Fleet and his staff could also derive some operational training, and the U.S. Fleet could be trained as a tactical unit to operate as it might have to do in accordance with the ORANGE War Plan, a four day period for special exercises was provided between the two major phases of the Fleet Problem. During this period of special exercises, the Fleet, in the main, operated as a single tactical unit under the Commander-in-Chief. For some of the special exercises, enemy units were represented by a single ship or aircraft of each type, simulating the known strength and characteristics of the Japanese Navy in that particular type of ship or aircraft. These "enemy units" then made air, sub-

NH 77334

Admiral Richardson and his Operations Officer, Captain B. H. Bieri.

marine, destroyer, or battleline attacks on the U.S. Fleet. Or, all the units in the Fleet of a particular type were divided up and assigned to either attack or defense.

During Fleet Problem XXI, these special exercises included large-scale submarine attacks by our own submarines on the Fleet in various defensive formations, full-blown air attacks on the Fleet by all the normally offensive units of our carrier aircraft, and simultaneous defense of the Fleet by all the normally defensive units of our carrier aircraft, as well as night destroyer attacks by one half of Fleet destroyer strength, with the other half used defensively. They also included training in fueling destroyers at sea, in battleline tactics, and in taking and changing from antisubmarine cruising formations to battle formations or to antiaircraft cruising formations.

In our tactical training extending over the months prior to the Fleet Problem, the staff devised exercises which simulated combat operations which had actually occurred, or we believe might be planned for, in the war then going on between our future allies and enemies. For instance, on January 18, 1940, Fleet Exercise 108 was a replica of the situation when the German pocket battleship *Graf Spee,* on December 13, 1939, engaged the three British cruisers, *Exeter, Achilles,* and *Ajax,* in what was known as the Battle of the River Plate.

A preliminary doctrine had been drawn up for light cruiser tactics against a single major-caliber ship. In Fleet Exercise 108, this doctrine was tested, modified, and re-tested. Similarly, in Fleet Problem XXI, within the limitations of the general conditions layed down by Naval Operations, we tried to devise situations which would test certain features of our ORANGE War Plans.

The first major phase of Fleet Problem XXI placed in opposition two fleets of unequal but comparable strength, with one fleet concentrated and the other divided into detachments by considerable ocean spacing. This simulated the then contrasting situation of the United States and Japanese navies. The Japanese Navy, with the greater carrier strength, was concentrated in the southern islands (Marshalls and Carolines). The major U.S. naval strength (the U.S. Fleet) was divided between the East and West Coasts, and the West Coast units were further subdivided between the detachments in Hawaiian waters and those in Southern California waters. And the U.S. Fleet was weaker than the Japanese Fleet in seaborne air power.

The second major phase of Fleet Problem XXI was also designed to fit into our ORANGE War Plans. It involved the movement overseas of an expeditionary force (Fleet Marine Force) protected by a major task force of the Fleet, the seizure of a defended island base by the units of the Fleet Marine Force, and the subsequent defense of the base by the landing force and the naval task force against enemy attacks. All this was to be carried out against defending units of an enemy fleet and defending troops. It was an operation quite similar to that carried out at Tarawa and other islands in the Pacific by the U.S. Fleet and against the Philippines by the Japanese, except that the defending fleets did not show up to do their defending.

Both major phases of the Fleet Problem were designed to afford training in making estimates of the situation, in formulating subsequent plans and operation orders, in making air searches over a large ocean area, and in scouting and screening, in tests of communications, and in the coordination of all types of air and ship operations.

One of the greatest benefits derived from these Fleet Problems (no longer held simultaneously employing all Atlantic and Pacific Ocean resources, since the end of World War II) was the yearly training of so many senior officers in the making of thorough and formal written "Estimates of the Situation," and the formulation of detailed operation plans, involving, by and large, the whole naval resources of the United States. All Flag Officers in the Fleet were required to make these "Estimates of the Situation" and send them and their own supporting plans and orders up to their next senior in the chain of command. Other officers in command were encouraged to submit similar written appreciations, plans, and orders.

In this way, since Fleet Problems generally were along probable future war situations, the system made all senior seagoing officers think, at least once a year, about war situations of the whole Navy, and not just of war situations of individual fleets or parts of individual fleets. This, I believe, was fruitful training.

Communication Mobilization

Before I discuss the major phases of the Fleet Problem, I think it desirable to record that:

> Communication mobilization was made effective 25 March 1940, in order to simulate communication conditions which might obtain during a period of strained relations preceding actual hostilities. Mobilized communications continued through the problem and at the request of the Commander in Chief have been extended indefinitely.[35]

Credit should be given my Communications Officer, Commander M. E. Curts (now Admiral, USN), for this very worthy recommendation to continue communication mobilization after the end of the Fleet Problem.

If the Fleet Problem had resulted in no other advance in naval war readiness and in training, this major step alone would have justified all the money and effort put into the Fleet Problem. This was true because there were revealed major deficiencies in the current communication mobilization plans, which were correctable. But, "the above failure of Communication Plans to fit war conditions was in the opinion of the Commander-in-Chief the most valuable communication lesson learned in Fleet Problem XXI. Immediate steps are being taken to correct this situation. . . ."[36]

---

[35] CINCUS, serial 01059 of 18 June 1940, letter to CNO, CNOCF, NHD, Encl. A, p. 1.

[36] *Ibid.*, p. 3.

NH 77330

Admiral Richardson with his Communications Officer, Commander M. E. Curts.

I will now get back to the major phases. And it should be remarked here that since there were only three carriers available in the Pacific, an imbalance of seaborne air strength between any two forces had to be accepted, if all the three carriers were to participate in all possible training.

However this provided training under conditions of inferior carrier strength, which would be the initial situation were we soon to engage in war with the Japanese.

First Major Phase

The playing of this phase was to be done in the Eastern Pacific Ocean area. BLACK and WHITE were at war.

From the conditions of the problem for the first phase, it might be assumed now, although it was nowhere so stated or intimated then, that WHITE was the United States Fleet, and BLACK was the Japanese Fleet. This supposition finds support in the statement of the general situation, which is summarized as follows:

> The Commander of the WHITE Fleet then at Long Beach, California was informed that "during the latter part of March, BLACK has despatched a raiding force of heavy cruisers, one carrier and destroyers to raid WHITE shipping, and as opportunity offers, to bomb shore objectives in the Hawaiian Area."
>
> • • •
>
> To protect this raiding force, BLACK also advanced the BLACK COVERING FORCE, a large detachment consisting of all combatant fleet types and tankers, toward the San Francisco area.
>
> • • •
>
> BLACK bombs shore objectives in the Hawaiian Area.
>
> • • •
>
> The WHITE Fleet departs southern California bases for the mid-Pacific area in anticipation of cutting off the retirement of the BLACK RAIDING FORCE and for the better defense of the Hawaiian Islands. This departure of the WHITE Fleet is seen and reported to BLACK by a BLACK submarine operating off San Diego. The only carrier in the BLACK RAIDING FORCE (and a simulated one) was torpedoed by a WHITE submarine operating from Hawaii. The commander of the BLACK RAIDING FORCE, being without carrier aircraft support then decides to seek the protection of the BLACK COVERING FORCE now near San Francisco, California. This decision is transmitted by Commander BLACK COVERING FORCE to BLACK Navy Department.
>
> • • •
>
> These BLACK communications are transmitted by use of a compromised BLACK code and the WHITE Navy Department gives the information to the WHITE commander on the afternoon of 3 April.[37]

The commanders of the BLACK and the WHITE Fleets were each given

[37] This latter, reportedly, is what happened during the early stages of the Pacific war and through the Battle of Midway.

the information in the general situation set forth above and separate special instructions. Commander WHITE Fleet was directed to "Destroy BLACK Fleet in order to gain control of the North Pacific east of longitude one hundred sixty west, if practicable destroy BLACK Fleet detachments in detail." Commander BLACK Fleet was directed to "concentrate BLACK COVERING FORCE and BLACK RAIDING FORCE by two hours, six April, then engage WHITE Fleet decisively and destroy it in order to gain control of the North Pacific east of longitude one hundred sixty west."

Each commander being told to destroy the other, it could be anticipated that they would engage decisively.

In the continuing interest of economy, the highest formation speed of battleships permitted during this phase was 15 knots. All cruisers, carriers, and destroyers were limited to 24 knots, except when the carriers were launching or recovering aircraft, when they and their plane guards were allowed to use the speed required for safe landings.

The commander of the BLACK Fleet was Admiral C. P. Snyder, USN,

NH 34893

Opposing Fleet Exercise commanders confer with Admiral Richardson. Admiral C. P. Snyder is on the left and Vice Admiral W. S. Pye is on the right.

and the WHITE Fleet was commanded by Vice Admiral W. S. Pye, USN. WHITE (Pye) decided that his immediate task was "to defeat the BLACK COVERING FORCE before it can unite with the BLACK RAIDING FORCE in order to gain control of the North Pacific east of longitude one hundred sixty West." The WHITE Fleet was superior to the BLACK COVERING FORCE in number of aircraft carriers and carrier-based aircraft (two to one) and in heavy cruisers, light cruisers, and destroyers. He had the tactical offensive until the BLACK RAIDING FORCE joined the BLACK COVERING FORCE. WHITE was inferior in battleline strength and had a stern chase with only 1 knot greater speed.

WHITE (Pye) decided to use his superior aircraft and destroyer strength to conduct attrition tactics on BLACK, and to reduce BLACK COVERING FORCE's battleline speed, so that the rendezvous with BLACK RAIDING FORCE would be delayed. WHITE then could defeat the two BLACK detachments in detail.

WHITE also decided to organize his Fleet into three task forces—(1) the striking force, consisting of his carriers, heavy cruisers, and plane guard destroyers, (2) the night attack force of old light cruisers and 23 destroyers, and (3) his main body, consisting of battleships, new 10,000-ton light cruisers, and his 8 new destroyers with double-purpose guns.

WHITE's (Pye) plan of action was to (1) search for and locate BLACK, (2) attack with bombs, concentrating on two ships of the battleline (so as to slow down the overall BLACK speed of advance), (3) make repeated light cruiser and destroyer night torpedo attacks at the earliest opportunity and, (4) advance his main body at maximum speed to attack BLACK COVERING FORCE, prior to its rendezvous with BLACK RAIDING FORCE.

On the other hand, Commander BLACK Fleet (Snyder) knew that it would be most difficult for the BLACK COVERING FORCE to rendezvous with the BLACK RAIDING FORCE before the WHITE Fleet could make contact with the BLACK COVERING FORCE, even if this raiding force acquired no damage which reduced its speed.

The conditions of the problem allowed only a little over five hours leeway in the time required for a rendezvous, if BLACK COVERING FORCE and BLACK RAIDING FORCE headed directly towards each other from their assigned positions at the start of the problem, had good weather all the way, and, during each hour, made good their maximum speed of advance. Consequently, a radical detour to the north was barred.

BLACK (Snyder) could only hope for unfavorable flying weather for WHITE carrier aircraft operations, unfavorable sea conditions for WHITE seaplane operations and destroyer attacks, and the continuation of the normal direction of the trade winds, which would require WHITE to work to eastward during aircraft recovery operations and thus delay his catching up with BLACK. BLACK noted that sea conditions, which would prevent safe recovery of ship-based seaplanes in the ocean area assigned, could be expected 60 percent of the time.

Commander BLACK Fleet (Snyder) decided that his desired course of action was "to engage WHITE Fleet decisively with the concentrated BLACK Fleet." The task of concentrating before being defeated in detail was the meat of the task assigned to him. To accomplish this, Commander BLACK Fleet decided that he should avoid action with his stronger adversary as long as possible. He would detour as far to the north as his five-hour leeway permitted and then steam straight for the rendezvous. He believed that he had only a very modest chance of success, depending upon the gods of weather all being in his favor. BLACK decided to employ his carrier aircraft offensively in the early stages of a fleet engagement, but, prior to that, he decided to "avoid damage to carrier by stationing it [50 to 75 miles] on side of [BLACK] COVERING FORCE opposite from WHITE Fleet, employing in and out tactics, and taking advantage of dark periods."

In the actual playing of the problem, the weather was unseasonably good instead of unseasonably bad. WHITE search planes located BLACK COVERING FORCE near the end of the second day. By means of WHITE's superior speed, and attacks by his superior air and light forces (in relation to those of the BLACK COVERING FORCE only), he was able to severely damage BLACK's carrier and to slow down BLACK's battleline, so as to be able to interpose between the BLACK RAIDING FORCE and the BLACK COVERING FORCE and to be in a position to defeat each of them in detail.

The important tactical lesson which might be drawn from this first phase of the problem was the folly of stationing a carrier where it would not receive maximum protection from the antiaircraft gun resources of the task force of which it was a part. This folly was not easily blameable, because of the major aircraft operating difficulties created by the presence in the formation of battleships, with a top formation speed of not much over 18 knots. The presence of the battleship in the protective formation was almost essential, because it carried the heaviest antiaircraft armament.

The strategical lesson, reaffirmed in this phase, was the great difficulty of uniting two groups of a naval task force on the field of battle, where their combined strength would be greater than that of an opposing naval force stronger than either of the groups initially separated, and so positioned as to be able to bring either group of the divided force under attack.

Second Major Phase

The playing of this phase was to be done in the central Pacific Ocean area. MAROON and PURPLE were at war.

Since this phase covered the movement overseas of an expeditionary force and the seizure of island bases, it was an operation equally applicable to both the U.S. Navy and the Japanese Navy. Both navies frequently underwent training in the offensive and defensive features of such an operation. Because of the locale, however, it was possible to visualize that MAROON simulated the United States and PURPLE, Japan.

The statement of the general situation is summarized as follows:

> A PURPLE Expeditionary Force with strong supporting fleet units had departed for the mid-Pacific from the Far East. Detachments of the PURPLE Expeditionary Force occupied Samoa on April 15 and Wake on April 16.
>
> • • •
>
> A strong naval task force from the MAROON Fleet was in latitude 8° north and longitude 119° west on April 13 headed west.
>
> • • •
>
> Special instructions to the MAROON and PURPLE Commanders informed MAROON that PURPLE's intentions were to seize a fleet advanced base in the Hawaiian Islands.
>
> • • •
>
> MAROON was directed "to destroy units of PURPLE Fleet advancing eastward of the one hundred eightieth meridian in order to prevent seizure of an advanced base at Lahaina [Maui] by PURPLE."
>
> • • •
>
> PURPLE was given the tasks of advancing a strong expeditionary force to "seize and secure an advanced fleet base at Lahaina Roads [Maui], and to destroy the local defense forces of MAROON in the Hawaiian Area which might interfere therewith, in order to make the fleet base secure and to provide advanced bases for patrol planes."
>
> • • •
>
> The tasks assigned Commander PURPLE were for the purpose of furthering

> the overall PURPLE mission of conducting future operations against MAROON in the Eastern Pacific and against the MAROON homeland.

During this second major phase, speed restrictions on destroyers and submarines were lifted, and cruisers and carriers were permitted to use 27 knots. Large-scale safety precautions in the use of patrol planes were instituted, in addition to those usually imposed by Fleet Problem regulations. The Commander-in-Chief stated, "It is desired to have patrol planes operated in Fleet Problem XXI in a manner which will permit the development of their value for scouting and attack, but will also prevent imposing on, or accepting unnecessary risks to, the personnel and material involved. It is essential to reduce to a minimum the possibility of serious disruption of the operations of surface ships by the necessity of search and salvage operations in areas remote from those in which surface ships are actually operating."

The commander of the PURPLE Fleet was Admiral C. P. Snyder, USN, and of the MAROON Fleet, Vice Admiral Adolphus Andrews, USN.

The Commander PURPLE had the tactical offensive. The PURPLE Fleet had a general superiority of fleet strength, including a two to one superiority in carriers and in destroyers, as well as a superiority of troops (carried on transports) in the landing area, since the MAROON army troops on the island of Oahu would not be available for the defense of the island of Maui.

PURPLE's forces were divided at the start of the operation due to the almost simultaneous seizure of Samoa and Wake. PURPLE's other major weaknesses were that he had only a small minesweeping force (which would prolong his wait in the landing area), and his transports were very vulnerable to aggressive bombing or submarine torpedo attacks. His speed of advance would be slowed by essential zigzaging, and he had a dateline to keep.

The MAROON Fleet had a strong submarine force, a strong defensive mine force, and a three to two advantage in patrol planes, as well as strong fixed defenses and strong troop strength on the island of Oahu.

PURPLE's mission required the defeat of any MAROON forces which sought to interfere with the passage to, and establishment at Lahaina of PURPLE forces, the overcoming of any resistance at Lahaina, and the destruction of any MAROON forces in the Hawaiian area which threatened the establishment of the PURPLE base.

This mission was markedly similar to many World War II missions given our Fleet and task force commanders as they seized base after base in the Gilberts, the Marshalls, and the Marianas and moved westward and then northward in the Pacific.

PURPLE (Snyder) decided he could best accomplish his mission by concentrating his MAIN BODY and RAIDING FORCE at an early date, and taking a detouring course for Lahaina which would avoid detection by MAROON's patrol plane searches, for as long as practicable. PURPLE hoped to establish his own temporary patrol plane base at French Frigate Shoals and to deny Johnston Island to MAROON, by making early air attacks on MAROON local naval defense units and base facilities in the Hawaiian area. PURPLE would seek to destroy any MAROON MAIN BODY or other forces which threatened to interfere with the advance of PURPLE MAIN BODY.

The MAROON Fleet was initially divided into a Northern Detachment (near Unalaska, Alaska) and a Southern Detachment (500 miles north of the equator).

The Southern Detachment was the major force. The Maroon Commander (Andrews) decided:

> During the early phases of this campaign PURPLE possesses the initiative to which in a considerable degree, MAROON must adapt its operations.
>
> • • •
>
> It is the basic plan of Commander MAROON to engage the PURPLE Fleet in a decisive day action after SOUTHERN and NORTHERN MAROON Detachments are concentrated and in an area where carrier planes can utilize shore fields if necessary.
>
> • • •
>
> Until the final stages of the campaign, MAROON will husband his air strength, risking engagement only when decisive advantage can be gained at comparatively little cost. He expects, initially, to be very conservative in employing his carrier offensively.

The most unusual feature occurring during this second phase of the Fleet Problem was a major night engagement between the two fleets. This was the first unplanned night fleet engagement in my experience. It further strengthened my belief that this was an area where the U.S. Fleet needed much training.

My relief as CINCUS (Kimmel), in commenting on this phase of the Problem at the critique, opined:

> It is generally accepted that night engagements should be sought only by a weaker force, already committed by circumstances or orders to decisive engagements with a superior enemy. Yet here was a situation in which the night action was almost unavoidable. It is believed that the engagement which actually developed indicated there has been insufficient preparation for night work between capital ships. A command, thoroughly experienced in such night encounter, would welcome an opportunity to engage under similar conditions, particularly if it was known that his enemy was insufficiently trained. The development of general principles, standard practices, and thorough indoctrination for action in a night melee is indicated.
>
> In night action even more than day, victory or defeat, at least insofar as the individual ship is concerned, will depend upon early, accurate, and rapid fire on an enemy ship, and the ability to maintain it, even while being heavily hit.

If this principle, which was stated so well by the future Fleet Commander, and accepted as valid by so many other officers, had been recognized as the key principle which would open or close the door to success during the first major United States naval offensive in World War II (Solomons Campaign), I am sure it would have received greater corrective effort from myself and from my successor.

One more point should be made before I button up this chapter on the Fleet Problem.

In a report on radio intelligence during the Problem, I stated, "The Commander-in-Chief feels that the potentialities of radio intelligence are, in general, insufficiently appreciated in the Fleet."[38] This was true, partly as a result of the rigid secrecy exercised by the Department regarding cryptanalysis efforts, even extending to the Fleet Commander himself. In my letter to the Department, I pointed out the need for the Fleet to be knowledgeable in regard to all aspects of radio intelligence and approved a recommendation of Commander Scouting Force that in the future:

> The activities of the radio intelligence organization should extend, under the direction of the Exercise Fleet Commander to every aspect of the work, including direction finding, interference, deception, radio intelligence and cryptanalysis, applying to these tasks the maximum concentration of effort and talent permitted by existing circumstances.

Had the Department found this recommendation acceptable, and had it been applied to the Department's own work, Pearl Harbor would not have found the Pacific Fleet Commander uninformed in regard to cryptanalysis results on Japanese codes and ciphers.

[38] CINCUS, serial 0898 of 27 May 1940, letter to CNO, CNOCF, NHD.

Chapter XIV

War Plans

In my reading of serious books dealing with World War II in the Pacific, the proceedings of the Joint Committee on the Investigation of the Pearl Harbor Attack, as well as some of the many books which deal with the events leading up to that attack,[1] it has seemed to me that the very real part our pre-Pearl Harbor War Plans played in the Pacific war has never been sufficiently pinpointed. Furthermore, I believe that students of naval history have an interest in the war-planning effectiveness of our Navy in the pre-Pearl Harbor period. Perhaps, that interest will be nurtured in this chapter.

Modern Development of War Plans

In the Spanish-American War period, just before I entered the Navy, there was no War Plans Division in the Navy Department to prepare contingent war plans of any kind. In 1896, William W. Kimball (1869), with twenty-seven years of naval experience, but still only a lieutenant

[1] More particularly, the following books were written by professionals or under the aegis of professionals; Samuel E. Morison, *The Rising Sun in the Pacific,* Vol. III of *History of United States Naval Operations in World War II* (Boston: Little Brown and Co., 1948); Maurice Matloff and Edwin M. Snell, *Strategic Planning for Coalition Warfare 1941-1942* in subseries *The War Department,* Office of the Chief of Military History, Department of the Army series *The United States Army in World War II* (Washington, D.C.: GPO, 1951); Mark Watson, *Chief of Staff: Prewar Plans and Preparations* in subseries *The War Department,* Office of the Chief of Military History, Department of the Army series *The United States Army in World War II* (Washington, D.C.: GPO, 1950); King and Whitehill, *Fleet Admiral King;* Knox, *A History of the United States Navy*; Husband E. Kimmel, *Admiral Kimmel's Story* (Chicago: Henry Regnery Co., 1954); RADM Robert A. Theobold, *The Final Secret of Pearl Harbor: The Washington Contribution to the Attack* (Old Greenwich, Conn.: The Devin-Adair Co., 1954); LT Grace P. Hayes, "The War Against Japan," Vols. I and II of "The History of the Joint Chiefs of Staff in World War II" (Washington, D.C.: Historical Section, Joint Chiefs of Staff, 1953–1954), WWIICF, NHD.

in rank, had developed a plan of operations to be undertaken should a war with Spain occur. And, on his own initiative, he submitted the plan to the Secretary of the Navy. This plan recommended a simultaneous attack on Spanish possessions in the Caribbean (Cuba) and in the Pacific (Philippines).

A Naval War Board, with advisory powers only, was created in March 1898 by the Secretary of the Navy. The Assistant Secretary of the Navy, Theodore Roosevelt, was designated to head the Board with Rear Admiral Arent S. Crowinshield (1864), Chief of the Bureau of Navigation, as its senior naval officer. Captain Albert S. Barker (1863) and Commander Richardson Clover (1867) were named as additional members. None of these officers were given orders to this duty. They were informally asked to serve and did serve.

Rear Admiral Montgomery Sicard (1851), after having been relieved by Rear Admiral William T. Sampson in command of the North Atlantic Squadron, was ordered to the Secretary of the Navy's Office and became President of the Naval War Board, and Captain Alfred Thayer Mahan (1855), USN, (Ret.) was ordered to active duty and reported for duty on the Board on May 9, 1898.

Lacking more attractive alternative naval war plans, Lieutenant Kimball's privately developed War Plan was approved by the Secretary of the Navy in early 1898. This casual arrangement in regard to naval war planning led Captain Mahan, when he wrote the "History of the Naval War Board of 1898," to remark that the Naval War Board of 1898 owed its creation to "The Secretary's lack of professional experience together with the non-existence of a General Staff to supply that lack. . . ." In my opinion, this remark by this author made it a matter of historical record that the Navy had no system of war planning and no promulgated war plans when the Spanish-American War commenced.[2]

The lack of war plans at the start of the Spanish-American War must have aroused the ire of Admiral George Dewey, who occupied a preeminent position in our Navy from the end of the Spanish war until his death in 1917. In any case, Admiral Dewey, as Chairman of the General Board of the Navy, inaugurated in 1901 a series of War Plans studies. Over the

[2] CAPT Alfred T. Mahan, "History of the Naval War Board of 1898," General Board No. 401-2, 20 June 1906, GB Files, NHD, p. 3; John D. Long, *The New American Navy* (New York: The Outlook Co., 1903), p. 162.

years, these studies evolved into useful educational, but not executive, documents.

There is now extant the original copy of the "Strategic Section" of a "War Plan for War with Japan," approved by the Executive Committee, General Board on February 25, 1914, and signed by Admiral George Dewey. This Plan was approved by the whole General Board on March 14, 1914. Five copies of this War Plan were prepared in March 1916, and the extant one placed in War Portfolio No. Two. No approval by any authority higher than the General Board is shown, and the Plan contains no orders for anyone to do anything to prepare for the war possibility, or after the war started. It does contain an excellent exposition entitled "The Strategy of the Pacific," and a very fine "Estimate of the Situation," in addition to well thought out "Administrative" and "Logistic" sections. The General Board also developed a "Base Plan for a War in the Atlantic."

This work was done, despite the fact that, until the Office of the Chief of Naval Operations was authorized by the Congress in 1915, after years of pleading by naval officers for some such arrangement, there was no official or office in the Navy Department charged by law with (1) the preparations of Naval War Plans or (2) the preparation and training of the Fleet for war.

The action of the Congress in creating the Office of the Chief of Naval Operations and setting forth the duties of the Chief of Naval Operations was a logical and essential step for the defense of the nation; it was made possible only by the commencement, in Europe in 1914, of World War I, which gave potency to the merits of professional naval arguments and permitted Congressional overriding of the bitter and strong opposition by the Secretary of the Navy, Josephus Daniels, and the President, Woodrow Wilson, to the creation of the Office of the Chief of Naval Operations.

The question of whether any actual war plans for war with the German-Austrian Forces existed in April 1917, at the time of our entry into World War I, was disputed publicly between the Secretary of the Navy (Josephus Daniels) and various naval officers during a Congressional investigation of the Navy in 1920; the Secretary saying War Plans existed, the naval officers strongly denying the fact. The Secretary showed, by his testimony before Congress, that he did not know or recognize the difference between war planning studies and War Plans, bearing the stamp of approval of the Secretary of the Navy or the President, and requiring execution by subordinates of essential preparedness measures.

Admiral Mayo, the Commander-in-Chief of the Atlantic Fleet during World War I, succinctly summed up the Secretary's error, when he testified:

> The General Board is charged with the preparation of plans of campaign. . . . The General Board has no executive functions.[3]

Vice Admiral William S. Sims, the author of the letter which set off the Congressional investigation, testified:

> All these witnesses have called your attention to the base plan of the General Board for a War in the Atlantic. . . . This base Plan related, however, not to any action on our part in the present war [World War I], but rather to the general strategical situation in the Atlantic and the steps which the Navy would have taken to mobilize, and the general strategy that would have been followed in event of our being engaged single handed against a European Power. . . . All of the witnesses agreed that this base plan was not referred to or used in the . . . war. Nor has any evidence been presented to show that this base plan of the General Board was ever officially approved by the department.

Developed War Plans, approved by the President or the Secretary of the Navy and distributed for appropriate action to the principal officers afloat and ashore, did not exist in 1917–1918, and, the Secretary ". . . rejected or failed to act upon recommendations which were made to him . . . to draw up adequate and officially approved [war] Plans."[4]

This sad record did little to lessen the opposition of later civilian Secretaries of the Navy to war planning during the early years after World War I ended in 1918. From 1919 thru the early and middle 1930's, the whole subject of war planning was a tabu one with the American people. They wanted the Army and the Navy to be 1,000-percent ready if war should suddenly come upon them, but they didn't want their Military Services to plan for war, for fear that the mere planning for it would bring war nearer.

Of course, exactly the opposite was true.

In order to keep the Navy as a whole from knowledgeable violation of this peculiar isolationist and pacifist tabu, the very existence of our Naval

[3] U.S., Congress, Senate, Subcommittee of the Committee on Naval Affairs, *Naval Investigation Hearings*. (66th Cong., 2nd sess., 30 Mar. 1920) (Washington, D.C.: GPO, 1920), p. 614.

[4] ADM Sims testimony, "Naval Investigation Hearings," 27 May 1920, as cited in "Naval Administration: Selected Documents on Navy Department Organization 1915-1940," Navy Department Library, NHD, Part III-A, pp. 32-33.

War Plans was a very closely held secret within the Naval Service during the period 1919–1937. Until 1937, there had never been an officer exclusively assigned to work on War Plans on the staff of the Commander-in-Chief, United States Fleet. And, it was not until 1939, when World War II was upon us, that there was a war plans officer detailed by the Navy Department, as such, to this most important command afloat. Up until the time these orders were issued and published, the number of officers in the active duty Navy, who knew any of the details of specific Naval War Plans, was probably never many more than 100. The Navy, at large, was kept ignorant of the details of War Plans, although not of the need for the development of specific and detailed plans at all levels of command.

I was never assigned to a billet where my duties were exclusively war planning, but I held a number of billets where there was a definite responsibility for knowing what our War Plans were and acting to further them. Particularly was this true during my duties as Budget Officer, 1934–1935; as Chief of Staff to the Commander-in-Chief, U.S. Fleet, 1935–1936; as Assistant Chief of Naval Operations, 1937–1938; and as Chief of the Bureau of Navigation, 1938–1939.

So, for the five-year period prior to my going to sea in June 1939, I had been quite close to our war planning, and was reasonably familiar with the status of our War Plans.

In the twenty-year period between the end of World War I and the time I was designated to command the Battle Force of the United States Fleet, our War Plans, insofar as they related to the Navy and to war with Japan, had never been feasible War Plans. I state this as a fact, because I believe it to be such. A little later, I will discuss in which respects these War Plans were unrealistic and how they got that way.

And, when I left Washington for the Pacific in June 1939, this unreality of our Naval War Plans was one of my major items of concern, since I believed that, in the two-year period ahead, I might be called upon to implement a major part of at least one of them, as the Basic ORANGE Plan had stated: "The Commander-in-Chief U.S. Fleet is the principal naval agent . . . for bringing the war to a successful conclusion."[5]

At that time, the up-to-date and controlling document for the Navy and for war with Japan was the Joint Army and Navy Basic War Plan—

[5] "Basic War Operating Plans, WPL-9" (hereafter cited as WPL-9), Vol. II, CNO, 29 Feb. 1924, Plan File, NHD, Part III, p. 20.

ORANGE, generally known as the ORANGE Plan. Japan was ORANGE; the United States was BLUE.

Before the present Joint Chiefs of Staff organization was brought into being, the Joint planning of the Army and Navy was accomplished by the Joint Board, an agency created by and responsible to the Secretaries of War and the Navy. This Joint Board of the Army and Navy had the primary responsibility for the development of Joint War Plans.

For a war with Japan, they developed three distinct plans during the period 1923–1939. These were approved jointly by the Secretary of War and the Secretary of the Navy in June 1923, in June 1928, and in February 1938.[6]

Flowing from the Joint Army and Navy Basic War Plan—ORANGE was a Navy Basic War Plan—ORANGE,[7] and flowing from the latter, but required to conform to it, were the War Plans of the Operating Forces of the Navy, known as O-1-ORANGE, O-2-ORANGE, etc.

Any unreality in an operational requirement in the Joint Basic War Plan ballooned and became more difficult to keep pace with (just as with skaters "cracking the whip" on ice) when it was restated in greater detail in the Navy Basic War Plan and then in final detail in the United States Fleet War Plan (O-1-ORANGE).

Pre-World War II Planning Systems

In our immediate pre-World War II planning practices, a basic war plan in the Navy had two major parts: one major part was for the fighting elements, called the Strategic Plan; the other major part was for the shore-side support elements, called the Logistic Plan. Both major parts were drafted to be in accord with a list of basic assumptions in regard to world, national, and military situations.

The Strategic Plan contained:

(a) a broadly stated Strategic Concept for conducting the war
(b) missions assigned to each of the Military Services in support of this Strategic Concept

---

[6] "Joint Army and Navy Basic War Plan ORANGE," Joint Board serial nos. 208, 280, and 618 of June 1923, June 1928, and Feb. 1938, respectively, Joint Board (JB) Files, File 325, NHD.

[7] Initially (in 1923), the "Basic War Plans" consisted of "Basic Readiness Plan, WPL-8" and "Basic War Operating Plan, WPL-9."

(c) tasks which needed to be accomplished by each of the Military Services
(d) a delineation of the theaters of operations
(e) an establishment of the command for the various theaters of operations and, in some instances the chain of command in the theater
(f) an allocation or assignment of forces to support the Strategic Concept, and needed to permit accomplishment of the assigned missions and tasks

The Logistic Plan contained the necessary planning directives, in five distinct and prescribed steps, to provide logistic support of the Strategic Plan. The five steps were:
(a) take CONDITION B
(b) take CONDITION A
(c) mobilize
(d) prosecute the war
(e) augment the operating forces

The Naval Logistic Plan also set forth a "Peacetime Ship Building Program," a "Peacetime Building Program for the Shore Establishment," and a "Maintenance Readiness Policy for the Shore Establishment."

War Planning in the Early 1920's

It is my intention to briefly relate the development of the ORANGE War Plan during the period 1923 to 1940 and to point out its strong and weak points, as I saw them.

The first post-World War I Naval War Plans were promulgated in June 1923 by Admiral R. E. Coontz (1885), USN, Chief of Naval Operations. These War Plans were in two volumes. One volume was the Basic Readiness Plan setting forth the "Standards of Readiness for the Fleet and Shore Establishment" to maintain in time of peace. The second volume set forth Basic War Operating Plans for handling four possible foreign emergencies or wars, as well as for the handling of domestic catastrophies.

By 1929, the Navy Basic War Plan—ORANGE, alone, was in four volumes totalling 800 pages and the United States Fleet War Plan (0-1-

ORANGE) eventually ran to another two volumes of similar length. Consequently, this chapter cannot deal in detail with many of the features of the ORANGE War Plans.

Of these four possible wars, naval planners generally considered that a war with Japan would be the most difficult to win, and was the most likely of the four to occur. So, gradually, the planning for this war received overriding attention from the planners.

Back in 1923, it had been appreciated by many seasoned naval officers that Japan's drive for expansion would probably take a two-pronged direction—westward to Manchuria and southward to Southeast Asia and the Netherlands East Indies.

It had also been appreciated that United States military operations against the flanks of these two movements would probably bring disaster to Japanese arms more quickly, and much more cheaply in terms of human lives, than a direct attack on the Japanese mainland, particularly with the means then available, or likely to be available in the foreseeable future.

For the 1923 Navy to operate on the flanks of these Japanese movements, a large base for Fleet Operations was required, in the Philippines if possible, but if not possible there, then at the harbor of Guam or some large protected anchorage amongst the many Japanese-mandated islands in the Marshall and Caroline groups.

The development of such a base in the Western Pacific was prohibited to the United States by the 1921 Washington Treaty for the limitation of naval armaments. Even if the requisite base could be developed at Manila or Guam between the then terminal date of the Washington Treaty (1936) and the commencement of war, the retention of this base, in the early days of an ORANGE War by the United States military strength likely to be available in the Western Pacific, was questionable.

Since a base for Fleet Operations was a fundamental need, and it could not be developed at the available fixed locations in the Western Pacific area, it was correctly reasoned that the base had to be mobile and brought into the area when needed.

This thinking led to the development, by the War Plans Division in the Office of the Chief of Naval Operations, of a Mobile Base Project in the Navy Basic War Plan. The objective was to obtain the necessary tenders, repair, ammunition, oiler, and supply ships for the Fleet Train and the necessary large floating drydocks and other shoreside material needed for the advanced base, which would be required to support Fleet operations in the Western Pacific. This advanced base became known as the Western Base and will be so referred to herein.

Western Base Project

Initial planning for the Western Base Project called for obtaining, from the Congress, appropriations for the necessary logistic support ships and material which would make feasible the following operations in a war with Japan:

1. The overseas movement of a specially designated Naval Task Force from the Hawaiian Islands, to Manila Bay in the Philippines, fourteen days after the day of the outbreak of war. This Task Force was to be at least 25 percent superior to the total Japanese naval strength.

   (a) The Task Force was to accompany and to protect (1) an Expeditionary Force and (2) the necessary logistic support ships and personnel needed to establish the Western Base.

   (b) 50,000 Army troops in troop ships, and 22,000 Marines in troop ships, were to comprise the Expeditionary Force.

2. A subsequent westward supporting movement from the Hawaiian Islands, by the remainder of the U.S. Fleet not later than sixty days after the declaration of war. This Task Force was to protect and accompany:

   (a) The remaining logistic support units of the Western Base.

   (b) Aircraft in crates or on the decks of ships to provide an overwhelming air superiority in the main theater of operations, the Western Pacific.

3. The maintenance of the entire U.S. Fleet, portions of the Naval Transportation Service and the 16th Naval District Forces in operating condition at the Western Base (Manila Bay or other suitable anchorage area) for one year after arrival.

   (a) The Western Base to be provided was required to include the following characteristics:

   (1) A Main Base with facilities for emergency repairs and docking of the U.S. Fleet, Naval Transportation Service ships, and Local Defense Forces, as well as for the routine upkeep and dock-

The Philippine Islands.

ing of the U.S. Fleet and Local Defense Forces. Docking and repair facilities capable of undertaking any underwater or other structural, engineering, and ordnance repairs as would permit combatant units, damaged in action or by other attack, to regain their stations in the Fleet in the minimum of time, and in the maximum reasonable material condition.

(2) A Special Base with facilities for the operation and maintenance of smaller classes of ships, such as destroyers or submarines, and for aircraft.[8]

1923-1933 Events

With each passing year, the naval problem received continual and fruitful study at the Naval War College, and by the officers of the War Plans Division of the Office of Naval Operations.

In February 1924, missions had been assigned by the Joint (Army and Navy) Board to the Army and Navy "To hold Manila Bay;" for "An immediate naval advance with land reinforcements for Manila," and for "The development and use of Army and Navy air power overwhelmingly." These were all incorporated in the Basic ORANGE Plan.[9]

The assumptions of 1923 in the Mobile Base Project for a large overseas movement fourteen days after the outbreak of war and the pre-war acquisition and assembly of the floating drydocks and other material for the Western Base, became increasingly impractical assumptions during the 1923-1933 period, when war seemed so far in the distant future to the American people and their Congressional representatives. The scanty naval appropriations of the depression years (fiscal years 1931-1934) not only prevented any progress in building up the Fleet Train of supporting ships needed for this large overseas movement but, during these years, had caused the actual diminution of the Fleet Train.

When it came to a final showdown as to what ships could be kept in commission with the funds available, the high command of the Navy always put the emphasis on maintaining in commission combatant ships rather than ships of the Fleet Train. It was hoped that the supporting and

---

[8] "Basic Readiness Plan, WPL-8" (hereafter cited as WPL-8), Vol. I, CNO (E. W. Eberle), 15 Sept. 1923, Plan File, NHD, Appen. F; "Navy Basic Plan—ORANGE, WPL-13" (hereafter cited as WPL-13) Vol. I, CNO, 1 Mar. 1929 (C. F. Hughes), Plan File, NHD, p. 13.

[9] WPL-9, Part III, p. 13.

troop ships, in part, could be improvised from our merchant shipping. It was a known fact that personnel training in combatant ships was far more efficient in preparing officers and men for war than training in ships of the Fleet Train.

I believe that the pacifist and isolationist groups in the country and in the Congress thought that they could make war less likely if they tied the United States Fleet to the coasts of the United States, by denying to it a Fleet Train. They realized, or were told, that a large Fleet Train was the *sine qua non* of overseas operations.

The strong belief by many Americans that our military forces should have a capability and be prepared "for defense only" was a high barrier for sound reasoning to hurdle. As a consequence, only the limited number of new combatant ships which the President allowed the Navy to request from Congress generally were authorized or appropriated for. The new Fleet Train ships requested were almost always eliminated by the President or dropped out of the naval authorization or appropriation bills at some stage in the Congressional struggle, as a last-ditch concession to the pacifist and isolationist groups. Their opposition, plus the Navy's own published preferences for combatant types of ships, made this choice almost inevitable.

Actually, of course, this lack of a Fleet Train made war with Japan much more likely. The military leaders of Japan, who were also the political leaders, recognized this fundamental weakness in our naval strength. They recognized that, if they planned their war moves boldly and moved quickly at the start of a war, they could achieve major successes toward accomplishment of their objectives in Southeast Asia, before our Fleet could be moved to the Western Pacific to stop them.

In the period between 1923 and 1928, subordinate commands and activities in the Navy developed their areas of the ORANGE Plan, disclosing a number of matters needing correction or change. The Joint Board developed a new Joint ORANGE Plan. Consequently, a new Navy Basic War Plan—ORANGE, based on the new Joint Plan was worked up and, when approved by Curtis D. Wilbur, Secretary of the Navy, was issued in early 1929.

The two major changes made by this plan were that the initial westward movements of the Fleet and the Expeditionary Force from Hawaii were postponed from a joint departure "14 days after the outbreak of war" to the Fleet departing "as soon after the outbreak of war as possible . . ." and the Expeditionary Force "ready to sail 30 days after the start of the war." A new basic provision was that United States naval power should be established in the Western Pacific in strength superior to that of ORANGE at the earliest practicable date after the declaration of war.[10]

1933-1939 Events

During the period (September 1935-June 1936) when I was Chief of Staff to the Commander-in-Chief, United States Fleet, the ORANGE Plan was subject to continued study from the Fleet viewpoint. The previous Commander-in-Chief, Admiral D. F. Sellers, USN, had shown his interest by reporting to the Chief of Naval Operations:

> All tactical exercises of the Fleet are based on situations which probably would arise in the execution of . . . [Fleet War Plan ORANGE].[11]

And again four months later he reported:

> To date the Fleet has held four cruising exercises, all of which have closely simulated tactical situations which might occur in an Orange war.[12]

On August 26, 1933, the Commander-in-Chief United States Fleet submitted to the Chief of Naval Operations the proposed ORANGE Plan for Fleet war operations. I can find no record of any previous Fleet (0-1-ORANGE) Plan based on the 1929 revision of the Basic Plan.

In the O-1-ORANGE Plan, issued by Admiral Sellers on January 1, 1934 (which also was the first actual Fleet ORANGE Plan widely distributed to unit commanders of the United States Fleet, as far as the records go), he had stated as the major tasks of the U.S. Fleet:

> The BLUE Fleet must arrive in the Philippines before ORANGE can securely garrison the principal actual or potential bases in that area and build up a large shore based Air Force.[13]

The Plan called for an advance of the Fleet from Hawaii to the Marshall Islands twenty days after war started, and the Commander-in-Chief stated:

---

[10] WPL-13, pp. 14, 21.

[11] CINCUS (D. F. Sellers), serial 2871 of 13 Oct. 1933, letter to CNO, Plan File, NHD.

[12] CINCUS (D. F. Sellers), serial 676 of 17 Feb. 1934, letter to CNO, Plan File, NHD, p. 3.

[13] "O-1-ORANGE" Plan, CINCUS, 1 Jan. 1934 superseded a 1927 "O-1-ORANGE" Plan.

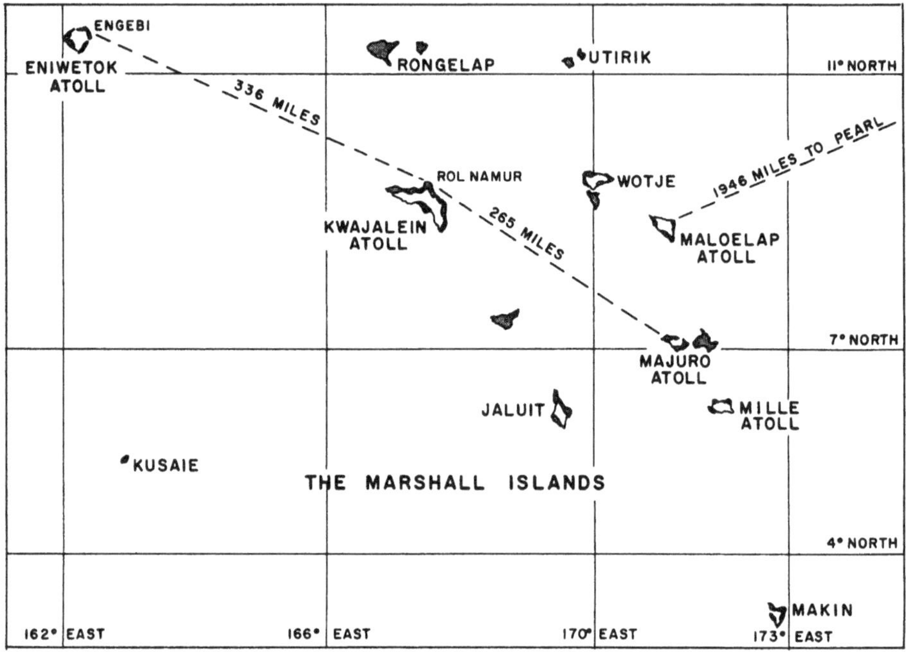

The Commander-in-Chief considers that the advance of the U.S. Fleet into Area H [Marshall Group] is a strictly practicable operation which can be carried out regardless of enemy movements. The U.S. Fleet should arrive there about 27M and be entirely refueled by 30M. This will be a small compact force, composed exclusively of vessels that have been in full commission and have been maintained at the highest degree of readiness. It includes a detachment of 68 patrol planes. These planes may be carried on the vessels of the Fleet or may fly from Base 41 [Oahu] via base 17 [Johnston Island] to Area H [Marshall Group], as is considered preferable at the time. The train will be kept to an absolute minimum.

It is the confident hope of the Commander-in-Chief that it will be practicable for him to advance between 30M and 40M from Area H [Marshall Group] to Area X [Philippines]. Under certain circumstances it may be best to advance on 30M without effecting a junction with the Supporting Detachment. It may be desirable to effect a junction with the Supporting Detachment at sea about 37M and then proceed in company to Area X [Philippines]. It may be desirable for the Supporting Detachment to join the Fleet in Area H [Marshall Group] about 37M, fuel, and proceed in company about 40M. The Commander-in-Chief's temporary mission will be the establishment of the Fleet in a secure base in Area X, but, should opportunities be presented to inflict severe losses on the Orange Fleet, they will be grasped with vigor and determination in the endeavor to gain an early decisive success. Should Orange success in Area S [Northern Philippines] make it impracticable to proceed to Base 49 [Manila], the Fleet will first secure Base 15 [Dumanquilas].

My boss, and the new Commander-in-Chief, Admiral J. M. Reeves, USN, some eight months later had written to the Chief of Naval Operations and pointed out that:

(b) ORANGE control over the Mandated Islands has given her potential bases which can be used as strong flank positions for operation of submarines and aircraft against BLUE passage to the Western Area.

(c) The rapid strides made in aviation, resulting in the effective use of long range shore-based patrol, bombing, and torpedo planes has enhanced the strength of ORANGE in the Western Pacific.

(d) The ratio of strength of the ORANGE and BLUE navies in all classes except capital ships has been materially altered since the Washington Treaty.

(e) The stipulation of the Washington Treaty to maintain the status quo of 1921 insofar as further protection to our outlying Pacific possessions is concerned, has weakened BLUE's position in the Western Pacific.[14]

He asked for further enlightenment on the phrase "at the earliest practicable date," when the Fleet and Expeditionary Force were to move to the Western Base. The Chief of Naval Operations replied that the phrase "to establish in the Western Pacific" and "at the earliest practicable date" should be used in conjunction with the phrase "in strength superior to that of ORANGE" and the move timed accordingly.[15]

It was during this period that the Chief of Naval Operations (Admiral W. H. Standley, USN), in commenting on a draft of the United States Asiatic Fleet Operating Plan, O-2-ORANGE, directed that the following paragraph be incorporated in that officer's plan:

That in the event of war between ORANGE and BLUE, hostilities will be initiated by ORANGE in the Far East without Warning.[16]

By 1935, Joint planning with the Army had brought agreement that the U.S. Fleet and the U.S. Asiatic Fleet would be merged into one task force which, together with the Army units of the Expeditionary Force, would be designated the U.S. Joint Asiatic Force, and whose commander would be the Commander-in-Chief of the U.S. Fleet.

[14] CINCUS (J. M. Reeves), serial 3836 of 24 Aug. 1934, letter to CNO, Plan File, NHD, p. 2.

[15] CNO (W. H. Standley), 10 Dec. 1934, letter to CINCUS, Plan File, NHD, p. 1.

[16] CNO (W. H. Standley), serial 3037 of 27 Nov. 1935, letter to Commander-in-Chief, Asiatic Fleet, Plan File, NHD, p. 3.

Modification of the original "through ticket to Manila" concept had also been brought about, so that the Director of the War Plans Division of the Office of Naval Operations could inform the Assistant Chief of Staff, War Plans Division, Army General staff that:

> 1. In the formulation of the Plan O-1-ORANGE of the Commander-in-Chief, U.S. Joint Asiatic Force, it has been decided that:
>
> The western advance of the U.S. Joint Asiatic Force will be a progressive movement through the Mandates.
>
> 2. Under this decision, it has also been further decided that the first offensive operations will be:
>
> To eject ORANGE from Marshalls and Eastern Carolines and to establish a base in that area preparatory to further operations against the Middle Carolines (Truk).
>
> It is considered at this writing that the best position for the Marshall Island base is at Wotje; that BLUE will also desire to operate planes from Rongelap, Eniwetok and Ponape.[17]

Six months later, the Director of the War Plans Division again reported to his opposite number in the Army General Staff:

> The O-1 Plan calls for (1) ejecting ORANGE from Marshalls and Eastern Carolines, (2) ejecting ORANGE from Middle Carolines, (3) establishing a base in southern Philippines, which may require ejecting ORANGE, (4) ejecting ORANGE from western Carolines, and (5) preparing to operate offensively in the Western Pacific, which may be expected to require the ejection of ORANGE from a succession of places necessary for the offensive operation of the Fleet or to the security of such places. The first of these steps alone may require upwards of eight Joint landing operations of varying difficulty.[18]

And shortly thereafter, the same officer reported:

> The Marine Corps has completed plans for attacks upon Wotje, Maloelap, and Majuro; has nearly completed plans for attack on Eniwetok, Rongelap and Jaluit, and is working on plans for Ponape and Truk.[19]

The scheme of planning of which this procedure was a part was stated to be as follows:

> The capture of these enemy positions is the focal point about which must be centered all plans for the conduct of this campaign. Plans for each of the

---

[17] DWPD (W. S. Pye), 29 Jan. 1935, letter to Assistant Chief of Staff, War Plans Division (ACSWPD).

[18] DWPD, 19 Jul 1935, letter to ACSWPD.

[19] DWPD, 30 July 1935, letter to ACSWPD.

actual landings must prescribe the expeditionary forces and supporting operations decided upon for this crucial phase. After thus having arrived at the size of troop convoys, and the ultimate distribution, BLUE will then plan the earlier phase which will include the overseas movement, the covering operations, and the operations for information. And in turn work back to the preparation phase, wherein at West Coast ports there will be an orderly loading of the necessary transports and cargo carriers and the preparation and assembly of the combatant vessels.[20]

The reasons for acquiring bases in the Marshalls and Carolines were set forth in the following War Plans Division "Estimate of the Situation:"

BLUE's earlier decision concerning his operations in the Marshalls in his western advance becomes for this campaign his

Mission:

To eject ORANGE from Marshalls and Eastern Carolines and to establish a base in that area preparatory to further operations against Middle Carolines in order to establish at the earliest practicable date the BLUE Fleet in superior strength in Western Pacific.

Analysis of Mission:

BLUE desires control of this area primarily to strengthen the defense system of his trans-Pacific supply line. By this control BLUE will:

(a) Acquire for own use position(s) from which to support BLUE supply line.

(b) Deny ORANGE use of such positions from which to operate against the BLUE lines.

At the same time BLUE will be laying the foundation for:

(a) further operations against Middle Carolines.

(b) isolation of ORANGE by denying enemy commerce from transiting this area.[21]

In July 1937, when I was Assistant Chief of Naval Operations, the Western Base concept, which, since 1929 had envisaged in addition to the major Western Base, minor operating and supply facilities at Dumanquilas Bay and at Malampaya Sound, was further altered to provide for three other advanced bases of major size, in addition to the Western Base. These new bases were designated Base ONE (Marshalls), Base TWO (Carolines or Palau), and Base THREE (destination to be assigned later).[22]

[20] *Ibid.*

[21] "Marshall Islands Campaign," study, CNO, OP-12B of Jan. 1935.

[22] WPL-13, Part II, Chap. III, Sec. 6, Para. 2362; "Navy Basic Plan ORANGE, WPL-16." (hereafter cited as WPL-16), CNO, 1 Mar. 1921, Plan File, NHD, Appen. VII, p. 1; WPL-16, Change No. 5 of 10 July 1937, Plan File, NHD, Appen. VII, p. 2.

The first progress in many years toward building up the Fleet Train was made soon thereafter, as evidenced by the Secretary of the Navy's 1937 Annual Report, which noted:

> Since the end of the [1937] fiscal year legislation has been enacted by the . . . Congress which authorizes the construction of six auxiliary vessels. However, funds have been made available for only two of these vessels.
>
> • • •
>
> It is hoped that Congress will appropriate funds for the other four ships in the near future and that authorization will be obtained and funds appropriated for additional construction of auxiliaries in subsequent years, following a consistent plan to supply the urgent need for these vessels. Nearly all of our auxiliaries are slow and over age, the newest one having been commissioned in 1926. Most of them are unable to perform . . . their peacetime duties.[23]

However, further changes in the ORANGE Plan were needed, and in the words of the official history of the War Department of World War II:

> . . . on 19 January 1938 two distinguished authorities on Pacific matters, Maj. Gen. Stanley D. Embick and Rear Adm. (later Admiral) J. O. Richardson, were directed to make further Pacific study. This led to a new Orange Plan accepted by the Joint Board on 21 February and approved by the Secretaries of War and Navy a week later. It was to implement this plan that the Navy proposed a 20 percent increase, which the President recommended to Congress and which in May 1938 was adopted.[24]

Just before I went over from OPNAV to become Chief of the Bureau of Navigation, five advanced Fleet air bases (Unalaska, Adak, Midway, Johnston Island, and Wake Island) were added to the logistic planning requirements.[25]

Altogether, the 1929 Plan was subjected to major changes (of which I am cognizant) in July 1932, November 1934, September 1935, September 1936, March 1937, March 1938, April 1938 and March 1939. Through these changes, the timing of the initial westward movement of a major task force of the U.S. Fleet and an Expeditionary Force had passed through the following stages of development:

(a) Ready to move 14 days after declaration of war (movement at discretion of CINCUS)

---

[23] SECNAV (Claude A. Swanson), *Annual Report*, 1937, pp. 1-2.

[24] Watson, *Chief of Staff, Prewar Plans and Preparations*, p. 92.

[25] WPL-16, Appen. VII, Sec. II; WPL-16, Change No. 6 of 23 Apr. 1938, Plan File, NHD, Appen. VII, pp. 2, 79.

(b) Sail 20 days (approximately) after declaration of war (at discretion of CINCUS)
(c) Ready to move 30 days after declaration of war (movement at discretion of CINCUS)
(d) A concentration at Pearl Harbor 30 days after the declaration of war
(e) Adequate concentration on the Pacific Coast of ships of the Fleet to safely convoy Expeditionary Forces to Hawaii ready at:
    (1) Mobilization 12 days
    (2) Mobilization 20 days

Then it became a full concentration of the Fleet at Pearl Harbor and westward movement at "the earliest practicable date."

The westward movement to Manila Bay from Pearl Harbor had passed through the following stages of development:

> (a) A direct movement from Pearl Harbor to Manila
> (b) A movement via the Mandated Islands
> (c) A progressive movement via the Mandated Islands to the Southern Philippines (Dumanquilas Bay and Malampaya Sound)
> (d) The establishment, at the earliest practicable date, of the United States Joint Asiatic Force in the Marshall Caroline Island Area in strength superior to that of ORANGE, and ready for further advance to the Western Pacific in condition to operate offensively in that area.

Each of these stages of development in the Strategic Plan was a considerable improvement in what was practical, feasible, and realistic over the previous plan.

In his "Plan Dog" memorandum of November 12, 1940 Admiral Stark summed up accurately the ORANGE Plan, as follows:

> . . . in a nutshell, it envisages our Fleet's procedure westward through the Marshalls and the Carolines, consolidating as it goes, and then on to the recapture of the Philippines. Once there, the Orange Plan contemplates the eventual economic starvation of Japan, and, finally, the complete destruction of her external military power. Its accomplishment would require several years, and the absorption of the full military, naval, and economic energy of the American people.
>
> In proceeding through these Mid-Pacific islands, we have several subsidiary objectives in mind. First, we hope that our attack will induce the Japanese to expose their fleet in action against our fleet, and lead to their naval defeat. Second, we wish to destroy the ability of the Japanese to use these positions

as air and submarine bases from which to project attacks on our lines of communication to the mainland and to Hawaii. Third, we would use the captured positions for supporting our further advance westward.[26]

A few words also should be given to the Logistic Plan.

Logistic Plan

The Navy Basic War Plan—ORANGE, WPL-13 contained the following two paragraphs as part of the Logistic Plan:

> The Plan of mobilization as laid down in . . . [this Navy Basic Plan—ORANGE] is based upon the assumptions that War with ORANGE will be precipitated without notice, and that conditions as they may exist upon such sudden entry into war must be the basis for estimating the Time required for mobilization.
>
> • • •
>
> Prior to the outbreak of war, a period of strained relations with ORANGE may exist, perhaps followed by a period of acute relations. In this event, conditions may permit of taking certain preparatory Mobilization Measures. To take full advantage of this latter contingency, each OPERATING PLAN and each CONTRIBUTORY PLAN will provide for a Step by Step Mobilization, in accordance with the Scheme laid down in this CHAPTER.

The procedures for carrying out the "Step by Step Mobilization" were detailed in subsequent paragraphs, as follows:

> When the NAVY DEPARTMENT is informed by the PRESIDENT that war with ORANGE is considered possible, the NAVY DEPARTMENT will send a Secret ALNAV Despatch:
>
> "TAKE CONDITION B FOR ORANGE WAR"[27]

All Operating Plans and Contributory Plans were required to make provision for taking the measures which, if undertaken upon receipt of the above ALNAV, would expedite mobilization. The provisions to be accomplished were many; they varied from the fitting out for war services (except for personnel and commissioning) of nearly all ships and aircraft out of commission to the assembling at mobilization bases of the mobilization supplies for all ships and aircraft units.

---

[26] CNO, serial 0025 of 12 Nov. 1940, memo, to SECNAV, Plan File, NHD, p. 4.

[27] WPL-13, pp. 76-77.

The Basic War Plan further provided:

> When war appears probable in the near future, and when authorized by the PRESIDENT, the NAVY DEPARTMENT will send a Secret ALNAV despatch:
>
> "TAKE CONDITION A FOR ORANGE WAR"[28]

Upon receipt of this second despatch, the Navy was to take all legally permissable measures to assume the war organization for an ORANGE War. It was further stated:

> that under present dispositions and personnel deficiencies, preliminary orders to the Naval Establishment should be issued 40 days prior to Zero Day for an ORANGE WAR.[29]

Strategic Concept

I should make it clear here and now that I, and a lot of other senior officers, fully concurred in the general Strategic Concept set forth in our War Plans of how to win the war with ORANGE. To win, we had to move the Fleet to the Western Pacific and there hammer and throttle ORANGE.

In the words of the official plan, the "Concept of the War" was:

> AN OFFENSIVE WAR OF LONG DURATION, PRIMARILY NAVAL THROUGHOUT, UNLESS LARGE ARMY FORCES ARE EMPLOYED IN MAJOR LAND OPERATIONS IN THE WESTERN PACIFIC, DIRECTED TOWARD THE ISOLATION AND EXHAUSTION OF ORANGE THROUGH CONTROL OF HER VITAL SEA COMMUNICATIONS AND THROUGH OFFENSIVE OPERATIONS AGAINST HER ARMED FORCES AND HER ECONOMIC LIFE.[30]

By and large, this concept was implemented during World War II and the war won thereby. Moreover, the Strategic Concept supported the National Mission which was:

> NATIONAL MISSION
>
> National Mission: To impose the will of the UNITED STATES upon ORANGE by destroying ORANGE Armed Forces and by disrupting ORANGE economic life, while protecting AMERICAN Interests at home and abroad.[31]

[28] *Ibid.*, p. 80.
[29] WPL-8, Part 1, p. 16.
[30] WPL-13, p. 45.
[31] *Ibid.*, p. 12.

I believed that the missions for the Armed Forces and the Navy also were soundly stated. They were as follows:

ARMED FORCES MISSION

MISSION FOR THE ARMED FORCES: To gain and exercise command of the sea, and as necessary of the air, and to operate offensively against ORANGE Armed Forces, Bases of Operation, and Economic Life, in order to isolate, exhaust and subdue ORANGE, while protecting AMERICAN Territory and AMERICAN Interests.[32]

NAVAL MISSION

MISSION FOR THE NAVY: To gain and to exercise command of the sea, and with the Army, to operate offensively against ORANGE Armed Forces, Bases of Operation and Economic Life, especially War Industries.[33]

Similarly, I had no objection to the delineation of the theaters of operation or to the designation of the Navy as being responsible for the co-ordination of all Armed Forces operating in the Western Pacific.

U.S. Fleet's Naval Mission And Required Operations

The Primary Naval Mission for the United States Fleet was:

TO ESTABLISH, AT THE EARLIEST PRACTICABLE DATE, UNITED STATES NAVAL POWER IN THE WESTERN PACIFIC IN STRENGTH SUPERIOR TO THAT OF ORANGE AND TO OPERATE OFFENSIVELY IN THAT AREA.[34]

The offensive operations delineated as required to carry out this Fleet Mission included:

(c) The movement to the WESTERN PACIFIC of a combined Naval and Military Expedition as soon after the outbreak of war as possible, and the seizure of an Advanced Fleet Base in that area. The Naval Forces in this initial movement must be superior to the Naval Forces available to ORANGE, and the Expeditionary Forces should be of sufficient strength to overcome all anticipated hostile resistance.

(d) The establishment of an Advanced Fleet Base at Manila Bay, or at some other location.

(e) The organization and earliest possible development of the Advanced Fleet Base, or bases, for defense, and for the maintenance and supply of the UNITED STATES Forces in the . . . [Western Pacific].

[32] *Ibid.*

[33] *Ibid.*

[34] *Ibid.*, p. 14.

(f) The establishment and maintenance of secure Lines of Communication between the UNITED STATES and the Advanced Fleet Base including the seizure, occupation and defense of Subsidiary Bases.

• • •

(l) The seizure, occupation and defense of additional Advanced Bases successively closer to the ORANGE MAIN ISLANDS.[35]

• • •

[THE DESTRUCTION OF] . . . ORANGE NAVAL, MILITARY AND AIR BASES, AND ACTIVITIES ENGAGED IN THE PRODUCTION AND TRANSPORTATION OF WAR NECESSITIES, BY INTENSIVE AIR ATTACKS.[36]

The principal Defensive Tasks included:

TO HOLD THE MANILA BAY AREA AS LONG AS POSSIBLE WITH THE MILITARY AND NAVAL FORCES IN THE WESTERN PACIFIC AT THE OUTBREAK OF WAR AND TO DENY THIS AREA . . . AS A NAVAL BASE IN CASE WE CANNOT USE IT OURSELVES.[37]

There was a very definite string attached to the westward movement, as set forth in the following paragraph:

TO START THE INITIAL COMBINED TRANS-PACIFIC MOVEMENT OF THE UNITED STATES FLEET AND SUPPORTING EXPEDITIONARY FORCES TO THE WESTWARD OF THE HAWAIIAN ISLANDS ONLY UPON THE AUTHORIZATION OF THE PRESIDENT OF THE UNITED STATES.[38]

It was apparent that to accomplish successfully the mission assigned to the Commander-in-Chief, it would be necessary to:

Destroy or contain the ORANGE FLEET or subdivisions thereof . . . [that might attempt to interfere with the movement of the Expeditionary Forces to the Western Base].

• • •

Seize, prepare, defend, and operate from, air bases sufficiently close to the ORANGE . . . [homeland] from which intensive air attacks may be launched against objectives in . . . [ORANGE homeland].[39]

This seemed logical to me and apparently to my successors who carried out the war with Japan, for this is what they did. It might be further added,

---

35 *Ibid.*, pp. 14-15, 17.
36 *Ibid.*, p. 17.
37 *Ibid.*, p. 50.
38 *Ibid.*, p. 19.
39 *Ibid.*, pp. 57, 59.

as a precursor of the Navy's seizure of Iwo Jima and Okinawa in World War II, that these actions seemingly had been in the cards a long time (since 1923). Thus, the Basic ORANGE Plan stated:

> To make effective the general concept of the war an advanced base within about 500 miles of Tsushima Straits will probably be required.[40]

Before getting down to my criticism of the ORANGE War Plan, I should say that:

(1) It generated a lot of worthwhile thinking in regard to a war with Japan.
(2) It helped in maintaining standards of readiness for the Fleet and the Shore Establishment and in providing objectives in budget planning and appropriation requests.
(3) It generated a sound Strategic Concept in regard to a war with Japan as well as a sound plan to carry out the concept, once the forces were available.
(4) The soundness of the Strategic Concept of the ORANGE War Plan led to marked professional advances in naval material and naval techniques required for the actual war, fought in the Pacific from 1941 to 1945. A few of these developments were:
  (a) fueling-at-sea techniques
  (b) new type landing boats, landing craft, and attack transports
  (c) survey ships capable of producing on the spot charts
  (d) net layers for protecting atoll anchorages
  (e) package base units, later expanded into LIONS and CUBS, for quickly bringing advanced bases to operational efficiency, and such useful equipment for these units as portable evaporators

Despite these virtues, and they were very real, I thought the ORANGE plans were not feasible, so it is desirable to ask and answer these two questions:

(a) In 1939-1940, in what respects were our ORANGE Naval War Plans unrealistic?

(b) Why were they unrealistic?

The first question is a lot easier to answer than the second.

---

[40] WPL-9, p. 32.

In What Respects Were Our Orange War Plans Unrealistic in June 1939?

In the larger sense, the ORANGE War Plans were predicated upon the following unrealistic assumptions:

(1) The war would take place between only the United States and Japan, and the rest of the countries of the world would either be friendly neutrals or unfriendly neutrals. This was most doubtful because of the alliances existing and developing in Europe and the similarity of interests between Japan and Germany, in that both desired the weakening of the power of Great Britain and the United States.

(2) The five to three comparative ratio of naval strength, existent in 1923 or even 1933, still existed. The strength of the Navy of Japan had been markedly increased in relation to our own Navy, and in at least one type, carriers, exceeded our Navy's. A small but effective German Navy had been created and was now an ally of Japan.

(3) Our "Navy was ready to fight" at the start of a war. This condition of readiness could not be reached, when a very large percentage of the people of the country did not want the United States to get into any kind of fight, and would not support the measures necessary to prepare the Navy for actual fighting.

(4) In order to obtain logistic readiness before a war was suddenly started against us, the President would accept the responsibility for such decisive action as informing the Navy Department and the Navy that "war was possible" and that "war appeared probable in the near future," so that logistic preparedness measures could be taken, particularly since some features of logistic preparedness always have to be taken in public view.

In more detailed naval professional matters, the ORANGE War Plans were unrealistic because:

(5) They were based upon an assumption that our ships were fully manned with qualified personnel and ready to fight.

(6) They were based upon the availability of ships to be placed back in commission at rigidly scheduled intervals after mobilization,

or some stage of mobilization, was ordered. These recommissioning intervals were thirty, sixty, and ninety days when World War II started in Europe and were too short for realization.

(7) Ships long out of commission when the war started were scheduled to sail for the war zones of the Western Pacific forty to fifty days after recommissioning. A ship out of commission for many years could not be worked up to realistic war readiness in this period.

(8) The movement of the Fleet to the Western Pacific required logistic support ships and facilities which did not exist, and could not be created within the stated periods, before they were scheduled to be used by the operating forces.

My predecessor as CINCUS had listed the deficiencies in ships and equipment needed by the Fleet to establish an advanced fleet base or to conduct an expeditionary force overseas, as follows:

> (a) Lack of [floating] docking facilities. . . .
> (b) Lack of distilling ships. . . .
> (c) Lack of fast mine sweepers. . . .
> (d) Lack of submarine nets and net laying vessels. . . .
> (e) Lack of suitable landing boats. . . .
> (f) Lack of equipment for rapid construction of landing fields. . . .
> (g) Lack of suitable store ships. . . .
> (h) Lack of high speed oilers. . . .
> (i) Lack of antiaircraft guns and fire control equipment for auxiliaries. . . .[41]

These deficiencies were not those that could be corrected overnight, or cured by waving a wand at the Presidential or Congressional level. In summary, my principal objections were centered on the;

(a) timing of the initial operations in the overseas movement to the Western Pacific

(b) Non-availability of adequate combatant and logistic forces to fight the early stages of the war

(c) Non-availability of adequately trained enlisted personnel

That these latter unrealities might exist seems to have been recognized by the early planners themselves as the 1923 War Plan said:

---

[41] CINCUS, "Annual Report," 1939, p. 25.

The greatest difficulty in executing all phases, lies in logistics.[42]

These difficulties had continued down through the years.

In my opinion, the very distinct deficiencies in these respects vitiated completely the prospects of a successful campaign, if the ORANGE Plan was adhered to.

Why Were Our Orange War Plans Unrealistic?

This is a difficult question to supply a fully complete and informative answer.

A war plan, to be realistic, must be based on using:

(1) what actually is in existence when the war starts, which means what is in hand at the time the plan is written or can logically be forecast as being in hand in the very immediate future
(2) what can be created and brought to hand as the war progresses

I believe that the officers who prepared our Naval War Plans in the peacetime era of 1923–1939 were fully aware of these principles, because they referred to them in the ORANGE Plan. But, in their actual detailed planning, they seemed to me to err on the side of forecasting that always the maximum forces which possibly could be available, would be available, rather than forecasting that what would be available was that average of forces, learned from long-time naval experience. To illustrate, we had sixteen battleships in commission. All sixteen were considered to be available and were scheduled for certain westward movments. But, experience told me that generally three of the sixteen had to be in navy yards for overhaul at all times, in order to keep them operating fifteen months out of every eighteen-month cycle.

In other words, the War Plans were predicated on the Navy the planners would like to have had, rather than on the Navy they actually had, and on what the planners would like to have occur in the event of war, rather than on what more likely would occur.

It should be said, in defense of the planners, that this latter scheme of things had the merit that things certainly wouldn't occur at a highly accelerated rate if this wasn't at least tried for.

[42] WPL-9, p. 27.

1940 Events

Having outlined some of the features of our War Plans, as they existed in 1939, it appears desirable to outline some of the things that were done and recommended to be done, during the short thirteen months that I was in command of the United States Fleet.

Just three weeks after taking command of the United States Fleet, on January 26, 1940, I wrote my immediate superior, Admiral H. R. Stark, Chief of Naval Operations and the officer responsible for the War Plans of the Navy, to give my thoughts in regard to the ORANGE War Plan.

Within this letter, I covered (3), (6), (7), and (8) of the unrealistic aspects of our ORANGE Plan listed above. The letter read:

> I have always thought our Orange Plan was chiefly useful as an exercise in War Planning, to train officers in War Planning and to serve as a basis for asking for appropriations, and as a guide for developing our Navy and its shore facilities. As to actually executing *the O-1 plan* I hope we will never be called upon to do that unless the Administration fully realizes the probable cost [human and physical resources] and duration of such a war and unless our people are prepared to support an expensive war of long duration.
>
> Even *if we could take Truk* what would we have[?] A secure anchorage, nothing else, several thousand miles from our nearest drydock and adequate repair facilities and still hundreds of miles from the enemy country. Of course it could not be taken without some underwater damage. To actually put on real pressure we would have to have a real base that would take many years and much money. We ought not to go into a thing like this unless we expected to see it through.
>
> I hesitate to write you because the written word is so easily misunderstood, *also I do not know what your ideas are,* what you are telling the boss,[43] what is the meaning of our diplomatic moves, or our Senators talks, or our neutrality patrol. But you are the *principal and only Naval advisor to the boss* and he should know that our Fleet can not just sail away lick Orange and be back at home in a year or so. Also the probable cost [human and physical resources] of any war should be compared [with] the probable value of winning the war.
>
> When we commissioned the San Diego DD's we used the facilities of San Diego Base, active DD Tenders, working parties from active DD's and their Tenders and Mare Island yard. I think that an excellent job was done but if it had been a real mobilization, all of these activities would have been [otherwise] fully occupied. How long would it have taken San Diego Base to have done this

[43] He is referring to the President of the United States.

and its other mobilization work without any outside assistance? A war plan if it is to be executed should be based on realities.

All of this letter may be needless but I know that if you do not tell the boss what you really know and feel about the probable cost and duration of an Orange War *NOBODY WILL.*

I would hate to see our leaders make a move from which they could not gracefully withdraw, and which would eventually force us into a war, half heartedly supported by our country. In other words before the Nation takes a step I hope we will carefully examine the direction we are heading, where we eventually go and be prepared to resolutely pursue the course whatever the cost.[44]

I should say here that it always was a source of great concern to me, lest President Roosevelt, blithely inspired by his own impetuosity and urged on by the clamor of the American people to "do something," might ignore the restraints, written into the ORANGE War Plan over a period of fifteen years, and order the Fleet to proceed to the Western Pacific without benefit of the necessary preparations or consideration for the necessity of having superior strength over the Japanese Navy.

The above personal letter I considered to be highly important and most secret. So, I wrote it longhand and sent it to Admiral Stark in the personal custody of an officer of my staff. I do not have any record of a reply, and I do not believe it was replied to.

The following copy of a digest of a conference held in the Office of the Chief of Naval Operations on May 1, 1940 shows the state of thinking of many of the senior officers of that date in respect to the ORANGE Plan better than any words of mine would.

DIGEST OF CONFERENCE HELD ON MAY 1, 1940 IN THE OFFICE OF THE CHIEF OF NAVAL OPERATIONS

PRESENT:

Admiral Stark [Chief of Naval Operations]
Admiral Sexton [Chairman, General Board]
Admiral Greenslade [Member, General Board]
Admiral King [Member, General Board]
Admiral Anderson [Director of Naval Intelligence]
Admiral Leary [Director of Fleet Training]
Admiral Ghormley [Assistant Chief of Naval Operations]

[44] U.S., Congress, *Hearings Before the Joint Committee on the Investigation of the Pearl Harbor Attack* (hereafter cited as *Pearl Harbor Hearings* with Part) (79th Cong., 1st sess., Part 14, Joint Committee Exhibits nos. 9 through 43, pursuant to S. Con. Res. 27, 79th Cong.) (Washington, D.C.: GPO, 1946), pp. 924-26.

Captain [R. S.] Crenshaw [Director of War Plans]
Captain [W. A.] Lee [Member, Fleet Training Division]
Captain [C. M.] Cooke [Member, War Plans Division]
Captain [C. J.] Moore [Member, War Plans Division]
Captain [H. W.] Hill [Member, War Plans Division]
Captain [O. C.] Badger [Secretary, General Board]
Commander [Forrest] Sherman [Member, War Plans Division]

Admiral Stark stated that the purpose of this meeting was to continue the discussion held in The General Board the previous week regarding the Commander-in-Chief's O-1 Plan (ORANGE). He stated that he wished to develop further the details of this plan—that while he was open minded on the subject, there appeared to be considerable doubt in the minds of many senior officers, including his own, regarding the practicability and advisability of projecting major fleet operations [too far] west of HAWAII.

Captain Crenshaw outlined the basic purpose of war planning, and emphasized the fact that plans, such as the O-1 Plan, were primarily for the purpose of providing logistic and other support for operations of this nature, so as to provide the Commander-in-Chief with adequate forces so that he has complete freedom of action, as he moves westward, to take full advantage of any opportunity to take the initiative and inflict damage on ORANGE.

Captain Cooke then described the lack of practical operating plans which had existed prior to the preparation of the O-1 Plan in 1927, and the benefits which had already resulted from the existence of such a plan. He pointed out that these operating plans were neither decisions nor orders, and quoted paragraphs 112-3, of WPUSF-44, which calls attention to the fact that this plan is based upon a certain set of assumptions, and that the actual situation existing at the time the plan became effective may require operations very different from those outlined in this plan.

Captain Cooke outlined the need for more realistic training along certain lines envisaged in the war plans. He recommended that future fleet problems provide for actual capture and establishment of an island base. He further recommended that a permanent task force be established in the fleet, whose function would be to seize and establish Advanced Bases.

Captain Cooke and Captain Hill described more in detail certain features of the plan illustrating its effect in providing facilities for prompt movement from the West Coast bases, and also the advantages accruing in the event that, during these early stages of the war, the military support of England and/or Holland could be enlisted. It was pointed out that the decision regarding seizure of bases in the MARSHALLs or CAROLINEs depended entirely upon the results of submarine and air reconnaissance of those areas as the fleet moved westward which would indicate whether the risk involved would be justified by the benefits to be attained. Risks must be taken, and losses anticipated. But by ***rapid movement*** in force to this area, when ORANGE was primarily engaged in taking the Philippine Islands and Guam and safeguarding her vital trade routes to the southward, it was probable that ORANGE forces might be stretched quite thinly throughout the MARSHALLs and CAROLINEs. If so, seizure of a base here would isolate the islands to the eastward of it and cause their eventual fall, thus denying them as bases for enemy operations against our vital Hawaiian trade, and making them available as bases from which BLUE operations could be conducted in defense of its line of communications. If TRUK could be taken, the eventual occupation of all the MARSHALLs by BLUE would provide a barrier safeguard for his lines of communication. Should the war develop into a RAINBOW No. 2 or RAINBOW No. 3 situation, the denial of these islands to ORANGE would remove a tremendous threat flanking the BLUE line of communications to the EAST INDIES.

It was stressed that the Commander-in-Chief considered it futile to attempt to make operating plans for more than 60 days. It was also pointed out that the preliminary planning and preparation of materials and facilities for seizing and establishing an Advance Base were extremely valuable, and tended to strengthen every plan now being contemplated by the War and Navy Departments. It was pointed out that the Navy Department has a very definite responsibility in providing, in time of peace, the means for the Commander-in-Chief to accomplish the probable task which may be assigned him in the early stages of the war.

Certain immediate needs of the Fleet, if this plan is to function, were cited. Among them being the following items which can be accomplished without Congressional authority:—

(a) Actual training with transports by both the Fleet Marine Force and the Army.

(b) Practical study of problem of fitting out transports in 4 to 6 days.

(c) Need for landing boats and for means of stowing them on transports.

(d) Need for landing boat crews and equipment.

(e) Need for test of ability to convert oil tankers to fresh water carriers.

(f) Need for means to make an Advanced Base secure—such as indicator nets, magnetic loops, etc.

(g) Means of quick and adequate survey of a poorly charted atoll.

(h) Need for more destroyer troop transports.

(i) Get the Fleet filled up with ammunition allowance.

(j) Staff Situation CINCUS. [hand written]

Admiral Stark directed that a list of such items be prepared in more detail.

During the general discussion which followed Admiral Anderson recommended that in an ORANGE War consideration be given to immediate initiation of cruiser warfare against ORANGE trade routes throughout the world, even if it involved immobilization of the Fleet at Hawaii.

Admiral Greenslade pointed out that the war could not be won in this manner,—that decisive results could not be achieved except by taking offensive action and projecting BLUE's sea power westward of HAWAII. Admiral King also stressed the need for taking the initiative.

Admiral Sexton and Admiral Leary pointed out the lack of time and Staff available to the senior commanders afloat for adequate war planning, the need for these officers to become "war plan conscious". At the present these officers are overburdened with other administrative duties, from part of which they should be relieved. They stressed the absolute necessity for the Commander-in-Chief, U.S. Fleet, who will have the responsibility for fleet operations in time of war, to devote a large portion of his own effort and the effort of the major portion of his Staff to the development of operating plans to meet emergencies which might develop under existing world conditions. It was pointed out that this would require the elimination of certain detailed administrative functions assumed by the Commander-in-Chief in recent years, and might involve changes in Navy Regulations. All senior officers in the conference concurred.

Concrete suggestions were made for remedy of this defect, and Admiral Stark requested Admiral Sexton to draft proposed changes in the Navy Regulations to improve the situation.[45]

The Rainbow War Plans

While my thoughts and interests lay primarily in the Far East, and in the continuing aggressive moves of Japan in that area, the events of the European war were drawing the overriding attention of the Navy's planners in Washington.

I am sure that my constant harping on the unrealistic aspects of the ORANGE Plan, dating back to my time as Assistant Chief of Naval Operations, was only one very small factor in the working up of a new series of War Plans which, in July 1941, led to the placing of the ORANGE Plan on the shelf. The events of World War II in Europe provided the real urge and necessity for a change.

The first major development was a War Plan known as RAINBOW ONE. Since it was premised on a situation where the United States was at war with a number of nations, the new series designation of RAINBOW was particularly appropriate, considering the former practice of designating War Plans with a single nation and with a single color—ORANGE, PURPLE, GREEN, RED, YELLOW, etc. Work on this RAINBOW Plan

---

[45] "Digest of Conference Held on 1 May 1940 in the Office of the Chief of Naval Operations," CNO, 2 May 1940, CNOCF, NHD.

was undertaken in the Joint Board, when I was Chief of the Bureau of Navigation.

Rainbow No. One

Although the RAINBOW no. ONE Joint Basic War Plan had been drafted by the Joint (Army and Navy) Board (the precursors of the Joint Chiefs of Staff) and approved by the Secretaries of War and the Navy before World War II even started, it was not to be promulgated for many months to subordinate naval commanders and planning officers.

The initial version of RAINBOW no. ONE was subject to major revision in April 1940, based on world-wide developments occurring since its preparation and approval.

On April 9, 1940, the Joint Planning Committee of the Joint Board had submitted a new general estimate of the world situation, as it might affect American defense plans and preparations for war, with a recommendation for revision of existing plans, and for the development or completion of new plans of the RAINBOW series. The Joint Board approved these recommendations on April 10, 1940.[46]

I believe that I knew little about the details of the final version of the RAINBOW no. ONE Plan until my visit to the Navy Department on July 8, 1940, just four days before the plan was approved for printing and appropriate naval distribution by the Chief of Naval Operations.[47] I believe that RAINBOW no. ONE was promulgated on a crisis basis, a crisis brought on by the overwhelming successes of Germany in overrunning Belgium, the Netherlands, and France in May and June of 1940.

The general assumption of RAINBOW no. ONE was that Great Britain and France had been defeated, and the United States was forced to defend, without allies, the integrity of the Monroe Doctrine and her interests in the Pacific. The general situation was stated as follows:

> *General Situation:*
>
> At the time this directive is issued, a European War is in progress, which may involve other nations and expand the field of military action. There is an

---

[46] "Joint Army and Navy Basic War Plans—RAINBOW," Joint Board No. 325, serial 642 of 9 Apr. 1940, JB Files, NHD.

[47] "Basic War Plan, RAINBOW No. 1, WPL-42" (hereafter cited as WPL-42), CNO, 12 July 1940, Plan File, NHD.

ever present possibility of the United States being drawn into this war. There is also the possibility that peace in Europe may be followed by a situation in which the United States will be forced to defend, without Allies, the integrity of the Monroe Doctrine and her interests in the Pacific.

Joint plans were to be prepared for the effective employment of the forces of the U.S. Army and U.S. Navy under the following circumstances:

> *Special Situation:*
>
> The termination of the war in Europe is followed by a violation of the letter or spirit of the Monroe Doctrine in South America by Germany and Italy. This is coupled with armed aggression by Japan against United States' interest in the Far East. Other nations are neutral.

The Joint Board was directed to prepare Joint plans for the effective employment of the U.S. Army and U.S. Navy.

> *Purpose of the Plan:*
>
> To provide for the most effective use of naval and military forces to defeat enemy objectives, particularly those in the territory and waters of the Western Hemisphere north of the approximate latitude thirteen degrees South.[48]

Under the assumption, the primary concern of those in charge of the United States war effort was the prevention of hostile German and Italian expeditionary forces being established in the Caribbean area, Panama, or the northern part of South America. The major naval task was to:

> ". . . deny to the enemy [Germany, Italy, and Japan] all overseas communications to the Western Hemisphere that would permit the extension of enemy influence to that part of the Western Hemisphere north of latitude 13 degrees South" in order to, "Maintain the integrity of the Monroe Doctrine in areas from which the security of the Panama Canal can be threatened and to defeat the enemy." [49]

---

[48] *Ibid.*, p. 4.

[49] *Ibid.*, pp. 9, 13; I believe that Samuel E. Morison creates quite an erroneous impression as to the strategic concept of the effective War Plan RAINBOW No. One and the reason for the assumption in this plan of the non-availability of a "Battle Fleet of the Royal Navy" in the Pacific. Morison, *The Rising Sun*, p. 49. The reason that no "Battle Fleet of the Royal Navy" would be available in the Pacific was the assumption in the plan that Great Britain had been defeated and was neutral at the time the special situation of the RAINBOW No. One arose. This error is carried over into Drummond's *The Passing of American Neutrality*, p. 93. He gives Morison as his authority. See also Admiral Stark's letter to Admiral Richardson of 22 May 1940, partially quoted below.

A restriction had been placed on the planners by some higher authority, which limited the overseas transfer of U.S. Army forces to the American continents and outlying islands, north of 13 degrees south latitude, and to Unalaska and Midway and United States territory or possessions in the Pacific east thereof. The Naval Mission in the Joint Plan was a limited one, the only one of a strictly offensive nature being "To destroy enemy sea forces operating in the Atlantic or in the Westrn Hemisphere." [50]

All this seems now to me to be pretty far removed from reality, but it reflected some of the fears and concerns which existed in my own mind and at high levels in Washington at the June 1940 stage of World War II, as the following extracts from my personal letters will show.

On May 13, 1940, three days after Germany had invaded the Netherlands, Belgium, and Luxembourg and the day before the Germans broke thru the French lines at Sedan, France, and commenced moving rapidly towards the English Channel, I wrote to Admiral Stark:

> It seems that, under present world conditions, the paramount thing for us is the security of the Western Hemisphere. This, in my opinion, transcends everything—anything certainly in the Far East, our own or others' interests.
>
> South America is the greatest prize yet remaining to be grabbed. Until the outcome in Europe can be more clearly seen, the security in the Western Hemisphere, seems to be the most important consideration for us.
>
> I feel that any move [by the Fleet] west means hostilities. I feel that at this time, it would be a grave mistake to become involved in the West, where our interests, although important, are not vital and thereby reduce our ability to maintain the security of the Western Hemisphere, which is vital.[51]

This letter brought a prompt reply from Admiral Stark on May 22, 1940, in which he said:

> I agree with the tenor of your letter and you will be glad to know I had already expressed myself. . . .
>
> I wish you would keep constantly in mind the possibility of a complete collapse of the Allies, including the loss of their Fleets. A very probable development of such a catastrophe is visualized in the RAINBOW ONE PLAN.
>
> • • •
>
> The situation in some of the South American countries gives real cause for concern—and I say this advisedly. If Germany should win—then what?? [52]

---

[50] WPL-42, Appen. I, pp. 2, 9.

[51] ADM Richardson, letter, 13 May 1940, to ADM Stark, as cited in *Pearl Harbor Hearings*, Part 14, p. 935.

[52] ADM Stark, letter, 22 May 1940, to ADM Richardson, as cited in *Pearl Harbor Hearings*, Part 14, p. 938.

I do not believe that my two-man war plans staff ever had enough time to prepare a Fleet Operating Plan to support the RAINBOW ONE War Plan before more obviously urgent RAINBOW plans arrived at Fleet Headquarters to be worked on. At least, I have been informed that there is no copy of a United States Fleet RAINBOW no. ONE War Plan presently in the Registered Publications Library of the Office of the Chief of Naval Operations, nor in the files of the Commander-in-Chief, Pacific Fleet, the Naval War College, the National War College, nor in the files of the current War Plans Division of the Office of the Chief of Naval Operations. My War Plans Officer, Commander V. R. Murphy, USN (now Vice Admiral, Retired), states that no finished Fleet RAINBOW ONE was ever promulgated by me or my successor.

Whatever else RAINBOW no. ONE did or didn't do, it considerably stirred up the War Plans sections of those naval districts whose commandants had additional duty under the Commander-in-Chief of the U.S. Fleet. These War Plans sections had been inadequately staffed for years on end, with the result that the logistic support by these naval districts of the "Two Ocean Navy" for war operations, had not been thoroughly estimated at the local level. Whatever the defects of RAINBOW no. ONE for other purposes, the plan served the Navy well at the Naval District level.[53]

Rainbow No. Two

On May 11, 1940, I received a despatch from the Department reading as follows:

> TENTATIVE RAINBOW NUMBER TWO TASKS AND DISTRIBUTION OF FORCES OUTLINED IN COMMANDER IN CHIEF MEMORANDUM DELIVERED DEPARTMENT BY CAPTAIN HILL TENTATIVELY APPROVED WITH MINOR EXCEPTIONS WHICH WILL BE FORWARDED.

It should be explained that Captain Harry Hill had been Admiral Bloch's War Plans Officer and had been held over after the change of command to assist in the tremendous workload in the CINCUS war plans section,

[53] Commandant 13th Naval District (COM 13), serial CFS-SE of 27 Sept. 1940, letter to CNO, CNOCF, NHD; CINCUS, serial 01715 of 25 Oct. 1940, letter to CNO, 1st End. to CFS-SE of 27 Sept. 1940; CINCUS, serial 01393 of 14 Aug. 1940, letter to COM 12, CNOCF, NHD.

which at that time had only one officer assigned to it. When Captain Hill left, he went to the Navy Department for duty and en route served as an officer messenger to carry certain highly classified letters back to the Department.

On 22 May, 1940, Admiral Stark, in the personal letter mentioned above, said:

> With regard to the specific questions raised in your letter of 13 May, the Joint Plan for Rainbow Two is about complete, and a copy of it, including the studies upon which it is based, will go to you shortly by officer messenger. This Joint Plan embraces in general all the basic assumptions listed in the memorandum Hill [Captain Harry W. Hill, USN, now Admiral, (Ret.)] brought East. The joint tasks of this plan will require the operation of the Fleet in general [accordance] with the Fleet tasks set up in Hill's memorandum.
>
> I think these assumptions are about the best upon which a basic plan of this nature can be premised, although in any preliminary operating plan which you may prepare at present, I think you should assume the present strength and disposition of the Fleet, in order to develop the problem from a practical basis.
>
> As you get time in these strenuous days, I believe it would be advisable for you to go ahead with the preparation of a tentative Fleet Operating Plan for Rainbow Two, as we are most anxious to have the benefit of your detailed study of the difficulties involved, and the logistic and other requirements.[54]

The Strategic Concept behind RAINBOW no. TWO called for the United States and allied democratic powers to fulfill the requirements of RAINBOW no. ONE and, in addition, to sustain the authority of the democratic powers in the Pacific area by the immediate projection of U.S. forces into the Western Pacific. It assumed that the British Empire and Navy were going concerns and that the Netherlands was an ally.

However, with the war situation in Europe changing and Japan continuing to move southward in the Far East, the assumptions of RAINBOW no. TWO lost their validity. In my letter of October 22, 1940 to the Chief of Naval Operations, quoted below, I stated that RAINBOW no. TWO was:

> "Inapplicable to the present situation and present state of development of the Naval Establishment", and "the assumptions of neither of these plans—RAINBOW NO. 1 and RAINBOW NO. 2—are applicable to the present situation, nor, to the knowledge of the Commander in Chief, is the assistance

[54] ADM Stark, letter, 22 May 1940, to ADM Richardson, as cited in *Pearl Harbor Hearings*, Part 14, p. 938.

from Allies visualized in the tentative draft of RAINBOW NO. 2 a likely possibility."[55]

The Commander-in-Chief, U.S. Fleet received the tentative draft of the RAINBOW no. TWO Plan in the summer of 1940. I do not believe this tentative draft was ever finalized by the Chief of Naval Operations.

I have been informed that there is currently no copy of RAINBOW no. TWO in the Registered Publications Library of the Office of the Chief of Naval Operations, and that the records of that office state that WPL-43—the number assigned to it—was never issued. The latter assertion is contained in a memorandum of Lieutenant Charles McCarthy, Registered Publications Officer, dated January 10, 1945.

Rainbow No. Three

While I was in Washington, in October 1940, there was considerable discussion between my War Plans Officer and the War Plans Division of Naval Operations in regard to the current world politico-military situation, and the War Plans that should be available to meet the fast-changing situation. Similarly, I discussed this matter with Admiral Stark and other senior officers.

Upon returning to my flagship from Washington in mid-October 1940, I drafted the following official letter to the Chief of Naval Operations:

From: The Commander-in-Chief, U.S. Fleet
To: The Chief of Naval Operations
Subject: War Plans—Status and Readiness of in view of the current international situation.

1. Since the return of the Commander-in-Chief, U.S. Fleet, from his recent conference in Washington, and in view of conversations that took place there, additional thought and study have been given to the status and readiness of the U.S. Fleet for war operations. As a result of this study, the Commander-in-Chief, U.S. Fleet feels it to be his solemn duty to present, for the consideration of the Chief of Naval Operations, certain facts and conclusions in order that there may be no doubt in the minds of higher authority as to his convictions in regard to the present situation, especially in the Pacific.

2. In order to bring out more clearly all the aspects of this situation, it is

[55] CINCUS, 22 Oct. 1940, letter to CNO.

necessary to review certain factors affecting it and to discuss them in the light of present events.

3. On the occasion of his first visit to Washington, in July, and in personal letters to the Chief of Naval Operations, the Commander-in-Chief stressed his firm conviction that neither the Navy nor the Country was prepared for war with Japan. He pointed out that such an eventuality could only result in a long drawn out, costly war, with doubtful prospects of ultimate success. He left Washington with three distinct impressions:

First. That the Fleet was retained in the Hawaiian area solely to support diplomatic representations and as a deterrent to Japanese aggressive action;

Second. That there was no intention of embarking on actual hostilities against Japan;

Third. That the immediate mission of the Fleet was accelerated training and absorption of new personnel and the attainment of a maximum condition of material and personnel readiness consistent with its retention in the Hawaiian area.

4. On the occasion of his second visit to Washington, in October, 1940, an entirely different impression was obtained. It is true that the international situation, between the two visits, had materially changed, principally in that the danger of invasion of the British Isles was considerably less imminent, with consequent reduced chances of the loss or compromise of the British Fleet; in that the United States had more closely identified itself with Great Britain; in that Japanese aggression had progressed to the domination of Indo-China and gave signs of further progress toward the Dutch East Indies; and, in the open alliance between Germany, Italy and Japan, reportedly aimed at the United States.

5. As a result of these changes, it now appears that more active, open steps aimed at Japan are in serious contemplation and that these steps, if taken now, may lead to active hostilities. It is in connection with this eventuality that the Commander-in-Chief is constrained to present his present views.

6. The present O-1 Plan (ORANGE), WPUSF 44 and WPUSF 45, in the light of the present international situation, is believed beyond the present strength of the U.S. Fleet and beyond the present resources of the U.S. Navy. This is believed true for the following reasons:

(a) The present strength of the U.S. Fleet is not sufficient "to establish, at the earliest practicable date, the United States Joint Asiatic Force in the Marshall-Caroline Islands area in strength superior to that of ORANGE and ready for further advance to the Western Pacific in condition to operate offensively in that area."

While recognizing the qualifying phrase "at the earliest practicable date," it is firmly believed that we cannot, at this time, even with Great Britain assuming responsibility for our Atlantic interests, denude that ocean of sufficient forces to protect our coastal trade and to safeguard our more vital interests in South America. Nor can we neglect the protection of our own and the interdiction of Japanese trade in the Southeastern Pacific. With these commitments adequately cared for, our remaining force is barely superior to ORANGE, *at the beginning* of our westward campaign. It will undoubtedly be subject to attrition losses enroute.

(b) The Army is not now prepared and will not in the immediate future, be prepared to support our western advance. The Fleet Marine Force is not sufficient to support the necessary operations alone.

(c) The capture of BASE ONE is a major military operation requiring detailed knowledge of the area, detailed planning based on such knowledge, and the taking over, conversion, manning, training and organization of a large number of merchant ships. The establishment of the BASE, after its occupation, requires: (a), the transport of large quantities of materials; (b), the organization, transport and maintenance of construction units capable of accomplishing the necessary development; and (c), the defense and supply of the base during the construction period. The Plan requires the completion of this BASE forty-five days after the arrival of the first material at the site.

We do not, at present, have the detailed knowledge of the area requisite for proper planning of these manifold activities. It is true that some knowledge possibly sufficient for *initiation* [author's italics] of operations and general planning for the attack, may be obtained by reconnaissance after hostilities have commenced, and the Plan provides for such operations. However, it is not known, nor can it be determined, until *after* [author's italics] actual occupation, whether or not the hydrography of the area permits the establishment of a fleet anchorage, what construction is possible on land areas under consideration and whether or not adequate defensive installations, particularly air fields for land-based aircraft, can be established. Granting that the base seized offers possibilities for the establishment of these facilities, it appears certain that the assembly of material and the organization for construction must await the actual occupation. To the knowledge of the Commander-in-Chief, no material has yet been assembled for this purpose, nor have any but the vaguest ideas for the ultimate accomplishment of this objective been advanced.

Present Fleet plans, due chiefly to lack of sufficient knowledge as a basis, and partly to the preoccupation of staffs of the forces afloat with routine matters of administration and training, have been most general in nature and have extended chiefly to the assignment of tasks and forces. Only tentative ideas (based largely on unsupported assumptions) for the actual accomplishment of the objectives, have been advanced.

(d) The time element, in the present Plan, is believed greatly out of proportion to the tasks to be accomplished. While a definite time limit does not actually appear (except for the forty-five day limit mentioned above), it is strongly implied in the tables and Appendix II of WPL 14 and throughout the O-1 Plan itself, that the operations visualized up to the establishment of BASE ONE can be accomplished in a period of some sixty to ninety days after mobilization.

It is the firm belief of the Commander-in-Chief, U.S. Fleet, that even if energetic, single-purpose steps toward the first objective (BASE ONE) of the plan were initiated promptly, a period of some six months to one year would be required for its accomplishment. With the knowledge now available, the time required for subsequent operations can not even be guessed at. It is believed to be in the order of years rather than months.

(a) I know of no flag officer who wholeheartedly endorses the present ORANGE Plan. It is the general conception that the Plan had its inception primarily in the desirability of having a guiding directive for the development of the Naval Establishment to meet any international situation that might be thrust upon it. It is my belief that the impracticabilities of the ORANGE Plan, in the absence of a better one, have been periodically overlooked in order that the Department might have for budget purposes and presentation to Congress the maximum justification for the necessary enlargement of the Navy. In my opinion, the development of the Naval Establishment has not yet proceeded to the point essential to the successful prosecution of the Plan.

7. In addition to the ORANGE PLAN, the Commander-in-Chief has available to him an approved Navy Basic War Plan, Rainbow No. 1, and a tentative draft, not as yet approved, of a Joint Army and Navy Basic War Plan, Rainbow No. II. The assumptions of neither of these Plans are applicable to the present situation, nor, to the knowledge of the Commander-in-Chief, is the assistance from allies visualized in the tentative draft of Rainbow No. II a likely possibility.

8. The foregoing considerations are set forth in some length in order to focus attention upon the fact that the Commander-in-Chief finds himself, in what he is lead to believe may suddenly become a critical situation, without an applicable directive. He cannot, in the absence of a clear picture of national policy, national commitments and national objectives, formulate his own plans other than for obvious measures of security and defense and for accelerated preparation for further eventualities. He is of the firm belief that successful operations in war can rest only on sound plans, careful specific preparation and vigorous prosecution based upon confidence in the success of the course being pursued.

9. There is no intention or desire on the part of the Commander-in-Chief to evade his legitimate responsibilities nor is it desired that anything in this letter be so construed. It is fully realized that no plan can foresee or provide for every possible situation, and that adjustments and re-estimates must be made to fit the actual situation presented. At the same time, it is most strongly

believed that the Commander-in-Chief must be better informed than he is now as to the Department's plans and intentions if he is to perform his full duty.

10. The foregoing is briefly summarized as follows:

(a) Unsuitability of ORANGE Plan in present situation and present development of Naval Establishment;

(b) Inapplicability of other Plans available to the Commander-in-Chief, U.S. Fleet (Rainbow Nos. 1 and II);

(c) Vital necessity for (1) new directive (possibly Rainbow No. III) based on present realities, national objectives and commitments as far as these are known or can be predicted at the present time; (2) coordination of plans development with National Policy and steps to be taken to implement that policy;

(d) In the light of information now available to him, the Commander-in-Chief is of the conviction that the elements of a realistic plan should embody:

(1) Security and defense measures of the Western Hemisphere;

(2) Long-range interdiction of enemy commerce;

(3) Threats and raids against the enemy;

(4) Extension of operations as the relative strength of the Naval Establishment (may be influenced by allied strength and freedom of action) is built up to support them.

11. Please acknowledge receipt of this letter by despatch.

12. It is hereby certified that the originator considers it to be impracticable to phrase this document in such a manner as will permit a classification of this document other than secret.

13. The exigency of the delivery of this document is such that it will not reach the addressee in time by the next available officer courier. The originator, therefore, authorizes the transmission of this document by registered mail within the continental limits of the United States.[56]

J. O. RICHARDSON

Admiral Stark's next personal letter to me (dated November 12, 1940) which, as indicated in paragraph 3 thereof, was written subsequent to the receipt of my extremely critical official letter of October 22, 1940, was non-committal but not uncordial. In this letter he said:

Dear J.O.: You may think I have been unusually silent for the last couple of weeks, — and so I have. Truth of the matter is that a great part of this time was spent in making up an estimate of the international situation, together with a number of officers in Naval Operations and two from the General Board. As a start on this I sat down one early morning and drew up a twelve page rough estimate, working on up till two o'clock the next morning, this in

---

[56] CINUS, serial 01705 of 20 Oct. 1940, letter to CNO, as cited in *Pearl Harbor Hearings*, Part 33, pp. 1190-92.

the effort to clear my own mind, as I sometimes do by drawing up a paper. After I finished the rough notes, I then got together Ingersoll, Turner, Savvy, Charlie Wellborn, Forrest Sherman, Hill, Sexton, Moore and Oscar Badger and we went to it, day and night, Saturdays and Sundays, for about ten consecutive days. The product which no one claims is perfect is now in the hands of the President. I am hoping he will give you some definite pronouncement on it in order that I may send you something more authoritative than I otherwise could do.

You know that we have no definite commitments. Perhaps none can be made. The direction which things finally take may be forced upon us.

For example, as you stated in a recent letter:— Upon your first visit here you found us of the opinion that in the event of war, we should not become involved in the Pacific, and that any major effort we might make would be in what we considered the most vital theater, namely, in the Atlantic. I have never changed my viewpoint on that and I may say that so far as I know, neither has the State Department. I believe the Secretary of the Navy also holds this view. But no appeasement.

Nevertheless, we can not afford to neglect the possibility of hostilities in the Pacific and that is why in so many of my letters I always mention keeping a weather eye to the Westward.

I think the study which was made when you were here, has been highly beneficial; studies of this sort always are, whether or not they are implemented.

I had hoped before this to get to you the Navy end of RAINBOW III as a more thoroughly considered directive to meet the possibilities of the present situation in the Pacific. This RAINBOW III plan is nearing completion now and I expect to send it to you in a few days. I trust that you will find the tasks assigned to you are within your power. We will await your comment.

When nearly two months had gone by and no official answer to my official letter of October 22, 1940 had been received from the Chief of Naval Operations, I sent my War Plans Officer (Commander V. R. Murphy) to Washington. He arrived back in Pearl on December 21, 1940 with the official reply (dated December 17, 1940) and also bearing advance copies of RAINBOW no. THREE. The official reply read as follows:

1. In reply to your recommendation in the above letter that a new war plan be issued, you are informed that Navy Basic War Plan—Rainbow No. 3 (W.P.L. 44) has recently been completed. Four advance copies have been forwarded to you by officer messenger. The finished copies of this plan, plus such revisions of WPL-42, Navy Basic War Plan—Rainbow No. 1, as have been found desirable for making parts of that plan usable with Rainbow No. 3, will be distributed as soon as practicable through the Registered Publication Section.

2. War Plan Rainbow No. 3 is designed to provide against the most imminent and difficult war situation which may confront the United States in the near future. It is, therefore requested that the Commander in Chief prepare as soon as practicable the operating plans for a war envisaged by Rainbow No. 3.

3. The Chief of Naval Operations has, in the past, kept the Commander in Chief advised as to all matters within his own knowledge which related to current national policy and pending national decisions. This past practice will be continued in the future. However, the Commander in Chief is doubtless aware that the changing world military situation will continue to affect policy, and thus will influence plans for the war operation of the naval forces. It is, of course, impracticable to draw up and to issue new Navy Basic War Plans when merely minor changes in policy occur. The Chief of Naval Operations considers that Rainbow No. 3 is, in its major aspects, suitable for all probable situations which may arise in the near future where the principal portion of the national effort is directed westward. Under study now by the naval and army officials are plans based on assumptions requiring the exertion of the principal portion of the national effort to the eastward (Rainbow No. 5), and also a plan, somewhat similar to Rainbow No. 1, involving the defense of the entire Western Hemisphere against attack from both the east and the west (Rainbow No. 4). So far as now can be foreseen, these three basic plans should be adequate to guide mobilization, initial deployment, and initial operations under all contingencies which are foreseeable at present.

4. In view of the above, it is believed unnecessary to comment on the present applicability of the Orange War Plan, as that Plan was drawn up to guide the prosecution of a war under circumstances which do not now exist.[57]

Despite his later statement to the contrary, my own belief is that Stark was not in any way pleased by the receipt of my official letter (of October 22, 1940) laying the deficiencies of the existing and effective ORANGE War Plan on the line, and that his true feelings in the matter were far more correctly expressed in the very terse official reply of December 17, 1940, nearly two months after my October 22, 1940 letter, than in his testimony before various groups inquiring into the Pearl Harbor disaster. In this official letter, the punch line was in paragraph 4, where Stark said:

> It is believed unnecessary to comment on the present applicability of the ORANGE WAR PLAN, as that Plan was drawn up to guide the prosecution of a war under circumstances which do not now exist.[58]

Yet, that ORANGE War Plan was to be the only one available to the operating units of the Fleet in the Eastern Pacific for another seven months,

[57] CNO, 17 Dec. 1940, letter to CINCUS, as cited in *Pearl Harbor Hearings*, Part 14, p. 980.
[58] *Ibid.*

until July 1941, when the Commander-in-Chief of the Pacific Fleet, Kimmel, issued his O-1 RAINBOW no. FIVE Plan.

I believe that my official letter of October 22, 1940 in regard to the dismal state of the Navy's War Plans was probably one factor which made Stark accept with equanimity the President's urge to have me relieved.

Stark never seemed to realize that there was a six-to-eight-month time-lag between the time he "willed" a new War Plan and the time one would actually be available to the Operating Forces of the Navy. He was basing his letters to me on RAINBOW no. FIVE when he was still two months away from promulgating RAINBOW no. THREE and six months away from promulgating RAINBOW no. FIVE.

The Head of the War Plans Division in Naval Operations (Rear Admiral R. K. Turner, USN, later Admiral) told the Naval Court of Inquiry into the Pearl Harbor disaster that, when he took over the War Plans Division in Naval Operations on October 23, 1940, "the only War Plan in existence was the ORANGE War Plan which was most unrealistic." [59]

His further testimony was summarized by the Naval Court of Inquiry, as follows:

> Vice Admiral Turner referred to the letter written by Admiral Richardson to Admiral Stark and stated that, after its receipt, he immediately started the preparation of the War Plan which was known as Rainbow Three, and which was issued in January 1941. This he stated was not a Joint Army and Navy Plan, but was purely a naval plan, based on the concept of Japan attacking the Philippines and the Netherlands East Indies and Hawaii, and it involved sending a detachment of the Pacific Fleet out to join the Asiatic Fleet. That plan was thoroughly discussed by the principal officers in the office of the Chief of Naval Operations and with one or two members of the General Board, and agreed on and approved by the Chief of Naval Operations. . . .[60]

The "Narrative Statement of Evidence at Navy Pearl Harbor Investigation" states:

> Admiral Stark stated he was delighted to receive this letter [October 22, 1940] from Admiral Richardson and that he was in accord with most of what Admiral Richardson has to say, particularly in regard to the War Plans. Admiral Stark also said the very reasons given by Admiral Richardson in his criticisms

---

[59] *Ibid.*, Part 32, p. 609.

[60] *Ibid.*, "Narrative Statement of Evidence," p. 1011.

of the situation at that time were some of the causes for the subsequent development of RAINBOW WAR PLAN No. 5 WPL-46.[61]

In any case, the actual Navy Basic War Plan RAINBOW no. THREE,[62] was not approved officially by the Chief of Naval Operations until January 7, 1941, three weeks prior to my detachment as CINCUS.

The first assumption of the Navy Basic War Plan RAINBOW no. THREE, was that the United States, allied with the British Commonwealth, the Netherlands, China, and perhaps other nations would be at war against Japan, Germany, and Italy. The concept of the war was:

1. The principal effort of the British Commonwealth is an air, land, and sea defensive against Germany and Italy, combined with a sea and air offensive against their waterborne communications, and is confined to British Isles and adjacent waters, the eastern North Atlantic, the Mediterranean, and the Near East.

2. The secondary effort of the British Commonwealth, and the complete effort of the Netherlands East Indies, is defensive against Japan in Malaysia and Hong Kong. Holding the Malay Peninsula and a substantial portion of the Netherlands East Indies constitutes a principal part of the allied offensive against Japanese economic strength.

3. The principal offensive effort of the United States is directed toward the suppression of Japanese overseas communications and the support of the defense of Malaysia against Japan. A secondary offensive effort is the support, with minor naval forces, including air components, of the British Commonwealth in the Atlantic Ocean, British home waters, and possibly the Mediterranean. Both Great Britain and China are being supported by the supply of war materials.

4. The principal defensive effort of the United States is directed toward the protection of American and allied commerce; and of United States and Canadian territory (including the Philippines), the Panama Canal, and the Caribbean area. A secondary defensive effort is directed toward protection of other allied and neutral territory in the Western Hemisphere, including possible internal support of national governments.

5. The principal offensive effort of Japan is toward the eventual capture of the Philippines, Malaysia, and Hong Kong. The offensive against China is maintained on a reduced scale. Secondary offensive efforts are toward the interruption of American and allied sea communications in the Pacific, the Far East, and the Indian Ocean; and the capture of Guam and other outlying allied positions.

---

[61] *Ibid.*, p. 93.

[62] "Basic War Plan, RAINBOW No. 3, WPL-44" (hereafter cited as WPL-44), CNO, 7 Jan. 1941, Plan File, NHD.

8. The United States' operations in the Pacific and Asiatic Theaters are conditioned by the possible necessity for a rapid dimunition in scope, should eventualities require the transfer to the Atlantic Theater of a major portion of the effort of the United States.[63]

RAINBOW no. THREE provided that, ". . . the Plan will not contemplate the commitment of the United States' naval forces in the Pacific Theater in such a manner as to prevent the eventual transfer of the principal war effort of the United States to the Atlantic if circumstances so require."[64]

It estimated Japan's initial objective as:

1. Capture of Guam.
2. Establishment of control over the South China Sea, Philippine waters, and the waters between Borneo and New Guinea, by the establishment of advanced bases, and by the destruction of United States and allied air and naval forces in those regions, followed by capture of Luzon.
3. Capture of Northern Borneo.
4. Denial to the United States of the use of the Marshall—Caroline—Marianas area by the use of fixed defenses, and by the operation of air forces and light naval forces to reduce the strength of the United States Fleet.[65]

The initial United States strategic deployment included:

a. *Pacific Theater.*

1. Principal concentration in Hawaiian Area for: covering and supporting an initial sweep for the capture of Japanese merchant vessels and naval raiders; for supporting other offensive operations; and for covering United States', Canadian, and Latin-American sea communications and territory.
2. Assembly in Hawaii of the Asiatic Fleet Reenforcement.
3. Reenforcement of the defenses of Unalaska.
4. Assembly at Panama of a fleet detachment for the control of trade along the Pacific Coasts of Central and South America.

b. *Asiatic Theater.*

1. Principal United States' concentration in Manila area preparatory to raiding Japanese sea communications, destroying Japanese naval forces, and supporting the defense of Luzon; but prepared for a shift of base at discretion to British or Dutch ports.

NOTES:—For holding the Malay Barrier, it is anticipated that the

---

[63] *Ibid.*, pp. 16-17.
[64] *Ibid.*, p. 15.
[65] *Ibid.*, p. 17.

(a) Principal British Naval, land, and air concentration will be in the Malay Peninsula.

(b) Principal Dutch naval, land, and air concentration will be in Java, with outlying defenses in Borneo and Sumatra.

It is expected that the British will conduct a fortress defense of Hong Kong.

c. *Atlantic Theater.*

1. Principal concentration of United States in the Caribbean area prepared for the capture of Martinique, and for the occupation of Dutch and other French possessions in the Caribbean area; followed by an Atlantic coast deployment, with the principal part of the force centered in New England, the Maritime Provinces, or Newfoundland, for the defense of North Atlantic convoys and for covering sea routes.
2. Secondary concentration in the Caribbean of aircraft and light naval forces, for patrol of the southern portion of the theater.
3. Assembly of the British Isles Detachment in United States Atlantic Coast ports.
4. Assembly of Army Troops in Atlantic or Gulf ports for outlying garrisons, and as a strategic reserve for use in Latin-America.[66]

The general task of the Naval Establishment was:

a. Sever Japanese sea communications in the Pacific Ocean and the Bering Sea to the eastward of the 180th Meridian, and through the Malay Barrier; and raid Japanese sea communications in other areas in the Western Pacific, and South China Sea and contiguous waters, in order eventually to destroy the economic power of Japan to conduct offensive warfare;

b. Assist forces of the British Commonwealth and of the Netherlands East Indies in the defense of Malayasia in order to further the economic blockade of Japan and the protection of the economic and political interests of the United States;

c. Provide naval support to the British in the Atlantic Ocean in order to assist in the defeat of the Axis blockade of the British Isles;

d. Protect United States' and Canadian territory, and, within United States' naval theaters, protect the sea communications of the United States and its allies; and prevent the further extension of enemy military power in the Western Hemisphere, in order to guard United States' interests.[67]

In the December 17, 1940 letter from the Chief of Naval Operations, previously quoted, the Commander-in-Chief was told to prepare, as soon as practicable, the Fleet operating plans for a war envisaged by RAINBOW no. THREE. This work was undertaken immediately.

[66] *Ibid.*, pp. 20-21.
[67] *Ibid.*, p. 23.

On January 22, 1941, I received from the Chief of Naval Operations a despatch (212155), which also had been addressed to the Commander-in-Chief of the Asiatic Fleet, and to Commander Patrol Force, U.S. Fleet, my senior subordinate in the Atlantic Ocean. It read along the following lines:

> THE INTERNATIONAL SITUATION CONTINUES TO DETERIORATE X IT NOW APPEARS TO ME THAT IF WAR EVENTUATES ITS GENERAL CHARACTER WILL BE ACCORDING TO PLAN *DOG* MY MEMORANDUM TO THE SECRETARY X IF THIS ESTIMATE PROVES CORRECT I CONTEMPLATE ORDERING MOBILIZATION ACCORDING TO PLAN *RAINBOW* THREE WITH FOLLOWING MODIFICATIONS ATLANTIC FLEET PRINCIPAL CONCENTRATION NEW ENGLAND AND CANADA EXECUTE ALL TASKS EXCEPT AFFIRM EXPECT EARLY REENFORCEMENT FROM PACIFIC AND MUCH STRONGER BRITISH ISLES DETACHMENT X PACIFIC FLEET WAITING ATTITUDE OR EXECUTE ASSIGNED TASKS IN AREA EASTWARD OF 16 DEGREES EAST DEPENDING ON ACTION BY JAPAN X ASIATIC FLEET CAN NOT EXPECT EARLY REENFORCEMENT ALERT STATUS OR CARRY OUT TASKS ACCORDING TO CIRCUMSTANCES[68]

However, Plan Dog, which, as amplified, contained the preliminary concept, missions, and tasks for RAINBOW no. FIVE, also had been received, so I wrote Stark officially on January 25, 1941, as follows:

> In view of . . . [OPNAV secret despatch 212155 of January 1941] and some degree of urgency implied therein, it is considered that study of the new situation and preparation of plans therefore should take priority over the preparation of plans for Rainbow No. 3. Unless advice to the contrary is received, this will be done.[69]

This letter was prepared in collaboration with the prospective Commander-in-Chief, U.S. Pacific Fleet, Rear Admiral H. E. Kimmel, USN. It represented his, as well as my own, views. But, I learned later the CNO had directed work on RAINBOW THREE to continue to have highest priority. And that, on March 28, 1941, CINCPAC had forwarded a draft

---

[68] CNO, 212155 Jan. 1941, despatch to CINCUS as cited in *Pearl Harbor Hearings*, Part 17, pp. 2475-76.

[69] CINCUS, serial 0129 of 25 Jan. 1941, letter to CNO, as cited in *Pearl Harbor Hearings*, Part 33, p. 1349.

copy of the proposed operating plans of the Pacific Fleet under RAINBOW no. THREE.[70]

Despite this, no copy of a promulgated United States Fleet Operating Plan, RAINBOW no. THREE is currently available in the files of the Registered Publications Section of the Office of Naval Operations or in the War Plans Division of CNO, or the other depositories searched. A marked up draft copy is all that remains as a record of the Fleet effort to comply with CNO's directive.

Rainbow No. Four

RAINBOW no. FOUR was a basic hemispheric defense plan. It was largely a RAINBOW no. ONE plan, except that, in the Western Hemisphere, United States forces were not limited, as in RAINBOW no. ONE, to military action north of thirteen degrees south latitude. U.S. military action in the Pacific, however, was to be limited to the area east of a line from Unalaska to Midway. The Joint Basic War Plan, RAINBOW no. FOUR, was first submitted to the President on June 13, 1940, but no immediate action was taken by him. On July 12, 1940, the President sent the plan to the new Secretaries of War and Navy (Stimson and Knox) for their comments. On July 26, 1940, they returned RAINBOW no. FOUR to the President jointly, recommending its approval, and on August 14, 1940 it was approved by the President. When the war situation in Europe stabilized, the development of RAINBOW no. FOUR into a working plan was placed at the bottom of the priority list by the Joint Board, and I do not believe it was ever developed into a usable end product for the fighting forces and logistic agencies of the Army and Navy. In any case, its main assumptions (the German capture of the British and French Fleets and their violation of the Monroe Doctrine in South America) were proven false by world events.

Rainbow No. Five

RAINBOW no. FIVE was the outgrowth of a memorandum of the Chief of Naval Operations to the Secretary of the Navy (dated November

---

[70] CINCUS, serial 019W of 28 Mar. 1941, letter to CNO; CNO, serial 052512 of 13 May 1941, letter to CINCUS, CNOCF, NHD.

12, 1940 and partially quoted below), in which he outlined four possible war contingencies, (A), (B), (C), and (D) and possible Strategic Concepts to handle each one of these contingencies. He requested the Secretary to obtain from the President a decision as to which course he intended the United States to follow in order to accomplish certain basic national objectives. He said that such a decision was essential for the:

> . . . preparation and distribution of the naval forces of the United States, in cooperation with its military forces, for use in war in accomplishment of all or part of these national objectives.[71]

The Chief of Naval Operations also recommended that:

> . . . as a preliminary to possible entry of the United States into the conflict, the United States Army and Navy at once undertake secret staff talks on technical matters with the British military and naval authorities in London, with Canadian military authorities in Washington, and with British and Dutch authorities in Singapore and Batavia. The purpose would be to reach agreements and lay down plans for promoting unity of allied effort should the United States find it necessary to enter the war under any of the alternative eventualities considered in this memorandum.[72]

Stark's memorandum to the Secretary was submitted shortly after he had received from Rear Admiral Ghormley in London a copy of "The Bailey Committee Report," a study prepared in the Plans Division of the British Admiralty and dealing with various problems which would arise in British-U.S. naval cooperation, if the United States entered the war on the side of Britain.

In sub-paragraph (D), or "DOG" in naval parlance, of Stark's memorandum, he asked the question, "Shall we direct our efforts toward an eventual strong offensive in the Atlantic as an ally of the British, and a defensive in the Pacific?"[73] And, later on, he wrote that "alternative (D) is likely to be the most fruitful for the United States."[74]

This memorandum of Stark's was made available to CINCUS and the other principal naval commanders afloat for comments, and certain parts of the "Strategic Concepts" were redrafted in the light of these and other comments received. As sub-paragraph (D) of the memorandum became

[71] CNO, 12 Nov. 1940, memo "Plan Dog" to SECNAV, Plan File, NHD, p. 2.

[72] *Ibid.*, p. 11.

[73] *Ibid.*, p. 10.

[74] *Ibid.*, p. 11.

the chosen vehicle for the full development of the "Strategic Concept" for a war plan, the whole memorandum acquired the name of "Plan Dog" and was so referred to amongst the principal commanders and their planners in the Navy.

However, the major impetus for the rapid development of Plan Dog into RAINBOW no. FIVE, in my opinion, came from the informal military staff conversations between the military and naval officers of Great Britain and the United States, held in London, commencing in September 1940. These conversations were transferred to Washington, reopening there on January 27, 1941, and lasted well beyond January 31, 1941, when I was relieved as CINCUS.

The holding of these talks had the approval of the Secretaries of War and Navy and the tacit consent of the President. The President sought to avoid any personal political risk, by refusing to personally authorize or prohibit the talks, which seemed to be a direct shirking of a responsibility inherent in the office of President and Commander-in-Chief of the Army and Navy.[75]

RAINBOW no. FIVE was based on the broad strategic objective of defeating Germany and her allies (either including or excluding Japan), with the major offensive effort of the United States in the Atlantic and on the continent of Europe, and a defensive United States military effort in the Far East. It was designated WPL-46.

WPL-46 was placed in effect for war purposes on December 7, 1941, and was immediately subject to major changes. As COMINCH put it:

> The entry of the United States into the war required immediate changes in the planned expansion of the naval establishment and redistribution of naval forces.[76]

Comment on the Rainbow Series

I believe the following lessons can be learned from this recital of my experience in the war planning efforts of the Navy prior to World War II:

---

[75] CAPT Tracy B. Kittredge, USNR, "U.S.-British Naval Cooperation, 1940-1945," 2 Vols., WWIICF, NHD, Sec. III, Part A, Chap. 10 and Part D, Chap. 13, pp. 314-318.

[76] Commander-in-Chief, United States Fleet (COMINCH) (E. J. King), serial 01350 of 12 July 1942, letter to Vice Chief of Naval Operations, CNOCF, NHD, p. 1.

(A) The Strategic Plan must be within the capabilities of the Logistic Plan.

(B) War Plans take many months, from the initial conception at the highest levels, before the officers at the fighting, operating, and logistic levels have a workable document which they can use to plan to accomplish effectively the desires of their superiors.

(C) War Plans must be in being prior to a period of strained relations or a war crisis, to cover a variety of assumptions and concepts. It is much more expeditious to adjust a War Plan to meet a variation of concept, assumptions, missions, or tasks than it is to develop a completely new plan.

My opinion, in regard to RAINBOW no. ONE, is that it was a good first step in the reorientation of our planners from a limited war to a world war. It alerted the President to the nation's military weaknesses. While the concept was pretty far removed from the actual capabilities of German and Italian sea power, at the time, at least, it seemed within the bounds of Axis psychological warfare capabilities. The Axis success in getting fascist-type political movements organized in South America was beyond my expectations.

My opinion, in regard to RAINBOW no. THREE, is that, except for certain omissions, it was a very good second step in the reorientation of the tasks of the United States Fleet from those which every naval officer would have liked to have it able to accomplish to tasks which appeared more nearly within its capabilities in a war with Japan or in a world war.

It should be pointed out again that it took over six months from the time world conditions indicated the necessity for a RAINBOW no. THREE War Plan before the Commander-in-Chief of the United States Fleet received an actual document which he could use to allot tasks to his subordinate commanders for actual war operations.

A similar experience followed with RAINBOW no. FIVE. The planners were first set to work on this by the Chief of Naval Operations in November 1940. The document was not available for issue for Navy-wide use until May 1941. The Commander-in-Chief of the Pacific Fleet did not issue his supporting and operating plan until July 25, 1941—over eight months after the initial decision of the Chief of Naval Operations that such a War Plan was necessary.

Major Omissions from Rainbow Three and Five

I do not know whether, the closer we got to war with Japan the less our principal naval commanders and their planning staffs were concerned with the fundamentals, or whether certain omissions in their plan resulted from pure oversight, but I believe it is very worthwhile recording that neither the Navy Basic War Plans—RAINBOW no. THREE or RAINBOW no. FIVE nor the U.S. Pacific Fleet Operating Plan—RAINBOW FIVE[77]—carries as an assumption that:

> War with ORANGE will be precipitated without notice.[78]

Our ORANGE War Plans from 1923 thru 1940 had carried this very, very important assumption.

And again, nowhere in RAINBOW no. THREE nor RAINBOW no. FIVE was any assumption that, "War will be preceded by a period of strained relations which will develop into actual hostilities before a formal declaration of War." This statement had been in the ORANGE Plans for many years and was carried over into RAINBOW no. ONE and then dropped.[79]

However, in my opinion the most vital omission was of a warning of an attack on Pearl Harbor and of an order in regard to the degree of readiness thereat which had been in our War Plans since 1937. Change no. six to WPL-13, issued March 26, 1937, introduced into the Basic ORANGE War Plans this strong warning regarding Pearl Harbor as a likely Japanese objective, and the degree of readiness to be maintained thereat.

> The Army and Naval Forces stationed in the HAWAIIAN ISLANDS will be prepared at all times to defend Oahu against all forms of surprise attack, including the following:
>
> (a) Gun, torpedo, and bombing raids, mining operations, and a possible landing of minor forces.
> (b) Attempts to enter PEARL HARBOR or HONOLULU HARBOR, or to close those harbors by blockships.
> (c) Sabotage or armed insurrection.[80]

For reasons quite unknown to me, Admiral Stark did not see fit to have

[77] WPL-44; "Navy Basic War Plan, RAINBOW No. 5, WPL-46," CNO, serial 060512 of 26 May 1941, Plan File, NHD; "U.S. Pacific Fleet Operating Plan, RAINBOW No. 5, WPPac-46" (hereafter cited as WPPac-46), CNO, 9 Sept. 1941, Plan File, NHD.

[78] WPL-13, pp. 11, 76.

[79] WPL-42, Appen. I, p. 6.

[80] WPL-13, Change No. 6 of 26 Mar. 1937, Plan File, NHD, pp. 17-17a.

these requirements carried over into the RAINBOW no. FIVE Plan, which was in effect when war started.

I would here point out that, in failing to carry forward this warning, Admiral Stark failed to follow the advice of his one-time principal commander afloat, for, in my final letter on War Plans to him, dated January 25, 1941, I outlined certain assumptions upon which the action of the U.S. Fleet in the Pacific should be predicated. There were seven in number, and number six was:

> Japanese attacks may be expected against shipping, outlying possessions or Naval units. Surprise raids on Pearl Harbor, or attempts to block the Channel are possible.[81]

I believe one of the reasons "Why Pearl Harbor Happened" lies in these omissions in CNO War Plans directives issued to my successor.

And, I believe that another of the reasons "Why Pearl Harbor Happened" is because my successor afloat in his War Operating Plan so markedly changed my number six assumption of Japanese intentions to read:

> Possibly raids or stronger attacks on Wake, Midway and other outlying United States positions.[82]

CINCPAC then stated, "The initial Japanese deployment is therefore estimated to be about as follows:

> Raiding and observation forces widely distributed in the Pacific, and submarines in the Hawaiian area.[83]

It was not until CINCPAC had assigned twelve other tasks to his subordinates, to be accomplished by his task forces during Phase I (that is, before Japan was in the war), that he issued the warning:

> Guard against surprise attacks by Japan.[84]

It was not until CINCPAC listed the tasks with "Japan in the war" (Phase 1A Tasks) and patrol plane searches had been established with ". . . facilities . . . available at the time operations commence" that he

---

[81] CINCUS, serial 0129 of 25 Jan. 1941, letter to CNO, as cited in *Pearl Harbor Hearings*, Part 33, p. 1350.

[82] WPPac-46, p. 22.

[83] *Ibid.*

[84] *Ibid.*, p. 26.

indicated, ". . . that enemy action in the area subject to our patrol plane search will comprise:

(a) Submarine raids and observation off Oahu. . . .

(b) Surface raids on our lines of communications.

(c) Surface and air raids against Wake and possibly against Midway, Johnston, Palmyra and Canton.

(d) Possibly carrier raid against Oahu.[85]

Summary

By and large, career naval officers are fairly literal-minded people. If you give them a written order, the chances are more than good that it will be observed or carried out in a conscientious manner.

Admiral Kimmel was known throughout the Naval Service for his highly conscientious performance of duty. I had the highest opinion of his capabilities. I still have.

I am sure that if he had received an order as definite as that quoted above (Change Number Six to the ORANGE Plan) from his superior, Admiral Stark, that, subsequent to the "War Warning" despatch of Novem- 27, 1941, Pearl Harbor would have been protected by an adequate seaplane patrol to the full limit of the resources available.

Any influence that I might have had on our War Plans ceased when on June 11, 1941, the ORANGE War Plans, RAINBOW no. ONE and RAINBOW no. THREE War Plans, were placed in an inactive status by the Chief of Naval Operations. Concentration of planning effort on WPL-46, RAINBOW no. FIVE was directed.[86]

RAINBOW no. FIVE was the plan which was to have these two unexplained and unexplainable omissions.

---

[85] *Ibid.*, pp. 42-43.

[86] CNO, serial 063712 of 11 July 1941, letter, CNOCF, NHD.

Chapter XV

The Basing of the Fleet at Pearl Harbor After the Fleet Problem

Before discussing the matter, some of the basic data in regard to basing the Fleet in Hawaiian waters should be put into the record.

The major portion of the United States Fleet, less the Atlantic Squadron and the Hawaiian Detachment, left the Pacific coast on Tuesday, April 2, 1940, to carry out Fleet Problem XXI. The schedule, approved by the Chief of Naval Operations, called for this portion of the Fleet to remain in the Hawaiian area until Thursday, May 9, 1940 and then to return to normal West Coast bases, arriving about May 17, 1940.

On April 29, 1940, I received from the CNO a despatch reading about as follows:

> IN VIEW OF THE POSSIBILITY OF ITALY BECOMING AN ACTIVE BELLIGERENT IN MAY, YOU MAY RECEIVE INSTRUCTIONS TO REMAIN IN HAWAIIAN WATERS WITH THE SHIPS OF THE FLEET THEN IN COMPANY WITH YOU X CHANGES IN SCHEDULED MOVEMENTS INDIVIDUAL UNITS PRIOR NINE MAY NOT CONTEMPLATED X UTMOST SECRECY IS DESIRED FOR THE PRESENT X ACKNOWLEDGE X

On May 1, 1940, I sent off the following letter:

> Dear Betty:
>
> I gave up the idea of visiting Midway and Alaska because I want to arrive on the Pacific Coast with the Fleet.
>
> As soon as practicable after I arrive on the Coast I want orders for Commander Murphy and myself to proceed to Washington on temporary duty for a few days in order that I may talk to you, and the President if you approve, about the present war situation, the possibility of our being drawn in, and

our existing War Plans.

Because of the difficulty of discussing such things in correspondence, the possibility of being misunderstood, and the secret nature of the subjects, I feel that it is highly inadvisable for me to attempt to write what I feel it my duty to say.

It is my firm conviction that we urgently need a reestimate of the situation of the United States in world affairs and a reconsideration of our basic war plans based on such an estimate. I strongly believe that such a reestimate and reconsideration will result in a firm determination to remain out of the present conflict in Europe and Asia.

I hope that nothing will delay the arrival of the Fleet at its normal bases on the Pacific Coast, that you will have orders issued for Murphy and me to proceed to Washington on temporary duty, and that you can give me an undisturbed opportunity to talk to you.

On May 4, 1940, I received from the Chief of Naval Operations a despatch reading, "IT LOOKS PROBABLE BUT NOT FINAL THAT THE FLEET WILL REMAIN IN HAWAIIAN WATERS FOR SHORT TIME AFTER MAY 9TH. WILL EXPECT TO APPRISE YOU FURTHER MONDAY OR TUESDAY NEXT [May 6th or May 7th]."

The important news arrived on Tuesday, May 7, 1940. It was contained in the following despatch, released by HRS (Stark) and receipted by JOR (Richardson):

CINCUS—HRS

CINCUS MAKE IMMEDIATE PRESS RELEASE IN SUBSTANCE AS FOLLOWS. I HAVE REQUESTED PERMISSION TO REMAIN IN HAWAIIAN WATERS TO ACCOMPLISH SOME THINGS I WANTED TO DO WHILE HERE X THE DEPARTMENT HAS APPROVED THIS REQUEST.

PARAGRAPH—DELAY FLEET DEPARTURE HAWAIIAN AREA FOR ABOUT TWO WEEKS PRIOR TO END OF WHICH TIME YOU WILL BE FURTHER ADVISED REGARDING FUTURE MOVEMENTS X CARRY OUT REGULARLY SCHEDULED OVERHAULS OF INDIVIDUAL UNITS, MOVEMENTS OF BASEFORCE UNITS AT YOUR DISCRETION.

7 May 1940

JOR — to be acknowledged

Release

L.N.

[Despatch hand written][1]

[1] ADM Stark, despatch, 7 May 1940, to ADM Richardson, microfilm NRS No. 1M, NHD.

I had not requested that the Fleet remain in Hawaiian waters, and there was no logical reason for me to make such a request. This was the second time the Department had put the Commander-in-Chief of the United States Fleet in a completely false position, with a requirement that he announce to the public something which, on its very face, every tyro ensign would recognize as a phony. I did not resent being told to do something by orders from above, but I did resent being told how to do it, particularly when that "how" made a perfect "nitwit" out of me.

Let us examine this requirement for me to announce that I requested "permission for the Fleet to remain in Hawaiian waters to accomplish some things I wanted to do while here."

The Fleet had just completed its annual Fleet Problem, the culmination of a year's tactical training. The two most logical things that needed to be done were:

> (1) to undertake further tactical training of senior officers to (a) overcome tactical deficiencies revealed by the Fleet Problem or to (b) explore new tactical problems or developments
>
> (2) to continue at a high but steady rate, fundamental seagoing and technical training of all officers and all men to keep the battle efficiency of the Fleet from slipping backwards. Such a backward slip was beginning to be reported to me and was logical due to the influx of young reserve officers and large numbers of recruits. The Fleet was experiencing a tremendous personnel turnover, as demands were met from the Navy Department for officers and men for new ship and air activities of the expanding Navy. The Fleet's state of efficiency was far from being fully stable.

Tactical training of the senior officers of the Fleet could well be continued in the Hawaiian area, but the fundamental training of officers and men, particularly in air and surface gunnery, required a large-scale ammunition supply and surface and air target services, available only from West Coast naval bases.

The important decision required of me at the moment, as I indicated later at the Congressional Hearings on the Pearl Harbor attack, was how to keep the fundamental training of the personnel of the Fleet rolling along in high gear during this period of temporary indecision in Washington.

When the Fleet went to the Hawaiian area at the end of the Fleet Problem, we did not take with us tugs, targets, target rafts, target planes, towing planes, or repair ships. If the Fleet was to be retained in the Hawaiian area, it was essential, in order that it could be usefully employed, that I know that we were going to remain there long enough to justify bringing out all of the target gear which was necessary for gunnery training of the ships and aircraft.

I was much concerned that I might start all these target ships, planes, and equipment toward Hawaii at towing speed and then, before or about the time they arrived, some sixteen to twenty days later, the Fleet would be ordered to return. Then we would have to wait for several weeks for all this target equipment to get back to normal bases on the West Coast, before the Fleet could again continue its essential training.[2] Our yearly training schedule was so tight that we could not afford to lose three to six weeks out of the training year.

In mid-May 1940, the Fleet was nearing the end of its competition year in gunnery, damage control, communications, and engineering. No officer wanted to lose out on any of the scheduled training exercises, which were looked upon as a requisite for maintaining battle efficiency. The experimental gunnery practices for each year, essential for steady year-to-year advancement in the field of gunnery, were largely fired in May and June of each competition year. The ammunition for these practices and the essential target services were available only at the West Coast ammunition depots and bases. Every tyro ensign knew all of the above. So, I believe it was quite undesirable to couple the decision to keep the Fleet in Hawaiian waters with an announced cover plan which was so obviously a phony.

The May 7 despatch had said, "DELAY FLEET DEPARTURE HAWAIIAN AREA FOR ABOUT TWO WEEKS," and my letter from Admiral Stark, dated May 7, 1940, said:

> When the Fleet returns to the Coast (and I trust the delay will not be over two weeks, but I cannot tell) the President has asked that the Fleet schedule be so arranged that on extremely short notice the Fleet [will] be able to return concentrated to Hawaiian Waters.[3]

So, during the first week, everyone expected the Fleet to start back at the end of two weeks. Even I was hopeful that the duration of the Fleet's stay in Hawaiian waters would be only "about two weeks" longer than

---

[2] *Pearl Harbor Hearings*, Part I, p. 260.
[3] *Ibid.*, Part 14, p. 934.

originally planned. My hopes were short-lived, for late on the 15th of May, the two-week stay in Hawaiian waters was lengthened to "for some time" in the following long-winded and diversive despatch:

> FROM: OPNAV
> TO: CINCUS
>
> SOME BRITISH AUTHORITIES FEEL THAT ITALY MAY JOIN GERMANY IN ACTIVE PARTICIPATION IN IMMEDIATE FUTURE X THIS FEELING IS NOT SHARED BY OTHER CLOSE OBSERVERS X OUR STATE DEPARTMENT INCLINED TO DISAGREE X REGARDING DUTCH EAST INDIES JAPAN HAS MADE TWO STATEMENTS WHICH IF TAKEN AT THEIR FACE VALUE STATE THEY WISH STATUS QUO PRESERVED X GREAT BRITAIN HAS STATED SHE HAS NO INTENTION OF INTERFERING WITH STATUS QUO AND THERE IS AN UNCONFIRMED REPORT THAT THE FRENCH FOREIGN OFFICE HAS ISSUED A SIMILAR STATEMENT X PRESENT INDICATIONS ARE THAT FLEET WILL REMAIN HAWAIIAN WATERS FOR SOME TIME X HOPE TO ADVISE YOU MORE DEFINITELY NEXT WEEK X

In each of the despatches and letters, I was given indefinite information, with a promise of more definite information shortly thereafter. So, there was always a reason to wait a little longer to receive the more definite word. It was tantalizing and aggravating and quite to be expected in an emergency period.

And, on May 22, the indefiniteness became the standard, when I was informed by despatch: "NOTHING MORE DEFINITE REGARDING MOVEMENTS [of] FLEET."

I wish to point out that, in all these early despatches, the Chief of Naval Operations either intentionally or unintentionally committed a fundamental military error, in that he failed to inform the CINCUS why the Fleet was retained in Hawaiian waters, thus depriving the CINCUS of a firm basis for formulating plans or courses of action in support of his superior's orders.

The Two-Week Delay Period

Starting immediately after the original public announcement of the change in Fleet schedule, steps had to be taken in regard to the many sets of Departmental orders for officers and enlisted men which called for their detachment from the ships of the Fleet upon arrival back on the West Coast, on or about May 17, 1940. These orders had been ground out by the Chief of the Bureau of Navigation ever since the latter part of January. On January 16, 1940, the Chief of the Bureau of Navigation had requested the Chief of Naval Operations to inform the Director of Officer Personnel, Bureau of Navigation, of the units of the U.S. Fleet which would remain in the Hawaiian area at the conclusion of the coming Fleet Problem as replacements for ships in the Hawaiian Detachment.

On the promise that the delay in reaching the West Coast was to be only a couple of weeks beyond that previously contemplated, I sent this despatch for action to the Bureau of Navigation, and for information to "all ships of the U.S. Fleet present Hawaiian Waters: "

> PROPOSE TO HOLD IN ABEYANCE THE DETACHMENT FROM SHIPS NORMALLY BASING ON WEST COAST OF ALL OFFICERS WHOSE PRESENT ORDERS CALL FOR THEIR DETACHMENT UPON ARRIVAL ON THE WEST COAST ON OR ABOUT 17 MAY X UNITS RETURNING TO WEST COAST IN ADVANCE OF FLEET EXCEPTED X OFFICERS WHOSE COMMISSIONS ARE BEING TERMINATED IN THE NAVAL SERVICE EXCEPTED

And, after receiving qualified approval of this proposal from the Bureau, the following was sent to all ships except the carriers:

> HOLD IN ABEYANCE DETACHMENT ALL OFFICERS EXCEPT THOSE AUTHORIZED BY CINCUS X EXCEPTIONS INCLUDE THOSE AUTHORIZED TO TAKE PASSAGE IN THE *CALIFORNIA,* THE *SAN FRANCISCO,* AND THE *LOUISVILLE* X OFFICERS WHOSE COMMISSIONS ARE BEING TERMINATED X SPECIAL CASES THAT HAVE BEEN GIVEN SEPARATE CONSIDERATION X

The instructions to the carriers were more restrictive:

> DO NOT DETACH ANY OFFICER UNLESS RELIEF OR REPLACEMENTS HAVE REPORTED AND FULLY QUALIFIED IN DUTIES ASSIGNED X FOR PILOTS THIS INCLUDES QUALIFIED IN CARRIER OPERATIONS

My restrictions regarding naval aviators were short-lived. Before the month was out, the Depatment laid down the law:

> At Pensacola Florida, the situation in regard to instructors is now critical. . . . Detach all Naval aviators under orders to Pensacola at this time whose reliefs have reported, and at the earliest practical date, detach all Naval aviators under orders whose reliefs are proceeding to report, but have not yet arrived.

This indicated that the needs of the Shore Establishment training activities were judged in the Department to be more essential than the fighting efficiency of the air arm of the Fleet. Since this information in regard to the carrying out of officers' orders all of which were completely unclassified, was bound to become known to the Japanese intelligence activities, it was a sure giveaway to the Japanese that the U.S. Governmental positioning of the Fleet in Hawaii was one of bluff, and not one of early combative action.

I proposed handling enlisted men in the following manner:

> COMMANDER-IN-CHIEF IS RETURNING TO WEST COAST BY IMMEDIATE AVAILABLE GOVT TRANSPORTATION THE FOLLOWING CLASSES OF MEN X THOSE GOING TO SERVICE SCHOOLS X THOSE ORDERED BY BUNAV TO SHORE DUTY AND SHORT TIMERS X IN ORDER TO UTILIZE FULL CAPACITY OF THE *NITRO* ON VOYAGE TO EAST COAST SHORT TIMERS WHOSE ENLISTMENTS EXPIRING THROUGH 30 JULY ARE BEING SENT X TOTAL NUMBER OF MEN INVOLVED ABOUT TEN FIFTY X DOES BUREAU DESIRE ANY CHANGE IN THIS POLICY

The "For Some Time" Period

When the "stay in Hawaiian waters for some time" despatch arrived on May 15, longer-range plans than just delaying detachments of officers, or speeding up the return to the States of sailormen whose enlistments were about to expire, had to be made.

The major immediate questions that had to be settled involved navy yard overhaul of ships, interim docking, target practice, and mobilization loads of ammunition and oil. A few quotes from my despatches to the Chief of Naval Operations outline these major problems:

> THERE IS ON HAND HERE IN PEARL 13,400 GALLONS ANTI-FOULING, 16,000 GALLONS ANTI-CORROSIVE BUT PRACTICALLY NO PLASTIC [paint]. THE FOLLOWING SHIPS INCLUDING THOSE ON THE WEST COAST REQUIRE DOCKING: 7 CL, 8 CA, 7 BB, 2 CV, 43 DD, 7 SUBS AND 26 MISCELLANEOUS CRAFT. UNDER NORMAL OPERATIONS, PEARL IS CAPABLE OF DOCKING 15 SHIPS PER MONTH ON MARINE RAILWAY. IN GRAVING DOCK UNDER SAME CONDITIONS CAN DOCK NO VESSELS IN JUNE, 2 CRUISERS IN JULY AND 2 BB OR 3 CL AND 2 [destroyer] LEADERS IN AUGUST, IN ADDITION

TO SHIPS NOW SCHEDULED. DUE TO LACK OF DOCKING KEEL BLOCKS, NO CARRIERS OR BATTLESHIPS CAN BE DOCKED BEFORE THE FIRST OF JULY. BY USING 3 SHIFT, 7 DAY WEEK, THE NUMBER ON THE RAILWAY CAN BE INCREASED 20%, AND IF THE *CUTTLEFISH* AND *CACHALOT* ARE DEFERRED, 10 CRUISERS CAN BE TAKEN IN JUNE, 5 BBS IN JULY, AND 2 BBS AND 1 CV IN AUGUST.

• • •

IF THE FLEET CONTINUES TO OPERATE IN THIS AREA IT IS ESTIMATED THAT 200,000 BBLS OF FUEL OIL WILL BE REQUIRED MONTHLY, IN ADDITION TO QUANTITIES FLEET TANKERS CAN DELIVER. IT IS NOW REQUESTED THAT THE PRESIDENT GRANT AUTHORITY TO ISSUE 100,000 BBLS FROM RESERVE. IF FLEET MINUS HAWAIIAN DETACHMENT REMAINS LONGER THAN 25 MAY, COMMERCIAL DELIVERY OF 100,000 BBLS BEFORE 10 JUNE AND AN EQUAL QUANTITY BEFORE 17 JUNE IS RECOMMENDED, BUT IF IT LEAVES FOR THE COAST BEFORE 25 MAY, FLEET OILERS CAN MAKE REPLACEMENT BY 30 JUNE.

The reserve fuel oil mentioned in the foregoing despatch was that currently in the oil storage farm at the Pearl Harbor Naval Base.

My recommendations in regard to docking and my question in regard to ammunition supply were contained in the following despatch:

FROM: CINCUS
TO: OPNAV

THE FOLLOWING SCHEDULE OF DOCKING SHIPS IS MY RECOMMENDATION:

A. AT MARE ISLAND NAVY YARD: 21 DD'S, 1 HEAVY CRUISER; 5 LARGE AUXILIARIES; 2 LIGHT CRUISERS.

B. AT THE NAVY YARD PEARL HARBOR: 9 DD'S; 7 SMALL AUXILIARIES; 2 LARGE AUXILIARIES; 8 SS; 3 LIGHT CRUISERS; 8 HEAVY CRUISERS.

C. AT SAN DIEGO: 11 SMALL AUXILIARIES AND 9 DD'S.

D. AT BREMERTON NAVY YARD: 9 DD'S; 3 CL'S; 1 BB; and 3 CARRIERS.

E. AT HUNTERS POINT DRY DOCK: 7 BB'S.

WHEN THIS SCHEDULE IS GIVEN APPROVAL I PROPOSE TO DESPATCH ONE FOURTH OF THE SHIPS DOCKING IN THE MAINLAND. AT THE PROPER INTERVALS, SIMILAR GROUPS WILL FOLLOW.

FOLLOWING SHIPS WILL COMPRISE THE FIRST GROUP TO DEPART 18 MAY:

A. NYD PUGET SOUND: 2 DD, *BROOKLYN* AND *YORKTOWN.*
B. FOR SAN DIEGO: 2 DD.
C. FOR HUNTERS POINT: *COLORADO* AND *WEST VIRGINIA.*
D. FOR MARE ISLAND: 5 DD AND THE *PHOENIX.*

INFORMATION IS REQUESTED AS TO WHETHER A FULL MOBILIZATION SUPPLY OF AMMUNITION IS TO BE TAKEN. THIS IS ASKED BECAUSE THIS PRECLUDES THE CARRYING OF TARGET AMMUNITION. ON COMPLETION OF SHIPS DOCKING, RECEIVING THEIR STORES AND THEIR AMMUNITION, THEY WILL PROCEED TO SAN PEDRO, FUEL, AND DEPART IN 2 GROUPS WITHIN 2 DAYS. WHEN I RECEIVE APPROVAL I WILL GIVE THE COMPOSITION OF THE OTHER GROUPS USING AIRMAIL.

The personnel in the Office of the Chief of Naval Operations were most appreciative of the problems caused by the major change in Fleet basing. Quick approval of many of my recommendations was received.

As soon as our stay in Hawaiian waters was made indefinite, all hands both in the Department and in the Fleet, seemed to realize that it was essential to get the ships docked, filled up with their mobilization supply of ammunition, and stripped of all gear and equipment not essential to war operations, and all efforts were cheerfully directed toward that end.

On May 16, 1940, I asked the Department, in regard to the ships currently scheduled to join the Pacific Ocean units of the Fleet:

WILL THE FOLLOWING VESSELS PROCEED TO WEST COAST; *ST LOUIS, HELENA, OMAHA, RANGER* AND CRUDIV SEVEN X IF THEY DO, I RECOMMEND THEIR DOCKING ON THE EAST COAST OR THE CANAL ZONE X I RECOMMEND CONSIDERATION AND REQUEST DECISION ON THIS POINT, SHALL SHIPS NOW UNDERGOING OVERHAUL AND THOSE SOON DUE FOR OVERHAUL, BE SPEEDED UP OR GIVEN ONLY LIMITED AVAILABILITY.

This despatch elicited some useful information and showed how the wind was blowing in Washington:

FROM: OPNAV
TO: CINCUS

PRESENT INTENTION TO RETAIN IN ATLANTIC THOSE UNITS NOW THERE EXCEPT NEW CONSTRUCTION DESTROYERS AND SUBMARINES X SHIPS UNDERGOING SCHEDULED OVERHAULS AND THOSE SOON DUE SHOULD HAVE WORK EXPEDITED AND COMPLETION DATES ANTICIPATED AS MUCH AS PRACTICABLE

However, the Department was still playing a game of blindman's buff with the Japanese and the personnel of the Fleet, as the following despatches indicate:

FROM: CINCUS
TO: OPNAV

IF THE DEPARTMENT DESIRES I SUGGEST THAT IT MAKE THE PRESS RELEASE REGARDING THE RETURN OF THE FIRST GROUP FOR DOCKING X I HAVE GIVEN IT NO PUBLICITY

• • •

FROM: OPNAV
TO: CINCUS

THE PRESENT INTENTION OF THE DEPARTMENT IS TO MAKE NO PRESS RELEASE IN REGARD TO THE RETURN OF UNITS OF THE FLEET TO WEST COAST PORTS X IN RESPONSE TO QUESTIONS WHICH WILL RESULT FROM THE OBSERVATION OF UNITS DEPARTING FROM THE HAWAIIAN AREA OR THEIR ARRIVAL IN THE MAINLAND PORTS ON THE PACIFIC COAST WE PLAN TO SAY THAT OVERHAULS AND DOCKINGS OF VESSELS IN THE FLEET WILL BE CONTINUED IN THE CUSTOMARY MANNER X IT IS DESIRED THAT YOU MINIMIZE PUBLICITY REGARDING RETURNING TASK GROUPS

The 5″38-caliber antiaircraft ammunition shortage in the Fleet was particularly large, and the Fleet was in no condition to move west of Hawaii because of this critical shortage. Ammunition ships were not assigned to the U.S. Fleet, but operated directly under the Chief of Naval Operations, in the Naval Transportation Service. So, the only thing I could do was to point out the considerable and most urgent needs of the Fleet, and request that OPNAV take suitable action. With only two ammunition ships in commission in the Navy, Naval Operations was limited by that reality, in what action it could accomplish promptly, but it sent a cheering despatch:

FROM: OPNAV
TO: CINCUS

THE SHORTAGE OF 5 INCH 38 CALIBER AMMUNITION IN THE FLEET IS BEING REMEDIED BY URGENT STEPS TAKEN HERE

Besides sending official despatches, I mentioned the 5″38-caliber AA ammunition shortage in a personal letter to Stark on May 13, 1940.[4] On May 22, he informed me that 20,000 rounds of 5″38-caliber AA would be sent via the ammunition ship *Pyro* (AE-1).[5] This was very good news.

The target practice ammunition situation was also critical. The situation did not return to normal until late September, as the following despatch shows:

FROM: OPNAV
TO: CINCUS 24 JUNE 1940
INFO: BUORD / NAVAMMDEP / PUGET SOUND / NAVAMUNDEP MARE ISLAND / *PYRO*

REFERRING TO YOUR DESPATCH OF 19TH AND PERSONAL LETTER OF CINCUS TO CHIEF OF NAVAL OPERATIONS OF 9TH X WHEN *PYRO* COMPLETES JULY TRIP IT IS INTENDED THAT VESSEL MAKE EXTRA TRIP BETWEEN PACIFIC COAST AND THE HAWAIIAN AREA FOR TRANSPORTATION BALANCE 1941 AMMUNITION FROM WEST COAST DEPOTS X THE *PYRO* SHOULD REACH HAWAIIAN AREA APPROXIMATELY 15 AUGUST WITH AMMUNITION FOR BATTLESHIPS, *SARATOGA,* AND *LEXINGTON,* ALSO SOME CRUISERS X *NITRO* WITH ENTIRE BALANCE FLEET TARGET AMMUNITION SCHEDULED LEAVE NORFOLK ABOUT AUGUST 21 X SPECIAL TRIP OF *PYRO* WILL ALLOW *NITRO* GO DIRECT HAWAIIAN AREA, REACHING THERE APPROXIMATELY 16 SEPTEMBER

Delay, inherent in the limitations of only two ammunition ships, in getting mobilization ammunition to the Fleet is shown by the following despatches:

FROM: CINCUS 14 OCT 1940
TO: BUORD
INFO: COMBATSHIPS / COMBATFOR / COMBATDIV 3

I DESIRE TO BE ADVISED AS TO THE PLANS OF THE PRESENT CONCERNING DELIVERY OF 14 INCH MOBILIZATION SUPPLY BATTLESHIP DIVISION 3

---

[4] ADM Richardson, letter, 13 May 1940, to ADM Stark, as cited in *Pearl Harbor Hearings,* Part 14, p. 935.

[5] ADM Stark, letter, 22 May 1940, to ADM Richardson, as cited in *Pearl Harbor Hearings,* Part 14, p. 938.

FROM: COMCRUBATFOR 1 NOV 1940
TO: BUORD
INFO: *NASHVILLE* / NAVAMUNDEP MARE ISLAND / NAVAMUN-DEP OAHU

IT IS NOW REPORTED BY *NASHVILLE* THAT THE FIRST INCREMENT OF HER 5 INCH MOBILIZATION SUPPLY HAS NOT BEEN RECEIVED X IN ACCORDING YOUR ...... AND THE SAME AS THE *BOISE* AND *SAVANNAH* REQUEST SHE BE ISSUED 600 ROUNDS

Proper Basing for Preparing for War

As soon as the most urgent logistical problems of the Fleet had been brought to the attention of the Department, I wrote on May 13, 1940 to Stark:

> When Hill was detached last January he took with him to Washington some ideas, largely Bloch's, as to what might be acceptable to the Commander-in-Chief, (under the assumptions then made), to serve as a start from which Op-12 would develop basic assumptions to be officially transmitted, within a few weeks, to the Commander-in-Chief for use in making plans.
>
> • • •
>
> The assumptions under which the Hill memorandum was drawn up and under which all other operations in the Western Pacific have previously been considered, are today all different. Previous assumptions and estimates of the situation no longer hold.
>
> It seems that, under present world conditions, the paramount thing for us is the security of the Western Hemisphere. This, in my opinion, transcends everything—anything certainly in the Far East, our own or other interests.
>
> South America is the greatest prize yet remaining to be grabbed. Until the outcome in Europe can be more clearly seen, security in the Western Hemisphere seems to be the most important consideration for us.
>
> I feel that any move west means hostilities. I feel that at this time it would be a grave mistake to become involved in the West where our interests, although important, are not vital, and thereby reduce our ability to maintain the security of the Western Hemisphere which is vital.
>
> If the Fleet is to go west it can only start, properly prepared, from the West Coast where it can be docked, manned, stocked and stripped, and a suitable train assembled.
>
> Rest assured that although I am entirely without information I realize your position, and I want you to know that if the situation becomes such that higher authority decides we should go West, all of us are ready to give all we have.

These are some of the things I wanted to talk to you about, and since I can not see you, I feel that I am duty bound to write you.[6]

In Stark's reply of May 22 to my letter of May 13 he stated, "I agree with the tenor of your letter," and "I think it [blitzkrieg events in Europe] has made more remote (for the moment at least) the question of a westward movement of the Fleet." My letter had dealt with many subjects, including the assumptions to be used in future war plans, and our national objectives in future war plans, as well as the westward movement of the Fleet in accordance with the current ORANGE War Plan, and with where the Fleet could best be prepared for war. It now seems clear that there were plenty of specific details of my opinions on these four subjects with which Stark disagreed.

The same day, May 22, I decided to try to elicit definite information on our stay in Hawaiian waters and accordingly wrote Stark:

Dear Betty:

As you no doubt well appreciate, I now must plan the Fleet schedule and employment for the next few months. To do this intelligently, however, it is necessary to know more than I know [now] about why we are here and how long we will probably stay. I realize that the answer to the second question is largely dependent upon the first, and probably also upon further developments, but nonetheless I should have something to go on. For instance, carrying out even a curtailed gunnery schedule will require wholesale movements of targets, tugs, utility planes, etc., from the Coast. The following are pertinent questions:

(a) Are we here primarily to influence the actions of other nations by our presence, and if so, what effect would the carrying out of normal training (insofar as we can under the limitations on anchorages, air fields, facilities and services) have on this purpose? The effect of the emergency docking program and the consequent absence of task forces during the training period must also be considered.

(b) Are we here as a stepping off place for belligerent activity? If so, we should devote all of our time and energies to preparing for war. This could more effectively and expeditiously be accomplished by an immediate return to the West Coast, with "freezing" of personnel, filling up complements, docking and all the rest of it. We could return here upon completion.

As it is now, to try and do both (a) and (b) from here and at the same

[6] *Pearl Harbor Hearings,* Part 14, pp. 935-36.

time is a diversification of effort and purpose that can only result in the accomplishment of neither.

If we are here to develop this area as a peacetime operating base, consideration should be given to the certain decrease in the efficiency of the Fleet and the lowering of morale that may ensue, due to inadequate anchorages, air fields, facilities, services, recreation conditions, for so large a Fleet. If only peacetime training is involved should the Bureau of Navigation and I not be advised so we may remove restrictions on officer details? [7]

Stark's reply to this letter, on the 27th of May, was one of the most direct replies to any of my letters to him, although it was far from being as definite as I would have liked:

Why are you in the Hawaiian Area?

Answer: You are there because of the deterrent effect which it is thought your presence may have on the Japs going into the East Indies. In previous letters I have hooked this up with the Italians going into the war. The connection is that with Italy in, it is thought the Japs might feel just that much freer to take independent action. We believe both the Germans and the Italians have told the Japs that so far as they are concerned she, Japan, has a free hand in the Dutch East Indies.

• • •

The above I think will answer the question "why you are there". It does not answer the question as to how long you will probably stay. Rest assured that the minute I get this information I will communicate it to you. Nobody can answer it just now. Like you, I have asked the question, and also—like you—I have been unable to get the answer.

• • •

You asked whether you are there as a stepping off place for belligerent activity? Answer: obviously it might become so under certain conditions but a definite answer cannot be given as you have already gathered from the foregoing.

I realize what you say about the advantages of returning to the West Coast for the purpose of preparation. At this time [it] is out of the question. If you did return it might nullify the principle reasons for your being in Hawaii. This very question has been brought up here. As a compromise, however, you have authority for returning ships to the Coast for docking, taking ammunition, stores, etc., and this should help in any case.

As to the freezing of personnel:—Nimitz has put the personnel problem before you. I will touch on it only to the extent that I have been moving Heaven and Earth to get our figure boosted to 170,000 enlisted men (or even

[7] *Ibid.*, p. 940.

possibly (172,300) and 34,000 marines. If we get these authorized I believe you will be comfortable as regards numbers of men for this coming year. I know the convulsion the Fleet had to go through to commission the 64 destroyers and some other ships recently. I am thankful that convulsion is over. I hope the succeeding one may be as light as possible and you may rest assured that Navigation will do everything it can to lessen this unavoidable burden on the Forces Afloat.

• • •

You were not detained in Hawaii to develop the area as a peacetime operating base but this will naturally flow to a considerable extent from what you are up against.

As to the decrease in the efficiency of the Fleet and the lowering of morale due to inadequate anchorages, air fields, facilities, service, recreation conditions, for so large a Fleet;

I wish I could help you. I spent some of my first years out of the Naval Academy in the West Indies,—I remember the last port I was in after a 22 month stay and where we didn't move for 6 months; and there was not even one white person in the place. The great antidote I know is WORK and homemade recreation such as sailing, fishing, athletics, smokers, etc. You can also move Task Forces around a good deal for seagoing and diversion; just so you be ready for concentrations should such become necessary. We will solve the oil situation for you for all the cruising you feel necessary.[8]

On June 22, 1940, Stark wrote me that, "Tentatively decision has been made for the fleet to remain . . . where it is. This decision may be changed at any time."[9]

As soon as practicable after May 15, temporary modified employment schedules were issued for the ships in Hawaiian waters. These were further modified as time passed and the indefinite news from Washington continued. Reference to the CINCUS modified employment schedules for the various types of ships, for the last quarter of the 1940 fiscal year and the first quarter of the 1941 fiscal year, show that a rather sharp decrease in gunnery practices resulted from the shift to Hawaiian waters amongst the major combatant ships of the Fleet during this six-month period.[10]

---

[8] *Ibid.*, pp. 943-44.

[9] *Ibid.*, Part 1, p. 262.

[10] "First Quarter Fiscal 1941 Employment Schedule," CINCUS, serial 1484 of 30 Apr. 1940, box 20, CINCUS Files, RG 313, NA; "First Quarter Fiscal 1941 Employment Schedule, Revised," CINCUS, serial 1770 of 28 May 1940, box 21, CINCUS Files, RG 313, NA. The revised employment schedule of May 28, 1940 reduced the previously scheduled 4-week gunnery time for carriers to 1½ weeks, and for heavy cruisers to 2 weeks. Time for independent training operations by Commanding Officers was correspondingly increased.

By and large, the people of the Hawaiian Islands welcomed the prolonged stay of the Fleet and took many steps to make off-duty hours more pleasant for officers and men alike. For this, I was grateful.

The local fishermen in Hawaii suffered because of the very large numbers of ships and naval aircraft in the area, conducting gunnery and bombing practices, and they complained frequently. The Army soon found a large part of the seagoing Navy sitting in its lap, and it took some time for both Services to adjust to this situation, but both did so good-naturedly although occasionally quite strenuously, as the following despatch of Commander Battle Force will indicate:

> ARMY REPORTS THAT MANY NAVY PLANES OF PRACTICALLY ALL TYPES FOULED AREA VICTOR 7 FORENOON 26 AUGUST THUS INTERFERING SCHEDULED AA FIRING. TAKE DRASTIC AND POSITIVE STEPS TO PREVENT FURTHER VIOLATIONS. AFTER INVESTIGATION TODAYS OFFENSES TAKE NECESSARY DISCIPLINARY MEASURES AND REPORT TO ME.[11]

In mid-August, Stark finally obtained approval from the President for my proposals for sending detachments of ships to the coast, so that married men could visit their families, if they were living in the western states. CNO said: "Heartily approve your letter dated August twelfth about visit of three task forces to West Coast," and I notified the Fleet as follows:

> NAVY DEPARTMENT HAS APPROVED THE RECOMMENDATION OF THE COMMANDER-IN-CHIEF THAT SHIPS OF THE FLEET LESS SHIPS PERMANENTLY DETAILED TO THE HAWAIIAN DETACHMENT AND SHIPS NORMALLY BASED ON PEARL HARBOR BE SENT TO HOME PORTS IN THREE TASK GROUPS FOR LEAVE AND LIBERTY X EACH TASK GROUP WILL REMAIN AT HOME PORTS FOR TWO WEEKS THE FIRST DEPARTING PEARL ABOUT 23 SEPTEMBER X DETAILED SCHEDULES WILL BE ISSUED LATER

This message was enthusiastically greeted throughout the Fleet, and I was grateful to Stark for his obtaining the approving Presidential nod.[12]

Nine months later, in commenting on these home-port visits, a force commander wrote, "The beneficial results from such cruises in regard to

[11] COMBATFOR, 270700 Aug. 1940, despatch to Air Commands Hawaiian Area; Commander Hawaiian Detachment, serial 1437 of 27 May 1940, letter to CINCUS.

[12] CINCUS, serial 2568 of 17 Aug. 1940, letter to Force and Type Commanders, box 35, CINCUS Files, RG 313, NA.

morale cannot be over emphasized." Besides that factor benefits are obtained by operating under conditions of low visibility, cold weather, rough seas, and sufficiently long periods out of sight of land to require celestial navigation." [13]

This is next to the last reference I have available in which the subject of the Fleet remaining in Hawaiian waters was mentioned by Stark to me. On November 12, 1940, he wrote me, "As you know, the matter of withdrawing the Fleet from Hawaii is delicate, and could hardly be accomplished without a certain amount of preparation in Washington. It does not now appear that we can withdraw it without some good pretext." [14]

During 1940, my opinion was that Stark had agreed with me that the Fleet should not have been retained in the Hawaiian Islands. I stated to the Joint Congressional Committee investigating the Pearl Harbor Attack that, ". . . from all that he said to me, and from all that he wrote to me, I gathered that he was fully in sympathy with me." [15]

Stark also testified in answer to a direct question at the hearings of the Congressional Committee on the Pearl Harbor Attack, that for some time he was in agreement with me.[16]

Despite what I believe was Stark's initial agreement with my opinion that the Fleet could best be prepared for war at the West Coast naval bases, he felt otherwise by the time I was relieved. Just when his opinion changed I do not know, but I believe he had come to willingly support the President's decision by the time of my October 1940 visit to Washington, although Stark's only direct statement known to me regarding when he changed his mind is, "I would say that by the time Admiral Kimmel had command of the fleet [1 February 1941], we had practically wiped out of our minds, or at least we no longer considered and talked about bringing the fleet back." [17]

Also, when I visited Washington in October 1940, neither Mr. Knox nor Stark raised the matter with me.

The original of my memorandum of September 12, 1940 to Secretary Knox (with Stark's pencilled comments thereon) was photographed and

[13] COMSCOFOR, "Annual Report," 1941, p. 9.
[14] *Pearl Harbor Hearings,* Part 14, p. 971.
[15] *Ibid.,* Part 1, p. 290.
[16] *Ibid.,* Part 5, p. 2189.
[17] *Ibid.*

published in the *Hearings before the Joint Committee on the Investigation of the Pearl Harbor Attack.* I now note that the paragraph on the subject of the Fleet being based in Hawaiian waters has "yes and no" written on the margin of most of the subparagraphs, and a question mark is alongside another subparagraph.

One reason I now think that Stark had changed his mind in regard to the Fleet remaining in Hawaiian waters, before October 1940, arises from my discussions with Secretary Knox when he was in the Fleet in September 1940. Mr. Knox was opposed to having the Fleet withdraw to West Coast bases, but did not amplify to any marked extent his objections. It may have been that he was most loyally supporting both his boss, the President, and his senior naval subordinate, Stark, in their opinions on the matter. And it is possible that he did not desire to be drawn into a professional discussion of the matter due to his then limited knowledge of the Naval Establishment.

Herewith is that part of the above memorandum which relates to the retention of the Fleet in the Hawaiian area. It is dated September 12, 1940, and I consider it important as a record of my views in regard to the basing of the Fleet at Pearl Harbor, four months after this action had been directed by the President.

4. *OPERATIONS*

A) *Retention of the Fleet in the Hawaiian Area.*

(a) From a purely Naval point of view there are many disadvantages attached to basing the fleet in this area, some of which are:

(1) Difficulty, delay and cost of transporting men, munitions, and supplies.

(2) Inadequacy of Lahaina as operating anchorage due to lack of security.

(3) Inadequacy of Pearl Harbor as operating anchorage due to difficulties of entry, berthing and departure of large ships.

(4) Congested and restricted operating areas, in the air and on the surface.

(5) Inadequate facilities for fleet services, training, recreation and housing.

(6) Prolonged absences from mainland of officers and men in time of peace adversely affects morale.

(7) In case of war, necessary for Fleet to return to mobilization

NH 77331

The Fleet at Lahaina Anchorage.

ports on West Coast or accept partial and unorganized mobilization measures resulting in confusion and a net loss of time.

(b) If the disposition of the Fleet were determined solely by Naval considerations the major portion of the Fleet should return to its normal Pacific Coast bases because such basing would facilitate its training and its preparation for war.

(c) If factors other than purely Naval ones are to influence the decision as to where the Fleet should be based at this time, the Naval factors should be fully presented and carefully considered, as well as the probable effect of the decision on the readiness of the Fleet. In other words, is it more important to lend strength to diplomatic representations in the Pacific by basing the Fleet in the Hawaiian Area, than to facilitate its preparation for active service in any area by basing the major part of it on normal Pacific Coast bases?

(d) In case our relations with another Pacific Nation deteriorate, what is the State Department's conception of our next move? Does it believe that the Fleet is now mobilized and that it could embark on a campaign directly from Hawaii or safely conduct necessary training from the insecure anchorage at Lahaina which is 2000 miles nearer enemy submarine bases than our normal Pacific Coast bases?[18]

The disadvantages stated by me in this memorandum should probably be buttressed a bit with the official statements of some of the other senior commanders who were in Hawaiian waters at the time. The situation in regard to Fleet training in the Hawaiian area was aptly summarized by Commander Scouting Force, the Commander Hawaiian Detachment, in his 1940 Annual Report to the Commander-in-Chief. He stated that the disadvantages were:

(a) A lack of adequate services.

(1) A need for large high speed sled targets and for more utility planes capable of towing large sleeves has been particularly noted.

(2) Facilities for providing ships quickly with fuel oil, gasoline, and water have been improved but are still inadequate.

(b) The recognized tendency of ships' bottoms to foul rapidly in Hawaiian Waters. This condition is being met by shortening the docking interval. The bottoms of ships' boats in some cases have been damaged by teredos. The limited dry docking facilities of Pearl Harbor are well known.

(c) The crowded facilities at [the] Naval Air Station Pearl Harbor for shore basing planes. Excellent facilities at Pearl Harbor were available at the

[18] *Ibid.*, Part 14, pp. 955-57. Paragraphs (a) and (b) and subparagraphs a-4, a-5, a-6, and a-7 bear handwritten "yes and no" comments in the margin. Paragraph (c) has a question mark in the margin.

Naval Air Station until the arrival of the Fleet, at which time the increased load at that station necessitated the curtailment of its use to actual emergencies or urgent repairs.

(d) The lack of tender facilities for cruisers. . . .

(e) The inadequacy of rifle and machine gun range facilities.

(f) There is no range finder calibration range available. . . .

(g) A disinclination on the part of enlisted men to reenlist on board ships of the Hawaiian Detachment. . . .

(h) Inadequate athletic and recreational facilities in the vicinity for the families of enlisted men. . . .

(i) The insufficiency and unsuitability of housing facilities in the vicinity for the families of enlisted men. . . .

(j) The difficulties attending the granting of leave. . . .[19]

[19]COMSCOFOR, "Annual Report," 1940, pp. 25-26.

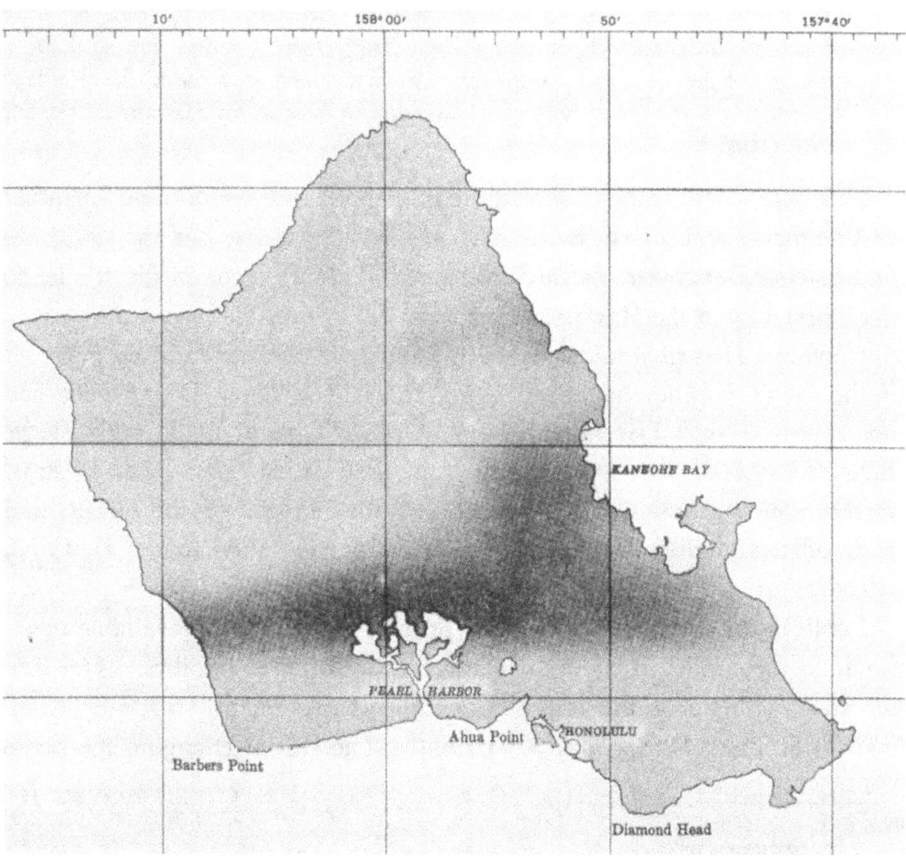

Pearl Harbor and the Island of Oahu.

I believe it also would not be amiss to mention the adverse effect that establishment of the Hawaiian Detachment and the retention of the Fleet in Hawaiian waters had upon the reenlistment rate in the Navy. A high reenlistment rate was and is a basic essential factor in the efficiency of the Navy. During the fiscal year 1939, the reenlistment rate was 80.81 percent. The Hawaiian Detachment was established during fiscal year 1940. The reenlistment rate fell to 75.45 percent. And, in the fiscal year 1941, despite a strenuous effort throughout the Fleet to get every man to reenlist and obtain the benefits which would come from riding the crest of war expansion, only 71.49 percent reenlisted.

I stated the case as follows:

> Enlisted men, as a rule, do not desire duty in the Hawaiian Area. This dislike may be attributed in a large measure, especially in the case of petty officers, to the necessity of being away from their families for so long a time. It is believed that by securing to as many men as possible the privilege incident to the change of home port, aversion to duty in the Hawaiian Area can be mitigated.[20]

I am sure it will come as something of a shock to the Honolulu Chamber of Commerce and, of course, it may not be true today, but in 1940, the Commander Destroyers, Battle Force stated "Enlisted men, on the whole, do not desire duty in the Hawaiian Area."[21]

However, Hawaii would have been a lot more popular for duty purposes if the men's families had been living there. The Navy Department had not approved until December 29, 1939, the change of home ports of the ships of the Hawaiian Detachment from their West Coast bases to Pearl Harbor. Such action would have entitled the families of the officers and petty officers of these ships to government transportation to the Hawaiian Islands.

I believe this delay was occasioned primarily by a lack of available naval funds to accomplish this very expensive movement of families.[22] The conservative estimate of the initial cost for this movement (made by Commander Scouting Force) was $594,720.00. The cost of changing the home

[20] CINCUS, serial 1783 of 29 May 1940, letter to CNO, box 26, CINCUS Files, RG 313, NA, p. 1.

[21] COMDESBATFOR, serial 2351 of 17 May 1940, letter to CINCUS, box 26, CINCUS Files, RG 313, NA, p. 2.

[22] CNO, serial 938 of 4 Jan. 1940, letter to CINCUS, box 22, CINCUS Files, RG 313, NA.

port of all ships of the Fleet based in Hawaiian waters would have been many millions of dollars, but I came to believe that it would be money well spent if a high reenlistment rate could be maintained.

However, the Chief of Naval Operations did not change the home ports of the ships of the Fleet to Hawaii. He passed on to the CINCUS a recommendation, by the Chief of the Bureau of Yards and Docks (Ben Moreell) to the Secretary of the Navy, to bar the families of Fleet personnel from the Hawaiian area, and asked for comment thereon. My reply was:

> The loss of morale to the Fleet which would result from barring the families of its officers or men from the Hawaiian Area, with the United States at peace, amidst constant reiteration by its principal officers of a desire to remain at peace, would be considerable, and the Commander-in-Chief recommends strongly against any such step at this time.[23]

Army War Plans Opinion

I did not learn until recently that the War Plans Division of the War Department General Staff opposed the retention of the U.S. Fleet in Hawaiian waters during the May-June period of 1940. This is set forth in the official Army history of World War II, as follows:

> The U.S. Fleet, which had moved to Hawaii in April 1940 to conduct its yearly exercises, received orders to remain at Pearl Harbor instead of returning to the west coast, as it normally did. On 27 May, in answer to a question from Admiral James O. Richardson, the fleet commander, Admiral Stark stated that the fleet would continue there until further notice, with the purpose of dissuading the Japanese Government from moving southward to take advantage of the defeat of the Netherlands and the desperate situation of France and Great Britain. The specific move that seemed imminent, as the battle of France drew to its disasterous end, was the occupation of French Indo-China.
>
> The War Department staff believed that a show of strength in the Pacific might be taken by the Japanese Government as an occasion to open hostilities. On this ground the Army planners strongly objected to leaving the Pacific Fleet at Pearl Harbor. Though it might perhaps strengthen the hand of men in the Japanese Government who favored a long-range policy of avoiding conflict with the United States, the measure was not strong enough to bring

---

[23] CINCUS, serial 01901 of 9 Dec. 1940, letter to CNO in reply to CNO, serial 052930 of 16 Nov. 1940, letter to CINCUS, CNOCF, NHD.

about—it was of course not meant to bring about—a showdown decision on long-range Japanese policy. Its effect on short-range policy was to give the Japanese Government the option of ignoring the implied challenge or of accepting it on the most favorable terms. The Army planners believed that the United States should either withdraw the fleet from Pearl Harbor or prepare seriously for hostilities, consciously deciding "to maintain a strong position in the Pacific," and "in order to do so, to avoid any commitment elsewhere, the development of which might require the weakening of that position." The retention of the fleet in the Pacific might cause Japanese leaders to review and revise their plans, but it would act as a deterrent "only so long as other manifestations of government policy do not let it appear that the location of the fleet is only a bluff." [24]

In my discussions in Washington, both within the Navy Department and within the White House, it was constantly asserted that the presence of the Fleet in Hawaiian waters was exerting a restraining influence on the Japanese. Since I did not then have access to the cryptographic decodes of Japanese despatches of that period and I do not have any such information now, it is of course true that the statement might have had a factual basis, as ascertained from a reading of Japanese diplomatic traffic being decoded. But, it has always seemed odd to me that such an affirmative statement has not been made in the intervening years by some Japanese military officer occupying an important position in the Japanese governmental structure during that period.

There is the statement, of course, by our Ambassador to Japan, Joseph C. Grew, that the Japanese Foreign Minister in June 1940, had said to him ". . . that the continued stay of our Fleet in those waters (Hawaiian) constitutes an implied suspicion of the intentions of Japan vis-a-vis the Netherlands East Indies and the South Seas. . . ." Ambassador Grew added his own interpretation of this statement; "The emphasis which the Minister placed upon this matter is an indication of the important effect on Japanese consciousness of the stay of our naval forces in Hawaii." [25]

It should be remembered that Ambassador Grew was not listening to the voice of the military clique running the Japanese Government. Grew was listening to the voice of a Japanese foreign minister, who was only very partially informed of what the dominant clique was planning and

[24] Matloff and Snell, *Strategic Planning for Coalition Warfare*, pp. 15-16.

[25] *Pearl Harbor Hearings*, Part 2, pp. 602-603.

doing, and why they were planning and doing it. As Mr. Grew himself said, ". . . I do not think the Japanese military people or naval people were taking any civilian into their confidence. The Foreign Office was always looked on askance by the Japanese military. . . ." [26]

That there had been an immediate Japanese reaction to the public announcement that the Fleet would prolong its current stay in Hawaiian waters, I did know. The Commandant 14th Naval District had in his Pearl Harbor headquarters a unit which took radio-direction bearings and analyzed the plain-language call-signs of the radio traffic of the Japanese Navy. This was not a cryptographic unit. On May 13, 1940, this unit reported:

> INFORMATION INDICATES ON 10 MAY FOURTH FLEET ORDERED TO MANDATED ISLANDS AND TO PROCEED TO OR BASE IN VICINITY PALAU THIS FORCE JUST RETURNED TO JAPAN FROM MANDATED ISLANDS AREA AFTER COVERING OUR FLEET PROBLEM PERIOD COMBINED FLEET RETURNED TO BASES AT SAME TIME AND ARE NOW LOCATED FIRST FLEET YOKOSUKA SECOND FLEET SASEBO

Washington reacted to this despatch immediately and directed:

> SEND LATEST INFORMATION COMPOSITION FOURTH FLEET X DEPT IS PARTICULARLY INTERESTED IN LEARNING OF ORANGE INTENTIONS OR THREATS AGAINST DUTCH EAST INDIES X REPORT ALL MOVEMENTS OF ORANGE FORCES BY DISPATCH X

Nowhere, in any of my letters or despatches of that period (now available), can I find any statement by me that the Fleet would have had greater security if at West Coast bases rather than in Hawaiian waters.

Yet, it was almost axiomatic in the 1940 state of the art of naval warfare that, as the distance between two naval forces increased, the opportunity of attack lessened and, because of fuel considerations, the difficulties of an attack increased. So, if I had been asked the question, in 1940, I am sure that I would have stated as a belief that the West Coast bases offered greater security than the Hawaiian area—but in no way, absolute security. In fact, in my Pearl Harbor testimony, I stated that the Japanese ". . . would quite likely have been able to deliver the same attack on Puget Sound." [27]

---

[26] *Ibid.*, p. 601.

[27] *Ibid.*, Part 1, p. 300.

I was not looking for a secure place to hide the Fleet. I wanted the Fleet to be positioned where it would have the higher state of readiness for its war missions.

There is not much more for me to add to this discussion. On July 2, 1940, I lunched with Clarence E. Gauss (Consul General at Shanghai and later our Ambassador to China) and Bloch. Gauss, having just come from Washington, opined that, "FDR and Hornbeck are handling the Far Eastern Policy and the disposition of the Fleet." My own later visits to Washington convinced me there was much truth in that statement. Certainly, the Navy wasn't determining where the Fleet would be prepared for war.

Basing the Fleet at Pearl Harbor in May of 1940 was undertaken under a completely false premise, in my opinion. The false premise was that the Fleet so positioned would exercise a restraining influence on the actions of Japan.

Since the same situation may, in the history of our country, arise again, I want to make the point crystal clear. If I am a small man, and after an unfriendly argument my big-man opponent takes a threatening position in regard to me, I may be restrained thereafter in what I say or do. If however, the man with whom I have had my unfriendly argument is smaller than I am and known to be less capable in the manly art of fisticuffs than I, then his moving in close may well be welcomed by me as an opportunity to settle the matter by a quick punch to his jaw.

In 1940, the policy making branch of the Government in foreign affairs —the President and the Secretary of State—thought that stationing the Fleet in Hawaii would restrain the Japanese. They did not ask their senior military advisers whether it would accomplish such an end. They imposed their decision upon them.

And yet, the advice of their military leaders was more likely to accurately reflect the true results. Japan had a military government. Would moving a Fleet that was undermanned, unprepared for war, and without a Fleet Train closer to where the Japanese could get at it, be a move calculated to impress the Japanese military government? That part of the United States Fleet in the Pacific, in its state of unpreparedness and in a peace posture, was the small man vis-a-vis the Japanese Fleet. This was true because the Japanese Fleet was superior to the Pacific contingent of the

U.S. Fleet in all categories, except possibly battleships, and was in a war posture as a result of its continuing war operations against China. This superiority continued right up to the time of the attack on Pearl Harbor, by which time the Japanese Fleet was markedly superior to that part of the U.S. Fleet in the Eastern Pacific (the U.S. Pacific Fleet), especially in aircraft carriers.

As I have indicated in an earlier chapter, I believe the decision of the President to send the Hawaiian Detachment to base at Pearl Harbor was a faulty decision, but a natural preliminary to the same faulty reasoning that led to moving the whole Fleet to Hawaii.

The leaders of every nation, in their dealing with other nations whose objectives are at cross-purposes with their own nation's, must give weighty consideration to the elements of military strength of the other nations.

It seemed to me that President Roosevelt and Secretary Hull evaluated the Japanese leaders in terms of themselves. Military moves, which were valueless from the hard realities of war and just window dressing, were assigned great weight. The President and Mr. Hull never seemed to take it into consideration that Japan was being led by military men, who would evaluate military moves largely on a military basis.

As the Army planners wrote, the location of the Fleet in Hawaiian waters would act as a deterrent to the Japanese only so long as its positioning did not appear to the Japanese as solely a bluff.

Chapter XVI

Security of the Fleet

As I have stated in the previous chapter, the security of the Fleet could not be as great operating from the ports and anchorages in the Hawaiian area, as it could be operating from the major West Coast naval bases.

This is not to say that a Fleet exists only to operate under secure conditions. It exists to operate where necessary. But, when the Fleet ceases its seagoing operations (over, on, and under the sea) and returns to base, the defense of the base should be such that the ships and aircraft may be maintained and logistically supported, and the personnel rested, all under reasonable conditions of security.

When the Fleet is at sea, it has a considerable amount of built-in security, gained from its movement, its disposition, and the interlocking protection provided by the various types of ships, aircraft, weapons, and equipment.

When the Fleet is berthed in port, it loses this advantage of movement, as well as its closely interwoven protective capabilities, since the ships' berthing basically must conform to the natural configuration of the port.

In the Hawaiian area, from May 1940 thru January 1941, the Fleet operated either from the open roadstead at Lahaina, or from the base at Pearl Harbor.

The Lahaina open roadstead offered no protection to the Fleet to augment its own protective resources, except that small protection provided by the natural arrangement of the surrounding islands. There were no logistic support facilities of any kind at Lahaina.

The Pearl Harbor Base was landlocked, and thus there was considerable natural security to the Fleet berthed therein, from both surface-ship and submarine torpedo attacks. However, if the Pearl Harbor Base was to

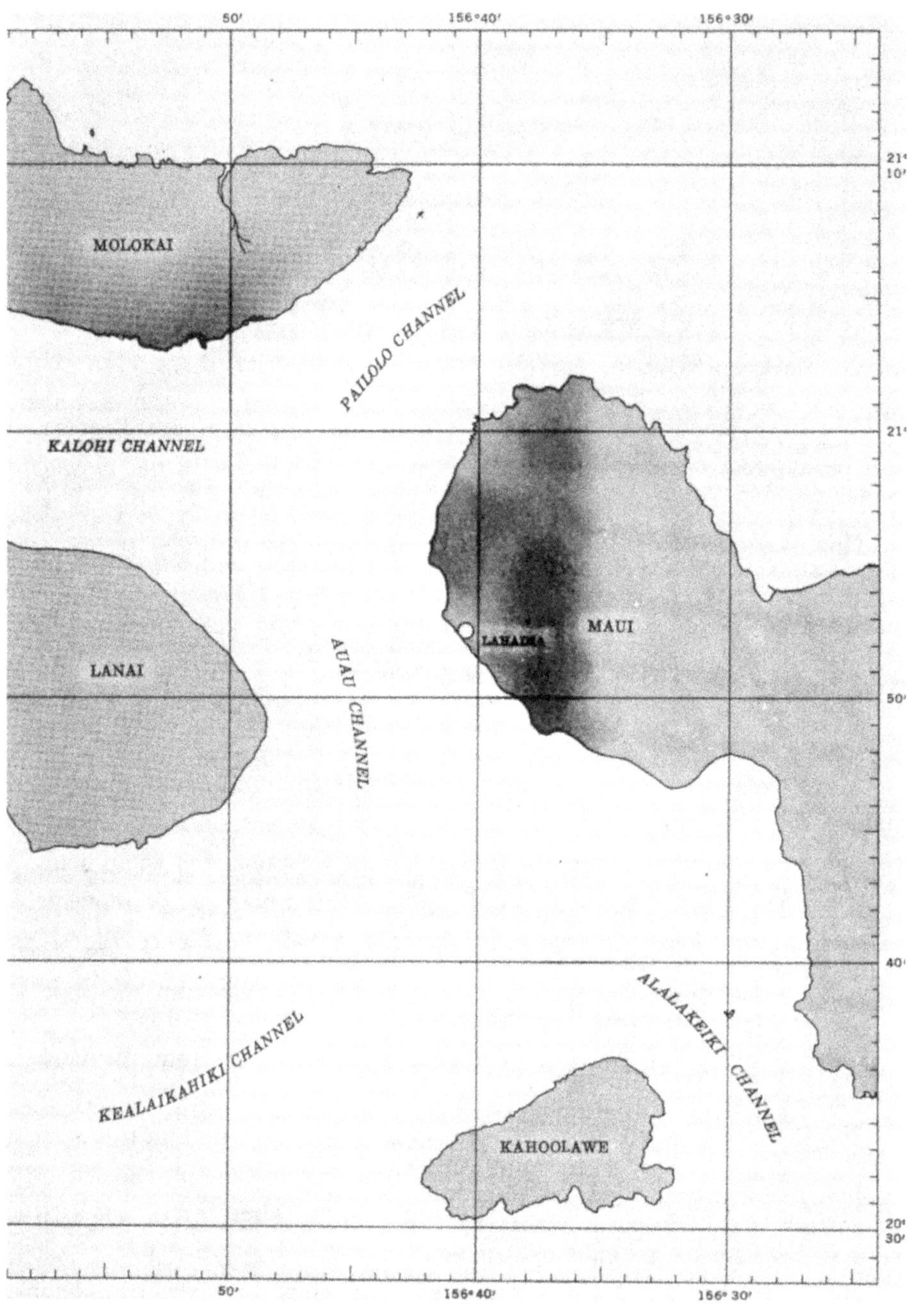

Lahaina Anchorage Area.

provide really adequate security to the Fleet, it needed to receive some man-made augmentation in these aspects of its security, and completely man-made security against air attacks. The logistic support facilities of the Pearl Harbor Base were in the process of moving from a Secondary Naval Base standard to a Primary Naval Base standard.

I will discuss several of the matters relating to the security of the Fleet which were particularly the direct responsibility of the Commander-in-Chief of the Fleet.

Under a sound assignment of tasks—I believe, still in effect today (1956) —the Army, in 1940, was responsible for the ". . . defense of all permanent naval bases"[1] and the ". . . defense against aerial attack of all military and naval facilities ashore within a harbor area."[2] The controlling document, *Joint Action of the Army and Navy,* which, by agreement between the Secretaries of the War and Navy Departments, assigned tasks to the Army and Navy, specifically provided that ". . . coastal frontier defense [must] be so effectively conducted as to remove any anxiety of the Fleet in regard to the security of its bases."[3] There was no inter-Service dispute about this point. On February 7, 1941, General Marshall wrote to Lieutenant General Short in Hawaii, ". . . we are keeping clearly in mind that our first concern is to protect the Fleet."[4]

This is not to say that the whole chore of defense of naval bases belonged to the Army. Amongst the assignment of tasks to the Navy by *Joint Action of the Army and Navy* was one that the Navy ". . . would provide and operate a system of offshore scouting and patrol to give timely warning of an attack. . . ."[5]

During the time I was Commander-in-Chief, ship-borne aircraft could be counted upon to search out to about 150–250 miles and yet, retain a reasonable measure of fuel-supply safety for the aircraft. Our shore-based patrol aircraft were good for considerably longer distances, and a 700–800 mile radius was considered safely within their capabilities.

In 1940, all aircraft built for patrol and scouting were assigned to the

[1] *Joint Action of the Army and the Navy 1935* (as revised after 1935), Joint Board No. 350, serial 514 of Nov. 1935 (Washington, D.C.: GPO, 1936), p. 2.

[2] *Ibid.,* p. 49.

[3] *Ibid.,* p. 42a.

[4] *Pearl Harbor Hearings,* Part 32, p. 566.

[5] *Joint Action of the Army and the Navy 1935,* p. 15.

Fleet, and therefore, the responsibility for providing the naval "system of off-shore scouting and patrol to give timely warning of an attack" rested with the Fleet commander, even though the detailed task might be delegated by him to a subordinate shore-based commander.

During the early 1930's, the Fleet security problem receiving the most attention had been one of providing internal security to the individual ship. The Fleet was always open to the public in port on Sundays, which were "general visiting days." The Communist Party was active at the Fleet bases. As the after-play of these visiting hours, it was a regular procedure to root out communist literature and "throw sheets" in crew's wash rooms, on the tops of lockers, and along the overhead where they were found tucked into mess tables and mess benches.

Then, as the years moved along, the development of the midget submarines and the two-man torpedoes directed attention towards the danger of surprise underwater attack on ships at Fleet bases. And, the very marked development of our own Fleet aviation and its expanding use in tactical exercises and Fleet Problems, drew everyone's attention to the danger of surprise air attacks on ships at Fleet bases.

It had been the practice in the Fleet to have a general Fleet security order covering both internal and external security measures to be taken (1) at sea and (2) at base and then, as the Fleet moved from base to base, to tighten up or relax the basic instructions, as was believed appropriate to the particular operating area or base. On August 26, 1939, my predecessor as Commander-in-Chief had ordered all ships to "maintain an alert internal security" and thus set the initial standard in the area of internal security for the World War II period.[6]

Soon after I took over, I issued a general letter to the Fleet covering such security matters as visitors on board ship, safeguarding of confidential and secret matter, observation of shore boats and small craft, scrutiny of packages brought aboard ship, disclosure of classified matter, photographing of ships, reporting of movements of foreign ships, providing special protection for powder magazines, requiring armed personnel on watch, and similar measures. Special internal security measures were prescribed also

[6] CINCUS, serial 0025-1306 of Aug. 1939, letter to Fleet; CINCUS Fleet Letter 3L-40, serial 555 of 10 Feb. 1940, letter to Fleet, WWIICF, NHD, p. 1. The letter listed eight letters issued by the previous CINCUS's on the subjct of security, during 1934-1939.

in a desire to prevent sabotage and subversive activities.

All these measures were based on the assumption set forth in the general letter to the Fleet that ". . . positive steps may be taken by a skillful and determined enemy, foreign or anti-government, to damage ships of the Fleet, singly or in groups."[7]

With the Fleet at sea, external security measures to safeguard against surprise attacks by aircraft, submarines, and surface craft had to be carried out, and when in water under 200 fathoms, mines had to be guarded against. In 1940 (in the pre-radar era), it was considered that at sundown the air attack danger diminished considerably, and the possibility of surprise torpedo attack from destroyer or surfaced submarine increased considerably. Accordingly, at sundown, ships greatly increased their watertight integrity, set additional watches at the torpedo defense batteries, and increased their lookouts.

Nowadays, it is easy to make light of the surface-ship menace, but in the United States Navy, during World War II, of the 23 large combatant ships (i.e., battleships, aircraft carriers, heavy cruisers, light cruisers, and "jeep" carriers) lost thru enemy acton, 10 of our ships were sunk by enemy aircraft, 10 were sunk thru surface-ship gun or surface-ship torpedo fire, and 3 were sunk by torpedoes from submarines.

So, during the 1939–1941 period, external security from each of these weapons received marked attention.

Offshore Scouting and Patrol

I do not know for how many years the air patrol around the Hawaiian Islands had been provided as a training measure in external security during Fleet concentrations there, but I am sure that the orders directing and providing for it went back far prior to 1938.[8] The patrol normally was discontinued after the Fleet critique, but prior to the breaking up of the Fleet

[7] CINCUS Fleet Letter 3L-40, serial 555 of 10 Feb. 1940, letter to Fleet, WWIICF, NHD; CINCUS Fleet Letter 3L-40 (revised), serial 2676 of 24 Aug. 1940, letter to Fleet, WWIICF, NHD, p. 1; CINCUS Fleet Letter 19L-40, serial 3277 of 26 Oct. 1940, letter to Fleet, WWIICF, NHD; CINCUS serial 2614 of 20 Aug. 1940, letter to Fleet, box 70, CINCUS Files, RG 313, NA.

[8] CINCUS, 620 of 5 Feb. 1938, letter; "Operation Plan 1-38," COMBASEFOR, serial 1411 of 1 Mar. 1938, microfilm NRS No. 1M, NHD.

concentration and the return of the various ships and aircraft to their normal peacetime bases. This would have occurred in the spring of 1940, except for the ambiguous order retaining the Fleet in Hawaiian waters "for a short period," and the developments of World War II.

My story in regard to security of the Fleet in Hawaiian waters really starts on January 12, 1940, when I wrote officially to the CNO and said, "Unless it is contrary to the wishes of the Navy Department, the Commander-in-Chief will, during the stay of the Fleet at Lahaina and Pearl Harbor, institute security measures similar in scope to those taken during Fleet Problem XIX [held in 1938]." [9]

The CNO replied, "The proposal of the Commander-in-Chief regarding the security measures to be taken during the stay of the Fleet at Lahaina and Pearl Harbor is quite satisfactory to the Navy Department." [10]

In early March 1940, before the Fleet sailed for the Hawaiian Islands and its eventual retention there, and in order to provide for training exercises to fulfill the Navy's responsibilities under *Joint Action of the Army and Navy,* I directed the Commander Base Force (Rear Admiral W. L. Calhoun, USN), to prepare and execute plans for security of the U.S. Fleet while berthed in the general Pearl Harbor area. He was to work in cooperation with the Commandant 14th Naval District, who also had certain naval responsibilities for security of the Fleet, in accordance with *Joint Action of the Army and Navy.*

The basic assumption of my directive to Calhoun was, "That submarines, air, and/or surface vessels, including small craft and merchant vessels, of a determined and resourceful foreign power, may execute an attack on ships of the United States Fleet while in anchorages outside Pearl Harbor and off Honolulu." [11] 1,600 copies of the resulting order by Calhoun were distributed to the Fleet.

The important part of Calhoun's order, as it relates to this discussion, is that it required a seven-day-a-week daylight-to-dark naval air patrol of the outer sea area around the Hawaiian Islands. Specifically, it was an

[9] CINCUS, serial 068 of 12 Jan. 1940, letter to CNO, box 91, CINCUS Files, RG 313, NA.

[10] CNO, serial 03416 of 1 Feb. 1940, letter to CINCUS, CNOCF, NHD.

[11] "Operation Order No. 2-40 (revised)," U.S. Fleet, serial 073 of 15 Jan. 1940, Plan File, NHD; "General Order No. 118," in *Navy Department General Orders: Series of 1935* (Washington, D.C.: GPO, 1940); "Operation Plan No. 2-40," COMBASEFOR, serial 0476 of 21 Mar. 1940, box 32, CINCUS Files, RG 313, NA.

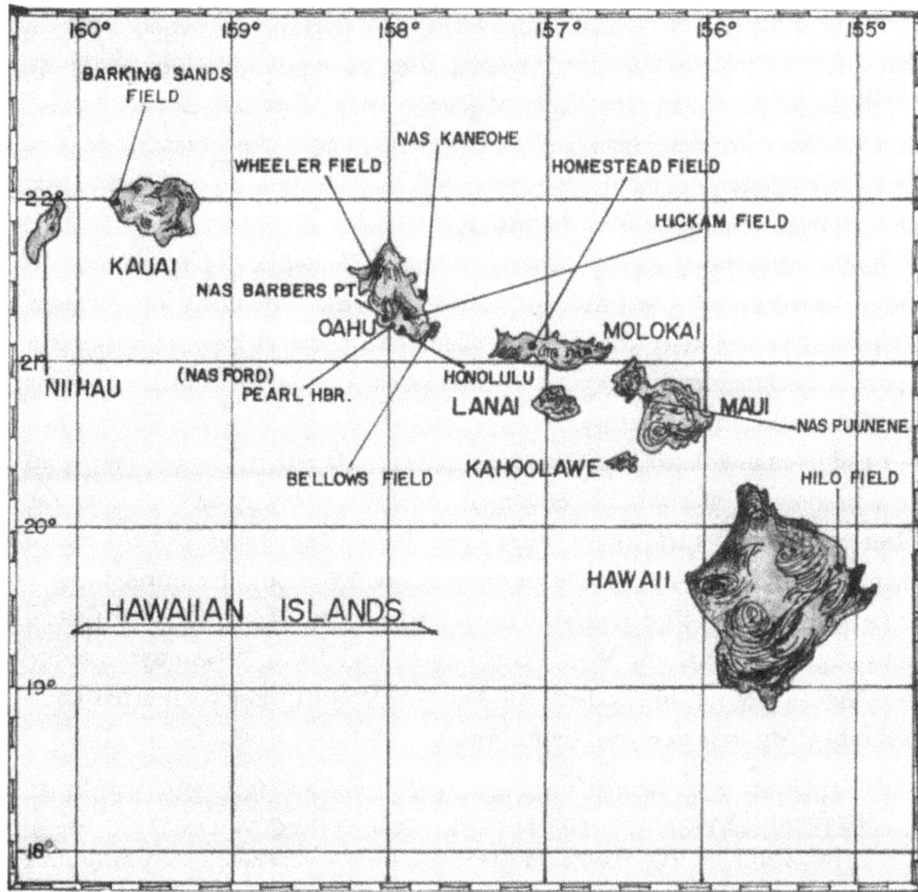

area bounded by a circle of 180 miles radius with its center at Ahua Point, close by the eastern entrance to Pearl Harbor Channel. Commander Patrol Wing Two—the local commander of naval patrol aircraft—was directed to use twelve aircraft daily for this search. When the Fleet was in the Lahaina area, the outer naval air patrol was to be centered on Lahaina, Maui, and flown by ship-based seaplanes.

When questioned, the local base commander at Pearl (Commandant 14th Naval District) said he believed the Commander Base Force Operation Plans were "sufficient for Fleet security purposes under present conditions." [12]

[12] COM14, serial 065 of 14 Feb. 1940, letter to COMBASEFOR, box 22, CINCUS Files RG 313, NA. This letter comments on COMBASEFOR Operation Plans 1-40, 2-40, and 3-40. These plans were slightly revised and reissued as a result of comments received.

These security orders had been carried out during the period between the arrival of the Fleet in the Hawaiian area on April 10, 1940 and June 17, 1940. On this date, the Chief of Staff of the Army sent out an "alert" to the Army in the Hawaiian Department. This "alert" lasted, in one form or another, for about six weeks, and as it created quite a stir at the time is worth recording and discussing.

Just a week prior to this "alert," while at Lahaina, I had listened to the re-broadcast of the President's address at the University of Virginia. I recorded in my diary that the President had come as near to making a personal declaration of war on the Axis powers as a President could. This gave me cause for concern.

I had been unable to find out why the Fleet was retained in the Hawaiian area or how long it would remain. At that time, my guess was that the Fleet would not return to the West Coast before September 1940. I feared that the President would order an overt act which would bring on war.

On June 13, 1940, I had sent a despatch to the Chief of Naval Operations suggesting that my War Plans Officer and I visit Washington, since the same suggestion in my letter of May 1, 1940 had not been acted upon favorably. My despatch read as follows:

> BELIEVE CHANGED WORLD CONDITIONS DEMAND REORIENTATION NATIONAL AND NAVAL POLICY IN CONSONANCE WITH OUR ABILITY TO SUPPORT THEM. IF MY ABSENCE FROM FLEET NOT INCOMPATIBLE WITH PRESENT PURPOSES BELIEVE IT WOULD BE CONDUCIVE TO MUTUAL UNDERSTANDING AND POSSIBLY SERVE TO SUPPORT YOUR REPRESENTATIONS IF I WERE ORDERED TO WASHINGTON VIA AIR. CAN START 18 JUNE ACCOMPANIED BY MURPHY.

On June 14, 1940, while operating off the Lahaina roadstead, I received orders authorizing the two of us to proceed to Washington on or about June 18 via Pan American Airways. On June 17, 1940, I shifted my flag to the *USS Colorado,* and started in to Pearl Harbor to take the plane to Washington when radio news arrived that France had capitulated. Soon thereafter, the CNO informed me that my trip to Washington was held in abeyance. The despatch said:

> INTERNATIONAL SITUATION SO SERIOUS THAT REDISTRIBUTION US FLEET BETWEEN ATLANTIC AND PACIFIC WILL BE MADE VERY

SOON I HAVE THEREFORE REQUESTED BUNAV TO HOLD YOUR ORDERS TO WASHINGTON IN ABEYANCE

I returned to my regular flagship.

On June 18, 1940, while in the Lahaina area, I received news by special seaplane mail of the Army "alert" of the Hawaiian Department. The June 17 despatch from the Chief of Staff of the Army to the Commander Hawaiian Department, Lieutenant General Charles D. Herron, USA, started off with these invigorating words:

IMMEDIATELY ALERT COMPLETE DEFENSIVE ORGANIZATION TO DEAL WITH TRANS PACIFIC RAID. . . .[13]

After directing the necessary initial steps in his own command, Lieutenant General Herron immediately took this despatch to show to his opposite naval number in the local coastal defense organization, Rear Admiral C. C. Bloch, Commandant 14th Naval District. In order to discuss further the action that should be taken, Bloch visited Vice Admiral Adolphus Andrews, USN, in his flagship. Andrews was the "Senior Officer Present" of the Fleet units at that moment in Pearl Harbor.

The latter promptly directed the Commander Base Force, Rear Admiral Calhoun, to initiate an inner naval air patrol from Pearl Harbor. The outer naval air reconnaissance currently was being flown from the Lahaina, Maui, roadstead area from which the Fleet was operating. Andrews, by special seaplane letter on the next day, June 18, 1940, outlined the information he had received from Bloch and requested my decision as to whether another naval air patrol should be established from Pearl to cover the Western Sector (from north thru west to south) to a distance of 300 miles.

I sent a message to Bloch and asked him whether Herron's request for additional air patrol was part of an Army exercise or was based upon information from the War Department. At 0945 on the 19th, Bloch informed me that the request was based on a directive received from the War Department.[14]

I then directed that the distant naval air patrol be initiated, and wondered why Andrews had waited to get my decision, if it had been such

[13] War Department, 17 June 1940, despatch to Commander Hawaiian Department, as cited in *Pearl Harbor Hearings*, Part 1, p. 271.

[14] *Ibid.*, p. 271, Part 14, pp. 949-50.

an open-and-shut case. I also wondered why the Navy Department did not alert the Fleet and the 14th Naval District, as the Army had been alerted.

The whole Fleet was at sea and, I believed, with the long-range air patrols being flown, was reasonably secure from surprise air attack.

Three days passed without my receiving from the Navy Department any despatch relating to the Army "alert." Then, on June 20, 1940, the following despatch came in from Naval Operations:

> RELIABLE SOURCES PERSISTENTLY REPORT ANY MOVEMENT IN FORCE BY MAJOR FLEET UNITS TOWARD ATLANTIC WILL OCCASION EXTENSIVE SABOTAGE IN CANAL X ARMY THERE INFORMED AND IN ALERT STATUS X DESIRE YOU MAKE TEST ON OR ABOUT 24 JUNE BY HAVING MAJOR PORTION OF FLEET IN COMPANY PUT TO SEA WITHOUT PREVIOUS ANNOUNCEMENT BUT YOU ARRANGING FOR LEAK TO EFFECT THAT PROBABLE DESTINATION IS CANAL AND THIS NOT DENIED BY AUTHORITIES X PROCEED TOWARD CANAL FOR APPROXIMATELY TWO DAYS THEN RETURN HAWAIIAN PORTS X MAINTAIN RADIO SILENCE EXERCISING AT YOUR DISCRETION X ANTICIPATE ORDERING YOU TO WASHINGTON FOR CONFERENCE ON YOUR RETURN [15]

On June 21, 1940, I flew from Lahaina to Pearl, and conferred with Bloch and Herron. Herron told me he did not know whether the "alert" was a real one or a drill. He was taking action as though it were an honest alert.

I decided it was a drill, as it did not seem possible that the Navy Department and the War Department could be so far out of step with each other, or out of touch with each other, that a world-crisis situation, suggesting an alert to one Department, would not suggest the same to the other Department.

If it were a drill, I could not understand why the drill status was not made clear to General Herron.

On the next day, I could stand the uncertainty no longer, so I sent off a despatch to the Navy Department, which paraphrased said:

> WAR DEPARTMENT HAS DIRECTED COMMANDING GENERAL HAWAIIAN DEPARTMENT TO PLACE HIS FORCES ON ALERT

[15] CNO, 20 June 1940, despatch to CINCUS. Another paraphrase is cited in *Pearl Harbor Hearings*, Part 3, p. 1409.

AGAINST RAID BY HOSTILE TRANSPACIFIC FORCES. PATROL SQUADRONS OF NAVY ARE PARTICIPATING. ASSUME THAT THIS IS A DRILL SINCE NO INFORMATION HAS BEEN RECEIVED FROM THE NAVY DEPARTMENT.[16]

I should have added to this despatch a question as to whether the Department desired naval forces to be alerted on a war basis as well.

The reply received (as paraphrased) stated:

REQUEST YOU CONTINUE TO COOPERATE WITH ARMY IN REGARD TO THEIR DIRECTIVE CONCERNING ALERT X THIS DIRECTIVE WAS ISSUED AFTER CONSULTING WITH THE DEPARTMENTS OF STATE AND NAVY X REASON IS FOR A MEASURE OF PRECAUTION.[17]

This despatch was sent from the Navy Department about ten o'clock at night, and was received by me shortly after 5:00 p.m. Honolulu time on Saturday, June 22, 1940. If the State Department and the War Department had deemed that a measure of precaution was necessary, it seemed to me a "poor way to run a railroad" for the Navy Department not to deem that such a measure of precaution should apply to the Navy.

Since the Fleet was to be at sea, commencing Monday the 24th, and since Herron was already receiving orders from the War Department to "walk back the cat" on his "alert," I was reluctant to accept the CNO's statement that the alert had been for a "measure of precaution." In fact, I never did accept it as such.

As a result of what I considered a certain degree of fiasco in the handling of this matter in Washington, I wrote to Stark and said:

As a similar situation may again arise, I believe a remedy would be to insure that where possible, when joint action is involved, even in drills, that the Commanders of the Army and Navy be jointly informed, with definite information to me as to whether the alarm is real or simulated for purposes of training.[18]

But, on December 7, 1941, when an alerting message was sent to Hawaii, the CNO still did not follow this sound principle. Only one despatch was sent, and that by the Army. And, the Army despatch got off to a slow start and faltered along the way.

---

[16] CINCUS, 22 June 1940, despatch to CNO. Another paraphrase is cited in *Pearl Harbor Hearings*, Part 1, p. 312.

[17] *Ibid.*

[18] *Ibid.*, Part 14, p. 948.

When I was asked the question, at the Congressional Inquiry into the Pearl Harbor Attack, in regard to this "alert" on June 17, 1940, ". . . can you account for the fact that the Navy was not alerted and the Army was alerted?" I answered, "That passes my comprehension." It still does.[19]

I have only one other thing to add in regard to the Army's "alert" of June 17, 1940. When I visited Washington in early July 1940 and had lunch with General Marshall, I asked him about the matter, as some phases of the "alert" were still being maintained in Hawaii. He told me that it had been instituted as a training measure exercise. He said the reason that the Commander Hawaiian Department had not been informed that it was a drill was because he (Marshall) wanted to ensure that things were not simulated in Hawaii, and all preparations were carried out completely. I recorded this statement in my diary, and I told my War Plans Officer (Commander V. R. Murphy) of it.

When General Marshall testified at the Congressional Hearings on the Pearl Harbor Attack, he denied that this alert was an exercise and denied talking with me about it.[20] My memory of my conversation with him is still firm and definite. I think that Senator Ferguson, at this point in the hearings, missed an opportunity in his questioning of the general. He should have said, "When you sent your message to Herron, it was clear and definite, and produced the results you sought to attain. Why didn't you send the same kind of a message to Short?"

However, the "alert" added a bit of ammunition to previously-made arguments in regard to the state of readiness at Pearl Harbor for actual war-making, and did, therefore, serve a partial purpose. In connection therewith, the Commandant 14th Naval District reported to the Commander-in-Chief:

> The local defense forces have no destroyers attached and it is my opinion that there should be destroyers on hand for District patrol purposes to be used in case of actual or approaching hostilities, and that the District should not have to be forced to wait until destroyers could be sent from some distant place to perform duties which will be more necessary at the beginning of hostilities than at any other time.

---

[19] *Ibid.*, Part 1, p. 313.
[20] *Ibid.*, Part 3, p. 1055.

• • •

There appears to be no answer to the fact that Army planes composing the inshore patrol are untrained in submarine detection, submarine bombing and the identification of Naval vessels.

C. C. Bloch.[21]

Cruise Towards Panama

The June cruise of the Fleet towards Panama, referred to above, had its humorous aspects. Actually, only 5 battleships, 7 cruisers, and 17 destroyers participated. We sailed on June 24, 1940 which was the day the Germans granted the request of the French for an armistice.

On the assumption that the Japanese regularly analyzed the Fleet's radio traffic, as we did theirs, it seemed logical to us that, if the Fleet were to be suddenly ordered to Panama, there would be a vastly increased amount of radio traffic between the Fleet and the local naval commander at the Panama Canal in connection with this movement, with most messages of very high priority.

Accordingly, in order to contribute toward encouraging the Japanese to believe the Fleet actually had sailed for Panama, a lot of dummy radio traffic from the Fleet and force flagships was sent to the Commandant 15th Naval District at Panama via Navy Radio, Pearl Harbor. My Fleet Communications Officer and Fleet Intelligence Officer started this dummy traffic flowing on the 19th, right after the initial movement order came in from the Department. The Commandant 15th Naval District kept dummy answers rolling back, and the traffic was worked up to a crescendo late on the 23rd. After sailing, radio silence was maintained by the Fleet.

I don't know whether this traffic helped fool the Japanese, but it fooled at least one office of our Navy Department, although its reaction was slow. On the 27th, in the midst of the Fleet radio silence, OPNAV requested that I break radio silence and inform that office of the reason for the heavy dummy radio traffic to Panama.

My Flag Secretary (Commander George C. Dyer) had tipped-off a newsman just before sailing that Panama might be our destination, and so the story received distribution. By listening to news broadcasts, I learned that Stark had told newsmen they would have to ask Sumner Welles about

[21] COM14, serial 269 of 1 July 1940, letter to CINCUS, microfilm NRS No. 1M, NHD.

the Fleet movement, and Secretary Hull was reported to have said he had no official information. As a further indication that some of the offices of the Navy Department were not in step with the CNO, I listened to a news broadcast in which it was stated the Navy Press Officer had said the Fleet was not leaving the Hawaiian area.

The Japanese Consul at Honolulu reported to Tokyo about the seaward movement of the task force. The radio call-sign traffic analysis group at Pearl Harbor reported that Tokyo had issued long orders to the main Japanese Fleet, Japanese Naval Air Force, and the China Coast Fleet. The Japanese Second Fleet was reported at Saipan, and a carrier and other ships were reported at Palau practicing landing exercises.

On June 27, the CNO ordered us to remain at sea until Saturday, June 29. On the 28th, the following despatch was received:

NH 77042

Captain Elwin F. Cutts, Commanding Officer, USS Pennsylvania, *welcomes* Neptunus Rex *on board his command on crossing the Equator during the cruise towards Panama in May 1940. Left to right, Captain Bernhard H. Bieri, Captain Sherwoode A. Taffinder, Admiral Richardson, Captain Cutts,* Neptunus Rex, *unidentified seaman, and Commander John L. McCrea, Executive Officer of the* Pennsylvania.

IF YOU CAN CONTINUE REASONABLE DOUBTS AS TO FLEET WHEREABOUTS, REMAIN AT SEA UNTIL SUNDAY MORNING 30 JUNE, OTHERWISE RETURN PORT AT DISCRETION.

The Fleet arrived back at Lahaina Roads at 0930 on Sunday, and my Flag Secretary informed the same newsman as before that the Fleet was back in Hawaiian waters. There was no sabotage at the Panama Canal.

In view of the length of time it would have taken the Fleet to reach Panama—about eighteen days—the test was hardly a realistic one, since we were at sea only six days. It seems to me that in order for saboteurs in Panama to get the information that the Fleet was headed towards Panama and then to get organized to do a realistic sabotage job of the Panama Canal, it would have taken much longer than the six days allowed by Washington. But, they were happy, as the final message from the Department on this operation read as follows:

THIS MESSAGE CONSISTS OF ONLY TWO WORDS X WELL DONE X AND THEREFORE TAKES CONSIDERABLE PADDING.

Naval-Air Long-Range Reconnaissance

I have felt that the basic factors governing the maintenance of an adequate naval-air long-range patrol reconnaissance from Pearl Harbor have never been adequately set forth to the younger generation of naval officers, even for those who make the effort to read the various investigations into the Pearl Harbor Attack. So, I intend to set forth a few facts and make a few personal comments.

Before detailing the specifics of the Hawaiian area naval-air long-range reconnaissance, it seems desirable to state the overall responsibility of the Commander-in-Chief, United States Fleet, in 1940 and early 1941, for naval-air long-range reconnaissance. During my tenancy as CINCUS, responsibility for both the Atlantic and Eastern Pacific Ocean areas was joined, and all patrol plane squadrons in the Navy were assigned to either the U.S. Fleet or the U.S. Asiatic Fleet.

Some idea of the extent of the need for naval patrol planes for long-range air reconnaissance from an overall hemispheric-defense-plan basis may be gleaned from the chart reproduced on the next page.

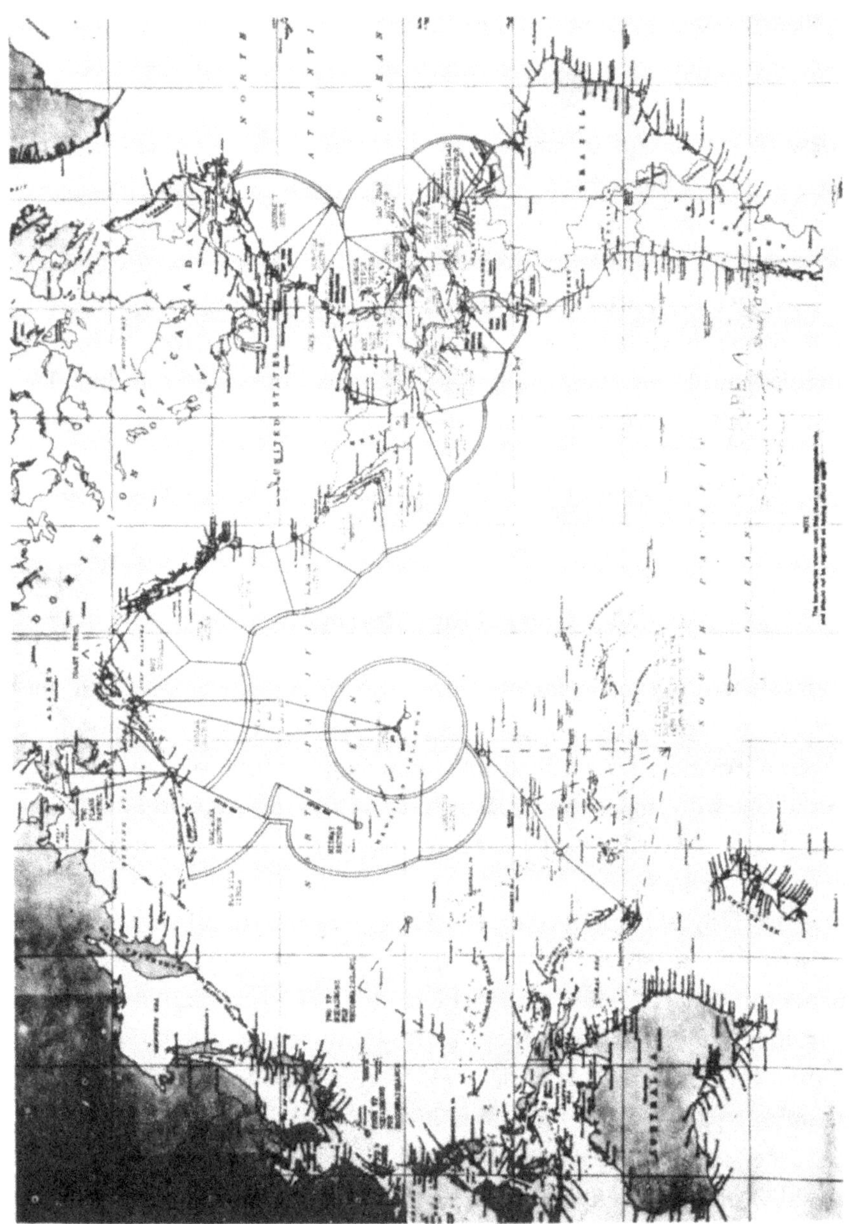

Captain Bellinger's plan for long-range air reconnaissance in the Atlantic and Pacific Ocean areas.

Marked on the chart area of this plate are the necessary patrol areas, as visualized in June of 1940 by the patrol plane type commander, Commander Aircraft, Scouting Force, U.S. Fleet (Rear Admiral A. L. Bristol, USN).[22] By and large, his vision of the need, and the actual requirements under war conditions were not too far apart. For, nearly all the sea areas shown on this chart as needing coverage by daily patrol plane search, were covered by such search after December 7, 1941 and as soon as the necessary patrol plane resources became available to the Navy.

In any consideration of the naval-air long-range reconnaissance from Hawaii during 1940 or 1941 there are two other things which should be kept in mind; firstly, that the naval aeronautical organization was strained to the utmost by its expansion program of planes and pilots, which required a tremendous pilot training program and secondly, that the pilot training process was a lengthy one. Building a new patrol plane took not less than six months after production was in full swing, but developing a first pilot of a patrol plane took sixteen to twenty-four months, depending on when the aviator was first ordered into patrol planes and the "J" factor for the individual pilot.[23]

My predecessor as CINCUS had informed the Chief of Naval Operations that "a general increase in Fleet patrol plane strength is considered to be urgently necessary" and recommended emergency procurement for an immediate increase of strength from 209 to 444 of operating patrol aircraft for the Fleet.[24] In response to this letter, the CNO initiated the emergency procurement of 200 patrol planes of a modified PBY-4-type, deliveries to begin during April 1940.[25]

As soon as this welcome news was received, CINCUS became vitally concerned with the future assignment of these new patrol plane squadrons, as well as with the steps to be taken to provide and train the necessary flight and ground personnel in time to have them ready to man the new

---

[22] COMAIRSCOFOR, serial 0454 of 8 June 1940, letter to CNO, box 89, CINCUS Files, RG 313, NA; CINCUS, serial 01276 of 27 July 1940, letter to CNO, box 78, CINCUS Files, RG 313, NA. The subject of this letter is patrol plane requirements to patrol sea approaches of the continental United States and its principal outlying possessions, including general requirements of bases, aircraft, personnel, and tenders to implement plans.

[23] CINCUS, "Annual Report," 1939, p. 27.

[24] CINCUS, serial 01352 of 19 Sept. 1939, letter to CNO.

[25] CNO, serial 6224 of 10 Oct. 1939, letter to CINCUS, CNOCF, NHD.

planes.[26] It was these planes, which were being received and worked up into new squadrons, which kept the whole patrol plane organization (AIRSCOFOR and AIRPATFOR) in a constant state of transition during the last six months of the calendar year 1940, and early 1941.

A policy had been established before I took over as CINCUS of ordering pilots to patrol plane duty only after they had acquired approximately 450 hours total flight time. 700 hours of flight time was required before qualification as first pilot of a patrol plane. 900 hours flight experience was required prior to qualification as a patrol plane commander.[27] These high pre-World War II standards were subject to several modifications during the "Emergency Period," and, by September 1940, graduates of Pensacola with 225 hours of flight time were being sent directly to patrol planes. Minimum flight time for patrol plane commanders was reduced to 600 hours, and for first pilots to 400 hours.[28]

The large elementary patrol plane pilot training program by Fleet-assigned patrol aircraft commands was in constant conflict with the overall operational and security requirements of the Fleet.

Soon after the large-scale, daily long-range reconnaissance flights were inaugurated in the Atlantic, the Type Commander of patrol aircraft had insisted that patrol planes of the units engaged in large-scale patrol activities, either in connection with neutrality duties or security patrols, should conduct, in addition, such gunnery training as would continue to maintain the individual proficiency of the personnel in the use of the bombsight and free machine guns.[29] This was a large order, and it was issued despite the approval of CNO given to an earlier recommendation that the primary mission of the patrol-type aircraft be changed from one of battle efficiency to that of ". . . training new personnel and that gunnery training requirements be reduced as required during this period. . . ."[30] As

[26] CINCUS, serial 01457 of 17 Oct. 1939, letter to COMAIRSCOFOR, box 110, CINCUS Files, RG 313, NA; CINCUS, serial 01533 of 26 Oct. 1939, letter to CNO; CNO, serial 6896 of 17 Nov. 1939, letter to CINCUS.

[27] COMAIRSCOFOR (A. B. Cook), serial 0637 of 30 Sept. 1939, letter; COMAIRSCOFOR, serial 0656 of 12 Oct. 1939, letter.

[28] COMAIRSCOFOR Letter 15L-40, 27 Sept. 1940, letter to AIRSCOFOR.

[29] COMAIRSCOFOR, serial 0781 of 28 Nov. 1939, letter to CINCUS, box 38, CINCUS Files, RG 313, NA.

[30] CNO, serial 6896 of 17 Nov. 1939, letter to CINCUS, CNOCF, NHD, p. 4.

time went on, the pressure from the Bureau of Aeronautics and from the CNO to produce more rapid results in the training field increased.

Eight months after insisting that gunnery training must go forward, COMAIRSCOFOR had worked around to a complete reversal and was advising his subordinates that "COMAIRSCOFOR desires to emphasize the importance of noninterference with the primary mission (flight training and qualification)," and the Commander Patrol Aircraft, in his Annual Report for the year ending June 30, 1940, reported "The state of training of patrol aircraft has steadily lowered during the last year" and "There has been no improvement in patrol aircraft gunnery and bombing training, and there has been a lessening in efficiency in navigation, scouting, and radio training." [31]

The point I wish to make is that it was against this pressure from the CNO and the Bureau of Aeronautics, both discouraging any diversion of effort from flight training, that the security patrols by long-range patrol planes were carried out from Pearl Harbor by the orders of the Commander-in-Chief. CNO continued to accentuate the overriding nature of the flight training requirements and to deprecate war-training tasks involving security of the Fleet and the fighting efficiency of the aircraft in Fleet air units. As late as August 1940, the CNO stated, ". . . in the expanded flight training program first priority is to be given to training. . . ." The pious hope was then expressed that this could be done ". . . without effecting to any appreciable degree the fighting efficiency of the Fleet." [32]

The security patrols required a large increase of hours in the air for the patrol planes.

The patrol wing commanders were not loath to point out to their superiors the heavy aircraft maintenance loads which their subordinates constantly carried, and their superiors relayed the reports to me. Reports of the burdensome nature of my requirements for long-range patrol plane reconnaissance also reached me thru the staff aviator (Commander A. C. Davis). There also was a belief that this particular part of the air arm of the Fleet was carrying a much heavier burden than justified by the

[31] COMAIRSCOFOR, serial 0529 of 26 July 1940, letter to PATWINGS, box 39, CINCUS Files, RG 313, NA, p. 3.

[32] CNO, serial 07438 of 31 Aug. 1940, letter to COMBATFOR, CNOCF, NHD.

personnel resources available. A couple of letters will suffice to illustrate the point:

July 3, 1940

From: Commander Patrol Wing TWO
To: Commander Scouting Force

1. Patrol Wing TWO is carrying out a daily security patrol consisting of six planes each flying an average of 8.5 hours. This totals in excess of 1500 hours each month for the Wing and increases by over 50% the normal monthly flying time. It is believed that conditions will require the present patrol to be maintained indefinitely with the probability it may be increased. Commander Patrol Wing TWO is particularly concerned regarding the amount of engine time being accumulated together with the concomitant overhaul load.

A. W. FITCH[33]

---

14 December 1940

From: Commander Patrol Wings, U.S. Fleet
To: Commander-in-Chief, U.S. Fleet
Via: Commander Scouting Force

The first thirty-six PBY-5 airplanes will be delivered without leak-proof gasoline tanks and without armor protection. . . .leak-proofing and armor will be procured for these airplanes, to be installed by the squadrons. . . .

A. L. BRISTOL[34]

During my tenure as CINCUS, I always felt that the Hawaiian area was well down on the Navy Department's priority list for receipt of additional patrol squadrons. Priority was being given, in late 1939 throughout 1940, to assignment in the Atlantic areas, or to the sale of patrol planes to our future allies.[35] Since these assignments resulted from direct Presidential pressure, it can be understood why the Pacific areas did not begin to have their patrol plane needs fulfilled.

I continued to pressure the Department to fill the needs of the Pacific Ocean areas, but with a marked lack of success. The best I was able to

---

[33] COMPATWINGS (A. L. Bristol), serial 1693 of 3 July 1940, letter to COMSCOFOR.

[34] COMPATWINGS, serial 0756 of 14 Dec. 1940, letter to CINCUS, CNOCF, NHD.

[35] "The succeeding seven airplanes originally assigned to Patrol Squadron Fourteen have been diverted to the British Government;" ". . . up to December 1, 1941, there were 2,000 bombing planes sent under Lend-Lease by the United States in connection with the war against Germany and the Axis in Europe." COMPATWINGS, serial 0756 of 14 Dec. 1940, letter to CINCUS, as cited in *Pearl Harbor Hearings*, Part 9, p. 4289.

get out of CNO was a statement, in July 1940, that "New pilots will not begin reaching the patrol wings in quantity until after October 1941," and later that "the order of commissioning and allocation of patrol wing squadrons will depend upon the international situation and strategic considerations at the time the planes become available."[36]

Between July 1, 1940, and June 30, 1941, the patrol plane strength of the Fleet was scheduled to increase from 198 operating planes to 324 operating planes. Despite this sizable increase in strength, only 12 of the additional 126 planes were to be assigned to the Hawaiian area, and they were not due to arrive until June 1941.[37] The story, at the working level in the Navy Department, was:

> The present plans indicate that one additional patrol plane squadron for Patrol Wing Two [based at Pearl] will be commissioned about June 1941. After that no additional Patrol Wing Two squadrons are scheduled to be commissioned until about June 1944. Four inshore patrol squadrons for Pearl Harbor, and two for Kaneohe Bay are scheduled for June 1943.[38]

Such letters indicated that the Navy Department viewed with considerable equanimity the inadequate patrol plane situation at Pearl.

It is against this background of definite Departmental frowning on diversion of effort from training in the patrol plane squadrons, Departmental equanimity about patrol plane strength in the Hawaiian area, and frequent reports from the local patrol wing commanders about the overly burdensome peacetime workload which their forces were operating under, that the actual patrol plane reconnaissance carried out from Pearl Harbor in late 1940 should be related.

On November 1, 1940, Captain P. N. L. Bellinger took over command of Fleet Patrol Wing Two based at Pearl Harbor. Bellinger was unhappy about the patrol plane situation in the Hawaiian area. He set forth his views as follows:

---

[36] CHBUAER (J. H. Towers), 8 June 1940, letter to CNO, with End. by COMAIRSCOFOR (A. B. Cook), serial 0461 of 17 June 1940, COMSCOFOR (Adolphus Andrews), serial 1697 of 21 June 1940, and CNO (H. R. Stark), serial 05638 of 16 July 1940, box 110, CINCUS Files, RG 313, NA.

[37] COMAIRSCOFOR, "Annual Report," 1940.

[38] CHBUAER, 29 Nov. 1940, letter, 6th End. of COMAIRBATFOR, serial 0744 of 20 Aug. 1940, letter to CINCUS, box 134, CINCUS Files, RG 313, NA, p. 4. The subject is Aviation Facilities in the Hawaiian Area.

I arrived here on October 30, 1940, with the point of view that the International situation was critical, especially in the Pacific, and I was impressed with the need of being ready today rather than tomorrow for any eventuality that might arise. After taking over command of Patrol Wing TWO and looking over the situation, I was surprised to find that here in the Hawaiian Islands, an important naval advanced outpost, we were operating on a shoestring and the more I looked, the thinner the shoestring appeared to be.[39]

Commander Scouting Force had this to add in his endorsement:

The Commander Scouting Force appreciates that the efforts of the Department toward the completion of adequate defense measures must necessarily be based upon the development of the entire Naval Establishment rather than concentration upon one point. He believes, however, that the importance of Pearl Harbor as the spear-head of our defenses in the Pacific, and the essential role of Patrol Wing TWO not only in the defense of Pearl Harbor but also in any operations to the westward, warrant early and full attention to the needs cited by the Commander of that Wing.

Commander Scouting Force has, since his arrival in this area as Commander Hawaiian Detachment, been much concerned at the lack of adequate material and facilities for proper and efficient operation of Patrol Wing TWO in war. He has effected such remedial measures as lay within his power, and has urged upon the Department such matters as the enlargement of the originally-planned installation at Kaneohe Bay and the provision of gasoline and lubricating oil reserve supplies at outlying-island bases so that these bases might be utilized temporarily without awaiting the arrival of tenders.

In view of the location of Pearl Harbor and the island bases, and the functions of Patrol Wing TWO in war in the Pacific, the Commander Scouting Force therefore recommends strongly that measures toward fulfilling the needs cited by Commander Patrol Wing TWO be given the highest priority in the Department's program and accomplished at the earliest practicable moment.[40]

And, my final effort is contained in the endorsement which I placed on this very excellent letter on the day before my detachment. It read, in part, as follows:

It is the Commander-in-Chief's opinion, however, that the basic letter, summarizing as it does the entire patrol plane situation in the Hawaiian area, presents a very valuable picture of the overall requirements that are urgently needed if the potentialities expected of patrol planes are to be even approxi-

---

[39] COMPATWINGTWO, serial 022 of 16 Jan. 1941, letter to CNO, as cited in *Pearl Harbor Hearings,* Part 37, pp. 961-65; *Pearl Harbor Hearings,* Part 26, p. 542.

[40] *Ibid.,* Part 26, pp. 544-45; COMSCOFOR, serial 035 of 21 Jan. 1940, letter to CINCUS, 1st End. to PATWINGTWO, serial 022 of 16 Jan. 1941, letter to CNO, CNOCF, NHD.

mately realized. Therefore, full review of the subject, accompanied by appropriate action toward expediting or initiating needed developments, is urged. Attention is particularly invited to:

(a) The desirability of better priority in the delivery of improved patrol planes to Patrol Wing TWO.

(b) The great importance of increased bomb and torpedo supply, including not only bulk storage, but also ready storage at Naval Air Station Pearl Harbor, together with suitable handling and loading equipment at the Air Station, and improved transportation from bulk storage. In this connection, provision at the Naval Air Station should include two "fills" for five patrol plane squadrons and *one aircraft carrier group.*

(c) The vital necessity of expediting the readiness at outlying island developments of the basic essentials: gasoline and oil storage, bomb and ammunition storage, parking area, ramps and dredged approaches thereto. This latter subject has been discussed informally with representatives of the Commandant Fourteenth Naval District and is understood to be receiving full consideration. Departmental support, if and as needed, is urged.[41]

Bellinger was also unhappy about the daily reconnaissance. He pointed out to me that it required fifty ready naval patrol planes each day to search an 800-mile, 360-degree-circle area from Pearl, and that he had only sixty-odd VPB planes altogether, and that planes and crews could fly only every second or third day.

That Bellinger's estimate of patrol plane requirements was conservative is evidenced by the fact that Major General F. L. Martin, USA, Commanding General Hawaiian Air Force with headquarters at Hickam Field, Oahu, submitted a study on August 20, 1941 stating that seventy-two ready planes of the B-17D-type airplane would be required to make a 360-degree search for 833 miles.[42]

Bellinger believed that the shorter outer air patrols that were being flown—300 miles—by six to twelve planes each day constituted such an inadequate protective search that, in view of the very extensive replacement patrol plane crew training program directed by the Navy Department, they constituted an unacceptable burden on the patrol plane resources and patrol plane crew resources available to him.

It should be noted, moreover, that, during periods when the major

---

[41] CINCUS, serial 0178 of 31 Jan. 1941, letter to CNO, 2nd End. to PATWINGTWO, serial 022 of 16 Jan. 1941, letter to CNO, CNOCF, NHD.

[42] *Pearl Harbor Hearings,* Part 4, p. 1025.

portion of the Fleet was at sea for training or exercises, the shore-based patrol plane air patrols were discontinued and Fleet-based search aircraft patrols were flown. This uneven workload in security patrols tended to disrupt the continuity of Patrol Wing Two flight training schedules. The shore-based patrols also were discontinued, or markedly reduced, during periods when the patrol wing commander reported that he was unable to provide even the six planes required for the minimum search. This happened whenever new-type planes replaced old planes, as well as at other times when the pilot training schedule was particularly overriding or, as illustrated by the following letter:

7 November 1940

From: The Commander Patrol Wing Two
To: The Commander Scouting Force
Subject: Outer air patrol, request for temporary modification of
Reference: (a) COMBASEFOR Operation Plan 6-40
(b) COMBATFOR despatch 210026 of October
(c) Approved operating schedule second quarter

1. In order to increase the training involved and permit maximum participation in the advance base operations scheduled by reference (c), authority is requested to temporarily modify the outer air patrol now being conducted in accordance with references (a) and (b). It is desired to substitute a search by planes returning from Johnston Island on 4, 5, 6 and 7 December. This search will effectively cover the sector 133° true to 330° true from Barbers Point to a distance of 180 miles and also the triangle based on this circle with its vertex at Johnston. If it is not considered expedient to use the same search on four consecutive days, authority is requested to make the above substitution on 4 December.

P. N. L. BELLINGER [43]

From the Fleet viewpoint, it was apparent that what we were actually carrying out in the Hawaiian area, insofar as naval-air patrol plane searches were concerned, was a questionable compromise between peacetime security measures for training purposes and wartime security measures for security purposes. If the effort being put into these air search security measures was for training purposes only, perhaps it was too great, because

[43] CINCUS, serial 0404 of 15 Sept. 1940, letter to COMBASEFOR; COMPATWINGTWO, serial 2786 of 7 Nov. 1940, letter to COMSCOFOR.

all other types of training for these long-range patrol aircraft and crews was being adversely affected. It also was quite obvious that the security provided the Fleet from surprise air attack from enemy carriers by the 300-mile reconnaissance in the Western Sector was quite limited.

On November 22, 1940, the CNO had written me that, "By far the most profitable object of sudden attack in Hawaiian waters would be the Fleet units based in that area. Without question the safety of these units is paramount and imposes on the Commander-in-Chief and the forces afloat a responsibility in which he must receive the complete support of Commandant Fourteen, and of the Army. I realize most fully that you are giving this problem comprehensive thought." [44]

At this time, a revision of my earlier (July) security order for the Fleet was in its draft form. The draft revision tightened up external security in many respects, and continued to prescribe that long-range air reconnaissance by Fleet patrol planes be carried out. When the order was issued, this latter provision was not included. The background for this important change is now given.

While my security directive of December 5, 1940[45] still was in the draft stage, I wrote to Stark on November 28, in reply to his letter of November 22, and told him that I had come to the conclusion that "wartime measures of security must be carried out in the Hawaiian Area," and sent him the tentative draft of my security directive—offering him an opportunity to comment in regard to it. As I noted above, the draft submitted to Stark called for continuing the daily long-range naval aircraft reconnaissance from Pearl. I learned by letter from my War Plans Officer, Murphy (temporarily in Washington), of Stark's point of view verbally expressed to him, that "wartime measures of security" were not required as yet, and that "continuous air patrols" were not necessary. So, the requirement for long-range naval patrol plane reconnaissance was stricken out of my order, and it was issued otherwise unchanged. In addition to the disinclination of my boss to approve the daily long-range air reconnaissance, I knew that my senior patrol wing commander considered this the most burdensome of the external security requirements, and, with the very modest

[44] *Pearl Harbor Hearings,* Part 14, p. 973.

[45] CINCUS, serial 01898 of 5 Dec. 1940, letter, microfilm NRS No. 1M, NHD ("Security of Fleet Units Operating in the Hawaiian Area").

naval long-range patrol aircraft resources available, it was obviously only partially effective.

Stark's adverse point of view toward daily long-range reconnaissance was confirmed in his letter to me of December 23, 1940, when he said, ". . . while the extent of security measures required is increasing, it has not yet reached the demands of full war time security. As I discussed with Murphy [my War Plans Officer], there will be an advantage in making occasional sweeps by aircraft and surface craft, but it is not yet necessary *to make these continuous.*" (author's italics) [46]

The receipt of my boss's opinion did not change my opinion, even though it changed my action.[47]

If any reenforcement is needed that it was still my point of view that this long-range naval-air reconnaissance was necessary, such reenforcement is contained in a letter written by me to the CNO on January 25, 1941, only six days before my detachment on February 1, 1941.

In commenting upon Plan Dog (as modified, it became RAINBOW FIVE), and stating the security measures necessary, *"before Japan entered the war,"* my letter stated that amongst the measures necessary, one was to "Expand patrol plane search to the maximum, reenforcing Patrol Wing Two [at Pearl] wtih units from Patrol Wing One [then based at San Diego, California]." [48]

However, I should make clear the difference between my believing the patrol was necessary, and carrying it out when my immediate superior said it wasn't necessary. My security order was conditioned by my immediate superior's advice and my juniors' desires, and I am sure my successor's order was similarly conditioned.[49]

Kimmel's order on security, which he issued on February 15, 1941, two weeks after taking command, was not markedly different from mine. It had been in tentative draft form within the staff before my relief, and

---

[46] *Pearl Harbor Hearings,* Part 14, p. 980.

[47] CINCUS Fleet Confidential Letter 8CL-40, serial 01988 of 30 Dec. 1940, letter to Fleet, WWIICF, NHD. This dealt with the security of units operating in Hawaiian waters.

[48] *Pearl Harbor Hearings,* Part 14, pp. 994-95.

[49] My last Security Order was U.S. Fleet Confidential Letter 8CL-40. Kimmel's first Security Order was CINCUS Fleet Confidential Letter 2CL-41, 15 Feb. 1941, letter to Fleet, WWIICF, NHD.

Kimmel had been shown Stark's letter to me in regard to my tentative order.[50]

So, I believe that some of the responsibility for the failure to have daily long-range air reconnaissance as part of the daily routine in 1941 at Pearl Harbor lies directly on the doorstep of the CNO. Having been told by the Commander-in-Chief that daily long-range reconnaissance would be carried out, he said it "was not yet necessary."

Torpedo Baffles in Pearl

This discussion, up to now, has been about air reconnaissance.

There is another aspect of the security of the Fleet at Pearl Harbor, on which my staff and I faulted pretty completely, and I do not wish, by omitting mention of the matter, to dodge the issue or avoid my share of the responsibility, if there were such.

The British had made a very successful night-aircraft torpedo attack on the heavy ships of the Italian Fleet at anchor in the harbor of Taranto, on November 11-12, 1940. When the extent of this success became known, several members of my staff gathered together the meagre data available on the individual attacks, including height of planes and depth of water at launching point, length of torpedo runs before reaching target, and angles of torpedo entry into water, and the matter was considered in relation to the security from torpedo attack of our own Fleet at anchorages at Lahaina and at Pearl. It was quite obvious that the Lahaina anchorage was very vulnerable from every consideration. This was the major factor which caused me to reduce to practically zero the time the Fleet spent at anchor at Lahaina, after the middle of November 1940. It seemed to me to be best that the Fleet should either be underway at sea, or berthed inside Pearl Harbor.

In Pearl Harbor, it was a fact that torpedoes, with the characteristics of the then available or projected United States air-carried torpedoes, could not be used effectively against berthed ships. Our then operating air torpedoes dove very deep when launched, and took some hundreds of yards before rising to their desired running depth. They did not arm until about

[50] *Pearl Harbor Hearings,* Part 1, p. 326.

NH 77062

USS West Virginia (*BB-48*) *entering Pearl Harbor and making the turn at Hospital Point.*

back at running depth.[51] In the Fleet staff there was no knowledge or intelligence of Japanese aircraft torpedoes which were operable under the limiting condition in Pearl Harbor of only 35-45 feet of water at possible launching points. Hindsight indicates that a sounder decision would have been to press home an independent investigation as to whether such torpedoes were a possibility, and not to dismiss the matter on the grounds that we had no intelligence of Japanese or other foreign torpedoes of such a capability. It was erroneous to assume that since a torpedo attack on berthed ships in Pearl was beyond our own torpedo capabilities, it was also beyond the capabilities of the Japanese. Such an investigation might have revealed that the British had made an air torpedo attack on the French battleship *Richelieu* at Dakar, in July 1940, and "The charted depth at the dropping position was only 7 fathoms."

As a result of our review of the matter, on November 28, 1940, I dismissed the air torpedo threat with these words in a letter to CNO. "I think torpedo nets within the harbor [Pearl] are neither necessary nor practicable. The area is too restricted and ships, at present, are not moored within torpedo range of the entrances." [52]

Shortly after this (February 15, 1941), the Chief of Naval Operations, in a lengthy letter,[53] presented to my successor some basic data available to the Department in regard to torpedo capabilities and anti-torpedo baffles, and requested his recommendation in regard to the installation of anti-torpedo baffles in Pearl Harbor. The information presented was no different from that which had been available to me, and my successor's recommendation, unfortunately, was much the same as mine.

---

[51] "A minimum depth of water of seventy-five feet may be assumed necessary to successfully drop torpedoes from planes. One hundred and fifty feet of water is desired. The maximum height planes at present experimentally drop torpedoes is 250 feet. . . . Desirable height for dropping is sixty feet or less. About two hundred yards of torpedo run is necessary before the exploding device is armed, but this may be altered." For the successful attacks at Taranto " . . . *the depths of water* in which the torpedoes were launched were between 14 and 15 fathoms." CNO, serial 09330 of 15 Feb. 1941, letter to CINCPACFLT, as cited in *Pearl Harbor Hearings,* Part 26, pp. 523-24. "The depth of water in and alongside available berths in Pearl Harbor does not exceed 45 feet." This is in reply to CNO, serial 010230 of 17 Feb. 1941, letter to COM14.

[52] *Pearl Harbor Hearings,* Part 14, p. 975; *Ibid.,* Part 26, pp. 523-24; *Ibid.,* "Narrative Statement of Evidence," p. 231.

[53] *Ibid.,* Part 26, pp. 523-25.

General Security of the Fleet at Pearl

During December 1940, I gave a lot of thought in regard to the security of the Fleet at Pearl Harbor. I had my staff do a lot of checking in regard to it. The members of the staff worked in conjunction with officers of the 14th Naval District.

Early in December, and in company with General Herron, I visited all the Army units whose primary duty was defense of the Naval Base. I met the commanders of these units and discussed their forces and equipment available and their most pressing needs. I made a personal accounting of the aircraft and antiaircraft guns. I personally drafted a tentative letter for my old boss, Bloch, to send to the Department. I turned all my data over to Bloch, and urged upon him the necessity of bringing it to the Department's attention, because of his basic base defense responsibilities.

At the end of December, Bloch did forward a comprehensive letter to the Chief of Naval Operations via me, including the pertinent information obtained by myself and by both staffs. My endorsement on this letter,[54] which repeated my previous adverse recommendation in regard to installing torpedo nets, was otherwise a pretty sound and vigorous letter. It was later used as the basis of a letter from the Secretary of the Navy to the Secretary of War. According to the voluminous testimony in regard to it, during the Pearl Harbor Investigation, including that of the Chief of Naval Operations and the Chief of Staff of the Army, it led to some additional ships, aircraft, guns, and equipment being promised in the future for the Hawaiian area.

The difference between the actual results and the promises are detailed by Admiral Kimmel, who said:

> Much has been made of the fact that Secretary Knox warned of an air attack on Pearl Harbor in a letter to the Secretary of War in January 1941. This was a timely letter, instigated by my predecessor Admiral Richardson in an attempt to induce the War and Navy Departments to improve the totally inadequate defensive power against an air attack on the fleet base at Pearl Harbor.
>
> Largely as a result of Richardson's efforts the War Department allocated 180 B-17 flying fortresses to the Hawaiian Department and the Navy allocated more than 100 PBY patrol planes to the Commandant of the 14th Naval District.

[54] *Ibid.*, Part 14, pp. 985-92.

These were the types of planes the local base defense forces had to rely upon to locate and destroy enemy aircraft carriers.

On December 7, 1941, as we have seen, the Army Hawaiian air force had twelve B-17 flying fortresses out of the 180 promised in the Spring of 1941 and the command of the 14th Naval District had not received a single patrol plane.[55]

Assumptions for Attack on Fleet

One more point of interest to future naval commanders should be made. In March 1940, for training purposes, a basic assumption of the security orders for the Fleet in the Hawaiian Islands was that "a determined and resourceful power may execute an attack on ships of the Fleet by submarine, air, and/or surface vessels, including small craft and merchant vessels." But, in July 1940 and again in December 1940, when Fleet orders on the subject of "Security of the Fleet units operating in the Hawaiian Area" were issued for actual security purposes, the basic assumption was that "No responsible foreign power would provoke war, under then existing conditions, by attacks on the Fleet or Base." Despite this basic assumption, long-range naval-air reconnaissance patrols were flown a major portion of the time, and were not finally discontinued until December 5, 1940 on the advice of the CNO.[56]

It is my present belief that one of the reasons that the Fleet security order did not continue to state the training assumption, which was most realistic, was that no responsible military commander in the 1940 period, with the then existing climate of American public opinion, dared to make an assumption which might reach the public, that in the foreseeable future he expected the United States Fleet to be the recipient of a surprise air attack from the Japanese Navy. The American people didn't even like to have any thoughts of war intruded upon their pleasurable living.

---

[55] Kimmel, *Admiral Kimmel's Story,* p. 16.

[56] CINCUS, serial 01898 of 5 Dec. 1940, letter, microfilm NRS No. 1M, NHD; "Operation Plan Nos. 1-40, 2-40, 3-40," serial 0475, 0476, 0477 respectively of 21 Mar. 1940, No. 5-40, serial (none) of 22 May 1940, and No. 6-40, serial 0727 of 12 July 1940, COMBASEFOR, box 32, CINCUS Files, RG 313, NA.

Subversive Activities

Before closing out this chapter, there is one rather odd aspect of the security of the Fleet which occurred. Several weeks after Secretary Knox had visited the Fleet, in September 1940, the following letter arrived:

From: The Secretary of the Navy.
To: All Ships and Stations
Subject: Subversive activities.

1. I am concerned over the possibility of subversive activity and sabotage aboard ships and at shore stations.

2. I desire that Fleet Commanders, Commandants of Naval Districts and Commanding Officers of Units not attached to Fleets or Districts take the utmost precautions to eliminate subversive elements and to prevent sabotage.

3. While I have the highest respect for our personnel, I feel it necessary to call attention of all concerned to the possibility of subversive elements and saboteurs joining the Navy at this time of great expansion.

FRANK KNOX.

The letter had obviously been generated in the Secretary's Office, because it was unnumbered, undated, and distributed to every command in the Navy, although calling for action only by a very limited number of officers in command.

The only incident which, to my knowledge, had occurred in the Fleet which might have aroused the Secretary's concern had occurred in August 1940, when there was a fast-circulating rumor that the enlisted men in the Fleet Flagship, the *Pennsylvania,* had shown disrespect to the officers at the movies. I had promptly issued the following order:

From: Commander-in-Chief, United States Fleet.
To: Units of the Fleet present in Hawaiian Area
Subject: Subversive Activities in the Fleet, measures to guard against.

Reference: (a) U.S. Fleet Letter 3L–40.

1. In an obvious attempt to create trouble and bring discredit upon officers and men, rumors have been circulated regarding unmilitary behavior of men at movies aboard ships of the Fleet. The *PENNSYLVANIA* has been most frequently mentioned. These rumors have no foundation in fact. The conduct of the crew of the *PENNSYLVANIA* has been exemplary at all times.

2. The persistence of these rumors indicate the presence of an organized subversive element or activity in the Hawaiian Area engaged in spreading

malicious gossip. Officers and men who repeat this gossip are harming the Navy and themselves.

3. It is an all hands job to get at the source of this kind of propaganda. Every officer and man in the Fleet should immediately bring to the attention of competent authority any information in this connection which comes to his attention, either afloat or ashore.

4. Publish this letter at quarters and bring it to the attention of all recruits as they join the Fleet.

J. O. RICHARDSON [57]

Unofficial letters to the naval intelligence activities of the Department failed to reveal the source of Secretary Knox's concern.

I always had the greatest trust in the fundamental loyalty of the American sailorman, and considered that our Navy was particularly fortunate in its freedom from conscious subversion. I trust that the great growth of communism, which has taken place since I left active duty, has not changed the situation.

---

[57] CINCUS, serial 2614 of 20 Aug. 1940 Letter to Fleet (in Hawaiian area), box 70, CINCUS Files, RG 313, NA.

Chapter XVII

Visits of the Secretaries of the Navy to the Fleet

It was my belief that visits to the Fleet of the Secretary of the Navy and his civilian assistants were generally of marked value to the seagoing part of the Navy. Secretaries generally get their noses pretty well buried in the day-to-day problems of the Navy Department. All too frequently, they forget that the reason for the existence of the Navy Department is to assist in ensuring that the Fleet is ready and able to do its share in producing victory in war, when victory is desired.

Also, all too frequently, the Secretaries forget that the officers they see in their daily work are only a small portion of the first-rate officers in the Navy. A visit to the Fleet tends to restore their sense of proportion. So, although visits meant a great deal in the way of "fuss and feathers" for the Fleet, still, in my book, they were much more than just worthwhile.

During my thirteen months in command, the Fleet had the benefit of a visit by Secretary of the Navy Charles Edison and by his successor, Secretary of the Navy Frank Knox. Mr. Edison visited the Fleet from April 1 to April 14, 1940, Mr. Knox from September 6 to September 15, 1940.

Mr. Edison had been Assistant Secretary of the Navy when I was Assistant Chief of Naval Operations in 1937, and later when I was Chief of the Bureau of Navigation, in 1938-1939. I knew him reasonably well. Mr. Knox had been in the Navy Department less than two months, and I knew him only slightly.

Both of these visits were useful; Mr. Edison's suffered from the fact that he was a "short timer," soon to leave the Office of Secretary.

Mr. Edison was accompanied by Rear Admiral E. J. King, his two aides, Captain M. L. Deyo and Lieutenant R. H. Rice, and a Mr. Arthur Walsh, later a Senator from New Jersey. Mr. Knox was accompanied by Captain Deyo, Colonel W. J. Donovan, the Head of the Office of Strategic Services during World War II, and Mr. John F. O'Keefe, Special Assistant to the Secretary.

Visit of Mr. Charles Edison

The following letter tells the story of Mr. Edison's visit better than my memory could.

Admiral H. R. Stark, U.S. Navy,
Chief of Naval Operations,
Navy Department,
Washington, D.C.

Dear Betty:

Just before the Secretary arrived my steward was transferred to the San Diego hospital with double pneumonia, but fortunately Admiral Calhoun sent me the best steward I have seen this cruise.

The Secretary arrived on board at 1400 on Monday, 1 April, where all of the Flag Officers present were presented to him.

About 1445 we went ashore and inspected Reeves Field, the new athletic field adjacent to Reeves Field, the Navy landing in San Pedro, Trona Field, and the Naval Reserve Air Base. Then I took the whole party to my apartment before we returned to the ship. At the athletic field in Long Beach I had the Mayor of Long Beach and the members of the Harbor Commission meet the Secretary, and at my suggestion he impressed upon them the need for recreational facilities for the men. The City of Long Beach told Bloch that if the Navy would acquire title to Reeves Field, Long Beach would present to the Navy the 40 acres which adjoin it. Long Beach is now making three baseball diamonds and a few tennis courts on this field.

At 1930 on 1 April all the Flag Officers came on board for dinner with the Secretary.

The Secretary apparently enjoyed his stay on the *PENNSYLVANIA* very much. At each meal I had a different member of my Staff sit next to him and the Secretary was very talkative and asked many questions. He was taken all over the ship, saw turret loading drill, broadside battery loading drill, seaplanes catapulted, smoke screens, air attacks, and all of Part III of the Fleet Problem.

He was outspokenly opposed to aircraft carriers on account of their vulnerability. He appeared to believe that we had too many men on board ship,

NH 77044

Admiral Richardson and Secretary of the Navy Charles A. Edison during the latter's visit to the United States Fleet, April 1940.

but I believe that members of my Staff corrected this viewpoint. He freely discussed the reorganization of the Navy Department, but was permitted to bring up the subject himself each time. He discussed at length the advantages of the enormous useless battleship, which he strongly favors. He appeared highly pleased with his trip, gained some in weight, and appeared much rested when he was transferred to the *WARRINGTON* at 1000 yesterday. He was much impressed by the fueling, and the smartness of the *WARRINGTON* in coming alongside.

Today we are in whites for the first time and have a fresh breeze, but the *WARRINGTON* apparently had no trouble in transferring the Secretary to the *YORKTOWN* by going alongside.

The Fleet will not reach Lahaina until about 1600 on the 10th and the Secretary wanted to reach Pearl Harbor about 1400, therefor I have ordered the *YORKTOWN* and the *INDIANAPOLIS* to anchor at Lahaina by 0900 tomorrow, when the Secretary's party will be transferred to the *INDIANAPOLIS* and Andrews will take them in to Pearl Harbor.

This will afford Andrews an opportunity to inform the Secretary regarding conditions in the Hawaiian Area, and particularly our needs for recreation, housing, and Fleet facilities, where he is not interrupted by official calls and entertainment.

Due to the detachment of Murfin [Commandant 14th Naval District] on the 11th, I felt that Andrews could probably give the Secretary more information than anyone available.

King appeared to enjoy his stay on the *PENNSYLVANIA,* and as far as I observed, was always ready to answer the Secretary's questions, but never volunteered any advice or opinion. The presence of King in the party was far more pleasant than I anticipated. I think Mr. Arthur Walsh thoroughly enjoyed his visit and should say that he gained about 5 pounds while he was on board.[1]

Due to bad weather we lost some time, and in an effort to make up a little time I set the Fleet speed at 15 knots, but found that the *PENNSYLVANIA,* who has been out of dock 9 months, required almost full power, and that the *CALIFORNIA* could not make 15 knots. . . . Thompson informs me that the *CHICAGO* requires an increase of 110% in fuel consumption to make 27 knots. There is a belief in the Fleet that this has been an unusually severe year insofar as fouling is concerned. It seems to me that unless the new paint is a great improvement, we will be forced to adopt a six months docking period.

I seriously question the value of any [of our present] logistic war plans for providing the Fleet with fuel on an extended cruise, because I do not believe that anyone has taken into consideration the full affect of fouling. I am certain that the battle line speed of our Fleet cannot exceed 15 knots, and I question

[1] Perhaps my comment regarding King in the above letter needs a word of explanation. I believe that Stark thought King should have had the CINCUS billet at the time that it was given to me, as King was my natural senior. It seemed an unusual thing to me that King should be attached to the Secretary's party as an observer, by Stark.

the wisdom of any plan that takes the Fleet to an operating area far removed from any possible docking facilities.

With kindest regards and best wishes.

Sincerely,

J. O. RICHARDSON

P.S. On 9 April I sent Andrews with a detachment in to simulate a raiding force against Pearl Harbor, to serve as an object for attack by our patrol planes and Army bombers. Andrews reported sighting Navy patrol planes, but he did not see any Army bombers.

Today we were picked up by our patrol planes about 0630, but we did not see any Army bombers. However, our submarines made several successful attacks from fairly short ranges. We had a heavy swell with white caps so that it was difficult to see the submarines.

While the Secretary was on board, one of the *SARATOGA's* fighting planes had a forced landing close aboard. The plane sank, but the Reserve Ensign was recovered without his even getting his feet wet.

Today one of the *LEXINGTON* bombing planes (SBU) had a forced landing. The plane sank, but the pilot and passenger were recovered with slight injuries.

The *PENNSYLVANIA* should anchor in Lahaina about 1700.

J.O.R.[2]

After leaving the Fleet, Mr. Edison returned to the West Coast in the *USS Nashville,* Captain R. S. Wentworth, Commanding. There, he visited the naval activities around San Francisco Bay. During this period, Captain E. F. Cutts commanded the Fleet Flagship, the *USS Pennsylvania.* Her executive officer was Commander J. L. McCrea. The *Yorktown* was skippered by Captain E. L. Gunther and her executive was Commander A. W. Radford. The destroyer *Warrington,* which was chosen as she had recently stripped ship of all gear thought unnecessary for wartime operations, was captained by Commander F. G. Fahrion and his executive officer was Lieutenant Commander D. C. Varian. It so happened that all these officers became Flag Officers except one, and so I believe Mr. Edison had the opportunity to talk to a professionally well-grounded group of officers.

[2] RADM O. G. Murfin, USN, Commandant 14th Naval District
VADM Adolphus Andrews, USN, Commander Scouting Force, U.S. Fleet
RADM William L. Calhoun, USN, Commander Base Force, U.S. Fleet
RADM E. J. King, USN, General Board, Navy Department
CAPT R. R. Thompson, USN, Fleet Engineer, U.S. Fleet

When he arrived, Mr. Edison was very much more interested in the problem of the reorganization of the Navy Department than he was interested in the Fleet, and I believe, despite my efforts and that of other officers, his interests were still so centered when he left.

During the several previous months, a proposal had been advanced by the Secretary for the reorganization of the Navy Department. This proposal, contained in a House Naval Affairs Committee print of June 23, 1939, did away with the long-established Bureaus of the Navy Department. It created more than double this number of new divisions of the Navy Department in the place of the Bureaus, and then distributed the functions of the Bureaus to these new divisions. It created a Chief of Shore Operations who was to be next in seniority to the Assistant Secretary of the Navy, and placed him in command of the materiel side of the Navy. The Chief of Shore Operations was to be a civilian, a naval engineer, or a naval constructor. By this arrangement, the shoregoing Staff Corps officers of the Navy would take over the managing of the Navy, and the Fleet would play second fiddle.

The Secretary of the Navy plugged for the new arrangements strongly. However, the President effectively intervened with the following memo, which was written during Mr. Edison's absence from Washington.

THE WHITE HOUSE
Washington
April 3, 1940

Memorandum for
THE ACTING SECRETARY OF THE NAVY

(1) I think there must be some mistake in regard to the suggested Naval Reorganization Bill. Before the Secretary of the Navy left, I made certain matters extremely clear.

I am willing to accept;

(a) A clause to legalize the Bureau of Ships with a Rear Admiral at its head under a status similar to that of other Bureau Chiefs, together with two assistants, one of whom may carry the rank of Rear Admiral, where the Chief of the Bureau of Ships belongs to the other branch of the Service. In other words, if the Bureau Chief is a constructor, he may have as an assistant an Engineer Officer or vice versa.

(b) A clause to create an Under Secretary of the Navy with such duties as the Secretary shall assign to him.

(c) Language making it clear that C. N. O. can control priorities where such priorities relate to Navy Yard work on operating Naval vessels or Naval vessels out of commission, or in reserve which C. N. O. determines shall be put into the status of full commission.

Outside of these, which I made clear at least three weeks ago, I want no other legislation.

For your information, and that of the Secretary in regard to the setting up of an Office of Shore Establishments, it is my desire that this part of Navy Work, i.e. materiel, shall be handled by the Assistant Secretary of the Navy, this duty being assigned to him by the Secretary. I have no objection to having detailed to him any Officer or Officers of any rank desired to carry out supervision of Shore Establishment work.

F.D.R.

The seagoing part of the Navy had been called upon to comment in regard to Mr. Edison's Reorganization Bill, and their comments had been strongly adverse to many of its features. I believe Mr. Edison was disturbed by the strength of some of the verbal comments on the same subject, which he heard in the Fleet. In any case, when he left the Fleet, he did not shower down accolades upon either the Fleet or its boss.

Under date of May 7, Mr. Edison wrote to me, "I found the Department going full speed as is usual with Congress in session. I have a little additional ammunition to get me through busy days because of the very enjoyable cruise I have just had with the Fleet, and which will always be a most happy remembrance."

Nazis in Uruguay

In June 1940, about midway between the visits of Mr. Edison and Mr. Knox, there were a number of large headlines in our newspapers in regard to the discovery, in Montevideo, Uruguay, of an incriminating document in the home of a local Nazi, and the subsequent arrest of twelve Nazis.

The document was reported by the newspapers to indicate that Germany had decided to use Montevideo as a headquarters for subversive action in South America. The German Minister to Uruguay protested the arrests, and added fuel to the newspaper fire.

At this time, the *USS Quincy* (CA-39), one of our new heavy cruisers was en route to Buenos Aires, Argentina, on a good-will visit. The Navy Department informed me that she was being diverted to Montevideo, upon the request of the State Department, in order to make plain to all the South American nations that the United States was closer to them, in all ways, than Germany.

In any case, the *Quincy* made the headlines by arriving three days after the arrest of the twelve Nazis. Her personnel had a pleasant visit, the ship's company made a good impression and kept out of trouble, and the State Department reportedly was well pleased.

I believe that such visits as these, and those related in the earlier chapters of this book, are at least one reason why the United States should never put all its national defense effort into land-based air power. The Navy can do a diplomatic job, which, due to the nature of air power and land power, can not be done by either the Army or the Air Force.

Visit of Mr. Frank Knox

When I was apprised of the pending visit of Mr. Knox, I decided to make a full effort to have him see as much as possible of the Fleet's operations, to provide the opportunity for him to talk to as many officers and men as possible, and to try to arouse his full interest in the major problems of the Fleet.

Since he was flying to Hawaii in a naval plane, it seemed desirable to set up a large plane guard organization so as to be able to rescue him from the drink, if misfortune should come upon his plane. Under Commander Aircraft, Scouting Force, twelve plane guards, from a heavy cruiser to a small seaplane tender, were strung along the 2,000-mile route at regular intervals.[3] Special naval aerologists were flown to San Francisco from Hawaii to outguess the weather. All went well, except at the last minute the Secretary advanced the day of his departure from the West Coast by one, which highly complicated the plane guard positioning, and then he did the same thing in Honolulu, cancelling a submarine dive and dummy torpedo firing on the last day. But, this time we had the plane guards on station forty-eight hours in advance, which was expensive in fuel con-

[3] The ships were the *Boggs, Brazos, Chandler, Childs, Hulbert, Lamberton, Memphis, Louisville, Neches, Pelican, Swan,* and *Wright.*

80-G-26186

Admiral Richardson with Secretary of the Navy Frank Knox.

sumption but safer for a Secretary who changed his schedule with each passing day.

Mr. Knox arrived at the Naval Air Station, Pearl Harbor on Friday, September 6, 1940, and in the Office of the Commandant 14th Naval District exchanged calls with the senior naval officers in the area, and with Lieutenant General Herron, USA, Major General Wilson, USA, and with Mayor Crane of Honolulu.

On September 7, 1940, Mr. Knox exchanged calls with the Governor of Hawaii and various naval officials. In the afternoon, he inspected the new Kaneohe Naval Air Station, which was in the process of being built.

During Mr. Knox's visit, the aircraft carrier *Enterprise* (CV-6) was serving as flagship of the Fleet. Upon anchoring that evening, I had all the Flag Officers present in the Fleet, aboard for dinner. Mr. Knox was intensely interested in his job and anxious to learn about the Fleet. He talked freely to all the Flag Officers at dinner that evening. Mr. Knox said, in effect, that we had had an understanding to support Great Britain for some time. He strongly favored the U.S. destroyer for British bases deal, just in the process of consumation.

On September 8, 1940, Mr. Knox embarked in the *Enterprise,* and she proceeded to Lahaina. On this particular day, September 8, Mr. Knox expressed the opinion to all the assembled Flag Officers that we would be in the war by March 15, 1941. This was just one further indication to me of how the top officials in Washington all believed and stated privately that we were headed for participation in the war, but publicly were still denying this belief to the people at large.

Mr. Knox observed air operations and overall Fleet operations from the *Enterprise,* and then he was shifted to other types of ships—big and little—including battleships, cruisers, and destroyers, to observe inter-type and single-ship operations. The Fleet carried out air and submarine attacks, day and night destroyer attacks, and various air exercises and gunnery firing for him to observe.

I made a real effort to see that Secretary Knox had an opportunity to talk to all the Flag Officers in the Fleet. I was particularly careful to see that he had the opportunity to talk fully with Admiral Snyder, my number one subordinate; Vice Admiral Andrews, who was a particular friend of the President's; Rear Admiral Kimmel, whom I believed was one of the best of the younger admirals; and a young destroyer Commanding Officer, Commander T. H. Binford, whose knowledge and judgment I thought of a high order. Snyder was in the *New Mexico* (BB-40), Andrews in the *Indianapolis* (CA-35), Kimmel in the *Boise* (CL-47), and Binford in the *Clark* (DD-361).[4]

On the 14th of September, the Fleet was back in Pearl, and Mr. Knox made an excellent talk before the Honolulu Chamber of Commerce. On the 15th, Bloch, Andrews, and I played golf with the Secretary and, before he left at 1600 that day for his return to Washington, I gave him my memorandum of recommendations and comments.

On 8 and 9 September, while he was on board the *USS Enterprise,* I fully and frankly expressed to the Secretary my views as to the urgent need for a greatly increased enlisted personnel, my opposition to retaining

[4] *USS Enterprise*—Captain: C. A. Pownall, USN; Executive: F. B. Stump, USN
USS Indianapolis—Captain: E. W. Hanson, USN; Executive: C. T. Joy, USN
USS Boise—Captain: S. B. Robinson, USN; Executive: E. J. Moran, USN

the Fleet in the Hawaiian area, my belief that the people were not being prepared for the war that was fast approaching, and my fear that there was not full understanding and satisfactory cooperation between the State, War, and Navy Departments. On 12 September, I prepared for the Secretary a memorandum of the points which I had attempted to cover. On 15 September, I gave this memorandum to the Secretary, stating at the time that he had undoubtedly heard the views of many senior officers, and I had prepared this memorandum because I wanted him to remember which views were mine.

I think I should note here what I believe Mr. Knox's reaction was to my expressed views.

He was not in accord with my views as to the retention of the Fleet in Hawaii. He favored an increase in personnel, but stated that the bottleneck was the lack of adequate facilities at the training stations, and that this condition could not be corrected until the passage of the next Naval Deficiency Appropriation Bill.

To this I said, "Mr. Secretary, the President, without any legislative authority, has started to construct an enormous air base in Jacksonville. If he was really interested in personnel, and since he has a large fund available to him, he could, with legislative authority, expand our naval training stations."

Mr. Knox appeared to feel that the people would support the administration as the war situation developed. I gathered from his comments to others, later repeated to me, that he felt that I put undue stress on adequate personnel, and that there was lack of "war-mindedness" in the Fleet.[5] Bloch told me that the Secretary said that I was obsessed with the personnel problem.

I also learned that I was too social-minded. This comment arose after a reception which Bloch and I gave for the Secretary. Since the Secretary was new to the Navy, I thought he would like to meet a large number of the senior officers of the Fleet, so that he could establish that personal

[5] As an indication of the contrary viewpoint, I quote the following letter: COMCRUBATFOR, serial 2659 of 17 June 1940, letter to CRUBATFOR, box 180, CINCUS Files, RG 313, NA, p. 1: "In these days of unexpected attacks and undeclared wars, Unit Commanders and Commanding Officers should have positive and rapid means of bringing their ships into a condition for opening fire with service ammunition."

touch so essential to good leadership in any organization. Initially, Bloch thought that he also should give a reception so that Mr. Knox could meet the many officers of the Shore Establishment in Hawaii. We decided to combine the two receptions, and Bloch very kindly offered his quarters for the joint venture.

But, the Secretary evidently did not value his opportunity to meet and talk with large numbers of his subordinates, and thought the reception inappropriate to the "war-mindedness" he desired to find in the Fleet.

To go back to my memorandum to the Secretary, I have set forth elsewhere in this book part of my recommendations in regard to basing the Fleet in Hawaii. One other part of that memorandum is worth repeating:

COOPERATION BETWEEN EXECUTIVE, STATE, WAR, AND NAVY DEPARTMENTS.

(a) Whether justified or not, I can not escape the feeling that the coordination and mutual understanding between the above departments of the government is not as close as is necessary for effective action.

(b) Before reaching a decision as to the disposition and movements of the Fleet, or units thereof, is the Navy Department consulted, are its views frankly and forcibly presented, and are its representations thoroughly understood and considered?

(c) Present policy appears to be headed towards forcing our will upon another Pacific Nation by diplomatic representations supported by economic measures, a large material Navy in process of construction, and the disposition of an inadequately manned *Fleet in being.* Can this be done and are we prepared to face war or the inevitable loss of prestige if it cannot? Have the objectives of such a war been formulated, and its costs considered and compared with the value of victory? Can such a war be won by defensive measures or by a people trained to believe that the Navy is for defensive purposes only, and that their whole obligation to their country can be met by the payment of taxes?

(d) The Commander-in-Chief has no responsibility for the formulation of National policy, but he has a definite responsibility for the efficiency of one arm upon which the government relies to enforce National policy, when its aims can not be secured by diplomatic means. He must be concerned over the question as to whether the strength and efficiency of the Fleet are commensurate with the aggressive policy of the administration in the Pacific. Especially so if there is a possibility that this policy will require implementation.

(e) Are objectives being formulated and plans made for our active participation in the European War? We cannot long remain half in and half out of such a war. We should decide now on definite objectives and plans and should not assume that we will fight this one like we did the last, i.e., by sending aviation and light forces for active participation and utilizing our heavy ships, in *Secure* home bases, largely as training ships. Such a course would immobilize our heavy ships which are most certainly going to be needed either in the Atlantic or the Pacific, depending on the progress of the war.[6]

I mailed a copy of this memorandum to Stark and, in a personal letter dated September 18, 1940, he stated:

Thanks ever so much for the dope you handed out to the Secretary. I have read it very carefully and will be prepared to back you up. As far as personnel goes I do not think you could have stressed it too much.

I think it is worth recording that the pencilled CNO comments alongside subparagraph (b) of the original letter, containing the above quote, reads "Yes and No."

I sent a copy of this part of the memorandum to Stanley Hornbeck in the State Department.

There is one other part of my comments on the then current naval publicity that is as true today as it was in 1940. It said:

Practically all Navy publicity, hearings before committees, speeches in Congress and handouts from the Navy Department have stressed. . . . The Fleet is fully manned, fully trained and ready to fight at the drop of a hat.

All I know now about the condition of the Fleet today is what I read in the papers, and what young officers tell me. But, I suspect that just as conditions in 1940 were less than perfect, there may be a few gaps in the manning, training, and readiness of the Fleet in the year of our Lord 1957. Such publicity is wrong if it tends to lull the public into a false sense of security.

I do not have any written record of Mr. Knox's views of his Fleet visit, other than in a personal note of thanks from his aide, which said:

The Secretary was pleased with the very efficient organization of units of the Fleet; the business like and serious attitude of the officers and men, and the high type of personnel.[7]

One thing I told him, however, I know stuck with him, at least until he reached Washington. I told him that the President had two hobbies—

[6] *Pearl Harbor Hearings,* Part 14, pp. 958-59.

[7] Aide to SECNAV, letter, 1940, to ADM Richardson, CINCUS Files (En 1), RG 313, NA.

stamp collecting and playing with the Navy, and that in this second hobby he frequently sent for subordinate officers in the Navy Department and talked with them about official naval business without going through the Secretary of the Navy. I stated that I had been so sent for when I was Budget Officer, Assistant Chief of Naval Operations, and Chief of the Bureau of Navigation, and it had been my practice, in each instance, to report to the Secretary of the Navy prior to visiting the White House and subsequent to my return. I added that it was my opinion that not all officers had observed this nicety, so that frequently previous Secretaries had learned the news long after their subordinates knew it.

I learned that, upon his return to Washington, Mr. Knox issued an order providing that the procedures I had followed be compulsory in all cases of Presidential beckoning.

Chapter XVIII

My Two Trips to Washington

My first visit to Washington was made after my requesting such a visit, and only authorized to be carried out after I repeatedly urged its desirability upon the CNO.

My second visit to Washington (only three months later) was made in compliance with the wishes of the Secretary of the Navy, and against my strongly expressed desires in the matter.

I lost my official head during my second visit, but I didn't discover that disagreeable fact until three months later.

FIRST TRIP

JULY 5, 1940—JULY 17, 1940

On May 1, 1940, I wrote Stark suggesting the desirability of my going to Washington and stating that I wanted orders for myself and my War Plans Officer to visit the Navy Department, as soon as the Fleet Problem was over and the flagship had returned to the West Coast.

My visit was not actually ordered until I again raised the question, and was not consumated until weeks after it was first ordered. I had asked Stark if I should travel incognito. This query was not answered, but the Bureau of Navigation had the Clipper transportation reserved in the names of Mandley and McCleary, so I traveled as Mandley and my War Plans Officer (Murphy) traveled as McCleary.

We left Pearl on Friday, July 5, 1940 and arrived in Washington on Sunday afternoon. Rear Admiral Nimitz (Chief of the Bureau of Navigation) and Lieutenant W. R. Smedberg, USN (Personal Aide to Admiral

Stark), formed the reception committee. The President, the Secretary of the Navy, and the Chief of Naval Operations were all out of Washington for the weekend.

I learned en route that the President, on July 5, had invoked the Export Control Act against Japan by prohibiting exportation, without license, of strategic minerals and chemicals, aircraft engines, parts, and equipment. Vichy France broke off diplomatic relations with Great Britain on the same day.

I had an agenda of three points.

(a) To ascertain definitely why the Fleet remained in Hawaii and the probable duration of its stay
(b) To urge that additional enlisted personnel be provided the Fleet and that there be greater stability in officer detail
(c) To urge that the ORANGE War Plan be brought up to date, and developed into a practical war plan

On Monday, July 8, I visited the offices of both Stark and Nimitz and talked at great length on my agenda, although it was natural that my conversations with Nimitz were more oriented to personnel problems. Both said they were doing all they could to secure adequate enlisted personnel.

I had lunch with President Roosevelt. He said we would not send the Fleet to the Far East under any foreseeable conditions. I told him that (a) the Navy could not fight so far from bases, that (b) war with Japan would be long and expensive in men and resources, and that (c) there was an urgent, immediate need for an increase of naval personnel.

The evening of July 8 I had dinner with the Starks, and the Nimitzs were present. After dinner, the men talked until 2330. Stark tried to convince me that he had done all that could be done to secure more men for the Navy.

I learned that the "Proposed Operating Force Plan for Fiscal Year 1942 for use in preparation of budget estimates . . ." had just been approved by the Secretary of the Navy for budgetary planning, and issued by the Chief of Naval Operations.[1] It called for only a 193,000 "maximum" naval enlisted strength and 38,600 Marine enlisted strength. It carried

[1] "Proposed Operating Force Plan, Fiscal Year 1942," CNO, serial 104338 of 1 July 1940, box 13, CINCUS Files, RG 313, NA.

forward the combatant ships of the Fleet, less submarines, at only 90 percent complement. The Fleet overall was to have only 91.6 percent of its complement.

On July 9, I saw Secretary of State Hull and Under Secretary Sumner Welles. I fully stated my view that (a) our ORANGE War Plan was useless, and that (b) the timetable therein was silly and could not be carried into execution because of the lack of men, material, a fleet train, training for large overseas operations, and adequate information of the enemy-held Western Pacific islands. I considered the ORANGE War Plan useful only to fulfill the law that we must have a plan and to serve as a basis upon which to build a Navy. It seemed to me that Secretary Hull's basic views were that the United States should take a position of strong opposition to every move of Japan. The Under Secretary, Sumner Welles, seemed less inclined to this view.

I had lunch with General Marshall and discussed the June 17 "alert" of the Hawaiian Department.

On July 10, the air battle of Britain began with the first large concentrated German air attacks. There were many who believed so strongly in the Douhet-Mitchell theory of air power that they stated that Britain would go under because of these attacks.

On the same day I saw Senator James Byrnes, whom I believed exercised great power in determining the size of the Navy through his control of the Congressional purse strings. I strongly stressed the need for more men in the Navy.

On July 11, I talked from 1030 to noon with Stanley Hornbeck. It was my opinion then, that he was the strong man in the State Department on the Far East, and the major advisor who believed that the Fleet should be kept on in Hawaiian waters. I was rather surprised that Hornbeck was never called before the Congressional Inquiry to discuss his part in basing the Fleet in Hawaiian waters.

Also during my stay, I paid a courtesy call on Colonel Knox, who took office as Secretary of the Navy on July 11, 1940.

I left Washington late on the 11th and was back aboard my flagship on the 17th.

The objective of my conversations was to develop as fully as possible the ideas or policies which underlay the retention of the Fleet in Hawaii;

to put forth the view that its retention inevitably involved considerable risk of war, and that, in my view, we were not taking, at the same time, the vital measures made necessary by the degree of risk involved. It was particularly my concern that the ships of the Fleet be brought up to their war complements (they were then at about 85 percent, with considerable numbers of new personnel due to replacement of trained personnel transferred to the recommissioned and recently constructed ships); that the antiaircraft defenses of the ships be augmented and improved; that all the ships in the Reserve Fleet be fully mobilized; that personnel, particularly officers, be frozen in their billets (as opposed to the customary summer shifts for training and rotation); and that our War Plans be revised to conform to the situation as it then appeared likely to eventuate. I requested also that we should at once obtain and train additional officers and men who would be required to man a rapidly expanding Fleet in the event of war.[2] I expressed the view also that our people, particularly psychologically, were not being prepared for war, but, on the contrary, were being told that we would not become involved. I considered this particularly detrimental to the attainment of that unity of purpose and effort that I knew would be required to prosecute a global war.

Both specifically and generally, I got the impression, from my various conversations, that the top flight of officials in Washington believed that Japanese aggression could be restrained by a strong attitude on the part of the United States; that the retention of the Fleet in Hawaii was a reflection of this strong attitude. There was a considerable body of opinion in Washington to the effect that the Japanese could be "bluffed."

I was told that the Fleet would remain in Hawaii indefinitely—as long as required to support our diplomatic activity—and that I should move out to Hawaii the necessary training services, and should proceed with intensified training activities to increase the readiness of the Fleet. I was told that every effort would be made to increase the personnel; that the current

[2] The new Naval Expansion Act was about to become law (signed July 19, 1940). It provided for a 70% expansion of the Fleet and an increase of aircraft from 10,000 to 15,000. The increase from 3,000 to 10,000 aircraft had been authorized only on June 15, 1940, five weeks before. Two years before, on May 17, 1938, 3,000 aircraft had been authorized for the Navy, but the 3,000 aircraft were to be attained only by 1945.

War Plans were under review; and that key personnel would be frozen in their current billets.

I came away with the impression that, despite his spoken word, the President was fully determined to put the United States into the war, if Great Britain could hold out until he was reelected.

I had no more than reached my flagship, after days of mulling over the seriousness of the United States embarking on a course of bluffing the Japanese, when the following despatch arrived:

FROM: OPNAV
TO: CINCUS

THE STATE DEPARTMENT HAS OFFERED THE SUGGESTION THAT, FOR REASON OF INFLUENCING THE JAPANESE ATTITUDE, THE JAPS BE ALLOWED TO TRACK BY RADIO DIRECTION FINDER BEARINGS YOUR FURTHEST WESTERN DETACHMENT WHILE IT IS HEADING WESTWARD. YOU ARE AUTHORIZED TO PROCEED IN ACCORDANCE WITH THIS SUGGESTION, AT YOUR DISCRETION, AND IF YOUR EXERCISES AS PLANNED ARE NOT INTERFERED WITH. THE REASON FOR THIS IS THAT CONSIDERABLE TROUBLE IN SETTLING THE JULY SEVENTH INCIDENT, CONCERNING THE ARREST OF JAP GENDARMES FOUND IN THE AMERICAN DEFENSE SECTOR OF SHANGHAI, HAS BEEN EXPERIENCED BY THE CO OF THE 4TH MARINES, AND THEIR STRONG ATTITUDE IS BELIEVED TO RESULT FROM A BELIEF OF THEIRS THAT AMERICANS ARE UNDER DEFINITE ORDERS TO REACH A SETTLEMENT.

We had a detachment headed towards Midway in connection with the build-up at our island bases in the Western Pacific.

I did not believe that the hard headed Japanese Army in China, engaged in waging a full-scale war with the Chinese, would be bluffed by a few dummy radio intercepts. We were certainly playing with fire, for if anything started, the Japanese would be ready for it, and we wouldn't.

But, I sent the following order:

FROM: CINCUS
TO: COMSCOFOR

SUGGESTIONS CONTAINED THIS REFERENCE ARE TO BE CARRIED OUT BY YOU X COMPLY UNTIL DEPARTURE MIDWAY AND AFTER THAT KEEP RADIO SILENCE UNTIL MONDAY AT SUN-UP

On the way back to Hawaii, I had thought a great deal about the various talks I had had with the responsible officials in Washington. I wondered if I could make a contribution to our national effectiveness and naval state of readiness in what so obviously was a critical period, by conveying my thoughts to Stark. So, on July 20, I composed the following letter, of which I still retain the pencil draft:

Air Mail July 20, 1940
Personal
Confidential

Dear Betty:

After carefully thinking over my visit to Washington, I would like to present to you some of my impressions:

a. It seems to me that there is not as close contact and cooperation, in exchange of views and mutual understanding, between the higher ups in the Department of State, War, and Navy as the seriousness of the situation demands.

b. I do not know, but it appeared to me that the Fleet was held, and is retained here on the advice of the State Department without adequate consideration as to how its indefinite retention here affects its readiness, training and preparation for War, or its morale.

c. It seems to me that the State Department should have stated the impression it wished to create, the gesture it wished to make, and leave to the Navy Department some choice as to how it could best be done.

d. As our complete entrance into the war appears to draw nearer, the contact between the military heads of the Army and Navy and the President should become closer and he should look to them for advice rather than to diplomats and politicians.

e. In regard to adequate enlisted men the President and Mr. Byrnes seemed uninterested and unconvinced of the need for additional men in training. The C.N.O. and Chief of BUNAV seemed to be satisfied with what they had done and were doing. I felt that, at the time I could do no more than strongly support the recommendations of the Chief of BuNav, but I keenly feel that the recommendations, if approved, will not produce results soon enough, hence my recent official letter. We need men and we need them *now,* but all we really have is a promise from a candidate for the Presidency as to what he will do if elected, and inaugurated. In order to be sure of adequate numbers we should reach the appropriated strength before the end of the calendar year so that he can make good his promise before he goes out of office.

Soon after we embarked on this gigantic program of National Defense I feared that this move had been decided upon as the only one by which enor-

> mous appropriations could be secured, and there was at least as much interest in government spending as there was in National Defense. The unwillingness to make provision for an enlisted strength commensurate with the material expansion of the Navy seemed to confirm this fear.
>
> Now I am beginning to believe that there is a strong possibility, if not an affirmative determination on the question of our getting into the War soon after the national elections. If there is a reasonable basis for this belief we should have many additional men as soon as we can get them, and the Fleet should be so based as to facilitate its preparation for employment in the Atlantic.

I wrote this letter, but I believe that I decided that sending it would serve no useful purpose. In any case, I did not send it.

On July 26, the President put aviation gasoline and certain classes of scrap iron on the control list. This further decreased the possibility of any amicable settlement with the Japanese. This embargo action seemed to me a good indication that the political leaders in the United States were more and more intent on war with Japan, unless Japan was willing to back down pretty completely. I did not believe that the people of the United States were being prepared for this contingency.

Talk to the Senior Officers of the Fleet

About two weeks after my return from Washington, I assembled all the Flag Officers of the Fleet, the commanders of all squadrons and divisions, and all Commanding Officers of ships or units of the Fleet present, and addressed them on August 3, 1940 in the Submarine Base Theater at Pearl Harbor. This was an attempt at indoctrination of all my principal subordinates, immediately available, so they could plan and act intelligently in support of the policies of the Navy Department and the President (as I knew them), and of my own policies.

This talk touches on a number of matters alluded to in other chapters, but I believe it important to this chronicle. So, in the main, here it is:

> I asked you to be here this morning because I have a few things which I want to say to you, and what I have to say is only *for you,* although parts of it are to be transmitted to your subordinates, but it is not for general discussion or dissemination among any other people than officers and men of the Navy.
>
> First, I will tell you about my trip to Washington. I was ordered to Wash-

ington as a result of a suggestion I made that I thought it was time the Commander-in-Chief had an opportunity to talk to the "Powers that Be" in Washington regarding the present situation, employment of the Fleet, and existing war plans. Those that I talked with were:

The President
Secretary of State
Secretary of the Navy, Colonel Knox
Undersecretary of State, Sumner Welles
Chief of Naval Operations
Chief of Staff of the Army
Chief of the Bureau of Navigation
Governor, Canal Zone
Senator Byrnes of the Appropriation Committee of the Senate
Dr. Hornbeck, Advisor to the State Department on Far Eastern Affairs,
and with the President again.

There were four questions that I hoped to get answers to:

First, why is the Fleet retained in this area: The answer is that the Fleet is here as a result of our Naval Policy in the Pacific. The President and the State Department are convinced that the presence of the Fleet here has had and is continuing to have a restraining influence on nations interested in the Pacific area.

The next question, how long will the Fleet remain in this area? When I left here I hoped to return with a fairly definite idea as to when we might expect the major portion of the Fleet to return to Pacific Coast bases. I came back with the conviction that no one knows how long the Fleet will stay here. Its stay is certainly indefinite, and by 'indefinite' I mean that it may leave next week, next month, or six months from now, nobody can say. But I have the definite impression that it will remain here until the situation in the Pacific clearly improves, or until the situation in the Atlantic deteriorates materially.

The third question, what can be done in regard to numbers and permanency of officers? I was told that Flag officers at sea, except those now under orders, will be frozen in their billets. I hope that none of them are actually *frozen* there as I want them to be very active. I was assured that shifts of officers for their own convenience or to round out their careers have been stopped. I was told that on large ships, battleships, cruisers, and carriers, the junior officers in training for specific billets will not be detached. On these ships where officers are assigned to specific duties, either to fill them now, or in preparation to fill them later, the Bureau of Navigation will not detach them. I think you have, or you will, receive a letter from the Bureau of Navigation telling you the manner of accomplishing that aim, and it is to be handled as 'confidential', between the Captains of the ships and the Detail Officer.

Before I left here, I learned that we were receiving newly graduated Ensigns by commercial transportation and that Heads of Departments and senior officers were being held for government transportation on the Coast. The Bureau of Navigation immediately sent a despatch to the Commandants of the 11th and 12th Naval Districts telling them that Heads of Departments and above were not to be retained awaiting government transportation.

I found that the Bureau of Navigation was badly in need of aviators to undertake the training of new aviators. That is why I modified the order I had issued about retaining aviators until it was certain that their reliefs were qualified.

There is one question that I have listed that has already been settled, the question of commissioning officers into the Line of the Navy from sources other than the Naval Academy. However we feel about that individually, it is an accomplished fact and law that aviators from sources other than the Naval Academy will be commissioned in the line of the Navy. If we are to have an aeronautical organization of the size we have contemplated, it is incumbent upon us to accept into the line of the Navy these young aviators and make Naval officers out of them.

The next [fourth] question, when may the Fleet get adequate enlisted personnel? I found that the Bureau of Navigation was not as concerned regarding enlisted men as I am. I hope that everybody in Washington is more concerned about it now. At present they are enlisting about between 1000 and 1200 recruits each week. They are adding to the Class A acceptable list somewhat more than that number, so that the present indications are that we can continue to secure adequate numbers of men on a voluntary basis.

There is now in process of construction in the four training stations additional barracks to add to the training facilities a capacity of about 4,000 men in addition to the capacity now existing. We will reach the number of men for which appropriations were made, that is 172,000, about the middle of January, and at that time under normal procedure we would stop enlistments, but I tried to impress upon the present Secretary, and Senator Byrnes, who handles the purse strings, the Chief of the Bureau of Navigation, and the Chief of Naval Operations, that:

(1) We are now building a large number of ships;

(2) we can complete a destroyer in 22 months;

(3) it takes 24 months to make a petty officer third class out of a fairly bright recruit;

(4) on every destroyer in addition to petty officer third class we have second class, first class, and chief petty officers, and

(5) it takes at least six years to make a chief petty officer.

Therefore, we should have on board ship *now* every man that we can find a place for to sleep, not because we need him to man the ships now in commission but in order that we may train men and have them ready for new ships.

The President agreed that when the appropriated strength was reached we would continue the recruiting of enlisted men until we had in the Navy all the men that we could immediately enlist. Under the law the President can create a deficiency for pay of men. He can also, under existing law, recruit up to 191,000. I told the President that nobody could foresee the number of men that we needed, that I did not ask for a definite number of men at any time but what I wanted was to keep the training stations filled at all times to get the men to the Fleet as soon as they could, and keep up that procedure until every ship was filled with men so that they could not stow men on board.

I told the same thing to Secretary Hull and Mr. Welles. I told them that they were concerned with the number of men in the Navy and with their ability because they must know the adequacy of the Navy to support the National Policy. I called upon them to help the Navy and keep ever before the President and before Congress the need for men.

Just before I left Washington they were considering the Draft Bill. Colonel Knox told me that if that law were enacted it would be incumbent upon the Navy to train its proportionate share of these men. That is a serious question because there is danger that in training of draftees it will interrupt and interfere with the training of the permanent men of the Navy. Also, for the Bureau of Navigation there is a serious question in the manner in which these draftees should be trained, whether they should be trained on board ship or whether they should create a separate training squadron for them, whether they should be handled at the regular training stations, or whether they should be handled at separate training stations. There is one thing that is essential if the law is enacted. That is, every one of these men leave the service with a kindly feeling towards the Navy, because many of them may be influential later in national affairs and it would be unfortunate for the Navy if they were embittered with their short experience in it.

Coming close to home, I want to again warn you and through you all officers that there should be no idle talk about the movements of the Fleet. For example, when the Fleet left here it was reported and rumored that the Fleet was bound for the Canal Zone. There were definite reasons for its leaving, there was a definite reason for the rumors and there was an absolutely sound reason for the Navy not to talk about it. I will tell you the reason but do not repeat it. The reason for this movement was that the Navy Department, State Department, and the War Department received so many rumors of possible sabotage to the Canal in case the Fleet attempted to return to the Atlantic that the Administration believed that it was advisable to simulate a move towards the Canal and if such subversive activities were planned they might be undertaken and the people apprehended. It would have destroyed the purpose of the movement entirely had it been generally reported here that the Fleet had gone out to sea and would return in 4 or 5 days.

In giving advice to your families as to movements, any officer is, of course, clearly within his rights to advise his family when his advice is based on information available to all, when it is based on his own estimate of the possible situation. But when he suddenly advises his family to do something because of information that has come to him through a secret or confidential source, the result may jeopardize the purpose for which the move was planned.

I want all of you to be cheerful, because your attitude is reflected in the attitude of the men. I want you to be cheerful, I want you to work hard, I want you to keep up your own morale and keep up the morale of your men, because whatever you do influences the attitude of the men. I want you to impress on all men the opportunity for advancement in rating because in May, of the rating quota issued to the Fleet there were 11,000 ratings that could not be filled because the men had either not enough time, or other necessary qualifications. You must impress on all men that they should not waste their present opportunities to learn a trade.

Likewise, every officer here should fully prepare himself to do the utmost to his capacity, not only his own job, but the bigger job. No one can tell when you will be called upon to do it.

The next thing I have to say is somewhat critical, that is criticism of you. It is apparent that, or at least I am impressed with the fact, that in some cases officers hesitate to take disciplinary action, and my feelings are: No leader that is so chicken hearted that he fails to take appropriate disciplinary action through fear of hurting an officer's record can be expected to direct operations in war that will surely result in loss of life. Another thing I have had brought to my attention is cases where officers were subject to disciplinary action and it was recommended that these officers be transferred to the *RELIEF* for observation and safe keeping for the major reason that it was possible that they might commit suicide. We are in a profession where many people are going to be killed. Why not do your own job and why try to wish on the *RELIEF* a job that she is not prepared to do? Also Captains of ships have recommended that officers on their ships be transferred to Commandants ashore for court-martial. You cannot have discipline until you do your part to maintain it.

Mission of the Fleet:

The first thing is to maintain and improve its efficiency. We have no direct responsibility regarding the number of officers and men on our ships. That responsibility belongs elsewhere, but we have a very definite responsibility to do the best that can be done with what we have. So it is incumbent upon all of us to exert our utmost to train officers and men—what we have—and the normal peacetime performance of routine duties and routine target practice is not enough. Everyone out here ought to become war-minded. Whether we ever enter the war or not, no one can say, but every sensible man knows that in case we do enter the war we will be better prepared to do so if we exert our utmost efforts to get ready. If in the next 8 months we do everything that is humanly possible to do to prepare our crews and ships for war, we will have the satisfaction of knowing that we are ready to the maximum of our ability, and that is all anyone can expect of you. I want every ship to see that the ship is materially prepared so far as is possible. On the *PENNSYLVANIA,* there is an example which might not be true on other ships, but in manning the ammunition gear they found that bunks had been installed which would interfere with handling ammunition in time of war, but peacetime target practice could go through without any interruption. That is what I want to impress on you.

I am not crying "war" because I do not know anything about it, but I do know this, that if we don't get ready we may be sorry. If we do get ready and we have no war we will not have wasted one stroke of work. We will only have performed our simplest duties.

I sent a copy of this talk to both Stark and Nimitz. They did not enjoy my remarks, and Stark wrote:

I read very carefully your talk to your officers and thought it splendid. I did feel, however, that your statement to the Fleet that

"I tried to impress upon—the Chief of Naval Operations that we are now building a large number of ships, etc. etc." [author's indenture]

and in general your following remarks on personnel were such that anyone listening could hardly fail to get the impression that we were not fully alive to the situation here.

After having worked almost literally day and night on the subject of personnel from the moment I got here, having been laughed at (at first) in the White House for the size of my requests for personnel; having been told when before the House Appropriations Committee that no one had ever talked to them as I had and wanting to know if I was not starting something brand new in making such extensive personnel demands, full complements plus a pool, etc.; having been told by Byrnes, after working with him for months, that I was the most persistent man on personnel he ever knew; having preached the same thing in the State Department to get their support on personnel if any opportunity came to them; I thought the Department could hardly be said to be showing lack of concern of this vital subject.

In a year's time for example we have at least obtained authority to increase the number of men in the Fleet from 116,000 to 191,000. The President's plan had been to give us an increase of only 6,000. The Marines have been increased from 18,000 to 43,000 when originally the President had insisted 1,000 was all they could have. This particular job of filling up the Fleet had been one of my ambitions for a long time. I think also that I have made at least some dent against the generally accepted theory of only 85% complement (which incidentally is now over 90% on the old basis). Before I came to this job and when I knew that I was coming, I sounded out personnel officers in the Fleet, stating that if I did nothing else as Chief of Naval Operations, I at least hoped to get the Fleet manned and, as you know, I had written you on this subject when you were Chief of Bureau of Navigation, and before you, I had written Andrews, etc. etc. Therefore it did seem to me the implications of your address that we had not been so concerned in this respect were somewhat unwarranted, and that the Fleet might get the impression the Department was not doing its utmost. We shall continue to press in every way possible, for full complements plus a pool for training. We are trying to get the President to approve a bill running up our authorization to approximately 500,000 and have drawn up a bill to that effect.

"I do not need to tell you that Nimitz is just as keen on this situation as I am, and that we have been working together like two brothers on it.

"My first reaction to your letter was to say nothing and let it go; on second thought, I decided it was due you to know my reaction;—so—that's that.

This about buttons up the story of my first trip to Washington. I felt that the trip had been very much worthwhile, for it had brought me abreast of Washington thinking, even though I had not been particularly successful in obtaining answers agreeable to me in regard to the items on my agenda.

SECOND TRIP
OCTOBER 7, 1940—OCTOBER 11, 1940

On September 18, 1940, I wrote to Stark as follows:

While the Secretary was on board the *ENTERPRISE* he said to me, "Admiral, will you come to Washington in early October while you are on the Pacific Coast?" I replied, "I can not come to Washington except under orders, but if Stark wants to see me I suppose I will be ordered."

Just before leaving Pearl Harbor the Secretary said, "Admiral, I will talk to Stark and it is possible that we may want you to come to Washington for a conference." I replied, "I will be glad to come any time I am wanted."

I do not know of any benefit to the Navy that would accrue from my coming to Washington as I fully and frankly expressed my views to the Secretary on all points where I felt that such expression might help the Navy or the Nation. I also gave him a memorandum which covered the more important points discussed with him. Nevertheless, if you or the Secretary want me to come I will be pleased to do so.

• • •

P.S. As far as I know I have nothing to take up with the Department that can not be handled by correspondence but if I am wanted in Washington I am ready to come on arrival at San Pedro.[3]

Stark replied on September 24, as follows:

[3] *Pearl Harbor Hearings,* Part 14, pp. 952-53.

P.S. Just received yours with regard to your coming East and will take it up with the Secretary. Unless there is something you feel you want to talk about or that crops up after your arrival on the Coast, I will tell the Secretary I see no need of your coming East, at least for the moment.[4]

On the 27th, he wrote:

The Secretary just came back from a cabinet meeting; rushed in for a minute and left on his way to New Hampshire. He asked me to tell you he would like to have you come East at your convenience, while you are on the West Coast, hence my despatch of this afternoon.

And again on October 1:

The Secretary wants very much to see you. I told him of your letter. However, one of the things he wanted to talk to you about is the possibility of sending a detachment to the Far East; it is being urged here by some. I have opposed it and so has Ingersoll. Your thoughts are likely to be determinative. . . . In addition the Secretary says he would just like to talk to you anyway, so there you are.

Personally, I am looking forward as always to seeing you. I will keep the decks clear and will arrange our evenings according to your desires.

• • •

For next Tuesday, October 8, I am tentatively slating the following for dinner: The Secretary, Comdr. Murphy, Admirals Sexton, Robinson, Nimitz, Ingersoll, Towers, Furlong, Moreell and General Holcomb.[5]

The "Destroyers for Bases" agreement between the United States and Great Britain was announced on September 3. On September 6, the first eight destroyers hauled down their United States flags, and broke the Union Jack. As a horse trade, I viewed this agreement as having much merit, but it tied the destinies of the United States more closely to those of Britain than I wished. It seemed to me that by giving somwhat more than she received, Great Britain had ensured her alliance with us for the duration.

---

[4] *Ibid.*, p. 961.

[5] *Ibid.*, p. 962;
RADM Walton R. Sexton, USN, Chairman, General Board
RADM Samuel M. Robinson, USN, Chief of the Bureau of Ships
RADM Chester W. Nimitz, USN, Chief of the Bureau of Navigation
RADM Royal E. Ingersoll, USN, Assistant Chief of Naval Operations
RADM John H. Towers, USN, Chief of the Bureau of Aeronautics
RADM William R. Furlong, USN, Chief of the Bureau of Ordnance
RADM Ben Moreell (CEC), USN, Chief of the Bureau of Yards and Docks
MG Thomas Holcomb, USMC, Commandant of the Marine Corps

NH 77094

USS Idaho (*BB-42*), *a battleship of the* New Mexico *class at anchor, Lahaina, Maui, about 1940.*

In any case, on September 20, 1940, the Fleet flag was shifted to the *New Mexico,* and, on September 23, the *New Mexico* sailed for the West Coast. While en route to the coast, on September 22, the Japanese attacked Dong Dang on the French Indochina border, 120 miles north of Hanoi. This seemed a preliminary to Japanese occupation of Hanoi. On September 27, 1940, Germany, Italy, and Japan bound themselves more closely together by means of the Tripartite Pact signed at Berlin.

I made the note in my diary on this day; "Only a question of time until we are at war in both oceans." The *New Mexico* arrived at Long Beach on September 30. At 1230 on Sunday, October 6, Murphy and I set off for Washington on the American Air Lines, arriving at 0700 the next morning.

I learned upon my arrival in Washington that, on October 4, 1940, CNO had issued a new Operating Force Plan based on raising the enlisted personnel strength to 240,000. The plan provided 99.5 percent of complement for the ships of the Fleet.

On October 5, the Secretary of the Navy had placed the Organized Naval Reserves on short notice for call to active duty.

On October 7, I talked with Mr. Knox, Stark, Yarnell, and Nimitz. I had lunch with the President. My conversation with the President is detailed in a later chapter.

At the dinner at Stark's on Tuesday evening, at which Mr. Knox, Sexton, Nimitz, Furlong, C. M. Cooke (Captain in the War Plans Division), Irish (Captain in the Bureau of Ships), Moreell, and Towers were present, the Secretary asked about our War Plans for an ORANGE War. All hands expressed opinions. I opined that, "We had better have a plan, or ideas for one, or some cockeyed plan would be forced on us from above."

On October 9, I talked with Stanley Hornbeck again, who now, surprisingly enough, was unwilling to accept the responsibility for retaining the Fleet in Hawaii.

On October 10, I talked with Congressman Carl Vinson (Chairman, House Naval Affairs Committee), who asked my opinion as to the advisability of having Leahy (retired CNO, then Governor of Puerto Rico) come to Washington as an advisor to the President. Vinson stated that he believed Stark was not adequately presenting the naval view to the President. I concurred in the idea of Admiral Leahy being brought to Washington in a duty assignment because of his influence with President Roosevelt.

About 1700 on October 10, Mr. Knox sent for Stark and me. Some of the details of that meeting are set forth in the following extract from the Congressional Pearl Harbor Investigation.

Senator FERGUSON. Did you discuss with anyone the question of a patrol line from Hawaii to the Asiatic coast?

Admiral RICHARDSON. Yes, I did.

Senator FERGUSON. Will you tell us whom you discussed such a matter with?

Admiral RICHARDSON. Mr. Chairman, may I read a memorandum on that subject which I prepared several weeks ago, thinking that I might be asked that question?

The CHAIRMAN. Yes. The committee will be very glad to have it, Admiral. May the Chair ask what sort of a line that was you were inquired about?

Admiral RICHARDSON. A patrol line.

In presenting this, I would like to state that my war plans officer accompanied me to Washington, and I discussed with him most of the things that were talked about. He was a man whose judgment I held in very high esteem, and when I prepared this he went over it so that I discussed with him what I might present here as part of my testimony, and I did it in the interest of accuracy.

On October 10, the day that I had reservations to return to the west coast by plane—

The CHAIRMAN. That is 1940?

Admiral RICHARDSON. 1940; October 10, 1940.

About 5 p.m. Colonel Knox, the Secretary of the Navy, sent for me and Admiral Stark to come to his office. I was accompanied by Commander Vincent R. Murphy. Admiral Stark was accompanied by Admiral Ingersoll, and Capt. C. M. Cooke, who is now, I think, perhaps a vice admiral.

The Secretary stated that he had important information bearing on the employment of the fleet. He stated that he had just talked to the President, and that the President was concerned as to the Japanese reaction to the British on the reopening of the Burma Road scheduled for October 17. In the event the Japanese took drastic action, he, the President, was considering shutting off all trade between Japan and the Americas, and to this end was considering establishing a patrol of light ships in two lines [one] extending from Hawaii westward to the Philippines, and [the other extending] from Samoa toward the Dutch East Indies.

The question was raised—I do not recall by whom—as to whether this included stopping Japanese ships as well as others, and the view was expressed that this [stopping Japanese ships] would be an act of war, and I asked whether the President was considering a declaration of war.

The Secretary stated that the President hadn't said, and that all he, Knox, knew was what he was told.

I was amazed at the proposal and stated that the fleet was not prepared to put such a plan into effect, nor for the war which would certainly result from such a course of action, and that we would certainly lose many of the ships.

Parenthetically, I had seen that thing tried in the war plans, and it didn't work.

There was some further discussion that a line of light ships as proposed would entail such dispersal as to expose the ships to destruction in detail, and that the best way to accomplish the President's purpose was to control the source of the trade by a patrol [off] of the relatively few ports involved.

The Secretary appeared displeased at the general reaction and mine in particular, and said:

"I am not a strategist; if you don't like the President's plan, draw up one of your own to accomplish the purpose."

The conference closed with the understanding that Stark and I, with our war plans officers, would draw up a statement of assumptions, proposed decisions, and tentative plan of operation in connection with the reopening of the Burma Road.

An outline plan was drawn up. It envisaged the transfer [from the Atlantic] to the Pacific of additional patrol planes, an aircraft carrier, some destroyers, and possibly a cruiser or two.

Admiral Stark was not prepared to approve these transfers, and stated that he would talk the matter over with the President and let me know later what decisions were arrived at.

When the plan was completed, the Secretary and the President were away from Washington, and I returned to the west coast on the 11th.[6]

Mr. Knox was really incensed with me when I spoke after he originally outlined the patrol line scheme. His feelings were not softened when I said the execution of such a plan would result in war.

My War Plans Officer, Murphy, worked all that night, along with Captains C. M. Cooke, Carl J. Moore, and Harry W. Hill, and by late next afternoon had drafted an agreed upon statement of assumptions, proposed decisions, and required naval operations should Japan react strongly to the opening of the Burma Road on October 17. A copy of this memorandum was sent to Admiral Hart, Commander-in-Chief of the Asiatic Fleet.

Nothing came of all this planning and furor, and I would not discuss it at this length, had it not been for pointing out that the administration's attitude was one of taking steps that were acts of war, but when anyone mentioned "war" tempers flared and harsh words flowed. Perhaps, with ships

[6] *Ibid.*, Part 1, pp. 305-306.

deployed all over the Pacific Ocean, the "Japanese would make a mistake and we would enter the war."

Since Secretary Knox died during World War II, he never had a chance to tell his story to the Joint Congressional Committee investigating the Pearl Harbor Attack. Perhaps this is a good place to say that I liked Secretary Knox very much. As Secretary of the Navy, I think he did an excellent job for the Navy and the country. He worked long and hard for the Navy, without apparent thought of advancing his own interests. He was impatient and given to snap judgments. When he got into the strategical field of naval operations, he was ignorant. Fortunately, after the war started, he stayed out of that field quite completely.

On my return to Long Beach, I told my staff that the United States would be in the war soon. I told the same thing to Rear Admirals Friedell, Russell Willson, Kimmel, and to Captain Cortlandt C. Baughman, the skipper of the acting flagship, the *USS New Mexico.*

Selective Military Service

The first peacetime draft bill in the United States was made law on September 16, 1940. Four months before this, on May 28, 1940, I had written the following to Stark:

> The American people appear to believe that every situation in life can be adequately met either by enactment of a law or the expenditure of money. Unquestionably we need to spend plenty of money for preparedness, but what we need more and what nothing has been said about is the preparation of our people. We need a united people, imbued with self-reliance, courage, stamina and fortitude. We fill the air and the papers about spending money and about material things, but no mention is made of preparation of the spirit, and in my opinion all the material and equipment in the world will not render us safe unless we stress the preparation and training of our people. As soon as it can be done I would like to see all of us rendered liable for compulsory military service. If all of our people realize the cost of preparedness and were made to feel that they had to bear their part in money, sweat, privation and hardship, they would be more interested and our Country would be better prepared.

I believe that, in their seventeen years of operation, the several draft bills have accomplished much in improving the knowledge of the younger generations of Americans in regard to their personal responsibility for preparedness. It has spread a greater awareness of the fundamentals of citizenship responsibilities through all the various strata of American society. If the American people are wise enough to keep in effect some form of widespread military service, throughout the years ahead, I do not believe we will ever approach another world crisis in as great ignorance or unreadiness as we did in 1939.

On October 16, 1940, the register of men required by the Draft Act took place, and some 16,000,000 men registered. It was a big step forward in our preparedness, but it was still just a step, when we should have been running at full stride.

On October 28, I heard that the *Kiplinger Letter* had said that I might be detached because of my opposition to war with Japan. And, on the next day, I recorded in my diary that I had a letter from Nimitz agreeing with me that King would relieve me, if I had to be taken out. Since Stark had told me that he thought the two best officers in our Navy at that time were King and Kimmel, I thought that King, the senior, would be the man who would in due time relieve me.

Despite what the *Kiplinger Letter* had said, I did not have any real foreboding of a blow about to fall upon me personally, when I arrived back in Pearl Harbor, in the *USS New Mexico,* on December 6, 1940, and prepared to shift back to the regular Fleet Flagship, the *USS Pennsylvania.* I looked forward to the year 1941 with the great hope that it would be a year of fast-improving readiness of the Navy for war.

Chapter XIX

While Others Were Packing My Sea Bag for Me

Training Detachment—Atlantic Squadron—Patrol Force

One of the constantly recurring problems during 1939 and 1940 was the pressing need for greater naval strength in the Atlantic.

The ORANGE War Plan against Japan was based on having the full U.S. Fleet strength available in the Pacific for early movement westward. This full Fleet strength was less than adequate for the job. Every transfer of ship strength from the Pacific to the Atlantic further jeopardized the ability to carry through the early stages of that war plan.

And yet, the practicalities of the unneutral Neutrality Patrol were such that more and more ships and aircraft were needed in the Atlantic to carry out necessary naval tasks, or those considered necessary at the political level. The Martinique Patrol absorbed much naval strength and effort.

The Chief of Naval Operations was under tremendous pressure from the President and the State Department to make major transfers of strength from the Pacific to the Atlantic Ocean. I resisted these to the best of my ability when these pressures were passed on to me, but many times quite unsuccessfully. My point of view was that when war did come to the United States, the offensive naval fighting tasks would be principally in the Pacific Ocean, and the defensive naval fighting tasks would be principally in the Atlantic Ocean. I believed that as long as we were limited to a "One Ocean Navy," most of that Navy and the newer units should be where the offensive naval tasks were to be carried out. As ships came off the ways in 1940-1941 and a "Two Ocean Navy" began to assume shape as a reality, I considered it practical to assign more strength (although I considered that they should be from older naval units) to the Atlantic.

I also opposed large transfers of naval strength to the Asiatic Fleet, believing that whatever was transferred to that area would be lost in the early days of the war.

Any decision the CNO might make in the matter was bound to leave his major subordinates afloat feeling disappointed, as the tasks needing to be done were well beyond the naval resources available to the CNO for distribution to the several ocean areas.

A glance at Appendix A (United States Fleet Organization, Fleet Notice 47N-40) and previous Fleet Notices 22N-39 and 1N-40 will show the great growth of the Atlantic Squadron from June 30, 1939 through October 1, 1940, when the Atlantic Squadron was renamed the Patrol Force. This growth continued on through February 1, 1941, when the Patrol Force became the Atlantic Fleet.

But perhaps, the shift of naval strength to the Atlantic is more dramatically illustrated in the yearly planned assignment of naval aircraft. The total naval aircraft available for assignment were distributed as follows:

	Total assigned	*Afloat*	*Ashore*
Fiscal year 1938	1,480	927	553
" " 1939	1,583	1,030	553
" " 1940	1,912	1,117	795
" " 1941	3,590	1,219	2,371

The U.S. Fleet planes were assigned as follows:

	Battle Force	*Scouting Force*	*Atlantic Squadron (Patrol Force)*	*Base Force*
Fiscal year 1938	485	71	0	250
" " 1939	573	302	0	35
" " 1940	501	288	106	52
" " 1941	413	213	319	63

By December 1940, the submarine forces in the Atlantic and Pacific were getting highly out of balance. Of the 93 submarines, 63 were in the Atlantic and only 30 in the Pacific. There was a lack of sufficient submarines to man all the patrol stations for the initial stages of an ORANGE War. I added my urging to that of Commander Submarines, Scouting Force (W. L. Friedell) and Commander Scouting Force (Adolphus Andrews) to try to get the CNO to redistribute the available strength on a basis more appropriate to probable war tasks.[1]

In the Atlantic excellent training for antisubmarine warfare was being obtained during 1940. In the Pacific, the antiaircraft training was much stronger. Marked effort was made to accomplish rapid interchange of information in these two areas of readiness. I wanted to get the whole Fleet up to the best standard of any part of it.

Whether the organization of naval ships in the Atlantic might be called the Atlantic Squadron, the Patrol Force, or the Atlantic Fleet, it was a fact of life that its principal officers could drop in on the Department any day, from Norfolk or Newport, and air their needs and views. For the rest of the U.S. Fleet, in Hawaii, talking matters over with the "powers that be" in Washington was quite more difficult a matter.

Many times, the CINCUS learned of the Atlantic events, and decisions taken in connection therewith, long after they had taken effect. Sometimes this was necessary, particularly in operational matters, which, in the Neutrality Patrol, were subject to White House wand-waving.

The evolution of the naval force in the Atlantic to a major independent command, directly under the CNO, was slow but inevitable, given the geography and turn of events.

Escort of *Chaumont*

In January 1941, toward the last of the month, the Chief of Naval Operations sent a despatch directing the Commanders-in-Chief of the United States Fleet and of the United States Asiatic Fleet to provide an escort for a naval transport, the *USS Chaumont* (AP-5), proceeding from Honolulu to Guam to Manila.

As I remember it, the Commander-in-Chief of the U.S. Fleet was directed to provide the escort for the *Chaumont* between Honolulu and Guam, and the Commander-in-Chief of the U.S. Asiatic Fleet to provide the escort between Guam and Manila.

Up to the then current stage of World War II, no escorts had been provided in the Pacific Ocean for any of our Army or Navy transports or

[1] Commander Submarine Force, serial C46 of 10 Dec. 1940, letter, and endorsements thereon.

merchant ships. I was completely in the dark as to why a change should be necessary on an overall basis or in this particular instance. No reason was assigned in the despatch.

This order put me in the analogous position of having to assign an escort commander to this duty without being able to give him adequate information (intelligence) or instructions.

I had always believed very strongly myself, and it was a standard part of our War College training that a seasoned subordinate always should be informed of the purpose for which a naval operation or a new naval procedure or policy was undertaken, rather than ordering him, peremptorily, to carry out the naval operation, new procedure, or policy.

Since my boss hadn't informed me, I could not tell whether or not the despatch orders inaugurated the start of a new policy for the escort in the Western Pacific of all transports, or possibly of all American flag merchant-type ships. I wished to be prepared to start to do this escorting if such were the Department's desires. Accordingly, I sent a despatch to CNO and asked two questions:

> REQUEST REPLY TO THE FOLLOWING TWO QUESTIONS. DOES THE ESCORT OF THE U.S.S. *CHAUMONT* INVOLVE A SIMILAR ESCORT FOR THE ARMY TRANSPORT *GRANT* SAILING FOR HONOLULU, GUAM AND MANILA ON THE 31ST OF JANUARY?
>
> WILL THE ESCORT OF U.S. GOVERNMENT SHIPS LEAD TO THE ESCORT OF MERCHANT SHIPS UNDER THE AMERICAN FLAG?

I was no wiser when the reply was received, for all OPNAV said was "NEGATIVE IN REPLY TO BOTH YOUR QUESTIONS."

I have since been told by an officer in high command afloat at that time (Thomas C. Hart), but do not know of my own knowledge, that the *Chaumont* was carrying a cryptographic decoding device for the use of the Commander-in-Chief of the Asiatic Fleet.

Upon my return to duty in Washington, I inquired of the Assistant Chief of Naval Operations, Rear Admiral Ingersoll, in regard to this escort job. He informed me, " . . . it was rumored that there were German raiders operating in the mid-Pacific area within the Marshall Islands or North thereof. You were directed to escort the *Chaumont* to protect her against possible attack by German raiders."

It seems to me that, were this a true reason, there was a professional military lapse, in failure to give this intelligence to the Commander-in-Chief in the Pacific. He was denied intelligence of a military situation in his area of naval responsibility. It also should be pointed out that the same prudence which would have required escorting the *Chaumont* would have been applicable to the Army transport *Grant* soon to traverse the same waters.

If the failure to inform the Commander-in-Chief of the U.S. Fleet, arose from an unwillingness to let him know that Japanese despatches were being read in Washington, and would be read by CINC Asiatic in Manila when the cryptographic decoding machine arrived there, then this decision is one more link in the long chain of disastrous violations of sound military principles, in regard to intelligence matters, by the high naval command in Washington.

Admiral Kichisaburo Nomura, IJN Stops off at Honolulu En Route to Washington

One of the interesting events occurring while my sea bag was being packed for me was the stopover in Honolulu of Admiral Kichisaburo Nomura, IJN. He was en route to Washington, D.C., where he was to be the Japanese Ambassador to the United States.

I had known Nomura for a good many years, as he had been Japanese Naval Attache′ to Washington when I was on duty there. When I was Director of Officer Personnel in 1928, Admiral Nomura had brought the Japanese Midshipmen's Training Squadron to the East Coast of the United States. I was directed to order a liaison officer to assist Admiral Nomura with the port arrangements of his visit, and this liaison officer reported back to me at the end of his duty.

In 1927, the Geneva Naval Disarmament Conference was meeting. Progress in reaching a meeting of minds was negligible, and eventually the negotiators agreed to disagree and go home. One of the major reasons for the breakdown was a reluctance of the British to consent to an arrangement permitting the United States to build long-legged heavy cruisers with 8″ guns. Admiral Nomura in discussing the British objections with his assigned liaison officer, gave as his opinion:

A war between the United States and Great Britain is impossible. Yet there is much anti-British sentiment in many parts of the United States, and many Congressmen delight in twisting the lion's tail.

NH 77328

Commander-in-Chief, U.S. Fleet greets Admiral Kichisaburo Nomura, IJN, the prospective Japanese Ambassador to the United States.

If the British did not object to the United States' building 8″ heavy cruisers, I doubt whether the United States Congress would authorize them. Look at the great difficulty and delays in getting the 6″ light cruiser building program authorized a few years back. If the British continue to object, I believe that your Congress will authorize the largest heavy cruiser building program in the history of the U.S. Navy up to now.

The soundness of Nomura's reasoning was indicated by later events. The British did continue to object to our building 8″ heavy cruisers, although in 1930, they yielded in part (on the size of the gun but not on a displacement greater than 10,000 tons), as provided for in that year's Naval Limitation Treaty. And, the U.S. Congress did authorize a large, modern heavy cruiser building program.

In January 1941, instructions from the Navy Department in regard to Nomura's visit to Honolulu were unusually specific. I was ordered to:

(a) Provide a destroyer escort for the merchant ship which Nomura was on, while it was approaching Honolulu
(b) Call on Nomura when his ship docked
(c) Invite Nomura to luncheon or dinner
(d) Find occasion to make a speech welcoming him, expressing pleasure at his appointment, and wishing him all success in his mission.

I did all these things with pleasure, as Nomura was an intelligent and friendly person. My remarks at the luncheon given for Nomura were as follows:

It affords me great personal pleasure to be the first United States official to have the honor of greeting and welcoming to America the newly appointed Japanese Ambassador to the United States, Admiral Kichisaburo Nomura, an officer so greatly distinguished in the life of his nation, not only through his own efforts but through the confidence of his Emperor.

He is not a new-comer to our shores having served with distinction as Naval Attache in Washington and having visited Hawaii and both the East and West Coasts of the United States in command of the Japanese Midshipmen Training Squadron.

The Ambassador has shown by his past accomplishments in the field of diplomacy, as well as in the field of action, that he possesses those high traits of character which are most needed at this critical time in world affairs.

Admiral Nomura, I speak for the officers of the United States Navy when

I express the professional gratitude which we feel in having a Japanese Naval Officer appointed to such a high diplomatic post.

We hope that your mission to the United States will be fully successful.

Admiral Nomura made an extremely apt reply. He said that the first time he had come to the United States, he had come as a young midshipman just learning the rudiments of being a professional naval officer. He had been back to the United States several times subsequently, each time more fully qualified professionally than before. But, this return found him again as a midshipman, in the diplomatic profession, just learning the rudiments of his profession.

Mid-Pacific Island Bases

One of the matters of considerable concern to me in January 1941 was that our mid-Pacific island air bases were still unready for war use, although knowledge of the need for action in connection therewith was widespread at all levels of government. Many people had done much in an effort to change their quite barren condition of 1938 and 1939. But, development of the mid-Pacific islands for naval use had proven slow, difficult, and costly.

Several times previously, I have referred to the importance of these mid-Pacific island bases in the carrying out of our war plans against Japan. From them, long-range air patrols could be flown, which would provide the Commander-in-Chief with much needed information in connection with either the movement eastward of Japanese forces, or his own planned advance to the Marshall Islands.

There was no disagreement between the Forces Afloat and the Navy Department in regard to the urgent need for these bases, but there was always the problem of where the Pacific island bases should be placed in the overall Navy Department priority list of urgent naval base development, and of allocation of funds. The island bases in the Atlantic, which we had acquired from Great Britain in the "Destroyers for Bases" trade, were held in very high priority in Washington because of the requirements of the Neutrality Patrol. It could be said of these Atlantic bases that they were needed right now, while the mid-Pacific bases would be needed only if and when war came at some time in the future.

During fiscal years 1939 and 1940, naval appropriations from the Congress for building bases were far larger than in previous years, but still inadequate to meet all the pressing needs of two-ocean naval base development in the Navy. In the Pacific, the initial island base developments had been undertaken with a view to their use only as seaplane bases. As these projects proceeded, it became quite apparent that it was a military necessity to provide for the operation of land-based aircraft from these islands, primarily for defensive purposes. A further expansion of overall naval air strength was quite obviously necessary, and was sought and obtained from Congress.

The approval by the Congress of the recommended expansion of the naval aeronautical organization to 10,000 planes (from 3,000 planes) quite altered the prospects for additional money from Congress for the development of the mid-Pacific air base facilities.[2] But, obtaining authorizations from Congress for specific base projects took days and weeks, and, after that, appropriations had to be obtained, taking more days and weeks. As aptly said some four months later by the Chief of the Bureau of Aeronautics, "The scope of the projects currently in progress has, of necessity, been limited by the amount of money available." [3] And, that was still far from unlimited.

By mid-October 1940, the status of patrol plane operations in the mid-Pacific was reported to be as follows: "patrol planes can be operated at the present time from Palmyra and Johnston Islands with the assistance of tenders, and from Midway either with the assistance of tenders or with the cooperation of the Pan American Airways organization." [4]

Still needed were better shore-side seaplane facilities and defensive resources, including land planes, antiaircraft batteries, Marine defense battalions, and support facilities.

The mid-Pacific developments received a considerable impetus after a subcommittee of the House Naval Affairs Committee made an inspection trip to Midway, Johnston, and Palmyra Islands in early October 1940.

---

[2] CNO, serial 017912 of 27 June 1940, letter to CINCUS, CNOCF, NHD; CNO, serial 021912 of 22 July 1940, letter to CINCUS, CNOCF, NHD.

[3] BUAER, 29 Nov. 1940, letter to CNO.

[4] COMBATFOR, serial 01031 of 19 Oct. 1940, letter to CINCUS, box 134, CINCUS Files, RG 313, NA.

Whoever in the Navy Department brought this trip to fruition deserves an accolade from the Navy.

At this time, not one of the islands visited had any landing fields. The fact that Vice Admiral Halsey, who at that time commanded the carrier aircraft in the Fleet, took time off to accompany the Congressmen on their tour, probably was a major assist in future development of land-type aircraft facilities on these islands, particularly Midway, for he was an enthusiast for land-type naval aircraft.

On November 17, 1940, I stated to the Department:

> The Commander-in-Chief . . . is keenly interested in the provision of facilities for landplane operations at Pacific island bases. As a matter of emphasis, he reiterates the opinion . . . that it would be unduly optimistic to suppose that it would be more than rarely possible to improvise, when needed, suitable landing areas in such places with sufficient rapidity. Therefore, the provision of landplane facilities, where this is practicable, should not be postponed until an emergency arises but should be definitely planned and accomplished as a part of the development of these bases.[5]

This was a restatement of views expressed earlier the same month.

During December 1940, the efforts of the Fleet to get airfields established on the mid-Pacific islands started to bear fruit. On December 4, 1940, the Chief of the Bureau of Aeronautics summed up the current status as follows:

> In the Midway . . . group, the development of a landing field on Eastern Island and a landing strip on Sand Island is being undertaken. . . . Work . . . has started, or is about to start. . . .
>
> Landing fields at Palmyra and Johnston Islands have been approved by the Shore Station Development Board, but no funds have as yet been made available to accomplish this work.
>
> A landing field has been included in the program for the development of Wake Island. . . . Funds are available and the work on the Wake Island development is expected to start in December 1946.[6]

At least partially as a result of the representations made during and after the Congressional visit, funds for landing fields at Palmyra and John-

[5] CINCUS, serial 01835 of 17 Nov. 1940, letter to CNO, box 134, CINCUS Files, RG 313, NA; CINCUS, serial 01790 of 5 Nov. 1940, letter to CNO, 3rd End. to COMPATWINGTWO, serial 2095 of 22 Aug. 1940, letter to CINCUS, CNOCF, NHD.

[6] CHBUAER, serial C57 of 4 Dec. 1940, letter to CNO, 3rd End. to COMAIRBATFOR, serial 0894 of 8 Oct. 1940, letter to CINCUS, CNOCF, NHD.

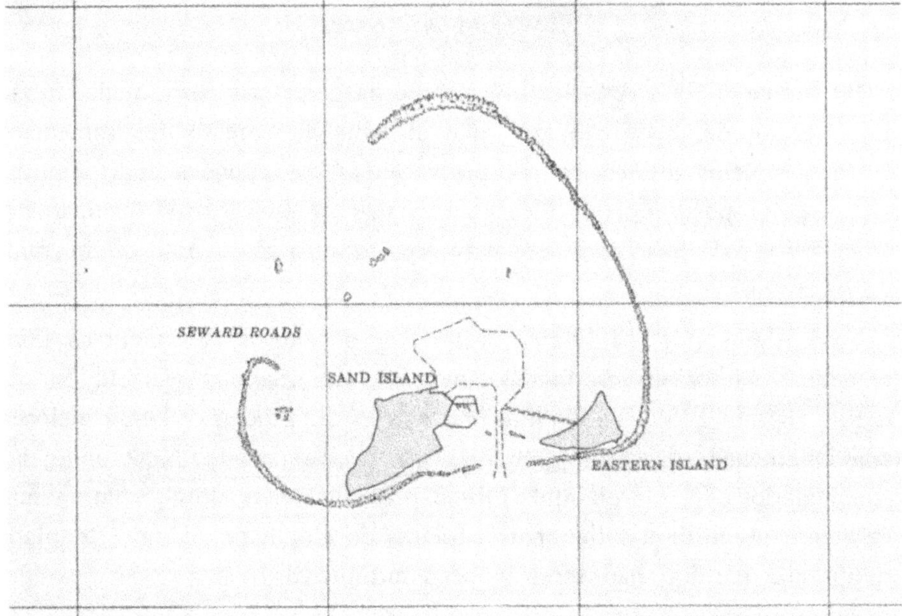

The Midway Islands.

ston were included in the Fourth Supplementary Deficiency Bill fiscal 1941. And, in one of the letters received in the week prior to my detachment, the Bureau of Yards and Docks promised to expedite the work on Midway in an effort to complete the land-plane runway on Eastern Island, Midway, by June 30, 1941.[7]

The part that the 1940-1941 development of aircraft facilities on Midway played in the success of the Pacific Fleet at the Battle of Midway in 1942 was an important one, and is a matter of history. Assembly of advanced base equipment and material for Midway was ordered on August 15, 1940.[8] A Marine Defense Battalion was ordered to depart for American Samoa prior to January 15, 1941.[9] But, it was not until January 17, 1941, that base work had proceeded far enough for the Chief of Naval Operations to direct that a permanent Marine Defense Battalion be established at Midway, Johnston, and Palmyra.[10]

[7] Bureau of Yards and Docks, serial YD of 9 Jan. 1941, letter to CNO, box 63, Bureau of Yards and Docks Confidential Correspondence, 1918-1941, Record Group 71, NA.

[8] CNO, serial 027112 of 15 Aug. 1940, letter, box 78, RG 313, NA.

[9] CNO, serial 054530 of 29 Nov. 1940, letter to all Bureaus, CNOCF, NHD, p. 2.

[10] CNO, serial 0638 of 17 Jan. 1941, letter to CINCUS, CNOCF, NHD.

Hawaiian Air Bases

By January 1941, considerably greater progress had been made in the air bases for the Hawaiian area, due in some measure to the immediacy of the problems created by the presence for the previous eight months of a large proportion of the Fleet in Hawaiian waters. I could detail to my relief the accomplishments here with less concern than those of the mid-Pacific islands.

Ford Island in Pearl Harbor was being developed as rapidly as Congressional authorizations, money, material, and manpower could be obtained. By late 1940, the landing mat was in the process of being widened and lengthened. A warming-up platform was underway. New living accommodations for officers and enlisted personnel were slowly coming into existence. A million-dollar patrol plane development of new seaplane ramps and parking had recently been authorized.

The land for the new major naval air base at Barbers Point, Oahu was being bought, and the planning for the facilities thereon was getting underway. The mooring mast field for lighter-than-air was well along to completion. Seaplane facilities at Kaneohe Bay, Oahu had been brought along rapidly, and the base was now in commission. Additionally, small air facilities had been established on the islands of Maui and Molokai, and were being expanded.[11]

The work of the development of the air bases and other facilities on all islands was a direct responsibility of the Shore Establishment, and the detailed work was primarily to be accomplished under the direction of the Commandant 14th Naval District.

For a Navy accustomed to operating overall on an annual 400-million-dollar budget, the total of 82 million dollars worth of public works projects in the Hawaiian area and mid-Pacific islands seemed almost unbelievable, but such was the total available in the fall of 1940.[12]

---

[11] CINCUS, serial 01775 of 1 Nov. 1940, letter to CNO (and endorsements thereto), box 134, CINCUS Files, RG 313, NA. Aviation facilities in the Hawaiian area is the subject of this letter.

[12] COM14, serial 4070 of 26 Sept. 1940, letter to CINCUS, box 119, CINCUS Files, RG 313, NA, p. 4.

Army-Navy Cooperation

In view of the questions which have been raised in regard to the co-operation of the Army and Navy in the Hawaiian area prior to the Pearl Harbor Attack, I wish to record my belief that such cooperation during my tenure in that area was excellent.

But, the point should be made that, because cooperation was excellent, it does not mean that Joint operational effectiveness was excellent. Joint operational effectiveness was certainly spotty when the first Joint exercises after the arrival of the Fleet in Hawaiian waters were held in May and June of 1940. A typical report of that period reads as follows:

> Joint operations with the Army have been conducted and the results have not been wholly satisfactory. The need for closer cooperation and for more frequent Joint operations is proven by the results attained. It is urgently recommended that such Joint operations with the Army be conducted at least once each month in the interests of increasing efficiency, safety of operations, and mobility of units.[13]

This recommendation was concurred with, except that exercises more frequent than monthly were deemed necessary. A regular schedule of various types of exercises was arranged with the Army and carried out. Operational effectiveness improved but was far from the perfection desired by "all hands."

I think the following despatch may illustrate the many fallacies that crept into public print in regard to Army-Navy cooperation.

> REFERRING TO ARTICLE "HOW TO BUILD AIR POWER" BY W. B. COURTNEY IN COLLIERS FOR 17 AUGUST 1940, I HAVE CONFERRED WITH LIEUTENANT GENERAL HERRON, COMMANDING HAWAIIAN DEPARTMENT AND REAR ADMIRAL BLOCH, COMMANDANT 14TH NAVAL DISTRICT REGARDING STATEMENT THAT QUOTE THE NAVY WASN'T PLAYING UNQUOTE WHEN A GENERAL BLACKOUT WAS RECENTLY HELD. BOTH AVER THAT STATEMENT IS A LIE WITHOUT QUALIFICATION. GENERAL HERRON WHO OBSERVED THE EXERCISE FROM THE AIR STATES THE NAVY GAVE GENEROUS AND COMPLETE COOPERATION AND THAT HE IS ENTIRELY WILLING TO BE SO QUOTED. CINCUS WAS AT SEA DURING EXERCISE

[13] "Annual Report of the Commander Patrol Wing Two (A. W. Fitch)" for the fiscal year 1940, 1 July 1940.

AND DID NOT WITNESS IT, BUT U.S. FLEET LETTER 1L40 GOVERNING BLACKOUT PROCEDURE WAS IN EFFECT AND CARRIED OUT.[14]

As late as January 1941, the Commandant 14th Naval District, in commenting on a Joint exercise, said:

> The communications between Army aircraft and naval vessels functioned well throughout the exercise. No issue is taken with the conclusion of the Commanding General, Hawaiian Air Force that the B18 type airplane is unsuitable for submarine search.

Lieutenant General Herron, USA, Commanding General Hawaiian Department, in commenting on the same exercise, said:

> I believe this exercise was of considerable value in bringing out some of the problems that will arise whenever Army aircraft are called upon to establish an antisubmarine patrol.

My comment on this read as follows:

> 2nd ENDORSEMENT January 22, 1941
> From: Commander in Chief, U.S. Fleet
> To: Commandant 14th Naval District
> Subject: Exercise S10 of 8 November 1940, Report of Army Participation
>
> 1. Returned. The Commander in Chief notes with gratification the continued cooperation, and the benefits therefrom. Every effort will be made to provide further occasion for such training.
>
> J. O. Richardson [15]

Not only were senior officers thinking of Army-Navy cooperation in the immediate day-by-day training, but they were thinking of active cooperation on a long-range basis. I quote from the letters of two of my many distinguished subordinates, who were discussing planning of additional aviation facilities in the Hawaiian area.

> This entire subject [of aviation facilities] is naturally viewed from the standpoint of national defense, and not merely that of the Navy. In the event of a Pacific campaign there would obviously be vast increases in the numbers of both Army and Navy planes in these Islands, and at the present time these could not be adequately based and serviced. Any money put into the necessary facilities is therefore well and wisely expended. I would recommend,

[14] CINCUS, 0020-0052 of 8 Sept. 1940, despatch to OPNAV.

[15] CINCUS, 22 Jan. 1941, letter to COM14.

however, that at an early date the appropriate agencies of the Army and Navy forces here present take joint action in setting up a further program of development, all with a view to mutual needs and use as circumstances may dictate.[16]

Admiral Peck Snyder said:

In a Pacific Campaign, the Army and Navy air elements in the Hawaiian Islands will undergo tremendous expansion. Close cooperation, mutual understanding, and joint employment of facilities will be essential. A program of aviation construction and activities is already underway. Commander Battle Force considers that the Local Joint Planning Committee, . . . is the appropriate agency to coordinate such Army and Navy development steps as are assigned to it for study and recommendations.[17]

Upon learning of my prospective detachment, General Herron was kind enough to write me on January 10, 1941.

Presumably, there is something of overwhelming importance to be done in Washington or they would not be taking you back there, but the Army infinitely regrets the going of a kindly and understanding friend. It has been the greatest of pleasures to work with you, and you go with the knowledge that under your regime an unprecedented and most timely cooperation between the Army and Navy has been achieved.

My reply of January 14, 1941 to General Herron contained this paragraph:

There is a bond between us and I might add that I have felt that bond of interest, understanding and respect growing from the commencement of our association in the Hawaiian Area. It has been a pleasure to work with the Army, through you, as Commanding General.

It is my belief that the picture which the newspapers paint of the Military Services at loggerheads with each other is more frequently wrong than right.

Repair Ships and Tenders

During the final few weeks, the failure of the CNO, up to that time, to plan to provide proper repair ships and tenders for the growing Fleet was pointed out for the last time. I said:

---

[16] COMAIRBATFOR (W. F. Halsey), serial 0744 of 20 Aug. 1940, letter to CINCUS, box 134, CINCUS Files, RG 313, NA, p. 4. This deals with aviation facilities in the Hawaiian area.

[17] COMBATFOR (C. P. Snyder), serial 0873 of 28 Aug. 1940, letter to CINCUS, box 134, CINCUS Files, RG 313, NA.

> During the Calendar Year 1941 thirty-eight large ships . . . will be added to the Forces Afloat. No additional repair ships will be available to take care of this load. During 1942 six large ships will be added. . . . One repair ship is provided during this year. During 1943 twenty-one large ships will be added. . . . One repair ship is provided during this year. During 1944 nineteen large ships will be added. . . . No repair ship is provided. During 1945 twenty-two large ships will be added. . . . No repair ship is provided.[18]

This letter, and an earlier one [19] dealing with inadequate planning for repair ships to help the smaller ships of the Fleet, were each based on data taken from the authorized and approved building programs of the Navy.

The Navy, in December 1940, was in the process of building 17 battleships, 12 carriers, 3 battle cruisers, 48 cruisers and 168 destroyers. Only 2 repair ships and 6 destroyer tenders were to be provided for all these ships. I recommended that the Navy Department provide 1 repair ship for each 20 large ships and 1 destroyer tender for each 18 destroyers. This was a conservative recommendation, and I believe that war damage experience led to an increased number of repair ships and tenders. But, had the action recommended been taken fore-handedly, it would have been a long step in the right direction.

Readiness of PATWING TWO

One of the last matters which concerned me while I was packing my sea bag was the ability of Patrol Wing Two at Pearl to meet sudden enemy action, or an emergency search for the enemy in an area up to 1,000 miles from the Hawaiian Islands. I communicated my wishes to Commander Scouting Force, who was the appropriate senior, and he undertook to obtain an immediate answer.

28 Jan 1941

CONFIDENTIAL
From: The Commander Patrol Wing Two.
To: The Commander Scouting Force.
Subject: Readiness of Patrol Wing Two for immediate action.

1. In reply to your question the following report as to the state of readiness for immediate action of Patrol Wing TWO is submitted. As your question is

[18] CINCUS, serial 0126 of 25 Jan. 1941, letter to CNO, CNOCF, NHD.

[19] CINCUS, serial 031 of 8 Jan. 1941, letter to CNO, CNOCF, NHD.

understood, the information desired primarily concerns the time required to act in case of a sudden emergency using personnel and material now available, and this report has been confined to that phase. Existing deficiencies in personnel, supplies, materials, equipment and supply facilities needed for a prolonged effort or campaign have been covered in detail in other correspondence.[20]

In succeeding paragraphs, the time required to initiate searches in areas within 250, 500, and 1,000 miles of the Naval Base at Pearl Harbor, by the patrol aircraft, was given. It was assumed (a) that no armament was required in the planes, except machine guns, or (b) planes were to be armed with 500 or 1,000-pound bombs. It was pointed out that only by "radically reducing present training work and keeping a definite number of planes in ready Standby Status" could a 500-mile or 1,000-mile search be started in less than two or three hours, respectively, and that searches by armed planes would require an hour to two hours more to initiate.

This report, available to my relief, was further evidence, if any were needed, of the very great advantages of a daily, routine long-range reconnaissance over one to be undertaken under emergency conditions of sudden orders, arising from reports of enemy or possible enemy action.

I wish now that, on December 5, 1940, I had not stopped these daily long-range naval-air reconnaissance flights. Once stopped, my successor found it unnecessary to restart them. Perhaps if I had kept them going, and he had kept them going, despite CNO's disbelief of their necessity, they would have served a very useful purpose on December 7, 1941.

Ordered Relieved on 31 January 1941

When my orders came thru directing my relief from command of the Fleet, in about three weeks, there were dozens of matters of importance to the Fleet in quite an unfinished condition. It became a matter of urgency for me and my staff to try to finish up the paper work end of as many as practicable, so as to be able to turn over a reasonably clean slate to my successor. I told my staff that, during the period I was packing my sea bag

---

[20] COMPATWINGTWO, serial 037 of 28 Jan. 1941, letter to COMSCOFOR.

for the last time, I wanted my successor, Admiral Kimmel, and the senior members of his staff to be brought into the discussion of all appropriate pending matters. In those matters dealing with war plans, an affirmative statement that this had been done was made in various letters to the Navy Department.[21]

My orders had been a real shock to me.

I was deeply disappointed in my detachment, yet there was some feeling of prospective relief, for I had never liked to work with people whom I did not trust, and I did not trust Franklin D. Roosevelt.

When the order relieving me of command of the Fleet was published, I received many letters from old friends and associates; but the most surprising and heartening one was from my only surviving sister, aged sixty-seven, a retired head of the Department of English in a Texas college, who knew little about the Navy, except that a Commander-in-Chief usually served in that billet two or more years.

This letter had a profound influence on my later life. I quote it here.

Canyon, Texas
January 10, 1941

Dear Brother:

One Sunday morning, forty years ago, I came down to breakfast to find the sitting room empty and the Paris [Texas] Morning News spread on the table.

We had been eagerly watching to see the publication of the Paris public school teaching staff, which had been delayed.

When I saw that, I read it and found my name omitted. At the foot, the notice said, "Miss M. Moss Richardson, on account of poor health and in recognition of her excellent service as a teacher, has been granted a leave of absence."

I was stunned, but I went on into the dining room quietly. Mamma said, "Moss, did you see the paper?"

"Yes."

"Did you ask for a leave of absence?"

"No."

"Did you know you were to have one?"

"No."

"Had anyone ever said anything about a leave of absence for you?"

"No."

Papa said, "Well, Moss, Mr. Wooten [school superintendent] has not done anything to you, that you would not have done to him. You never have

[21] *Pearl Harbor Hearings,* Part 14, pp. 993-99.

approved of him, and I suppose he knows it. If you could, you would have dropped him."

I thought Papa was wonderful. I think so yet. I knew that I had said to God several weeks before, "God, I can't do my best work here in Paris. I can do better work where I can have approval. If your judgment is the same as mine, move me, roughly and rudely if you must, but move me; and I'll never say a word." *And I never did.*

I was powerless to move, but God had me in charge. I have placed you and America daily in the care of God. You will be used.

Love to both you and May.

Devotedly,
Moss

Chapter XX

I Get Out of Step with the President

Reason for My Early Relief as Commander-in-Chief, U.S. Fleet

When I went to sea duty in June of 1939, I was due to become CINCUS in January 1940. I expected to stay on at sea at least until June 1941 and more probably until about January 1942, as, during recent years, the "custom of the Service" had been for officers to serve as CINCUS for eighteen to twenty-four months.[1] I was relieved at the end of January 1941, after thirteen months as CINCUS, and after having been assured, in October 1940, by the Chief of Naval Operations and the Chief of the Bureau of Navigation that I could count on a twenty-four month tour in that billet.

My early detachment was a shock to me and, I have been told by many people, a considerable surprise to the Naval Service.

There was and still is much speculation in regard to the cause for my detachment and the effect this decision of President Roosevelt's had on the location of the Fleet on December 7, 1941.

My knowledge of the matter is one-sided and, for that reason, incomplete. But, it appears desirable that my knowledge, in full, should be placed on record.

Secretary Knox Parries the Question

Upon my relief as CINCUS and my return to Washington in March 1941, and since my orders directed me "to report to the Secretary of the

[1] ADM C. C. Bloch, USN, CINCUS—January 1938 to January 1940 (24 months)
ADM A. J. Hepburn, USN, CINCUS—June 1936 to January 1938 (18 months)
ADM J. M. Reeves, USN, CINCUS—June 1934 to June 1936 (24 months)

Navy for duty," I so reported to Colonel Frank Knox on March 24, 1941.

After my saying, "I report for duty," I said to the Secretary "I have never known a Commander-in-Chief to be detached in such a summary manner as I have been, and I feel that I owe it to myself to inquire as to the reason for my peremptory detachment."

Colonel Knox said, "Why, Richardson, when you were here in Washington last October, you hurt the President's feelings by what you said to him. You should realize that. But, I am sure that someday soon, the President will send for you and have a talk."

I did not believe that the President would send for me because it had been my observation that Franklin D. Roosevelt took pains to avoid personal meetings and discussions with those with whom he had differed sharply—or had dropped from his team. To illustrate, Admiral King told me that Stark wasn't told that King was to be CINCUS until several days after the decision was made.

I did not ask "Betty" Stark at this time why I had been relieved, and I have never asked him since. He had not written to me in regard to this during the period between the time of the issuance of my orders and my detachment (twenty-five days). This I thought very, very strange. He has never, to this day, brought up the subject in our many meetings during the fifteen years since that date. In view of what happened to our Fleet at Pearl Harbor on December 7, 1941, I believe he may have a few regrets as to his part in the matter.

The Official Record

During the 1945 Congressional Pearl Harbor Investigation, I was asked a number of questions. To the best of my knowledge, I answered all of them completely, except one. That question dealt with my conversation with the President on October 8, 1940. What I said was truthful. I omitted one important exchange of views with the President.

The record reads as follows:

> Mr. MITCHELL. Well, the White House records show that on October 8, 1940, you had lunch with the President and with Governor Leahy at 1 p.m. Do you remember that?
>
> Admiral RICHARDSON. That is correct.

Mr. MITCHELL. Governor Leahy or Admiral Leahy?

Admiral RICHARDSON. Admiral William E. [sic] Leahy.

Mr. MITCHELL. He was then Governor of Puerto Rico.

Admiral RICHARDSON. Yes. We did not go to the White House office in company. I was invited by the President through the Chief of Naval Operations to lunch at 1 o'clock. When I arrived there I found Admiral Leahy there.

Mr. MITCHELL. Will you state in your own way, Admiral, just what occurred at that meeting and what was said about any of these matters we have been referring to?

Admiral RICHARDSON. The President talked to Admiral Leahy about Puerto Rican affairs, and as I was not interested, I remember little of what was said; but I have a vague recollection that one subject under discussion was the question of housing.

The President asked Admiral Leahy his opinion about strengthening the Asiatic Fleet and my recollection is that Admiral Leahy said that whatever you sent out will be lost, therefore I would send the least valuable combatant ships we have, the 7,500 ton cruisers, but I recommended, I personally recommended that none be sent. A decision to send none was reached.

Mr. MITCHELL. Admiral Leahy had been Chief of Naval Operations previously?

Admiral RICHARDSON. He had been Chief of Naval Operations. He was Chief of Naval Operations when I was the Assistant.

Mr. MITCHELL. Then proceed, Admiral, with your statement of what occurred there.

Admiral RICHARDSON. The following statement, because of its importance, I have written out. I wrote it out several weeks ago when it appeared certain, in my mind, that I would, unfortunately, be called before this committee. And with the permission of the Chairman I would like to read this statement—

The CHAIRMAN. Yes.

Admiral RICHARDSON. Which I prepared in the quiet of my home, where I could think and refresh my memory to a maximum extent possible.

The CHAIRMAN. You may proceed, Admiral, to do that.

Admiral RICHARDSON. I took up the question of returning to the Pacific coast all of the fleet except the Hawaiian Detachment.

The President stated that the fleet was retained in the Hawaiian area in order to exercise a restraining influence on the actions of Japan.

I stated that in my opinion the presence of the fleet in Hawaii might influence a civilian political government, but that Japan had a military government which knew that the fleet was undermanned, unprepared for war, and had no Train of auxiliary ships without which it could not undertake active operations. Therefore, the presence of the fleet in Hawaii could not exercise a restraining influence on Japanese action.

I further stated we were more likely to make the Japanese feel that we meant

compliments of ***Life*** **Magazine**

Admiral Richardson taking the oath before the Joint Congressional Committee investigating the Pearl Harbor Attack.

business if a Train were assembled and the fleet returned to the Pacific coast, the complements filled, the ships docked, and fully supplied with ammunition, provisions, stores, and fuel, and then stripped for war operations.

The President said in effect, "Despite what you believe, I know that the presence of the fleet in the Hawaiian area, has had, and is now having, a restraining influence on the actions of Japan."

I said, "Mr. President, I still do not believe it, and I know that our fleet is disadvantageously disposed for preparing for or initiating war operations."

The President then said, "I can be convinced of the desirability of returning the battleships to the west coast if I can be given a good statement which will convince the American people and the Japanese Government that in bringing the battleships to the west coast we are not stepping backward."

This is embarrassing.

Later I asked the President if we were going to enter the war. He replied that if the Japanese attacked Thailand, or the Kra Peninsula, or the Dutch East Indies we would not enter the war, that if they even attacked the Philippines he doubted whether we would enter the war, but that they could not always avoid making mistakes and that as the war continued and the area of operations expanded sooner or later they would make a mistake [2] and we would enter the war.[3]

Mr. MITCHELL. Does that complete your statement of the conversation?

• • •

Admiral RICHARDSON. That is about all of it.

• • •

Mr. MITCHELL. Admiral Richardson, in the correspondence which you have (at his witness desk) there appears to be a memorandum to the Chief of Naval Operations dated October 9, 1940, made by you. That was the day following this visit with the President?

---

[2] This caused me to think that he meant sooner or later the Japanese would commit an overt act against the U.S., with the result that the citizens of the United States would be willing to enter the war.

[3] It should be noted that only the first part of this statement of the President's was in consonance with the following political promises he had made just a month before at the Teamsters Union Convention in Washington, and was to make again three weeks later in Philadelphia, on October 23, 1940, when he opened his campaign for a third term: "We will not participate in foreign wars, and we will not send our Army, naval, or air forces to fight in foreign lands outside of the Americas, except in case of attack."

His public statements, of course, did not state what I consider were his real intentions or beliefs in the matter, which were that we would be at war with Japan in due time, and that he was willing for some ship of the Navy to be the victim of a Japanese "mistake." And, these intentions showed how deceiving were the words in his October 23, 1940 campaign speech: "It's for peace that I have labored, and it is for peace that I shall labor all the days of my life." *War—And Aid to Democracies,* Vol. 9 of *The Public Papers and Addresses of Franklin D. Roosevelt,* Samuel L. Rosenman, ed. (New York: The MacMillan Co., 1941), pp. 415, 495.

Admiral RICHARDSON. It was.

• • •

Mr. MITCHELL. You made that memorandum of October 9, 1940, following your visit the day before with the President?

Admiral RICHARDSON. I did. In order that the Chief of Naval Operations might be informed as to the decisions of the President and as to his views as expressed to me.[4]

• • •

Confidential *October 9, 1940*

MEMORANDUM FOR THE CHIEF OF NAVAL OPERATIONS

Points covered in talk with the President:

1. Go ahead with assembly of Train.

2. Have we fuel oil in Samoa adequate to fill four (4) old light cruisers?

3. Give me a chart showing British and French Bases or possible bases for surface ships, submarines or airplanes in Islands in the Pacific, east of the International Date Line.

4. The British Ambassador stated that Ghormley was busy transmitting to the Department information regarding technical materials, and the British Admiralty felt that they should have officers prepared for staff conferences.

5. The British believe the Germans will attempt to occupy Dakar from Spain overland through Africa.

6. I (F.D.R.) can be convinced of the desirability of retaining the battleships on the West Coast if I can be given a good statement which will convince the American people, and the Japanese Government, that in bringing the battleships to the West Coast we are not stepping backward.

7. The President indicated that he might approve sending a Division of old Light Cruisers to visit Mindinao [sic] as a gesture. He did not appear favorably disposed toward sending a stronger force.

J. O. RICHARDSON[5]

Mr. MITCHELL. The first item on that memorandum is: "Go ahead with assembly of Train."

What does that mean?

Admiral RICHARDSON. There had been some discussion as to assembling auxiliary vessels, transports, repair ships, supply ships. I had urged that it be done as one evidence of our intention to be prepared. The President stated that we would go ahead with the assembly of a Train.

Mr. MITCHELL. Item 2 is: "Have we fuel oil in Samoa adequate to fill four old light cruisers?"

Is that a question the President asked, or one you wanted to know about?

[4] *Pearl Harbor Hearings,* Part 1, pp. 265-68.

[5] ADM Richardson, 9 Oct. 1940, memo. to CNO, CNOCF, NHD.

Admiral RICHARDSON. The President asked me. I knew we did not have it. So I wanted the Chief of Naval Operations informed that he might find it necessary or advisable to have a supply of fuel oil in Samoa.

Mr. MITCHELL. Item 3:

"Give me a chart showing British and French bases or possible bases for surface. ships, submarines, or airplanes in islands in the Pacific east of the international date line."

Was that another request from the President?

Admiral RICHARDSON. No. That was a request by me, as I remember it.

Mr. MITCHELL. Then, in paragraph 4, you stated:

"The British Ambassador stated that Ghormley—"

That is Admiral Ghormley, is it?

Admiral RICHARDSON. It is Admiral R. L. Ghormley.

Mr. Mitchell. (reading):

"—was busy transmitting to the Department information regarding technical materials, and the British Admiralty felt that they should have officers prepared for staff conferences."

Were you reporting a thing that the President had said to you?

Admiral RICHARDSON. I was.

Mr. MITCHELL. No. 5:

"The British believe the Germans will attempt to occupy Dakar from Spain overland through Africa."

Under that, in brackets, "F.D.R."

What does that mean?

Admiral RICHARDSON. "F.D.R." belongs to the next paragraph. The first is a bit of information. The next, the sixth paragraph is intended to read:

"I, Franklin D. Roosevelt, can be convinced of the desirability, because that is what the President stated to me.

Mr. MITCHELL. (reading):

"I can be convinced of the desirability of retaining the battleships on the west coast if I can be given a good statement which will convince the American people, and the Japanese Government, that in bringing the battleships to the west coast we are not stepping backward."

That was informing the Chief of Naval Operations what the President had said?

Admiral RICHARDSON. That is true. I was at that time, just before going to Washington, on board a flagship on the west coast with approximately one-third of the battleships. We had returned to the west coast for replenishment and for recreation and for overhaul and, if my memory serves me correctly, I was at that time flying my flag in the *NEW MEXICO.*

Mr. MITCHELL. Item 7, the last on the memo, is this (reading):

"The President indicated that he might approve sending a Division of old

Light Cruisers to visit Mindinao [sic] as a gesture. He did not appear favorably disposed toward sending a stronger force."

That was just passing on to the Chief of Naval Operations an item of information?

Admiral RICHARDSON. It was.[6]

Senator Ferguson of Michigan returned to my conversation with the President during his period for questioning me, and the following colloquy took place:

Senator FERGUSON. When you gave yesterday the conversation that you had at the White House with the President and Admiral Leahy did you finish reading your entire statement?

Admiral RICHARDSON. I did.

Senator FERGUSON. Can you recall anything more that took place at that conversation?

Admiral RICHARDSON. No. In a conversation of the length of 2 hours, some of it about Puerto Rico, some of it about the fleet, some of it about a selection system, some of it about retiring officers, it is impossible to remember more than what impressed one at the time as being of grave import.

Senator FERGUSON. You had some very definite opinions on the subject that you were discussing with the President, did you not?

Admiral RICHARDSON. I did.

Senator FERGUSON. And he had some very definite opinions on the subject that he was discussing with you?

Admiral RICHARDSON. He did.

Senator FERGUSON. Well, now, will you tell us—or, first, you told us, as near as you can state it, what the President had said. Will you state, as near as you can, what you said to the President? Did you make a written memo based on that? I thought that you—

Admiral RICHARDSON. I read that for you yesterday. Shall I read it again?

Senator FERGUSON. What you said to the President?

Admiral RICHARDSON. I did.

Senator FERGUSON. Have you anything to add to that?

Admiral RICHARDSON. No.

Senator FERGUSON. Well, then, did you hear from the President on that subject again?

Admiral RICHARDSON. I never heard from the President again and never saw him again.[7]

---

[6] *Pearl Harbor Hearings,* Part 1, pp. 268-69.

[7] *Ibid.,* pp. 310-11.

Why the Senator's Question Was Not Answered More Fully

I believe a statement is essential as to why I did not respond more completely to Senator Ferguson's question "Can you recall anything more that took place at that conversation?"

A full answer to that question would have required me to inform the committee of the statement I made to the President during our October 8 conversation, which I believe led to my early detachment from CINCUS.

It was my belief then, and it is my belief now, that few committees of Congress are interested in ascertaining the factual truths in a matter under investigation.

The members are primarily interested in obtaining from witnesses statements that can be used to the political advantage of their political party (Democratic or Republican).

I think this was particularly true of the Joint Committee investigating the Pearl Harbor Attack.

As Senator Lucas (Democrat of Illinois) said, "When I know the background of this thing [the Congressional Investigation into the Pearl Harbor Attack], when I know of the statements made upon the floor of Congress, long before hearings were started, and then when I hear about a non-partisan investigation dealing with facts alone, I am tempted to laugh. . . . I, too, want the facts, but there are some folks who want political facts."[8] And, I was completely unwilling to lend myself to making unnecessary statements which could be used to the political advantage of either political party.

In fact, I told the first General Counsel to the Committee, William D. Mitchell, that, while on the witness stand, I would volunteer no information and I would limit myself to answering questions as tersely as possible. And further, I had taken a vow to myself that I would not discuss my conversation with the President on that eighth day of October any further than required to do so.

The Joint Committee had been given the mission by the Congress to:

> . . . make a full and complete investigation of the facts relating to the events and circumstances leading up to or following the attack made by Japanese

[8] *Ibid.*, Part 9, p. 4287.

armed forces upon Pearl Harbor in the territory of Hawaii on December 7, 1941, and shall report to the Senate and the House of Representatives . . . the results. . . .[9]

A full answer to Senator Ferguson's question would have gone into matters which, in my opinion, bore no relation to the Committee's mission and the Pearl Harbor Attack.

For these reasons, the answer was given as stated in the Congressional Investigation of the Pearl Harbor Attack.

The October 1940 Conference

I had not wanted to come east to Washington for that October conference, but when I was ordered to come, I made up my mind that it was my duty to my country and my personal responsibility to the President, to the whole Navy, and particularly to officers and men who manned the ships of the Fleet, to state the facts frankly as I saw them.

This I had done.

In the Congressional Investigation of the Pearl Harbor Attack, there is a copy of a memorandum, dated September 12, 1940, that I had given Secretary of the Navy Frank Knox near the completion of his September visit to the Fleet. It said:

(B) *Enlisted Personnel.*

(a) While the (Navy's overall) enlisted strength increased 11,349 between 23 May and 15 August, the Fleet in the Pacific made a net gain of only about 600. Our enormous expenditures for material may prove futile unless there is a prompt and commensurate personnel expansion.

(b) The bottleneck of the training stations, limiting the rate of acceptance of new men, should be eliminated *at once* and emergency expansion should begin *now* without awaiting deficiency appropriations. We have not waited for specific appropriations in providing material expansion, and it is difficult to understand or explain to the Fleet why we are unable or unwilling to meet even more vital problems of personnel (involving the imperative necessity of making ready what we *already have* as well as training men for new construction) with equally direct and effective action. I estimate the time necessary to make a modern man-of-war's-man at 4 years. You can see the necessity of getting started on this training right away.[10]

---

[9] *Ibid.*, Part 1, p. 4.
[10] *Ibid., Part* 14, pp. 954-55.

One result of the personnel deficiency problem, which bothered me a great deal, in fact probably more than any other, was that it kept many of my senior subordinates in the Fleet from being as war-minded as I would have liked, since they reasoned, "surely the President isn't going to put us into war with only partially manned ships." Secretary Knox had told Admiral Bloch that I didn't seem very war-minded, and this concerned me. So, it seemed to me that if the Fleet was to be fully war-minded, I just had to get more men into the Navy and thus to the Fleet.

This condition was referred to by me in the Congressional Investigation of the Pearl Harbor Attack, when I testified:

> I did everything within my power to make the officers and men of the fleet become war-minded, and one great deterrent of my effective accomplishment of that aim was the fact that many officers who were long-time friends would say, in effect, "Joe, we cannot be on the verge of war, otherwise they would give us enough men to man the ships!" [11]

Much had happened in the four months of June, July, August, and September of 1940 to affect the future materiel strength of the Navy. To list some of the major occurrences:

> On June 14, 1940, the President had signed the "11% Naval Expansion Act," increasing the carrier, cruiser, and submarine tonnage of the Navy by 167,000 tons, and that of auxiliary ships by 75,000 tons.
>
> On June 15, 1940, the President had signed the act increasing the naval aeronautical strength from 3,500 to 10,000 planes.
>
> On July 1, 1940, the Navy had awarded contracts for forty-four new ships.
>
> On July 19, 1940, the President had signed the Naval Expansion Act, providing for a "Two Ocean Navy" and expanding the Fleet by 70 percent.
>
> On September 9, 1940, the Navy had awarded contracts for 210 new ships, including 12 aircraft carriers and 7 battleships.

But through all these materiel changes, expanding the Navy very markedly during this four-month period, naval enlisted strength of the regular

---

[11] *Ibid.*, Part 1, p. 327.

Navy remained at 145,000.[12] Only on September 28, 1940 had the buildup to 224,000 men been initiated.[13] It was not until nine months later, on June 21, 1941 that a buildup of the Navy to 369,000 was authorized.[14] In my opinion 369,000 was a realistic figure for the Navy to be seeking in October 1940.

So, when I had the opportunity, on October 8, 1940, to talk to the President again, I went all over the personnel situation in much the same manner as I had covered it during my conversation with him on July 8, 1940. He continued to maintain, as he had done on July 8, 1940, that men in mechanical trades in civil life could be quickly inducted and made adequate sailormen, if their services were suddenly required.

I insisted that a seasick garage mechanic would be of little use at sea, and that it took time for most young men to get their sea legs.

I said it was essential that the enlisted personnel of the Fleet should be markedly increased immediately. This was in order that the men required to man the ships then building could be given some prior training in the Fleet, and so that the Fleet would have 100 percent of complement left in it, when these men were transferred out, to put the new ships in commission.

The discussion waxed hot and heavy.

I could not help but detect that reelection political considerations, rather than long-range military considerations, were the controlling factor in the President's thinking. It was less than a month before the 1940 Presidential Election, and the President was reluctant to make any commitment to increase the number of men in the Navy, which, due to the location of naval ships in foreign waters, would seem to run counter to his third-term campaign statements.

In Washington, D. C., on September 11, 1940, at the Teamster's Union Convention, he had pledged that:

> We will not participate in foreign wars, and we will not send our Army,

[12] "Revised Operating Force Plan, Fiscal Year 1940," CNO, serial 238 of 5 Jan. 1940, WWIICF, NHD, p. 2a.

[13] "Revised Operating Force Plan, Fiscal Year 1941," CNO, serial 150638 of 28 Sept. 1940, WWIICF, NHD, p. 2a.

[14] "Operating Force Plan, Fiscal Year 1942," CNO, serial 205338 of 21 June 1941, WWIICF, NHD, p. 2a.

naval, or air forces to fight in foreign lands outside of the Americas, except in case of attack.'[15]

He repeated this pledge in Philadelphia on October 23, 1940,[16] and paraphrased it on October 30, 1940, when he said in Boston:

> I have said this before, but I shall say it again and again and again: Your boys are not going to be sent into any foreign wars.[17]

Finally, when it became fully apparent that he had no intention of accepting my recommendations, I said to him very deliberately:

> Mr. President, I feel that I must tell you that the senior officers of the Navy do not have the trust and confidence in the civilian leadership of this country that is essential for the successful prosecution of a war in the Pacific.

The President, with a look of pained surprise on his face, said:

> Joe, you just don't understand that this is an election year and there are certain things that can't be done, no matter what,until the election is over and won.

I had prepared the above statement, which I made to the President after long thought and deliberation, and prior to my departure from my flagship for Washington.

I had believed for some time that Admiral Stark, the Chief of Naval Operations and the President's principal naval advisor (both in accordance with the law and in fact), was not succeeding in inducing the President to accept the naval point of view in regard to naval matters. I also believe that Stark realized not only this, but that the Navy was not ready for war, due to Presidential decisions made for party political reasons, rather than on the basis of what was good for the country.

Congressman Vinson had spoken to me of this failure when I was in Washington in July 1940, and sought my advice as to how to remedy it.

It seemed to me that the President's great love for the Navy led him, on occasion, to rationalize that, since he loved the Navy as much or more than the naval officers with whom he was dealing on naval matters, this love raised his technical judgment in regard to these matters to a par or above that of his really informed advisors.

I thought the President's policies would get us into a shooting war—sooner than they did actually.

---

[15] Rosenman, *War—And Aid to Democracies,* p. 415.

[16] *Ibid.,* p. 495.

[17] *Ibid.,* p. 517.

I thought the Navy's deficiencies were such as to make very doubtful its successfully carrying out the approved War Plans for a war with Japan.

I thought the President's disregard of the recommendations of his principal naval advisers would lead to naval failures or disasters in this war for which he and the country were completely unprepared.

I thought that the President could be shocked into either changing his policies, or providing adequate implementation of them.

I thought that it was worth my own official neck to get this accomplished. For I believed it was either my neck now, or that of the Navy in the months ahead. I thought I had but this one chance, and this one choice.

I thought that what I believed to be the true opinion of many senior naval officers, in regard to the civilian leadership of the country, would be a real shock to the President.

I can state with complete accuracy that, when the President heard my statement, he looked and acted completely crushed. He *was* shocked.

Unfortunately, the shock did not lead to a change of Presidential policies or the naval implementation of them. I believe it did lead to my being relieved of my duties as Commander-in-Chief of the U.S. Fleet.

I could not end this story without adding the statement I made to the Congressional Committee at the conclusion of my testimony, on November 21, 1945:

> Mr. Chairman, I thank you for this opportunity to state that I never bore any resentment toward President Roosevelt because of my detachment from command of the United States Fleet.
>
> He was the constitutional Commander in Chief of the Army and Navy. I was one of his senior subordinates; there was a difference of opinion; each of us frankly expressed his views; neither could induce the other to change his opinion; I was relieved of command of the Fleet. Had I been constitutional Commander in Chief of the Army and Navy, I would have taken the same action.
>
> Because of this conviction, on January 28, 1941, 4 days before I was relieved of command of the Fleet with orders to proceed to Washington for duty, I sent to the Chief of Naval Operations by an officer, the following oral message: "The day I was made Commander-in-Chief I realized then and thereafter that the same power which made me commander in chief could unmake me at any time. When I arrive in Washington I shall keep my lips sealed and my eyes in the boat and put my weight on the oar in any duty assigned.[18]

[18] *Pearl Harbor Hearings,* Part 1, pp. 339-40.

Chapter XXI

Picking up the Loose Ends

Telling the Public the Facts

It takes great intestinal fortitude for a military officer to report to his senior that some of the units of his force are not ready for war. Too frequently such a report results in his detachment and the ordering to his billet of some officer whose abilities are thought to be of a higher order, or, in case the truth is offensive to the seniors affected, the ordering of someone whose conscience is more elastic, or standards of readiness markedly lower.

In June of 1940, the commander of the Atlantic Squadron of the United States Fleet had reported to me:

> The Primary War Mission of the Squadron is to defend and further our interests in the Atlantic. The present composition of the Squadron is quite inadequate to cope with the forces which the progress of events in Europe may soon release to operate against it.
>
> The battleships of Battleship Division Five are not ready for war.
>
> • • •
>
> The destroyers of the Squadron are not ready for war. They require additional trained personnel both commissioned and enlisted. They require tactical training and an opportunity to acquire skill and proficiency in the use of the weapons with which armed. Many of them require considerable repair before they can be considered reliable at high speeds.[1]

I passed this report on to the Secretary of the Navy and further stated:

> The strength of the Fleet is only adequate for a purely defensive mission in the northern half of the Western Hemisphere under naval alignments that exist today.[2]

[1] "Annual Report of the Commander Atlantic Squadron" (H. E. Ellis), for the fiscal year 1940, serial C-329, WWIICF, NHD, p. 6.

[2] CINCUS, June 1940, letter to SECNAV.

After all this, I was very much surprised, and not a little upset, to find in the Secretary's Annual Report to the President no caution because of these basic facts, but the statement "On any comparable basis, the United States [Navy] is second to none." [3]

I did not foresee the unenviable position in which the Navy would be placed in the eyes of the American public at the start of the war in the Pacific. But, as sound compliance was the general prudential rule of all seamen, I thought that the "Powers that Be" in Washington would do the country, the Navy, and themselves a better service by telling the public the truth about the many deficiencies that needed correction, rather than proclaiming from the tree tops "a second to none" condition for the Navy.

FDR as Assistant Secretary

During the period of great expansion of the Navy, President Franklin D. Roosevelt frequently developed a great passion for having a particular feature worked into the design of new ships, such as having destroyers carry an aeroplane, or for getting the Navy Department to adopt some particular piece of equipment for an already designed ship. He had pursued a similar policy when he was Assistant Secretary of the Navy under Josephus Daniels.

I had a good knowledge of some of these earlier skirmishes between the Assistant Secretary and the various officers in the Navy Department. I think they illustrate well enough how his mind worked, to justify the inclusion of one of these incidents in this book.

Prior to World War I, the Navy was authorized by the Congress to build some much needed subchasers for coastal antisubmarine patrol. The Navy finally decided that a 110-foot wooden-hulled subchaser was the minimum length hull which could carry the available antisubmarine equipment, keep to sea, and do its job in the rough weather so frequent in our coastal waters. The wooden hull pleased Assistant Secretary Roosevelt very much, because, as a yachtsman, he had a strong prediliction for wooden hulls. However, he argued long and hard for a 65-foot subchaser. Some naval officers, including myself, believed that his arguments were conditioned by the fact that a relative of his had an interest in an engine which would adequately power a 65-foot subchaser, but could not adequately power a

[3] SECNAV, *Annual Report*, 1940, p. 1.

110-foot subchaser, since the necessity of building a subchaser that would take this particular engine was frequently mentioned by the Assistant Secretary.

When the question as to whether this engine would be satisfactory for the 110-foot subchaser was submitted officially to the Bureau of Engineering, my classmate, J. O. Fisher, was handling the internal combustion engine desk in the Bureau. He submitted an adverse report on the engine.

A few days later, FDR met me in the corridor and said, "J. O., I am going to have your friend Joe Fisher ordered to Guam." I said, "Surely Mr. Secretary you are not going to establish Guam as a penal colony or punish an officer for doing what he believed to be his duty."

Captain Hugh Rodman was on duty with the General Board during the period this skirmish was taking place. He told me that one evening, as he was leaving the Department, FDR's civilian aide, Louis McHenry Howe, came up to him and said, "Captain, I understand that the question of building 65-foot subchasers is before the General Board. You will find it to your advantage to recommend this program be adopted." Hugh Rodman's reply was typical of the man; "You dirty little SOB; I will not make any recommendation unless I think it to the advantage of the Navy."

In any case, the Navy built many 110-foot subchasers, and no 65-foot subchasers, and did not use the particular engine advocated by FDR.

During the service of FDR as Assistant Secretary of the Navy, I came in close contact with him. I knew quite well most of the other officers below Flag rank whose official duties in the Navy Department also required them to work closely with the Assistant Secretary.

FDR had great personal charm, and attracted people to him. Those naval officers who worked for him had a certain bond of association, even during the twelve years that FDR was away from the Washington scene. Upon his return to the government as President, FDR found that this group had moved along in the Navy under their own power, and in the intervening years had become captains and Flag Officers. As President, he was in a position to create opportunities for their further advancement, and he took pleasure in doing so.

From February 1941 On

In order to complete the story of my active service in the Navy, it should be recorded that I served on the General Board from the date of

80-G-703464

Presentation to Mr. Clarence Dillon of a Certificate of Merit for his services to the Navy Relief Society. Left to right, Fleet Admiral Chester W. Nimitz, Secretary of the Navy James Forrestal, Mr. Dillon, Fleet Admiral Ernest J. King, and Admiral Richardson, Executive Vice President of the Navy Relief Society.

my reporting to the Navy Department in March 1941 until May 25, 1942, when I was assigned by the Secretary of the Navy to duty with the Navy Relief Society as Executive Vice President.

During my service with the Navy Relief Society, I prepared the first "Manual for the Navy Relief Society," which I hoped would serve the same constructive purpose for the Navy Relief Society as the occasional codification of our federal laws serve the legal branch of our government.

In 1941, I was made the senior member of the Special Committee for Reorganization of National Defense. This committee was established by the Joint Chiefs of Staff to consider and make recommendations regarding unification of the Army and Navy. I disagreed heartily with the report, which recommended a single department with a "Commander of the Armed Forces" who would serve as Chief of Staff to the President, besides exercising military command over the Army, the Navy, a newly created Air Force, and the commanders of areas, theaters and independent commands. I expressed my disagreement in a minority report which foretold some of the problems that would be created, not solved, by unification.

And then, after World War II was over, I appeared as a witness of the United States Navy during the trial of the alleged Japanese war criminals before the International Military Tribunal for the Far East, sitting in Tokyo.

I was finally relieved from active duty on January 2, 1947, after nearly forty-nine years of active naval service.

The day after the attack on Pearl Harbor, I went down to the General Board rooms. Everybody was sitting around giving their views in regard to the whys and wherefores of the attack. The President of the General Board finally said, "Joe, you haven't said a word up to now. What are your views?" I said, "All I have to say is that every day from now on, I am going to pray for two things. The first is for the success of our arms; the second is that I shall keep my mouth shut."

I did not "lay down the bricks" after reporting to the General Board on March 25, 1941 (and I haven't laid them down yet). I was still anxious to be useful to the Navy and to the country, insofar as my talents could be employed. Fortunately, during the next five years, I worked among and with friends, in the professional part of the Navy at least, and there is no work so rewarding as working with friends.

There are two matters which occurred during that period which I believe may have some permanent naval interest and should be mentioned:

(A) Drafting of authority of Chief of Naval Operations and Commander-in-Chief of the United States Fleet

(B) Drafting of regulations for temporary promotion of officers in time of war

Drafting of Authority for Chief of Naval Operations and Commander-in-Chief of the United States Fleet

One Sunday, in early March 1942, when I was on the General Board, and King was Commander-in-Chief of the United States Fleet, upon his request, I drafted the Presidential Executive Order which reorganized the

Navy Department. King came to the General Board rooms, and asked Sexton and me, who were present together, to draft the order, and Sexton, my senior by five years, turned the job over to me.

This order established in one officer, who was to serve as both Commander-in-Chief of the United States Fleet and Chief of Naval Operations, broad authority over not only the Forces Afloat, but those ashore. As drafted, the order gave King the supreme command of the Operating Forces. It also gave King responsibility for the preparation, readiness, and logistic support of the Operating Forces and, more importantly, the necessary authority to coordinate and direct the efforts of Bureaus and offices of the Navy Department to this end.

This drafting job was done to King's complete satisfaction, and is an indication of the high respect which we had for each other. With the addition of only two words, suggested by me, and accepted by King, the President signed the order the way it was originally drafted.

As an indication of how FDR treated those who ceased to be useful to him, I relate the followng incident. When King asked Sexton and me to draft an "Executive Order" making him Commander-in-Chief, U.S. Fleet and Chief of Naval Operations, I asked him what was to become of Stark. He said: "The President said that he did not give a damn what happened to Stark so long as he was gotten out of Washington as soon as practicable."

I then asked if Stark knew about the impending change, and, when King said "no," I said that I thought that in all decency Stark should be informed to which King agreed. Stark was not retired, but was ordered to command our Naval forces in Europe, with his Headquarters in London.

Regulations for Temporary Promotion of Officers in Time of War

In 1942, I was appointed by the Chief of the Bureau of Naval Personnel as the senior member of a board to draft regulations (for signature by the President) to govern the temporary promotion of all naval officers during the war.

It was my opinion that, in time of war, the temporary promotion of all officers in the Navy should be kept in step with that of those officers (both reserve and regular) who are in the Operating Forces and actually fighting the war. I do not believe that officers in Washington, close to the Secretary or Assistant Secretaries, should have special preferment over those outside of Washington. I do not believe that reserve officers deserve or need faster promotion than regular officers. They are definitely not qualified to have such promotion.

So, I drafted the regulations to provide that promotions could be made only one grade at a time, and, except under very limited circumstances, only in step with one's contemporaries and at reasonable intervals. These regulations were recommended for approval as they were passed up the naval chain of command to the Secretary of the Navy. They were approved by him and sent to the President.

The next thing I knew was that I read in the paper, that the drafted regulations were unsatisfactory to the President. I learned then that he had said to Secretary Knox, "Richardson has hamstrung you and me so that we can't promote whom we want to."

So, the drafted regulations were brought back to the Navy Department and changed so that reserve officers could be appointed from civilian life into the Navy in the highest permissible grade (lieutenant commander) on one day, and immediately promoted the next day to the next higher grade. And, this was done for the favored few by the Secretary.

Nowadays (1957), I hear that the Navy has been for some years promoting seagoing Line officers to the rank of captain after about 18 years service and to Flag rank after about 26 years service. These officers have 5 to 8 years less service than most officers of my era had in which to gain the knowledge and seagoing or flying experience necessary to fully qualify them for the difficult tasks which captains and Flag Officers have always had to face at sea, in peace, as well as in war.

I do not doubt the advantage of the additional pay and prestige to the individual officer. But, I do wonder whether the Government and the Navy are getting a fair break from the tax payers' dollar when they go out and hire these 18-year captains en masse.

I believe that the Navy gets a harder, longer, and more effective try from the individual officer if he isn't permitted to catch the Flag Officer "carrot" held in front of him from the day he enters the Naval Academy, until he is past fifty. Dropping the captain "carrot" in officers' mouths at ages of 38 to 40, distinctly lowers the average officer effort which is put into the U.S. Navy during the age bracket 40 to 50.

Battleship Admiral

It wasn't until about a year ago, when I had been off active duty for ten years, that I ever heard myself referred to as a "battleship admiral."

I had always prided myself on the fact that I was a small-ship sailorman. So, merely to set the record straight, I point out that, when I became Commander-in-Chief after thirty-eight years of service, I had not been attached to a battleship during the previous twenty years. My service in the *Delaware* and the *Nevada* (the only two battleships I was ever attached to) was less than five years out of nearly twenty-one years of sea service.

However, during my service on the *Delaware,* I had the advantage of serving under four captains (Charles Gove, John Hood, Hugh Rodman, and William L. Rodgers), all of whom were promoted to Flag rank; and on the *Nevada* under four captains (Joseph Strauss, A. T. Long, T. P. Magruder, and W. C. Cole), all of whom were promoted to Flag rank; and, when I became Commander Battle Force, the three senior officers in the U.S. Fleet (Bloch, Snyder, and Richardson) had served on the *USS Delaware* during my service on that battleship.

But, as for the battleship, she served the Navy and the country extremely well over a period of sixty years. I trust that her successor, the aircraft carrier, and the aircraft carrier's successor—whatever that may be—will do as well for the Navy, and leave her place as the spearhead of the naval attack with as fine a war record, and no less willing an exit, than the battleship.

Aviation in the Navy

During the period that the Naval Aeronautical Organization was expanding rapidly, quite a number of seagoing Line officers of established reputation, varying in age from their late thirties to early fifties, were urged to try for qualification as naval aviators or naval aviation observers at Pensacola. In Bill Halsey's book, he writes:

> In the spring of 1930, the Chief of the Bureau of Navigation, Rear Adm. James O. Richardson, wrote me that he understood I was interested in aviation, and asked if I would like to take the course at Pensacola. I jumped at the chance. Shortly before this, all line officers had been required to take the full aviation physical examination, and I had passed easily. But now, for the first time in my career, I failed, on my eyes. I had never noticed anything wrong

NH 77103

Naval aircraft operating with the Fleet.

> with them beyond normal age reactions, and I was confident that the disability was temporary. I let a week go by, then took the exam again; still no dice. I had to accept defeat.[4]

Actually, I was a captain and the Director of Officer Personnel in 1930. As I remember the incident, the circumstances were about as follows. When I came to the Bureau of Navigation in the summer of 1928, I was informed by my predecessor that all of the captains due for sea duty in the next six months had been slated for appropriate sea billets, except R. F. Zogbaum and William F. Halsey, Jr., and that there were no prospective billets at sea for them. Halsey had been ashore at the Naval Academy since January 25, 1927, so his return to sea duty was not overly urgent. Zogbaum was ordered to Pensacola to take the course as a student naval aviator, and I

[4] FADM William F. Halsey and LCDR J. Bryan III, *Admiral Halsey's Story* (New York: McGraw-Hill Book Co., Inc., 1947), pp. 52-53.

slated Bill Halsey as Commandant Naval Station, Guantanamo, Cuba, which service was counted as sea duty for rotation purposes.

When Bill was informed that he was slated for Guantanamo, he seriously objected to this assignment because of the physical condition of his wife. So, he was continued on at the Naval Academy. Somewhat later, and with the approval of the Chief of the Bureau of Aeronautics, Admiral Moffett, I offered Bill the opportunity to go to Pensacola as a student naval aviator. He was delighted at the alternative but could not qualify physically. So, in June 1930, he was ordered in command of a destroyer squadron. Four years later, in 1934, he went to Pensacola as a student naval observer.

Bill Halsey refers to himself as "Bill" Halsey, but he more frequently is called "Bull" Halsey in the newspapers today. The nickname "Bull" was really earned by and tagged to his father. During part of the period when I was a midshipman, the elder Halsey was the Executive Officer of the midshipman training ship, the *USS Monongahela,* a three-masted square-rigged sailing ship.[5] The elder Halsey would stand on the bridge of the *Monongahela* and, in a strong wind, roar so loudly that the midshipmen on the royal yards would hear the command. From this capability came the nickname "Bull."

No one of my vintage called Bill Halsey "Bull" in the pre-World War II era.

During the period when Ernie King was Chief of the Bureau of Aeronautics and I was Budget Officer of the Navy Department, he tried to persuade me to go to Pensacola and take the course as an aviation observer. However, I was fifty-seven by that time, and thought that, since my defective vision precluded my being an aviator, I had better stick to my last.

Franklin D. Roosevelt Memorial Foundation

In September 1948, I received a letter from Miss Grace G. Tully, Executive Secretary of the Franklin D. Roosevelt Memorial Foundation, asking that I prepare a detailed memorandum of my recollections of my relationship with the Government during the period 1933 to 1945, for deposit in the Franklin D. Roosevelt Library at Hyde Park.

Miss Tully said, "I believe your association with President Roosevelt

[5] Later, the elder Halsey was Commanding Officer of the *Chesapeake,* a steel square-rigger.

dated back to the years when he was Assistant Secretary of the Navy. During his Administration as President you were one of our top naval officers, and I know he always enjoyed his visits with you. Your recollections of experiences in the Navy and your association with President Roosevelt would add a very interesting and valuable chapter to the comprehensive history of this era." [6]

I gave considerable thought to this letter. However, I declined the invitation and stated that my decision was due to a "firm belief, that should I succeed in maintaining a purely objective point of view, the product would prove unacceptable to the Director of the Foundation." [7]

Miss Tully did not yield. In a second letter, she said, "the reasons you state for not wishing to undertake this work, are in the opinion of the Foundation, the very reasons why we are anxious for your contributions" and asked for a reconsideration.[8]

But, at the time, I stuck to my guns. Now that this document has been prepared, perhaps Miss Tully will consider that her polite requests have been fulfilled.

---

[6] Grace Tully, letter, 13 Sept. 1948, to ADM Richardson.
[7] ADM Richardson, letter, 30 Sept. 1948, to Grace Tully.
[8] Grace Tully, letter, 21 Oct. 1948, to ADM Richardson.

Chapter XXII

Retrospect

I am seventy-nine now. [1957]

I am beyond rancor or any feeling of "sour grapes." I believe my shipmates and associates will attest to this.

My God, my country, and my Navy have been extremely good to me, and I am deeply appreciative. I have given much thought to our Navy, and to its part in World War II, but particularly to the events that occurred in the 1939-1941 period. I have read many of the books that have been published about this period.

I believe that many of the honest opinions, which those of us who served in the Navy have in regard to this period, have not been placed on paper as yet. It has been my intention in this book to rectify my previous omissions in this respect.

Treatment of Kimmel

When I turned over the command of the United States Fleet to Admiral Husband E. Kimmel, I did so with these words:

> On taking command of the fleet over a year ago I called on you to join me in working together as a team.
>
> I asked that each member be imbued with a cooperative spirit, mutual respect, good-will, understanding, and a determination to voluntarily contribute the last bit to his assigned task.
>
> This you have done!
>
> All of you can take pride in the work accomplished under trying conditions. The path ahead is not easy. There is much to be done.
>
> My regret in leaving you is tempered by the fact that I turn over this command to Admiral Kimmel, a friend of long standing, a forthright man, an officer of marked ability and a successor of whom I am proud.

> Under his leadership I know that you will continue to so perform your duties as to justify the confidence with which the nation places its security in your hands.

I stand by my words.

I consider that, after Pearl Harbor, Admiral Kimmel received the rawest of raw deals from Franklin D. Roosevelt and, insofar as they acquiesced in this treatment, from Frank Knox and "Betty" Stark.

I consider "Betty" Stark, in failing to ensure that Kimmel was furnished with all the information available from the breaking of Japanese despatches, to have been to a marked degree professionally negligent in carrying out his duties as Chief of Naval Operations. This offense was compounded, since in writing he had assured the Commander-in-Chief of the United States Fleet twice (both myself and Kimmel) that the Commander-in-Chief was "being kept advised on all matters within his own [Stark's] knowledge" and "You may rest assured that just as soon as I get anything of definite interest, I shall fire it along."[1]

The Navy had been expecting and planning for a Japanese surprise attack for many years. However, the subordinates in a military organization can not stand with their arms raised in protective alertness forever. Some superior has to ring a bell that moves the subordinate members of the organization, trained, ready, and expecting a fight, but in the corners of their fighting ring, out to the center of the ring.

That bell was never rung by Kimmel's superiors in Washington.

I consider that "Betty" Stark, in failing to pick up the telephone and give Kimmel a last-minute alert on the morning of Pearl Harbor, committed a major professional lapse, indicating a basic absence of those personal military characteristics required in a successful war leader. I believe his failures in these respects were far more important derelictions than those of any of his subordinates.

I do not assert that Kimmel was without blame for some of the naval aspects of the Pearl Harbor debacle, but his blame was less than that of his superiors.

I feel that, throughout this affair, Stark utterly failed to display the

---

[1] "The Chief of Naval Operations has, in the past, kept the Commander in Chief advised as to all matters within his own knowledge which related to current national policy and pending national decisions. This past practice will be continued. . . . " *Pearl Harbor Hearings,* Part 14, p. 980; *Ibid.,* Part 16, pp. 2174, 2182, 2239.

loyalty downward that every subordinate has a right to expect from his superior officer. I have known Stark well all of his life in the Navy, and I hold him in high esteem. I know that he is an honorable man, and I can not conceive of how he could have treated Kimmel as he did, unless he was acting under the mistaken impression that he owed no loyalty except upward, or what I think is more likely, his failure to obey his natural impulse was due to influence or possibly direct orders from above.

I am impelled to believe that sometime prior to December 7 the President had directed that only Marshall could send any warning message to the Hawaiian area. I do not know this to be a fact and I cannot prove it. I believe this because of my knowledge of Stark, and the fact that his means of communication with Kimmel were equal to, if not superior to, those available to Marshall for communication with Short. He made no effort to warn Kimmel on the morning of December 7, but referred the matter to Marshall.

Prophecy Come True

I think I have rather fully developed in Chapter Fourteen, on War Plans, the fact that the seasoned officers of the Navy over a twenty-year period, had correctly diagnosed the aspirations and intentions and war habits of the Japanese.

I submit just one more piece of evidence—in reality a prophecy and a coincidence.

On December 7, 1941, at breakfast, I said to my wife, "We are on the verge of war which may break out any minute. About eight years ago, while a student at the War College, I wrote a thesis on Japanese policy. After breakfast, I shall find that thesis and read it to see if my opinions then expressed have changed."

The thesis was found and read that forenoon. Soon after lunch, that same Sunday, when I answered the telephone, a voice said, "Joe, turn on your radio." When this was done, the report of the Japanese attack on Pearl Harbor was heard.

The subject of this thesis, which was submitted on February 1, 1934, was:

THE RELATIONSHIP BETWEEN JAPANESE POLICY AND STRATEGY IN THE CHINESE AND RUSSIAN WARS, AND ITS LESSONS TO US

The following are the concluding pages of this thesis:

However well coordinated and harmonized the policy and the strategy of the Japanese in these Chinese and Russian Wars, the finest examples of complete harmony and effective strategy are not to be found in the wars, but in the preparations for these wars and in her participation in conferences, peace and otherwise. This will probably continue to be true of the future, for example, at the next Naval Conference Japan will demand, and probably secure, parity with the United States, either by agreement or by expiration of the Treaty. In either case, the United States will have sunk her modern fleet and bound herself not to fortify any possessions west of Hawaii for no permanent compensating advantage. Of course, she will then be legally and ostensibly free to fortify her Far Eastern possessions, but although the Treaty will have expired, its implications will remain to serve as a basis upon which pacifists and fanatical peace societies will rest their propaganda that any appropriation for fortification is an aggressive act conducive to war.

Lessons to Us

As Naval Officers we are on sure ground in believing:

(a) That Japanese foreign policy aims to establish the supremacy of Japan in Eastern Asia.

(b) That Japan will resist, by force, any attempt on the part of any nation to thwart her aspirations in that area.

(c) That she will have a well prepared and well trained Army and Navy when she enters any future war.

(d) That she will have comprehensive and accurate information regarding the strength, efficiency, capabilities and dispositions of the armed forces of her prospective enemy.

(e) That she will have a well considered plan of operations, and that the objectives of her strategy will be the objectives of her policy.

(f) That, in the preparation for and the conduct of the war, there will be complete harmony between policy, strategy and available resources.

(g) That every effort will be made to strengthen her position diplomatically and financially prior to the outbreak of any war.

(h) That treaties, agreements and international law will be mere scraps of paper if they even appear to conflict with what she considers to be to her interest or advantage.

(i) That should it appear to her advantage to do so, she will strike viciously, effectively and unexpectedly prior to any declaration of war.

(j) That the war will be vigorously prosecuted, and heartily supported by, an entirely homogeneous intensely patriotic, and thoroughly valorous [Japanese] people, who will be convinced that it is a crucial struggle for existence.[2]

In connection with the above, it is worth noting that, having demanded naval parity at the conference table, and it having been refused, the government of Japan gave notice, on December 29, 1934, of its intention to terminate the Treaty for the Limitation of Naval Armaments, to take effect December 31, 1936, and the treaty was so terminated under its terms. It is also worth noting that the initial step in the pre-World War II development of Guam as a naval base (dredging the harbor of Apra) was defeated in Congress by the pacifists and isolationists, who, as predicted, argued that any such work would be an aggressive act conducive to war with Japan.

The Roberts Commission

I have been told, and I believe, that Justice Frankfurter suggested to the President the creation, under a carefully drawn precept, of a mixed commission composed of officers of the Armed Forces, with a civilian counsel, and headed by a member of the Supreme Court, to investigate the attack on Pearl Harbor. His objective was to have a commission which would not be limited by the rules of evidence governing either a civilian court or a military court of inquiry. I was also told that the Chief Justice (Harlan F. Stone) was requested to serve, but refused the assignment.

In the impression that the Roberts Commission created on the minds of the American people, and in the way it was drawn up for that specific purpose, I believe that the Report of the Roberts Commission was the most unfair, unjust, and deceptively dishonest document ever printed by the Government Printing Office.

I cannot conceive of any honorable man being able to recall his service as a member of that commission without great regret and the deepest feeling of shame. The military members of the Roberts Commission (Admiral William H. Standley, USN (Ret.), Rear Admiral Joseph M. Reeves, USN (Ret.), Major General Frank R. McCoy, USA (Ret.), and Brigadier

---

[2] James O. Richardson, "The Relationship Between Japanese Policy and Strategy in the Chinese and Russian Wars, and its Lessons to Us" (dissertation, Naval War College, 1 Feb. 1934).

General Joseph T. McNarney, USA (Ret.)) were later rewarded for their services by favorable assignment and promotion, or employment after retirement, but I cannot believe that such rewards were adequate compensation for their supine service to the President. Its procedures should have outraged every American.

Its findings had been decided on before it ever met, for the decision to relieve Kimmel and Short was made prior to the initial meeting of the Roberts Commission. Had the Roberts Commission been intended to do a factual job, such a removal would have been untimely, to say the least, since it presented to the Commission a finding of culpability.

A more disgraceful spectacle has never been presented to this country during my lifetime than the failure of the civilian officials of the Government to show any willingness to take their share of responsibility for the Japanese success at Pearl Harbor.

Before the Roberts Commission, the leaders of the Armed Forces of the United States, who were the victims of the initial attack in this aggressive war by the Japanese, were not given a trial, were not permitted to introduce evidence in their behalf, and were not allowed counsel. Yet, these leaders were found guilty of dereliction of duty by the Commission, and were crucified in the public press and at the bar of public opinion in the United States.

I have known Admiral William H. Standley for a long time. I know that he is an honest, fair-minded, sincere man, and I value his friendship. I believe that he was made a member of the Roberts Commission to induce the United States Navy to have confidence in the justness of its findings, and I have had sympathy for him because of the position in which he was placed as a member of that commission.

At a time when it was essential that the people of the whole country be united in the war effort and imbued with confidence in its leadership, Admiral Standley was faced with the necessity of deciding whether he should join in signing what he conceived to be an unfair, misleading report or submit a minority report wth the resultant inimical effect on the unity and confidence of the country.

Nevertheless, my sympathy for him was somewhat lessened by my knowledge that he knew President Roosevelt and the majority of his fellow members of the Commission. He should have foreseen the outcome, and he could have avoided service on the Commission.

It may be surprising to have any senior officer state that a brother officer could have avoided accepting assignment to duty. I believe he could have. This opinion is fortified by the following incident. The Secretary of the Navy sent for me and told me that he was not satisfied with the report of the Naval Court of Inquiry on Pearl Harbor or with any preceding inquiry, and that he had so stated to the press, adding that he would have another investigation made.

He then stated that he would like to have me undertake this investigation for him. I said, "Mr. Secretary, I am sorry but I am not available for such assignment, because I am prejudiced and I believe that no prejudiced officer should undertake the inquiry."

The Secretary asked what I meant by the statement that I was prejudiced, and I replied, "I am prejudiced because I believe that any fair and complete investigation will result in placing a part of the blame for the success of the attack upon the President." Mr. Forrestal replied substantially, as follows: "In this case, the President was to blame only to the extent of being a poor judge of men." The Secretary amplified his remarks by naming one or more officers whose retention in high office for some time indicated bad judgment on the part of the President, but he did not mention Kimmel.

I was not ordered to conduct the investigation.

It is my firm belief that, when the President realized the extent of the damage done by the attack on Pearl Harbor, he lost his nerve and lost his head, and ordered the convening of the Roberts Commission, believing that he could best protect his own position by focusing public attention on Pearl Harbor.

At that time, and increasingly so since, I thought that the wisest course of action for the President, from all points of view, would have been to send a despatch to those in command at Pearl Harbor, along the following lines:

> DESPITE THE RESULT OF THE DASTARDLY UNPROVOKED ATTACK OF THE JAPANESE ON PEARL HARBOR THE AMERICAN PEOPLE AND I HAVE CONFIDENCE IN OUR ARMY AND NAVY. WE SHALL BE AVENGED.

Instead of sending out the Roberts Commission to muddy the waters, the reliefs of Kimmel and Short should have been despatched as soon as possible. The Army and Navy and everyone else would have understood and approved this action, because all would have recognized that, regardless of where the blame lay, no armed force should remain under the command of a leader under whom it had suffered such loss.

Had this been done, many hours of labor, thousands of gallons of ink, and tons of paper which were wasted in fruitless inquiries and newspaper reports on them, would have been saved, and the public would have been much better served.

Also, those opposed to the President would have had far less reason to question his integrity and fair-mindedness.

I am convinced that the President would have been quite willing to approve, without qualification, the induced requests of Kimmel and Short for retirement, except for the furor aroused by the publication of the Report of the Roberts Commission.

The publication of this report led the uninformed public to believe that Kimmel and Short were largely, if not wholly, responsible for the success of the Japanese attack. They, and the worshippers of Roosevelt, naturally insisted that Kimmel and Short should not be placed on the retired list with retired pay, but should be tried by General Court Martial or otherwise, to determine what if any punishment, less than summary execution, should be inflicted upon them.

The very small number of informed persons and those politically opposed to Roosevelt were firmly convinced that the truth had not been told, and that Kimmel and Short had not been accorded a fair hearing by the Roberts Commission. Therefore, the majority of even this group insisted upon a trial by General Court Martial or otherwise, not because of interest in fair play for the officers concerned, but because they believed that evidence prejudicial to Roosevelt would be adduced in any fair and complete hearing of the case.

Insofar as I know, the overwhelming majority of senior naval officers were convinced that any trial during the war would have been prejudicial to national interests.

Faced with this situation and knowing that any fair trial would be prejudicial to his leadership and to national unity, the President found no acceptable alternative to encouraging these officers to retire under a threat of future disciplinary action which, I believe, he had no intention of taking.

Pre-1941 Policy of Navy Department Re Japan

When Admiral W. H. Standley, American Ambassador to Russia, was in Washington about November 1942, he told me that:

(a) Secretary Hull was somewhat perturbed by hearing and reading an assertion that the attitude of the State Department toward Japan, prior to Pearl Harbor, had been one tending toward appeasement.

(b) Admiral Leahy was doing quite a little talking about how, as Chief of Naval Operations, he had favored taking a strong position vis-a-vis Japan early in the Chinese Incident, to the extent of greatly strengthening the U.S. Asiatic Fleet, but that he could not secure the support of the State Department.

(c) The remarks of Admiral Leahy, in his then current position as Chief of Staff to the Commander-in-Chief of the Army and Navy, were resented by Secretary Hull, who did not believe that they were entirely in accord with fact or represented the views of the Navy Department or those of thinking senior naval officers at the time in question, and that the Secretary would like to have some ammunition with which to combat Leahy's statement.

(d) He had told Secretary Hull that I was Assistant Chief of Naval Opèrations during part of this time, and that I would be able and probably willing to throw some light on the matter.

(e) Secretary Hull had some hesitancy about asking my views, but he had informed the Secretary that I would probably be quite willing to call and give him what information I could.

(f) He had advised the Secretary to send for me and he wanted to know if I would call on the Secretary, if I were requested to do so.

I told Admiral Standley that I doubted whether I could throw much light on the matter, but, that I would certainly call and talk to the Secretary if I were invited.

On January 3, 1943, the newspapers announced the publication of the State Department paper *Peace and War, United States Foreign Policy 1931-1941,* the so called "White Paper," and stated that it would be available for distribution on Monday, January 4, 1943. On January 6, 1943, the office of the Secretary of State telephoned me and stated that the Secretary of State would like to have a talk with me, and an appointment was made for 11:30 a.m., January 8, 1943.

When I called on Mr. Hull, he was most cordial and said, "Admiral, I have not seen you since you were last in Washington as Commander-in-Chief of the Fleet." I said, "Mr. Secretary, I saw you the first time I came to

Washington as Commander-in-Chief of the Fleet, but I was not so fortunate as to see you the second time I came." Mr. Hull said, "Oh, yes, I saw you when you were at the White House having a conference with the President when I was present." I do not believe that Mr. Hull saw me at the White House in October 1940 and my diary fails to show that he was present when Admiral Leahy and I conferred with the President."

Mr. Hull mentioned the recently issued State Department paper *Peace and War.* I said that I had been unable to read this paper, because it had not been ready for issue by the Government Printing Office on Monday, and that I had just procured a copy the day before. Mr. Hull said, "Why, you should have asked us for a copy."

Mr. Hull spoke generally of the attitude of the press, the recurrent comment on the alleged appeasement policy of the Department, and his surprise that the press had apparently exaggerated the importance of Ambassador Grew's report on January 27, 1941 that "Japanese military forces planned a surprise mass attack at Pearl Harbor in case of 'trouble' with the United States."

Mr. Hull said that this report of Grew's was of no importance and many such messages had been received and, furthermore, it was not nearly as specific and as official as the warning of the Navy Department to the War Department in its letter of January 24, 1941, reference to which was made in the report of the Roberts Commission. I explained to Mr. Hull my connection with the initiation of the correspondence which resulted in the Navy Department's letter of January 24, 1941. He stated that he was most interested and was pleased that I had given him the information.

The Secretary stated that he did not recall that the Navy Department or naval opinion favored a stronger position with respect to Japan than that taken by his Department. He stated that he had been looking over reports of speeches made by naval officers in responsible positions and hearings before committees of Congress for evidence of a feeling on the part of the Navy that it was prepared to support a more aggressive course of action, and that he would be pleased if I could now, or by looking up such matters, bring to his attention any material that would further enlighten him.

I told him that I was exceedingly busy as Executive Vice President of the Navy Relief Society and that I did not have any spare time, but that there were several naval officers of high rank, long experience, and some personal knowledge of the subject, whose time was not fully occupied and who might be able to assist him. I mentioned Admiral Hart and Admiral Bloch, both members of the General Board.

I told Mr. Hull that for several years I had been of the opinion that the attitude of the State Department vis-a-vis Japan, as expressed in statements and correspondence, had been stronger than the power of the Navy to support such a position.

I thought, *but did not say,* "Japan has talked peace as she made war, while the words of the United States have been strong but her actions weak."

As an example of what I mean, with much publicity we loudly prohibited the shipment of aviation gasoline and steel scrap to Japan, but we quietly defined aviation gasoline by its octane rating, 87 or above as I remember. Upon the request of Japan, we permitted the shipment to her of millions of gallons of gasoline of 86.5-octane rating in *steel* drums of 50 gallons capacity, when few if any laboratories could measure the difference between an 86 and an 88-octane rating. This information was given me by Mr. Homer DeFriest of the Socony Vacuum Co. Also, we permitted the shipment of high-quality lubricating oil in specially made drums of heavy-gauge steel, which were probably designed for use later as mine cases.

During my talk with Mr. Hull, the name of Mr. Walter Lippmann was mentioned, and Mr. Hull appeared to be most resentful of Lippmann's attitude. He said that Lippmann had wanted to represent the United States in relations with the French, or at least guide our policies with relation to the whole Mediterranean area. He also said that, since he had refused Mr. Lippmann's offer of service, he had become highly critical of the State Department.

He stated that all his conversations with me had been personal and confidential

During the course of our conversation, I told Mr. Hull of my reading, on the morning of December 7, 1941, the thesis that I had written at the Naval War College (1933-1934) on the Russian-Japanese war and the Chinese-Japanese war. I gave him a copy of my conclusions as to lessons we might learn by the study of Japanese policy and strategy, as exemplified in these two wars.

The afternoon of the day I saw Mr. Hull, I read the paper *Peace and War.* I thought of writing him my view that this paper left the impression that it was an alibi for the State Department and frankly expressing my opinion that, while the attitude of the State Department, as exemplified by despatches and public statements, had been so strong as not to be in consonance with the existing naval and military power of the United States, the actions of the administration in dealing with Japan had been far more conciliatory than the written and spoken word.

A few days later, I saw Admiral Thomas C. Hart and asked his opinion of the White Paper. He was strongly of the opinion that it was an alibi for the State Department and that it was issued to create the impression that, regardless of what other Executive Departments made mistakes prior to Pearl Harbor, the State Department had a clear record. He stated that he had explained his views to Secretary Knox and had urged him to take the matter up with the President in order to prevent the creation of a false impression, contrary to fact and prejudicial to the good name of the Navy and the Navy Department. He said that he felt a personal interest in the matter, as he had been Commander-in-Chief of the U.S. Asiatic Fleet during part of the period covered by the White Paper. Hart stated that Colonel Knox told him that the matter had been mentioned at a Cabinet meeting, and that it had been stated at the meeting that Elmer Davis would arrange a press conference for Mr. Hull, at which prepared questions would be asked Mr. Hull by the gentlemen of the press. In reply, Mr. Hull would clarify the purpose for which the White Paper had been compiled and issued, and thereby remove any possible implication that the records of other Executive Departments were not as good.

Hart said that no such press conference had been held, and he suggested that I speak to Colonel Knox about the White Paper and urge him to do something about it. I replied that I was not in a particularly good position to do that effectively, but that Admiral H. R. Stark was in the city, and since he had a personal interest in the matter, I suggested that Hart urge him to speak to Colonel Knox. Hart did not speak to Stark about this matter before Stark returned to London.

In the course of this conversation, Hart said that upon his return from the Asiatic Station he had gone to the White House in company with some other person (King, I think), and that the President said in effect, "Well, Tommy, you were not fooled by the Japs or mistaken about their ability." He continued to the effect that the Army had told him that it could hold the Philippines and added, "Why, I could have stalled the Japs off for about one year longer."

On January 31, 1943, at the home of Admiral David F. Sellers, I saw

Dr. Stanley K. Hornbeck and I spoke to him about the White Paper. He explained that the paper was published to show the record of the State Department and the gradual change of public opinion in the United States away from one of isolation. I said that I thought that the average person would consider the Grew report of January 27, 1941, regarding the planned mass attack at Pearl Harbor, the most newsworthy thing in the White Paper.

Dr. Hornbeck said in effect, "Of course the Department received many such warnings, but why should any special importance be attached to this report when the Navy Department made a much more definite report three days before in its letter to the War Department, as mentioned on page five of the Report of the Roberts Commission?"

I mentioned that I had seen in the newspapers that Mr. Anthony Eden had congratulated Mr. Hull on the White Paper. Dr. Hornbeck apparently had not heard of the Eden message, but on 1 February he sent me a copy of the State Department press release on the subject, stating in his note, "I find this item on my desk this morning."

My Judgment Regarding the Japanese War

I have frequently heard it said that the Japanese violated the rules of the game the same way, at Pearl Harbor, as they had done with the Russians at Port Arthur. I should like to point out the difference which, to a military commander looking for an alarm, was a very real difference.

The Japanese commenced acts of war with Russia in 1904, after breaking off diplomatic relations, but before a formal declaration of war. At Pearl Harbor, they commenced acts of war before even breaking off diplomatic relations.

I believe that both the President and the Secretary of State consistently viewed the Japanese thru rose-colored glasses, when they did not actually misread their intentions.

I believe the President consistently overestimated his ability to control the actions of other nations whose interests opposed our own.

I believe the President's responsibility for our initial defeats in the Pacific was direct, real, and personal.

Tribute to Secretaries of the Navy

I have, in various places in this book, paid my tribute to the many fine officers I served under, and who served under me. I was fortunate in this respect.

The record would not be complete without reference to two of the civilian heads of the Navy. During my service, I came to know two Secretaries of the Navy particularly well: Josephus Daniels and Claude Swanson. As a whole, the Navy heartily disliked and feared the former and loved and respected the latter. But, I liked both of them, and tried my best to serve them well.

Josephus Daniels

In my opinion, Josephus Daniels was a hard-working, conscientious, and honest man, who had a great yearning to make over the Navy into a greater and finer seagoing clan. He was devoted to what he believed were the interests of the government, and applied his energies vigorously to all aspects of the Navy, *except* its war-making readiness and capabilites.

Claude A. Swanson

When Claude A. Swanson (Senator from Virginia) was appointed Secretary of the Navy, he was seventy-one and too old, by any normal standard, to assume the responsbilities of that office. I believed that he was appointed to repay a political obligation by making possible the appointment of the Honorable Harry F. Byrd to the Senate by the Governor of Virginia and to enable F. D. R. to enjoy being the *de facto* Secretary of the Navy.

During the early years of Mr. Swanson's Secretaryship, there was less friction in the Navy Department than I have ever known, largely because he was so esteemed by all hands, that the higher echelon composed their differences, rather than disturb the Secretary by referring disagreements to him.

The Secretary treated me as a son. I had an affectionate esteem for him. If space permitted, I could cite many instances showing his wisdom, kindness, sense of humor and of fair play, trust in and loyalty to his subordinates, as well as amusing experiences during my service with him and in his long life in public service.

Until he was striken ill, he rendered great service to the Navy in its relations with Congress and in building up the Navy prior to World War II.

I think that Secretary Swanson's manner of conducting business with the other Departments and personalities of the Government was about as successful as any governmental administrator I had the good fortune to observe. He illustrated his general approach to this complex problem by the following occurrence, which he related to me one day when we were en route to Mount Vernon. As recorded in my diary, Secretary Swanson said, "The other day, the Judge Advocate General [who handled correspondence between the Navy and the Comptroller General's office] came into my office with a letter addressed to the Comptroller General [McCarl], which protested vigorously a decision affecting the Navy. I asked him 'You would like to have me sign this letter?' The JAG said 'Yes Sir.' I asked him 'Long after I sign this letter, McCarl will still have the power to make other decisions adversely affecting the Navy, will he not?' The JAG answered 'Yes Sir.' So I said to him 'Take this letter back and couch it in more temperate language, because no sane man would slap a tiger in the face when his other hand is in the tiger's mouth.' "

Congressman Carl Vinson

I have known the Honorable Carl Vinson since 1914, and I can not forego the opportunity to pay my respects to him, because I firmly believe that his service to the Navy and the nation renders him one of the great living Americans.

During his long service on the Naval Committee and the Armed Services Committee of the House, he has heard the views of officers of the Navy on practically all proposed legislation affecting the Navy, with the result that he probably knows more about the Navy than any single officer in the Naval Service.

Prior to Pearl Harbor, of his own volition, he introduced and secured the enactment of bills increasing the authorized strength of the Navy; and, because of his firm belief that aircraft carrier operations would play a major role in the approaching war, he induced, or perhaps forced the Navy to start the construction of many carriers, by stating to the Chief of Naval Operations that he would not support a building program including even one battleship unless the program provided for a commensurate number of carriers. The result was that, although Japan was superior to the U.S. in carriers when Pearl Harbor was attacked, the U.S. had sufficient carriers under construction so that her carrier force was soon far superior.

Beyond Self

I learned a long time ago that in the things I had to say, no one was too much interested in the things which concerned me alone; however, everyone was intensely interested in the things I said which affected him, his friends, or his enemies. And so, I record my present thoughts on a few naval personalities with whom I touched stays.

Helping Hands for the long Pull

During my early and middle career, four officers under whom I served were very helpful to me, and I want to record my gratitude to them. John Hood, Albert W. Grant, Hugh Rodman, and Andrew T. Long. All of them became Flag Officers and served the Navy well.

Rear Admiral John Hood

Perhaps the officer who exercised the greatest influence on me was John Hood (1879). He had been an instructor when I was a cadet at the Naval Academy. He was in the *Solace* on her passage to Manila when I also was on board en route to the Asiatic Station. He was Commanding Officer of the Station Ship at the Naval Academy, the *Reina Mercedes,* when I was at the Postgraduate School, and finally, he was my captain in the *Delaware.*

He was intelligent, handsome, proud, and taut. More than any other officer I knew, he manifested complete loyalty downward.

Vice Admiral A. W. Grant

I was never shipmates with Albert W. Grant (1887). He was an instructor at the Naval Academy and the executive officer of one of the practice cruise ships when I was a naval cadet; he was on the Asiatic Station in the *Frolic* during my service in that area. He was Chief of Staff to the Commander-in-Chief of the Atlantic Fleet when I was commander of the Third Division of the Atlantic Fleet Torpedo Flotilla, and later he was again the head of an academic department at the Naval Academy when I was at the Postgraduate School there. He was vigorous, impetuous, and a hard-working driver, but a completely fair and just man.

Admiral Hugh Rodman

I served with Hugh Rodman (1881) while he was Executive Officer of the *New Orleans*, and later when he was commanding the *Delaware*. He was one of the best ship handlers, and the best cribbage player that I ever saw. He was a rugged, hard-working, and hard-hitting type of naval officer. He would ride over a junior roughshod unless one stood up to him. If you did this a couple of times, you were likely to find him on your side. I doubt that, after he reached the grade of lieutenant, he ever read a professional book.

Rear Admiral Andrew T. Long

I name Andrew T. Long, not only for what he did for me, but for what he let me do in training myself.

During my service as navigator and then as Executive Officer of the *Nevada*, I served under four Commanding Officers, and with four or five heads of every department, and enough watch officers and men to man at least two battleships.

Joseph Strauss (1885), the first of the four Commanding Officers, was an officer of the highest personal integrity, a hard-working officer, and a meticulous navigator, who taught me much.

Andrew T. Long (1887), who relieved Strauss, was a polished, courtly gentleman, who went further on less work, than any officer I ever knew.

He allowed me to handle the ship, under his supervision, when leaving or entering port—an invaluable experience. I shall always remember his statement, "Richardson, I have never known any investment which paid such high dividends as a little investment in courtesy."

Long was largely responsible for my becoming Assistant Chief of the Bureau of Ordnance.

Other officers whom I knew well, particularly during my more mature years, were Bill Leahy and Claude Bloch.

Fleet Admiral William D. Leahy

William D. Leahy (1897) was Executive Officer of the *Nevada* while I was navigator. When I was Assistant Chief of the Bureau of Ordnance, Leahy was Director of Officer Personnel. While I was Director of Officer Personnel, he was Chief of the Bureau of Ordnance. When I was Budget Officer, he was Chief of the Bureau of Navigation. Later, when he was Chief of Naval Operations, I was his Assistant for one year. Over a period of ten years, we lunched together every working day, whenever possible. He probably did more to advance my interests than any other officer in the Navy, and I am grateful.

I could not have lunched with Bill Leahy as frequently as I did without then having sincere regard for him as a friend and respect for his many great abilities as a naval officer. He was a successful student of human nature, astute in regard to the "Washington Scene," and a skilled negotiator in naval matters. He could be depended upon to assess correctly all the various factors bearing on the problem, and then play his own cards accordingly. He was ambitious, loved power and the inside knowledge which went with it. On occasion, fortunately for the Navy only a rare occasion, I thought that because he felt that it weakened his position to be turned down by his superior officers, against very strong opposition, he yielded rather than risk defeat.

I believe Stark and later Denfeld were recommended by Leahy to the President to be Chiefs of Naval Operations, because Leahy believed that, in each instance, the proposed appointee would serve the President and the Secretary in the same manner that he had, and that he would have a willing recipient of his advice in the office.

Admiral Claude C. Bloch

Claude C. Bloch (1899) and I were shipmates in the *Delaware.* I was Bloch's assistant when he was Chief of the Bureau of Ordnance, and we have been lifelong friends.

In appearing before a committee of Congress, Bloch always did a superior job. Any officer could have profited by observing his performance. He was also highly skilled in many other aspects of the naval officer's profession. It was generally believed in the Navy that, no matter where Bloch was assigned, he and his command would do a superior job.

Bloch was largely responsible for my being Budget Officer of the Navy.

Bloch was Commandant 14th Naval District, with headquarters at Pearl Harbor, on December 7, 1941. I believe some measure of Bloch's great competence and skill as a naval officer may be obtained, when it is recalled that he and his command were practically alone in escaping any strong criticism or censure from one or more of the many investigating officers or bodies inquiring into the Pearl Harbor disaster.

Admiral Joseph M. Reeves

As Commanding Officer of the *USS Langley,* Admiral Joseph M. Reeves (1894), then captain, probably did more to develop the operation of planes from carriers than any other individual in any Navy. He had tremendous energy, drive, and single-purposeness.

In his long service in the Naval Aeronautical Organization, by his example and his indoctrination, he imbued naval pilots with the firm conviction that, if any one of them were forced down, either in peacetime exercises or in war operations, no effort would be spared in the endeavor to rescue him. This indoctrination paid high dividends during the war.

During the later years of his life, he appeared to believe that he owed his highest loyalty to President Roosevelt; and, as liaison officer between Mr. Harry Hopkins and the Navy Department, he was instrumental in giving to Russia, under Lend-Lease, untold millions of dollars worth of naval material.

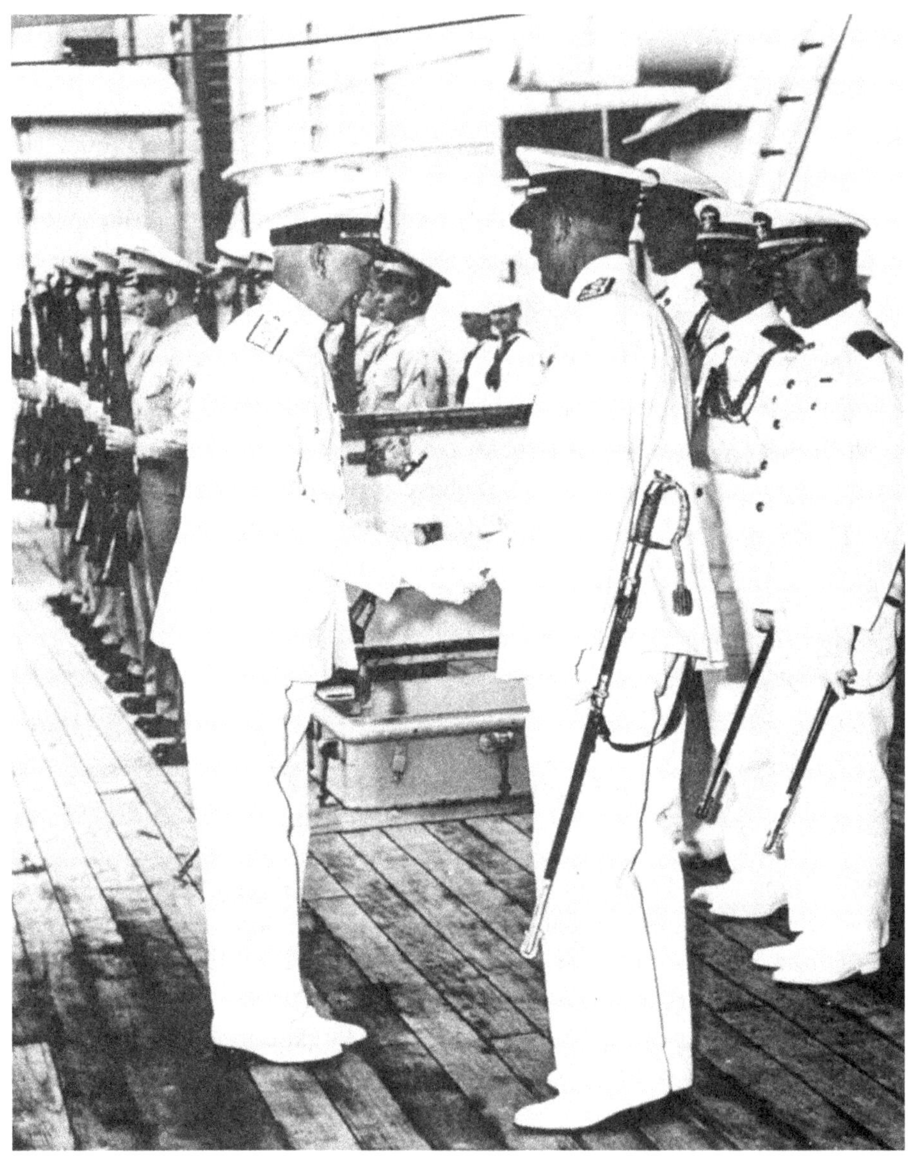

NH 77335

Admiral Richardson with the Commandant, 14th Naval District, Rear Admiral C. C. Bloch.

Rear Admiral John H. Upshur

I remember with pleasure knowing and playing bridge with a distinguished and courteous gentleman, the sixty-fourth graduate of the Naval Academy, John H. Upshur (1847), who retired in 1885 and died in 1917 at age ninety-three. He was a fine link with, what my generation called, the Old Navy, the Navy of sails, incipient steam, and smooth-bore guns.

Captain Laurance F. Safford

There is one officer, considerably junior to me, to whom I wish to pay special tribute. His name is Laurance F. Safford. Safford was of the Naval Academy class of 1916, and early in his career, he became interested in cryptanalysis, and soon became an expert in the field.

What is accomplished in this field is a closely guarded secret within the Naval Service, and there is a galaxy of regulations and laws against public disclosure of specifics in regard to the making or breaking of codes and ciphers. So, I write guardedly.

I was on a Selection Board to select lieutenant commanders to commanders back in 1936. Safford at that time was a lieutenant commander. The Selection Board the previous year evidently had had no knowledge of Safford's real accomplishments in the field of cryptanalysis and had passed him by. I undertook it as my mission to inform the members of the Board, on which I sat, of the great future value to the Navy of Safford's continued promotion in the Navy.

Part of the statement I made at that time to the eight other Flag Officers on the Selection Board has often recurred to me.

> Should the United States become involved in war, in the Pacific, what this officer has done and can do will probably contribute more to bring victory to our Navy than the efforts of any or all us who are serving on this Board.

In view of the disclosure, in the Pearl Harbor Investigations, in regard to our knowledge of Japanese codes and ciphers up thru the Battle of Midway, I believe the statement was borne out by events.

Anyhow, Safford was selected by nine votes, and continued to serve the Navy with distinction in his chosen field for many years. His country and his Navy owe him a great debt of gratitude, which neither has fully paid.

Naval Personnel

During all my service in the active-duty Navy (forty-nine years), I was deeply interested in and, for many years, actively concerned with the permanent officer corps of the Navy.

I believe that the Navy can be no better than its officers, and that the officer corps, as a whole, will always be less well qualified than its hard core of permanent officers.

I believe that many early Americans were influenced by Ben Franklin's aphorisms. I wish more of our present-day Americans were so influenced, as I feel myself to have been. In any case, some of my thoughts in regard to naval personnel are well expressed in the following aphorisms:

(1) In addition to what you may learn from seniors, one can learn much from younger officers and from enlisted men who serve under you.
(2) A Navy can be no better than its officers' conception of duty.
(3) No man is so important that he can afford to be discourteous.
(4) Few people will perceive that you are an ass, if you refrain from braying.
(5) In delicate matters, those who know, don't talk and those who talk, don't know.
(6) The bane of the Navy is a contented admiral.
(7) He who considers everything, decides nothing.
(8) In a lifetime of experience with men, I have found no substitute for brains.

I can say quite frankly that, whatever success I may have attained in the Navy has been due to good luck, a strong sense of duty, hard work, and many good friends, and in spite of a tendency to be somewhat insubordinate by nature.

I have frequently advised young officers that they should not remain in the Navy if they do not love the Service, if they are not willing to work hard, and if they are not prepared to bear up and carry on under what they conceive to be a grave injustice. I believe this to be good advice.

Another strong belief that I have voiced again and again thru my naval service is that "simple obedience to orders is not enough."

> However far the orders go, there is always the last touch that cannot be commanded, but can only be given. All the difference between effective and ineffective war-making lies in the success of government or command in enlisting this free contribution of the man to his defined duty.[3]

Before I left home in Texas for the Naval Academy, my step-mother gave me a motto to observe that I believe was of much help to me in my naval career. I have told it to many of the officers who served with me. I tried to follow it all my life.

I believe so strongly that its general observance would make for effectiveness, contentment, and even happiness amongst the personnel in the Navy, that I repeat it herewith:

> The wise man seeks to outshine himself. The fool seeks to outshine others.

And as a final word, I recall the following verse from James Russell Lowell's "The Present Crisis:"

> Truth forever on the scaffold
> Wrong forever on the throne;
> Yet that scaffold sways the future
> And behind the dim unknown
> Standeth God within the shadow
> Keeping watch above His own.

---

[3] William E. Hocking, *Morale and Its Enemies* (New Haven: Yale University Press, 1918), pp. 20-21.

Appendix A

UNITED STATES FLEET
U.S.S. NEW MEXICO, Flagship

Long Beach, California,
15 October 1940.

FLEET NOTICE 47N-40

From: Commander-in-Chief, United States Fleet.
To: FLEET.
Subject: United States Fleet Organization, Second Quarter, Fiscal Year, 1941.
Reference: (a) Fleet Notice 38N-40.

1. Reference (a) is hereby cancelled as of 1 November 1940.

2. The following organization of the UNITED STATES FLEET for the Second Quarter, Fiscal Year 1941, is effective as ordered for individual units, complete organization to be effective 1 November, 1940.

UNITED STATES FLEET

(1) (BB38) PENNSYLVANIA — Flagship
1 VOS plane — Flag Unit

BATTLE FORCE, UNITED STATES FLEET

(BB44) CALIFORNIA — Flagship
1 VOS plane — Flag Unit

BATTLESHIPS, BATTLE FORCE, UNITED STATES FLEET

(BB48) WEST VIRGINIA — Flagship

BATTLESHIP DIVISION ONE

(BB39) ARIZONA (F)
(BB36) NEVADA
(1) (BB38) PENNSYLVANIA (FF)
(VO-1) Observation Squadron One, RED (Solid) (9 VOS).

BATTLESHIP DIVISION TWO

(BB43) TENNESSEE (F)
(BB37) OKLAHOMA
(BB44) CALIFORNIA (FF)
(VO-2) Observation Squadron Two, WHITE (Solid) (9 VOS).

BATTLESHIP DIVISION THREE

(BB42) IDAHO (F)
(BB41) MISSISSIPPI
(1) (BB40) NEW MEXICO
(VO-3) Observation Squadron Three, BLUE (Solid) (9 VOS).

BATTLESHIP DIVISION FOUR

(BB48) WEST VIRGINIA (F)
(BB45) COLORADO
(BB46) MARYLAND
(VO-4) Observation Squadron Four BLACK (Solid) (9 VOS)

NOTE:

(1) NEW MEXICO temporary fleet flagship during navy yard overhaul of PENNSYLVANIA.

CRUISERS, BATTLE FORCE, UNITED STATES FLEET

(CL48) HONOLULU — Flagship

CRUISER DIVISION THREE

(CL10) CONCORD (F)
(CL5) MILWAUKEE
(CL6) CINCINNATI
(CL11) TRENTON
(VCS-3) Scouting Squadron 3, RED (Double Stripe) (8 VSO).

CRUISER DIVISION EIGHT

(CL41) PHILADELPHIA (F)
(CL40) BROOKLYN
(CL42) SAVANNAH
(CL43) NASHVILLE
(VCS-8) Scouting Squadron 8, BLACK (Double Stripe) (16 VSO).

CRUISER DIVISION NINE

(CL48) HONOLULU (F)
(CL46) PHOENIX
(CL47) BOISE (RF)
(CL50) HELENA
(CL49) ST. LOUIS
(VCS-9) Scouting Squadron 9, GREEN (Double Stripe) (20 VSO).

DESTROYERS, BATTLE FORCE, UNITED STATES FLEET

(CL8) DETROIT — Flagship
2 VSO planes—Ship Unit
BLUE (Double Stripe)

DESTROYER FLOTILLA ONE

(1) (CL7) RALEIGH — Flotilla Flagship
2 VSO planes—Ship Unit
BLUE (Double Stripe)
(1) (AD3) DOBBIN — Tender, Squadrons 1 and 3
(AD4) WHITNEY — Tender, Squadrons 5 & 9

DESTROYER SQUADRON ONE

(DD360) PHELPS — Squadron Flagship

DESTROYER DIVISION TWO

(DD355) AYLWIN (F)
(DD348) FARRAGUT (RF)
(DD353) DALE
(DD354) MONAGHAN

DESTROYER DIVISION ONE

(DD349) DEWEY (F)
(DD351) MACDONOUGH (RF)
(DD352) WORDEN
(DD350) HULL

DESTROYER SQUADRON THREE

(DD361) CLARK — Squadron Flagship

DESTROYER DIVISION SIX

(DD370) CASE (F)
(DD365) CUMMINGS (RF)
(DD373) SHAW
(DD374) TUCKER

DESTROYER DIVISION FIVE

(DD372) CASSIN (F)
(DD371) CONYNGHAM
(DD369) REID
(DD375) DOWNES (RF)

DESTROYER SQUADRON FIVE

(DD356) PORTER — Squadron Flagship

DESTROYER DIVISION TEN

(DD376) CUSHING (F)
(DD378) SMITH
(DD379) PRESTON (RF)
(DD377) PERKINS

DESTROYER DIVISION NINE

(DD366) DRAYTON (F)
(DD368) FLUSSER
(DD367) LAMSON (RF)
(DD364) MAHAN

DESTROYER SQUADRON NINE

(DD358) McDOUGAL — Squadron Flagship

DESTROYER DIVISION EIGHTEEN

(DD395) DAVIS (F)
(DD396) JOUETT
(DD383) WARRINGTON
(DD381) SOMERS

DESTROYER FLOTILLA TWO

(CL8) DETROIT .... Flotilla Flagship

2 VSO planes—Ship Unit
BLUE (Double Stripe)

(AD11) ALTAIR .... Tender, Squadrons 4 and 6
(AD14) DIXIE .... Tender, Squadrons 26 and 8

DESTROYER SQUADRON FOUR

(DD357) SELFRIDGE — Squadron Flagship

DESTROYER DIVISION EIGHT

(DD389) MUGFORD (F)
(DD393) JARVIS (RF)
(DD392) PATTERSON
(DD390) RALPH TALBOT

DESTROYER DIVISION SEVEN

(DD391) HENLEY (F)
(DD386) BAGLEY
(DD388) HELM
(DD387) BLUE (RF)

DESTROYER SQUADRON SIX

(DD363) BALCH — Squadron Flagship

DESTROYER DIVISION TWELVE

(DD384) DUNLAP (F)
(DD398) ELLET
(DD397) BENHAM
(DD385) FANNING (RF)

DESTROYER DIVISION ELEVEN

(DD380) GRIDLEY (F)
(DD400) McCALL
(DD382) CRAVEN
(DD401) MAURY (RF)

DESTROYER SQUADRON EIGHT

(DD359) WINSLOW — Squadron Flagship

DESTROYER DIVISION THREE

(DD411) ANDERSON (F)
(DD405) ROWAN
(DD413) MUSTIN
(DD412) HAMMANN

DESTROYER DIVISION FIFTEEN

(DD399) LANG (F)
(DD408) WILSON
(DD407) STERETT (RF)
(DD406) STACK

DESTROYER SQUADRON TWENTY-SIX

(DD249) HOPKINS — Squadron Flagship

DESTROYER DIVISION FIFTY-TWO

(DD207) SOUTHARD (F)
(DD208) HOVEY (RF)
(DD206) CHANDLER
(DD209) LONG

DESTROYER DIVISION FIFTY-ONE

(DD340) PERRY (F)
(DD339) TREVER
(DD338) WASMUTH
(DD337) ZANE (RF)

(2) DESTROYER DIVISION FIFTY

(DD113) RATHBURNE (F)
(DD114) TALBOT
(DD116) DENT (RF)
(DD115) WATERS

NOTES:

(1) Permanent change of home port due to assignment to Hawaiian Detachment.

(2) In reduced commission; assigned special duty with underwater training school; operates directly under Comdesflot TWO.

AIRCRAFT, BATTLE FORCE, UNITED STATES FLEET

(CV5) YORKTOWN .... Flagship
4 VM Planes—Flag Unit
3 VM Planes—Fleet Aircraft Tactical Unit

CARRIER DIVISION ONE

(CV3) SARATOGA (F)
2 VM Planes—Flag Unit
(CV2) LEXINGTON

CARRIER DIVISION TWO

(CV5) YORKTOWN (F)
(CV6) ENTERPRISE

SARATOGA AIR GROUP

(WHITE, Solid)
Group Command Plane
(1 VSB plane)
(VB3) Bombing Squadron Three
(18 VB planes)
(1) (VF3) Fighting Squadron Three
(18 VF planes plus 1 VSB, 2 VM planes)
(VS3) Scouting Squadron Three
(18 VSB planes)
(VT3) Torpedo Squadron Three
(18 VTB planes)

YORKTOWN AIR GROUP

(RED, Solid)
Group Command Plane
(1 VSB plane)
(VB5) Bombing Squadron Five
(18 VSB planes)
(1) (VF5) Fighting Squadron Five
(18 VF planes plus 1 VSB, 2 VM planes)
(VS5) Scouting Squadron Five
(18 VSB planes)
(VT5) Torpedo Squadron Five
(18 VTB planes)

LEXINGTON AIR GROUP

(YELLOW, Solid)
Group Command Plane
(1 VSB plane)
(VB2) Bombing Squadron Two
(18 VB planes)
(1) (VF2) Fighting Squadron Two
(18 VF planes plus 1 VSB, 2VM planes)
(VS2) Scouting Squadron Two
(18 VSB planes)
(VT2) Torpedo Squadron Two
(18 VTB planes)

ENTERPRISE AIR GROUP

(BLUE, Solid)
Group Command Plane
(1 VSB plane)
(VB6) Bombing Squadron Six
(18 VSB planes)
(1) (VF6) Fighting Squadron Six
(18 VF planes plus 1 VSB, 2 VM planes)
(VS6) Scouting Squadron Six
(18 VSB planes)
(VT6) Torpedo Squadron Six
(18 VTB planes)

UTILITY UNITS

3 VSO, 2 VJ planes SARATOGA
3 VSO, 2 VJ planes YORKTOWN
3 VSO, 2 VJ planes ENTERPRISE
3 VSO, 2 VJ planes LEXINGTON

NOTE:

(1) Complement to be increased from 18 to 27 VF about 1 January, 1941.

MINECRAFT, BATTLE FORCE, UNITED STATES FLEET

(CM4) OGLALA ..... Flagship

MINE SQUADRON ONE

MINE DIVISION ONE	(1) MINE DIVISION TWO	MINE DIVISION FIVE
(DM22) PRUITT (F)	(AM5) TANAGER	(DM17) MONTGOMERY
(DM19) TRACY	(AM15) QUAIL	(DM15) GAMBLE (F)
(DM20) PREBLE	(AM21) LARK	(DM16) RAMSAY
(DM21) SICARD	(AM35) WHIPPOORWILL	(DM18) BREESE

NOTE:

(1) No division commander.

SCOUTING FORCE, UNITED STATES FLEET

(1) (2) (CA35) INDIANAPOLIS Flagship
1 VSO plane — Flag Unit

CRUISERS, SCOUTING FORCE, UNITED STATES FLEET

(CA29) CHICAGO ..... Flagship

(2) CRUISER DIVISION FOUR

(CA29) CHICAGO (F)
(CA24) PENSACOLA
(CA25) SALT LAKE CITY
(3) (CA30) HOUSTON (RFF)
(1) (CA35) INDIANAPOLIS (FF)
(VCS-4) Scouting Squadron Four
BLUE (Single Stripe)
(16 VSO).

CRUISER DIVISION FIVE

(CA26) NORTHAMPTON (F)
(CA33) PORTLAND
(VCS-5) Scouting Squadron Five
YELLOW (Single Stripe)
(8 VSO)

(2) CRUISER DIVISION SIX

(CA36) MINNEAPOLIS (F)
(CA34) ASTORIA
(CA32) NEW ORLEANS
(CA38) SAN FRANCISCO
(VCS-6) Scouting Squadron Six
BLACK (Single Stripe) (16 VSO).

NOTES:

(1) Assigned to Crudiv Four for administration, inspection, tactics.
(2) Permanent change of home port due to assignment Hawaiian Detachment.
(3) To be assigned as Flagship, Commander-in-Chief, Asiatic Fleet in November 1940.

AIRCRAFT, SCOUTING FORCE, UNITED STATES FLEET

(AVD6) HULBERT .... Flagship

PATROL WING ONE

Normally bases San Diego

Squadrons

(VP-11)	Patrol Squadron Eleven	BLUE	(Double Horizontal Stripe)	(12 VPB)
(VP-12)	Patrol Squadron Twelve	RED	(Double Horizontal Stripe)	(12 VPB)
(VP-13)	Patrol Squadron Thirteen	BLUE	(Single Vertical Stripe)	(6 VPB)
(VP-14)	Patrol Squadron Fourteen	BLACK	(Single Vertical Stripe)	(12 VPB)

1 VSO plane, 2 VM planes—Utility Unit

Tenders

(AVD 6) HULBERT (Also Flag Comdr. Aircraft Scouting Force).
(AVP 4) AVOCET
(AVP 6) PELICAN

PATROL WING TWO

Normally bases Pearl Harbor

(AV1) WRIGHT Flagship

2 VSO Planes—Ship Unit

Squadrons

(VP-22)	Patrol Squadron Twenty-two	YELLOW	(Solid)	(12 VPB)
(VP-23)	Patrol Squadron Twenty-three	BLUE	(Solid)	(12 VPB)
(VP-24)	Patrol Squadron Twenty-four	ALUMINUM	(Solid)	(12 VPB)
(VP-25)	Patrol Squadron Twenty-five	BLACK	(Solid)	(12 VPB)
(VP-26)	Patrol Squadron Twenty-six	GREEN	(Solid)	(12 VPB)

1 VSO plane, 2 VM planes, 1 VPB—Utility Unit

Tenders

(AV 1) WRIGHT (F)
(AVP 7) SWAN
(AVD 7) WILLIAM B. PRESTON

PATROL WING FOUR

Normally bases Seattle - Sitka

(AVD2) WILLIAMSON Flagship

Squadrons

(VP-41)	Patrol Squadron Forty-one	BLUE	(Checker)	(6 VPB)
(VP-42)	Patrol Squadron Forty-two	RED	(Checker)	(6 VPB)
(VP-43)	Patrol Squadron Forty-three	YELLOW	(Checker)	(6 VPB)
(VP-44)	Patrol Squadron Forty-four	BLACK	(Checker)	(6 VPB)

1 VSO, 2 VM planes—Utility Unit

Tenders

(AVD 2) WILLIAMSON (F)
(AVP 5) TEAL

PATROL WING SIX

Normally bases Alameda

Squadrons

(1)	(VP-61)	Patrol Squadron Sixty-one	(9 VPB)
(2)	(VP-62)	Patrol Squadron Sixty-two	(6 VPB)

1VOS, 1 VM plane—Utility Unit

Tenders

Will be assigned later.

NOTES:

(1) VP-61 (ex-VP-44) will transfer to Patrol Wing SIX about 21 Feb. 1941 and will expand from 6 to 9 plane strength.

(2) Will commission about 21 May 1941.

SUBMARINES, SCOUTING FORCE

(CL9) RICHMOND .... Flagship

2 VSO planes—Ship Unit

RED (Double Stripe)

SUBMARINE SQUADRON FOUR, SUBMARINE BASE, PEARL HARBOR

(SM1)	ARGONAUT	Squadron Flagship
(AM30)	SEAGULL	Tender
(ASR1)	WIDGEON	Submarine Rescue Vessel
(DD336)	LITCHFIELD	

SUBMARINE DIVISION SEVEN

(SS128) S-23 (F)
(SS123) S-18
(SS139) S-34
(SS140) S-35

SUBMARINE DIVISION THIRTEEN

(SS174) SHARK (F)
(SS170) CACHALOT
(SS171) CUTTLEFISH
(SS179) PLUNGER
(SS180) POLLACK
(SS181) POMPANO

SUBMARINE DIVISION TWELVE

(SS168) NAUTILUS (F)
(SS167) NARWHAL
(SS169) DOLPHIN
(SM1) ARGONAUT (FF)

SUBMARINE DIVISION SEVENTEEN

(SS194) SEADRAGON (F)
(SS195) SEALION
(SS196) SEARAVEN
(2) (SS197) SEAWOLF

SUBMARINE SQUADRON SIX

(Normally operates with Battle Force)

(SS188) SARGO .... Squadron Flagship
(AS3) HOLLAND .... Tender
(ASR5) ORTOLAN .... Submarine Rescue Vessel

SUBMARINE DIVISION SIXTEEN

(SS185) SNAPPER
(SS186) STINGRAY
(SS187) STURGEON
(SS191) SCULPIN (F)
(2) (SS192) SAILFISH
(SS193) SWORDFISH

SUBMARINE DIVISION FIFTEEN

(SS182) SALMON
(SS183) SEAL
(SS184) SKIPJACK
(SS188) SARGO (FF)
(SS189) SAURY
(SS190) SPEARFISH (F)

(1) EXPERIMENTAL DIVISION TWO

(SS132) S-27
(SS133) S-28

NOTES:

(1) Assigned special duty with underwater sound training school.
(2) Upon reporting.

BASE FORCE, UNITED STATES FLEET

(AS10) ARGONNE .... Flagship
(AD13) RIGEL .... also Receiving Ship, San Diego

TRAIN, BASE FORCE

(AS10) ARGONNE .... Flagship

	(AF1)	BRIDGE		(AO5)	NECHES	
	(AF7)	ARCTIC	(1)	(AO16)	LARAMIE	
	(AF9)	YUKON	(1)	(AO17)	MATTOLE	
	(AG10)	ANTARES		(AO21)	TIPPECANOE	
	(AG16)	UTAH	(5)	(AO22)	CIMARRON	
	(AH1)	RELIEF		(AO23)	NEOSHO	
	(AM3)	ROBIN		(AO24)	PLATTE	
(2)	(AM13)	TURKEY		(AR1)	MEDUSA	
(2)	(AM16)	PARTRIDGE		(AR4)	VESTAL	
	(AM20)	BOBOLINK		(ARD1)	FLOATING DRYDOCK	
	(AM24)	BRANT		(AT12)	SONOMA	
(2)	(AM25)	KINGFISHER		(AT23)	KALMIA	
	(AM26)	RAIL		(AT33)	PINOLA	
	(AM31)	TERN		(AT34)	ALGORMA	
	(AM43)	GREBE		(AT64)	NAVAJO	
	(AM52)	VIREO	(1)	(AT65)	SEMINOLE	
	(AO1)	KANAWHA	(1)	(AT66)	CHEROKEE	
	(AO3)	CUYAMA	(1)	(DD90)	MC KEAN	(3)
	(AO4)	BRAZOS	(1)	(DD83)	STRINGHAM	(3)

MOBILE TARGET DIVISION ONE
(DD117) DORSEY (F)
(DD146) ELLIOT
(AG19) BOGGS
(AG21) LAMBERTON

(1) SUBCHASER DIVISION THIRTY-ONE
PC 451 (F)
PC 449
PC 450
PC 452

BASE

Destroyer Base, San Diego

(4) UTILITY WING (RIGEL)

(4) (VJ-1) Utility Squadron One GREEN (Solid) (11 VJ, 11 VJR, 1 VM)
(4) (VJ-2) Utility Squadron Two YELLOW (Solid) (11 VJ, 11 VJR, 1 VM)
(VJ-3) Utility Squadron Three ALUMINUM (Solid) (4 VJ, 4 VJR, 9 VM)

NOTES:
(1) When directed by Chief of Naval Operations.
(2) Permanent change of home port due to assignment to Hawaiian Detachment.
(3) Classification to be changed to (APD).
(4) Includes Hawaiian Utility Detachment assigned KINGFISHER.
(5) Operating under direction Opnav.

PATROL FORCE, UNITED STATES FLEET

(1) (BB35) TEXAS Flagship
(2) (CA31) AUGUSTA Flagship
(3) (CL13) MEMPHIS

BATTLESHIPS, PATROL FORCE, UNITED STATES FLEET
BATTLESHIPS DIVISION FIVE

(BB35) TEXAS (F)
(BB33) ARKANSAS
(BB34) NEW YORK
(VO-5) Observation Squadron Five
YELLOW (Solid) (9 VOS).

CRUISERS, PATROL FORCE, UNITED STATES FLEET
CRUISER DIVISION SEVEN

(CA45) WICHITA (F)
(CA37) TUSCALOOSA
(CA39) QUINCY
(CA44) VINCENNES
(CA27) CHESTER
(CA28) LOUISVILLE
(VCS-7) Scouting Squadron Seven,
GREEN (Single Stripe) (24 VSO)

DESTROYERS, PATROL FORCE, UNITED STATES FLEET

(5) (CL4) OMAHA .... Flagship
(6) (DD394) SAMPSON .... Flagship
(AD12) DENEBOLA .... Administrative Flagship and Mobile Tender (mid-Atlantic Area)
(AD2) MELVILLE .... Tender (Caribbean Area)
(AD15) PRAIRIE .... Tender, Squadrons 2 and 7

(7) DESTROYER SQUADRON TWO

(DD362) MOFFETT .... Squadron Flagship

DESTROYER DIVISION FOUR

(DD410) HUGHES (F)
(DD414) RUSSELL
(DD415) O'BRIEN
(DD416) WALKE

DESTROYER DIVISION SIXTEEN

(DD402) MAYRANT (F)
(DD403) TRIPPE
(DD404) RHIND
(DD409) SIMS

NEW CONSTRUCTION DESTROYERS

(DD418) ROE
(DD420) BUCK
(DD431) PLUNKETT
(DD423) GLEAVES
(DD424) NIBLACK

DESTROYER SQUADRON TWENTY-SEVEN

(DD341) DECATUR .... Flagship

DESTROYER DIVISION FIFTY-THREE

(DD126) BADGER (F)
(DD128) BABBITT
(DD158) LEARY
(DD159) SCHENCK

DESTROYER DIVISION FIFTY-FOUR

(DD160) HERBERT (F)
(DD130) JACOB JONES
(DD147) ROPER
(DD157) DICKERSON

DESTROYER SQUADRON THIRTY

(DD199) DALLAS .... Flagship

DESTROYER DIVISION SIXTY

(DD154) ELLIS (F)
(DD152) DuPONT
(DD153) BERNADOU
(DD155) COLE

DESTROYER DIVISION SIXTY-ONE

(DD145) GREER (F)
(DD118) LEA
(DD142) TARBELL
(DD144) UPSHUR

DESTROYER SQUADRON THIRTY-ONE

(DD220) MacLEISH .... Flagship

DESTROYER DIVISION SIXTY-TWO	DESTROYER DIVISION SIXTY-THREE
(DD239) OVERTON (F)	(DD223) McCORMICK (F)
(DD240) STURTEVANT	(DD210) BROOME
(DD245) REUBEN JAMES	(DD221) SIMPSON
(DD246) BAINBRIDGE	(DD229) TRUXTUN

AIRCRAFT, PATROL FORCE, UNITED STATES FLEET

(8) (CV4) RANGER .... Flagship

1 VSO, 1 VSN, 1 VPB Planes—Flag Unit

CARRIER DIVISION THREE

(CV4) RANGER (F) (CV7) WASP

RANGER AIR GROUP (GREEN, Solid)		WASP AIR GROUP (BLACK, Solid)	
	Group Command Plane (1 VSB plane)		Group Command Plane (1 VSB plane)
(9) (VB4)	Bombing Squadron Four (18 VSB planes)	(VF71)	Fighting Squadron Seventy-One (18 VF Planes) (1 VSB Plane) (2 VM Planes)
(9) (VF4)	Fighting Squadron Four (18 VF Planes) (1 VSB Plane) (2 VM Planes)	(VF72)	Fighting Squadron Seventy-Two (18 VF Planes) (1 VSB Plane) (2 VM Planes)
(9) (VS41)	Scouting Squadron Forty-One (18 VSB planes)	(VS71)	Scouting Squadron Seventy-one (18 VSB Planes)
(VS42)	Scouting Squadron Forty-two (18 VSB planes)	(VS72)	Scouting Squadron Seventy-two (18 VSB Planes)
	3 VSO, 2 VJ—Utility Unit		3 VSO, 2 VJ—Utility Unit

PATROL WINGS — PATROL FORCE
PATROL WING THREE

(AVD4) CLEMSON .... Flagship

Squadrons

(VP-31)	Patrol Squadron Thirty-one	GREEN	(Single Horizontal Stripe)	(12 VPB)
(VP-32)	Patrol Squadron Thirty-two	RED	(Single Horizontal Stripe)	(12 VPB)
(VP-33)	Patrol Squadron Thirty-three	BLACK	(Single Horizontal Stripe)	(12 VPB)

1 VSO plane, 2 VM planes—Utility Unit

Tenders

(AVD4) CLEMSON (F)
(AVP1) LAPWING
(AVP9) SANDPIPER

(10) PATROL WING FIVE

(AVD5) GOLDSBOROUGH .... Flagship

Squadrons

	(VP-51)	Patrol Squadron Fifty-one	YELLOW	(Solid)	(12 VPB)
(11)	(VP-52)	Patrol Squadron Fifty-two	BLUE	(Solid)	(12 VPB)
	(VP-53)	Patrol Squadron Fifty-three	RED	(Solid)	(12 VPB)
	(VP-54)	Patrol Squadron Fifty-four	GREEN	(Solid)	(12 VPB)
(12)	(VP-55)	Patrol Squadron Fifty-five	ALUMINUM	(Solid)	(9 VPB)
(13)	(VP-56)	Patrol Squadron Fifty-six	ALUMINUM	(Solid)	(9 VPB)

1 VSO, 2 VM planes—Utility Unit

Tenders

(AVD5) GOLDSBOROUGH (Flagship Patrol Wings, Patrol Force)
(AVD3) THRUSH
(AVP3) GANNET
(AVP8) GEORGE E. BADGER

(14) (4) PATROL WING SEVEN

(VP-71)	Patrol Squadron Seventy-one	WHITE	(Double Vertical Stripe)
(VP-72)	Patrol Squadron Seventy-two	RED	(Double Vertical Stripe)

SUBMARINES, PATROL FORCE, UNITED STATES FLEET
SUBMARINE SQUADRON TWO, SUBMARINE BASE, NEW LONDON

(ASR2) FALCON .... Submarine Rescue Vessel

SUBMARINE DIVISION FOUR

(SS91) R-14 (F)
(SS79) R-2
(SS81) R-4
(SS87) R-10
(SS88) R-11
(SS90) R-13 (RF)

EXPERIMENTAL DIVISION ONE

(AG24) SEMMES
(SS125) S-20
(SS127) S-22
(SS130) S-25
(SS134) S-29

SUBMARINE SQUADRON THREE, SUBMARINE BASE, COCO SOLO

(SS155) S-44 .... Flagship
(ASR4) MALLARD .... Submarine Rescue Vessel

SUBMARINE DIVISION ELEVEN

(SS153) S-42 (F)
(SS154) S-43
(SS155) S-44 (FF)
(SS156) S-45
(SS157) S-46
(SS158) S-47

BEING COMMISSIONED OR RECOMMISSIONED

SUBMARINE DIVISION EIGHTEEN

(SS198) TAMBOR
(SS199) TAUTOG
(SS200) THRESHER

SUBMARINE DIVISION NINETEEN

(SS201) TRITON
(SS202) TROUT
(SS203) TUNA
(SS209) GRAYLING

SUBMARINE DIVISION FORTY-TWO

(SS80) R-3 (F)
(SS78) R-1
(SS82) R-5
(SS83) R-6
(SS89) R-12
(SS93) R-16

SUBMARINE SQUADRON TWENTY

BEAVER .... Tender

SUBMARINE DIVISION NINE

(SS163) BARRACUDA
(SS164) BASS
(SS165) BONITA

SUBMARINE DIVISION FORTY-FOUR

(SS136) S-31 (F)
(SS105) S-1
(SS126) S-21
(SS129) S-24
(SS131) S-26
(SS135) S-30
(SS137) S-32
(SS138) S-33

TRAIN, PATROL FORCE, UNITED STATES FLEET

(AG17) WYOMING

TRANSPORTS

(AP11) BARNETT (F)
(AP10) McCAWLEY
(APD1) MANLEY
(4) (APD2) COLHOUN
(4) (APD3) GREGORY
(4) (APD4) LITTLE

SPECIAL ASSIGNMENT

(DD141) HAMILTON

(DD343) NOA
(Ship Unit—1 VOS)

(18) DESTROYER DIVISION SEVENTY-FIVE

(DD178) HOGAN (F)
(DD161) PALMER
(DD179) HOWARD
(DD180) STANSBURY

MISCELLANEOUS

(4)	(AF1)	BRIDGE	(4)	(AM67)	CARDINAL
(15)	(AF9)	YUKON	(4)	(AM68)	CATBIRD
(4)	(AH2)	SOLACE	(4)	(AM69)	CURLEW
(4)	(AM66)	BULLFINCH	(4)	(AM70)	FLICKER
(4)	(AM71)	ALBATROSS			

U.S. Naval Mobile Base Hospital No. 1—Guantanamo Bay, Cuba.

Utility Squadron

(16)	(VJ4)	Utility Squadron Four	(6 VJ, 5 VJR)
(17)		Utility Wing Detachment	(2 JRS, 3 J2F)

NOTES:

(1) Until relieved by AUGUSTA.
(2) To report during Third Quarter.
(3) Operate under Commander Cruiser Division SEVEN; permanent assignment to be made at later date.
(4) On reporting.
(5) On reporting to become flagship ComDesRolFor.
(6) Until relieved by OMAHA.
(7) Temporarily assigned ComRolFor.
(8) Flagship ComAirRolFor — ComCarDiv-3.
(9) Effective about 1 January 1941: Present VS-41 will be assigned VF instead of VSB planes and become VF-42. VF-4 will become VF-41. VB-4 will become VS-41.
(10) Upon receipt of new planes by Patwing-5, tail markings will be changed to conform to Fleet Letter 13L-40.
(11) To expand from 6 to 12 plane strength during 2nd Quarter, 1940.
(12) To transfer to Patwing-1 about 1 March becoming VP-12.
(13) Ultimate assignment to be determined later.
(14) VP-71 and VP-72 to be commissioned about May 1941.
(15) Until reporting to ComBaseFor.
(16) Commission about 15 November. Base ship GANNET.
(17) Discontinued on reporting VJ-4.
(18) Converted to High-Speed Minesweepers.

The following ships are assigned as a part of the Defense Forces of the Naval Districts indicated. They are not a part of the U.S. Fleet. This assignment is published for information only.

Eleventh Naval District
DESTROYER DIVISION SEVENTY

(DD109) CRANE (F)
(DD164) CROSBY
(DD137) KILTY
(DD138) KENNISON

Fourteenth Naval District
DESTROYER DIVISION EIGHTY

(DD103) SCHLEY (F)
(DD106) CHEW
(DD139) WARD
(DD66) ALLEN

Fifteenth Naval District

ERIE

DESTROYER SQUADRON THIRTY-THREE

(DD215) BORIE Squadron Flagship

DESTROYER DIVISION
SIXTY-SIX

(DD148) BRECKINRIDGE(F)
(DD149) BARNEY
(DD150) BLAKELEY
(DD151) BIDDLE

DESTROYER DIVISION
SIXTY-SEVEN

(DD248) BARRY
(DD247) GOFF
(DD125) TATTNALL
(DD156) J. FRED TALBOTT
(DD187) DAHLGREN

Twelfth Naval District
DESTROYER DIVISION
EIGHTY-THREE

(DD250) LAWRENCE (F)
(DD236) HUMPHREYS
(DD242) KING
(DD243) SANDS

Thirteenth Naval District

(PG51) CHARLESTON — Flagship
Commander Alaskan Sector.

DESTROYER DIVISION
EIGHTY-TWO

(DD233) GILMER (F)
(DD231) HATFIELD
(DD232) BROOKS
(DD234) FOX
(DD235) KANE

FLEET MARINE FORCE
MARINE CORPS BASE, SAN DIEGO

FORCE TROOPS

Headquarters Company, FMF
1st DEFENSE BATTALION
2nd DEFENSE BATTALION
6th DEFENSE BATTALION (to be organized)

2ND MARINE BRIGADE

BRIGADE SPECIAL TROOPS:

Headquarters Company
4th Tank Company
2nd Transport Company
2nd Chemical Company
2nd Service Company (to be organized)
2nd Signal Company (to be organized)

1st Medical Company
2nd Medical Company
Company "A", 2nd Engineer Battalion

6TH MARINES: (Infantry)

Headquarters and Service Company
1st Battalion
2nd Battalion
3rd Battalion (to be organized)

8TH MARINES: (Infantry)

Headquarters and Service Company
1st Battalion
2nd Battalion
3rd Battalion (to be organized)

10TH MARINES: (Artillery)

1st Battalion (to be organized)
2nd Battalion

MARINE AIRCRAFT WING

Headquarters Squadron

2ND MARINE AIRCRAFT GROUP

Headquarters and Service Squadron Two
Base Air Detachment Two

VMJ-2: 1 JO-2, 1 JRS-1, 1 SBC-4, 1 BG-1,
3 J2F-4, 1 R3D-2.
VMB-2: 6 BG-1.
VMF-2: 18 F3F-2, 1 SBC-4, 1 SU-4.
VMS-2: 8 SOC-3.

NAVAL STATION, GUANTANAMO BAY, CUBA
1ST MARINE BRIGADE

BRIGADE SPECIAL TROOPS:

Headquarters Company
1st Chemical Company
1st Tank Company
3rd Tank Company
1st Transport Company

1st Signal Company (to be organized)
1st Service Company
1st Medical Battalion
Depot Supply Detachment
Company "A", 1st Engineer Battalion

5TH MARINES: (Infantry)

Headquarters and Service Company
1st Battalion
2nd Battalion
3rd Battalion

7TH MARINES: (Infantry) (to be organized)

11TH MARINES: (Artillery)

1st Battalion
2nd Battalion (to be organized)

1ST MARINE AIRCRAFT GROUP

Headquarters and Service Squadron One
VMF-1: 20 F3F-2; 1SBC-4.
VMB-1: 18 SBD-1.
VMS-1: 21 BG-1.
VMJ-1: 1 JRS-1; 2 BG-1; 1 SBD-1;
1 JO-2; 3 J2F-4; 2 R3D-2.
VMO-1: 6 BG-1; 1 J2F-4.

ST. THOMAS, VIRGIN ISLANDS
Base Air Detachment, Bourne Field
VMS-3: 6 J2F-2A; 1 JRF-1A.

MARINE BARRACKS, PARRIS ISLAND, S. C.
4th Defense Battalion
5th Defense Battalion (to be organized)

MARINE BARRACKS, PEARL HARBOR, T. H.
3rd Defense Battalion

NAVAL AIR STATION, DUTCH HARBOR, ALASKA
Advance Detachment, Marine Defense Force

STATIONS OF FLAG AND COMMANDING OFFICERS

UNITED STATES FLEET

40 Admiral J. O. Richardson	Commander-in-Chief, U.S. Fleet
131 Rear Admiral S. A. Taffinder	Chief of Staff
336 Captain B. H. Bieri	Assistant Chief of Staff

FORCE COMANDERS AND THEIR CHIEFS OF STAFF

24 Admiral C. P. Snyder	Commander Battle Force
250 Captain C. W. Magruder	Chief of Staff
32 Vice Admiral A. Andrews	Commander Scouting Force
260 Captain T. S. Wilkinson	Chief of Staff
31 Rear Admiral H. Ellis	Commander Patrol Force
258 Captain R. R. M. Emmet	Chief of Staff
73 Rear Admiral W. L. Calhoun	Commander Base Force
198 Captain C. W. Crosse	Chief of Staff
12009 Major General W. P. Upshur	Commanding General, Fleet Marine Force
12077 Colonel J. M. Arthur	Chief of Staff

FLEET TYPE COMMANDERS AND THEIR CHIEFS OF STAFF

35 Vice Admiral W. S. Pye	Commander Battleships, Battle Force—Battleships
123 Rear Admiral I. C. Kidd	Chief of Staff
57 Vice Admiral W. F. Halsey, Jr.	Commander Aircraft, Battle Force—Carriers and Carrier Aircraft
170 Captain J. H. Hoover	Chief of Staff
43 Rear Admiral E. J. Marquart	Commander Minecraft, Battle Force—Minecraft
458 Captain G. D. Hull	Chief of Staff
44 Rear Admiral G. J. Rowcliff	Commander Cruisers, Scouting Force—Heavy Cruisers
225 Captain W. K. Kilpatrick	Chief of Staff
55 Rear Admiral H. E. Kimmel	Commander Cruisers, Battle Force—Light Cruisers
384 Captain W. S. DeLany	Chief of Staff
69 Rear Admiral W. L. Friedell	Commander Submarines, Scouting Force—Submarines
438 Captain C. A. Lockwood, Jr.	Chief of Staff

111	Rear Admiral A. L. Bristol	Commander Aircraft, Scouting Force—Patrol Wings
1182	Commander D. Ketcham	Chief of Staff
116	Rear Admiral M. F. Draemel	Commander Destroyers, Battle Force—Destroyers
181	Captain H. J. Abbett	Chief of Staff

PATROL FORCE TYPE COMMANDERS AND THEIR CHIEFS OF STAFF

53	Rear Admiral A. C. Pickens	Cruiser Division Seven—Heavy Cruisers
54	Rear Admiral D. M. LeBreton	Battleship Division Five—Battleships
65	Rear Admiral A. B. Cook	Commander Aircraft, Patrol Force—Carriers, Carrier Aircraft and Patrol Wings
600	Comdr. R. E. Davison	Chief of Staff
121	Rear Admiral F. L. Reichmuth	Commander Destroyers, Patrol Force—Destroyers
390	Captain W. G. Greenman	Chief of Staff
167	Captain R. S. Edwards (R)	Commander Submarines, Patrol Force—Submarines

FLOTILLA, SQUADRON AND DIVISION COMMANDERS, SURFACE CRAFT AND SUBMARINES

35	Vice Admiral W. S. Pye	Battleship Division Four
57	Vice Admiral W. F. Halsey, Jr.	Carrier Division Two
36	Rear Admiral A. P. Fairfield	Battleship Division Three
37	Rear Admiral W. N. Vernou	Battleship Division Two
44	Rear Admiral G. J. Rowcliff	Cruiser Division Four
53	Rear Admiral A. C. Pickens	Cruiser Division Seven
54	Rear Admiral D. M. LeBreton	Battleship Division Five
55	Rear Admiral H. E. Kimmel	Cruiser Division Nine
65	Rear Admiral A. B. Cook	Carrier Division Three
68	Rear Admiral J. H. Newton	Cruiser Division Five
74	Rear Admiral R. Willson	Battleship Division One
114	Rear Admiral F. J. Fletcher	Cruiser Division Six
116	Rear Admiral M. F. Draemel	Destroyer Flotilla Two
135	Rear Admiral A. W. Fitch	Carrier Division One
143	Rear Admiral R. A. Theobald	Destroyer Flotilla One
151	Rear Admiral H. K. Hewitt	Cruiser Division Eight
157	Rear Admiral F. X. Gygax	Cruiser Division Three

145	Captain H. M. Jensen	Submarine Squadron Two and Submarine Base, New London
169	Captain I. H. Mayfield	Destroyer Squadron Three
179	Captain W. S. Farber	Destroyer Squadron Forty-one
186	Captain J. B. Earle	Destroyer Squadron Five
188	Captain T. A. Symington	Destroyer Squadron Nine
199	Captain W. F. Amsden	Destroyer Squadron Four
208	Captain S. F. Heim	Destroyer Squadron Thirty-three
234	Captain A. S. Carpender (D)	Destroyer Squadron Thirty-one
235	Captain J. L. Kauffman	Destroyer Squadron Thirty
257	Captain W. R. Carter (R)	Submarine Squadron Four and Submarine Base, Pearl Harbor, T.H.
282	Captain F. A. Daubin	Destroyer Squadron Six
284	Captain T. E. Van Metre	Destroyer Squadron Twenty-six
308	Captain F. S. Steinwachs	Submarine Squadron Six
319	Captain W. L. Ainsworth	Destroyer Squadron Two
321	Captain J. G. Ware	Transports, Patrol Force
349	Captain S. Picking	Submarine Squadron Three and Submarine Base, Coco Solo, C.Z.
388	Captain L. E. Denfeld	Destroyer Squadron One
440	Captain A. S. Merrill	Destroyer Squadron Eight
477	Captain L. H. Thebaud	Destroyer Squadron Twenty-seven
511	Commander R. L. Conolly	Destroyer Division Seven
524	Commander W. D. Baker (R)	Destroyer Squadron Thirty-one
560	Commander H. E. Paddock	Destroyer Division Six
563	Commander W. S. Popham	Destroyer Division One
567	Commander T. G. Peyton	Destroyer Division Eighteen
568	Commander S. P. Jenkins	Destroyer Division Eight
569	Commander C. W. Flynn	Destroyer Division Two
582	Commander N. M. Pigman	Destroyer Division Eleven
583	Commander H. D. Clarke	Destroyer Division Sixteen
585	Commander A. E. Smith	Destroyer Division Three
587	Commander H. E. Overesch	Destroyer Division Ten
589	Commander G. C. Kriner	Destroyer Division Nine
593	Commander R. W. Christie	Submarine Division Fifteen and Experimental Division Two—Ordered Submarine Squadron Twenty
596	Commander B. W. Chippendale	Destroyer Division Four
601	Commander D. P. Moon	Destroyer Division Fifteen
602	Commander R. S. Berkey	Mobile Target Division One
603	Commander G. F. Hussey, Jr.	Destroyer Division Fifty-one
604	Commander T. J. Keliher, Jr.	Destroyer Division Five
617	Commander C. H. Roper	Submarine Division Twelve

618	Commander E. P. Sauer	Destroyer Division Twelve
628	Commander A. DeG. Mayer	Mine Division One
638	Commander F. D. Kirtland	Destroyer Division Sixty-six
640	Commander A. D. Burhans	Destroyer Division Fifty
659	Commander H. B. Broadfoot	Destroyer Division Fifty-three
660	Commander T. V. Cooper	Destroyer Division Sixty-three
697	Commander M. Comstock	Submarine Division Thirteen
699	Commander J. B. Heffernan	Destroyer Division Sixty
710	Commander R. W. Fleming	Destroyer Division Eighty-two
713	Commander C. W. Brewington	Destroyer Division Sixty-one
731	Commander C. W. Styer	Submarine Division Sixteen
777	Commander V. C. Barringer, Jr.	Destroyer Division Eighty-three
806	Commander W. M. Percifield	Submarine Division Seventeen
807	Commander S. H. Hurt	Destroyer Division Fifty-two
809	Commander C. E. Eason	Destroyer Division Seventy-five
987	Commander H. J. Walker	Submarine Division Eleven
1198	Commander F. M. O'Leary	Submarine Division Seven
1339	Lt-Comdr. L. A. Thackrey	Destroyer Division Sixty-seven
1359	Lt-Comdr. W. A. Gorry	Submarine Division Four and Experimental Division One
1639	Lt-Comdr. H. W. Chanler	Destroyer Division Sixty-two
1785	Lt-Comdr. R. P. Wadell	Destroyer Division Fifty-four
1893	Lt-Comdr. W. J. Longfellow	Mine Division Five (Acting)

WING, GROUP AND SQUADRON COMMANDERS, AIRCRAFT

178	Captain E. D. McWhorter	Patrol Wing Five
211	Captain P. N. L. Bellinger	Patrol Wing Two
500	Commander W. K. Harrill	Patrol Wing One
635	Commander V. H. Ragsdale	Utility Wing
647	Commander J. D. Price	Patrol Wing Three
651	Commander A. C. McFall	Patrol Wing Four
1282	Commander J. L. Murphy	VJ-2
1291	Lt-Comdr. D. C. Allen	VP-24
1307	Commander A. J. Isbell	VP-54
1320	Lt-Comdr. W. L. Rees	YORKTOWN Air Group
1370	Lt-Comdr. G. B. H. Hall	WASP Air Group
1420	Lt-Comdr. S. B. Cooke	VP-13
1464	Lt-Comdr. E. P. Moore	LEXINGTON Air Group
1467	Lt-Comdr. E. C. Ewen	ENTERPRISE Air Group
1470	Lt-Comdr. W. C. Gilbert	VS-6
1504	Lt-Comdr. R. F. Hickey	RANGER Air Group
1507	Lt-Comdr. C. R. Brown	SARATOGA Air Group

1523 Lt-Comdr. W. P. Cogswell VP-22
1552 Lt-Comdr. R. E. Blick VB-3
1596 Lt-Comdr. H. S. Duckworth VF-2
1598 Lt-Comdr. A. R. Nash VP-42
1605 Lt-Comdr. L. P. Pawley VO-5
1650 Lt-Comdr. A. R. Brady VP-25
1652 Lt-Comdr. G. Van Deurs VP-23
1655 Lt-Comdr. J. W. Harris VP-11
1658 Lt-Comdr. C. F. Greber VO-4 and Observation Wing
1684 Lt-Comdr. C. W. Crawford VS-72
1685 Lt-Comdr. J. P. W. Vest VCS-5
1689 Lt-Comdr. J. B. Dunn VP-31
1692 Lt-Comdr. F. B. Johnson VP-41
1700 Lt-Comdr. J. W. King VS-2
1739 Lt-Comdr. T. T. Tucker VCS-6
1740 Lt-Comdr. T. B. Williamson VS-41
1743 Lt-Comdr. W. T. Rassieur VP-14
1745 Lt-Comdr. A. P. Storrs, 3rd VP-53
1755 Lt-Comdr. D. S. MacMahan VF-72
1763 Lt-Comdr. H. D. Felt VB-2
1776 Lt-Comdr. C. S. Smiley VS-5
1781 Lt-Comdr. H. L. Young VF-6
1794 Lt-Comdr. W. C. Holt VP-43
1797 Lt-Comdr. D. E. Wilcox VS-71
1813 Lt-Comdr. M. E. Arnold VB-5
1816 Lt-Comdr. P. R. Coffin VF-71
1833 Lt-Comdr. W. J. Mullins VP-51
1854 Lt-Comdr. C. E. Ekstrom Light Cruiser Scouting Wing and VCS-9
1875 Lt-Comdr. H. L. Hopping VCS-3
1885 Lt-Comdr. W. V. R. Vieweg VP-56
1890 Lt-Comdr. A. Handly VT-6
1891 Lt-Comdr. N. W. Ellis VF-5
1900 Lt-Comdr. W. V. Davis, Jr. VT-5
1902 Lt-Comdr. A. B. Vosseller VP-55
1904 Lt-Comdr. M. E. A. Gouin VB-6
1916 Lt-Comdr. T. A. Turner, Jr. VP-32
1917 Lt-Comdr. R. C. Sutliff VS-3
1942 Lt-Comdr. S. Teller VT-2
1945 Lt.-Comdr. B. D. Quinn VP-33
1950 Lt-Comdr. A. V. Magly VT-3
1957 Lt-Comdr. W. W. Harvey VF-3
1960 Lt-Comdr. E. C. Parker VF-4
1971 Lt-Comdr. H. V. Hopkins VB-4

1977	Lt-Comdr. G. C. Montgomery	VS-42
1979	Lt-Comdr. C. W. Oexle	VP-12
1982	Lt-Comdr. C. C. McDonald	VP-52
1986	Lt-Comdr A. N. Perkins	VP-26
1997	Lt-Comdr. W. L. Erdmann	VP-44
2001	Lt-Comdr. R. R. Waller	VCS-7
2176	Lt-Comdr. T. G. Richards	VJ-1
2644	Lt-Comdr. C. Briggs (R)	VCS-8
2656	Lt-Comdr. I. E. Hobbs	VO-3
2738	Lieut. J. M. Carson	VCS-4
2908	Lieut. C. H. Duerfeldt	VO-1
2942	Lieut. C. W. Haman	VO-2
4226	Lieut. R. F. Jones	VJ-3

COMMANDING OFFICERS, BATTLESHIPS

167	Captain R. S. Edwards (D)	COLORADO
177	Captain H. M. Bemis	CALIFORNIA
184	Captain S. B. McKinney	IDAHO
191	Captain C. N. Hinkamp	TEXAS
205	Captain C. C. Baughman	NEW MEXICO
207	Captain J. H. Ingram	TENNESSEE
217	Captain H. T. Markland	WEST VIRGINIA
221	Captain E. F. Cutts	PENNSYLVANIA
222	Captain E. J. Foy	OKLAHOMA
226	Captain F. W. Rockwell	NEVADA
237	Captain W. R. Munroe	MISSISSIPPI
251	Captain E. W. McKee	MARYLAND
273	Captain H. C. Train	ARIZONA
295	Captain L. E. Lindsay (R)	COLORADO
446	Captain D. E. Barbey	NEW YORK
468	Captain J. L. Hall, Jr.	ARKANSAS

AIRCRAFT CARRIERS

246	Captain A. H. Douglas	SARATOGA
299	Captain E. L. Gunther	YORKTOWN
310	Captain F. C. Sherman	LEXINGTON
320	Captain C. A. Pownall	ENTERPRISE
347	Captain J. W. Reeves, Jr.	WASP
422	Captain A. E. Montgomery	RANGER

HEAVY CRUISERS

197	Captain T. A. Thomson, Jr.	WICHITA
229	Captain A. M. R. Allen	SALT LAKE CITY
241	Captain C. M. Yates	SAN FRANCISCO
244	Captain J. R. Beardall	VINCENNES
259	Captain S. S. Payne	NORTHAMPTON
262	Captain D. I. Hedrick (D)	MINNEAPOLIS
265	Captain P. B. Haines	ASTORIA
266	Captain F. T. Leighton	LOUISVILLE
274	Captain L. P. Johnson	TUSCALOOSA
279	Captain M. C. Robertson	CHICAGO
281	Captain W. C. Wickham	QUINCY
298	Captain J. B. Oldendorf	HOUSTON
301	Captain C. E. Van Hook	PORTLAND
305	Captain A. H. Gray	NEW ORLEANS
339	Captain E. W. Hanson	INDIANAPOLIS
341	Captain F. J. Lowry (R)	MINNEAPOLIS
342	Captain J. H. Magruder, Jr.	AUGUSTA
363	Captain N. Scott	PENSACOLA
379	Captain M. S. Tisdale	CHESTER

LIGHT CRUISERS

261	Captain W. W. Smith	BROOKLYN
277	Captain M. B. DeMott	HELENA
287	Captain C. H. Morrison	ST. LOUIS
293	Captain V. D. Chapline	PHILADELPHIA
302	Captain A. McGlasson	MILWAUKEE
307	Captain J. R. Barry	TRENTON
318	Captain S. S. Lewis	CINCINNATI
325	Captain C. J. Bright	RICHMOND
373	Captain H. E. Fischer	PHOENIX
376	Captain A. C. Bennett	SAVANNAH
377	Captain H. Dodd	HONOLULU
378	Captain R. S. Wentworth	NASHVILLE
389	Captain S. B. Robinson	BOISE
414	Captain R. B. Simons	RALEIGH
436	Captain I. C. Sowell	CONCORD
453	Captain A. v. S. Pickhardt	DETROIT
473	Captain C. J. Parrish	MEMPHIS
475	Captain P. P. Powell	OMAHA

DESTROYERS

638	Commander F. D. Kirtland	BRECKINRIDGE (148)
642	Commander T. DeW. Carr	DAVIS (3[illegible])
660	Commander T. V. Cooper	McCORMICK [illegible]
667	Commander R. E. Dees	WINSLOW [illegible]
669	Commander F. G. Fahrion	WARRINGTON (383)
699	Commander J. B. Heffernan	ELLIS (154)
710	Commander R. W. Fleming	HATFIELD (231)
713	Commander C. W. Brewington	GREER (145)
714	Commander L. B. Austin	BALCH (363)
717	Commander G. W. Clark	JOUETT (396)
721	Commander C. W. Weitzel	PORTER (356)
729	Commander W. W. Warlick	MC DOUGAL (358)
743	Commander A. M. Bledsoe	PHELPS (360)
751	Commander G. W. Johnson	MOFFETT (362)
777	Commander V. C. Barringer, Jr.	LAWRENCE (250)
790	Commander L. P. Lovette	SELFRIDGE (357)
803	Commander W. K. Phillips	SAMPSON (394)
856	Commander J. C. Metzel	SOMERS (381)
1012	Commander F. L. Johnson	LANG (399)
1166	Commander J. E. Hurff	PATTERSON (392)
1204	Commander J. B. Carter	REID (369)
1219	Lt-Comdr. C. V. Lee	AYLWIN (355)
1221	Lt-Comdr. M. S. Pearson	CRAVEN (382)
1226	Lt-Comdr. T. B. Brittain	SHAW (373)
1232	Commander R. W. M. Graham	RALPH TALBOT (390)
1270	Commander T. H. Binford	CLARK (361)
1271	Lt-Comdr. P. E. Pendleton	LAMSON (367)
1277	Commander H. F. Gearing	TUCKER (374)
1303	Commander R. K. Davis	WORDEN (352)
1321	Lt-Comdr. J. H. Carter	DRAYTON (366)
1324	Lt-Comdr. E. G. Fullinwider	MC CALL (400)
1334	Lt-Comdr. R. D. Tarbuck	MAC DONOUGH (351)
1341	Lt-Comdr. C. R. Todd	CUMMINGS (365)
1350	Lt-Comdr. R. B. Tompkins	HENLEY (391)
1360	Lt-Comdr. W. B. Jackson, Jr.	CUSHING (376)
1362	Lt-Comdr. T. J. O'Brien	PRESTON (379)
1368	Lt-Comdr. F. X. McInerney	SMITH (378)
1380	Lt-Comdr. W. F. Fitzgerald, Jr.	CASSIN [illegible]
1386	Lt-Comdr. J. P. Womble, Jr.	DALE (353)
1389	Lt-Comdr. S. W. DuBois	DEWEY (349)
1390	Lt-Comdr. T. F. Darden, Jr.	BENHAM (397)

1394	Lt-Comdr. C. H. Bushnell	DUNLAP (384)
1399	Lt-Comdr. E. A. Tarbutton	HELM (388)
1401	Lt-Comdr. N. B. Va[illegible]ergen	MONAGHAN (354)
1408	Lt-Comdr. W. Craig	MUGFORD (389)
1409	Lt-Comdr. C. H. Sa[illegible]rs	WALKE (416)
1411	Lt-Comdr. W. Nyq[illegible]st	HULL (350)
1418	Lt-Comdr. J. S. Freeman	MUSTIN (413)
1422	Lt-Comdr. G. H. Lyttle	FLUSSER (368)
1444	Lt-Comdr. E. D. Snare	MAURY (401)
1446	Lt-Comdr. A. Macondray, Jr.	STERETT (407)
1447	Lt-Comdr. T. F. Wellings	PERKINS (377)
1448	Lt-Comdr. A. E. True	HAMMANN (412)
1449	Lt-Comdr. J. C. Pollock	RUSSELL (414)
1454	Lt-Comdr. W. R. Cooke, Jr.	FANNING (385)
1461	Lt-Comdr. W. A. Griswold	SIMS (409)
1525	Lt-Comdr. P. G. Hale	PLUNKETT (431)
1539	Lt-Comdr. E. A. Taylor	MAYRANT (402)
1545	Lt-Comdr. J. E. Craig	CONYNGHAM (371)
1554	Lt-Comdr. O. A. Kneeland	HOPKINS (249)
1569	Lt-Comdr. C. F. Espe	O'BRIEN (415)
1572	Lt-Comdr. J. H Leppert	MAHAN (364)
1580	Lt-Comdr C. H. Kimball	JARVIS (393)
1593	Lt-Comdr. E. A. Solomons	GRIDLEY (380)
1602	Lt-Comdr. I. Olch	STACK (406)
1620	Lt-Comdr. W. L. Freseman	BAGLEY (386)
1626	Lt-Comdr. G. R. Cooper	RHIND (404)
1630	Lt-Comdr. C. O. Comp	BLUE (387)
1631	Lt-Comdr. H. D. Smith	CASE (370)
1638	Lt-Comdr. E. E. Woods	DICKERSON (157)
1639	Lt-Comdr. H. W. Chanler	OVERTON (239)
1640	Lt-Comdr. E. H. Pierce	GLEAVES (423)
1645	Lt-Comdr. E. R. Durgin	NIBLACK (424)
1663	Lt-Comdr. R. G. Sturges	WILSON (408)
1686	Lt-Comdr. J. Y. Dannenberg	BROOME (210)
1695	Lt-Comdr. F. J. Mee	ELLET (398)
1707	Lt-Comdr. M. K. Kirkpatrick	DENT (116)
1720	Lt-Comdr. E. B. Strauss	BROOKS (232)
1728	Lt-Comdr. C. A. Chappell	WASMUTH (338)
1742	Lt-Comdr. G. W. Welker Jr.	FARRAGUT (348)
1750	Lt-Comdr. R. [illegible]	ROE (418)
1752	Lt-Comdr. W. E. Hennigar	BADGER (126)
1785	Lt-Comdr. R. P. Wadell	HERBERT (160)
1796	Lt-Comdr. D. N. Cone, Jr.	SIMPSON (221)

1802	Lt-Comdr. W. P. McCarty	LITCHFIELD (336)
1807	Lt-Comdr. A. D. Chandler	SOUTHARD (207)
1814	Lt-Comdr. W. M. Hobby, Jr.	ANDERSON (411)
1819	Lt-Comdr. H. C. Robison	BUCK (420)
1821	Lt-Comdr. T. H. Hederman	DOWNES (375)
1836	Lt-Comdr. B. R. Harrison, Jr.	ROWAN (405)
1841	Lt-Comdr. K. P. Hartman	BLAKELEY (150)
1853	Lt-Comdr. E. L. Woodyard	JACOB JONES (130)
1861	Lt-Comdr. R. L. Campbell, Jr.	TRIPPE (403)
1870	Lt-Comdr. E. W. Rawlins	TARBELL (142)
1926	Lt-Comdr. K. Earl	HOGAN (178)
1953	Lt-Comdr. P. V. Mercer	RATHBURNE (113)
1961	Lt-Comdr. E. Watts	LEARY (158)
1966	Lt-Comdr. D. J. Ramsey	HUGHES (410)
1969	Lt-Comdr E. P. Creehan	BAINBRIDGE (246)
1976	Lt-Comdr. H. B. Southworth	HUMPHREYS (236)
1992	Lt-Comdr. M. C. Stormes	TALBOT (114)
2004	Lt-Comdr. B. L. Doggett	GILMER (233)
2022	Lt-Comdr. A. C. Wood	MAC LEISH (220)
2024	Lt-Comdr. E. S. L. Goodwin (D)	NOA (343)
2313	Lt-Comdr. E. E. Berthold	KING (242)
2373	Lt-Comdr. J. A. Farrell, Jr.	FOX (234)
2393	Lt-Comdr. M. R. Peterson	BIDDLE (151)
2407	Lt-Comdr. J. H. Long	BARNEY (149)
2410	Lt-Comdr. J. S. Smith, Jr.	TREVER (339)
2594	Lt-Comdr. R. E. Elliott	PERRY (340)
2603	Lt-Comdr. S. P. Smith	CHANDLER (206)
2608	Lt-Comdr. G. C. Wright	BERNADOU (153)
2621	Lt-Comdr. R. D. Smith	WATERS (115)
2634	Lt-Comdr. J. S. Blue	PALMER (161)
2655	Lt-Comdr. J. C. Sowell	DECATUR (341)
2661	Lt-Comdr. H. D. Larson (R)	HAMILTON (141)
2680	Lt-Comdr. A. E. Jarrell	STURTEVANT (240)
2685	Lt-Comdr. T. H Tonseth	SCHENCK (159)
2690	Lt-Comdr. J. J. Laffan	DALLAS (199)
2755	Lt-Comdr. H. B. Heneberger	TRUXTUN (229)
2759	Lieut. J. E. Florance	HOVEY (208)
2760	Lt-Comdr. R. N. McFarlane	STANSBURY (180)
2879	Lt-Comdr. J. F. Newman, Jr.	SANDS (243)
2884	Lt-Comdr. C. Broussard	LEA (118)
2855	Lieut. C. F. Horne, Jr.	LONG (209)
2904	Lieut. E. M. Waldron	DU PONT (152)

2914 Lieut. J. J. Greytak — KANE (235)
2936 Lieut. H. L. Edwards — REUBEN JAMES (245)
2954 Lieut. W. K. Romoser — UPSHUR (144)
2961 Lieut. C. W. Moses — COLE (155)
2968 Lieut. F. L. Tedder — HOWARD (179)
2986 Lieut. J. K. Reybold — CLAXTON (140)
3016 Lieut. L. M. LeHardy — ZANE (337)
3177 Lieut. H. M. Briggs (D) — HAMILTON (141)
3198 Lieut. M. R. Stone (D) — DICKERSON (157)
3228 Lieut. E. T. Goyette — BABBITT (128)
3229 Lieut. J. F. Hines, Jr. — ROPER (147)
3296 Lieut. S. G. Hooper — BORIE (215)

MINECRAFT

965 Commander J. G. Atkins — OGLALA
1893 Lt-Comdr. W. J. Longfellow — BREESE
1905 Lt-Comdr. D. F. McLean — MONTGOMERY
2000 Lt-Comdr. A. M. Townsend — SICARD
2026 Lt-Comdr. J. H. Sides — TRACY
2107 Lt-Comdr. E. R. J. Griffin — TANAGER
2328 Lt-Comdr. H. M. Hayter — RAMSAY
2357 Lt-Comdr. J. H. Morrill — QUAIL
2735 Lt-Comdr. W. G. Beecher, Jr. — PRUITT
2747 Lt-Comdr. C. F. Chillingworth, Jr. — PREBLE
2437 Lieut. J. O. Jenkins — LARK
2451 Lieut. L. F. Blodgett — WHIPPOORWILL
3028 Lieut. D. A. Crandell — GAMBLE

SUBMARINES

1256 Commander N. S. Ives — NARWHAL (167)
1623 Lt-Comdr. L. D. Follmer — NAUTILUS (168)
1762 Lt-Comdr. L. N. Blair — STINGRAY (186)
1782 Lt-Comdr. M. M. Stephens — SALMON (182)
1872 Lt-Comdr. E. E. Yeomans — SARGO (188)
1879 Lt-Comdr. S. G. Barchet — ARGONAUT (SM1)
1894 Lt-Comdr. G. W. Patterson, Jr. — SAURY (189)
1910 Lt-Comdr. W. D. Wilkin — SCULPIN (191)
1935 Lt-Comdr. M. J. Tichenor — DOLPHIN (169)
2002 Lt-Comdr. G. E. Peterson — CUTTLEFISH (171)
2391 Lt-Comdr. F. K. Loomis — SKIPJACK (184)
2392 Lt-Comdr. J. W. Murphy, Jr. — TAMBOR (198)
2398 Lt-Comdr. R. G. Voge — SEALION (195)

2400	Lt-Comdr. W. A. Lent	TRITON (201)
2401	Lt-Comdr. S. P. Moseley	POLLACK (180)
2406	Lt-Comdr. P. D. Compton	SHARK (174)
2412	Lt-Comdr. F. B. Warder	SEAWOLF (197)
2601	Lt-Comdr. M. C. Mumma, Jr.	SAILFISH (192)
2607	Lt-Comdr. C. C. Smith	SWORDFISH (193)
2624	Lt-Comdr. L. S. Parks	POMPANO (181)
2637	Lt-Comdr. T. G. Reamy	SEARAVEN (196)
2651	Lt-Comdr. C. E. Tolman, Jr.	SPEARFISH (190)
2671	Lt-Comdr. K. C. Hurd	SEAL (183)
2672	Lt-Comdr. W. L. Wright	STURGEON (187)
2687	Lt-Comdr. W. N. Christensen	CACHALOT (170)
2693	Lt-Comdr. W. R. Headden	PLUNGER (179)
2745	Lieut. H. L. Stone	SNAPPER (185)
2772	Lieut. J. G. Johns	SEADRAGON (194)
2899	Lieut. W. L. Anderson	THRESHER (200)
2984	Lieut. J. H. Willingham, Jr.	TAUTOG (199)
3098	Lieut. W. R. Edsall	S-34
3226	Lieut. T. D. Jacobs	S-23
3233	Lieut. C. C. Burlingame	S-30
3280	Lieut. W. A. Saunders	S-24
3283	Lieut. G. D. Dickey	S-20
3286	Lieut. T. M. Dykers	S-35
3352	Lieut. W. R. Ignatius	S-22
3368	Lieut. M. P. Russillo	S-25
3397	Lieut. W. D. Irvin	S-29
3419	Lieut. G. R. Donaho	R-14
3451	Lieut. J. A. Bole, Jr.	S-21
3461	Lieut. W. J. Millican	S-18
3464	Lieut. E. C. Hawk	S-26
3583	Lieut. R. C. Lynch, Jr.	S-46
3586	Lieut. E. C. Folger, Jr.	R-11
3593	Lieut. O. G. Kirk	S-42
3602	Lieut. J. F. Davidson	S-44
3606	Lieut. E. R. Hannon	S-43
3642	Lieut. J. T. Hardin	R-4
3668	Lieut. D. F. Weiss	R-10
3669	Lieut. E. C. Stephan	S-28
3678	Lieut. C. A. Johnson	R-13
3684	Lieut. W. S. Stovall, Jr.	S-27
3786	Lieut. J. W. Davis	S-47
3874	Lieut. F. C. Lucas, Jr.	R-2
3934	Lieut. I. C. Eddy	S-45

AUXILIARIES—INCLUDING NAVAL TRANSPORTATION SERVICE

85	Captain B. McCandless	RIGEL, also Commanding Officer Destroyer Base, San Diego.
385	Captain E. P. Eldredge	DOBBIN
387	Captain D. F. Patterson	WYOMING
402	Captain L. S. Pamperin	BARNETT
412	Captain H. D. McHenry	McCAWLEY
430	Commander R. S. Haggart	PYRO
462	Commander P. Cassard	ARGONNE
464	Commander E. L. Vanderloot	WHARTON
466	Commander J. R. Palmer	UTAH
471	Commander W. E. Doyle	HOLLAND
480	Commander G. Hutchins	ALTAIR
485	Commander W. J. Larson	MELVILLE
501	Commander A. H. Balsley	NITRO
509	Commander J. G. Moyer	DIXIE
512	Commander W. A. Corn	WHITNEY
515	Commander J. B. W. Waller	PRAIRIE
516	Commander T. A. Doyle, Jr.	MEDUSA
518	Commander K. C. Christian	RELIEF
522	Commander R. A. Dyer, Jr.	DENEBOLA
539	Commander R. P. Luker	VESTAL
540	Commander O. O. Kessing	CHAUMONT
553	Commander J. M. Shoemaker	WRIGHT
650	Commander H. J. Redfield	CIMARRON
735	Commander P. L. Meadows	PLATTE
741	Commander C. A. F. Sprague	TANGIER
748	Commander J. D. Wilson	MATTOLE
796	Commander E. D. Gibb	SPICA
800	Commander M. L. Lewis	YUKON
847	Commander W. E. Hilbert	BEAVER
848	Commander H. W. Olds	TIPPECANOE
910	Commander A. L. Karns	ARD-1
924	Commander W. C. Vose	RAMAPO
936	Commander J. B. Noble	BRIDGE
958	Commander M. P. DuVal, Jr.	ANTARES
970	Commander J. R. Redman	HENDERSON
981	Commander W. N. Thornton	PATOKA
988	Commander J. H. Foskett	NECHES
1002	Commander W. E. A. Mullan	NEOSHO
1008	Commander C. B. Momsen	SIRIUS
1019	Commander D. Osborn, Jr.	CAPELLA

1097 Commander R. A. Dierdorff	Wm. W. BURROWS
1167 Commander J. P. Vetter	VEGA
1170 Commander R. J. Townsend	KANAWHA
1193 Commander J. E. Dingwell	TRINITY
1200 Commander J. F. Rees	CUYAMA
1205 Commander J. B. Mallard	RAPIDAN
1258 Commander S. J. Michael	GOLDSBOROUGH
1259 Commander C. S. Isgrig	BRAZOS
1289 Commander G. P. Kraker	SALINAS
1315 Commander B. B. Biggs	ARCTIC
1498 Lt-Comdr. J. V. Carney	HULBERT
1503 Lt-Comdr. F. J. Bridget	WILLIAM B. PRESTON
1548 Lt-Comdr. H. E. Regan	WILLIAMSON
1577 Lt-Comdr. J. P. Whitney	CLEMSON
1643 Lt-Comdr. F. Akers	GEORGE E. BADGER
1660 Lt-Comdr. A. L. Toney	ELLIOTT
1683 Lt-Comdr. J. L. Pratt	CHILDS
1703 Lt-Comdr. E. C. Loughead	MANLEY
1896 Lt-Comdr. H. L. Collins	DORSEY
1909 Lt-Comdr. W. D. Brown	GREGORY
1914 Lt-Comdr. E. T. Layton	BOGGS
1926 Lt-Comdr. K. Earl	LITTLE
2072 Lt-Comdr. J. S. Hawkins	SONOMA
2101 Lt-Comdr. C. B. Schiano	KINGFISHER
2138 Lt-Comdr. E. D. McEathron	GREBE
2159 Lt-Comdr. F. W. Beard	RAIL
2175 Lt-Comdr. S. E. Kenney	PARTRIDGE
2222 Lt-Comdr. L. M. Wise	BRANT
2226 Lt-Comdr. M. E. Thomas	NAVAJO
2246 Lt-Comdr. E. V. Raines	ROBIN
2263 Lt-Comdr. D. B. Candler	SEAGULL
2264 Lt-Comdr. H. R. Carson, Jr.	TURKEY
2343 Lt-Comdr. R. D. Williams	ALGORMA
2367 Lt-Comdr. F. J. Ilsemann	VIREO
2413 Lt-Comdr. D. R. Hull	SEMMES
2460 Lieut. I. B. Smith	KALMIA
2518 Lieut. W. B. Pendleton	TERN
2520 Lieut. H. C. Jones	BOBOLINK
2572 Lieut. A. A. Griese	PINOLA
2686 Lieut. W. L. Benson	LAMBERTON
3147 Lieut. H. R. Horney	LAPWING
3164 Lieut. A. Smith, Jr.	SANDPIPER
3256 Lieut. R. E. Dixon	AVOCET

3262	Lieut. P. A. Tague, Jr.	GANNET
3276	Lieut. H. J. Dyson	PELICAN
3295	Lieut. A. R. Truslow, Jr.	SWAN
3378	Lieut. J. J. McRoberts	THRUSH
3620	Lieut. L. T. Stone	ORTOLAN
3671	Lieut. H. J. McRoberts	TEAL
3683	Lieut. G. A. Sharp	FALCON
3811	Lieut. J. E. Stevens	WIDGEON
3845	Lieut. F. W. Laing	MALLARD
3987	Lieut. J. A. Webster	BULLFINCH
4277	Lieut. J. E. Smith	CARDINAL

FLEET MARINE FORCE

12157	Lt-Colonel Bert A. Bone	1st Defense Bn.
12083	Colonel Thomas E. Bourke	2nd Defense Bn.
12051	Colonel Harry K. Pickett	3rd Defense Bn.
12048	Colonel William H. Rupertus	4th Defense Bn.
12073	Colonel Lloyd L. Leech	5th Defense Bn.
12019	Brig-Gen. Hollard M. Smith	1st Marine Brigade
12091	Lt-Colonel Alfred H. Noble	5th Marines
12125	Lt-Colonel Charles T. Brooks	1st Battalion
12233	Major William J. Whaling	2nd Battalion
12230	Major George R. Rowan	3rd Battalion
12168	Lt-Colonel Galen M. Sturgis	1st Bn., 11 Mar.
12118	Lt-Colonel Field Harris	1st Marine Aircraft Group
12011	Brig-Gen. Clayton B. Vogel	2nd Marine Brigade
12086	Colonel Leo D. Hermle	6th Marines
12127	Lt-Colonel Oliver P. Smith	1st Battalion
12164	Lt-Colonel Lewis B. Reagan	2nd Battalion
12047	Colonel Henry L. Larson	8th Marines
12108	Lt-Colonel Franklin A. Hart	1st Battalion
12220	Lt-Colonel Elmer E. Hall	2nd Battalion
12025	Brig.-Gen. Ross E. Rowell	Marine Aircraft Wing
12167	Lt-Colonel John B. Wilson	2nd Bn., 10th Mar.
12140	Lt-Colonel Lewie C. Merritt	2nd Marine Aircraft Group
12201	Lt-Colonel Ford O. Rogers	Base Air Detachment, Bourne Field, St. Thomas, V.I.
12306	Major Augustus W. Cockrell	Advance Detachment, Marine Defense Force

NOTES:
(D) Ordered Detached.
(R) Ordered to Report.

George C. Dyer,
Flag Secretary.

J. O. RICHARDSON

Appendix B

Abbreviations Used

ACSWPD	Assistant Chief of Staff, War Plans Division
CHBUAER	Chief of the Bureau of Aeronautics
CHBUNAV	Chief of the Bureau of Navigation
CHBUSHIPS	Chief of the Bureau of Ships
CINCPACFLT	Commander-in-Chief, Pacific Fleet
CINCUS	Commander-in-Chief, United States Fleet
CNO	Chief of Naval Operations
CNOCF	Central Classified Records of the Secretary of the Navy/Chief of Naval Operations, 1940-1947
COM (followed by number)	Commandant, Naval District
COMAIRBATFOR	Commander Aircraft, Battle Force
COMAIRSCOFOR	Commander Aircraft, Scouting Force
COMBASEFOR	Commander Base Force, United States Fleet
COMBATFOR	Commander Battle Force, United States Fleet
COMBATSHIPS	Commander Battleships, Battle Force
COMCRUBATFOR	Commander Cruisers, Battle Force
COMCRUSCOFOR	Commander Cruisers, Scouting Force
COMDESBATFOR	Commander Destroyers, Battle Force
COMSCOFOR	Commander Scouting Force, United States Fleet
COMSUBFOR	Commander Submarines, Scouting Force
COMPATWINGS	Commander Patrol Wings, Patrol Force
COMPATWINGTWO	Commander Patrol Wing Two, Aircraft Scouting Force
DWPD	Director, War Plans Division
GB	General Board of the Navy
JB	Joint Army-Navy Board
JOR	Admiral James O. Richardson
NA	U.S. National Archives and Records Service
NHD	U.S. Naval History Division
NRS	Naval Records Special Microfilm File
RG	Record Group
SECNAV	Secretary of the Navy
WPL	War Plan
WWIICF	World War II Command File, 1935-1945

A Note on Sources

Unpublished Sources

Most of the unpublished materials used in this work are found in either the Modern Military Records Branch, U.S. National Archives, or in the Operational Archives of the Naval History Division. The former repository (abbreviated in the footnotes as "NA") contains the Records of Naval Operating Forces, Record Group 313, a group that includes the Commander-in-Chief, U.S. Fleet Correspondence Files, 1939-1940. This collection (cited as "CINCUS Files") is arranged according to the *Navy Filing Manual* and its contents are readily accessible. A group of pre-World War II files of operating forces (sometimes referred to as "Flag Files"), which until recently was at the Federal Records Center, Mechanicsburg, Pa., is also part of Record Group 313 and comprises more than 1,700 cubic feet of mostly unprocessed documents. The official correspondence of Battle Force subordinate commands, 1929–1940 ("BATFOR Files"), was the major section of these files used by the author.

The National Archives also holds in the Records of the Office of the Chief of Naval Operations (Record Group 38) some 24,000 microfilm reels of security-classified messages and despatches. Most of the messages used in this manuscript are believed to be located among these microfilms. Another segment in Record Group 38 used by the author is the general correspondence of the Fleet Training Division, 1914–1941.

Other relevant groups in the National Archives include the General Records of the Navy Department, 1917–1940, Record Group 80, and the Bureau of Yards and Docks Confidential Correspondence, 1918–1941, Record Group 71.

The Operational Archives of the Naval History Division contains the following major groups that provided documentation for this history: (1) The World War II Command File, 1935–1945 (cited as "WWIICF"), which contains a number of annual reports, organizational documents, and official correspondence pertinent to the period prior to the Pearl Harbor Attack; (2) The Plan File, 1935–1945, which includes a number of the operation plans and orders, as well as basic Joint Army-Navy and Naval War Plans of the interwar years; (3) The Central Classified Records of the Secretary of the Navy/Chief of Naval Operations, 1940–1947 ("CNOCF"); (4) Records of the General Board of the Navy, 1900–1951 ("GB Files"); and (5) Records of the Navy Secretariat of the Joint Army-Navy Board, 1903–1947 ("JB Files"). Additional documents used in writing this book are contained in the Naval Records Special ("NRS") microfilm files numbered 1M and 136/8, which were prepared by the Operational Archives at the time the original manuscript was completed.

Several letters that pertain to Admiral Richardson's early career can be found in his official naval file at the Military Personnel Records Center, St. Louis, Mo.

In the process of checking and editing this manuscript for publication, the Naval History Division sought to locate each document that was a source of information for the author. However, in the interval since this manuscript was completed in 1958 and the present time, a number of records have been moved from one repository to another. Further, certain documents (notably Admiral Richardson's diary and some of his other papers) are known to have been destroyed. For these reasons, there are a few instances in which quotations are not cited and some footnotes do not identify the location of documents.

Published Works

The published works used most extensively in this account were *Annual Report of the Secretary of the Navy for the Fiscal Year* (Washington, D.C.: Government Printing Office, 1902–1941), and the voluminous U.S., Congress, Joint Committee, *Hearings before the Joint Committee on the Investigation of the Pearl Harbor Attack.* (79th Cong., 1st and 2nd sess., 39 parts, 1946, pursuant to S. Con. Res. 27, 79th Cong.) Washington, D.C.: Government Printing Office, 1946.

Among other works consulted were:

Allen, Frederick Lewis, *Since Yesterday*. New York: Harper and Bros., 1939.

Angell, Norman, *Let the People Know*. New York: The Viking Press, 1943.

Beard, Charles A. and Mary R., *America in Mid Passage*. New York, The Macmillan Co., 1939.

Davis, Forrest and Ernest K. Lindley, *How War Came*. New York: Simon and Schuster, 1942.

Drummond, Donald F., *The Passing of American Neutrality 1937-1941*. Ann Arbor: University of Michigan Press, 1955.

Halsey, William F., and J. Bryan III, *Admiral Halsey's Story*. New York: McGraw-Hill Book Co., Inc., 1947.

Hocking, William E., *Morale and its Enemies*. New Haven: Yale University Press, 1918.

Jane's Fighting Ships. London: Sampson Low Marston and Co., 1908.

Jones, S. Shepard and Denys P. Myers, eds., *Documents on American Foreign Relations,* July 1939 to June 1940, Vol. II. Boston: World Peace Foundation, 1940.

Kimmel, Husband E., *Admiral Kimmel's Story.* Chicago: Henry Regnery Co., 1954.

King, Ernest J. and Walter Muir Whitehill, *Fleet Admiral King: A Naval Record.* New York: W. W. Norton and Co., Inc., 1952.

Knox, Dudley W., *A History of the United States Navy.* New York: G. P. Putnam's Sons, 1948.

Long, John D., *The New American Navy.* New York: The Outlook Co., 1903.

Matloff, Maurice and Edwin M. Snell, *Strategic Planning for Coalition Warfare 1941-1942* in subseries *The War Department,* Office of the Chief of Military History, Department of the Army series *The United States Army in World War II.* Washington, D.C.: Government Printing Office, 1951.

Morison, Samuel E., *The Rising Sun in the Pacific,* Vol. III of *History of United States Naval Operations in World War II.* Boston: Little Brown and Co., 1948.

Morley, Felix, *The Society of Nations: Its Organization and Constitutional Development.* Washington, D.C.: The Brookings Institution, 1932.

The New York Times, 1940.

Rosenman, Samuel I., ed., *War—And Aid to Democracies,* Vol. 9 of *The Public Papers and Addresses of Franklin D. Roosevelt.* New York: The Macmillan Co., 1941.

Shepardson, Whitney H. and William O. Scroggs, *The United States in World Affairs: An Account of American Foreign Relations* in series *Council on Foreign Relations.* New York: Harper and Bros., 1941.

Sherwood, Robert E., *Roosevelt and Hopkins: An Intimate History.* New York: Harper and Bros., 1948.

Sims, William L. and Burton J. Hendrick, *The Victory At Sea.* Garden City, New York: Doubleday, Page and Co., 1920.

Standley, William H. and Arthur A. Ageton, *Admiral Ambassador to Russia.* Chicago: H. Regnery Co., 1955.

Stimson, Henry L. and McGeorge Bundy, *On Active Service in Peace and War.* New York: Harper and Bros., 1947.

Theobold, Robert A., *The Final Secret of Pearl Harbor: The Washington Contribution to the Attack.* Old Greenwich, Conn.: Devin-Adair Co., 1954.

Turnbull, Archibald D. and Clifford L. Lord, *History of United States Naval Aviation.* New Haven: Yale University Press, 1949.

U.S., Congress, House Subcommittee of the Committee On Appropriations, *Navy Department Appropriation Bill for 1940.* (76th Cong., 1st sess., 1939) Washington, D.C.: Government Printing Office, 1939.

U.S., Congress, House, Subcommittee of the Committee On Appropriations, *Navy Department Appropriation Bill for 1942.* (77th Cong., 1st sess., 1941) Washington, D.C.: Government Printing Office, 1941.

U.S., Congress, Senate, Subcommittee of the Committee on Naval Affairs, *Naval Investigation Hearings.* (66th Cong., 2nd sess., 30 Mar. 1920) Washington, D.C.: Government Printing Office, 1920.

U.S., Navy Department, *Administration of the Naval Establishment of the United States (Naval Instructions)*, 1913 in *Regulations for the Government of the Navy of the United States (Navy Regulations)*, 1913. Washington, D.C.: Government Printing Office, 1913.

U.S., Navy Department, *Navy Department General Orders: Series of 1935*. Washington, D. C.: Government Printing Office, 1940.

U.S., Navy Department, *Navy Directory: Officers of the United States Navy and Marine Corps,* January 1939. Washington, D.C.: Government Printing Office, 1939.

Watson, Mark, *Chief of Staff: Prewar Plans and Preparations* in subseries *The War Department,* Office of the Chief of Military History, Department of the Army series *The United States Army in World War II.* Washington, D.C.: Government Printing Office, 1950.

Zimmern, Alfred E., *The League of Nations and the Rule of Law 1918-1935.* London: Macmillan and Co., Ltd., 1939.

Index

H

N

O

P

Q

R

T

Y

Z

☆ U.S. GOVERNMENT PRINTING OFFICE: 1974 O—492-042

www.ingramcontent.com/pod-product-compliance
Lightning Source LLC
LaVergne TN
LVHW080308110826
845155LV00023B/91
* 9 7 8 1 9 0 7 5 2 1 2 7 0 *